MANAGEMENT

THIRD

PR

MANAGEMENT THEORY AND PRACTICE

SEVENTH EDITION

GERALD A. COLE
PHIL KELLY

SOUTH-WESTERN
CENGAGE Learning™

Australia • Brazil • Japan • Korea • Mexico • Singapore • Spain • United Kingdom • United States

SOUTH-WESTERN
CENGAGE Learning

Management: Theory and Practice
Gerald A. Cole and Phil Kelly

Publishing Director: Linden Harris

Publisher: Brendan George

Development Editor: Jennifer Seth

Editorial Assistant: Charlotte Green

Production Editor: Adam Paddon

Production Controller: Eyvett Davis

Marketing Manager: Amanda Cheung

Typesetter: KnowledgeWorks Global, India

Cover design: Adam Renvoize

For product information and technology assistance, contact **emea.info@cengage.com**.

For permission to use material from this text or product, and for permission queries, email **clsuk.permissions@cengage.com**.

This work is adapted from *Management Theory and Practice*, 6th edition, published by South-Western a division of Cengage Learning, Inc. © 2004

British Library Cataloguing-in-Publication Data
A catalogue record for this book is available from the British Library.

ISBN: 978-1-84480-506-8

Cengage Learning EMEA
Cheriton House, North Way, Andover, Hampshire, SP10 5BE United Kingdom

Cengage Learning products are represented in Canada by Nelson Education Ltd.

For your lifelong learning solutions, visit
www.cengage.co.uk

Purchase your next print book, e-book or e-chapter at
www.cengagebrain.com

Printed in Singapore
1 2 3 4 5 6 7 8 9 10 – 13 12 11

CONTENTS

PART ONE: MANAGEMENT THEORY

PART TWO: MANAGEMENT IN PRACTICE

PART THREE: FUNCTIONAL MANAGEMENT-MARKETING, PRODUCTION, PERSONNEL AND FINANCIAL

LIST OF CASES

PREFACE

The aim of Management Theory and Practice 7ed is to provide an accessible introduction to the principal ideas and developments in management theory and practice. It is a holistic text covering a wide range of management topics. The book also aims to stimulate further reading and thinking about the subject of management by signposting a wide range of books and articles, and by providing opportunities for discussion and comment on important issues arising from the text. Chapter questions and associated video case studies are also useful in this respect, encouraging readers to set out their ideas in response to typical examination-type and review questions and compare their responses with the suggested answers supplied. Whilst targeted primarily at those studying a first degree or diploma in business and management, the book is also of use as a foundation text for higher degrees and courses.

Since management is a rather eclectic subject, drawing its subject matter from a variety of sources, the material in the book is presented in relatively short chapters, with numbered paragraphs for easy reference. Chapters are grouped by topic and arranged in a logical sequence, so that whilst the subject matter is wide-ranging, and sometimes quite complex, it is possible to see some development of the body of knowledge that we call 'management'.

The book can be used as a class-based textbook or as a practice manual for independent self-study. The glossary is intended to reinforce some of the definitions referred to in the main text, and may be especially helpful to overseas students unfamiliar with British practices. The basic elements of the book are the fifty-two short chapters which are grouped into fourteen topics, forming the major building blocks of the subject (see the model below). This enables readers to focus on particular topics, or to work through them all systematically, depending upon need or preference. The questions at the end of each chapter can be used to check understanding, or to raise issues with tutors and/or fellow students. Tutors may also use these questions to encourage students to apply this reading within their own organizations, or to develop their own ideas as to how management ought to be practised. The reading lists are founded on the many other texts referred to within the book, and it is hoped that readers will seek out these other texts, old and new, in order to see for themselves how key ideas have been expressed or developed by key management theorists. In this respect the current book is a guide to the work of other writers, and an encouragement to wider reading. Questions appear at the end of each chapter and suggested answers are available on the companion website, to help students focus on the salient points and assist with structured responses. There are also video case studies available on the companion website and referenced at the end of each chapter.

NOTES ON THE SEVENTH EDITION

Whilst the overall chapter structure of the book remains the same as the previous edition, significant updates and new materials have been added. At a general level, the pedagogical features have been improved in this latest edition. Every chapter now has defined learning outcomes, a glossary and reference list, a chapter introduction, text and conclusion. In addition, there are

FIGURE FM.1 Model for studying management theory and practice

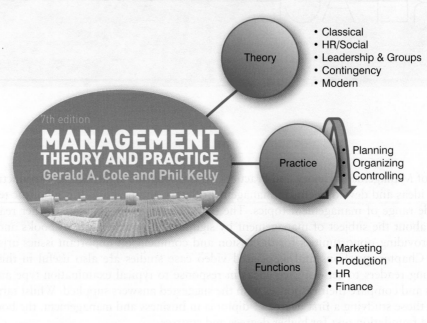

more figures, an ExamView test bank, new case studies (written and video) and vignettes. Using the glossary, students can now see, at a glance, which chapters make reference to a particular concept.

At a more specific level, many chapters have been updated and new content has been added. Content decisions were influenced by the Quality Assurance Agency for Higher Education (QAA) subject benchmark statements for general business and management (2007) which articulate the knowledge and skills expected of successful honours graduates in the field. The QAA recognize that the purpose of general business and management programmes includes the study of organizations, their management and the changing external environment in which they operate plus preparation for and development of a career in business and management. Studying organizations encompasses the internal aspects, functions and processes of organizations including their diverse nature, purposes, structures, governance, operations and management, together with the individual and corporate behaviours and cultures which exist within and between organizations and their influence upon the external environment. The 'external environment' encompasses a wide range of factors, including economic, environmental, ethical, legal, political, sociological and technological, together with their effects at local, national and international levels upon the strategy, behaviour, management and sustainability of organizations. Finally, 'management' encompasses the various processes, procedures and practices for effective management of organizations. It includes theories, models, frameworks, tasks and roles of management, together with rational analysis and other processes of decision making within organizations and in relation to the external environment. It is expected that graduates will also be able to demonstrate knowledge and understanding in the following areas:

–   Markets – the development and operation of markets for resources, goods and services

–   Customers – customer expectations, service and orientation

–   Finance – the sources, uses and management of finance; the use of accounting and other information systems for managerial applications

- People – the management and development of people within organizations

- Operations – the management of resources and operations

- Information systems – the development, management and exploitation of information systems and their impact upon organizations

- Communication and information technology – the comprehension and use of relevant communication and information technologies for application in business and management

- Business policy and strategy – the development of appropriate policies and strategies within a changing environment, to meet stakeholder interests

- Pervasive issues – sustainability, globalization, corporate social responsibility, diversity, business innovation, creativity, enterprise development, knowledge management and risk management.

Incorporating the QAA advice, the chapter about women in management and the entire book now consider a broad range of diversity challenges associated with the 21st century workplace. The chapter dealing with the international context of management discusses the processes of internationalization and the concept of globalization and the challenge of working in diverse and multicultural organizations. The planning chapters now refer to positioning and resource-based strategies and recognize emergent as well as planned approaches. The ethics and corporate social responsibilities aspects of policy have been strengthened in Chpater 17. Chpater 21 now contains more on business processes and business process management. In Chpater 24, managing change, there is greater emphasis on understanding and building the need for change and the use of change models. The section on control in management has a greater focus on quality management and the role of information technology has been developed to include more on how companies compete with information resources and the application of Net technologies. Furthermore Chpater 41, 'New technology in Manufacturing' now includes a thorough coverage of ERP systems. The marketing section has been improved to take greater account of globalization and the Internet and a greater emphasis on Supply Chain Management. Additionally, there is now more information about the marketing strategy. The HR section now contains much more on the strategic as well as the operational role for HR specialists. All of the HR legislation has been updated and the need for fairness in HR practice discussed. Managerial competencies and competencies generally are afforded more attention. Finally, the scope of the financial aspects of management section has also been broadened to include more on investment appraisal. These changes, with the new text and video case studies, should enhance the book's appeal, making it more useful to contemporary readers and management practitioners. Feedback on the content, style and pedagogical features is welcome – please email Dr Phil Kelly, p.kelly1@ljmu.ac.uk with your comments.

ACKNOWLEDGEMENTS

May I take this opportunity to thank all of those individuals whose insight, time and hard work have contributed to this book. Special thanks go to Jennifer Seth, the Development Editor at Cengage Learning, for her patience, support and management of the project. Exceptional thanks go to all of those in the formal review process; their feedback and suggestions for improvement helped shape the book. Numerous individuals contributed towards the thinking behind the book, through conversations, conferences, seminars and writings. Huge benefit has resulted from the views and experiences of business educators and practitioners from the UK and around the world. Personal appreciation goes to many individuals including: staff from Liverpool Business School (LBS) based within the Faculty of Business and Law, Alistair Beere in particular; staff from Kaplan Professional, Dr Yvonne Moogan in particular; Steve Fowler and staff at the Institute for Risk Management (IRM). May I also thank the LJMU business students and staff for trialling aspects of the text. Grateful thanks also to a variety of companies and publishers for permission to reproduce copyright material. Acknowledgements appear throughout the text as and when we use such material. Likewise, thank you to the various organizations who provided case study materials.

The Publisher would like to thank the following academics who supplied feedback on the original proposal and during the writing process:

Frank Auton, University of Westminster

Dr. Hugh Crozier, London Metropolitan University

Raymond Rogers, Coventry University Business School

The Publisher also thanks various copyright holders for granting permission to reproduce material throughout the text. Every effort has been made to trace all copyright holders, but if anything has been inadvertently overlooked, the Publisher will be pleased to make the necessary arrangements at the first opportunity (please contact the Publisher directly).

ABOUT THE AUTHORS

Gerald Cole worked and taught in a wide variety of organizations, both large and small, in the public and private sectors. He held two non-executive directorships and was also an external examiner in CMS and DMS courses at Middlesex University. His other books include Personnel Management, Strategic Management and Organizational Behaviour.

Dr Phil Kelly, formerly advisor to Asia's highest paid CEO, worked for over 20 companies in almost as many countries prior to becoming a Senior Lecturer at Liverpool Business School. Having completed his Doctorate in Business Administration, at one of Europe's leading business schools, he went on to establish himself in academia, teaching at a range of universities. An experienced lecturer, he has an MA (with distinction) in teaching and learning in Higher Education, and frequently teaches on a range of business courses. Phil has written several books, the last one, 'International Business and Management' is a popular text on a range of business degree programmes.

WALK-THROUGH TOUR

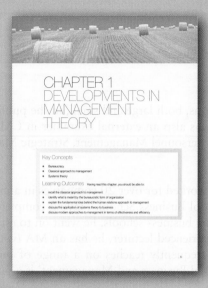

Key Concepts and Learning Objectives
Each chapter starts with a list of objectives to help you monitor your understanding and progress through the chapter.

Introduction
Each chapter starts with a comprehensive introduction that provides a complete overview of the key issues, helping you to assess your understanding and highlight key content.

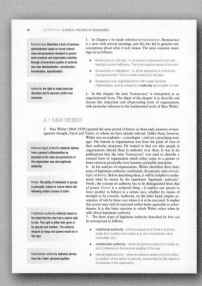

Margin glossary Terms
Key terms are highlighted throughout the text and explained in full in the margins as well as in a full glossary at the end of the book.

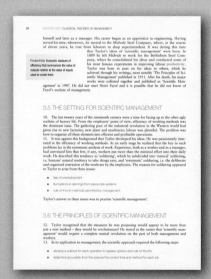

Accessible, concise structure
The clear and logical 'bite-sized chunks' are easy to navigate and gradually build up knowledge and understanding.

End of Chapter Questions

provided at the end of each chapter to help reinforce and test your knowledge and understanding, and provide a basis for group discussions and activities.

Useful Websites

a selection of useful web links and resources to complement and boost learning and revision.

Video Cases

relevant short video clips and activities are introduced at the end of each chapter, find them online at www.cengage.co.uk/colekelly.

Long Case Studies

Long cases discuss in depth the issues and principles encountered during the section.

About the website

The seventh edition of *Management Theory and Practice* is accompanied by a range of digital support resources. These resources have been carefully tailored by our experienced author to meet the needs of the reader. Collectively these resources are designed to engage students, encouraging critical thinking and an active and questioning approach to the subject of management. They can also be used to save important tutor time, whilst enhancing the quality of delivery.

To discover the dedicated digital support resources accompanying this textbook please go to:
www.cengage.co.uk/colekelly7

For students

- Multiple Choice Questions to test your learning
- Video Cases and Activity Work Book for each chapter
- Flashcards to test your knowledge
- Online Glossary to reinforce key definitions
- MP3 transcripts to help you revise

For lecturers

- Secure password protected site with teaching materials
- A downloadable Lecturer Teaching Guide
- PowerPoint Slides to be used in your lectures
- Video Cases and Tutor Notes to accompany each chapter
- ExamView Test Bank to accompany each chapter
- Answers to Chapter Questions

PART I
MANAGEMENT
THEORY

Every practising business manager who seeks to improve their skills and abilities should be concerned with the knowledge and application of management theories. Yet there exists this persistent view that management theory and practice are polar opposites. In any subject concerned with rational intervention in human affairs, theory must lead to practice; but practice is the source of theory: neither theory nor practice is prime (Checkland, 1985). Management is one of those bodies of theory and practice whose concern might be described as 'rational intervention in human affairs'. Checkland goes on to argue that any approach to rational intervention in human affairs has to accept that in studying purposeful human action and in trying to bring about change in human situations, it is not simply a matter of setting to work to discover 'laws' governing the phenomena in question. Autonomous human beings could, in principle, act deliberately in a way which could either confirm or refute any supposed 'laws' of human affairs. This means that the would-be rational intervener in human affairs cannot separate theory and practice in the

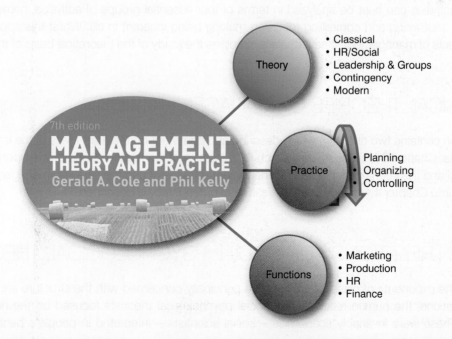

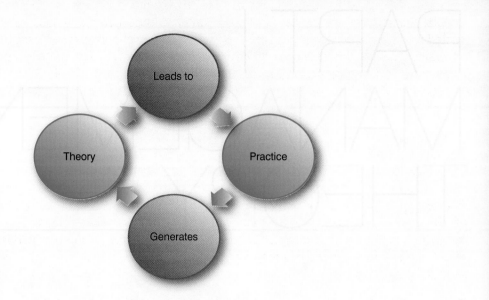

way that can be done by the natural scientist. Such intervention requires a steady interaction between theory and practice in a process of inquiry. The state of the subject, or discipline, is then best thought of as an account of the history and present state of that process. According to Checkland, 'theory' and 'practice' are NOT the concern of two different groups of people, namely 'academics' and 'practitioners'. 'Practitioners' need also to be reflective about their actions; 'academics' need also to engage in practice. This book, concerned with management (rational attempts to intervene in human affairs), and with the present state of that art-cum-science, will make sense of the history and help guide future managerial action. Recognizing that all practical action is theory-laden and that good theory underlies and improves practice, we start with theory in the first part of the book.

The two short opening chapters in this section of the book provide an overview of developments in management theory (Chapter 1), together with some discussion of key terms, especially that of 'management' (Chapter 2). The theoretical framework for Part One (Chapters 1–11) is based on the idea that management activities can best be analyzed in terms of four essential groups of activities, namely planning, organizing, motivating and controlling (decision-making being inherent in all). Whilst this approach omits some aspects of management, it nevertheless simplifies the study of the theoretical basis of the subject.

CLASSICAL THEORIES OF MANAGEMENT

This section contains two chapters which describe and comment on the main ideas of the leading classical theorists. Chapter 3 focuses on the search for principles of management and draws upon the work of Henri Fayol and then considers scientific management (Taylorism) and the scientific management school. This leads into Chapter 4 where Max Weber's idea of bureaucracy is described.

HUMAN RELATIONS AND SOCIAL PSYCHOLOGICAL THEORIES

Whereas the exponents of classical theory were principally concerned with the structure and mechanics of organizations, the human relations and social psychological theorists focused on the human factor at work. These were invariably academics – social scientists – interested in people's behaviour in the workplace. They were particularly interested in human motivation, group relationships and leadership. Chapter 5 introduces the concept of 'motivation', and describes the famous Hawthorne Studies conducted in the United States almost seventy years ago. A brief outline of the ideas of Mary Parker Follett follow, then the chapter continues with an explanation of the ideas of several early contributors to motivation theory, in the 1950s and 1960s, notably Maslow, McGregor, Herzberg, Likert, Argyris and McClelland. Chapter 6 summarizes the work of later theorists, including Vroom's so-called 'expectancy theory', and the contributions of Locke, Kelley and Skinner.

THEORIES OF LEADERSHIP AND GROUP BEHAVIOUR

This section of the book examines some leading concepts in the related fields of leadership and group behaviour. Chapter 7 describes different ways of looking at leadership, discusses the tensions between concern for the task and concern for people, and summarizes a number of important theories of leadership. Chapter 8 looks at crucial aspects of the workplace, behaviour of people in groups and examines some features of the working of groups, including the effect of competition and the task of team-building.

SYSTEMS AND CONTINGENCY APPROACHES TO MANAGEMENT THEORY

The dominance of first the Classical School and second the Human Relations/Social Psychological Schools has been overtaken by a more comprehensive approach to the study of management in organizations. This more recent approach views the organization as a system of interrelated sets of activities which enable inputs to be converted into outputs (a transformational process). The approach enables theorists to study key elements of organization in terms of their interaction with one another and with their external environment. Whereas, in the past, the explanations were in terms of structures or people, now it is possible to identify theories which seek to explain or predict organizational behaviour in a multi-dimensional way by studying people, structure, technology and environment at one and the same time. The most recent formulations of systems theories tend to be labelled contingency theories because they emphasize the need to take specific circumstances, or contingencies, into account when devising appropriate organizational and management systems. Chapter 9 introduces the concept of 'systems' as applied to organizations, and describes some of the major developments in the growth of systems theory whilst Chapter 10 summarizes developments in contingency theories.

MODERN APPROACHES TO MANAGEMENT THEORY

Part One ends with a single short chapter, outlining a number of key issues facing modern organizations, and identifies a selection of the theorists helping practising managers address these issues. All the issues to which we refer are dealt with in various chapters throughout the remainder of the book.

REFERENCES

Checkland, P. (1985) 'From Optimizing to Learning: A Development of Systems Thinking for the 1990s', *The Journal of the Operational Research Society*, 36:9 April 1985 (Sep., 1985), p. 757–767.

Section One
Introduction

CHAPTER 1
DEVELOPMENTS IN MANAGEMENT THEORY 1910–2000

Key Concepts

- Bureaucracy
- Classical approach to management
- Systems theory

Learning Outcomes   Having read this chapter, you should be able to:

- recall the classical approach to management
- identify what is meant by the bureaucratic form of organization
- explain the fundamental idea behind the human relations approach to management
- discuss the application of systems theory to business
- discuss modern approaches to management in terms of effectiveness and efficiency

1.1 INTRODUCTION

1. Prior to discussing the 'developments in management theory' we ask, what is management theory? First, let us consider what is meant by the term a theory. A theory can be a well-substantiated explanation, accepted knowledge, a collection of concepts, an expectation of what should happen or should be, an acceptable general principle or body of principles explaining phenomena, a particular conception or view of something to be done or of the method of doing it and a system of rules or principles. Theories help us to understand causes and relationships. However, theory is generally speculation. This book is about theory and practice and we may draw a distinction between the two – the former is more about a proposed explanation – in some cases theory can be thought of as a model of reality – whilst the latter is more about action, translating an idea into action – engaging in an activity. Theories are analytical tools for understanding, explaining, and making predictions about a given subject matter. In our case, that subject matter is management within the context of organizations.

2. Briefly, and for now, we may think of management as the act of getting people and transformational resources together to accomplish desired goals and objectives – management comprises planning, organizing, resourcing (encompasses the deployment and manipulation of human, financial, technological, and natural resources), leading or directing, and controlling an organization; since organizations can be viewed as systems, management can also be defined in terms of design. A more thorough explanation of what is meant by the term management is developed in the next and subsequent chapters. For now we note that there are many management theories which will be outlined in this chapter and discussed further in the remaining Part One of this book. Management theories, or approaches to management, tend to be clustered and several major categories are recognized (see Figure 1.1). Collectively, each contributes to our overall understanding of management.

3. The earliest contributors to our understanding of management theory included practising managers as well as social scientists. More recent theorists have tended to be academics or management consultants. The early theorists can be divided into two main groups – the practising managers, such as Taylor and Fayol, and the social scientists, such as Mayo and McGregor.

4. The practising managers tended to reflect upon, and theorize about, their personal experiences of management with the object of producing a set of rational principles of management which could be applied universally in order to achieve organizational efficiency. The resultant 'theories' of management were concerned primarily with the structuring of work and organizations, rather than with human motivation or organizational culture, for example. The label generally ascribed to these theorists is 'Classical', or, in some cases, 'Scientific Managers'. Their

FIGURE 1.1 **Management theory – the building blocks**

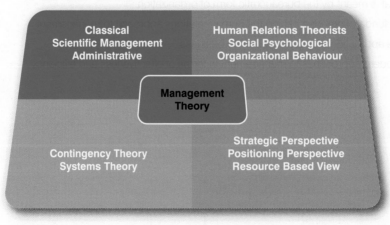

approaches were generally prescriptive, i.e. they set out what managers ought to do in order to fulfil their leadership function within their organization.

5.   The social scientists, by contrast, were academics, whose starting point was research into human behaviour in the workplace. At first most of their studies were also linked to concerns about efficiency, including the effects of physical working conditions on employees. Subsequent theorists were more interested in the human factor at work, and thus concentrated their attention on issues such as employee motivation, interpersonal communication and leadership style. Their focus was as much on individual satisfaction as on the efficient use of resources. Typical labels that have been assigned to these early social scientists include 'Human Relations Theorists' and 'Social Psychological School'. They were concerned primarily with social relationships and individual behaviour at work.

6.   Another group of social scientists, whose work was grounded in the idea of organizations as social systems, produced a more comprehensive view of the behaviour of people at work, based on the interaction of a number of variables, such as structure, tasks, technology and the environment. Later theorists of this school were given the label 'Contingency Theorists', since their ideas were based on what was appropriate in given circumstances, i.e. Where the effect on people of one variable was contingent on its relationship with one or more others.

7.   Towards the end of the 20th century, business management came to consist of branches, such as: human resource management, operations management or production management, strategic management, marketing management, financial management and information technology management – responsible for management information systems. Theorists of management, such as Mintzberg, Porter, Peters and Moss Kanter, adopted a strategic perspective, involving several key organizational factors. These have embraced such factors as organization mission, vision, culture and values, organizational structure, leadership, the external environment, and customer satisfaction (including both internal as well as external customers). Not surprisingly, these approaches build on the work that has gone before. They generally adopt a comprehensive view of organizations, and in many ways may be regarded as modern exponents of contingency theory. Their concern has been to predict which conditions are the most likely to produce organizations capable of meeting the competing demands of their various stake-holders. The contribution of the academics among them has been more objective than that of the management consultants (e.g. Peters), who are inclined to be prescriptive in their approach.

8.   Complementing the work of Porter and others, who looked for means to attain competitive (and sustainable) advantages by focussing on the organizations' external environment – competitive positions/ positioning perspective – scholars such as Barney turned to the internal environment, developing a perspective on strategy that emphasizes the importance of capabilities (sometimes known as core competences) in determining sustainable competitive advantage.

9.   In the 21st century scholars and practitioners find it increasingly difficult to subdivide management into functional categories. As an alternative, people think in terms of the various processes, tasks and objects subject to management.

1.2 CLASSICAL THEORIES

10.   The classical approach to management was primarily concerned with the structure and activities of formal, or official organization. Issues such as the division of work, the establishment of a hierarchy of authority, and the span of control were seen to be of the utmost importance in the achievement of an effective organization. The two greatest exponents of classical theories were undoubtedly Henri Fayol (1841–1925) and F.W. Taylor (1856–1915). Between them these two practising managers laid the foundations of ideas about the organization of people at work and the organization of work itself. At first these ideas were developed

Classical approach to management The organization is thought of in terms of its purpose and formal structure and this approach aims to identify how methods of working can improve productivity. Emphasis is placed on the planning of work, the technical requirements of the organization, principles of management and the assumption of rational and logical behaviour

separately, Fayol in France and Taylor in the United States. By the 1930s their work was being promoted and developed by writers such as L.F. Urwick and E.F.L. Brech on both sides of the Atlantic. The work of these contributors to classical theories of management is described in Chapter 3.

1.3 BUREAUCRACY

Bureaucracy Describes a form of business administration based on formal rational rules and procedures designed to govern work practices and organization activities through a hierarchical system of authority (see also standardization, centralization, formalization, specialization).

11.   While Fayol and Taylor were grappling with the problems of management, a German sociologist, Max Weber (1864–1924), was developing a theory of authority structures in which he identified a form of organization to which he gave the name 'bureaucracy'. The distinguishing features of a bureaucracy were a definition of roles within a hierarchy, where job-holders were appointed on merit, were subject to rules and were expected to behave impartially. Weber's ideas and their impact upon modern organization theory are discussed in more detail in Chapter 4.

1.4 HUMAN RELATIONS AND SOCIAL PSYCHOLOGICAL SCHOOLS

12.   The fundamental idea behind the human relations approach to management is that people's needs are the decisive factor in achieving organizational effectiveness. The leading figure of human relations was Professor Elton Mayo, whose association with the so-called 'Hawthorne Studies' between 1927 and 1932 provided an enormous impetus to considerations of the human factor at work. A summary of the Hawthorne Studies and their impact on industrial psychology is contained in Chapter 5.

13.   Many of the issues raised by Mayo and his colleagues were taken up in the post-war years by American social psychologists. An early major influence here was Abraham Maslow's work on motivation, based on a hierarchy of human needs, ranging from basic physiological needs (food, sleep, etc) to higher psychological needs, such as self-fulfilment. Other important contributors included McGregor, Argyris, Likert and Herzberg. The work of these theorists and the results of their research are covered in Chapter 5. Later theorists of motivation (e.g. Vroom) are summarized in Chapter 6.

1.5 SYSTEMS AND CONTINGENCY APPROACHES

14.   By the late 1960s another group of theories began to challenge the dominance of human relations and psychology. These were theories that viewed organizations as complex systems of people, tasks and technology. The early work on this approach was conducted by British researchers from the Tavistock Institute of Human Relations, who, despite their title, recognized that human or social factors alone were not the most important consideration in achieving organizational effectiveness. They recognized that organizations were part of a larger environment within which they interacted and in particular were affected by technical and economic factors just as much as social factors. They coined the phrase 'open socio-technical system' to describe their concept of a business enterprise. An 'open' social system is one that interacts with

its environment, e.g. a commercial enterprise, a 'closed' social system is self-contained, e.g. a strict monastic community. This approach is described in greater detail in Chapter 9.

15.   Arising out of the open systems approach is an essentially pragmatic 'theory' which argues that there is no one theory at present which can guarantee the effectiveness of an organization. Management has to select a mix of theories which seem to meet the needs of the organization and its internal and external pressures at a particular period in its life. This has been termed a contingency approach to management. Notable exponents of this approach are Pugh and colleagues in the United Kingdom, and Lawrence and Lorsch in the United States. A summary of their work appears in Chapter 10.

> **Open system** Considers the organization's structures, systems, processes and external environment to be interrelated and able to affect one another

1.6 MODERN APPROACHES TO MANAGEMENT

16.   The emphasis in management theorising in the latter part of the twentieth century was on organizational effectiveness, with its focus on strategic issues. This emphasis implies more than just efficiency, which is concerned with 'doing things right'. Effectiveness is primarily a question of 'doing the right things' even more than performing them efficiently. Thus, the concerns of such theorists have been topics such as developing strategic mission and implanting organizational values/culture (i.e. doing the right things) as well as managing change, promoting quality management, achieving organizational excellence, facilitating personal empowerment and optimizing stakeholder relationships. Some of the leading ideas in these areas of interest are described in Chapter 11.

> **Efficiency** Doing things right

> **Effectiveness** Doing right things

CONCLUSION

17.   The task of management is carried out in the context of an organization. Over the past century or so the development of coherent theories to explain organizational performance has moved away from approaches that relied purely on a consideration of structural or human relations issues, in favour of more comprehensive perspectives. Early ideas about management were put forward at a time when organizations were thought of as machines requiring efficient systems to enable them to function effectively. The emphasis, therefore, was on the efficient use of resources, especially human resources, in the service of a mechanistic model of organizations. Later theorists modified this approach by taking account of social and environmental as well as technical factors in the workplace. Their emphasis was as much on employee satisfaction as on organizational effectiveness. Modern approaches to the analysis of organizational effectiveness do not necessarily rule out the ideas put forward by earlier theorists, but emphasize that they must be evaluated in the context of an organization's overriding need for flexibility in responding to change in its external and internal environment, in order to meet the competing demands of all its various stakeholders – customers, suppliers, employees and shareholders, etc.

QUESTIONS

1   Discuss the developments in Management Theory, contrasting and evaluating various approaches put forward in the twentieth and twenty first century.

2   In your own words explain what Management Theory is. In your answer you should identify major contributors to a theory of management and discuss the origin of their contribution. You should contrast different ideas about management that have evolved over time.

3   Critically compare the classical with the human relations approach to management.

4   Discuss management's preoccupation with effectiveness and efficiency. Evaluate the importance of effectiveness and efficiency to the scientific managers (bureaucrats), systems/contingency theorists and contemporary managers – which of the concepts features greatest in their theories?

USEFUL WEBSITES

The Institute of Management: **www.managers.org.uk**

Management Guru: **www.mgmtguru.com/mgt301/ 301_Lecture1Page2.htm**
Brief history of early management thinking

CHAPTER 2
DEFINITIONS OF MANAGEMENT

2.1 INTRODUCTION

Organization A group of people with a common purpose who work together to achieve shared goals (see formal organization and informal organization)

1.   In the previous chapter we provided a tentative definition for management. Not unexpectedly, the variety of approaches to the theoretical background of management has produced several versions of what is meant by such key words as 'management' and 'organization'. This chapter looks at the most typical interpretations of these words, and offers some explanations.

2.2 THE MEANING OF MANAGEMENT

Management Coordinated activities (forecasting, planning, deciding, organizing, commanding) to direct and control an organization

2.   There is no generally accepted definition of 'management' as an activity, although the classic definition is still held to be that of Henri Fayol. His general statement about management, in many ways, still remains valid after almost a century and has only been adapted by more recent writers, as shown below:

> 'To manage is to forecast and plan, to organize, to command, to coordinate and to control.'
>
> *Fayol (1916)*

> 'Management is a social process... the process consists of... planning, control, coordination and motivation.'
>
> *Brech (1957)*

> 'Managing is an operational process initially best dissected by analyzing the managerial functions...The five essential managerial functions (are): planning, organizing, staffing, directing and leading and controlling.'
>
> *Koontz and O'Donnell (1984)*

> 'Five areas of management constitute the essence of proactive performance in our chaotic world: (1) an obsession with responsiveness to customers, (2) constant innovation in all areas of the firm, (3) partnership – the wholesale participation of and gain sharing with all people connected with the organization, (4) leadership that loves change (instead of fighting it) and instils and shares an inspiring vision, and (5) control by means of simple support systems aimed at measuring the "right stuff" for today's environment.'
>
> *Peters (1988)*

The definitions proposed by Brech, Koontz and O'Donnell represent changes of emphasis rather than principle. For example, Fayol's use of the term 'command' is dropped in favour of 'motivation' (Brech), or 'directing and leading' (Koontz & O'Donnell). Tom Peters' view of management, by comparison, shifts the emphasis away from describing what management is about and stresses what it is that managers need to do. Nevertheless, even his enthusiastic prescriptions for dealing with chaos are tempered by references to 'participation' (i.e. motivating), 'leadership' and 'control'.

3.   It has to be recognized that the above definitions are extremely broad. Basically, what they are saying is that 'management' is a process enabling organizations to set and achieve their objectives by planning, organizing and controlling their resources, including gaining the commitment of their employees (motivation). Several writers (e.g. Stewart, Mintzberg) have attempted to move away from this generalized approach towards a more detailed and behaviour-oriented analysis of what managers actually do.

4.   Mintzberg (1973), for example, in reporting his major study of managerial work, highlights a number of key roles appearing regularly in such work. He describes these roles as 'organized sets of behaviours identified with a position', and gathers them into three main groupings, as follows:

Interpersonal roles	Informational roles	Decisional roles
Figurehead	Monitor	Entrepreneur
Leader	Disseminator	Disturbance handler
Liaison	Spokesman	Resource allocator
		Negotiator

Recognizable though these ten role-models may be, they are still defined very generally, and there is the additional problem that some of them apply equally to non-managerial jobs (e.g. Monitor, negotiator).

5.   Stewart (1994), in reviewing efforts to define management, shows how difficult it is to produce a sufficiently focused and yet comprehensive answer. She points out that in fact there is not just one but three categories of management position: the first level entails a direct responsibility for other people, the second entails a responsibility for other managers and the third entails responsibility for multiple functions (the 'general manager'). In each of these situations the job-holder is faced with some crucial concerns:

–   learning what it means to be a manager at that level (i.e.what role has to be played),

–   learning how to improve the ability to judge others (because one is going to have to rely on others as work and tasks are delegated),

–   learning to understand more about one's own capacities and weaknesses, and

–   learning how to cope with stress.

6.   Stewart considers that managerial jobs, in particular, are affected by the extent of, and the relationship between, the following:

–   the core of the job (i.e. the personal responsibilities of the jobholder which cannot be delegated), which she terms the 'demands' of the job,

–   the 'constraints' of the job (e.g. limited resources), and

–   the 'choices' available to the job-holder by way of different work from another person (e.g. different amounts of time spent on operational as opposed to strategic matters).

In her research Stewart found that managerial jobs could vary considerably in the size and impact of each of these three factors.

7.   The search for a comprehensive definition of 'management' that is not over-generalized still proceeds. In the meantime, this book deals with management as a collection of activities involving planning, organizing, motivating and controlling (see below). This approach is helpful in enabling the work of management to be analyzed for study purposes (management, as a concept, is also considered in Chapters 3 and 46).

2.3 ADMINISTRATION

8.   At this point it will be helpful to distinguish the concept of 'management' from that of 'administration'. At one time these concepts were more or less inter-changeable. Fayol himself

used the French word administration to mean what we now would understand as 'management', in his original treatise on the subject, and so did Lyndall F. Urwick (see next chapter). For the last forty years however, the term 'management' has been understood as encompassing much more than 'administration', which has tended to embrace the narrower process of developing and maintaining procedures, e.g. As in office administration. That is to say 'administration' is seen primarily as an aspect of organizing. 'Management', by comparison, is also concerned with planning, controlling and motivating staff.

2.4 WHAT IS ORGANIZATION AND WHAT IS AN ORGANIZATION?

9.   Whatever view is preferred concerning the definition of management, it is clear that it can only be discussed within the context of an organization. Brech (1965) once described organizations as 'the framework of the management process'. It must be recognized, however, that this 'framework' can be described in several different ways. The first distinction is between the use of the word 'organization' to describe the process of organizing, and its use to describe the social entity formed by a group of people. Organization structure is dealt with later (Chapter 22).

10.   As yet there is no widely accepted definition of an organization. Nevertheless, as the following quotations suggest, there are some commonly accepted features of organizations such as purpose, people and structure.

'Organizations are intricate human strategies designed to achieve certain objectives.'

Argyris (1960)

'Since organizations are systems of behaviour designed to enable humans and their machines to accomplish goals, organizational form must be a joint function of human characteristics and the nature of the task environment.'

Simon (1976)

'Organizations are systems of inter-dependent human beings.'

Pugh (1990)

Formal organization The collection of work groups that has been consciously designed by management to maximize efficiency and achieve organizational goals

'Organizations are set up to achieve purposes that individuals cannot achieve on their own. Organizations then provide a means of working with others to achieve goals ... likely to be determined by whoever is in the best position to influence them.... A key characteristic of organizations is their complexity.'

Stewart (1994)

Informal organization The network of relationships between members of an organization that form of their own accord on the basis of common interests and friendship

11.   An organization, then is a group of people with a common purpose who work together to achieve shared goals. The collection of work groups that has been consciously designed by management to maximize efficiency and achieve organizational goals is referred to as the formal organization (see Chapters 4 and 22). However, scholars also recognize the informal organization, the network of relationships between members of an organization which form of their own accord, on the basis of common interests and friendship. The study of the structure, functioning

and performance of organizations and the behaviour of groups and individuals within them is often termed organization theory (see also organizational behaviour).

12.   Like discussions about management theory, approaches to organization theory tend to follow the pattern of classical, human relations and systems perspectives. The classical approach concentrates attention on the organization structure and all that is required to sustain it (organization charts, procedures, communication channels, etc). Brech and Urwick are good examples of writers who see organizations in this way. The human relations approach, by comparison, says, in effect, that people are the organization. Therefore it is vital to give first consideration to issues of group and individual needs before such other issues as structure, authority levels, and decision-making, for example. Job enrichment is a typical example of a human relations approach to organizational design. The systems approach aims to describe organizations in terms of open systems, responding to external and internal influences in developing, and ultimately achieving, their objectives. Key areas of attention for systems theorists include the relationship between formal and informal (or unofficial) organizations, the external environment, the question of boundaries, the organization's culture and the impact of technology. Finally, the contingency approach aims to develop systems theory by balancing a number of key organizational variables within a given context (both external and internal). This latter approach is the one that is adapted by practically every modern theorist in their search for the optimum organizational profile – structure, strategy, staffing, etc.

2.5 RELATIONSHIP BETWEEN MANAGEMENT AND ORGANIZATION THEORY

13.   The impact of the behavioural sciences on the study of people at work has led to the ascendancy of organization theory over purely management theory. Management is no longer seen as the controlling factor in work organizations. Instead it is seen as a function of organizations. Its task is to enable the organization's purposes to be defined and fulfilled by adapting to change and maintaining a workable balance between the various and frequently conflicting pressures at work in the organization.

14.   Handy (1993), sums up the new relationship very neatly. In a discussion on the role of the manager, he suggests that the key variables a manager has to grapple with are:

- people
- work and structures
- systems and procedures.

Organization theory The study of the structure, functioning and performance of organizations and the behaviour of groups and individuals within them (see also organizational behaviour)

Organizational behaviour The study of the structure, functioning and performance of organizations and the behaviour of groups and individuals within them

Human relations approach A school of management thought which emphasizes the importance of social processes at work (emphasizes the informal organization)

Classical approach The organization is thought of in terms of its purpose and formal structure and this approach aims to identify how methods of working can improve productivity. Emphasis is placed on the planning of work, the technical requirements of the organization, principles of management and the assumption of rational and logical behaviour

Systems approach A management approach which is focused on the total work of the organization and the interrelationships of structure and behaviour and the range of variables within the organization. The organization is viewed within its total environment and emphasizes the importance of multiple channels in interaction

Contingency approach An extension of the systems approach that implies organizational variables (e.g. strategy, structure and systems) and its success or performance is dependent upon environmental influences (forces). There is, therefore, no one best way to structure or manage organizations; rather it must be dependent upon the contingencies of the situation

These variables cannot be dealt with in isolation but within the constraints of an environment in which Handy sees three crucial components:

– the goals of the organization

– the technology available

– the culture of the organization (its values, beliefs, etc.)

All six factors mentioned interact with each other and change in one of them will inevitably lead to change in one or more others. To manage successfully is to balance these factors in a way that meets the needs of the organization at a particular period in time, which essentially represents a contingency approach to management.

Systems theory The study of the behaviour and interactions within and between systems

2.6 THE PROCESS OF MANAGEMENT

15.   The systems approach to organizations (see Chapter 9) is based on the three major elements of inputs, throughputs/conversion (transformation) and outputs. The process of management is concerned with all three of these elements and especially with the transformation processes of organizations. As Drucker (1955) first described it, over fifty years ago, management is concerned with the 'systematic organization of economic resources' and its task is to make these resources productive. The following paragraphs introduce the idea of management as a transformation process, describe its principal elements and emphasize that management is oriented towards results as well as towards action.

16.   Management is not an activity that exists in its own right. It is rather a description of a variety of activities carried out by those members of organizations whose role is that of a 'manager', i.e. someone who either has formal responsibility for the work of one or more persons in the organization or who is accountable for specialist advisory duties in support of key management activities. These activities have generally been grouped in terms of planning, organizing, motivating and controlling activities. These groupings describe activities which indicate broadly what managers do in practice, primarily in terms of their inputs. They apply to supervisory and junior management positions as well as to middle and senior management roles.

17.   The groupings of management activities can be summarized as follows:

– planning: deciding the objectives or goals of the organization and preparing how to meet them

– organizing: determining activities and allocating responsibilities for the achievement of plans; coordinating activities and responsibilities into an appropriate structure

– motivating: meeting the social and psychological needs of employees in the fulfilment of organizational goals

– controlling: monitoring and evaluating activities, and providing corrective mechanisms.

These traditional groupings – the POMC approach – are the ones chosen to represent the framework for this book. It is appreciated that they do not tell the whole story about what constitutes management, but they are a convenient way of describing most of the key aspects of managerial work in practice. Inherent in each activity is decision making (Chapter 19).

18.   Before moving on to look at each of these groupings in detail, it will be useful to consider some of the shortcomings of the POMC approach, in order to make allowance for it in the chapters that follow. As stated above, the approach focuses on the actions (inputs) of managers

rather than on results (outputs). It also ignores the role elements of a managerial job, and does not take into account the different levels of management job.

19.   Firstly, let us turn to the question of results. One particularly influential writer on the subject of managerial effectiveness, Professor Bill Reddin of the University of New Brunswick, considers it essential for the job of management to be judged on output rather than by input, and by achievements rather than by activities. In his book *Managerial Effectiveness* (1970) he argues that we tend to confuse efficiency with effectiveness. Efficiency is the ratio of output to input. However, although 100% efficiency can be obtained by high output in relation to high input, the same result can be achieved where both output and input are low. Effectiveness, as Reddin defines it, is the extent to which a manager achieves the output requirements of his position. This assumes that the outputs have been identified and made measurable. Examples of differences between 'efficient' managers and 'effective' manages, according to Reddin, are that 'efficient' managers seek to solve problems and reduce costs, whereas 'effective' managers seek to produce creative alternatives and increase profits. On this basis, the POMC approach is more concerned with efficiency than 'effectiveness'.

20.   It has to be recognized that the POMC approach is essentially a leader-centred approach to management. It does not take account of the variety of roles that managers can be called upon to play. We saw above that Mintzberg's analysis of managerial roles identified key roles, which clearly encompass more than just planning, organizing, motivating and controlling. Other crucial, albeit lower-key roles, include liaison activities and disturbance-handling, for example. Kotter (1996) takes the view that, where change is concerned, success is mostly down to leadership rather than management. The former, in his view, enables change to happen, often with long-term results. The latter enables predictability and order, and can produce short-term results. Kotter believes there is too much emphasis on managing organizations, and too little on providing them with effective leadership.

2.7 PLANNING

21.   **Planning** is an activity which involves decisions about ends (organizational aims/objectives), means (plans), conduct (policies) and results. It is an activity taking place against the background of (1) the organization's external environment, and (2) the organization's internal strengths and weaknesses. Planning can be long term, as in strategic and corporate planning, or short term, as in the setting of annual departmental budgets. Long term usually implies a time horizon of about five years, although this may be ten or twenty years in certain industries (oil extraction, pharmaceuticals, etc). Short term can be any period from the immediate future (crisis management) up to about one year. In summary, planning is the formalization of what is intended to happen at some time in the future; concerns actions taken prior to an event, typically formulating goals and objectives and then arranging for resources to be provided in order to achieve a desired outcome. Chapters 16–21 describe the major aspects of planning.

Planning The formalization of what is intended to happen at some time in the future; concerns actions taken prior to an event, typically formulating goals and objectives and then arranging for resources to be provided in order to achieve a desired outcome

2.8 ORGANIZING

22.   Plans have to be translated into operation – determining activities and allocating responsibilities for the achievement of plans; coordinating activities and responsibilities into an appropriate structure. This involves detailed organization and coordination of tasks and the human and material resources needed to carry

Organizing Determining activities and allocating responsibilities for the achievement of plans; coordinating activities and responsibilities into an appropriate structure

them out. A key issue here is that of formal communications. Various aspects of organizing are dealt with in Chapters 22–27.

2.9 MOTIVATING

Motivating Activating the driving force within individuals by which they attempt to achieve some organizational goal

23.   Motivating is about activating the driving force within individuals by which they attempt to achieve some organizational goal. We consider some of the most significant theories of motivation in Chapters 5 and 6. The motivating activities of managers, however, are essentially practical in their intent for, in setting plans and executing them, managers have to gain the commitment of their employees. This is primarily a question of leadership, or style of management, and Chapter 7 outlines the principal options available to managers in practice.

2.10 CONTROLLING

Controlling Ensuring plans are properly executed; assuring the organization functions as planned

24.   Controlling ensures plans are properly executed; assuring the organization functions as planned; activities are concerned essentially with measuring progress and correcting deviations. The basic functions of control are to establish standards of performance, to measure actual performance against standards and to take corrective actions where appropriate. Control activities act as the feedback mechanism for all managerial activities. Their use is, therefore, crucial to the success of management. Key aspects of control are discussed in Chapters 28–30.

CONCLUSION

25.   In this chapter we explained what is meant by 'management' and 'organization'. There is no generally accepted definition of 'management' but we consider it to be coordinated activities (forecasting, planning, deciding, organizing, commanding) to direct and control an organization. We distinguished the concept of 'management' from that of 'administration', recognizing that the term 'management' has been understood as encompassing much more than 'administration', which has tended to embrace the narrower process of developing and maintaining procedures, e.g. as in office administration. That is to say 'administration' is seen primarily as an aspect of organizing. 'Management', by comparison, is also concerned with planning, controlling and motivating staff. Similarly there is no widely-accepted definition of an organization. Nevertheless, there are some commonly-accepted features of organizations such as purpose, people and structure. An organization, is a group of people with a common purpose who work together to achieve shared goals. The collection of work groups that has been consciously designed by management to maximize efficiency and achieve organizational goals is referred to as the formal organization.

QUESTIONS

1 What do you understand by the terms 'management' and 'organization'? Explain, using your own words.

2 Broadly in what ways does a classical approach to organizations differ from a human relations approach?

3 What are the key organizational variables that might confront a manager in a typical organization? Which are more likely to need frequent revision, and why?

4 What is the advantage to the student of management of considering managerial roles rather than managerial functions in analyzing the process of management?

5 Why do you think the current emphasis on satisfying the customer leads organizations to adopt particular management priorities?

6 Organizations employ various resources (e.g. finance, raw materials, people, plant and equipment) in order to achieve objectives. Discuss the role of management in an organization and assess the relative importance of management as a resource. (ICSA MPP)

7 Synthesize and defend (argue) your own definition of management. In your answer you should draw on the work of leading management scholars from the past century.

USEFUL WEBSITES

HRM Guide: **www.hrmguide.co.uk/history/classical_ organization_theory_modified.htm** Classical organization theory – Henri Fayol

Institute of Business Consulting: **www.ibconsulting.org.uk/** The Institute of Business Consulting is the professional body for all consultants and business advisers.

Chartered Management Institute: **www.managers.org.uk/ listing_with_description_1.aspx?id=10:255&id= 10:63&id=10** Certificate in Management Consulting

Department of Business Innovation & Skills: **www.bis.gov.uk**

VIDEO CASES

Now take a look at the online video cases – visit the companion website to work through real world business problems associated with the concepts presented within this chapter.

113 Introduction to PoM – Management
Through its leaders and managers, organizations seek to do the right thing (effectiveness) as reflected in the organizational

mission and goals and to do those things efficiently, thus keeping costs to a minimum. In doing so, the organization will achieve its purpose. In this case study, we ask what management is, giving consideration to the types of manager and management functions.

REFERENCES

Argyris, C. (1960) 'Understanding Organizational Behaviour', Tavistock.

Brech, E. F. L. (1957) 'The Principles and Practice of Management',

Brech, E. F. L. (1965) 'Organization – the Framework of Management', Ed. 2. Longman.

Drucker, P. (1955) 'The Practice of Management', Heinemann.

Fayol, H. (1949) 'General and Industrial Management', Pitman.

Handy, C. B. (1999) 'Understanding Organizations', Ed. 4. Penguin.

Handy, C. B. (2002) 'What's a Business For?' Harvard Business Review, Dec 2002, Vol. 80 Issue 12, p. 49–56.

Koontz, H. and O'Donnell, C. (1984) 'Management', Ed. 8. McGraw-Hill.

Kotter, J. (1996) 'Leading Change', Harvard Business School Press.

Mintzberg, H. (1973) 'The Nature of Managerial Work', Harper & Row.

Peteraf, M. A. (1993) 'The Cornerstones of Competitive Advantage: A Resource-Based View', Strategic Management Journal, Vol. 14, No. 3. (Mar., 1993), p. 179–191.

Peters, T. (1988) 'Thriving on Chaos – Handbook for a Management Revolution', Macmillan.

Pugh, D. S. (1997) 'Organization Theory', Ed. 4. Penguin.

Reddin, W. (1970) 'Managerial Effectiveness', McGraw Hill.

Simon, H. A. (1976) 'Administrative Behaviour', Ed. 3. Collier Macmillan.

Stewart, R. (1994) 'Managing Today and Tomorrow', Macmillan.

Section Two
Classical Theories of Management

CHAPTER 3
THE SEARCH FOR PRINCIPLES OF MANAGEMENT

Key Concepts

- Management, principles of
- Scientific management
- Span of control
- Specialization

Learning Outcomes   Having read this chapter, you should be able to:

- identify the general principles of management defined by classical theorists
- evaluate the principles of Scientific Management
- evaluate Urwick's principles of management

1. The search for universally applicable principles of management began in the industrial heartlands of Europe and America in the last years of the nineteenth century. This chapter firstly describes the most important ideas on management proposed by the Frenchman, Henri Fayol, at the beginning of the twentieth century. Particular attention is paid to his definition of management, and to his general principles of management, which may then be compared with similar principles proposed by other classical writers. The chapter continues with an account of Taylor's ideas concerning 'scientific management' in the workplace, together with some brief references to other individuals sharing his viewpoint. The chapter ends with summaries of the ideas of two latter-day scientific managers, Urwick and Brech, who developed many of the ideas of Fayol and Taylor in the period following the Second World War.

Scientific management A school of classical management theory, dating from the early twentieth century, based on the application of work study techniques to the design and organization of work in order to maximize output – increased productivity (to find the 'one best way' of performing each task); it is a form of job design theory and practice which stresses short, repetitive work cycles; detailed, prescribed task sequences; a separation of task conception from task execution; and motivation based on economic rewards (see also Taylorism, after Frederick Taylor who was influential in founding its principles)

3.1 HENRI FAYOL

2. Henri Fayol (1841–1925), the celebrated French industrialist and theorist, began his working life as a young mining engineer at the age of nineteen. He spent his entire working life with the same company, rising to Managing Director at the age of forty-seven, and only retiring after his seventy-seventh birthday! Under his leadership the company grew and prospered despite its near-bankrupt state when he took over. His entrepreneurial successes won him considerable fame and popularity, and when, in 1916, he published his major work on management, he ensured himself a place in the annals of industrial history.

3. The publication of 'Administration Industrielle et Generale' in 1916 brought to light the distillation of a lifetime's experience of managerial work. In one English translation by Constance Storrs, the foreword was provided by none other than Urwick (see below). Urwick questioned the appropriateness of the title, in which the French 'administration' had been translated as 'management'. His fear was that with such a title, Fayol's work would be seen as relevant only to industry, whereas, in Urwick's view, it was just as applicable to central and local government as well. History has shown that he need not have worried, since Fayol's ideas have had a major influence on the world of organizations.

3.2 FAYOL'S DEFINITION OF MANAGEMENT

4. Fayol prefaced his famous definition of management by stating what he considered to be the key activities of any industrial undertaking. He outlined six such key activities, as follows:

1) Technical activities, e.g. production.

2) Commercial activities, e.g. buying and selling.

3) Financial activities, e.g. securing capital.

4) Security activities, e.g. safeguarding property.

5) Accounting activities, e.g. providing financial information.

6) Managerial activities, e.g. planning and organizing.

Fayol accepted that the first five were already sufficiently well known, but recognized at the outset that the sixth group of activities would require further explanation for his readers. Whilst the other activities were all interdependent to some extent, there was no single one which was concerned with broad planning and resourcing. It was vitally necessary to isolate these last mentioned activities, said Fayol, and it is these to which he gave the name 'managerial'.

5.   To manage, said Fayol, is to 'forecast and plan, to organize, to command, to coordinate and to control'. He saw forecasting and planning as looking to the future and drawing up a plan of action. Organizing was seen in structural terms, and commanding was described as 'maintaining activity among the personnel'. Coordinating was seen as essentially a unifying activity. Controlling meant ensuring that things happen in accordance with established policies and practice. It is important to note that Fayol did not see managerial activities as exclusively belonging to the management. Such activities are part and parcel of the total activities of an undertaking. Having said this, it is equally important to point out that Fayol's general principles of management take a perspective which essentially looks at organizations from the top downwards. Nevertheless, they do have the merit of taking a comprehensive view of the role of management in organizations. Thus, Fayol's analysis has more far-reaching implications than Taylor's ideas on scientific management, which were centred on the shop floor.

Management Coordinated activities (forecasting, planning, deciding, organizing, commanding) to direct and control an organization

3.3 FAYOL'S PRINCIPLES OF MANAGEMENT

Management, principles of 14 elements of what being a manager involved, developed by Fayol

6.   In his book Fayol lists fourteen so-called 'principles of management'. These are the precepts which he applied the most frequently during his working life. He emphasized that these principles were not absolutes but capable of adaptation, according to need. He did not claim that his list was exhaustive, but only that it served him well in the past. The fourteen 'principles' listed below in Figure 3.1 are given in the order set out by Fayol, but the comments are a summary of his thinking on each point.

7.   Fayol's General Principles have been adopted by later followers of the classical school, such as Urwick and Brech. Present day theorists, however, would not find much of substance in these precepts. From our present day viewpoint, the following general comments may be made:

A The references to division of work, scalar chain, unity of command and centralization, for example, are descriptive of the kind of formal organization that has come to be known as bureaucracy. Fayol, in true classical fashion, was emphasizing the structural nature of organizations.

B Issues such as individual versus general interests, remuneration and equity were considered very much from the point of view of a paternalistic management. Today, questions concerning fairness, or the bonafide conflict of interests between groups, have to be worked out jointly between management and organized labour, often with third party involvement by the State.

Rational model of organization
A perspective which holds that behaviour within an organization is not random, but that goals are clear and choices are made on the basis of reason in a logical way. In making decisions, the objective is defined, alternatives are identified and the option with the greatest chance of achieving the objective is selected

C Although emphasizing the hierarchical aspects of the business enterprise, Fayol was well aware of the need to avoid an excessively mechanistic approach towards employees. Thus references to initiative and esprit de corps indicated his sensitivity to people's needs as individuals and as groups. Such issues are of major interest to theorists today, the key difference being that whereas Fayol saw these issues in the context of a rational model of organization structure, the modern organization development specialist sees them in terms of adapting structures and changing people's behaviour to achieve the best fit between the organization and its customers.

FIGURE 3.1 Fayol's principles of management

1. Division of work	Reduces the span of attention or effort for any one person or group. Develops practice and familiarity.
2. Authority	The right to give orders. Should not be considered without reference to responsibility.
3. Discipline	Outward marks of respect in accordance with formal or informal agreements between firm and its employees.
4. Unity of command	One man one superior!
5. Unity of direction	One head and one plan for a group of activities with the same objective.
6. Subordination of individual interests to general interest	The interest of one individual or one group should not prevail over the general good. This is a difficult area of the management.
7. Remuneration	Pay should be fair to both the employee and the firm.
8. Centralisation	Is always present to a greater or lesser extent, depending on the size of company and quality of its managers.
9. Scalar chain	The line of authority from top to bottom of the organisation.
10. Order	A place for everything and everything in its place; the right man in the right place.
11. Equity	A combination of kindliness and justice towards employees.
12. Stability of tenure of personnel	Employees need to be given time to settle into their jobs, even though this maybe a lengthy period in the case of managers.
13. Initiative	Within the limits of authority and discipline, all levels of staff should be encouraged to show initiative.
14. Esprit de corps	Harmony is a great strength to an organization; teamwork should be encouraged.

D Fayol was the first to achieve a genuine theory of management based on a number of principles which could be passed on to others. Many of these principles have been absorbed into modern organizations. Their effect on organizational effectiveness has been subject to increasing criticism over the last twenty years, however, mainly because such principles were not designed to cope with modern conditions of rapid change, flatter structures and increased employee participation in the decision-making processes of the organization.

3.4 TAYLOR AND SCIENTIFIC MANAGEMENT

8. The following paragraphs summarize the key ideas of the pioneers of 'Scientific Management' –Taylor, Gilbreth and Gantt – and comment on the main consequences of their work.
9. Frederick Winslow Taylor (1856–1915), like Fayol, was one of the early practical manager-theorists. Born in Boston, Massachusetts, in 1856, he spent the greater part of his life working on the problems of achieving greater efficiency on the shop floor (the concept of efficiency was also considered in Chapter 1). The solutions he came up with were based directly on his own experience at work, initially as a shop-floor worker

Efficiency Doing things right

himself and later as a manager. His career began as an apprentice in engineering. Having served his time, whowever, he moved to the Midvale Steel Company, where, in the course of eleven years, he rose from labourer to shop superintendent. It was during this time that Taylor's ideas of 'scientific management' were born. In 1889 he left Midvale to work for the Bethlehem Steel Company, where he consolidated his ideas and conducted some of his most famous experiments in improving labour productivity. Taylor was keen to pass on his ideas to others, which he achieved through his writings, most notably 'The Principles of Scientific Management' published in 1911. After his death, his major works were collected together and published as 'Scientific Management' in 1947. He did not meet Henri Fayol and it is possible that he did not know of Fayol's analysis of management.

Productivity Economic measure of efficiency that summarizes the value of outputs relative to the value of inputs used to create them

3.5 THE SETTING FOR SCIENTIFIC MANAGEMENT

10.   The last twenty years of the nineteenth century were a time for facing up to the often ugly realities of factory life. From the employers' point of view, efficiency of working methods was the dominant issue. The gathering pace of the industrial revolution in the Western world had given rise to new factories, new plant and machinery; labour was plentiful. The problem was how to organize all these elements into efficient and profitable operations.

11.   It was against this background that Taylor developed his ideas. He was passionately interested in the efficiency of working methods. At an early stage he realized that the key to such problems lay in the systematic analysis of work. Experience, both as a worker and as a manager, had convinced him that few, if any, workers put more than the minimal effort into their daily work. He described this tendency as 'soldiering', which he subdivided into 'natural' soldiering, i.e. humans' natural tendency to take things easy, and 'systematic' soldiering, i.e. the deliberate and organized restriction of the workrate by the employees. The reasons for soldiering appeared to Taylor to arise from three issues:

● fear of unemployment

● fluctuations in earnings from piece-rate systems

● rule-of-thumb methods permitted by management.

Taylor's answer to these issues was to practise 'scientific management'.

3.6 THE PRINCIPLES OF SCIENTIFIC MANAGEMENT

12.   Taylor recognized that the measures he was proposing would appear to be more than just a new method – they would be revolutionary! He stated at the outset that 'scientific management' would require a complete mental revolution on the part of both management and workers.

13.   In its application to management, the scientific approach required the following steps:

● develop a science for each operation to replace opinion and rule-of-thumb

● determine accurately from the science the correct time and method for each job

- set up a suitable organization to take all **responsibility** from the workers except that of actual job performance

- select and train the workers

- accept that management itself be governed by the science developed for each operation and surrender arbitrary power over workers, i.e. cooperate with them.

> **Responsibility** An obligation placed on a person who occupies a certain position in the organization structure to perform a task, function or assignment

14.   Taylor saw that if changes were to take place at the shopfloor level, then facts would have to be substituted for opinion and guesswork. This would be done by studying the jobs of a sample of especially skilled workers, noting each operation and timing it with a stop-watch. All unnecessary movements could then be eliminated in order to produce the best method of doing a job. This best method would become the standard to be used for all like jobs. This analytical approach has come to be known as Work Study, the series of techniques now utilized all over the world (see Chapter 40).

15.   In Taylor's time the most usual practice at the work organization level was for the management to leave working methods to the initiative of the workers – what Taylor called rule-of-thumb. His suggestion that managers should take over that role was certainly new. Not only that, it was controversial, for he was deliberately reducing the scope of an individual's job. Contemporaries said it turned people into automatons. Taylor argued that the average worker preferred to be given a definite task with clear-cut standards. The outcome for future generations was the separation of planning and controlling from the doing, or the fragmentation of work. McGregor's Theory X assumptions about people (see Chapter 5) are essentially a description of the managerial style produced by Taylor's ideas. In the last decade, ideas such as job enrichment and work design have been translated into practice precisely to combat the fragmentation effects of years of Taylorism. Another comment of Taylorism is that the gradual deskilling of work has been accompanied by a rise in educational standards, thus tending to increase worker-frustration even further.

> **McGregor's Theory X and Theory Y** Theory X managers consider workers as lazy and having to be driven to achieve performance. Theory Y managers consider workers enjoy the experience of work and have a desire to achieve high performance. McGregor believed that managers managed their staff on the basis of these beliefs, irrespective of actual employee approach to work

16.   Taylor felt that everyone should benefit from scientific management – workers as well as managers. He disagreed with the way most piece-rate systems were operated in his day, as the practice was for management to reduce the rates if workers earnings went up beyond an acceptable level. Taylor's view was that, having measured scientifically the workers' jobs and set rates accordingly, then efficient workers should be rewarded for their productivity without limit. The difficulty for most managers was that they lacked Taylor's expertise in measuring times and had to resort to arbitrary reduction in rates where measurements had been loose.

> **Taylorism** An approach to management based on the theories of F.W. Taylor. See also scientific management

17.   So far as the workers were concerned, scientific management required them to:

- stop worrying about the division of the fruits of production between wages and profits

- share in the prosperity of the firm by working in the correct way and receiving wage increases of between 30% and 100% according to the nature of the work

- give up their ideas of soldiering and cooperate with management in developing the science

- accept that management would be responsible, in accordance with the scientific approach, for determining what was to be done and how

- agree to be trained in new methods, where applicable.

18.   One of Taylor's basic theses was that adoption of the scientific approach would lead to increased prosperity for all. It was, therefore much more important to contribute to a bigger

cake than to argue about the division of the existing cake. Needless to say this kind of approach did not receive much favour with the trade unions at the time. Taylor saw them as a decidedly restrictive influence on issues such as productivity. In his view wages could now be scientifically determined, and should not be affected by arbitrary factors such a union power or management whim. His own experience had shown the considerable increase in earnings achieved by workers adopting their part of the scientific approach.

19.   In terms of work-organization, the workers were very much under the control of their management in Taylor's system. Taylor felt that this would be acceptable to them because management's actions would be based on the scientific study of the work and not on any arbitrary basis. It would also be acceptable, argued Taylor, because of the increased earnings available under the new system. He claimed that there were rarely any arguments arising between management and workers out of the introduction of the scientific approach. Modern experience has unfortunately shown Taylor's view to be considerably over-optimistic in this respect. The degree of trust and mutual cooperation, which Taylor felt to be such an important factor in the success of scientific management, has never been there when it mattered. As a result, although workers' attitudes towards Work Study have often been favourable, the ultimate success of work-studied incentive schemes has always been rather limited owing to workers' feelings that the management was attempting to 'pin them down' and to management's feelings that the workers had succeeded in 'pulling the wool over their eyes' concerning the timing of key jobs.

20.   In support of his Principles, Taylor demonstrated the benefits of increased productivity and earnings which he had obtained at the Bethlehem Steel Works. He described to his critics an experiment with two shovellers – 'first-class shovellers', in his words – whose efforts were timed and studied. Each man had his own personal shovel, which he used regardless of the type of ore or coal being shifted. At first the average shovel load was about 38 pounds and with this load each man handled about 25 tons of material a day.

21.   The shovel was then made smaller for each man, and the daily tonnage went up to 30. Eventually it was found that with smaller shovels, averaging about 21 pounds per load, the daily output rose even higher. As a result of this experiment, several different sizes of shovel were supplied to the workforce to enable each man to lift 21 pounds per load whether he was working with heavy ores or light coals. Labourers who showed themselves capable of achieving the standards set by the two 'first-class' shovellers were able to increase their wages by 60%. Those who were not able to reach the standard were given special training in the 'science of shovelling'. After a three-year period, Taylor and his colleagues reviewed the extent of their success at the Bethlehem Works. The results were impressive: the work of 400–600 men was being done by 140; handling costs per ton had been reduced by half, and as Taylor was quick to point out, that included the costs of the extra clerical work involved in studying jobs; and the labourer received an average of 60% more than their colleagues in neighbouring firms. All this was achieved without any kind of slave-driving which was no part of scientific management, at least so far as Taylor was concerned.

3.7 SCIENTIFIC MANAGEMENT AFTER TAYLOR

22.   Three important followers of scientific management were Frank and Lilian Gilbreth and Henry Gantt. All made significant contributions to the study of work.

23.   The husband-and-wife team of Frank and Lilian Gilbreth, who were somewhat younger than the pioneering Taylor, were keenly interested in the idea of scientific management. In his now famous Testimony to the House of Representatives Committee in 1912, Taylor describes how he was first approached by Frank Gilbreth who asked if the principles of scientific management could be applied to bricklaying. Some three years later Gilbreth was able to inform Taylor that as a direct result of analyzing, and subsequently redesigning, the working methods of typical bricklayers, he was able to reduce the number of movements in laying bricks from 18 per

brick to five per brick. The study of task movements, or 'motion study' as it was known, was a development of Taylor's ideas and represented the Gilbreths' major contribution to basic management techniques.

> **Time and motion studies** measurement and recording techniques which attempt to make operations more efficient

24.   A particular feature of the Gilbreths' work was its detailed content. 'Measurement' was their byword, and the Science of Management, as they put it, consisted of applying measurement to management, and of abiding by the results. They were convinced that it was possible to find the 'one best way' of doing things, and there is no doubt that they went a long way towards the ideal. As employers, the Gilbreths practised what they preached. They laid down systematic rules and procedures for the efficient operation of work and insisted upon adherence to these rules and procedures. In return, the employees were paid well above competitors' rates, and, into the bargain were freed from unnecessary effort and fatigue. With this approach, the separation of the planning from the doing was complete. The employees had no discretion whatsoever once the scientific process had determined how the job should be done. Although these ideas were challenged at the time, they could not be ignored by the new industrial age and its obsession with ideas of efficiency. Whilst few people were prepared to undertake the sheer details of the Gilbreths' methods, the basic techniques caught on, and today (as Method Study) they represent one of the key measures used by management to organize and control working methods in a wide range of industries.

25.   Two examples of the recording techniques used by the Gilbreths are 'therbligs' and process charting. Therbligs (Gilbreth spelt backwards, in effect) are the basic elements of on-the-job motions and provide a standardized basis for recording movements. They include such items as: search, find, grasp, assemble and inspect. A few items cover periods when no motion may be in evidence such as: wait-unavoidable, rest and plan. The most usual list of therbligs contains 18 items, and may be accompanied by appropriate symbols and colours to aid recording. Examples of Therbligs are shown below in Figure 3.2.

> **Flow chart** A pictorial summary that shows, with symbols and words, the steps, sequence and relationship of the various activities involved in the performance of a process

Flow process charts were devized by the Gilbreths to enable whole operations or processes to be analyzed. In these charts five symbols were utilized to cover Operation, Transportation, Inspection, Delay and Storage. **Flow chart** symbols used in the flow process charts are shown in Figure 3.3.

3.8 HENRY GANTT

26.   Gantt was a contemporary and colleague of Taylor's at the Bethlehem Steel Company. Whilst accepting many of Taylor's ideas on scientific management, Gantt felt that the individual worker was not given enough consideration. Although Taylor himself could not have been accused of making employees work unduly hard, in any way, his methods were used by less conscientious employers to squeeze as much production as possible out of their workforce. This was particularly true in respect of piece-rate systems. Gantt introduced a payment system where performance below what is called for on the individual's instruction card still qualified the person for the day-rate, but performance of all the work allocated on the card qualified the individual for a bonus. Gantt discovered that as soon as any one worker found that he could achieve the task, the rest quickly followed. Better use was made of the foremen, because they were sought after by individuals who needed further instruction or help with faulty machines. As a result, supervision improved, breakdowns were minimized and delays avoided by all concerned. Eventually individual workers learned to cope on their own with routine problems. Gantt's bonus system also allowed for the men to challenge the time allocated for a particular task. This was permitted because Gantt, unlike the Gilbreths, did not believe that there was a 'one best way', but only a way 'which seems to be best at the moment'. Gantt's approach to scientific

FIGURE 3.2 Therblig symbols

Therblig	Colour	Symbol/Icon	Therblig	Colour	Symbol/Icon
Search	Black		Use	Purple	
Find	Gray		Disassemble	Violet, Light	
Select	Light Gray		Inspect	Burnt Orange	
Grasp	Lake Red		Pre-Position	Sky Blue	
Hold	Gold Ochre		Release Load	Carmine Red	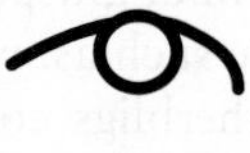
Transport Loaded	Green		Unavoidable Delay	Yellow Ochre	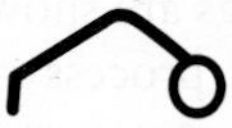
Transport Empty	Olive Green		Avoidable Delay	Lemon Yellow	
Position	Blue		Plan	Brown	
Assemble	Violet, Heavy	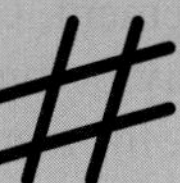	Rest for overcoming fatigue	Orange	

Gantt chart A graphical tool used to show expected start and end times for project activities, and to track actual progress against these time targets

management left some discretion and initiative to the workers, unlike those of his colleague, Taylor, and of his fellow theorists, the Gilbreths.

27. Although it was his ideas on the rewards for labour that made Gantt a notable figure in his day, he is best remembered nowadays for his charts. The Gantt chart was originally set up to indicate graphically the extent to which tasks had been achieved. It was divided horizontally into hours, days or weeks with the

FIGURE 3.3 **Flow chart symbols**

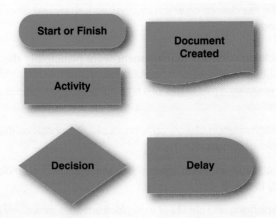

task marked out in a straight line across the appropriate numbers of hours or days, etc. The amount of the task achieved was shown by another straight line parallel to the original. It was easy from such a chart to assess actual from planned performance. There are many variations of the Gantt chart in use today, and an example is given below in Figure 3.4.

FIGURE 3.4 **Gantt chart**

Period	Week 1	Week 2	Week 3	Week 4
Planned Output	1000 units	1000 units	1000 units	1000 units
Actual Output	**850 units**	**900 units**	**1000 units**	**1100 units**
Weekly Actual				
Cumulative				

3.9 COMMENTS ON THE SCIENTIFIC MANAGEMENT SCHOOL

28.   The benefits arising from scientific management can be summarized as follows:

● its rational approach to the organization of work enabled tasks and processes to be measured with a considerable degree of accuracy

● measurement of tasks and processes provided useful information on which to base improvements in working methods, plant design, etc.

● by improving working methods it brought enormous increases in productivity

● it enabled employees to be paid by results and to take advantage of incentive payments

● it stimulated management into adopting a more positive role in leadership at the shop-floor level.

- it contributed to major improvements in physical working conditions for employees
- it provided the foundations on which modern work study and other quantitative techniques could be soundly based.

29.   The drawbacks to scientific management were principally the following:

- it reduced the worker's role to that of a rigid adherence to methods and procedures over which he had no discretion
- it led to the fragmentation of work on account of its emphasis on the analysis and organization of individual tasks or operations
- it generated a 'carrot-and-stick' approach to the motivation of employees by enabling pay to be geared tightly to output
- it placed the planning and control of workplace activities exclusively in the hands of the management
- it ruled out any realistic bargaining about wage rates since every job was measured, timed and rated 'scientifically'.

30.   Whilst it is true that business and public organizations the world over have benefited from, and are continuing to utilize, techniques which have their origins in the Scientific Management movement, it is also a fact that, in the West, at any rate, a reaction against the basic philosophy of the creed has taken place. Tasks and processes are being re-integrated, the individual is demanding participation in the key decision-making processes, and management prerogatives are under challenge everywhere by individuals and organized groups alike. Yet, as Chapter 15 points out, Japanese companies in particular have taken up many of the beneficial aspects of scientific management and combined them with other approaches to produce a highly successful production system (see Theory Z).

Theory Z The management style (characteristic of many Japanese companies) that combines various aspects of scientific management and behaviouralism; the characteristics include long-term employment, development of company-specific skills, participative and collective decision-making and a broad concern for the welfare of workers

31.   On balance, the most important outcome of scientific management was that it stimulated ideas and techniques for improving the systematic analysis of work at the workplace. It also undoubtedly provided a firm launch-pad for a wide variety of productivity improvements in a great range of industries and public services.

32.   Its major disadvantage was that it subordinated the worker to the work system, and so divorced the 'doing' aspects of work from the planning and controlling aspects. This led to:

Behaviouralism An approach to job design that aims to improve motivation hence performance by increasing job satisfaction

- the creation of boring, repetitive jobs;
- the introduction of systems for tight control over work; and
- the alienation of shop-floor employees from their management.

3.10 URWICK

33.   Lyndall Urwick was an enthusiastic and prolific writer on the subject of administration and management. His experience covered industry, the Armed Forces and business consultancy. He was strongly influenced by the ideas of Henri Fayol, in particular. Urwick was convinced the only way that modern man could control his social organizations was by applying principles, or universal rules, to them. In one of his best-known writings – 'The Elements of Administration' – published in 1947 he set out numerous principles which, in his view, could be applied to

organizations to enable them to achieve their objectives effectively. Like other classical writers, Urwick developed his 'principles' on the basis of his own interpretation of the common elements and processes which he identified in the structure and operation of organizations. On this basis, the principles represented a 'code of good practice', which, if adhered to, should lead to success in administration, or management as we would call it today.

34.   In 1952 Urwick produced a consolidated list of ten principles, as follows:

The Principle of

OBJECTIVE – the overall purpose or objective is the raison d'être of every organization.

SPECIALIZATION – one group, one function!

COORDINATION – the process of organizing is primarily to ensure coordination.

AUTHORITY – every group should have a supreme authority with a clear line of authority to other members of the group.

RESPONSIBILITY – the superior is absolutely responsible for the acts of his subordinates.

DEFINITION – jobs, with their duties and relationships, should be clearly defined.

CORRESPONDENCE – authority should be commensurate with responsibility.

SPAN OF CONTROL – no one should be responsible for more than five or six direct subordinates whose work is interlocked.

BALANCE – the various units of the organization should be kept in balance.

CONTINUITY – the structure should provide for the continuation of activities.

Source: L.F. Urwick, 1952, *Notes on the Theory of Organization*, AMA. Reproduced with permission.

> **Specialization** The degree to which an organization's activities are divided into specialist roles

> **Authority** The right to make particular decisions and to exercise control over resources

35.   As a statement of classical organization theory, Urwick's list would be difficult to better, concentrating, as it does, mainly on structural issues. Compared with Fayol's Principles of Management, Urwick's list is less concerned with issues such as pay and morale, for example. Its emphasis is very much upon getting the organizational mechanisms right.

36.   There is no doubting the rational appeal of Urwick's 'principles', especially in relation to the internal environment of the organization. Organizations, however, do not operate in a vacuum. They have to interact with their external environment. That is to say they are open systems. Where modern studies have found weaknesses in Urwick's 'principles' is precisely on this point. The 'principles' tend to assume that it is possible to exert control over the issues mentioned, but many current trends in Western society, in particular, run directly counter to several of the 'principles'. For example, attitudes towards greater sharing of authority at work are likely to clash with the Principle of Authority and the Principle of Correspondence. Similarly, attitudes towards the reintegration or enrichment of jobs will conflict with the Principle of Specialization, the Principle of Definition and the Span of Control.

> **Span of control** A measure of the number of employees who report to one supervisor or manager

37.   Organizations are not self-contained. They have to respond to the pressures of an external environment – social, technological, political, legal and economic. Urwick's 'principles', therefore, are not capable of being introduced easily into modern organizations. They can be, and are, adopted with modification in several cases, but will always be suspect because they fall into the category of 'what ought to be' rather than 'what actually is' in terms of the realities of organizations today.

38.   Urwick's ideas in general achieved considerable popularity with business organizations on both sides of the Atlantic because of their commonsense appeal to managers. In more recent times, however, Urwick's emphasis on purpose and structure has not been able to provide answers to problems arising from social attitudes, external market pressures and rapidly changing technology. His ideas are now a little archaic. They prescribe part, but only part, of what is needed for organizational health.

3.11 BRECH

39.   Brech wrote widely on management and organization issues. Whilst sharing Urwick's concern with the development of principles or general laws of management, Brech was also concerned with the development of people within the organization. His approach was basically a classical one, but tempered to some extent by the prevailing human relations theories of the 1950s and 1960s. He saw management as a process, a social process, for planning and regulating the operations of the enterprise towards some agreed objective, and carried out within the framework of an organization structure. Key issues for Brech in the formation of the structure were:

- defining the responsibilities of the management, supervisory and specialist staff

- determining how these responsibilities are to be delegated

- coordinating the execution of responsibilities

- maintaining high morale.

40.   Brech's own list of principles of organization overlapped considerably with those of Fayol and Urwick. It was less dogmatic in approach than the others, but was nevertheless concerned with the division of responsibilities, lines of communication, unity of command and the allocation of authority, to give just a few examples. Fundamentally, in his view, the principles exist to maintain a balance between the delegation of managerial responsibility throughout the organization and the need to ensure unity of action as well.

41.   Writing in the 1970s, Brech regretted that there was still no general agreement about a fundamental body of principles of management. Until such principles are developed, he argued, it will be impossible for management to gain recognition as a science, or indeed as a profession. He believed that such principles, or basic laws of management, could be deduced from an analysis of the nature of the management process, and this is what he himself attempted in the footsteps of Fayol, Urwick and others. However, he conceded that the development of principles would probably be acceptable only on the basis of first-hand research into management practices – a view which would undoubtedly have pleased researchers such as Henry Mintzberg (1973), Rosemary Stewart (1994) and others who believe that it is primarily through research into managerial behaviour that a body of relevant knowledge or fundamental truths may emerge.

42.   Brech's writings on principles are much more directed towards helping practising managers become more effective in their roles, than towards contributing to a general body of knowledge concerning the theory of management. In this respect his own contribution is that of a thoughtful management consultant aiming to improve management practice rather than that of an objective research worker seeking to test out hypotheses. Seen in this light, Brech's contribution has been considerably influential, especially in management training and development.

CONCLUSION

43.   This chapter considered early thoughts and important ideas on management – coordinated activities (forecasting, planning, deciding, organizing, commanding) to direct and control an organization – and the search for universally applicable principles of management; 14 elements of what being a manager involved, developed by Fayol. Several of these principles are considered later in the book. For example authority is considered in Chapter 4. Next, we considered Taylor's ideas concerning 'scientific management' considered later in Chapter 21.This is a school of classical management theory, dating from the early twentieth century, based on the application of workstudy techniques to the design and organization of work in order to maximize output – increase productivity (to find the 'one best way' of performing each task); it is a form of job design theory and practice which stresses a separation of task conception from task execution and motivation based on economic rewards (see also Taylorism). We introduced McGregor's Theory X, and Theory Y is considered later in Chapter 5, Theory Z is considered in Chapter 6. We also introduced the terms mechanistic system and specialization, considered later in Chapter 10. Finally, the chapter ended with summaries of the ideas of two latter-day scientific managers, Urwick and Brech, who developed many of the ideas of Fayol and Taylor in the period following the Second World War.

Mechanistic system A rigid system of management practice and structure which is characterized by a clear hierarchical structure, specialization of task, defined duties and responsibilities and knowledge centred at the top of the hierarchy

QUESTIONS

1 Identify the general principles of management defined by classical theorists

2 'Attempts to bring scientific methods into management merely show what an inexact art management really is'. Discuss. (ACCA)

3 Does the work of Taylor have any relevance to modern marketing management?

4 Develop your own principles or general laws of management and explain why they could be universally applicable.

5 Critically compare and contrast your principles with those proposed by others, particularly with management scholars who are regarded as classical writers.

We are grateful to the Association of Chartered Certified Accountants (ACCA) for permission to reproduce past examination questions.

USEFUL WEBSITES

Accel-Team: **www.accel-team.com/scientific/ scientific_02.html**
Reviews scientific management

VIDEO CASES

Now take a look at the online video cases – visit the companion website to work through real world business problems associated with the concepts presented within this chapter.
122 Principles of Management – an Introduction

This case considers what is meant by management from the perspectives of commercial and not-for-profit organizations. Similarities and differences are considered and arguments from two people presented over three short film clips.

REFERENCES

Mintzberg, H. (1975) 'The manager's job: folklore and fact', Harvard Business Review, Jul/Aug 75, Vol. 53 Issue 4.
Mintzberg, H. (1973) 'The Nature of Managerial Work', Harper & Row.

Stewart, R. (1994) 'Managing Today and Tomorrow', Macmillan.

CHAPTER 4
MAX WEBER AND
THE IDEA OF
BUREAUCRACY

Key Concepts

- Authority
- Bureaucracy
- Power

Learning Outcomes   Having read this chapter, you should be able to:

- describe and discuss the bureaucratic form of organization
- list and describe three types of legitimate authority
- distinguish power from the concept of authority
- list the main features of bureaucracy
- evaluate bureaucracy commenting on side-effects and dysfunctions

Bureaucracy Describes a form of business administration based on formal rational rules and procedures designed to govern work practices and organization activities through a hierarchical system of authority (see also standardization, centralization, formalization, specialization)

Authority the right to make particular decisions and to exercise control over resources

1.   In Chapter 1 we made reference to bureaucracy. Bureaucracy is a term with several meanings, and this has led to genuine misconceptions about what it truly means. The most common meanings are as follows:

● Bureaucracy is 'red tape', i.e. an excess of paperwork and rules leading to gross inefficiency. This is the negative sense of the word.

● Bureaucracy is 'officialdom', i.e. all the apparatus of central and local government. This is a similar meaning to red tape.

● Bureaucracy is an organizational form with certain dominant characteristics, such as a hierarchy of **authority** and a system of rules.

2.   In this chapter the term 'bureaucracy' is interpreted as an organizational form. The object of the chapter is to describe and discuss this important and all-pervading form of organization, with particular reference to the fundamental work of Max Weber.

4.1 MAX WEBER

3.   Max Weber (1864–1920) spanned the same period of history as those early pioneers of management thought, Fayol and Taylor, to whom we have already referred. Unlike them, however, Weber was an academic – a sociologist – and not a practising manager. His interest in organizations was from the point of view of their authority structures. He wanted to find out why people in organizations obeyed those in authority over them. It was in his publications that the term 'bureaucracy' was used to describe a rational form of organization which today exists to a greater or lesser extent in practically every business and public enterprise.

Rational-legal authority Authority derives from a person's office/position as bounded by the rules and procedures of the organization (see also legitimate authority)

4.   In his analysis of organizations, Weber identified three basic types of legitimate authority: traditional, charismatic and rational-legal authority. Before describing these, it will be helpful to understand what he meant by the expression 'legitimate authority'. Firstly, the concept of authority has to be distinguished from that of power. Power is a unilateral thing – it enables one person to force another to behave in a certain way, whether by means of strength or by rewards. Authority, on the other hand, implies acceptance of rule by those over whom it is to be exercised. It implies that power may only be exercised within limits agreeable to subordinates. It is this latter situation to which Weber refers when he talks about legitimate authority.

Power The ability of individuals or groups to persuade, induce or coerce others into following certain courses of action

5.   The three types of legitimate authority described by him can be summarized as follows:

Traditional authority Authority based on the belief that the ruler had a natural right to rule. This right is either God-given or by descent and tradition. The authority enjoyed by kings and queens would be of this type

● **traditional authority** – where acceptance of those in authority arises from tradition and custom (e.g. as in monarchies, tribal hierarchies, etc.)

● **charismatic authority** – where acceptance arises from loyalty to, and confidence in, the personal qualities of the ruler

Charismatic authority Authority derives from the 'rulers' personal qualities

● rational-legal authority – where acceptance arises out of the office, or position, of the person in authority, as bounded by the rules and procedures of the organization.

It is this last-mentioned form of authority which exists in most organizations today, and this is the form to which Weber ascribed the term 'bureaucracy'.

4.2 BUREAUCRACY

6.   The main features of a bureaucracy, according to Weber, are as follows:

- a continuous organization of functions bound by rules
- specified spheres of competence, i.e. the specialization of work, the degree of authority allocated and the rules governing the exercise of authority
- a hierarchical arrangement of offices (jobs), i.e. where one level of jobs is subject to control by the next higher level
- appointment to offices are made on grounds of technical competence
- the separation of officials from the ownership of the organization
- official positions exist in their own right, and job holders have no rights to a particular position
- rules, decisions and actions are formulated and recorded in writing.

7.   The above features of bureaucratic organization enable the authority of officials to be subject to published rules and practices. Thus authority is legitimate, not arbitrary. It is this point more than any other which caused Weber to comment that bureaucratic organization was capable of attaining the highest degree of efficiency and was, in that sense, the most rational known means of carrying out 'imperative control over human beings'.

8.   Weber felt that bureaucracy was indispensable for the needs of the large-scale organization, and there is no doubt that this form of organization has been adopted in one way or another by practically every enterprise of any size the world over. The two most significant factors in the growth of bureaucratic forms of organization are undoubtedly size and complexity. Once an organization begins to grow, the amount of specialization increases, which usually leads to an increase in job levels. New jobs are created and old jobs redefined. Recruitment from outside becomes more important. Relationships, authority boundaries and discipline generally have to be regulated. Questions of control and coordination became all-important. Thus a small, relatively informal, family concern can suddenly grow into quite a different organization requiring new skills and new attitudes from its proprietors. Although size almost inevitably implies complexity, there are also issues of complexity for smaller organizations. These can arise out of the requirements of sophisticated modern technology, for example. In such an environment specialized and up-to-date skills are required, the span of control has to be small, questions of quality control are vital and last, but by no means least, a keen eye needs to be kept on the competition. Add to all these points the rules and regulations of governments and supranational bodies, such as the European Union (EU) and the World Trade Organization (WTO), and the result is a highly complex environment, which can only be controlled in a systematic form of organization. Indeed, one of the challenges to modern managements is to maintain a 'lean' organization in such circumstances.

4.3 BUREAUCRACY AFTER WEBER

9.   Weber's contribution to our understanding of **formal organization** structures has been a major one. No subsequent discussion or debate on this topic has been possible without reference to his

Formal organization The collection of work groups that has been consciously designed by management to maximize efficiency and achieve organizational goals

basic analysis of bureaucratic organization. Nevertheless, without disputing the basic proposition that bureaucracy is the most efficient means of organizing for the achievement of formal goals, several researchers since Weber have established important weaknesses in the bureaucratic model. These researchers have identified a number of awkward side-effects or 'dysfunctions' of bureaucracy. These can be summarized as follows: Rules, originally designed to serve organizational efficiency, have a tendency to become all-important in their own right. Relationships between office-holders or roles are based on the rights and duties of each role, i.e. they are depersonalized, and this leads to rigid behaviour (predictability). Decision-making tends to be categorized, i.e. choices are previously programmed and this discourages the search for further alternatives, another form of rigidity. The effects of rigid behaviour are often very damaging for client or customer relations and also for management–worker relationships; customers are unable to obtain tailor-made services, but have to accept standardization; employees have to work within a framework of rules and controls which has been more or less imposed on them. Standardization and routine procedures make change and adaptation difficult when circumstances change. The exercise of 'control based on knowledge', as advocated by Weber, has led to the growth of experts, whose opinions and attitudes may frequently clash with those of the generalist managers and supervisors.

10.　One particularly well-known follow-up to Weber's theories was conducted by an American sociologist, Alvin Gouldner. He studied the effects of introducing a bureaucratic system into an organization which had been very informal and indulgent in its management style. The head office of a small gypsum (plaster of Paris) company had appointed a new manager to make the plant more efficient. His new approach led to the replacement of informal methods of working by formalized procedures such as workstudy and production control. These changes were resented by the workforce and the eventual outcome was a reduction, rather than an increase, in the efficiency of operations. In studying this situation, Gouldner identified three different patterns of bureaucracy operating within the one organization. These were as follows:

> MOCK BUREAUCRACY. This expression was applied by Gouldner to situations where the rules and procedures were imposed by an outside body (e.g. Head Office) and where they were either ignored, or were merely paid lip service to, by the employees concerned. In this situation a separate set of 'rules' (i.e. their own) was developed by these employees.

> REPRESENTATIVE BUREAUCRACY. In this case the rules were followed in practice because both management and employees agreed on their value.

> PUNISHMENT-CENTRED BUREAUCRACY. This description was applied to situations where either the management or the employees imposed their rules on the other. Disregard of the rules was seen as grounds for imposing sanctions. Each side considered its rules as legitimate, but there was no common position.

11.　Weber's thinking on bureaucracy was dominated by his view of how rational it was. Gouldner by contrast helped to indicate that opinions and feelings are also a key ingredient in the success of a bureaucratic form of organization. Whereas Weber emphasized the structural aspects of organization, Gouldner emphasized behaviour. He saw that rules not only generated anticipated responses e.g. obedient behaviour, but also unanticipated responses, e.g. minimum acceptable behaviour. Therefore, in any one organization, there will be a tendency to respond to the rules in any one of the three ways described above, depending on how and why the rules were introduced.

Role culture A form of culture that is based on logic and rationality and relies on the strength of the functions of specialists in, for example, finance or production. The interactions between the specialists is controlled by procedures and rules

12.　Handy (1999) describes bureaucracies as 'role cultures' based on logic and rationality. In the role culture, power comes from position power, i.e. the authority of the office, as determined by rules and procedures. Such a culture offers security and predictability to its members, but can be frustrating for those who are ambitious and results-oriented. Handy sees bureaucracy as a Greek temple, based on the firm pillars of its speciality departments and ideally constructed for stability. Its very stability is a drawback in times of change. The Greek temple is not designed for adaptability.

13.   However one chooses to describe a bureaucracy, there is little doubt that it is by far the most frequent form of organization in society, and the question that has to be asked is not so much 'is this organization a bureaucracy?' as 'to what extent is this organization a bureaucracy?' The evidence seems to suggest that there is something of the Greek temple in every organization!

4.4 EFFICIENCY AND EFFECTIVENESS

14.   Thus far, in this book, we have referred to two fundamental and generic objectives of organizations – to be effective (do the right thing) and to be efficient (do things right). In this chapter we have highlighted the crucial role of bureaucracy in organizational efficiency. When environments are relatively stable or placid, organizations need not concern themselves as much with their effectiveness (the right thing today will be the right thing in five or ten years time). Consequently, bureaucracy remained in favour throughout much of the twentieth century. However, significant changes in business environments as a result of deregulation (increased competition), globalization and technological change (travel, internet and mobile telecoms in particular) towards the end of the century increased environmental turbulence, necessitating continuous change within organizations. This presents a more constant 'effectiveness' challenge – organizations must constantly ask whether they are doing the right thing. Such a challenge calls for creativity, risk taking, entrepreneurial activity and the management of uncertainty; it requires dynamic, flexible, learning and adaptable organizations. Consequently, throughout the latter part of the twentieth century, many business scholars and practitioners argued that aspects of bureaucracy stifled the attitudes and behaviours required from employees. As a result, excessive formalization (red-tape) was often removed, generalists were favoured over specialists and decision-making was decentralized to improve responsiveness in many, or at least in parts of organizations. Less work was standardized and controlled and a more results-oriented or self-regulatory control framework favoured.

CONCLUSION

15.   It is important to recognize that organizations do not simply decide to be bureaucratic or not – all large organizations are bureaucratic to some degree. The question is – how much? Bureaucracy describes a form of business administration based on formal rational rules and procedures designed to govern work practices and organization activities through a hierarchical system of authority (see discussions on standardization, centralization, formalization, and specialization). It emphasizes efficiency. In the next chapter we will consider employee motivation (also a factor of productivity (efficiency) and effectiveness). In doing so, we will consider bureaucracy and its impact on motivation. We will also revisit a number of related concepts such as power and authority (such concepts also feature in Chapters 7, 22 and 23).

QUESTIONS

1 Compare and contrast Fayol's principles of management and Weber's description of bureaucracy.

2 Discuss the main advantages and disadvantages of the ideal-type of bureaucracy, as described by Weber.

3 Critically evaluate the contribution of the classical/ traditional school of management theorists to our understanding of organization. (CIMA)

4 List the main features of bureaucracy.

5 Evaluate bureaucracy, commenting on side effects and dysfunctions.

6 Briefly compare and contrast classical with human relations and social psychological theories.

7 What were the main conclusions of the Hawthorne studies?

8 Explain what is meant by motivation and why understanding human motivation is a complex matter?

9 Outline Maslow's theory of motivation commenting on needs and the central points of the theory. Briefly discuss any criticisms of Maslow's theory of motivation.

10 Use Hertzberg's theory of motivation to discuss the impact of scientific management and Taylorism on employee motivation. Evaluate the scientific management approach in terms of motivating workers.

VIDEO CASES

Now take a look at the online video cases – visit the companion website to work through real world business problems associated with the concepts presented within this chapter.

43 Work Design – flexibility and the contemporary workplace

Explores alternative work arrangements – considers technology and work organization.

58 Organization structure changes at Body Shop

There are many work tasks to be done in a large organization and consequently the work must be divided up and allocated. In this case we consider what is meant by organization structure and design; consider why it is necessary to structure human resources, discuss how we should set about this enormous challenge and ask how we can make efficient and effective use of human resources in order to attain goals and derive a sustainable competitive advantage. In particular we consider issues associated with bureaucracy and hierarchy. Body Shop grew and with it came particular design challenges.

REFERENCES

Handy, C. B. (1999) 'Understanding Organizations', Ed. 4. Penguin.

Pugh, D. S. (1997) 'Organization Theory', Ed. 4. Penguin.

Section Three
Human Relations and Social Psychological Theories

CHAPTER 5
MOTIVATION – THE EARLY THEORISTS

Key Concepts

- Content theories of motivation
- Hierarchy of Needs
- Motivation

Learning Outcomes Having read this chapter, you should be able to:

- explain what is meant by the term motivation (in the work place)
- compare the work of several prominent social scientists on motivation at work

1. This is the first chapter devoted to Human Relations and Social Psychological Theories. Whereas the exponents of classical theory were principally concerned with the structure and mechanics of organizations, the human relations and social psychological theorists focused on the human factor at work – people's behaviour in the workplace. They were particularly interested in human motivation, group relationships and leadership. Chapter 5 introduces the concept of 'motivation', and motivation theory. The chapter begins with an explanation of the basic concept of motivation, and follows this with a summary of different models of motivation proposed by Schein (1988). Next we provide an account of the celebrated Hawthorne Studies, conducted in the USA some seventy years ago. The chapter continues with an outline of the work of a number of American social scientists, namely Follett, Maslow, McGregor, Herzberg, Likert, Argyris and McClelland.

5.1 THE CONCEPT OF MOTIVATION

2. Human motivation studies aim, in essence, to discover what it is that triggers and sustains human behaviour (in the work place). Motivation is a driving force that encourages individuals to behave in particular ways as they seek to achieve a goal. Not all theorists focus on the proces of motivations. In fact, most of the early theorists were interested in the drives and/or needs of people at work, i.e. the content aspects of motivation.

3. A very basic and simplified model of motivation is shown in Figure 5.1. This suggests that a stimulus, such as hunger (physical) or the desire for company (social) gives rise to a response. This response takes the form of some kind of behaviour, which leads to an outcome, which is either satisfactory or unsatisfactory. Where the behaviour is appropriate, satisfaction is achieved. Where it is not, the stimulus remains in the form of frustration, and the process begins again.

Hawthorne studies A series of studies exploring aspects of group working within the Western Electric Company in the USA during the late 1920s and early 1930s

Motivation A driving force that encourages an individual to behave in particular ways as they seek to achieve a goal

Process theories of motivation These theories look at motivation as the outcome of a dynamic interaction between the person and their experiences of an organization and its management. Such processes depend critically on the sense individuals make of their experiences at work

Content theories of motivation These theories attempt to explain those specific things which actually motivate the individual at work and are concerned with identifying people's needs, the strength of those needs and the goals they pursue in order to satisfy those needs

FIGURE 5.1 **A basic model of motivation**

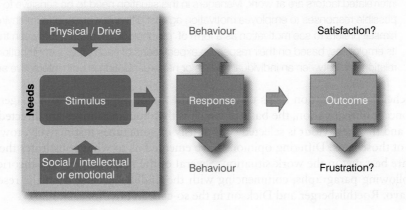

4.   Understanding human motivation is a complex matter. Sometimes a person's motives may be clear to themselves, but quite puzzling to others. In other situations both the individual and those affected by their behaviour understand what is driving them. In some situations, especially where stress is involved, the individual concerned may be totally unaware of their motives, whereas others may see them quite clearly. It is important for those in managerial and supervisory positions to be aware of these issues, and to take account of their own prejudices in this area of their work. This is because our efforts to understand others are coloured by our attitudes towards them and the assumptions we make about their behaviour. If we assume that a particular group of workers is hardworking and reliable, we tend to treat them with respect and trust; if, however, we see them as lazy and unreliable, we are likely to treat them as requiring close control and supervision.

5.   Schein, a professor at the MIT Sloan School of Management, has made a noteworthy mark on the field of organizational development and social psychology. He propounded a classification of managers' assumptions about people based on a review of earlier approaches to motivation. His classification follows a broadly chronological pattern as follows:

Rational-economic concept of motivation Motivational theory suggesting employees are motivated by their economic needs

- **Rational-economic** model. This view of human motivation has its roots in the economic theories of Adam Smith in the 1770s. It suggests that the pursuit of self-interest and the maximization of gain are the prime motivators. According to Schein, this view places human beings into two main categories: (1) the untrustworthy, money motivated, calculative masses, and (2) the trustworthy, more broadly motivated moral elite whose task it is to organize and control the masses. Such an approach is evident in the work of Taylor and the Gilbreths, and the entrepreneurs of mass production techniques.

- Social model. In the 'social model', Schein drew heavily on the conclusions of the Hawthorne researchers. This view sees people as predominantly motivated by social needs – the need for personal relationships. The implication for managers is that an emphasis on attending to people's needs over the needs of the task will lead to greater productivity as well as higher morale. Such a view, according to Schein, needs to be treated with some reservations.

- Self-actualizing model. This concept is based on Maslow's theory of human needs (see below), which whilst allowing for the influence of other needs, stresses the individual's need for self-fulfilment as the prime motivator. The implication for managers is that people need challenge, responsibility and autonomy in their work if they are to work effectively. There is some research evidence to support such a view, especially amongst professional and highly skilled employees.

- Complex model. Schein proposes this model of motivation as being fuller than the earlier models. It presupposes that understanding people's motivation is a complex business in which several interrelated factors are at work. Managers in this situation need to be sensitive to a range of possible responses to employee motivation against differing work and team environments. Schein himself prefers to see motivation as a form of 'psychological contract' between the organization and its employees, based on their respective expectations of each other's contribution. Ultimately, the relationship between an individual and his or her organization is both interactive and interdependent.

6.   Schein's classification helps us to relate the major approaches to management theory with the concept of motivation, the basis of which is that human motives are directed towards desired ends, and that behaviour is selected consciously or sometimes instinctively, towards the achievement of those ends. Differing opinions have emerged as to what constitutes these ends and how they are best met in the work situation. Several of the most well-known theories are outlined in the following paragraphs, commencing with the findings arising from the research carried out by Mayo, Roethlisberger and Dickson in the so-called Hawthorne Studies.

5.2 THE HAWTHORNE STUDIES

7.   Professor Elton Mayo is usually associated with the social research carried out at the Hawthorne plant of the Western Electric Company in Chicago, USA, between 1927 and 1932, and named the Hawthorne Studies. In these studies, the emphasis was on the worker rather than on work. Unlike Taylor and the scientific managers, the researchers at Hawthorne were primarily concerned with studying people, especially in terms of their social relationships at work. Their conclusions were that people are social animals – at work as well as outside it – and that membership of a group is important to individuals. Group membership leads to establishment of informal groups within the official, formal groupings as laid down in the organization structure.
8.   These conclusions gave rise to the idea of social man (now the social model) and to the importance of human relations. Elton Mayo has been described as the founder of the human relations movement, whose advocates stressed the need for managerial strategies to ensure that concern for people at work was given the highest priority. This movement, if it can be described as such, spanned the period from the mid-1920s to the mid-1950s, after which there was a gradual trend away from the social model, and its close relation – the self-actualizing model, towards the complex model, where people operate in highly variable organizational environments.

5.3 ELTON MAYO

9.   Elton Mayo (1880–1949) was an Australian by birth, a psychologist by training, and, according to some, a natural PR man by inclination! At the time of the Hawthorne studies he was Professor of industrial research at the Harvard Graduate School of Business Administration. He was already involved in a study of issues related to fatigue, accidents and labour turnover at work when he was approached by executives of the Western Electric Company for advice. The company, which prided itself on its welfare facilities, had begun a number of studies into the effects of lighting on production and morale. It had discovered, to its surprise, that the groups of workers who were the subject of study improved their productivity whether their lighting was improved or not. Clearly some factor other than the impact of physical improvements was at work. The company management decided to call in the experts.
10.   Their decision was to bring considerable fame to Mayo, in particular. His popularization of the results of the Hawthorne Studies made an enormous impact at the time. The social model was seen as a rebuttal of the ideas of scientific management, with its emphasis on the task and the control of work. Subsequent decades have also been greatly influenced by the findings at Hawthorne, and most of the credit has gone to Mayo.
11.   The studies were carried out over several years in a number of different stages, as follows: First Stage (1924–1927). This was conducted by the company's own staff under the direction of Messrs Pennock and Dickson. As mentioned above, this stage was concerned with the effects of lighting on output. Eventually two groups of comparable performance were isolated from the rest and located in separate parts of the plant. One group, the control group, had a consistent level of lighting; the other group, the experimental group, had its lighting varied. To the surprise of the researchers, the output of both groups increased. Even when the lighting for the experimental group was reduced to a very low level, they still produced more! At this point Pennock sought the help of Mayo and his Harvard colleagues.
12.   Stage two (1927–1929). This stage became known as the Relay Assembly Test Room. The objective was to make a closer and more detailed study of the effects of differing physical conditions on productivity. At this stage, it is important to note, there was no deliberate intention to analyze social relationships or employee attitudes. Six women workers in the relay assembly section were segregated from the rest in a room of their own. Over the course of the experiments the

effects of numerous changes in working conditions were observed. Rest pauses were introduced and varied; lunch times were varied in timing and in length. Most of the changes were discussed with the women before being implemented. Productivity increased whether the conditions were made better or worse. Later studies included altering the working week. Once again output increased regardless of the changes. By the end of stage two the researchers realized they had not just been studying the relationship between physical working conditions, fatigue, monotony and output, but had been entering into a study of employee attitudes and values. The women's reactions to the changes – increased output regardless of whether conditions improved or worsened – has come to be known as 'the Hawthorne Effect'. That is to say the women were responding not so much to the changes as to the fact that they were the centre of attention – a special group.

13.   Stage three (1928–1930). Before the relay assembly test had come to an end, the company had decided to implement an interview programme designed to ascertain employee attitudes towards working conditions, their supervision and their jobs. The interviews were conducted by selected supervisors, initially on a half-hour, structured basis. Eventually the interview pattern became relatively unstructured and lasted for ninety minutes. Despite this, the numbers interviewed reached over 20 000 before the programme was suspended. The wealth of material gained was used to improve several aspects of working conditions and supervision. It also became clear from the responses that relationships with people were an important factor in the attitudes of employees.

14.   Stage four (1932). This was known as the bank wiring observation room. In this study fourteen men on bank wiring were removed to a separate observation room, where, apart from a few differences, their principal working conditions were the same as those in the main wiring area. The aim was to observe a group working under more or less normal conditions over a period of six months or so. The group was soon developing its own rules and behaviour – it restricted production in accordance with its own norms; it short-circuited the company wage incentive scheme and in general protected its own sectional interests against those of the company. The supervisors concerned were powerless to prevent this situation. The group had clearly developed its own unofficial organization, run in such a way that it was able to protect itself from outside influences whilst controlling its internal life too.

15.   Final stage (1936). This stage was commenced some four years after stage four because of the economic difficulties of the depression. This final stage was based on lessons learned from the earlier studies. Its focus was firmly on employee relations and took the form of personnel counselling. The counsellors encouraged employees to discuss their problems at work and the results led to improvements in personal adjustments, employee-supervisor relations and employee–management relations.

16.   The official account of the Hawthorne studies was written not by Mayo but by a Harvard colleague (Roethlisberger) and one of the company's own researchers (Dickson). Their detailed descriptions of the research did not appear until 1939, some time after Mayo had already put the spotlight on the Studies in his popularized account published six years earlier.

17.   There have been many criticisms of the way the Hawthorne Studies have been interpreted. Mayo's references to them were included in writings, which propounded his theories about man and industrial society. As a result, his use of the studies was biased towards his own interpretation of what was happening. For the official evidence one must look to Roethlisberger and Dickson. Modern researchers point out that their Hawthorne colleagues overlooked important factors in assessing their results. They also adopted some unreliable methods for testing the evidence in the first place. However, everyone is agreed that the Hawthorne Studies represented the first major attempt to undertake genuine social research. Important lessons were learned, and, perhaps even more importantly, many questions were raised by these studies.

18.   The main conclusions to be drawn from the Hawthorne research are:

- Individual workers cannot be treated in isolation, but must be seen as members of a group.

- The need to belong to a group and have status within it is more important than monetary incentives or good physical working conditions.

- Informal (or unofficial) groups at work exercise a strong influence over the behaviour of workers.

- Supervisors and managers need to be aware of these social needs and cater for them if workers are to collaborate with the official organization rather than work against it.

19.   The Hawthorne experiment began as a study into physical conditions and productivity. It ended as a series of studies into social factors: membership of groups, relationships with supervision, etc. Its most significant findings showed that social relations at work were every bit as important as monetary incentives and good physical working conditions. They also demonstrated the powerful influence of groups in determining behaviour at work. By modern standards of social research, the Hawthorne studies were relatively unsophisticated in their approach. Nevertheless, they represented a major step forward for the social sciences in their study of work organizations. Also, by their model of 'social man', they did much to further the humanization of work.

5.4 MARY PARKER FOLLETT

20.   The ideas of Mary Parker Follett, an American social worker, management consultant and pioneer in the fields of organizational theory and organizational behaviour, were so far ahead of her time that most of them were ignored. The fact that she was a woman, trying to speak out in a man's world, was undoubtedly another factor. In her principal piece on the workplace, published after her death, Dynamic Administration (1941), she took forward the work of the Hawthorne researchers by concluding that human problems were not just important, but were central to the success of organizations. In particular, she argued the case for giving greater, not less, responsibility to people at work. She was aware of the importance of teamwork, and the role of the leader, which she saw in holistic and shared terms. The leader's role was to envision the future and to empower others to achieve that future. She herself did not use the modern expression empowerment, but that is clearly what she meant. Her idea of leadership meant gaining others' collaboration and respect, and reconciling conflicts. Such a leadership approach depended on the interaction of leader and followers, and her ideas on the significance of followers pre-dated Fiedler (see Chapter 7) by thirty years.

21.   Follett's view of conflict suggested there were basically three ways of dealing with it: by domination, by compromise, or by integration. Today we would refer to her integration as a 'win-win' solution. Domination implies a 'win-lose' outcome, and compromise a 'lose-lose' situation, in which neither side is content. She was strongly against the notion that conflict was a matter of 'either-or', as this meant that alternative solutions were restricted from the outset. Today, Follett's ideas are being acknowledged, as writers and historians look back across the twentieth century, free from prejudices.

22.   The concept of social man dominated the thinking of social researchers and practising managers alike in the wake of the Hawthorne studies. The emphasis on the employee's social and belonging needs, as opposed to the needs of the task, continued throughout the 1930s, and 1940s until the mid 1950s. If more attention had been paid to the ideas of Mary Parker Follett in those years, we might have moved forward earlier from the era of social man towards that of self-actualizing man.

23.   This is a suitable point to introduce what many commentators have described as the social psychological school of motivation. The emphasis is still on people as the most crucial factor in determining organizational effectiveness, but people who have considerably more than just physical and social needs. The dominant concept here is that of self-actualizing man, and the influential contributors here are the American social scientists Maslow, McGregor, Herzberg, Likert, Argyris and McClelland.

5.5 MASLOW'S HIERARCHY OF NEEDS

Hierarchy of Needs A theory of motivation developed by Maslow which states that people's behaviour is determined by their desire to satisfy a progression of physiological, social and psychological needs

24.   Maslow's studies into human motivation led him to propose a theory of needs based on an hierarchical model with basic needs at the bottom and higher needs at the top, as in Figure 5.2. This theory made a considerable influence on developments in management theory during the 1950s/60s due partly to the simplicity of the model and partly to the identification of higher-level needs.

25.   The starting point of Maslow's hierarchy theory, first published in 1954, is that most people are motivated by the desire to satisfy specific groups of needs. These needs are as follows:

- physiological needs – needs for food, sleep, etc.

- safety needs – needs for a stable environment relatively free from threats

- love needs – needs related to affectionate relations with others and status within a group

- esteem needs – needs for self-respect, self-esteem and the esteem of others

- **self-actualization** needs – the need for self-fulfilment.

Self-actualization The need for personal fulfilment, to develop potential, to become everything that one is capable of becoming

26.   The second and most central point of Maslow's theory is that people tend to satisfy their needs systematically, starting with the basic physiological needs and then moving up the hierarchy. Until a particular group of needs is satisfied, a person's behaviour will be dominated by them. Thus, a hungry person is not going to be motivated by consideration of safety or affection, for example, until after his hunger has been satisfied. Maslow later modified

FIGURE 5.2 **Hierarchy of needs**

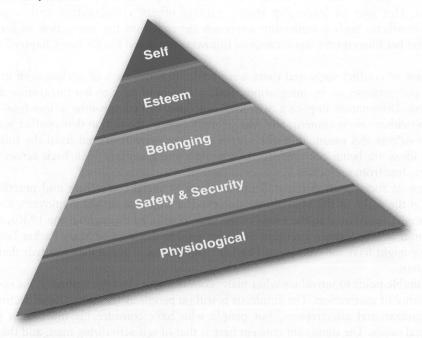

Source: Abraham H. Maslow, Robert D. Frager and James Fadiman, 1987, *Motivation and Personality 3rd edition.*
Adapted by permission of Copyright © Pearson Education, Inc., Upper Saddle River, NJ.

this argument by stating that there was an exception to the rule in respect of self-actualization needs. For this group of needs it seems that satisfaction of a need gives rise to further needs for realizing one's potential.

27.   Maslow's theory provided a useful early framework for discussions about the variety of needs people may experience at work, and the ways in which their motivation can be met by managers. One criticism of the theory is that systematic movement up the hierarchy does not seem to be a consistent form of behaviour for many people. Alderfer (1972), for example, argued that individual needs were better explained as being on a continuum, rather than in a hierarchy. He considered that people were more likely to move up and down the continuum in satisfying needs at different levels. He concluded that there were really only three major sets of needs – existence needs (i.e. The basics of life), relatedness needs (i.e. Social and interpersonal needs) and growth needs (i.e. Personal development needs). Drucker (1974) commented that Maslow had not recognized that when a want was satisfied, its capacity to motivate was changed. An initially satisfied want that was not sustained could, on the contrary, become counter-productive and act as a disincentive.

5.6 McGREGOR – THEORY X AND THEORY Y

28.   Like Schein's classification of managers' assumptions about people, McGregor's Theory X and Theory Y (refer back to Chapter 3) are essentially sets of assumptions about behaviour. In proposing his ideas, McGregor pointed to the theoretical assumptions of management that underlie its behaviour. He saw two noticeably different sets of assumptions made by managers about their employees. The first set of assumptions regards employees as being inherently lazy, requiring coercion and control, avoiding responsibility and only seeking security. This attitude is what McGregor termed Theory X. This is substantially the theory of scientific management, with its emphasis on controls and extrinsic rewards. Schein's rational-economic model (see para. 5 above) is very similar to that of Theory X.

> **Extrinsic motivation** a form of motivation that stresses valued outcomes or benefits provided by others, such as promotion, pay increases, a bigger office desk, praise and recognition

29.   McGregor's second set of assumptions sees people in a more favourable light. In this case employees are seen as liking work, which is as natural as rest or play; they do not have to be controlled and coerced, so long as they are committed to the organization's objectives. Under proper conditions they will not only accept but also seek responsibility; more, rather than less, people are able to exercise imagination and ingenuity at work. These are the assumptions of Theory Y. They are closely related to Maslow's higher-level needs and to Schein's self-actualizing model.

30.   Theory X and Theory Y have made their greatest impact in the managerial world rather than in the academic world. The two labels have become part of the folklore of 'management style', which will be looked at in the chapter on leadership (Chapter 7). They do help to identify extreme forms of management style, but there is a danger that they may be seen only as polar extremes representing an either/or style. In real-life a blend of the two theories is more likely to provide the best prescription for effective management.

5.7 HERZBERG'S MOTIVATION-HYGIENE THEORY

31.   Herzberg's studies of the mid-twentieth century concentrated on satisfaction at work. In the initial research some 200 engineers and accountants were asked to recall when they had experienced satisfactory and unsatisfactory feelings about their jobs. Following the interviews, Herzberg's team came to the conclusion that certain factors tended to lead to job satisfaction, whereas others led frequently to dissatisfaction (see Figure 5.3). The factors giving rise to

FIGURE 5.3 Factors affecting job attitudes

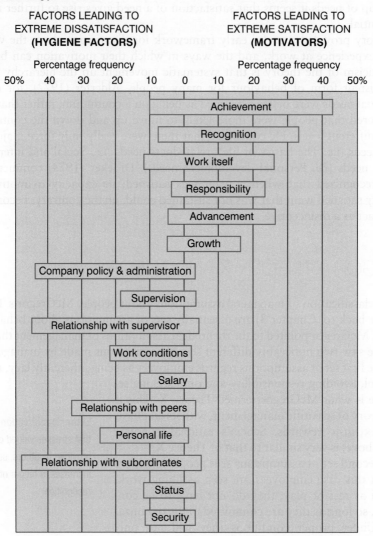

Note: The *length* of each 'box' denotes the frequency with which the factor occurred in the situation described by the respondents. The overlap of the boxes across the centre line indicates: a) that motivators have their *negative* aspects, e.g. lack of achievement can lead to dissatisfaction; and b) that hygiene factors have their *positive* aspects, e.g. salary can be a source of satisfaction.

Hygiene factors Aspects of work which remove dissatisfaction but do not contribute to motivation and performance, including pay, company policy, supervision, status, security and working conditions are known as Hygiene or context factors

satisfaction were called motivators. Those giving rise to dissatisfaction were called hygiene factors. These studies were later extended to include various groups in manual and clerical groups, where the results were claimed to be quite similar.

32. The most important motivators, or satisfiers, to emerge were the following:

● achievement
● recognition
● work itself
● responsibility
● advancement.

Herzberg pointed out that these motivators were intimately related to the content of work, i.e. With its intrinsic challenge, interest and the individual responses generated by them.

33.   The most important hygiene factors, or dissatisfiers, were as follows:

- company policy and administration

- supervision – the technical aspects

- salary

- interpersonal relations – supervision

- working conditions.

Herzberg noted that these dissatisfiers were more related to the context, or environment, of work than to its content. When in line with employee requirements, such factors could smooth the path of working life, but in a taken-for-granted way. When these factors were out of line with employees expectations, they could be a source of difficulty and complaint, and definitely provided grounds for dissatisfaction at work. This lack of a positive aspect to these factors led Herzberg to call them 'hygiene' factors, because whilst they contributed to the prevention of poor psychological health, they did not make a positive contribution to employees' sense of well being, at least not in any lasting way.

34.   The key distinction between the motivators and the hygiene factors is that whereas motivators can bring about positive satisfaction, the hygiene factors can only serve to prevent dissatisfaction. To put it another way, if motivators are absent from the job, the employee is likely to experience real dissatisfaction. However, even if the hygiene factors are provided for, they will not in themselves bring about substantial job satisfaction. Hygiene, in other words, does not positively promote good health, but only acts to prevent ill health.

35.   If we apply Herzberg's theory to the ideas and assumptions of earlier theorists, it is possible to see that Taylor and colleagues were thinking very much in terms of hygiene factors (pay, incentives, adequate supervision and working conditions). Mayo, too, was placing his emphasis on a hygiene factor, namely interpersonal relations. It is only when we consider the ideas of the neo-human relations school that motivators appear as a key element in job satisfaction and worker productivity.

36.   Herzberg's motivation-hygiene theory was generally well received by practising managers and consultants for its relatively simple and vivid distinction between factors inducing positive satisfaction and those causing dissatisfaction. It led to considerable work on so-called job enrichment, i.e. the design of jobs so that they contain a greater number of motivators (to be discussed in Chapter 21). The approach here is basically to counter the effects of years of Taylorism, in which work was broken down into its simplest components, and over which there was no responsibility for planning and control. Herzberg's ideas were less well received by fellow social scientists, mainly on grounds of doubt about (a) their applicability to non-professional groups and (b) his use of the concept of 'job satisfaction', which they argued is not the same thing as 'motivation'.

Job enrichment The process of vertically increasing the responsibilities of a job, by the addition of motivators, e.g. more discretion, improved job interest, etc.

5.8 LIKERT

37.   Likert's contribution to the concept of motivation, and its applicability to the world of work, came mainly from his work as Director of the Institute of Social Research at the University of Michigan, USA. These so-called 'Michigan studies' were described by Likert, in 1961, who theorized about high-producing and low-producing managers. The former, according to his research, were those who achieved not only the highest productivity, but also the lowest costs and the highest levels of employee motivation. The latter, by comparison, produced higher costs and lower employee motivation.

38.   Research indicated that the high-producing managers tended to build their success on interlocking and tightly knit, groups of employees, whose cooperation had been obtained by thorough attention to a range of motivational forces. These included not only economic and security motives, but also ego and creativity motives (self-actualization, in Maslow's terminology). Another key feature noted by the Michigan researchers was that, although the high-producers utilized the tools of classical management – work study, budgeting, etc. – they did so in a way that recognized the aspirations of the employees, by encouraging participative approaches.

39.   A dominant theme in Likert's discussion of these 'new patterns of management' is the importance of supportive relationships. Management can achieve high performance when employees see their membership of a work group to be 'supportive', that is to say when they experience a sense of personal worth and importance from belonging to it. High-producing managers and supervisors tended to foster just such relationships with, and within their groups.

40.   The idea of supportive relationships is built into Likert's view of the ideal organization structure. Supportive relationships lead to effective work groups which can interact with other effective groups in an overlapping form of organization. In this form of structure certain key roles perform a 'linking pin' function. A head of a section, for example, is a member not only of their own group but also of their managers' group. Their manager or supervisor, in turn, is a member of a further group higher up the organizational hierarchy, and so on. Such an organization still has the basic shape of a classical organizational pyramid, but operates in practice on the basis of interlocking teams, instead of separate specialisms. This form is shown diagrammatically in Figure 5.4.

41.   In reviewing his work on motivation, leadership and organization structures, Likert distinguished between four separate systems, or styles of management. These are founded on a number of differing assumptions about human behaviour and are useful to compare with Schein's classifications and McGregor's theory X – theory Y. The four systems are as follows:

– Exploitative-authoritative where power and direction come from the top downwards, where threats and punishment are employed, where communication is poor and team-work non-existent. Productivity is mediocre.

– Benevolent-authoritative is similar to the above but allows some upward opportunities for consultation and some delegation. Rewards may be available as well as threats. Productivity is fair to good but at the cost of considerable absenteeism and turnover.

– Consultative where goals are set or orders issued after discussion with subordinates, where communication is both upwards and downwards and where teamwork is encouraged, at least partially.

FIGURE 5.4 **Overlapping group form of organization**

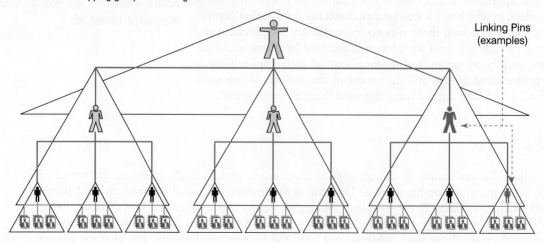

There is some involvement of employees, as a motivator. Productivity is good with only moderate absenteeism, etc.

– Participative-group is the ideal system. Under this system, the keynote is participation, leading to commitment to the organization's goals in a fully cooperative way. Communication is good both upwards, downwards and laterally. Motivation is obtained by a variety of means. Productivity is excellent and absenteeism and turnover are low.

42.   The Exploitative-authoritative system corresponds closely to Schein's rational economic model and McGregor's theory X. The benevolent-authoritative system can be considered as a similar, but softer, approach. The consultative system is fairly close to the idea of the social model. Finally, the participative-group system is more like Schein's self-actualizing model and very close to the idea of theory Y. The Exploitative-authoritative System, at one extreme, is highly task oriented, whilst the participative-group system is highly people oriented at the other.

5.9 ARGYRIS

43.   Professor Argyris was one of Likert's contemporaries. His initial interests, whilst at Yale University, were in the relationship between people's needs and the needs of the organization. He suggested the reason for so much employee apathy was not so much because of laziness, but rather because people were being treated like children. This led to what he called the immaturity-maturity theory, which suggests that the human personality develops from immaturity to maturity in a continuum, in which a number of key changes take place. These are shown in Figure 5.5.

FIGURE 5.5 **Immaturity–Maturity Theory**

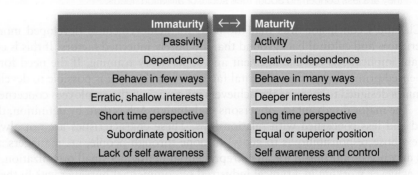

Immaturity	←→	Maturity
Passivity		Activity
Dependence		Relative independence
Behave in few ways		Behave in many ways
Erratic, shallow interests		Deeper interests
Short time perspective		Long time perspective
Subordinate position		Equal or superior position
Lack of self awareness		Self awareness and control

Source: Chris Argyris, 1957, *Personality and Organisation: The Conflict between System and the Individual* copyright © Harper & Row, Publishers, Inc. Copyright renewed 1985 by Chris Argyris. Reprinted by permission of HarperCollins Publishers.

44.   Against the above model of maturity, Argyris sets the features of the typical classical organization: task specialisation, chain of command, unity of direction and span of control. The impact of this type of organization on individuals is that they are expected to be passive, dependent and subordinate, i.e. they are expected to behave immaturely! For individuals who are relatively mature, this environment is a major source of frustration at work. This frustration leads to individuals seeking informal ways of minimizing their difficulties such as creating informal organizations that work against the formal hierarchy.

45.   The lessons for motivation are important. For the more we can understand human needs, the more it will be possible to integrate them with the needs of organizations. If the goals of the organization and the goals of individuals can be brought together, the resulting behaviour will be cooperative rather than defensive or downright antagonistic (a matter discussed by Ouchi, 1980). Argyris's ideas, therefore, favour a self-actualization model of man with some of the attributes of complex man too.

Need for achievement (nAch) A general concern with meeting standards of excellence, the desire to be successful in competition and the motivation to excel

5.10 ACHIEVEMENT MOTIVATION

46. Whilst many social psychologists have studied common factors in human motivation, others have focused on differences between individuals. One such researcher, whose work is well known, is McClelland of Harvard University. He and his team drew attention to three sets of needs in particular, as follows:

Need for power (nPow) The desire to make an impact on others, change people or events and make a difference in life

- the **need for achievement (n-Ach)**
- the **need for power (n-Pow)**
- the need for affiliation, or belonging (n-Aff).

McClelland isolated n-Ach as a key human motive, and one that is influenced strongly by personality and by environment.

47.   Persons with a high need for achievement tend to have the following characteristics:

- their need for achievement is consistent
- they seek tasks in which they can exercise personal responsibility
- they prefer tasks which provide a challenge without being too difficult and which they see as within their mastery
- they want feedback on their results
- they are less concerned about their social or affiliation needs.

McClelland's conclusion was that the need for achievement is developed more by childhood experiences and cultural background than by purely inherited factors. If this is correct it has important implications for management and supervisory training. If the need for achievement is influenced primarily by environmental factors, then clearly it is possible to develop training programmes designed to increase the achievement motive in the employees concerned.

48.   The major disadvantage of persons with high n-Ach is that, by definition, they are task oriented and less concerned with relationships. These characteristics are not always suitable for those whose responsibility is to get work done through people, i.e. managers and supervisors. This may not be a problem for an entrepreneurial figure in a small organization, but what of the high achiever working in a typical industrial or commercial bureaucracy? In the latter case high n-Ach can be frustrated by the constraints imposed by delegating responsibility. Nevertheless, McClelland's ideas were important as a contribution to our understanding of motivation at work, and how the concept of n-Ach might be applied in practice.

CONCLUSION

49.   The word 'motivation' is often used to describe certain sorts of behaviour. This (and the next) chapter is mainly concerned with the basic management and leadership problem of how we motivate or persuade others to do what we want them to do. Since it is part of a manager's job to get work done through others, managers need to understand why people do things (that is, what motivates them) so they can influence others to work towards the goals of the organization. The chapter began with an explanation of the basic concept of motivation, and was followed by a summary of different models of motivation; we provided an account of the Hawthorne Studies and continued with an outline of the work of a number of American social scientists, namely Follett, Maslow, McGregor, Herzberg, Likert, Argyris and McClelland.

QUESTIONS

1   What are the similarities between Schein's description of the Rational-Economic Model, McGregor's Theory X and Likert's System 1 (Exploitive-Authoritative)?

2   What is the 'Hawthorne Effect'? What are the implications of this for those undertaking research into human behaviour in the workplace? In your answer you should argue why the Hawthorne Studies were considered to be so important in their time.

3   What are the essential differences between motivators and hygiene factors in Herzberg's theory of motivation.

4   How can an understanding of the need for achievement be of use to managers in industry and commerce?

5   Discuss the major features and significance of the Hawthorne experience at Western Electric. (ACCA)

We are grateful to the Association of Chartered Certified Accountants (ACCA) for permission to reproduce past examination questions.

USEFUL WEBSITES

The Institute of Management: **http://www.managers.org.uk**
Harvard Business School library: **www.library.hbs.edu/hc/ hawthorne/intro.html**
Harvard Business School library information about the Hawthorne studies and human relations movement

Frederick Herzberg: **www.businessballs.com/herzberg.htm**
Frederick Herzberg motivational theory

VIDEO CASES

Now take a look at the online video cases – visit the companion website to work through real world business problems associated with the concepts presented within this chapter.

22 The Power of Recognition
Organizational performance is a broad concept that includes productivity, customer and employee satisfaction. Efficiency is about how the organization uses its resources to undertake activities and how some companies are able to get more out

of their resources than others. In the case of human resources, this is achieved through motivation. This case focuses on influencing the behaviour of employees in order to attain desired levels of performance. In particular, there is an emphasis on Motivator factors – aspects of work which lead to high levels of job satisfaction, motivation and performance, and include achievement, recognition, responsibility, advancement, growth and the work itself.

REFERENCES

Alderfer, C. (1972) 'Existence, Relatedness and Growth', Collier Macmillan.
Drucker, P. (1974) 'Management: Tasks, Responsibilities, Practices', Heinemann.
Kelly, P. P. (2009) 'International Business and Management', Cengage Learning EMEA.

Ouchi, W. G. (1980) 'Markets, Bureaucracies, and Clans', Administrative Science Quarterly – Ithaca, 25 (1), p. 129–141
Schein, E. (1988) 'Organizational Psychology', Ed. 3. Prentice-Hall.

CHAPTER 6
MOTIVATION – LATER THEORISTS

Key Concepts

- Attribution theory
- Equity theory
- Expectancy theory
- Goal theory
- Reinforcement
- Theory Z

Learning Outcomes Having read this chapter, you should be able to:

- explain the process theory of motivation
- recall the expectancy theory of motivation
- recall the equity theory of motivation
- recall the goal theory of motivation
- discuss Theory Z and its application to Western organizations
- discuss how attribution theory may help managers to motivate their employees

1.   The motivation theories discussed in the previous chapter have been labelled 'content theories' of motivation, because they focus on the needs, drivers or triggers of human behaviour in the workplace. This chapter examines some of the ideas proposed by those whose focus is mainly on the process of motivation rather than its content. Not surprisingly, these theories tend to be called 'process theories' of motivation. Process theories of motivation focus upon what people are thinking when they decide whether or not to place effort into a particular activity. One of the most well known of these is so-called Expectancy Theory, which is the first to be outlined. This is followed by a brief consideration of other later theories of motivation, including Equity, Goal, Attribution and Reinforcement Theory, and an analysis of Japanese motivational practices given the name of 'Theory Z'.

> **Reinforcement** The encouragement of particular behaviours through the application of positive and/or negative rewards

6.1 EXPECTANCY THEORY

2.   The development of this theory of motivation is based on the work of the American, Victor Vroom, during the 1960s. A key point of his theory is that an individual's behaviour is formed not on objective reality but on his or her subjective perception of that reality. The core of the theory (see Figure 6.1) relates to how a person perceives the relationships between three things – effort, performance and rewards. Vroom focused especially on the factors involved in stimulating an individual to place effort into something, since this is the basis of motivation. He concluded there were three such factors, each based on the individual's personal perception of the situation. These were:

> **Theory Z** The management style (characteristic of many Japanese companies) that combines various aspects of scientific management and behaviouralism; the characteristics include long-term employment, development of company-specific skills, participative and collective decision-making and a broad concern for the welfare of workers

EXPECTANCY, i.e. the extent of the individual's perception, or belief, that a particular act will produce a particular outcome.

INSTRUMENTALITY, i.e. the extent to which the individual perceives that effective performance will lead to desired rewards.

> **Perception** A mental process used to manage sensory data

VALENCE, i.e. the strength of the belief that attractive rewards are potentially available.

This approach to the concept of human motivation, with its emphasis on the psychological mechanisms that trigger effort, is quite different from that of the content theorists whose work was described in the previous chapter. The basic model developed by Vroom, indicating the components of effort that can lead to relevant performance and appropriate rewards, can be summarized in Figure 6.1.

3.   It is important to note that Vroom distinguishes 'valence' from 'value'. He does so by defining the former in terms of the anticipated satisfaction the individual hopes to obtain from the outcome or reward, and by defining 'value' in terms of the actual satisfaction obtained by the individual. According to Vroom the three factors – Expectancy, Instrumentality and Valence – combine together to create a driving force (Force), which motivates an individual to put in effort, achieve a level of performance and obtain rewards at the end. Vroom suggested that Force was a multiple of Expectancy and Valence (encompassing Instrumentality) in the formula: Force = Expectancy × Valence (or F = E × V)

4.   Effort alone, however, may not necessarily lead to effective performance. Other factors are involved, such as the individual's own characteristics (personality, knowledge and skills) and the way in which they perceive their role. For example, the prospect of promotion could be seen by a newly-appointed employee as an attractive prospect (valence), but their expectancy of gaining promotion could be low, if they perceive that promotion is attained primarily on length of

FIGURE 6.1 Expectancy Theory

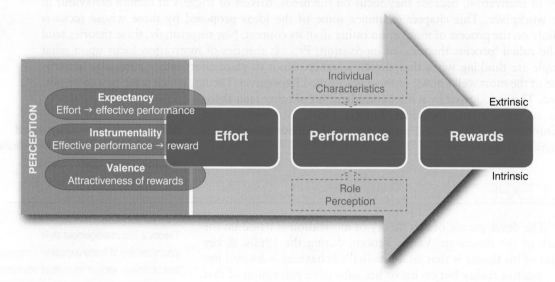

Source: Adapted from Vroom, V.H (1964) *Work and Motivation*. copyright © Victor Vroom. Reproduced with permission.

service. In such a situation, performance does not lead to rewards, so effort in that direction is not seen as worthwhile. In any case, effort does not necessarily lead to effective performance, if the individual has insufficient knowledge and skills, or if their perception of their role does not equate with that of their superior, for example.

5.   Other factors which are not shown may also affect performance, e.g. constraints of the job, organization style, etc. Effort, therefore, does not always result in effective performance. It is also true that effective performance may not always lead to the rewards anticipated by the individual. Nevertheless, on both counts, it is not the reality which spurs on the individual but the prospect of effective performance and/or desirable rewards. It is the individual's perception of the situation that is the vital part of this theory.

6.   Rewards may be classified in two categories – (1) intrinsic and (2) extrinsic. Intrinsic rewards are those gained from fulfilling higher-level personal needs, such as self-esteem and personal growth. The individual can exercise a degree of personal control over these. Extrinsic rewards, by comparison, are those provided by the organization, and thus outside the control of the individual, such as pay, promotion and working conditions. Several research studies have suggested the rewards associated with intrinsic factors are more likely to be perceived as producing job satisfaction. The extrinsic rewards are less likely to match individual expectations.

7.   Thus, Expectancy Theory is a process theory which argues that individual motivation depends on the valence of outcomes, the expectancy that effort will lead to good performance and the instrumentality of performance in producing valued outcomes. The main features of Expectancy Theory are, it:

> **Expectancy Theory** a process theory which argues that individual motivation depends on the valence of outcomes, the expectancy that effort will lead to good performance, and the instrumentality of performance in producing valued outcomes

- takes a comprehensive view of the motivational process;

- indicates that individuals will only act when they have a reasonable expectancy that their behaviour will lead to the desired outcomes;

- stresses the importance of individual perceptions of reality in the motivational process;

- implies that job satisfaction follows effective job performance rather than the other way round; and

- has led to developments in work redesign, where emphasis has been laid on intrinsic job factors, such as variety, autonomy, task identity and feedback.

6.2 EQUITY THEORY

8. Have you or a colleague ever been demotivated to find out that a similar employee has been getting better benefits than you (for the same or less work)? A theory of motivation which focuses on people's feelings of how fairly they have been treated in comparison with the treatment received by others is termed Equity Theory. The basis of this theory, in a work context, is that people make comparisons between themselves and others in terms of what they invest in their work (inputs) and what outcomes they receive from it. As in the case of Expectancy Theory, this theory is also founded on people's perceptions, in this case of the inputs and outcomes involved. Thus, their sense of equity (i.e. fairness) is applied to their subjective view of conditions and not necessarily to the objective situation. The theory states that when people perceive an unequal situation, they experience 'equity tension', which they attempt to reduce by appropriate behaviour. This behaviour may be to act positively to improve their performance and/or to seek improved rewards, or may be to act negatively by, for example, working more slowly (cf. Taylor-type soldiering) on the grounds of being under-rated or under-paid.

9. Buchanan and Huczynski (2010), in a review of research, suggests that when people perceive or seek to resolve an inequitable situation for themselves they can be predicted to make one of seven choices:

1   alter your inputs (e.g. not exerting as much effort)

2   alter your outcomes (e.g., persuade the manage to increase pay)

3   rationalize the inequity (e.g., 'I used to think I worked at a good pace but now I realize . . .')

4   compare with someone else (e.g. 'I may not be doing as well as my brother, but I'm doing better than our father did at my age.')

5   alter the comparison person's outcomes (persuade the manager to cut this persons pay)

6   alter the comparison person's inputs (e.g. leave the difficult tasks to them)

7   'leave' (i.e., quit their job).

10. Equity Theory suggests that people are not only interested in rewards as such, which is the central point of expectancy theory, but they are also interested in the comparative nature of rewards. Thus, part of the attractiveness (valence) of rewards in a work context is the extent to which they are seen to be comparable to those available to the peer-group. Such thinking, however, is best applied to extrinsic rewards, such as pay, promotion, pension arrangements, company car and similar benefits, since they (a) depend on others for their provision, and (b) have an objective truth about them. Equity Theory cannot apply in the same way to intrinsic rewards, such as intrinsic job interest, personal achievement and exercise of responsibility, which by their very nature are personal to the individual, entirely subjective and therefore less capable of comparison in any credible sense. Nevertheless, so far as extrinsic rewards are concerned, managers would be well advised to reflect on the ideas of Equity Theory, especially in recognizing that subjective perceptions are extremely powerful factors in motivation.

Equity Theory A theory of motivation which focuses on people's feelings of how fairly they have been treated in comparison with the treatment received by others

Goal Theory A theory of motivation that is based on the premise that people's goals or intentions play an important part in determining behaviour. Goals guide people's responses and actions and direct work behaviour and performance, leading to certain consequences or feedback

6.3 GOAL THEORY

11. **Goal Theory** is a theory of motivation based on the premise that people's goals or intentions play an important part in determining behaviour. Goals guide people's responses and actions and

direct work behaviour and performance, leading to certain consequences or feedback. The thinking behind Goal Theory is that motivation is driven primarily by the goals or objectives that individuals set for themselves. Unlike Expectancy Theory, where a satisfactory outcome is the prime motivator, Goal Theory suggests that it is the goal itself that provides the driving force. Locke (1967) first proposed the idea that working towards goals was in itself a motivator. His research indicated that performance improved when individuals set specific rather than vague goals for themselves. When these specific goals were demanding, performance was even better. General exhortations to 'do one's best' appear to be less effective than identifying specific targets and aiming for them.

12.   Goal theorists also argue that an individual's motivation is enhanced when feedback on performance is available. Other important factors include goal-commitment (i.e. the extent to which the individual is committed to pursuing the goal even when things get rough), and self-efficacy (i.e. the perception that one has the ability to achieve the goal). Goal commitment is likely to be enhanced when goals are made public and when they are set by the individual rather than imposed externally. Clearly, the concept of goal 'ownership' is important here. Self-efficacy is rather like the quality noted by McClelland as being at the core of those with a high n-Ach, i.e. a belief that they were capable of achieving their goals, which were set at a realistic, though challenging, level (see previous chapter).

6.4 ATTRIBUTION THEORY

13.   Managers frequently have to make judgements about employees and employees will frequently judge themselves and colleagues. They will often make attempts to determine the causes of behavioural outcomes (work performance). For example, expectancy and goal theory will often require a manager to reward an employee. The reward will normally only be given if the manager judges that desirable work outcomes arose as a consequence of the employees behaviour (motivation and work). In this chapter we have also discussed equity theory whereby employees make comparisons between themselves and others; in doing so, they will be judging themselves and others and attributing causes to behaviour. Attribution is the process by which we ascribe causes to events as well as to our own and others' behaviour. It is part of the overall perceptual process. Attribution Theory is used to explain aspects of discrimination within the organization and may also be used to explain aspects of motivation. When explaining or describing behaviour and its relationship with performance, people tend to consider internal and external forces. The internal forces relate to personal attributes such as ability, skill, amount of effort, etc whereas external forces may include environmental factors, organizational rules and policies, resources, etc. Attribution is an important process because the subsequent responses depend upon how individuals interpret the original causes. When judging subordinate performance, if the manager perceives the cause of outcome (e.g. work output) to be internal and based on employee behaviour (ability, skill, effort and motivation) then a reward is likely to be given. However, should the manager believe that external factors caused the outcome then rewards may be withheld. A number of theories have been proposed to explain whether managers are more or less likely to attribute cause to employee ability or the situation (external force). Self-serving bias describes a situation whereby individuals attribute success to their own abilities and failure to the situation. However, when we judge others we tend to assume that failure is due to lack of ability rather than caused by the situation (Actor–observer effect). Specific

Attribution Theory The way in which individuals make sense of other people's behaviour through attributing characteristics to them by judging their behaviour and intentions on past knowledge and in comparison with other people they know

Self-serving bias a situation whereby individuals attribute success to their abilities and failure to the situation

Actor–observer effect when we judge others we tend to assume that failure is due to their lack of ability rather than caused by the situation

conditions may determine when people judge behaviour to be intentional. The presence of a relevant goal, intention, possession of relevant skills, etc are likely to influence a judgement that considers internal forces to be at work in causing the outcome. Kelley (1973) suggests that when people make attributions, they do so with three major criteria in mind: Distinctiveness, i.e. How distinctive or different is the behaviour? How untypical? Consensus, i.e. How far is the behaviour typical of others in the same situation? Consistency, i.e. How consistent is the behaviour over time? Or is this an unusual piece of behaviour?

14.   Application of the theory to an issue such as an individual's lateness for work might result in the following thinking: Internal Attribution: Distinctiveness – Individual is considered to dislike work Consensus – Other people are usually on time Consistency – Individual is frequently late External Attribution Distinctiveness – Individual is not usually late to work Consensus – Other employees were also late Consistency – Individual is rarely late In the case of the internally caused behaviour, we would be likely to draw the conclusion that this person was an unmotivated individual who disliked his job, and therefore 'chose' to be late. Where the behaviour was seen as essentially caused by external factors, we would be likely to conclude that this was a one-off event caused by circumstances outside his control, such as a major traffic hold-up en route to work.

15.   Attribution theory has a number of implications for the manager and employees – errors can occur when we judge the performance of others. Such errors may impact upon motivation. Some employees are more likely to believe that they can influence their level of performance through their own abilities or skills. Others may believe that their performance is determined by external factors beyond their influence. Employees who do not meet targets or objectives may blame external factors/forces and as a result may reduce the level of future effort. In situations where the manager fails to give a reward, judging outcomes to have been caused by external forces, and the employees perceives their good performance to be due to their ability and effort then the lack of recognition and reward may well have a demotivating effect. Attribution Theory is as much an issue of perception between individuals as a theory of motivation. Nevertheless, by providing another way of looking at people's behaviour, it can add to our understanding of the motivational process. The theory clearly has connections with Achievement Theory, since people attributed with primarily internal sources of behaviour have strong similarities with those showing high n-Ach needs (i.e. Belief in their own internal strengths). People attributed with external causes of behaviour are likely to see their working lives dominated by external forces, such as the production system, actions of management, etc.

6.5 REINFORCEMENT THEORY

16.   Whereas Attribution Theory has strong links with ideas about human perception, Reinforcement Theory, as applied to motivation, has major connections with learning theory, and especially the work of the late American behaviourist, Burrhus Skinner. The Reinforcement Theory of motivation suggests that a given behaviour is a function of the consequences of earlier behaviour. Thus, it is argued, all behaviour is determined, to some extent, by the rewards or punishments obtained from previous behaviour, which has the effect of reinforcing current actions. In this sense all behaviour is caused by external sources, since we can have little control over the consequences of our actions. So, if an individual's efforts to contribute new ideas to a team are consistently met with an indulgent but apathetic approach by the management (i.e. Negative reinforcement), then the individual is likely to be discouraged from making further suggestions, and may even seek to change his or her job. Where, by comparison, the individual is encouraged to share new ideas and help to develop them (i.e. Positive reinforcement), then the person is likely to generate even more ideas.

17.   Strict Reinforcement Theory would argue that an individual's own understandings, emotions, needs and expectations do not enter into motivation, which is purely about the consequences of behaviour. However, modifications of the theory (e.g. Social Learning Theory) do

allow for the effect of individuals' perceptions of the rewards/punishments obtained by others as a contributor to motivation. Thus, an employee is not just affected by the consequences of his own actions at work, but is able to infer 'appropriate' behaviour from what he sees as the consequences for others of their behaviour. Reinforcement Theory is not concerned with what motivates behaviour, or how, and is not strictly a theory of motivation. It is more concerned with control of behaviour (i.e. Power over others).

18.   Supporters of Reinforcement Theory offer some important guidelines to those intending to use it as a motivating tool in the workplace. Typical suggestions include the following:

- positively reinforce desired behaviour

- ignore undesirable behaviour, so far as possible

- avoid using punishment as principal means of achieving desired performance

- provide reinforcement as soon as possible after the response

- apply positive reinforcement regularly

- assess positive and negative factors in the individual's environment

- specify desired behaviour/performance in quantifiable terms.

19.   The underlying assumption behind this approach is that people are there to be controlled, and that management's task is to provide the 'right' conditions to encourage high performance. This is not quite such a negative view of people as is suggested by McGregor's Theory X (see previous chapter), but Reinforcement Theory is not too far removed from that concept of human motivation.

6.6 THEORY Z – THE JAPANESE APPROACH

20.   The reference in the previous paragraph to McGregor's Theory X is timely, for it leads us into the last 'theory' in this chapter – 'Theory Z'. This describes an approach to employee motivation based on Japanese management practices. The phrase was coined by an American exponent of Japanese approaches to management, William Ouchi, who used it to describe attempts to adapt Japanese practice to Western firms. Theory Z is the management style that combines various aspects of scientific management and behaviouralism; the characteristics include long-term employment, development of company-specific skills, participative and collective decision-making and a broad concern for the welfare of workers.

21.   In the last quarter of the twentieth century, considerable attention was given to the success of Japanese manufacturing industries. One of the key factors in their success, according to Ouchi, has been their approach to their management of resources, especially people. Among the key features of Japanese industrial organizations, notes Ouchi, are the following personnel-related factors:

- There is a high degree of mutual trust and loyalty between management and employees.

- Career paths are non-specialized with life-long job rotation as a central feature of career development.

- Decision-making is shared at all levels.

- Performance appraisal is long-term (i.e. the first appraisal takes place ten years after joining the company).

- There is a strong sense of collective responsibility for the success of the organization, and cooperative effort rather than individual achievement is encouraged.

22.   Although Ouchi recognizes that many of the features of Japanese management cannot be translated into Western industrial society, he believes that certain features can be applied in a Western context. Despite the participative management style implied by the above theory, it is important to note that the Japanese have taken up many of the ideas of Taylor (see Chapter 3), but, in contrast to Western industrialized nations, they have emphasized the importance of the human resource element in achieving production efficiency using Taylor's methods. The acceptance of Taylorist approaches to manufacturing has enabled the Japanese to capture an enviable place in world markets for their manufactured goods. It is not that the Japanese are particularly innovative, but they have found the secret of achieving a standard of production control which ensures a consistently excellent product. This standard has been achieved because of thorough attention to human resource issues as well as to questions of technology, quality and cost control. Backed by financial policies aimed at long-term growth rather than short-term profits, and a worldwide view of product marketing, Japanese manufacturing companies have set a high standard for their competitors to follow. Critics of Japanese manufacturing companies have pointed to the slow processes of decision-making, the lack of risk-taking, the reliance on a myriad of small firms and part-time employees, the docile nature of the trade unions and the imprisoning effect of lifetime employment in one company. It is precisely because of such criticisms that Japanese management practices have to be adapted if they are to be employed successfully elsewhere. The whole point of Theory Z, as Ouchi himself was at pains to indicate, lies in the adaptation of Japanese approaches to Western production methods.

CONCLUSION

23.   In this and the previous chapter we have considered the problem of how we motivate or persuade others (employees etc.) to do what we want them to do. Motivation theories are important to managers and others seeking to be effective leaders. Whilst there is no all-encompassing explanation, the aforementioned theories (alongside those outlined in the previous chapter) are helpful in understanding motivation. Expectancy theory attempts to explain behaviour in terms of an individual's goals and choices and the expectation of achieving the objectives. In short, this theory suggests that employee motivation depends upon whether the employee wants the reward on offer for doing a good job and whether they believe more effort will lead to that reward. Therefore, in order to motivate people we must show them something desirable, indicate how straightforward it is to obtain it and then support their self-belief that they can complete the task and achieve the reward. Equity Theory is a process theory of motivation which argues that the perception of unfairness in an organizational setting leads to tension, which drives the individual to act to resolve that unfairness. The theory proposes that individuals who perceive themselves as either under-rewarded or over-rewarded will experience distress, and that this distress leads to efforts to restore equity within the relationship. People are motivated by what they consider a fair/equitable return for their efforts. Inequity is uncomfortable and tends to generate behaviour aimed at restoring equity, such as altering inputs (e.g. effort) or outcomes or cognitively distorting them, leaving the organization, attempting to distort the other person's perceptions of inputs or outcomes or changing the person used as a point of comparison. Goal setting is a powerful way of motivating people. Goal-setting theory states that goals can be a major motivational source at work. Goals, when accepted, lead to higher performance levels. We also discussed attribution theory, noting the importance of perception to many theories of motivation. We considered reinforcement theory and finished with a brief review of Theory Z. For Ouchi, Theory Z focused on increasing employee loyalty to the company by providing a job for life with a strong focus on the well-being of the employee. According to Ouchi, Theory Z management tends to endorse stable employment, high productivity and high employee morale and satisfaction.

QUESTIONS

1 Motivation of subordinates is an important aspect of a manager's job.

    a What do you think motivates a person to work well?

    b What steps can a manager take to motivate his subordinates? (ICSA)

2 In what respects is Expectancy Theory novel in its approach to motivation at work?

3 What is 'Theory Z', and to what extent can its underlying assumptions be transferred to non-Japanese manufacturing companies?

4 Compare and contrast process and content theories of motivation. In your answer you should (a) explain what a process theory of motivation is and then what a content theory of motivation is and (b) list and describe three examples of each.

5 Critically evaluate process theories of motivation and their application in the management of workplace behaviour – which do you consider to be the most important and why?

USEFUL WEBSITES

Institute for employment studies: **www.employment-studies.co.uk/consult/index.php?id=mwb&tab=work**
Motivation and well-being

REFERENCES

Buchanan, D. and Huczynski, A. (2010) 'Organizational Behaviour', Ed. 7. Financial Times Press.

Kelley, H. (1973) 'The processes of causal attribution', American Psychologist, 28(2), Feb 1973, p. 107–128.

Locke, E. (1967) 'Toward a theory of task motivation and incentives', Organizational Behaviour and Human Performance, Volume 3, Issue 2, p. 157–189.

Martin, J. and Fellenz, M. (2010) 'Organizational Behaviour and Management 4e', Ed. 4. Cengage Learning EMEA.

Mullins, L. (2010) 'Management and Organizational Behaviour', Ed. 9. Financial Times Press.

Skinner, W. (1974) 'The focused factory', Harvard Business Review, May/Jun 74, Vol. 52 Issue 3, p. 113–121.

Section Four
Theories of Leadership and Group Behaviour

CHAPTER 7
LEADERSHIP –
THEORY AND
PRACTICE

Key Concepts

- Appointed Leader
- Charismatic leadership
- Contingency theory of leadership
- Functional Leader
- Leadership
- Power
- Situational leadership
- Traits approach to leadership

Learning Outcomes   Having read this chapter, you should be able to:

- review the main theories of leadership
- discuss alternative styles of leadership
- compare various types of leader
- contrast the leader and manager roles

1.   Every manager and business leader must consider, as a matter of routine, the attainment of organizational goals and superior performance. This presents issues of effectiveness (strategy/goals) and efficiency (the use of resources). This chapter explores the concepts of leadership (and management) and will focus on the leaders' use of power to influence and persuade followers to act in ways which help the organization attain its goals. Chapter 7 describes a number of different ways of looking at leadership, discusses the tensions between concern for the task and concern for people, and summarizes a number of important theories of leadership. Leadership is a concept which has fascinated humankind for centuries, but only in recent years has any kind of theory of leadership emerged. This chapter describes and comments on a number of the theoretical and practical aspects of leadership in the work situation. A review of the main theories of leadership is followed by a discussion of the alternative styles of leadership available, in practice, to a person in a management or supervisory position.

7.1 WHAT IS LEADERSHIP?

2.   Before defining 'leadership', it would be appropriate to reflect briefly on the various types of leader which have been identified, and to consider some of the practical difficulties arising from these. The most important types of leader are as follows:

CHARISMATIC – gains influence mainly from strength of personality, e.g. Napoleon, Churchill, Richard Branson and others. The difficulty with **charismatic leadership** is that few people possess the exceptional qualities required to transform all around them into willing followers! Another issue is that personal qualities or traits of leadership cannot be acquired by training; they can only be modified by it.

TRADITIONAL – position is assured by birth, e.g. kings, queens and tribal chieftains. This is another category to which few people can aspire. Except in the small family business, there are few opportunities for traditional leadership at work.

SITUATIONAL – influence can only be effective by being in the right place at the right time. This kind of leadership is too temporary in nature to be of much value in a business. What is looked for is someone who is capable of assuming a leadership role in a variety of situations over a period of time.

APPOINTED – influence arises directly out of his position, e.g. most managers and supervisors. This is the bureaucratic type of leadership, where legitimate power springs from the nature and scope of the position within the hierarchy. The problem here is that, although the powers of the position may be defined, the job-holder may not be able to implement them because of weak personality, lack of adequate training or other factors.

FUNCTIONAL – secures their leadership position by what he or she does, rather than by what they are. In other words, functional leaders adapt their behaviour to meet the competing needs of the situation. This particular type will be looked at more closely later on in the chapter.

Leadership The process of influencing others to understand and agree about what needs to be done and how to do it, and the process of facilitating individual and collective efforts to accomplish shared objectives

Power The ability of individuals or groups to persuade, induce or coerce others into following certain courses of action

Styles of leadership Suggests that successful leadership is about the style of behaviour adopted by the leader, usually described as falling within an autocratic–democratic scale

Charismatic leadership The ability to exercise leadership through the power of the leader's personality

Traditional authority Authority based on the belief that the ruler had a natural right to rule. This right is either God-given or by descent and tradition. The authority enjoyed by kings and queens would be of this type

Situational leadership an approach to determining the most effective style of influencing

Appointed Leader A leader who influences others by virtue of their position

Functional Leader A person who leads by action rather than by position

PRINCIPLE-CENTRED – whose approach to leadership is influenced by moral and ethical principles, involving considerations of equity, justice, integrity, honesty, fairness and trust. This approach is associated with the ideas of Stephen Covey (see below).

3. Leadership, then, is something more than just an aspect of personality, tradition, opportunism or appointment. It is intimately connected with actual behaviour and attitudes towards oneself and others. Although leadership may involve empowering others, and sharing the leadership burden in many respects, it nevertheless cannot abdicate its final responsibility for a group's results. Any leader must ultimately accept personal responsibility for success or failure. The way in which the leadership is carried out is influenced strongly by cultural factors (see Chapter 13), and this is an important consideration for senior management given the extent of globalization in many industries. For present purposes, we can define 'leadership' as the process of influencing others to understand and agree about what needs to be done and how to do it, and the process of facilitating individual and collective efforts to accomplish shared objectives. Leadership is a dynamic process and there is no 'one best way' of leading – leadership is essentially about striking the right balance between the needs of people, task and goals in a given situation.

4. The main variables in the leadership process can be illustrated as shown in Figure 7.1.

FIGURE 7.1 **The key leadership variables**

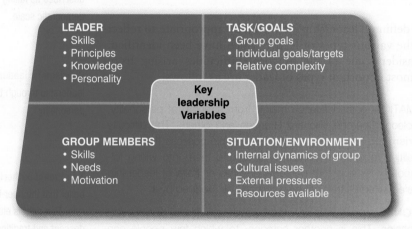

The critical variable in the above is the leadership role. Using his or her skills and knowledge, drawing on personal qualities and adhering to principles of integrity and trust, a leader has to make the best of the other three variables. Perhaps all three might be favourable at a particular time, but the likelihood is that one or other of task, group members and situation will be problematic, and thus the leader will be challenged. The task facing the leader and the group may be complex, and there will always be the need to consider individual goals or targets within the overall objective. The group members themselves may not always have the best blend of knowledge and skills, and they may need motivating to achieve the overall objective (see previous chapters). There will always be issues of group morale to be considered, as well as the needs of individuals. Finally, the situation or environment, both internal and external, are important. The interactions within the group and with the leader are major factors affecting outcomes. Cultural traditions may need to be considered where the group is not homogeneous. There will always be external pressures of one kind or another that may not be favourable to group progress, and there may be problems with insufficient resources to support the group in its efforts. The art of good leadership is to be able to make the best use of all the variables, even when they are unfavourable. If they are very unfavourable, part of the leader's role is to seek help on behalf of the group. Thus, a very important aspect of leadership is to recognize one's own dependence on others. At this point we might ask what, if any, is the difference between leadership and management?

7.2 LEADERSHIP AND MANAGEMENT

5. In the preceding chapters we have explored theories of management and asked what is meant by the term management. We drew on the work of Fayol to help us define what managing means (forecasting, planning, controlling, organizing, commanding and coordinating). We have also outlined ideas of power and authority (as separate concepts); we noted an emphasis on efficiency (scientific management) and discussed types of authority through Weber's idea of bureaucracy (Chapter 4). This chapter builds on previous chapters, with a discussion regarding what is meant by the terms leader and manager and continues with the theme of what leaders and managers are required to do. Leadership has been defined in terms of traits, behaviours, influence, interaction patterns, role relationships and occupation of organizational positions (**traits approach**). Most definitions of leadership infer a process whereby one-person influences another. In the case of organizational leadership, people are influenced to do what is beneficial for the organization. Gary Yukl, a leading American researcher with interest in leadership, power and influence, and motivation, defines leadership as the process of influencing others to understand and agree about what needs to be done and how to do it, and the process of facilitating individual and collective efforts to accomplish shared objectives. Typically associated with the concept of influence is motivation, discussed in the previous two chapters; leadership may be considered as the ability of an individual to influence, motivate and enable others to contribute towards the effectiveness and success of the organization.

> **Traits approach to leadership** assumes leaders are born and not made. Leadership consists of certain inherited characteristics, or personality traits, which distinguish leaders from followers. Attention is focused on the person in the job and not the job itself

6. However, managers must also motivate employees but more with an eye on efficiency. Historically, scholars have argued the leader and manager as different roles whilst others have deemed them synonymous. Leadership is essentially an influencing process; the process is ultimately aimed at goal achievement. The function of the leader is to ensure the organization does the right thing (effectiveness) whilst the manager ensures things are done right (efficiency); the leader is concerned with establishing direction, the vision and organizational goals and influencing followers to obtain commitment. Consequently, the leader must be a good communicator and able to influence others-motivating and inspiring. The manager ensures goals are attained through plans, budgets, resource allocation, organization and problem-solving. Many management scholars now share the view that leadership is one aspect of the management role. However, they note that being a good manager does not necessarily translate to being a good leader and vice versa. Yukl notes that a person can be a leader without being a manager and a person can be a manager without leading.

7.3 THEORIES OF LEADERSHIP

7. In this first part of the book our focus is on management theory. Leadership theories may focus on leader traits, behaviour (what the leader actually does), the power influence approach (the amount and type of power and how it is exercised), the situation or some combination thereof. Early leadership theories tended to be more universal in nature, i.e. applied to all types of situation, whereas more recently contingency theories of leadership have emerged, suggesting that certain aspects of leadership may apply to some situations but not others. For the first half of the 20th century, researchers believed they could identify personal attributes and qualities

such as personality traits required by leaders (trait spotting). This would make it possible to identify, select and promote such individuals into leadership positions. Whilst the authors of numerous studies have proposed a range of leadership traits and qualities, many of them are vague and of limited value in trying to identify leaders. Whilst researchers concluded that a person's predispositions can help predict behaviour, they then shifted their attention from trait identification to the study of leadership behaviour patterns and later, the identification of appropriate behaviours for different contexts. In the second half of the 20th century, leadership and management styles (behaviour patterns) became a major focus for research. Based on research, leadership behaviours tend to be grouped into those focussing on work (task-oriented behaviour) and those considering the follower (subordinate in many cases). Consideration behaviours are based on relationship building (relations-oriented behaviour), supporting, developing, recognizing and helping others. Specific task behaviours include planning work activities, clarifying roles and objectives and monitoring operations and performance – how things get done. The two key orientations (task and relationship building) reflect a concern for people and a concern for production, both of which are important for effective leadership. A person-oriented-behaviour may result in higher job satisfaction; build trust, respect and loyalty and organizational commitment whilst the task orientation may result in better coordination and the more efficient utilization of resources. Together, both are important for the overall performance of the organization. Consequently, both types of behaviour need to be embraced by an effective leader. A person (manager or leader) can emphasize one or both. Studies suggest that people (followers) preferred their leaders to be both considerate and performance- oriented as well. Subsequent research added a third orientation, behavioural set, based on approaches to change. Change-oriented behaviour is concerned with understanding the environment, finding innovative ways to adapt to it, and implementing major changes in strategies, products, or processes (see Chapters 24 and 25). Ideas about leadership in management roles range from the 'ideal' approaches of scientific management, the human relations and social psychological schools and Covey's **principle-centred leadership** to the pragmatic approaches of the contingency theorists. The leading theories will be examined briefly in turn.

Principle-centred leadership A leadership type based upon morals and ethical principles

7.4 TRAIT THEORIES

8.   As we saw earlier, in the discussion of classical management ideas, the debate was usually led by practising managers who were strong characters in their own right. Part of their success was undoubtedly due to personal qualities, and it is perhaps not surprising that the earliest studies undertaken into leadership focused their attention on the qualities required for effective leaders. However, it has proved an impossible task to identify the particular traits or characteristics separating leaders from non-leaders. Of those traits which do appear more frequently, intelligence, energy and resourcefulness are perhaps the most representative and these are certainly mentioned in Covey's ideas of 'principle-centred' leadership (see below).

7.5 STYLE THEORIES

9.   The interest in the human factor at work which was stimulated by the researchers of Human Relations, and taken up by the social psychologists who followed them, led logically to an interest in leadership as an aspect of behaviour at work, rather than of personal characteristics. Since the 1950s, in particular, several theories about leadership or management style have been proposed. These have tended to be expressed in terms of authoritarian versus democratic

styles, or people-orientation versus task orientation. In some cases, despite acknowledged inconsistencies in the theories themselves, style theories have led to quite useful devices for improving training for leadership. A selection of the best-known style theories is discussed below:

10.   *Authoritarian-Democratic.* Three examples of this approach to management style are as follows: McGregor's Theory X manager – tough, autocratic and supporting tight controls with punishment – reward systems – the authoritarian. The contrasting style is that of the Theory Y manager – benevolent, participative and believing in self-controls – the democrat. These styles flow from the assumptions about people that are the original basis of Theory X and Theory Y (see Chapter 5).

Likert's (see Chapter 5) four management systems:

Exploitive-authoritative system – the epitome of the authoritarian style

Benevolent-authoritative system – a paternalistic style

Consultative system – moves towards greater democracy and teamwork

Participative-group system – the ultimate democratic style

11.   *Tannenbaum and Schmidt's model of a continuum of leadership styles,* ranging from authoritarian behaviour at one end to democratic behaviour at the other, as illustrated in Figure 7.2.

FIGURE 7.2 **A continuum of leadership styles**

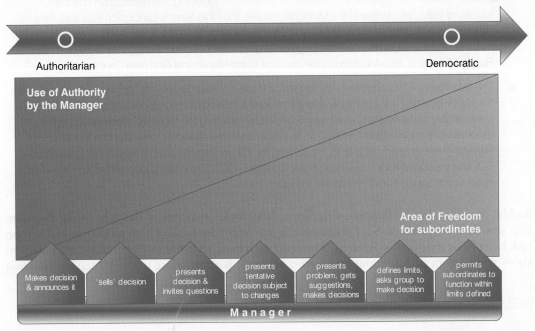

Source: Adapted from "How to Choose a Leadership Pattern" in *Harvard Business Review* (Mar/Apr 1958) by R. Tannenbaum and W. Schmidt (1957), copyright © Harvard Business Publishing, 1958. Reproduced with permission.

12.   The implication behind the above three approaches is that managers have a basic choice between being either authoritarian or democratic, and that the best style – the ideal – is a democratic one. In practice, the either/or choice proposed by the theorists may be somewhat artificial. Much will depend on the other elements of the leadership situation, as in Figure 7.2. In some circumstances an authoritarian style could be more effective than a democratic style, and vice versa. The suggestion that a democratic style is generally preferable to an authoritarian one has been criticized on the grounds that whilst this may apply to current trends in Western

industrialized nations, it need not apply at all in other cultures. The main weakness of these approaches is that they place too much emphasis on the leader's behaviour to the exclusion of the other variables in leadership, such as the internal dynamics of the group, the nature of the task and the competencies of group members.

13.   *People-Task Orientations.* Examples of approaches utilizing two of the leadership variables – people and tasks – are as follows:

- The Michigan Studies – these mid-twentieth century studies, analyzed a number of variables between managers of high-productivity groups and managers of low-productivity groups. The object was to see if any significant differences could be identified, thus providing some clues to leadership behaviour. In many respects (age, marital status, etc) there were no such differences between the two groups. However, one significant difference was noticed, and this was that the supervisors in charge of the high-producing groups tended to be employee-oriented while their opposite numbers in the low-producing groups tended, ironically, to be production-centred. The employee-oriented supervisors paid more attention to relationships at work, exercised less direct supervision and encouraged employee participation in decision-making. Production-oriented supervisors were more directive and more concerned with task needs than people needs. The two different orientations appeared to represent different ends of the same continuum, as shown in Figure 7.3. The Ohio Studies –conducted around the same time, also analyzed two distinct groupings of behaviour: 'Consideration' and 'Initiating Structure'. Consideration described behaviour that was essentially relationships-oriented; initiating structure referred to behaviour concerned with the organization of the work processes, including communication channels, allocating tasks, etc. Unlike in the Michigan studies, the Ohio team's conclusion was that the two dimensions of Consideration and Initiating Structures were separate dimensions. It was shown to be possible for a supervisor to score high on both dimensions. This finding was developed by Robert Blake and Jane Mouton in their concept of the Managerial Grid (see Chapter 46).

- The 3-D Theory – this approach, by Professor Reddin of New Brunswick University, Canada, takes the Blake-type grid a stage further and introduces a three-dimensional perspective. This adds considerably to the flexibility of leadership styles by including the factor of effectiveness in the dimensions. Reddin's Grid (Figure 7.4), is able to consider aspects of the situation in which leadership is exercised, as well as accounting for the concern for people (Relationship Oriented – RO) and the concern for production (Task Oriented – TO). The basic grid together with the eight styles which spring from it are shown in Figure 7.4.

Reddin describes the central grid as the set of basic styles available in the light of the Relationship and Task orientations. So, for example, a manager who focuses high on people and low on task has a basic style that is 'Related'. However each basic style has two alternative management styles arising from it, depending on whether the style is appropriate to the leadership situation

FIGURE 7.3 **The Michigan continuum**

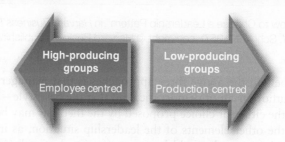

FIGURE 7.4 Reddin's 3-D Theory

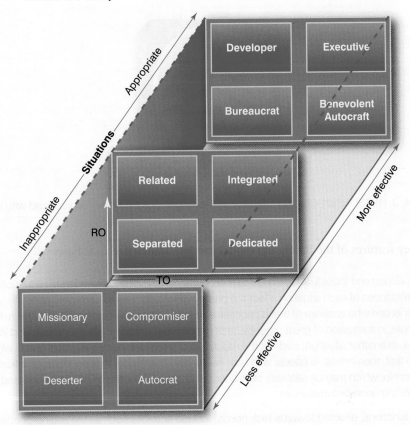

or not. Appropriate leadership tends to be more effective, i.e. achieves the output requirements for that particular managerial job. Thus, a 'Related' style that is used appropriately is called Developer, whilst an inappropriate style is called Missionary. The concept of effectiveness, added to the dimensions of relationships and task orientations, makes up the three-dimensional perspective. Unlike the Blake Grid, which has only one effective style (9,9), the Reddin Grid has four effective styles. Like the Blake Grid, however, Reddin's ideas have not been validated by research, and whilst useful for the purposes of management development, are not an authoritative answer to the question of what constitutes effective leadership.

7.6 CONTINGENCY APPROACHES

14. *Functional, or Action-centred Leadership.* This concept of leadership was developed in the United Kingdom by Professor John Adair. It is based on the theory that leadership is more a question of appropriate behaviour than of personality or of being in the right place at the right time. Adair's model of leadership (Figure 7.5) incorporates the concern for task and concern for people that has featured in all the theories previously mentioned. The functional model, however, distinguishes the concern for individuals from the concern for groups, and stresses that effective leadership lies in what the leader does to meet the needs of task, group and individuals. This takes the functional model nearer to the contingency approaches of modern theorists, whose concern is with the variety of factors – task, people and situation – which have a direct bearing on leadership and leadership styles.

FIGURE 7.5 Functional model of leadership

Source: Adair, J. (1973) *Action-Centred Leadership*. Copyright © John Adair. Reproduced with permission.

15.   The key features of the functional model can be summarized as follows:

- Task, Group and Individual Needs are fulfilled in the context of a total leadership situation. The circumstances of each situation affect the priority which attaches to each area of needs. An effective leader is one who is aware of these priorities and who can act in accordance with them. For example, in a situation of great urgency, task needs must predominate over group and individual needs. In another situation, such as the rebuilding of a football team, it is group needs which must come first, then individual needs, with task needs last. The model thus encourages a flexible style of leadership, which may be relatively task-oriented or group-oriented or individual-oriented, depending upon circumstances.

- Task functions, directed towards task needs, include activities such as the setting of objectives, the planning of tasks, the allocation of responsibilities and the setting of appropriate standards of performance.

- Group maintenance functions, directed towards group needs, include activities such as team-building and motivation, communication, discipline and acting as group representative to others outside the boundaries of the unit.

- Individual maintenance functions, directed towards the needs of individuals, include activities such as coaching, counselling, motivation and development.

Contingency theory of leadership a view which argues that leaders must alter their style in a manner consistent with aspects of the context

16.   Adair's concept of leadership is a **contingency theory of leadership**. It stresses that the leader's behaviour in relation to task, group and individual needs has to be related to the overall situation and, therefore, has to be adaptive.

17.   *Contingency Leadership.* The first theorist to use explicitly the label 'contingency' was Fiedler (1967). Fiedler named his leadership model 'the leadership contingency model'. In his view, group performance is contingent upon the leader adopting an appropriate style in the light of the relative favourableness of the situation. According to Fiedler, the three most important variables in determining the relative favourableness of the situation are Leader–member relations, Degree of structure in task and Power and authority of the position. These three situational variables can produce eight possible combinations of situation, of which the most favourable to the leader is when (1) there are good leader–member relations, (2) the task is highly structured and (3) the leader has a powerful position. By comparison, the least favourable conditions are when (1) the leader is disliked, (2) the task is relatively unstructured and (3) the leader has little positional power.

7.7 POWER & INFLUENCE

18.   As Kelly (2009: 172) notes, Effectiveness is influenced by the leader's power and influence – this is the essence of leadership. Leadership is about influencing the behaviour of others (followers). Power describes the ability to influence others, to get them to do things. In some cases the leader may influence subordinate or follower attitudes and in other cases their behaviour. Scholars have identified several types of power: reward, coercive, referent (Charisma), legitimate (position power), expert, informational, affiliation and group. Yet the exercise of power may be perceived by followers in either negative or positive terms. Rewards and praise are normally welcomed whilst punishment, penalties and sanctions are not. It is important to note that power is not a property of the leader but is a property of the relationship between the leader and follower; if followers do not believe the leader has a particular power base (such as knowledge or access to rewards) then they may not be compliant. Furthermore, the differing power bases are interrelated and may support each other. To be effective as the leader, it is necessary to influence people to carry out requests, support proposals and implement decisions. Whilst a variety of influence outcome may be described, we will focus on three: commitment (attitudes are influenced and agreement reached), compliance (a behavioural response, willing to make a minimal effort) and resistance (the subordinate is opposed to the proposal or request). The type of behaviour used intentionally to influence the attitudes and behaviour of another person is usually called an influence tactic. Influence tactics include:

RATIONAL PERSUASION – the use of explanations, logical arguments and factual evidence to show that a request for proposal is feasible and relevant for attaining task objectives.

PRESSURE – the leader persistently reminds the subordinate to carry out a request.

LEGITIMATING – the leader establishes authority by referring to rules, policies or a contract.

APPRISING – the leader explains how the subordinate will benefit personally as a result of carrying out the request or supporting a proposal.

CONSULTATION – encouraging involvement at an early stage.

INGRATIATION – the leader uses praise and flattery or may express confidence in the subordinate's ability to undertake a particular task.

PERSONAL APPEAL – the leader asks the subordinate for a personal favour.

EXCHANGE – the leader offers something specifically in return for the subordinates help.

COALITION – the leader gets others to persuade the subordinate to do something.

7.8 PRINCIPLE-CENTRED LEADERSHIP

19.   Leadership, according to Covey (1992), can be contrasted with management but he agrees the two are not mutually exclusive. Leadership derives its power from values and correct principles. Covey's view of leadership is based on the idea that effectiveness in a social role, such as management, depends upon how far a person adheres to certain principles of behaviour. He argues that the extent to which leaders recognize, and adhere to, principles such as fairness, justice, integrity and trust, determines their progress towards survival and stability, or to disintegration and destruction. He sees these principles as universal, objective and self-evident, just like the principle of gravity. He contrasts principles with values, which he argues are subjective, internal and derive mainly from our culture. The key issue, as Covey sees it, is for people to align their values to the 'correct' principles, of which there are four: trustworthiness, trust, empowerment and alignment.

20. Trustworthiness is essentially about a person's character and competence. We trust people for their honesty and reliability, for their character or integrity, and for their ability to carry out a role effectively, which is competence. Trust, in the sense of putting one's trust in others, is essential for effective team working and other personal relationships at work. A lack of trust is a major cause of failure in businesses and the public sector alike. Empowerment is the enabling of teams and individuals to assume responsibility for achieving the results they have agreed. It enables people to respond to the trust vested in them by their senior managers, who need to become sources of help, not measurers of performance. Where empowerment is practised, organizational structures and systems can be realigned, so that there is little hierarchy, a wide span of control and flexible systems. Alignment is the process of constantly reviewing the situation in the light of external conditions and the implementation of the other three principles.

21. Covey is effectively introducing a moral element into the practice of management. He identifies eight discernible characteristics of people whom, based on study, observation and personal experience, he would describe as 'principle-centred leaders'. Principle-centred leaders are continually learning, are service-oriented – they think of others, they need to serve, radiate positive energy, believe in other people, lead balanced lives, see life as an adventure, are synergistic and exercise for self-renewal. Covey's principles are essentially aimed at improving one's own outlook and personal competency, rather than about how to manipulate other people and situations in order to attain goals. They are intended to encourage an entirely new way of seeing the managerial role. In the work situation Covey sees the principles of trustworthiness, trust, empowerment and alignment operating at four different levels:

- personal (the relationship with oneself, where trustworthiness is the key principle),

- interpersonal (interaction with others, where trust is the key principle),

- managerial (getting a job done with others, where empowerment is the key principle), and

- organizational (building teams, developing structures, strategies and systems, where alignment is the key principle).

He argues that principle-centred leadership has to be grounded in all four levels. In other words the principles cannot be applied in a vacuum but have to be related to the people and tasks comprising the situation in which the leader has to operate. Covey's work on leadership further develops ideas introduced in his widely-read text The Seven Habits of Highly Effective People (1992), which is referred to in Chapter 27.

CONCLUSION

22. Organizational leadership is the ability of an individual to influence, motivate and enable others to contribute toward the effectiveness and success of the organizations of which they are members. A comparison between the various leadership theories is shown in Figure 7.6, which concludes this chapter. Leadership appears to be a critical determinant of organizational effectiveness – much of leadership is about influencing the behaviour of others. To be a successful leader, managers are likely to need a variety of cognitive (memory of detail and analytical ability), interpersonal (persuasive/good communicators) and technical skills. The function of the leader is to ensure the organization does the right thing (effectiveness) whilst that of the manager is to ensure things are done right (efficiency); the leader is concerned with establishing direction, the vision and organizational goals and influencing followers to obtain commitment. Consequently, the leader must be a good communicator and able to influence others-motivating and inspiring.

Leadership behaviours tend to be grouped into those focussing on work (task oriented behaviour) and those considering the follower. Consideration behaviours are based on relationship

FIGURE 7.6 Summary of Leadership Theories

Source	Title (if any)	Characteristics	Dimensions
D McGregor	Theory X/Theory Y	authoritarian versus democratic	'either/or'
R Likert	Systems 1–4	authoritarian versus democratic	'either/or'
Tannenbaum & C Schmidt	Leadership Continuum	authoritarian versus democratic	'either /or'
Michigan Studies	-	employee-centred vs production-centred	'either/or'
Ohio Studies	-	'consideration' and 'initiating structure'	both
Blake & Mouton	Managerial Grid	'concern for people' and 'concern for production'	both
W Reddin	3-D Theory	relationships and task orientations; effectiveness	all three
Harvard Studies	-	'task leaders' vs 'socio-emotional leaders'	'either /or'
J Adair	Functional Theory	task, group and individual needs; adaptive behaviour	multiple
F E Fiedler	Theory of Leadership Effectiveness	'favourableness of the situation'; adaptive behaviour	multiple
S Covey	Principle centred	adoption of key moral principles	multiple

building (relations-oriented behaviour), supporting, developing, recognizing and helping others. Specific task behaviours include planning work activities, clarifying roles and objectives and monitoring operations and performance – how things get done. The two key orientations (task and relationship building) reflect a concern for people and a concern for production, both of which are important for effective leadership. Subsequent research added a third orientation, behavioural set, based on approaches to change. Power describes the ability to influence others, to get them to do things. In some cases the leader may influence subordinate or follower attitudes and in other cases their behaviour. Scholars have identified several types of power: reward, coercive, referent (Charisma), legitimate (position power), expert, informational, affiliation and group. The type of behaviour used intentionally to influence the attitudes and behaviour of another person is usually called an influence tactic. Participative leadership involves effort by a leader to encourage and facilitate participation by others in making important decisions. Participative leadership, delegation and empowerment are concepts linking the power and behaviour approaches to leadership.

QUESTIONS

1   Contrast the leader and manager roles – do you believe a leader can also be a manager?

2   Review the main theories of leadership – in your answer, discuss limitations of the trait approach

3   The word leadership is sometimes used as if it were an attribute of personality, sometimes as if it were a characteristic of certain positions within an organization, and sometimes as an aspect of behaviour. Discuss.

4   Can a person be both a leader and manager at the same time? Contrast the roles of manager and leader identifying similarities and differences.

5   Evaluate the role of power in leadership theory. In your answer you should list and describe several types of power. You should also evaluate each type of power commenting on how it may be perceived by followers.

USEFUL WEBSITES

The Institute of Leadership & Management: **www.i-l-m.com/** Various resources for leadership

About.com Guide: **psychology.about.com/od/leadership/p/ leadtheories.htm** Leadership Theories – eight Major Leadership Theories

VIDEO CASES

Now take a look at the online video cases – visit the companion website to work through real world business problems associated with the concepts presented within this chapter.
9 Leadership: Management Lessons from McDonald's
Efficiency is about how the organization uses its resources to undertake activities and we note that some companies are able to get more out of their resources than others. In the

case of human resources, this is achieved through motivation.
74 Leadership – what is it
LEADERSHIP AND MANAGEMENT – the meaning of the concepts is explored through the terms effectiveness and efficiency.

REFERENCES

Covey, S. (1992) 'Principle-Centred Leadership', Simon & Schuster.

Kelly, P. P. (2009) 'International Business and Management', Cengage Learning EMEA.

Martin, J. and Fellenz, M. (2010) 'Organizational Behaviour and Management 4e', Ed. 4. Cengage Learning EMEA.

Northouse, P. G. (2010) 'Leadership, Theory and Practice', Ed. 5. SAGE Publications.

Tannenbaum, R. and Schmidt, W. H. (1958) 'How to Choose A Leadership Pattern', Harvard Business Review, Mar/Apr 58, Vol. 36 Issue 2, p. 95–101.

Yukl, G. (2010) 'Leadership in Organizations: Global Edition', Ed. 7. Pearson Higher Education.

CHAPTER 8
GROUPS AND
GROUP BEHAVIOUR

Key Concepts

- Group
- Team

Learning Outcomes   Having read this chapter, you should be able to:

- identify Tuckman's five stages of group development
- identify categories of group behaviour
- list characteristics of effective teamwork
- discuss Belbin's eight team roles

Group An association of two or more individuals who have a shared sense of identity and who interact with each other in structured ways on the basis of a common set of expectations about each other's behaviour

Group cohesiveness The extent to which members of a group interact, co-operate, are united and work together effectively. Generally, the greater the cohesiveness within a group, the more rewarding the experience is for the members and the higher the chances are of success

Group dynamics The behavioural interactions and patterns of behaviour that occur when groups of people meet

Team Implies a small, cohesive group that works effectively as a single unit through being focused on a common task

1.   The study of groups in work situations has been an important activity of behavioural scientists ever since the pioneering work of the Hawthorne Researchers almost a century ago. The outcome of numerous studies into different aspects of the behaviour of groups is a considerable store of useful and practicable knowledge about the working of groups. Typical areas of research have included the study of group effectiveness, inter-group competition, group formation methods and group cohesiveness and dynamics. The most important factors in the behaviour of groups are as indicated in Figure 8.1.

Previous chapters have dealt with various aspects of leadership, tasks and environment, motivation and whilst these factors cannot be ignored, this chapter focuses attention on the other factors, such as group norms, group cohesiveness and roles within groups. It concludes with a summary of recent research into teams and team building.

2.   Groups at work are formed as a direct consequence of an organization's need to differentiate itself. Differentiation, or specialization, involves not only the breaking down of the organization into functions, but also the formation of groups to support the tasks assigned to those functions. It is important to recognize that group tasks vary. For example an additive task is a type of task whose accomplishment depends upon the sum of all group members' efforts (e.g. tug-of-war). A conjunctive task is a task whose accomplishment depends upon the performance of the group's least talented member (e.g. running a relay race). Finally, a disjunctive task accomplishment depends upon the performance of the group's most talented member (e.g. a quiz). A group is basically a collection of individuals, sharing a common aim and identity. Thus, a group is more than an aimless crowd of people waiting in an airport lounge or at a bus stop. A group has some central purpose, temporary or permanent, and a degree of self-

FIGURE 8.1 Key factors in group behaviour

awareness as a group. In the work situation, most tasks are in fact undertaken by groups and teams, rather than by individuals. Groups are also widely used for solving problems, creating new ideas, making decisions and coordinating tasks. These group functions are what the organization itself needs to fulfil its purpose. However, individuals themselves need groups. Groups provide identity, stimulus, protection, assistance and other social and psychological requirements. Groups, therefore, can work in the interests of organizations as a whole as well as in the interests of individual members.

3. One of the earliest distinctions to be made between groups (arising from the Hawthorne investigations) was between formal and informal groups. Formal groups were those set up by the management of an organization to undertake duties in the pursuit of organization goals. Some writers have described formal groups as official groups, to avoid the confusion that can arise when describing groups operating in an informally structured organization (e.g. an organic type of organization). Such groups may be informal in the sense that they have few rules, enjoy participative leadership and have flexible roles. Nevertheless they are completely official. What is meant by informal organizations are those groupings which the employees themselves have developed in accordance with their own needs. These, of course, are unofficial. Every organization has these unofficial groups, and research has shown how important they are for organizational effectiveness. A second distinction made by some scholars is between groups and teams – we will revisit this issue later in the chapter. First we consider how groups are formed and develop.

8.1 GROUP FORMATION, DEVELOPMENT, NORMS & COHESIVENESS

4. Despite having different tasks, most group activities subscribe to the same basic model: groups are formed, they perform a task(s) and then disband. The way they are formed, their structure and the outcomes of group work are discussed here. Like selecting a football team, the coach or players may select the team (group members). It is generally assumed that selection by the players is more subjective, based on emotions, whilst selection by the coach may be more objective. Kelly (2008) argues that the group allocation process has important consequences. Firstly and directly, it determines the distribution of various structural variables within the group i.e. how many males or females there may be, their age, ability and nationality. Secondly and indirectly it impacts upon group cohesion and cooperative structures – the extent to which group members pull together. It is widely recognized that new groups are not 'born' as high performing groups but must develop the required cooperative structures.

5. A useful way of looking at the development of groups was devized by Tuckman (1965), who described groups as moving through four key stages of development. Later (1977) he added a fifth stage. The final model can be summarized as follows: Stage 1 Forming. Finding out about the task, rules and methods; acquiring information and resources; relying on the leader. Stage 2 Storming. Internal conflict develops; members resist the task at the emotional level. Stage 3 Norming. Conflict is settled, cooperation develops; views are exchanged and new standards (norms) developed. Stage 4 Performing. Teamwork is achieved, roles are

Forming The initial formation of a group and the first stage in group development

Storming The second stage of group development which involves members of the group getting to know each other and putting forward their views

Norming The third stage of group development during which members of the group establish guidelines and standards and develop their own norms of acceptable behaviour

Performing The fourth stage of group development during which the group concentrates on the performance of the common task

Adjourning When a group disperses after goals have been met

flexible; solutions are found and implemented. Stage 5 Adjourning. Group disperses on completion of tasks. See Figure 8.2

6.   Group norms can be seen to develop at Stage 3 in the above analysis. Norms, in this context, are common standards of social and work behaviour which are expected of individuals in the group. Once such norms have been developed, there are strong pressures on people to conform to them. Norms are influenced by organizational factors such as policies, management style of superiors, and rules and procedures. They are also influenced by individual employees, whose standards may or may not be in line with those of the official organization. For example, a group norm for the young men in an engineering workshop could be to follow a fashion of wearing long hair. This could conflict with organizational norms concerning the safety of employees in the workplace. Another example of a conflict between official and unofficial group norms can be drawn from a situation where a group itself decides to operate a certain level of output over a given time, regardless of targets set by the management in their search for increased efficiency and productivity. The ideal situation, from an organization's point of view, is attained when the unofficial norms of the group are in harmony with the official norms of the organization. There is no doubt that part of the leadership role of a manager is to secure this harmony in his or her own section.

7.   The key point made about group development is that effectiveness (see below) is an outcome which develops over time, as the group begins to understand what is required of it and how it can utilize the knowledge, skills and attributes of the individual members in fulfilling group and individual goals. On the way to achieving effectiveness, groups will undoubtedly face uncertainty, if not conflict, but these processes have to be seen as necessary costs of achieving both harmony and purposeful behaviour.

Group dynamics The behavioural interactions and patterns of behaviour that occur when groups of people meet

8.   Group cohesiveness describes the extent to which members interact (**group dynamics**), co-operate, are united and work

FIGURE 8.2 **Stages of group development**

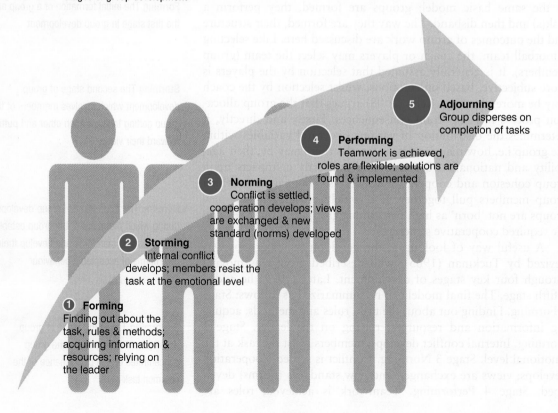

5 Adjourning
Group disperses on completion of tasks

4 Performing
Teamwork is achieved, roles are flexible; solutions are found & implemented

3 Norming
Conflict is settled, cooperation develops; views are exchanged & new standard (norms) developed

2 Storming
Internal conflict develops; members resist the task at the emotional level

1 Forming
Finding out about the task, rules & methods; acquiring information & resources; relying on the leader

together effectively. Generally, the greater the cohesiveness within a group, the more rewarding the experience is for the members and the higher the chance of success. A very cohesive group will demonstrate strong loyalty to its individual members and strong adherence to its established norms. Individuals who cannot accept these norms are cast out from the protection of the group. As Tuckman's analysis shows, cohesiveness develops over time. A newly-formed group has little cohesiveness. There are several factors which can help cohesiveness to develop in a group. These include the following:

● similarity of work

● physical proximity in the workplace

● the workflow system

● structure of tasks

● group size (smaller rather than larger)

● threats from outside

● the prospect of rewards

● leadership style of the manager

● common social factors (age, race, social status, etc.).

In general, the reasons why people do develop into closely knit groups are threefold: because of things they have in common, pressures from outside the group and because of their need to fulfil their social and affiliation needs.

8.2 GROUP EFFECTIVENESS

9. Group effectiveness has to be considered in at least two dimensions – effectiveness in terms of task accomplishment, and effectiveness in terms of the satisfaction of group members (affective outcomes). The two outcomes, are, however, related. When group members are happy to belong to a group they and the group tend to perform better. In his classic work, 'The Human Side of Enterprise' (1960), McGregor provided a perceptive account of the differences between effective and ineffective groups. A summary of the most important features he noted appears below, see Figure 8.3. McGregor's view of effective groups corresponds to Tuckman's Stages 3 and 4, i.e. Norming and Performing. The features of ineffective groups are closer to Tuckman's Stage 2, i.e. Storming. A difference between McGregor and Tuckman seems to be that the former sees some groups as fixed in their poor behaviour, whereas the latter implies that groups tend to move out of the ineffective stages into more effective behaviour.

10. An area of considerable interest to behavioural scientists for many years has been the process of interaction within groups. Over the past two decades several core structural variables such as group size, gender, ability, personality, nationality, age and experience have been researched and their impact upon performance ascertained (Group structure). Researchers have argued that variability in age can create conflict within workgroups, due to differences in training and experience which lead workers of different ages to disagree with one another about their jobs. The available evidence suggests that in mixed gender groups, males are (a) more active and influential than females, (b) more likely than females to engage in agentic activities (giving opinions and suggestions) but less likely to engage in communal activities and (c) more concerned than females about resolving issues such as status, power and wealth. Grouping on the basis of past performance has also been tried with varying success. The abilities of group members are the focus of many studies on the effects of group composition. Most of these studies reflect a desire to create successful groups by selecting people who can work together. Several scholars have

FIGURE 8.3 Differences between effective and ineffective groups

Effective groups	Ineffective groups
1. Informal, relaxed atmosphere.	1. Bored or tense atmosphere.
2. Much relevant discussion with high degree of participation.	2. Discussion dominated by one or two people, and often irrelevant.
3. Group task or objective clearly understood, and commitment to it obtained.	3. No clear common objective.
4. Members listen to each other.	4. Members tend not to listen to each other.
5. Conflict is not avoided, but brought into the open and dealt with constructively.	5. Conflict is either avoided or is allowed to develop into open warfare.
6. Most decisions are reached by general consensus with a minimum of formal voting.	6. Simple majorities are seen as sufficient basis for group decisions, which the minority have to accept.
7. Ideas are expressed freely and openly.	7. Personal feelings are kept hidden and criticism is embarrassing.
8. Leadership is not always with the chairman, but tends to be shared as appropriate.	8. Leadership is provided by chairman.
9. The group examines its own progress and behaviour.	9. The group avoids any discussion about its own behaviour.

asked whether there is such a thing as an optimum group size. Some suggest groups should be no larger that six because they are difficult to manage, there is a greater propensity for social loafing and coordination problems. Furthermore motivation problems are associated with larger groups. Not only is it more difficult to coordinate the efforts of the team as membership grows, but efforts may increase as individual contributions lose value in team decisions. Reduced effort may go unnoticed as team size increases, creating an incentive to free ride on the efforts of others (social loafing). The major influences on group effectiveness can be broken down into two main categories: (1) Immediate constraints, e.g. group size, nature of task, skills of members and environmental factors and (2) Group motivation and interaction. The basic difference between the two categories is that (1) represents things that cannot be changed in the short-term, and that (2) represents behaviour that (potentially) can be changed in the short-term. Let us now look at key points in each of these categories.

8.3 IMMEDIATE CONSTRAINTS

11.   There are four particularly influential constraints. These are as follows:

GROUP SIZE – small groups tend to be more cohesive than larger groups; small groups tend to encourage full participation; large groups contain greater diversity of talent.

NATURE OF TASK – in work-groups, the production system, including the type of technology used, has a major effect on groups, e.g. high-technology plant often disperses employees into isolated couples incapable of forming satisfactory groups. Where group tasks are concerned with problem-solving, decision-making or creative thinking, different member talents may be required along with a variety of leadership styles. A further aspect of task is the time factor, i.e. urgency tends to force groups to be task and action-oriented.

MEMBERSHIP – the personalities concerning the variety of knowledge and skills available cannot be changed overnight. A knowledgeable group, skilled at group working, are much more likely to succeed in their tasks, than an inexperienced group. Equally a group with a wider range of talents in its midst tends to be more effective than a group with a narrow range of talents.

ENVIRONMENTAL FACTORS – these include physical factors, such as working proximity, plant or office layout. In general, close proximity aids group identity and loyalty, and distance reduces them. Other environmental issues include the traditions of the organization and leadership styles. Formal organizations tend to adopt formal group practices. Autocratic leadership styles prefer group activities to be directed. More participative styles prefer greater sharing in groups. The important point about these immediate constraints is that they establish the scenario for the operation of the group. If the expectations and behaviour of the members match this scenario, then the group will tend to perform very effectively. By contrast, if there is a considerable mismatch, the chances of the group succeeding in its objectives will be slight.

8.4 GROUP MOTIVATION, INTERACTION (STRUCTURE/ DYNAMICS) & CONFLICT

12.   GROUP MOTIVATION – the level of motivation in the group will be a decisive factor in efficiency and effectiveness. High motivation can result from members' perception of the task, and their role in it, as being of importance. Standards of performance are essential to motivation, together with adequate and timely feedback of results. Individuals also need to feel satisfied with membership of the group. Where these features are absent, motivation will tend to be low.

13.   GROUP INTERACTION – this depends mainly upon factors such as leadership, individual and group motivation, and appropriate rules and procedures. As we saw in the previous chapter on leadership, the key to success in leadership is to obtain the best 'mix' of attention to task and attention to people, taking the total situation into account. The ability of a group leader to obtain the commitment of his team towards achieving the task (team spirit) will result in a high degree of collaboration. Where interaction is high people tend to be more open, and more comfortable with the pursuit of the task. All groups need some method of operating. This might consist of a few simple rules and procedures to control decision-making and conflict, for example. Alternatively, as in formal committees, quite complex procedures may apply in order to encourage or control interaction.

14.   One of the most useful attempts to develop categories of behaviour, especially verbal behaviour, in groups was that of the late Robert Bales, a Harvard professor who pioneered the development of systematic methods of group observation and measurement of interaction processes. In several studies of small groups, Bales and his colleagues were able to generate a list of frequent behaviour categories to enable them to observe behaviour in a way that was relevant and consistent. Some examples of the categories were as follows:

- shows solidarity
- agrees
- gives suggestion
- gives opinion
- asks for orientation
- asks for suggestion
- shows antagonism (dislike).

These categories were grouped according to whether they furthered the task functions or whether they aided interpersonal relations, or socio-emotional functions, as Bales called them.

15.   Bales' ideas have been adapted by a number of British researchers, notably Rackham and Morgan (1977), who have used their version as the basis for improving skills in interpersonal

relationships and for interaction process analysis. Their list utilizes the following categories of possible behaviour in groups:

- proposing (concepts, suggestions, actions)
- building (developing another's proposal)
- supporting (another person or his concepts)
- disagreeing
- defending/attacking
- blocking/difficulty stating (with no alternative offered)
- open behaviour (risking ridicule and loss of status)
- testing understanding
- summarizing
- seeking information
- giving information
- shutting out behaviour (e.g. interrupting, talking over)
- bringing in behaviour (involving another member).

Experience in the use of such categories can enable observers of group behaviour to give constructive and relevant feedback to group members, instead of rather generalized or anecdotal descriptions of what has appeared to have taken place.

16.   Categories of behaviour are a key element in distinguishing roles in groups. Feedback to groups can help the members to see what kind of role they played in the proceedings. Role is not quite the same as position (or job). The latter is concerned with the duties and rights attached to a particular job title. The former is concerned with how the job is performed, and is affected by the expectations of superiors, of organizational policies, of colleagues and subordinates as well as the expectations of the job holder himself. This web of relationships has been called the role-set.

17.   In any group activity a number of roles are likely to be performed – for example, the roles of 'leader', 'peacemaker', 'ideas person', 'humourist' and 'devil's advocate' to name but a few. In informal groups roles may emerge in line with individual personality and know-how. In formal groups many roles are already defined, such as chairman, secretary, visiting expert and others. Sometimes members of a group experience a conflict of roles. For example, a union representative may feel a conflict between his or her need to fulfil a spokesman role for constituents, and the need to act responsibly as an employee of the company. Sometimes the chairman of a committee stands down temporarily from the chair in order to express a deeply felt personal view about an issue in which he or she has an interest. This action prevents undue role conflict on the question of impartiality from the chair.

18.   The items discussed here are essentially about actual behaviour in a group. This behaviour is part of a dynamic, or constantly changing, process within the group, which can be influenced by individuals in response to issues that have occurred during task undertaking. Thus, even where the immediate constraints impose tight restrictions on behaviour, the group can still be effective if individuals can be motivated to work together to achieve their objectives.

8.5 COMPETITION & CONFLICT BETWEEN GROUPS

19.   So far we have been discussing behaviour within groups. Another important aspect of group behaviour is inter-group relations and the impact of the group on the individual. Since

every organization is made up of a number of different groups (e.g. IT, marketing, operations) of employees, the question of collaboration between groups is vital for obtaining an overall balance in the social system. As Lawrence and Lorsch were at pains to point out (see Chapter 10) integration is as crucial to organizational success as differentiation. Breaking an organization down into smaller units (work groups), in order to cope adequately with the diversity of tasks faced, creates opportunities to develop task interests and special know-how, but, at the same time, it also creates rivalries and competing interests which can be damaging to the organization's mission. An understanding of the consequences, good and bad, of intergroup competition can, therefore, be of considerable help to an organization's management.

20.   The first systematic study of intergroup competition was made many years ago by Sherif and colleagues in the United States. They organized a boys' camp in such a way that two deliberately created groups were formed for the experiment. Various devices were used to encourage the development of separate identities between the two groups. As the camp progressed, a number of interesting changes took place both within and between the groups. WITHIN GROUPS – Collections of individuals, with no special ties with each other, grew into closely-knit groups; the group climate changed from being play-oriented to work-oriented, and leadership tended to become more autocratic; each group became more highly structured and placed a much greater emphasis on loyalty and conformity. BETWEEN GROUPS – Each group began to see the other group as 'the enemy', hostility between groups increased whilst communication between them decreased; stereotyped opinions of the other side began to emerge, especially negative stereotypes.

21.   Conflict between groups and their members and employee behaviour can be explained, to some extent, by Social Identity Theory (SIT). Belonging to groups (both socially and at work) affects the way we think about and see ourselves (whom we are) and the way others think about and see us. Such thinking impacts upon behaviour, the way we behave and the way others behave in

Social identity Part of the self-concept which comes from our membership of groups

relation to ourselves and the groups to which we may belong. The way we view ourselves is determined in part by the groups to which we belong (social identity). Thus, social identity defines the person and appropriate behaviours for them. This typically happens through social comparison – individuals not only compare themselves with other individuals with whom they interact, but they also compare their own group with similar, but distinct, out-groups. We all see ourselves as members of various social groupings, which are distinguishable and hence different from other social groupings. According to SIT, people tend to classify themselves and others into various social categories, such as organizational membership, religious affiliation, gender and age cohort. As these examples suggest, people may be classified in various categories, and different individuals may utilize different categorization schemas. Categories are defined by typical characteristics abstracted from the members.

22.   According to Huczynski and Buchanan (2010), the consequence is that by identifying with certain groupings but not others, we come to see the world in terms of 'us and them'. Whilst group membership may have its benefits (self esteem, privilege) it can also be a source of conflict and may, through generalizations and stereotypes, determine inappropriate behavioural responses. The group can impact upon (1) perceptions of individual members; (2) individual performance; (3) individual behaviour and (4) individual attitudes. In social identity theory, a social identity is a person's knowledge that he or she belongs to a social category or group. A social group is a set of individuals who hold a common social identification or view themselves as members of the same social category. Through a social comparison process, persons who are similar to themselves are categorized with the self and are labelled the in-group; persons who differ from them are categorized as the out- group. The consequence of the social comparison process is people come to see themselves as members of one group/category (the in-group) in comparison with another (the out-group), and the consequences of this categorization include conflict and prejudice. SIT suggests that much inter-group conflict stems from the very fact that groups exist. More specifically, in SIT it is argued that (a) given the relational and comparative nature of social identifications, social identities are maintained primarily by inter-group comparisons and (b) given the desire to enhance self-esteem; groups seek positive differences between themselves and reference groups. This suggests groups have a vested interest in perceiving or

even provoking greater differentiation than exists and disapproving of the reference (out) group on this basis. Difference can determine the ability of people to work effectively and efficiently together in pursuit of common goals. We will revisit SIT later in the book when we discuss women in management (Chapter 14) and the international context of management (Chapter 15).

23.   Inter-group competition, as was noted above, has its advantages and disadvantages. The prime advantages are that a group develops a high level of cohesiveness and a high regard for its task functions. The main disadvantages are that groups develop competing or conflicting goals, and that inter-group communication and cooperation breaks down. Since the Sherif study, several researchers have followed up with studies of conflict resolution between groups. The general conclusions are that to reduce the negative side-effects of inter-group competition, an organization would need to: encourage and reward groups on the basis of their contribution to the organization as a whole, or at least, to large parts of it, rather than on individual group results; stimulate high interaction and communication between groups, and provide rewards for inter-group collaboration; encourage movement of staff across group boundaries for the purposes of increasing mutual understanding of problems; and avoid putting neighbouring groups into a situation where they are competing on a win-lose basis for resources or status, for example.

24.   Not all conflict is harmful. On the contrary, disagreement is an essential element in working through problems and overcoming difficulties. The conflict of ideas when put to the service of organization or group goals is in fact the sign of a healthy organization. What is to be avoided is the point-scoring conflict that develops between groups who see their relative success and status vis-a-vis their neighbours as being more important than the pursuit of the common good.

8.6 TEAMS, TEAM-BUILDING & VIRTUAL TEAMS

25.   A team implies a small, cohesive group that works effectively as a single unit through being focused on a common task. What, then, are the characteristics of effective teamwork? Research suggests that they are as follows:

- clear objectives and agreed goals

- openness and confrontation

- support and trust

- cooperation and conflict

- sound procedures

- appropriate leadership

- regular review

- individual development

- sound intergroup relations.

26.   Long-term research into management team-skills has been carried out by Dr. Meredith Belbin and colleagues. The result, after studying numerous teams at Henley Management College, showed that team behaviour fell into one or more of eight fairly distinct team roles, as follows:

Team-role A pattern of behaviour, characteristic of the way in which one team member interacts with another, where performance facilitates the progress of the team as a whole

- Chairman – An individual who can control and coordinate the other team members, who recognizes their talents but is not threatened by them, and who is concerned with what is feasible rather than what is exciting or imaginative.

- Shaper – This is another leader role, but one in which the role-holder acts much more directly to shape the decisions and thinking of the team.

- Innovator – This type of person provides the creative thinking in a team, even if a concern for good ideas overshadows his ability to be sensitive to other people's needs.

- Monitor/Evaluator – The strength of this role lies in the holder's ability to analyze issues and suggestions objectively.

- Company Worker – Whilst the first four roles provide the major inspiration and leadership, this role provides for implementation of ideas by the role-holders' ability to translate general ideas and plans into practice.

- Team Worker – This role meets the needs of the team for cohesiveness and collaboration, for role holders tend to be perceptive of people's needs and adept at supporting individuals.

- Resource Investigator – A person in this role looks for resources and ideas outside the team with the aim of supporting the team's efforts.

- Completer – This is an individual whose energies are directed primarily to the completion of the task, and who harnesses anxiety and concern towards getting the job done on time and to a high standard.

27. Individuals are likely to be predisposed (an individual's behavioural tendency in a team environment) to behaving in one predominant role, even though they may show tendencies towards others. The dominant role is closely linked to particular reasoning abilities and personality characteristics, but is also affected by the priorities and processes of a manager's job. An effective team is one that is likely to have a range of roles present in its make-up. Belbin concluded that the ideal team would be composed of one Chairman (or one Shaper), one Innovator, one Monitor Evaluator and one or more Company Workers, Team Workers, Resource Investigators or Completers. Since ideal conditions are rarely present, managers have to build their teams from amongst the people they have, and encourage a greater degree of role flexibility. However, a manager can benefit from understanding the distinctions between the roles and making an assessment of the role-strengths of his own staff. Knowing what to expect, as well as what not to expect, from colleagues enables the manager to head-off potential tensions or even group breakdown.

28. There are many types of group within the organization such as the functional, cross functional, self managed, task force, virtual and executive team. They vary in size and degrees and interdependence and consequently their need for communication, coordination, control and leadership. Each can vary in relation to degrees of autonomy, authority, diversity of membership, stability of membership and the duration of existence. Globalization, increased competition and improvements in communication technologies have driven many organizations to rely upon virtual teams – a team that uses mainly electronic interaction in order to achieve objectives without the need to function as a team in the traditional sense of the term. A further team type is now more common as a result of globalization – the multicultural team. As organizations globalize their operations, it is likely that the frequency with which employees will interact with people from different countries will increase. Further, domestic populations are becoming more diverse, suggesting that domestic organizations will also need to learn how to manage more heterogeneous workgroups than they have managed previously. Kelly (2009) warns us that diversity appears to be a double-edged sword, increasing the opportunity for creativity as well as the likelihood that group members will be dissatisfied and fail to identify with the group. A group that is diverse could be expected to have members who may have had significantly different experiences and, therefore, significantly different perspectives on key issues or problems. However, such differences can create serious coordination and communication difficulties for groups. He advises that we allocate more time to allow diverse groups to become cohesive.

CONCLUSION

In this chapter we recognized the important role of groups in helping organizations attain their goals but argued that not all groups are effective; they need to work at developing cooperative structures. Stages of development, group structures and dynamics were considered alongside tools to classify certain types of group behaviour and the roles group members may adopt. Aside from considering within group issues we also considered the challenges associated with inter-group working. We closed with a discussion about teams, recognizing there to be many types of team. More recently, as a result of social and technological forces, organizations have given increased attention and made greater use of virtual and multicultural teams.

QUESTIONS

1   How are group norms established, and why are they sometimes in conflict with the norms of the organization as a whole?

2   What are the implications of Belbin's research for team development or team building?

3   List the factors influencing effective teamwork. Take four of the factors and write a short paragraph on each.

4   Define what a group is and with reference to at least one stage model describe how groups develop.

5   Compare and contrast effective and ineffective groups – what makes a group effective?

USEFUL WEBSITES

Belbin Associates: **www.belbin.com/** Brief outline of Belbin Team Role Theory

Management Library: **managementhelp.org/grp_skll/teams/teams.htm** Team Building

VIDEO CASES

Now take a look at the online video cases – visit the companion website to work through real world business problems associated with the concepts presented within this chapter.
18 Team Composition
Discussion about the size and composition of successful teams. A video clip is used, more as a mini lecture to stimulate discussion, and explore team compilation problems

117 Groups and teams
Groups form a major part of any organizational activity. Using several short film clips we set out to explore why groups and teams are an important aspect of organizational activity and consider how such groups and teams are formed, their structure and associated performance issues.

REFERENCES

Buchanan, D. and Huczynski, A. (2010) 'Organizational Behaviour', Ed. 7. Financial Times Press.
Kelly, P. P. (2008) 'Achieving desirable group-work outcomes through the group allocation process', Team Performance Management, Volume: 14 Issue: 1/2, p. 22–38.
McGregor, D. M. (1960) 'The Human Side of Enterprise', McGraw-Hill New York.
Mullins, L.(2010) 'Management and Organizational Behaviour', Ed. 9. Financial Times Press.

Rackham, N. and Morgan,T. (1977) 'Behaviour Analysis in Training', McGraw Hill.
Tuckman, B. W. (1965) 'DEVELOPMENTAL SEQUENCE IN SMALL GROUPS', Psychological Bulletin, Vol. 63, No. 6, 3, p. 384–399.
Tuckman, B. W. and Jensen, A. (1977) 'Stages of Small-Group Development Revisited', Group and Organization Studies, 2 (4), p. 419–427.

Section Five
Systems and Contingency Approaches to Management Theory

CHAPTER 9
ORGANIZATIONS AS SYSTEMS

Key Concepts

- Socio-technical system
- System
- Systems approach
- Systems thinking

Learning Outcomes Having read this chapter, you should be able to:

- review the role of systems theory in understanding organizations
- list the main characteristics of open systems
- explain what a cybernetic system is
- identify the key variables considered in the systems approach to organizations
- list four types of environment
- discuss the five sub-systems at work in organizations

Organization A group of people with a common purpose who work together to achieve shared goals (see formal organization and informal organization)

System a set of elements connected together which form a whole, thereby possessing properties of the whole rather than of its component parts

Inputs The resources introduced into a system for transformation into outputs

Outputs The completed products or services of a system

Systems approach A management approach which is focused on the total work of the organization and the interrelationships of structure and behaviour and the range of variables within the organization. The organization is viewed within its total environment and emphasizes the importance of multiple channels in interaction

1. In Chapter 2 (Definitions of Management) we defined an **organization** as a group of people with a common purpose who work together to achieve shared goals. We also noted that like discussions about management theory, approaches to organization theory tend to follow the pattern of classical, human relations and **systems** perspectives. We have not yet explained the systems perspective. The dominance of first the Classical School and second the Human Relations/Social Psychological Schools has been overtaken by a more comprehensive approach to the study of management in organizations. This more recent approach views the organization as a system of interrelated sets of activities which enable **inputs** to be transformed into **outputs**. This view attempts to bring together the classical and human relations approach. The approach, which is described in more detail below, enables theorists to study key elements of organization in terms of their interaction with one another and, importantly, with their external environment. Whereas, in the past, the explanations were in terms of structures OR people, now it is possible to identify theories which seek to explain or predict organizational behaviour in a multi-dimensional way by studying people, structure, technology and environment at one and the same time. This chapter defines the characteristics of open social systems and summarizes the current theoretical position as a prelude to a discussion of the ideas of several outstanding theorists who have contributed to the growing understanding of organizations as systems. A **systems approach** is a management approach which attempts to reconcile the classical and human relations approaches, Mullins (2010). Attention is focused on the total work of the organization and the interrelationships of structure and behaviour and the range of variables within the organization. The organization is viewed within its total environment and emphasizes the importance of multiple channels in interaction.

9.1 SYSTEMS THEORY

2. Defined at its simplest, a system is a collection of interrelated parts which form some whole. Typical systems are the solar system, the human body, communication networks and social systems. Systems may be 'closed' or 'open'. Closed systems are those, which, for all practical purposes, are completely self-supporting, and thus do not interact with their environment. An example would be an astronaut's life-support pack. Open systems are those which do interact with their environment, upon which they rely for obtaining essential inputs and for the discharge of their system outputs. Social systems (e.g. organizations) are always open systems. A basic model of an open system is shown diagrammatically in Figure 9.1.

3. The three major characteristics of open systems are as follows:

● they receive inputs or energy from their environment

● they convert these inputs into outputs

● they discharge their outputs into their environment.

FIGURE 9.1 Basic model of an open system

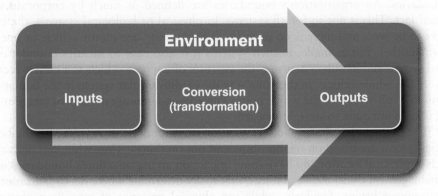

In relation to an organization, the inputs include people, materials, information and finance. These inputs are organized and activated so as to convert human skills and raw materials into products, services and other outputs which are discharged into the environment, as shown in Figure 9.2. Note that some scholars discuss inputs solely in terms of the raw materials required for the product/ service whilst others include the inputs used to make the product or service (see transformational resources – people, processes, knowledge, technology, etc.).

FIGURE 9.2 The organization as an open system

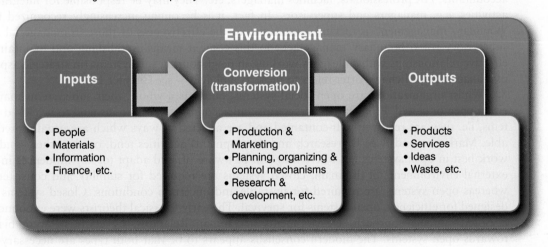

4.   A key feature of open systems is their interdependence on the environment, which may be relatively stable or relatively uncertain at a particular point in time. This feature is of considerable importance to business enterprises which need to adapt to the changing fortunes of the market place if they are to flourish. A classification of environments is given later in the chapter.

Sub-system One part of numerous interdependent elements that comprise the wider system

5.   Most systems can be divided into sub-systems. For example, the human body – a total system – encloses a number of major sub-systems, such as the central nervous system and the cardiovascular system, to name but two. Organizations have their sub-systems as well, e.g. production, marketing and accounting sub-systems. The boundaries between sub-systems are called interfaces. These are the sensitive internal boundaries contained within the total system, and they will again

be referred to shortly. In the meantime it is important to consider a few points about system boundaries. An organization's boundaries are defined as much by corporate strategy as by actual fact. This is not so for all systems. In physical or biological systems, the boundaries are there to be seen, and there is no problem distinguishing one motor vehicle or one human being from another. For example, in such systems it is also easy to identify boundaries between the total system and its sub-systems i.e. the gearbox of a motor vehicle is a clearly recognisable sub-unit of the whole vehicle. In the same way the cardiovascular system in the human body is a recognisable sub-system of the whole body. These boundaries are matters of fact. For organizations the issue is not quite so straightforward.

6.   The point is that the boundaries of an organization are not visible, for the boundaries of a social system are based on relationships and not on things. Thus while certain factual elements, such as physical location, do have some impact on an organization's boundaries, it is the results of management decisions, i.e. choices, that really determine where the organization ends and the environment begins. Similarly, while the physical presence of machinery, for example, may partly determine some of the internal boundaries of the organization, it is ultimately a matter of corporate, or departmental, strategy which decides where the production system begins and where it ends.

7.   In any organization, some employees work consistently at the external boundary. These are the people who have to deal with the inputs and the outputs to the system, e.g. those responsible for raising capital, purchasing from suppliers, identifying customer requirements, etc and those responsible for sales, distribution, etc. Other employees work consistently on internal boundaries, i.e. at the interfaces between the various sub-systems of the organization. These people may be responsible for the provision of services to others in the organization, e.g. management accountants, HR professionals, facilities managers, etc. They may be responsible for integrating activities, e.g. managers and supervisors. In fact, it is becoming increasingly recognized that 'boundary management' is of vital importance to the effectiveness of those in managerial and supervisory roles. Boundary management in this context means establishing and maintaining effective relationships with colleagues working in neighbouring sub-systems (in strategic aspects of management, Michael Porter refers to these as 'linkages' – see Chapter 16).

8.   Whilst organizations are open social systems, taken as a whole, their sub-systems may be either open or closed. Production sub-systems and accounting sub-systems tend to be closed systems, i.e. they are relatively self-contained and are affected in ways which are usually predictable. Marketing and R & D (research and development) activities tend, on the other hand, to work best in open systems i.e. where they can be aware of, and adapt to, key influences in the external environment. In the main, closed systems are required for stability and consistency, whereas open systems are required for unstable and uncertain conditions. Closed systems are designed for efficiency, open systems for survival. The early Classical theorists were expounding a closed systems approach. Developments in Human Relations, by contrast, were biased towards open systems. The modern consensus appears to be that both types are necessary for the maintenance and growth of successful organizations.

9.   The common characteristics of open systems as follows:

● inputs

● throughput or conversion (transformation), e.g. the processing of materials and organising of work activities

● output, e.g. of products or services

● cyclic nature, e.g. the returns from marketing the output enable further inputs to be made to complete the cycle of production

● feedback enables the system to correct deviations; Organizations tend to develop their own thermostats

- differentiation, e.g. the tendency to greater specialisation of functions and multiplicity of roles.

- equifinality – open systems do not have to achieve their goals in one particular way. Similar ends can be achieved by different paths and from a different starting point.

10.   Giving consideration to the aforementioned characteristics of open systems, the input–conversion–output model, shown in Figure 9.2, now needs to be expanded to take in the key factors of feedback. The result of including feedback from output to input is to produce a so-called 'closed loop' system. A closed loop system is basically a self-regulating system, such as a thermostat in a heating system or, to take a business example, a budgetary control system in a departmental operating plan. In each case, information fed back to the input side of the system enables corrective changes to be made to keep the system on course, i.e. in a steady state. The revised model of the organization as an open system can now be drawn as in Figure 9.3.

FIGURE 9.3 **The basic cycle of the organizational system**

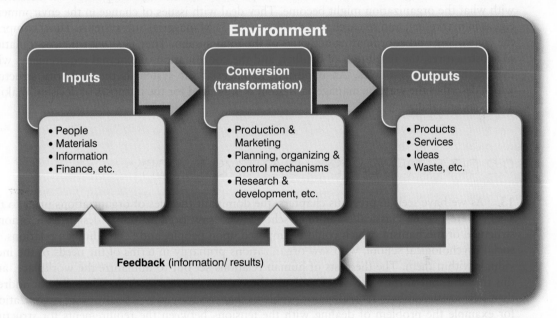

11.   The revised model shows the consequences of the outputs as information and results. The information can take many forms, e.g. sales volumes, new orders, market share, customer complaints, etc. and can be applied to control the inputs and conversion processes, as appropriate. The results are the revenues and profits which are fed back into the organization to provide further inputs, and so ensure the survival and growth of the system. An adaptive system, such as the one described above, is sometimes referred to as a 'cybernetic' system; the term 'cybernetics' in this context means the study of control and communication. Cybernetics was made famous by Norbert Wiener in the late 1940s, but is still very much a developing science. The essence of a cybernetic system is self-regulation on the basis of feedback information to disclose a shortfall in performance against standards and to indicate corrective action. The late Stafford Beer was a British theorist, consultant and professor at the Manchester Business School. He is best known for his work in the fields of management cybernetics. In the late 1950s he published his first book about

Adaptive system In general, an adaptive system has the ability to monitor and regulate its own performance. In many cases, an adaptive system will be able to respond fully to changes in its environment by modifying its behaviour

Cybernetic system a system with reference to the components and operation of feedback control (see self-regulation)

cybernetics and management, building on the ideas of Norbert Wiener especially for a systems approach to the management of organizations. Beer was arguably the first to apply cybernetics to management, defining cybernetics as the science of effective organization (see the viable system model).

12.   Katz and Kahn set out to describe their view of social systems and their related sub-systems. Advocating an open system approach, they identified five sub-systems at work in organizations. The five sub-systems they identified can be summarized as follows: 1) Production or Technical sub-systems. These are concerned with the accomplishment of the basic tasks of the organization (production of goods, provision of services, etc). 2) Supportive sub-systems. These are the systems which procure the inputs and dispose of the outputs of the production sub-system. They also maintain the relationship between the organization as a whole and the external environment. 3) Maintenance sub-systems. These are concerned with the relative stability or predictability of the organization. They provide for the roles, the rules and the rewards applicable to those who work in the organization. 4) Adaptive sub-systems. The first three systems above serve the organization as it is. The adaptive sub-systems by comparison are concerned with what the organization might become. They deal with issues of change in the environment, e.g. as in marketing, and research and development. 5) Managerial Sub-systems. These comprise the controlling and coordinating activities of the total system. They deal with the coordination of substructures, the resolution of conflict, and the coordination of external requirements with the organization's resources. An important managerial sub-system is the authority structure which describes the way the managerial system is organized for the purposes of decision-making and decision-taking.

9.2 DEVELOPMENTS IN SYSTEMS THEORY

13.   As we have seen in previous chapters, the dominant theories of organizations prior to the 1960s were (1) the classical/traditional school, who saw organizational design as a rational structure, or mechanism, which could be imposed upon people, and (2) the human relations, or social psychological school, who saw organizations primarily in terms of the needs of the individuals within them. The theorists of human relations set out to humanize the workplace, and this they did, but at the expense of studying the organization as a whole. They did not address themselves sufficiently to several major problems that can arise in practically every organization, for example the problem of dealing with the tensions between the requirements for structure and the needs of people. Questions of conflict tended to be dealt with in terms of avoiding it by attention to motivation and leadership. A further difficulty in the human relations approach was its emphasis on the practical application of ideas rather than on the conceptual development of organizational theory. This is not to deny the usefulness, to practising managers in particular, of the propositions of human relations, but it suggests the need to look elsewhere for a fuller explanation of behaviour in organizations.

14.   This is where we turn to theorists who see organizations as complex social systems, responsive to a number of interdependent and important variables. The key variables that are of greatest interest to those adopting a systems approach to organizations are as follows:

● people – as individuals and in groups

● organization structures

● environment – the external conditions affecting the organization

● technology – in terms of the technical requirements of work.

These variables are best-remembered by the acronym POET. Whereas earlier theorists looked at individual variables in isolation, the theorists of systems study the relationship between two or more of them. Initially, the Tavistock researchers, for example, looked at the relationships between people and technology, and between structure and environment. Later studies, such as those of Pugh and colleagues, have developed a more comprehensive and multi-dimensional approach, utilizing all the above variables. The principal developments in systems theories of organization design are discussed in the following paragraphs.

15. The researchers, so far, have indicated that there is no one best way of designing organizations to meet their current objectives. On the contrary, the evidence seems to suggest that the variables are so volatile that only a 'contingency' approach can prove practicable. This suggests that organizations can only be made viable when steps are taken to adapt them to a particular set of prevailing conditions. Naturally, this approach appeals more to theorists than practising managers, who must feel daunted by the need to be eternally adaptive. Nevertheless, it offers the best prospect to date of achieving the optimum organization design. Before looking at contingency approaches (in the next chapter) it is necessary to describe some of the earlier contributions to systems theory as applied to organizations, commencing with the Tavistock researchers.

9.3 THE TAVISTOCK GROUP

16. The Tavistock Institute of Human Relations in London has been engaged in various forms of social research for over sixty years. Despite its title, the Institute has developed its reputation for its contribution to systems theory. In particular, Trist and Bamforth introduced the concept of 'socio-technical' systems and Rice and Emery promoted several important ideas relating to open-systems theory and types of environment.

17. The Trist and Bamforth studies into changes in the method of extracting coal in British pits took place in the 1940s. The researchers were interested in the effects of mechanization on the social and work organization at the coal-face. Before mechanization, the coal had been extracted by small, closely knit teams working as autonomous groups. They worked at their own pace, often isolated in the dark from other groups. Bonds established within groups became important outside work as well as during the shift. Conflicts between competing groups were frequent and sometimes violent, but were always contained. This was the system which operated before the coal-cutters and mechanical conveyors were introduced. It was called the shortwall method.

18. The mechanized coal-face was completely different. It consisted of a long wall which required not small groups, but groups of between forty and fifty men plus their supervisors. These men could be spread out over 200 yards, and they worked in a three shift system. The new system (longwall method), was essentially a mass-production system based on a high degree of job specialization. Under the former shortwall method, each team had provided all the skills required, but in the longwall arrangement the basic operations were separated between the shifts. So, for example, if the first shift cut the coal from the face, the second shift shovelled it into the conveyor, and the third shift advanced the coal-face along the seam. Even within each shift, there was a high degree of task specialization.

19. The social consequences of the new method, arising from the breakdown of the previously closely integrated social structure were increased haggling over pay, inter-shift competition for the best jobs, the seeking of scapegoats in other shifts, and a noticeable increase in absenteeism. The results of the radical change in working methods and the miners' adverse response to them, led Trist and Bamforth to the conclusion that effective work was a function of the interdependence of technology (equipment, physical layout and task requirements) and social needs (especially

Socio-technical system A sub-division of the systems approach which is concerned with the interactions between the psychological and social factors and the needs, demands of the human part of organization and its structural and technological requirements

relationships within groups). It was not sufficient to regard the working environment as either a technical system or a social system. It was a combination of the two: a socio-technical system.

20. Eventually a so-called 'composite longwall method' was developed which enabled the needs of the social system to be met, whilst at the same time utilizing the benefits of the new mechanized equipment (the technical system). Tasks and working arrangements were altered so that the basic operations could be carried out by any one shift, and so that tasks within each group were allocated by the members. Payment was changed so as to incorporate a group bonus. The outcome of the composite methods was increased productivity, reduced absenteeism and a lower accident rate.

21. Alongside the coal-mining studies mentioned above, the reputation of the Tavistock group was also assured by Rice's studies into the calico mills at Ahmedabad, India. In his book Rice elaborated upon key aspects of systems theory as applied to organizations, two of which are selected for inclusion here: his concept of systems, and his views on work design.

22. Rice saw any industrial system (e.g. a firm) as an open system, importing various items from its environment, converting them into goods, services and waste materials, and then exporting them into the environment. Within the total system of the firm, he suggested, there existed two main systems: an operating system and a managing system. The operating system deals with the import, conversion and export of the product or service, whilst the managing system deals with the control, decision-making and communication aspects of the total system. Each system can have one or more sub-systems, which is why it is necessary to develop the managing system, so as to coordinate the interaction of all the systems and sub-systems.

Information system A set of people, procedures and resources that collects, transforms, and disseminates information in an organization – accepts data resources as input and processes them into information products as output

23. Rice's view of systems can be compared usefully with those of Handy who identified not only the operating system but also the adaptive, maintenance and information systems in activating the various parts of the total organization. It is these last three which come closest to making up the managing system formulated by Rice. On balance, the more modern analysis is the clearer of the two in helping to establish the prime focal points of the managing system.

24. The studies at Ahmedabad produced, among other things, some interesting conclusions about the design of work. These can be summarized as follows: (a) effective performance of a primary task is an important source of satisfaction at all levels of work; (b) the capacity for voluntary cooperation is more extensive than is often expected; (c) there is great benefit in allowing individuals to complete a whole task; (d) work groups of eight seem to have the best chance of success for achieving group tasks; (e) there is a clear relationship between work effectiveness and social relations and (f) where group autonomy has been established, unnecessary interference by supervisors will be counter-productive.

25. The above findings have been incorporated into current ideas on the design and redesign of work, so as to meet social and psychological needs of employees as well as the requirements of changing technology. They also share much common ground with Herzberg's ideas of motivation and job enrichment.

9.4 OPEN SYSTEMS AND THE ENVIRONMENT

26. The final example of the work of the Tavistock Group relates to another key factor in systems theory – the nature of the environment. Emery and Trist (1965) were the first to produce a classification of environments. They described four types of environment as follows: 1) Placid, randomized. This represents a relatively unchanging and homogeneous environment, whose

demands are randomly distributed. 2) Placid, clustered. This environment too, is relatively unchanging, but its threats and rewards are clustered. So, for example, in a monopoly situation, an organization's failure or success depends upon its continued hold over the market. 3) Disturbed, reactive. In this environment there is competition between organizations and this may include hindering tactics. 4) Turbulent field. This describes a dynamic and rapidly changing environment in which organizations must adapt frequently in order to survive.

27.   Emery and Trist were particularly interested in the last type, the turbulent field. This is an area where existing formal, or bureaucratised, structures are ill-suited to deal with their environment. According to the writers, more and more environments are becoming turbulent, and yet organization structures are not becoming correspondingly flexible. This important point is referred to in the next chapter – see the summary of the 'mechanistic organic structures' concept introduced by Burns and Stalker.

28.   Finally, we should note that viewing organizations as systems has limits and the systems approach and way of thinking is not without criticism. As has already been noted, organizations are more than simple physical systems and include people and the complex interactions between them. People have a free-will and their behaviour is not always predictable. Social systems are much more complicated than single human systems. Boulding (1956) presented a hierarchy of systems arguing the human level (level 7) where behaviour may be contemplated was followed by the social organization level (8). He noted that 'Adequate theoretical models extend unto about the fourth level, and that not much beyond'. The adoption of systems models can lead to mechanistic and overly rationalistic theories. That said, the systems approach and systems thinking has formed the backbone of organizational analysis.

> **Systems thinking** a holistic approach to analysis that focuses on the way a system's constituent parts interrelate and how systems work over time and within the context of larger systems

CONCLUSION

29.   In this chapter we have described the evolution of management and organization theory. Whereas the classical approach may be criticized for almost viewing organizations without any regard for their people and the human relations approach emphasized people without organizations (and neither particularly considered organizations in turbulent environments), the systems approach takes a holistic perspective, encouraging managers to view organizations both as a whole and as part of a larger environment (open system). The approach considers the interdependency of organization parts, changes in one part – technical or social – will affect other parts, a matter we build upon in the next chapter. The concept of socio-technical systems arose from the work of scholars at the Tavistock Institute – they first developed the concept of the organization as a system. The systems approach and systems thinking has formed the backbone of organizational analysis and can be applied to organizational design problems, strategy, change management, information systems and was later adapted in the concept of the learning organization.

QUESTIONS

1   What are the major differences, in each case, between the approach of the systems theorists and those of (a) the Classical theorists, and (b) the Human Relations theorists?

2   Discuss the major features and significance of the coal-mining research of the Tavistock Institute in the 1940s in Britain. (ACCA)

3   Review the role of systems theory in understanding organizations.

We are grateful to the Association of Chartered Certified Accountants (ACCA) for permission to reproduce past examination questions.

USEFUL WEBSITES

UK Systems Society (UKSS): **www.ukss.org.uk/**
The Society is committed to the development and promotion of 'systems' philosophy, theory, models, concepts and methodologies for improving decision-making and problem-solving for the benefit of organisations.

REFERENCES

Boulding, K. (1956) 'General Systems Theory – The Skeleton of Science', Management Science.

Buchanan, D. and Huczynski, A. (2010) 'Organizational Behaviour', Ed. 7. Financial Times Press.

Checkland, P. (1985) 'From Optimizing to Learning: A Development of Systems Thinking for the 1990s', The Journal of the Operational Research Society, 36:9 April 1985 (Sep., 1985), p. 757–767.

Emery, F. E. and Trist, E. L. (1965) 'The Causal Texture of Organizational Environments', Human Relations, Feb 65, Vol. 18 Issue 1, p. 21–32.

Johnson, G., Scholes, K. and Whittington, R. (2006) 'Exploring Corporate Strategy Enhanced Media Edition', FT Prentice Hall.

Kelly, P. P. (2009) 'International Business and Management', Cengage Learning EMEA.

Mullins, L. (2010) 'Management and Organizational Behaviour', Ed. 9. Financial Times Press.

O'Brien, J. A. (2002) 'Management Information Systems – Managing Information Technology in the E-Business Enterprise', Ed. 5. McGraw-Hill Higher Education.

Senge, P. M. (1996) 'Systems thinking', Executive Excellence, 13 (1), p. 15.

CHAPTER 10
CONTINGENCY
APPROACHES TO
MANAGEMENT

Key Concepts

- Contingency approach
- Differentiation
- Integration
- Mechanistic system
- Organic system
- Situational approach

Learning Outcomes Having read this chapter, you should be able to:

- discuss what is meant by the contingency approach to management
- contrast mechanistic and organic systems
- distinguish six primary variables of structure
- explain the congruence model of organizational behaviour based on the system paradigm
- evaluate the contribution of systems theory to theories of management and organization

1.   The most recent formulations of systems theories tend to be labelled contingency theories because they emphasize the need to take specific circumstances, or contingencies, into account when devising appropriate organizational and management systems. There is no clear distinction between the systems approach and the contingency approach to the management of organizations. The latter has developed out of the findings of the former. A systems approach highlights the complexity of the interdependent components of organizations within equally complex environments. A contingency approach builds on the diagnostic qualities of the systems approach in order to determine the most appropriate organizational design and management style for a given set of circumstances. Essentially the contingency approach suggests that issues of design and style depend upon choosing the best combination, in the light of prevailing (or forecast) conditions, of the following variables: (a) the external environment, (b) technological factors and (c) human skills and motivation.

Contingency approach An extension of the systems approach that implies organizational variables (e.g. strategy, structure, and systems) and their success or performance are dependent upon environmental influences (forces). There is, therefore, no one best way to structure or manage organizations; rather it must be dependent upon the contingencies of the situation

2.   The label 'contingency approach' was suggested by two American academics, Lawrence and Lorsch (1967). Their important contribution to this approach will be summarized shortly. Other British writers referred to within this chapter have adopted a contingency approach: Joan Woodward is noted for her important studies into the effects of technology on structure and performance; Burns and Stalker introduced the concept of mechanistic and organic types of structure and discussed them in relation to the environment; finally, the so-called Aston group (Pugh, Hickson *et al.*) have undertaken interesting studies into several of the technology-structure variables within organizations.

3.   Unlike the Classical and Human Relations approaches to the management of organizations, the contingency approach does not seek to produce universal prescriptions or principles of behaviour. It deals in relativities, not absolutes. It is essentially a situational approach to management. The contingency approach does not turn its face against earlier approaches, but adapts them as part of a 'mix' which could be applied to an organization in a particular set of circumstances. The following paragraphs look at several important research studies which have dealt with two or more elements of this 'organizational mix'.

Situational approach A viewpoint that emphasizes the importance of the environmental situation in determining (organization) behaviour

Differentiation the degree to which the tasks and the work of individuals, groups and units are divided up within an organization

10.1 LAWRENCE & LORSCH

Integration The required level to which units in an organization are linked together, and their respective degree of independence (Integrative mechanisms include rules and procedures and direct managerial control)

4.   These two Harvard researchers set out to answer the question what kind of organization does it take to deal with various economic and market conditions? They were concerned, therefore, with structure and environment as the two key variables in their study. Initially Lawrence and his colleague studied the internal functioning of six plastics firms operating in a diverse and dynamic environment. The results in these six firms were then compared with two standardized container firms operating in a very stable environment, and two firms in the packaged food industry, where the rate of change was moderate.

Specialization The degree to which an organization's activities are divided into specialist roles

5.   The major emphasis of their study was on the states of differentiation and integration within organizations. Differentiation was defined as more than mere division of labour or specialization. It also referred to the differences in attitude and behaviour of the

managers concerned. These differences were looked at in terms of (a) their orientation towards particular goals, e.g. issues of cost reduction are more important to production managers than to sales or research managers; (b) their time orientation, e.g. sales and production managers have short-term orientations whilst research managers have long-term orientations; (c) their interpersonal orientation, e.g. production managers tend to be less relationship-oriented than sales managers and (d) the relative formality of the structure of their functional units, e.g. the highly formalized production departments with their many levels, narrow span of control and routine procedures as contrasted with the relatively informal and flat structures of the research departments.

6.   Integration was defined as the quality of the state of collaboration that exists amongst departments. It was seen to be more than a mere rational or mechanical process, as in the Classical approach. Integration was a question of interrelationships, in the final analysis, said Lawrence and Lorsch. Inevitably the differences of attitude referred to within paragraph 5 above would lead to frequent conflicts about what direction to take. These conflicts were not adequately catered for within the Classical theories. A key interest of the two researchers, therefore, was to assess the way conflict was controlled within organizations.

7.   In approaching their studies, Lawrence and Lorsch took the view that there was probably no one best way to organize. What they could hope for was to provide a systematic understanding of what states of differentiation and integration are related to effective performance under different environmental conditions. In essence they were arguing about Environmental determinism – a perspective which claims that internal organizational responses are wholly or mainly shaped, influenced or determined by external environmental factors.

Environmental determinism a perspective which claims that internal organizational responses are wholly or mainly shaped, influenced or determined by external environmental factors

8.   Effective performance was judged in terms of the following criteria: change in profits over the past five years, change in sales volume over the same period and new products introduced over the period as a percentage of current sales. As it turned out, the firms selected for study encompassed a range of performance from high through medium to low performance when set against the chosen criteria.

9.   The main conclusions that Lawrence and Lorsch arrived at were as follows:

- The more dynamic and diverse the environment, the higher the degree of both differentiation and integration required for successful organization.

- Less changeable environments require a lesser degree of differentiation, but still require a high degree of integration.

- The more differentiated an organization, the more difficult it is to resolve conflict.

- High-performing organizations tend to develop better ways of resolving conflict than their less effective competitors. Improved ways of conflict resolution lead to states of differentiation and integration that are appropriate for the environment.

- Where the environment is uncertain, the integrating functions tend to be carried out by middle and low-level managers; where the environment is stable, integration tends to be achieved at the senior end of the management hierarchy.

10.   The research referred to above was based on a very small sample of firms, it relied on some rather subjective information, and several of the measures employed have been criticized as unreliable by subsequent researchers. Despite the criticisms, the Lawrence and Lorsch study represented a most important step forward in the search for a theory of organizations that could take account of the major variables affecting the structure of successful organizations.

10.2 BURNS & STALKER

11.   Another famous study of the environment–structure relationship was conducted by Burns and Stalker during the 1950s in Scotland and England. Some twenty firms in the electronics industry were studied from the point of view of how they adapted themselves to deal with changing market and technical conditions, having been organised initially to handle relatively stable conditions.

12.   The researchers were particularly interested in how management systems might change in response to the demands of a rapidly changing external environment. As a result of their studies, they devised two distinctive 'ideal types' of management system: mechanistic systems and organic systems. The key features of both systems are summarized below.

Mechanistic system A rigid system of management practice and structure which is characterized by a clear hierarchical structure, specialization of task, defined duties and responsibilities and knowledge centred at the top of the hierarchy

13.   Mechanistic systems are appropriate for conditions of stability. Their outstanding features are as follows: a specialized differentiation of tasks, a precise definition of rights, obligations and technical methods of each functional role, a hierarchical structure of control, authority and communication, a tendency for vertical interaction between members of the concern, a tendency for operations and working behaviour to be dominated by superiors, and an insistence upon loyalty to the organization and obedience to superiors.

Organic system A fluid and flexible system of management practice and structure which is characterized by the adjustment and continual redefinition of tasks, a network structure of control, authority and communication and where superior knowledge does not necessarily coincide with positional authority

14.   By contrast, organic systems are appropriate for conditions of change. Their outstanding features can be summarized as follows: individual tasks, which are relevant to the total situation of the concern, are adjusted and redefined through interaction with others, a network structure of control, authority and communication, where knowledge of technical or commercial aspects of tasks may be located anywhere in the network, a lateral rather than vertical direction of communication through the organization, communications consist of information and advice rather than instructions and decisions and commitment to the organization's tasks is seen to be more important than loyalty and obedience.

15.   Burns and Stalker did not see the two systems as being complete opposites, but as polar positions between which intermediate forms could exist. They also acknowledged that firms could well move from one system to the other as external conditions changed, and that some concerns could operate with both systems at once. They stressed that they did not favour one or other system. What was important was to achieve the most appropriate system for a given set of circumstances – a perfect expression of the contingency approach!

16.   The Burns and Stalker study was influential in the design of the Lawrence and Lorsch study mentioned earlier. Clearly, mechanistic systems are closely related to considerations of states of differentiation, and organic systems have much in common with the concept of integration. It is interesting to note, however, that whereas Burns and Stalker see organic systems as being more appropriate to changing conditions than mechanistic ones, their American counterparts see both systems as crucial to coping with diversity. The more dynamic and diverse the environment, the higher the degree of both differentiation and integration, say the Americans. Differentiation involves several of the features of the mechanistic systems, which Burns and Stalker see as being ill-adapted to conditions of change. This points to one of the major criticisms made against the mechanistic versus organic approach – it assumes that change can best be effected by organic types of structure, when this is not at all certain. Large organizations, however great their commitment to delegation, involvement and communication between groups, have to maintain a high degree of structure and formality, even when confronted by periods of change.

10.3 JOAN WOODWARD

17. The Woodward studies, conducted by a small research team from the South East Essex College of Technology during the period 1953–1958, were initially aimed at assessing the extent to which classical management principles were being translated into practice by manufacturing firms in the area, and with what success. Information on various aspects of formal organization was collected from 100 firms. About half the firms had made some conscious attempt to plan their organization, but there was little uniformity. In terms of structure, for example, the number of levels of management varied between two and twelve, and spans of control (the number of persons directly supervised by one person) ranged from ten to ninety for first-line supervisors. The conclusions drawn by the team were that there was little in common amongst the most successful firms studied, and there was certainly no indication that classical management principles were any more likely to lead to success than other forms of organization. At the time this was considered to be rather disconcerting, given the popularity of classical ideas.

18. Having had no positive conclusions from the first part of their studies, Woodward's team turned their attention to the technological data they had collected. The question they posed was as follows: is there any relationship between organizational characteristics and technology? In attempting to answer this question, the team made a lasting contribution to the theory of organizations by establishing the key role of technology as a major variable affecting organization structures.

19. Their first step was to find some suitable form of classification to distinguish between the different categories of technology employed by the firms concerned. Three main categories were eventually selected as follows: (1) Unit and Small Batch Production. This included custom-made products, the production of prototypes, large fabrications undertaken in stages and the production of small batches; (2) Large Batch and Mass Production. This encompassed the production of large batches, including assembly-line production, and mass production and (3) Process Production. This included the intermittent production of chemicals in multipurpose plant, as well as the continuous flow production of liquids, gases and crystalline substances.

20. When the firms in the study were allocated to their appropriate categories, and then compared by their organization and operations, some discernible patterns began to emerge. For example, it was seen that process industries tended to utilize more delegation and decentralization than large-batch and mass production industries. This was just one aspect of the link between technology and organization structure. Others included the following:

- The more complex the process, the greater was the chain of command, i.e. there were more levels of management in the process industries than in the other two categories.

- The span of control of chief executives increased with technical complexity, i.e. the number of people directly responsible to the chief executive was lowest in unit/ small-batch production firms and highest in process production.

- By contrast with the point above, the span of middle management decreased with technical complexity, i.e. fewer people reported to middle managers in process production than in large-batch/mass production firms, who in turn had fewer people than in unit/small-batch production.

21. As well as the differences mentioned above, there were also some interesting similarities. For example the average number of workers controlled by first-line supervisors was similar for both unit/small-batch and process production – and these were noticeably fewer in number than for mass production situations. Another similarity between unit/small-batch and process production was that they both employed proportionately more skilled workers than mass production categories. Woodward's team also found that firms at the extremes of the technical range tended to adopt organic systems of management, whereas firms in the middle of the range, notably the large-batch/mass production firms, tended to adopt mechanistic systems.

22.   Having established some definite links between organizational characteristics and technology, Woodward's team turned their attention to the relationship, if any, between these two factors and the degree of business success (profitability, growth, cost reductions achieved, etc). What they found was that the successful firms in each category were those whose organizational characteristics tended to cluster around the median figures for their particular category. So, for example, a process production firm would be better served by a taller, narrower structure backed up by an organic system of management rather than by a flatter, broader structure, operated mechanistically. On the other hand, a mass-production firm would appear to benefit from a flatter, broader structure, operated in a mechanistic way. Firms in either category which did not have their appropriate characteristics would tend to produce less than average results.

23.   Woodward concluded that the predominance given to the Classical theorists, especially in respect of the application of their ideas in practice (span of control, unity of command, definition of duties, etc), only made sense when viewed in terms of large-batch/mass production processes. Classical ideas did not seem appropriate for other categories of production. Her research strongly suggested that not only was the system of production a key variable in determining structure, but that also there was a particular form of organization which was most suited to each system.

24.   This contingency approach is very much in line with the conclusions reached by Lawrence and Lorsch. Woodward's conclusions also confirm the criticism of the Burns and Stalker study which has been made previously (see above). From her studies it would seem that mass production firms could not cope successfully with change if they adopted an organic system, i.e. an inappropriate system, according to her evidence.

10.4 THE ASTON GROUP

25.   The so-called Aston group – Pugh, Hickson and others – now dispersed, but originally at the University of Aston, Birmingham, began a major study into various aspects of structure, technology and environment in the late 1960s. Unlike the earlier studies of Woodward and Trist and Bamforth, for example, which did not break technology down into more than one variable, the Aston study attempted to discern the basic elements of technology by gathering data on several possible dimensions. These included features such as operating variability, workflow integration and line control of the workflow. Many of the results of the Aston study did not accord with those of the Woodward studies. One explanation put forward was that the Woodward studies were conducted into mainly smaller firms, whilst the Aston study had included several large companies. This was significant because Pugh and his colleagues had concluded that the impact of technology on organization structure must be related to size. In small organizations they said, technology will be critical to structure, but in large organizations other variables will tend to confine the impact of technology to the basic operating levels.

Standardization The degree to which an organization lays down standard rules and procedures

Formalization The degree to which instructions, procedures, etc. are written down

26.   The importance of the Aston group is that they adopted a multi-dimensional approach to organizational and contextual variables, i.e. they attempted to develop the idea of an 'organizational mix' which can be applied to an organization at a particular point in time in order to achieve successful results. This essentially contingency approach has provided the basis for further research into what represents the ideal structure for an organization in the light of a particular grouping of circumstances.

27.   The Aston study distinguished six primary variables of structure and considered them against a number of contextual variables. The structural variables were as follows: 1) Specialization (of functions and roles). 2) Standardization (of procedures and methods). 3) Standardization of employment practices. 4) Formalization

(extent of written rules, procedures, etc.). 5) Centralization (concentration of authority). 6) Configuration (shape of organization). These variables were considered in a number of different contexts including the following: – Origin and history. – Ownership (owner-managers, shareholders, parent company, etc.). – Size of organization. – Charter (i.e. Number and range of goods/services). – Technological features (in several dimensions). – Interdependence (balance of dependence between the organization and customers, suppliers, trade unions, etc.).

Centralization The degree to which the authority to make certain decisions is located at the top of the management hierarchy

28. Among the conclusions reached by the Aston team was the relevance of size to the structural variables. As an organization grows beyond the stage at which it can be controlled by personal interaction, it has to be structured more explicitly. Larger size tends to lead to a) more specialization, b) more standardization, c) more formalization but d) less centralization. Overall, the conclusion of the researchers was that it was possible to predict, fairly closely, the structural profile of an organization on the basis of information obtained about the contextual variables.

Configuration the shape of the organization's role structure – the structures, processes and relationships through which the organization operates

10.5 MODELS BASED ON THE SYSTEM PARADIGM

29. Whilst the systems perspective is valuable, systems theory by itself may be too abstract a concept to be a usable tool for managers. Consequently, a number of organizational theorists have attempted to develop more pragmatic theories or models based on the system paradigm. There are a number of such models now in use. The organizational system model proposed, in 1965, by Harold Leavitt, of the Carnegie Institute of Technology, is made of four major components: task (the organization's purpose), people (those who carry out the task), technology (tools and computers etc.) and structure. Leavitt argues the components are interdependent with one another and a change in any one of the components will result in change amongst the other three. This model is grounded in Systems thinking but is not based on open system theory i.e. forces in the external environment are not modelled. A decade later, Nadler and Tushman developed their congruence model for diagnosing organizational behaviour, see Figure 10.1. Recognizing the organization is influenced by its environment, their model took account of both systems and open system theory. Nadler and Tushman (1989) divided their model into inputs, process and outputs. Their (transformation or internal) process contained similar components to the model proposed by Leavitt. Inputs came from the environment including organizational history and current strategy which help define how people in the organization behave. Nadler and Tushman also argued a need for the transformational process components to be congruent or 'fit' with each other. Nadler and Tushman (1989) did however recognize that such congruence may present advantages and disadvantages. In the short-term, a system with high congruence is an effective and performing system however, such a system may be resistant to change. Their model suggests there is no one best way to organize. Rather, the most effective way of organizing is determined by the nature of the strategy as well as the work, the individuals who are members of the organization, and the informal processes and structures (including culture) which have emerged over time.

30. Aside from structure, organization theory and design, Contingency theories in terms of [A] determines [B] ('If-Then'), etc. have been applied in many areas, leadership (see Chapter 7) and change management (see Chapter 24) in particular. Martin (2010) suggests contingency theory applies to the leadership, motivation and structure areas within organizational behaviour and takes the view that the best style of leadership, form of motivation or organizational structure

FIGURE 10.1 Congruence model of organizational behaviour

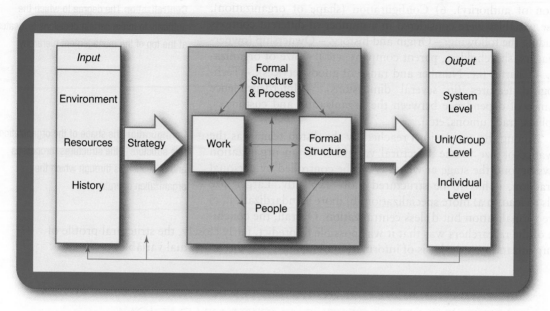

Source: "Organizational Frame Bending: Principles of Managing Reorganization" in *The Academy of Management Executive* by D.A. Nadler and M. Tushman. Copyright © 1989 by Academy of Management (NY). Reproduced with permission of The Academy of Management (NY) in Textbook format via Copyright Clearance Center.

depends upon the factors active in the situation. Kelly (2009) describes a contingency approach to management, the idea that there is no one best way to manage and to be effective, planning, organizing, leading and controlling must be tailored to the particular circumstances faced by an organization. Similarly, Huczynski and Buchanan (2010) define a contingency theory of leadership (see also situational leadership) as a perspective which argues that leaders must adjust their style in a manner consistent with aspects of the context.

Strategic choice The process whereby power-holders within organizations decide upon courses of strategic action

31. Like the other theories presented within this part of the book, contingency theory does not come without criticism. Child (1997) discusses the integrative potential of strategic choice theory within organization studies and examines its contribution to an evolutionary perspective on the subject. Strategic choice followed the 'determinism' theories (see structural determinism, the context factors and environmental determinism), the 'contingency' views, giving attention to organizational decision makers. 'Strategic choice' is a process whereby power-holders within organizations decide upon courses of strategic action (in this case, structure). The decisions of such managers are coloured by their values, attitudes and beliefs; the sources of which include culture (e.g. professional, corporate or national membership), experience and training. Values, attitudes and beliefs impact upon evaluations, cognitions, mental process and actions. Despite the criticism (it is an oversimplification), some scholars continue to defend and apply contingency theory, particularly in change management theory and practice. The contribution of the theory remains important and we will review contemporary management theory and developments in the next and final chapter of the theory elements of this book.

CONCLUSION

32. In summary the contingency approach is an extension of the systems approach that implies organizational variables (e.g. strategy, structure and systems) and its success or performance is dependent upon environmental influences (forces). There is, therefore, no one best way to

structure or manage organizations; rather it must be dependent upon the contingencies of the situation (see also environmental determinism). Figure 10.2 summarizes the principal systems and contingency approaches to organization and management theory. The dates refer to the first publication of the relevant theory or research report. The general model implicit in contingency theory is shown in Figure 10.3.

FIGURE 10.2 The principal systems and contingency approaches to organization and management theory

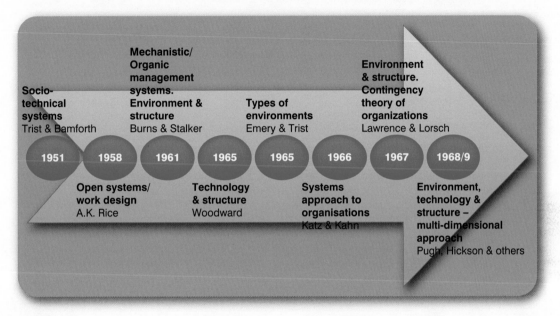

FIGURE 10.3 General model of contingency theory

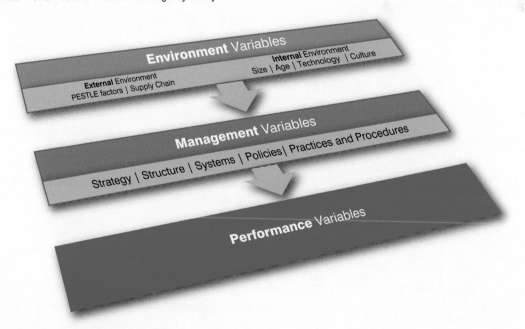

33.   Whilst the classical theorists argued for universal principles of administration, the simple idea behind Contingency theory is that organization structure should be dependent upon the organization context i.e. it should be regarded as a contingent variable. Organization theory is not therefore about one-best-way to manage but to guide managers through insights that enable the formulation of responses enabling their organizations to fit their specific internal and external context. The contingency approach emphasizes the need for flexibility. Later theorists (see Child in particular) developed the view that an organization's environment, market and technology is the result of senior management decisions (strategic choice).

QUESTIONS

1 In what ways is the concept of 'integration' important for organizations?

2 How would you summarize the principal contributions to organization and management theory of: Joan Woodward's Essex studies and the Burns and Stalker studies?

3 In what ways could the Aston group's study be said to have furthered understanding about the analysis of organizations?

4 In approaching their studies, Lawrence and Lorsch took the view that there was probably no one best way to organize. Discuss this viewpoint with reference to the contingency approach and the views of other theorists.

5 Discuss the contingency approach to organization design/structure.

6 List and briefly describe the most important factors that may influence organization design/structure.

7 **a** What are the main features of a bureaucratic organization?

b How effectively do bureaucratic organizations respond to changing circumstances in the environment? (ICSA MPP)

8 Discuss what is meant by the contingency approach to management.

9 Whilst the systems perspective is valuable, systems theory by itself may be too abstract a concept to be a usable tool for managers. Identify and explain the congruence model (proposed by Nadler and Tushman) based on the systems paradigm.

REFERENCES

Buchanan, D. and Huczynski, A. (2010) 'Organizational Behaviour', Ed. 7. Financial Times Press.

Child, J. (1997) 'Strategic choice in the analysis of action, structure, organizations and environment: Retrospect and prospect', Organization Studies – Berlin, 18 (1), p. 43–76.

Kelly, P. P. (2009) 'International Business and Management', Cengage Learning EMEA.

Lawrence, P. R. and Lorsch, J. W. (1967) 'Differentiation and Integration in Complex Organizations',

Administrative Science Quarterly, Vol. 12, No. 1. (Jun.,1967), p. 1–47.

Martin, J. and Fellenz, M. (2010) 'Organizational Behaviour and Management 4e', Ed. 4. Cengage Learning EMEA.

Mullins, L. (2010) 'Management and Organizational Behaviour', Ed. 9. Financial Times Press.

Nadler, D. A. and Tushman, M. (1989) 'Organizational Frame Bending: Principles for Managing Reorientation', Academy of Management Executive, Aug 89, Vol. 3 Issue 3, p. 194–204.

Pugh, D. S. (1997) 'Organization Theory', Ed. 4. Penguin.

Section Six
Modern Approaches to Management Theory

CHAPTER 11
MODERN APPROACHES TO MANAGEMENT

Key Concepts

- Learning organization
- Postmodernism

Learning Outcomes   Having read this chapter, you should be able to:

- explain how management theory has evolved
- identify and discuss the key management issues of the first decade of the 21st century
- list the main contributors to management theory over the past 25 years
- compare traditional with contemporary management approaches

1.   In our quest to identify management theories throughout this first part of the book we have identified four broad approaches: classical, human relations, systems and contingency approaches; collectively these approaches may define modern management. However, the term modern management is synonymous with the 1970s and 1980s and is not so resonant with managers of the present day. In this final chapter we will take a brief look at further subdivisions of these approaches that have evolved more recently and will also consider the tenets of a post-modern management theory. Since the 1990s and as a result of a variety of changes a more recent view of organizations and management is captured under the banner of post-modernism. Advocates of post-modernism are likely to reject rational approaches and question the possibility of any kind of complete and coherent theory of management. It may be argued that post-modernism is less a specific approach and more a generalized concept. In many ways it can be seen as a healthy challenge to traditional approaches. Today, interest in the management of organizations is as lively as it was throughout the twentieth century. The search for better and more efficient ways of utilizing people's knowledge and skills in providing goods and services for domestic and global markets has never been stronger. The desire to understand the external world of the organization and to learn how best to cope with change in the environment is more challenging now than it has ever been. The appreciation of the importance of human skills, ingenuity and motivation has grown, not diminished, with the arrival of new technologies. Technology and ICT in particular is transforming possibilities for Third World businesses to better compete with businesses in the developed nations. What, perhaps, has changed is the recognition that there will be an increasing international and multicultural dimension to both large and smaller business corporations, as they seek to find skilled labour or low-cost production facilities. The global economy is not too far away, as the various regional groupings begin to develop their own infrastructure, as in the European Union and the Asia-Pacific Rim. This short chapter summarizes current issues for management and identifies leading exponents of management theory whose more recent ideas have led us to the present position. The work of these theorists will be discussed in more detail in subsequent chapters.

11.1 MANAGEMENT THEORY TODAY

2.   Stuart Crainer, Executive Editor of *Business Strategy Review* wrote about one hundred years of management (2003). He suggests that the roots of modern management lie at the turn of the 20th century. At the turn of the 20th century, management lay largely undefined. Or, more accurately, the most convincing attempt at providing a definition for management was little known. This came from a somewhat surprising source, the French mining engineer called Henri Fayol (1841–1925). Fayol formulated a distinct managerial philosophy that was a major contribution to the management century. First, he recognized the universality of management. Management was as applicable to a mining company, to a hospital or to the post office. Second, Fayol identified management as a discipline in its own right. Fayol developed 14 'general principles of management', which, he said, were the universal characteristics of management. Fayol's 14 principles were what did – or should – concern managers. To ensure that they were implemented effectively in practice, Fayol said that managers needed to plan, organize, command, co-ordinate (lead) and control. Amongst all the early thinkers on the subject, Fayol's ideas have probably been the most enduring. Parallel to Fayol's career was that of Frederick Winslow Taylor (1856–1915). While Fayol wrestled with the broader theoretical question of the nature of management, it was scientific management that made Taylor one of the most influential figures of the 20th century. Even today, his influence remains strong on many businesses throughout the world. A 1997 Fortune magazine article noted: 'Taylor's influence is omnipresent: it's his ideas that determine how many burgers McDonald's expects its flippers to flip or how many callers the phone company expects its operators to assist'. Management expert Drucker has cited Taylor's thinking as 'the most lasting contribution America has made to Western thought

since the Federalist Papers'. The implications of Taylor's (rationalistic) philosophy were felt across the world; scientific management became the first international management theory. The need to produce more and in a more efficient way was taken as a first principle. In terms of management, Taylor's crucial contribution was to invent management as science. However, as with Bureaucracy, scientific management was not without its critics. The first downside of Taylor's thinking was that he placed efficiency before ethics, Crainer (2003). The theory was that scientific management increased productivity, lessened costs, enabled lower prices, and, as a result, more sales and greater profits. This was all very well until the competition did the same. Taylor's theories denied people their individuality. And, after initial enthusiasm, people did not like it. Thus, traditional management is essentially based on classical management and in some cases is used as a term synonymous with modern management. Modern management draws from the four key approaches (Classical, Humanistic, Systems and Contingency) discussed so far in this part of the book.

3. In the last quarter of the twentieth century, systems theory and systems thinking evolved (and contingency theory) further. The theory has been used by scholars of many management disciplines to investigate and explain specific aspects of organizations. For example, systems thinking forms the basis of many change management theories. Furthermore, the concept of the learning organization and organization learning is also based on systems and contingency theories. In the face of change, organizations must experiment with new ways of managing that respond more adequately to the demands of today's environment. Peter Senge is an American scientist and director of the Centre for Organizational Learning at the MIT Sloan School of Management.

Learning organization An organization skilled at creating, acquiring, and transferring knowledge, and at modifying its behaviour to reflect new knowledge and insights

He has had a great impact on the way we conduct business today. Senge believed in the theory of systems thinking which has sometimes been referred to as the 'Cornerstone' of the Learning Organization. Systems thinking is the process of understanding how things influence one another within a whole. In organizations, systems consist of people, structures and processes that work together to make an organization attain its goals or fail. Systems thinking has been defined as an approach to problem solving, viewing 'problems' as parts of an overall system, rather than reacting to a specific part. Systems thinking is based on the belief that the component parts of a system can best be understood in the context of relationships with each other and with other systems, rather than in isolation. The systems thinking approach incorporates several tenets which include: Interdependence, Holism, Goal seeking, Transformation of inputs into outputs, Regulation (feedback), Hierarchy – complex wholes are made up of smaller subsystems and Differentiation – specialized units perform specialized functions, Senge (1996). Whereas the traditional organization emphasized efficiency, the learning organization, in contrast, focuses on problem-solving and does this through broad participation (empowerment and employee involvement).

4. Buchanan and Huczynski (2010) describe the learning organization as an organizational form that enables individual learning to create valid outcomes such as innovation, efficiency, environmental alignment and competitive advantage. This reflects open systems theory and the challenges identified by Emery and Trist. Knights and Willmott's (2007) definition of the learning organization emphasizes the collective aspect of systems theory when they refer to it as a recent and managerially-fashionable term to describe organizations which value collective and not just individual learning; may be reflected in more participative structures and a managerial emphasis on continuous learning (i.e. organizational improvement). Similarly the definition provided by Johnson, Scholes and Whittington (2006) draws on systems theory (collection of parts in pursuit of a common goal) – a learning organization is capable of continual regeneration from the variety of knowledge, experience and skills of individuals within a culture which encourages mutual questioning and challenge around a shared purpose or vision. As was highlighted previously, in a changing environment the organization must seek out new knowledge constantly if it is to stay ahead of competition and perform value-adding activities in an efficient

and effective manner. The organization meets this challenge by learning and adapting, by trial and error (experience). We will revisit the concept of the learning organization in Chapter 44.

5.   Aside from separating open from closed systems, scholars – notably professor Peter Checkland of Lancaster University in the UK – differentiate between different types of systems problems. While soft systems thinking treats all problems as ill-defined or not easily quantified, hard systems approaches assume that the problems associated with such systems are well-defined, have a single, optimum solution and that a 'scientific' approach to problem-solving will work well. Hard system problems are often associated with aspects of computer based information systems whilst soft system techniques focus more on improvements to organizational problems. Developments in hard systems thinking began to emerge as a distinct philosophy in the 1950s and are based upon the idea that the world is considered to be systemic and is studied systematically. Like hard systems thinking, soft systems thinking can be characterized as having a desirable end, but the means to achieve it and the actual outcome are not easily quantified. Much of Checkland's work has had a great influence on business information systems (see Chapter 30). He is the developer of soft systems methodology (SSM): a methodology based on a way of systems thinking.

6.   Many scholars associate the classical theories (scientific management and bureaucracy in particular) with modern management. The classical theories in particular define the modern organization, a term typical in the 1980s. Clegg (1992) suggests that modernist organizations may be thought of in terms of Weber's bureaucratized, mechanistic structures of control, as these were subsequently erected upon a fully rationalized base of divided and de-skilled labour (see also Taylorism). By the 1970s this modernist model had begun to lose momentum but continued in the minds and organizations of many. The changing state of the 1980s and 1990s (globalization, deregulation, increased competition, technological changes such as the Internet,

Postmodernism A more recent view of organizations and management that rejects a rational, systems approach and accepted explanations of society and behaviour. Postmodernism places greater emphasis on the use of language and attempts to portray a particular set of assumptions or versions of the 'truth'

mobile telecomms, etc.) led to organizational responses and change – pioneered particularly in Japan argues Clegg. 'Post' comes after modern and postmodernism is a more recent view of organizations and management that rejects a rational, systems approach and accepted explanations of society and behaviour. Commenting and contrasting the post modern organization, Clegg questioned the most evident differences. Tomorrow's managers and workers will still have to face some of the same problems as did yesterday's. Where they will differ will be in their responses. It is by contrasting modern with postmodern responses to recurrent problems of organization that the nature of the changes required can be spelt out. These 'perennials' form a number of organizational imperatives: (1) articulating mission, goals, strategies and main functions; (2) arranging functional alignments; (3) identifying mechanisms of co-ordination and control; (4) constituting accountability and role relationships; (5) institutionalizing, planning and communication; (6) relating rewards and performance and (7) achieving effective leadership. Within the core enterprises and countries of postmodern organizational forms, control will become less authoritarian in the workplace as new forms of market discipline substitute for the external surveillance of supervision, changes fostered by extensive deregulation. Internal markets

Post-modern organization A networked, information-rich, delayered, downsized, boundary-less, high-commitment organization employing highly skilled, well-paid, autonomous knowledge workers

within large organizations will increasingly be created as cost-centres and profit-centres proliferate, and surveillance will be lessened as more flexible manufacturing systems are adopted within which workers become their own supervisors. Where modernist organization was rigid, postmodern organization is flexible. Where modernist consumption was premised on mass forms of consumption, postmodernist consumption is premised on niches. Where modernist organization was premised on technological determinism, postmodernist organization is premised on technological choices made possible through 'de-dedicated' microelectronic equipment. Where modernist organization and jobs were highly differentiated, demarcated and deskilled, postmodernist organization and jobs will be highly de-differentiated, de-demarcated and multiskilled. The post-modern organization is a networked, information-rich, delayered, downsized, boundary-less, high-commitment organization employing highly skilled, well-paid, autonomous knowledge workers.

7.   Daft (2009) contrasts traditional work (modernism) with the contemporary workplace (post-modernism) suggesting that in the traditional world of work, management was to control and limit people, enforce rules and regulations, seek stability and efficiency, design a top-down hierarchy and achieve bottom-line results. He suggests that the new workplace asks that managers focus on leading change, harnessing people's creativity and enthusiasm, finding shared visions and values and sharing information and power. Teamwork, collaboration, participation and learning are guiding principles that help managers and employees manoeuvre the difficult terrain of today's turbulent business environment. He therefore describes a new era of management. Daft also considers the evolution of management thinking.

8.   The strategic importance of management to national economies has grown considerably. This is largely on account of the increasing demands for higher living standards among national populations, together with a desire amongst developing economies to trade on more equal terms with their well-established counterparts worldwide. The principal factors involved in these changes include:

- the rapid advance of micro-electronic technology, which has revolutionized many of the processes by which goods and services are made available to customers

- the increased ability of firms to compete with each other due to the benefits of new technology and a sufficiency of trained labour

- the entry into world markets of new low-cost manufacturing firms from Asian countries who are successfully challenging established Western firms

- the increased expectations of customers for quality and variety in consumer goods and personal services

- the massive improvements in worldwide communication systems, especially the development of the internet, leading to better and more timely information for buyers, sellers and middlemen/agents

- the greater inter-connectedness of the world's people due to increased trade and cultural contact (e.g. via tourism and the internet), and by growth in air travel and transportation.

9.   What issues are raised for business organizations by this expanding economic activity throughout the globe? The following are issues that have been identified in management theories promoted during the latter part of the last century: the

- importance of establishing a vision, or mission, and sustainable competitive advantage for the organization

- clarification of organizational purpose and goals

- development of shared values in the organization (i.e. 'culture')

- continuing need for leadership that can see beyond the bounds of what is, to what might be

- development of organization structures that permit flexibility of action, but with relative stable core systems

- development of multi-skilled employees with relevant knowledge, skills and competence

- optimization of employee contribution through job challenge and empowerment

- continuing need to anticipate changes in the external environment – customers, competitors, suppliers, technological, economic and political trends – improvement of internal communication and decision-making channels

- use of new technology to communicate more effectively with markets and individual customers

- use of business processes and enterprise-wide information systems to integrate activity

- management of change in and about the organization

- development of standards of excellence throughout the organization

- development of a global strategy in the light of international trade

- need to balance global control and universal standards with the culture and practices of the local business unit.

10.   In diagrammatic form, the above issues can be seen in relation to each other, as in Figure 11.1.

11.   Of course, a diagram such as Figure 11.1 over-simplifies the situation, but it does help to break down the complexity of the challenge facing management, where each issue feeds off, or contributes to, the others; thinking about strategy, and devising a relevant mission and accompanying goals, triggers the kind of culture that will mark-out the organization in the marketplace. The drive towards creating a climate of excellence forms a key part of that culture. The external environment plays a pivotal role, because customers, competitors, suppliers, local communities and other external stakeholders all exert a crucial influence on how management will seek to achieve sustainable competitive advantage. Internally, the abilities and attitudes of employees, and the way in which their contribution is optimized is critical. The manner in which

FIGURE 11.1   Key management issues – 1970 to 2000

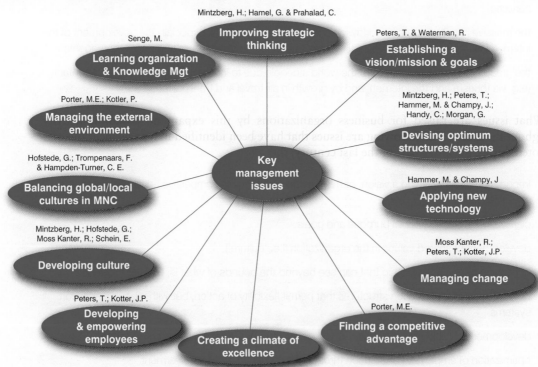

people are treated, the utilization of new technology, and the pressures arising from the external marketplace, are all aspects of the challenge of managing change. On top of all these factors are the organizational structures and systems that are a major part of the organization's fabric, linking all the various parts and processes together in a whole tapestry of organizational activity. Increasingly, for many firms, there is the issue of balancing global/international standards with those of local business units in differing cultures.

CONCLUSION

12.   Management is complex. Throughout this part of the book we have tried to arrange and organize the major (popular) approaches to management, successful throughout the twentieth century, see Figure 11.2. We have presented an overview of the ideas, theories and management philosophies that have contributed to making the workplace what it is today. The principles provide a foundation and framework for us to explore the practice of management and analyze organizations. In this chapter, we have considered more recent trends and approaches and built on our management understanding. Since no one management approach provides universally applicable principles of management, today's manager must take those ideas, from the different approaches, which best suit the particular requirements of their culture, organization and their job. In some cases the classical theories and principles along with systems theory and contingency approaches may be adopted whilst in other cases ideas from the human relations movement may be of more value. The different approaches are not generally in competition with each other and in many cases we can trace a progression of ideas, each building upon or complementing the other; all of the approaches discussed in this part of the book contribute to the blend that defines contemporary management. We should also recognize, particularly in complex and ever changing contexts, that many view management as much of an art as science. There are many aspects to management and we will attempt to illuminate some of the more important ones over the following chapters of this book.

FIGURE 11.2 Evolution of Management Theory

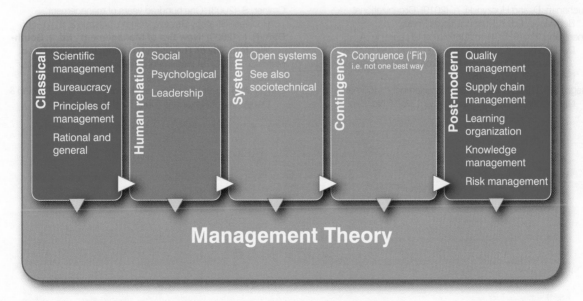

QUESTIONS

1 Critically evaluate the main traditional approaches to management (classical, humanistic, systems and contingency) and contrast them with post-modern ideas of management.

2 Explain how management theory has evolved over the past 100 years.

3 Discuss why it is important to understand both historic and contemporary theories of management.

4 Synthesize the fundamental differences between classical management and contingency theory.

5 Define what is meant by management – in your answer you should list and describe the popular approaches to management developed throughout the 20th century and discuss the evolution of management theory. Are the different approaches complimentary or in competition with one another? Explain your answer.

USEFUL WEBSITES

Chartered Management Institute: **www.managers.org.uk/** Chartered professional body in the UK dedicated to

promoting the highest standards in management and leadership excellence

REFERENCES

Buchanan, D. and Huczynski, A. (2010) 'Organizational Behaviour', Ed. 7. Financial Times Press.

Checkland, P. (1985) 'From Optimizing to Learning: A Development of Systems Thinking for the 1990s', The Journal of the Operational Research Society, 36:9 April 1985 (Sep., 1985), p. 757–767.

Clegg, S R. (1992) 'Postmodern Management?', Journal of Organizational Change Management, Vol. 5 No. 2, p. 31.

Crainer, S. (2003) 'One hundred years of management', Business Strategy Review, Volume 14 Issue 2, p. 41–49.

Daft, R. L. (2009) 'New Era of Management', Ed. 9. South-Western, Div of Thomson Learning; International ed.

Mullins, L. (2010) 'Management and Organizational Behaviour', Ed. 9. Financial Times Press.

Senge, P. M. (1996) 'Leading learning organizations', Training & Development Alexandria (Dec), 50 (12), p. 36–37.

PART II
MANAGEMENT IN PRACTICE

THE CONTEXT OF MANAGEMENT

Having examined some of the key theoretical aspects of management, we now turn to the practice of management. This section of the book considers some of the important contextual issues that lie behind the day-to-day operation of work organizations. Chapter 12 outlines the main types of business organization, with an emphasis on limited companies and introduces the idea of 'corporate governance'. Chapter 13 considers aspects of organizational value-building, i.e. the development of corporate culture. This is followed in Chapter 14 by consideration of key issues raised for women in management. Chapter 15 rounds off the contextual issues by briefly considering international aspects of management.

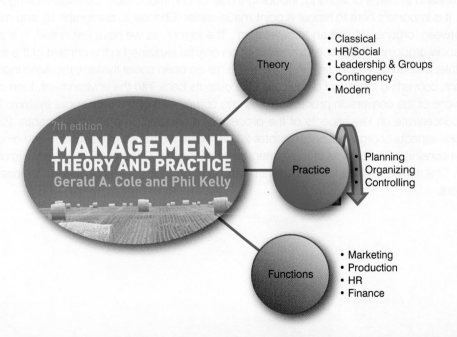

- **Theory**
  - Classical
  - HR/Social
  - Leadership & Groups
  - Contingency
  - Modern

- **Practice**
  - Planning
  - Organizing
  - Controlling

- **Functions**
  - Marketing
  - Production
  - HR
  - Finance

7th edition

MANAGEMENT THEORY AND PRACTICE
Gerald A. Cole and Phil Kelly

MANAGEMENT PLANNING

The following six chapters provide a basic introduction to the fundamental management activity of planning. No enterprise can be undertaken in a vacuum. It must have some purpose in mind, and the means to at least make a start towards achieving that purpose. Planning, in essence, is a process concerned with defining ends, means and conduct at every level of organizational life. It is a management activity, which starts by defining the aims and objectives of the organization, i.e. ends. Planning is also about taking steps (making plans) to agree on the resources, i.e. the means by which the aims and objectives may be fulfilled. Part of this process includes deciding the policies which will guide the implementation of the plans, i.e. the manner in which the organization will conduct itself. Planning is an essentially cyclical and ongoing process, in which aims and objectives are regularly reviewed, and where the progress of plans are subject to frequent review and updating in the light of results. The time perspective of planning is the future rather than the present or the immediate past. Chapter 16 summarizes some of the key issues involved at the strategic level of planning, where decisions are taken about the primary vision, goals, competitive situation and resourcing of the organization. Chapter 17 looks, in a little more detail, at the practical implications of setting goals, objectives and policies. Chapter 18 outlines important aspects of setting performance standards in the planning process. Chapter 19 examines the decision-making processes, and Chapter 20 summarizes the planning aspects of the organization's human resources. Finally, Chapter 21 considers aspects of 'grass-roots' planning, aimed at improving the ability of the organization to deliver its goals.

ORGANIZING FOR MANAGEMENT

If planning is considered as providing the route map for the journey, then organizing is the means by which we arrive at our chosen destination. Plans, as we saw earlier, are statements of intent, direction and resourcing. To translate intentions into effect requires purposeful activity, and this is where the role of the organizing function of management is introduced. Organizing is concerned, above all, with activity. It is a process for determining, grouping and structuring activities; devising and allocating roles arising from the grouping and structuring of activities; assigning accountability for results and determining detailed rules and systems of working, including those for communication, decision-making and conflict-resolution. It is important here to repeat a point made earlier (Chapter 2, paragraph 9), and make the distinction between 'organizing' and an 'organization'. The former, as we have just noted, is a process; the latter is a social grouping. The process, however, can only be explained in the context of the social grouping. If we take a systems view of an organization, i.e. as an open social system, receiving inputs from the environment, converting them and discharging the outputs back into the environment, then organizing is essentially one of the conversion processes. It is one component of the total social system. The next six chapters concentrate on key aspects of the process of organizing. In particular, Chapter 22 deals with the structural aspects of organizations, Chapter 23 highlights the issues of delegation and empowerment, Chapter 24 considers key aspects of the management of change, Chapter 25 looks at the implementation of change, Chapter 26 reviews formal communications in organizations and Chapter 27 deals with time management.

CONTROL IN MANAGEMENT

The control function in management rounds off the POMC process referred to at the outset of this book. Once the planning, organizing and motivating activities are underway, then they must be monitored and measured, i.e. controlled. The primary aim of the control function of management is to measure performance against aims, objectives and standards with a view to enabling corrective actions to be taken, where necessary, to keep plans on course. Control is essentially a question of developing feedback systems throughout the organization. It may be implemented both quantitatively and qualitatively. There are three chapters in this section of the book. The basic nature of the control function, together with its key methods and techniques, is outlined in Chapter 28. This is followed by a short chapter (Chapter 29) outlining some of the key elements of a Quality Management system. In Chapter 30, the role of Information Technology is discussed, especially in terms of its impact on office routines and procedures.

Section Seven
The Context of Management

THE CONTEXT OF MANAGEMENT

UNITED PARCEL SERVICE, UPS

Formed in 1907, United Parcel Service, UPS, well known for its brown trucks, is the world's largest package delivery company, in terms of both revenue and volume. UPS offers time-definite delivery of letters, documents and small packages via air and ground services to more than 200 countries and territories around the world. In 2009, the company delivered an average of 15 million pieces per day worldwide, or a total of 3.8 billion packages. This contributed to the generation of $45 billion in revenue. This was generated by approximately 408 000 employees, of whom 68 000 were located internationally, with 88 000 vehicles and the 11th largest airline. Major competitors include FedEx, an array of international operators, including Royal Mail, national postal services and air cargo handlers.

The company has made many changes in over 100 years of existence. Changes have been made to the business model in order to take account of various environmental and contextual forces (technological, social, political and economic), threats and opportunities. Starting out as a messenger company (with the advent of telegraphy), UPS moved into package delivery and then became a carriage business, becoming international in the mid-70s with a true international model by the 1980s. The business changed further with the advent of globalization and the Internet. The UPS strategy focuses on market penetration for growth. The company typically expands through mergers and acquisitions, alliances and partnerships; senior managers at UPS consider organic growth to be too slow. Markets are only considered if they pass three tests: (1) the market has to be of a good size, growing and attractive; (2) the company has to be able to leverage its existing skills, brand, technology and people resources; and (3) the initiative has to fit within the corporate strategy.

UPS's global presence grew out of its highly refined US domestic business. Europe is their largest region outside the United States – accounting for approximately half of their International revenue. UPS believe that both Europe and Asia offer significant opportunities for long-term growth. The company has built a strong international presence through significant investments over several decades. One recent acquisition and investment took place in 2008, when the company completed construction of a new hub in Tamworth, England, UPS's largest ground hub outside the US. It replaced three smaller facilities, and added more capacity and better efficiencies than existed with the three separate facilities.

In conducting their business UPS must contend with many challenges. General economic conditions and competition (see Para 1) could adversely affect their business, financial position and results of operations. Their business is subject to complex and stringent regulation. For example, as a result of concerns about global terrorism and homeland security, governments around the world have adopted or may adopt stricter security requirements that will result in increased operating costs. Furthermore, the company may be affected by global climate change or by legal, regulatory or market responses to such change. Concern over climate change, including the impact of global warming, has led to significant legislative and regulatory efforts to limit greenhouse gas (GHG) emissions. Efforts to regulate GHG emissions, especially aircraft or diesel engine emissions, could impose substantial costs on the company. These costs include an increase in the cost of the fuel and other energy they purchase and capital costs associated with updating or replacing aircraft or trucks prematurely. Even without such legislation or regulation, increased awareness and any adverse publicity in the global marketplace about the GHGs emitted by companies in the airline and transportation industries could harm reputation and reduce customer demand for services, especially air services.

There are other contextual challenges faced by the company. Operating internationally, they are exposed to risks associated with changes in exchange rates (in particular the Euro, British Pound and Canadian Dollar) or interest rates which may have an adverse affect on results. Strikes, work stoppages and slowdowns by employees could adversely affect business, financial position and results of operations.

Factors in the environment therefore determine many aspects of the way the company manages its business. In response to legislative and investor demands, UPS have adopted various business codes. Corporate Governance Guidelines exist for the Board Structure and the membership of the Board committees which include Audit, Compensation, Executive and Corporate Governance. UPS have implemented a written Code of Business Conduct that applies to all employees. The code asserts that the company 'treats each individual fairly' and that they 'do not discriminate against any applicant for employment or any employee in any aspect of their employment at UPS because of age, race, religion, sex, disability, sexual orientation, military status, pregnancy, national origin or veteran status'.

Much of the company's success is attributed to their distinctive culture. UPS believe that the dedication of their employees results in large part from their 'employee-owner' concept. The UPS employee stock ownership tradition dates from 1927, when the founders, who believed that employee stock ownership was a vital foundation for successful business, first offered stock (shares) to employees. To facilitate employee stock ownership, UPS maintain several stock-based compensation programs. The company also has a long-standing policy of 'promotion from within' which complements [their] tradition of employee ownership, and this policy reduces the need for [UPS] to hire managers and executive officers from outside UPS. The

majority of their management team began their careers as full-time or part-time hourly UPS employees, and have spent their entire careers with UPS. Many of the UPS executive officers have more than 30 years of service with UPS and have accumulated a meaningful ownership stake in the company. Therefore, UPS executive officers have a strong incentive to effectively manage UPS, which benefits all shareowners.

In 2010, UPS was named one of the best places to work for equality by the Human Rights Campaign (HRC). A range of non-discriminatory policies can be found within the employee handbook. Additionally, all employees are required to attend diversity training. An inclusive company, UPS was recently recognized as one of the best American companies for diversity. Their commitment to diversity is demonstrated by representation within the board of directors, employee base and senior management. Included within their diversity program are leadership development initiatives such as the Women's Leadership Development (WLD) scheme designed to provide an integrated and aligned series of tools and practices that brings talented women (and men) into higher levels of responsibility at UPS. Subsequent programs have been implemented to help attract, retain and develop diverse employees.

In summary, when practicing management, UPS must take account of important contextual (situational) issues. Such issues lie behind their day-to-day operations and explain many of the key decisions and initiatives they undertake.

Source: http://www.ups.com/

CHAPTER 12
BUSINESS ORGANIZATIONS AND CORPORATE GOVERNANCE

Key Concepts

- Corporate governance
- Enterprise risk management
- Limited company
- Partnership
- Public limited company (plc)
- Sole trader

Learning Outcomes
Having read this chapter, you should be able to:

- compare and contrast the most common types of business organization
- discuss the responsibilities of a company director
- identify the basic principles of good governance
- discuss the risk management process and its contribution to corporate governance
- discuss what is meant by the theory of the firm and contrast it with the triple bottom line

Management Coordinated activities (forecasting, planning, deciding, organizing, commanding) to direct and control an organization

1.   The subject-matter of this book is management. Many of the management issues touched upon are common to every kind of organization, be it business, state enterprise, public service, non-profit-making charity or private club. However, the full range of management theory and practice occurs mainly in what we call 'business organizations'. We introduced the general meaning of organization in Chapter 2 and in this chapter describe the main legal characteristics of such organizations.

2.   A business organization, in contrast to a public service organization or a charity, exists to provide goods or services usually at a profit. Making a profit may not necessarily be the sole aim of a business (see the theory of the firm and the triple bottom line at the end of the chapter), but it is certainly what distinguishes it from a non-business organization. In Britain, business organizations are mainly to be found in the private sector of the economy. The business organizations we are concerned with here range in size from the sole trader, through partnerships between two or more people working in collaboration, to large public limited companies (plcs) employing thousands of staff in a variety of locations. There are also cooperative enterprises, notably in retail distribution, but also in manufacturing on a small scale.

Sole trader A type of business entity which legally has no separate existence from its owner (the limitations of liability benefited from by a corporation, and limited liability partnerships, do not apply to sole traders) – the simplest form of business

3.   The most common types of business organization are as follows:

- limited companies
- sole traders
- partnerships
- cooperatives.

Public limited company (plc) A limited company whose shares may be purchased by the public and traded freely on the open market and whose share capital is not less than a statutory minimum (for the UK – a company registered under the Companies Act (1980) as a public company)

The following paragraphs summarize the principal features of these businesses, together with the main advantages and disadvantages for the parties concerned. We also introduce the concept of corporate governance and the related concept of risk management.

12.1 LIMITED COMPANIES

Corporate governance The system used to control and direct a company's operations

4.   When a limited company is formed, it is said to have become 'incorporated', i.e. endowed with a separate body, or person. The corporation so formed is treated in English law as a separate entity, independent of its members. The corporation, or 'company', as it is generally called, is capable of owning property, employing people, making contracts and of suing or being sued. Another important feature of a company is that, unlike a sole trader or a partnership, it does have continuity of succession, as it is unaffected by the death or incapacity of one or more of its members.

Limited company A corporation with shareholders whose liability is limited by shares

5.   The key feature of a 'limited' company is that, if it fails, it can only require its members (shareholders) to meet its debts up to the limit of the nominal value of their shares. The principle of legally limiting the financial liabilities of persons investing in business ventures was introduced by Parliament in the 1850s to encourage the wealthy to give financial support to the inventors, engineers and others who were at the forefront of Britain's Industrial Revolution. Without the protection of limited liability, an investor could find himself stripped of his home and other personal assets

Partnership When you go into business with someone else (more commonly associated with professional services such as accountants, solicitors and doctors)

in order to meet debts arising from the failure of any company in which he had invested his money.

6.   Since the turn of the twentieth century, various Company Acts have laid down the principles and procedures to be followed in the conduct of business organizations. Such legislation has been intended to minimize the risk to suppliers and customers as well as to shareholders, and to a lesser extent employees, arising from gross mismanagement of, or deliberate restriction of information about, a company. Legislation was consolidated into one Principal Act – the Companies Act, 1985 – as amended by the Companies Act, 1989. The Companies Act 2006 superseded the Companies Act 1985. The implementation of the Companies Act 2006 was fully completed in 2009. The Act provides a comprehensive code of company law for the United Kingdom, and made changes to almost every aspect of the law in relation to companies. The Act codifies certain existing common law principles, such as those relating to directors' duties and introduces various new provisions for private and public companies but otherwise amends or restates almost all of the Companies Act 1985.

7.   Limited liability companies fall into two categories: public limited companies (plcs) and private limited companies. The Memorandum of a plc must state that the company is a public company (i.e. its shares are available for purchase by the public) and the company name must end with the words 'Public limited company'. A private limited company, by comparison, may not offer its shares to the public, and is even restricted in the transfer of its shares between the private shareholders. The name of a private limited company must end with the word 'Limited'. Both kinds of company must have at least two members and one director. Once registered under the Companies Act, a private company can begin trading without further formality. A public limited company has to obtain a certificate of trading from the Registrar of Companies. All limited companies have to fulfil certain procedures before they can be incorporated. These include the filing of two particularly important documents: (a) the Memorandum of Association (purpose of the company etc.) and (b) the Articles of Association which regulate the internal affairs of the company. Companies are required to submit annual returns to the Registrar, and these are available for public inspection. The main advantages of limited liability can be summarized as follows:

- in the event of business failure, shareholders are protected against the loss of more than the nominal value of their shareholding.

- the separate legal person of the company exists independently of the members

- shares (in plcs) are readily transferable.

The disadvantages are primarily as follows:

- precisely because liability is limited, it may be difficult for small companies to borrow as extensively as desired, since banks and other financial institutions may be unable to recover their funds if the business fails.

- there are legal procedures involved in setting up a company, as well as the procedures incurred in publishing the various financial accounts of the company.

12.1.1 Company directors

8.   The directors of the company are, in law, its agents, and are accountable for the conduct of the company's affairs; they must act within their powers and abide by the terms of the **company's memorandum and articles of association** and decisions made by the shareholders. They are appointed by the shareholders/members to use their best endeavours to achieve the company's objectives. Every director has a duty to act honestly in the best interests

Company's memorandum and articles of associaton The documents needed to form a company. In the UK, a company must draw up a Memorandum of Association to document and record details of the firm. The memorandum provides basic information on a business or association in the United Kingdom and with the Articles of Association, forms the company's charter or constitution. The memorandum may be viewed by the public at the office in which it is filed

of the company (see fiduciary duties), to avoid possible conflicts of interest, and not to make a personal profit from the directorship other than what the company is prepared to pay by way of salary and fees, for example. Directors must act in a way that benefits the shareholders as a whole, but additionally must have regard for other matters such as the interests of employees, the impact on the community and the environment, etc.

9.   Directors may be executive, having operational as well as strategic responsibilities, or non-executive, having only board responsibilities. Executive directors are usually full-time employees, whereas non-executives usually work part-time for one or two days a month. Some non-executive directors serve on several different boards, and this has raised questions as to whether there should be restrictions on the number of such posts held by any one individual.

10.   In the UK the typical company board is a unitary board, composed of a majority of executive directors with a small number of non-executives. A few companies, especially those that are not-for-profit businesses, may have a majority of non-executive directors.

11.   Recently, non-executive directors have been encouraged to take the leadership of key board committees, such as the audit and remuneration committees. This means they, rather than their executive colleagues, are monitoring the company's financial audits and establishing the remuneration of the board members. There are a few who argue that the UK's so-called unitary boards are *de facto* two-tier boards, where one section is composed of full-time executive directors, fully in the picture about what is happening in the company, whilst the other, smaller section comprises the part-time non-executives, who are remote from most of the day-to-day events in the company.

Chief executive officer (CEO) The highest-ranking executive or administrator in charge of management; the singular organizational position that is primarily responsible for carrying out the strategic plans and policies of an organization

12.   The principal director is usually the chairman of the board, who may be full or part-time. The senior executive director is the person who holds the title of managing director or chief executive officer (CEO) and who is responsible for overall day-to-day operations, as well as for board duties. The CEO is responsible for implementing policies and strategy, as well as for helping to formulate them. He, or she, is responsible for building and motivating the senior management team, and for installing appropriate systems to ensure the smooth-running of the business. The chief administrative officer of the board is the company secretary, who is responsible for ensuring that the legal requirements for running meetings, appointing directors, voting and other procedures, are adhered to. The company secretary may, or may not, be a director. In a small company the CEO may act as company secretary.

13.   Directors' responsibilities include determining, and subsequently monitoring, the company's strategic goals and the policies under which they are to be achieved. They are also responsible for preparing and publishing the company's financial accounts for the shareholders/members. These accounts (see Chapter 51) have to include the balance sheet, showing the company's assets and liabilities as at the end of the trading year. They must include a profit and loss account (or income and expenditure account), showing the income received from trading activities, the cost of sales, the amount of profit, taxation, dividends paid and profits retained in the business. Most accounts also include a cash flow statement.

14.   Accounts may need to be audited by an external and independent firm of accountants, which has to state that the accounts represent 'a true and fair view of the state of affairs of the company'. Otherwise, the auditors have to qualify the accounts. It is the responsibility of the directors to recommend the appointment of the company's auditors, and to satisfy themselves that the latter are fulfilling their duties properly. In particular, directors need to pay attention to the way the company treats such issues as depreciation, stock valuation and financial provisions.

12.2 CORPORATE GOVERNANCE & RISK MANAGEMENT

15.   Businesses around the world need to be able to attract funding from investors in order to expand and grow, Mallin (2009). Before investors decide to place their funds in a particular

business, they will want to be as sure as they can be that the business is financially sound and will continue to be so in the foreseeable future. Investors therefore need to have confidence that the business is being well-managed and will continue to be profitable. The financial crisis which came to a head in 2008–09 triggered widespread reappraisal, locally and internationally, of the **governance** systems which might have alleviated it. The manner in which company directors promote and control their company's operations, that is the way they exercise their stewardship, is not just a matter of interest to their shareholders/members, but is a matter of public interest too. In the UK a number of codes of good practice have been developed over recent years, following criticisms of the behaviour of some boards and individual directors. The Financial Reporting Council published the UK Corporate Governance Code – formerly known as the **Combined Code** – on 28 May 2010. The new edition of the Code will apply to financial years beginning on or after 29 June 2010. The purpose of corporate governance is to facilitate effective, entrepreneurial and prudent management that can deliver the long-term success of the company. The Code's function should be to help boards discharge their duties in the best interests of their companies. The first version of the UK Code on Corporate Governance (the Code) was produced in 1992 by the Cadbury Committee. Its paragraph 2.5 is still the classic definition of the context of the Code: Corporate governance is the system by which companies are directed and controlled. Boards of directors are responsible for the governance of their companies. The shareholders' role in governance is to appoint the directors and the auditors and to satisfy themselves that an appropriate governance structure is in place. The responsibilities of the board include setting the company's strategic aims, providing the leadership to put them into effect, supervising the management of the business and reporting to shareholders on their stewardship. The board's actions are subject to laws, regulations and the shareholders in general meeting. Corporate governance is therefore about what the board of a company does and how it sets the values of the company, and is to be distinguished from the day to day operational management of the company by full-time executives.

> **Governance framework** The governance framework describes whom the organization is there to serve and how the purposes and priorities of the organization should be decided

> **Combined Code** A set of principles of good corporate governance and provides a code of best practice aimed at companies listed on the London Stock Exchange

16. The Code is not a rigid set of rules. It consists of principles and provisions. The Listing Rules (publicly listed companies have to abide by additional regulations called the 'Listing Rules'; traditionally set by the Stock Exchange itself but now administered by the Financial Services Authority (FSA) and effectively have the force of law) require companies to apply the main principles and report to shareholders on how they have adhered to these principles. The main principles of the code focus on LEADERSHIP – every company should be headed by an effective board which is collectively responsible for the long-term success of the company; EFFECTIVENESS – e.g. the board should be supplied in a timely manner with information in a form and of a quality appropriate to enable it to discharge its duties; ACCOUNTABILITY – the board is responsible for determining the nature and extent of the significant risks it is willing to take in achieving its strategic objectives. The board should maintain sound risk management and internal control systems; REMUNERATION – formal and transparent procedures on executive remuneration etc. and RELATIONS WITH SHAREHOLDERS – e.g. the board should use the AGM to communicate with investors and to encourage their participation.

12.3 RISK MANAGEMENT

17. An important aspect of the code and the duties of directors (and all employees for that matter) is the management of risk. The key principle to note here is that the board is responsible for determining the nature and extent of the significant risks it is willing to take in achieving its strategic objectives. The board should maintain sound risk management and internal control

systems. The Institute of Risk Management (IRM, 2002) welcomed the sharper focus on the proper management of risk in the revised code. In order to help organizations and the Board manage risk, a Risk Management Standard was published by the Institute of Risk Management (IRM, 2002), The Association of Insurance and Risk Managers (AIRMIC) and Alarm (The Public Risk Management Association) in 2002. Risk management is a rapidly developing discipline and there are many and varied views and descriptions of what risk management involves, how it should be conducted and what it is for. Risk can be defined as the combination of the probability of an event and its consequences (ISO/IEC Guide 73). In all types of undertaking, there is the potential for events and consequences that constitute opportunities for benefit (upside) or threats to success (downside). Risk Management is increasingly recognized as being concerned with both positive and negative aspects of risk.

18.   Risk management is a central part of any organization's management. It is the process whereby organizations methodically address the risks attached to their activities with the goal of achieving sustained benefit within each activity and across the portfolio of all activities. The focus of good risk management is the identification and treatment of these risks. Its objective is to add maximum sustainable value to all the activities of the organization. It marshals the understanding of the potential upside and downside of all those factors which can affect the organization. It increases the probability of success, and reduces both the probability of failure and the uncertainty of achieving the organization's overall objectives.

19.   The aforementioned standard contains a risk management process, depicted in Figure 12.1. A description of each activity, along with suggested methods, is provided within the standard which can be obtained from the IRM web site. The risk management process (RMP) starts with an understanding of the business context and is then followed by risk assessment. Risk identification sets out to highlight an organization's exposure to uncertainty. This requires an intimate knowledge of the organization, the market in which it operates, the legal, social, political and cultural environment in which it exists, as well as the development of a sound understanding of its strategic and operational objectives, including factors critical to its success and

FIGURE 12.1   **Risk Management Process**

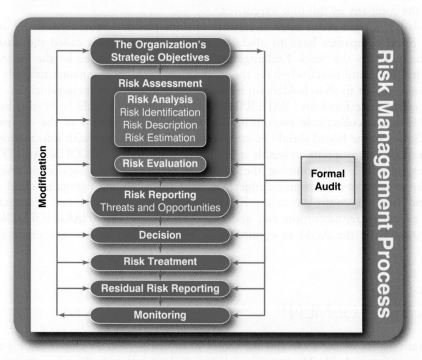

Source: Adapted from *A Risk Management Standard* (2002) Published by the Institute of Risk Management (www.theirm.org)
Reproduced with permission.

the threats and opportunities related to the achievement of these objectives. Risks are then described and estimated in terms of probability and impact in a structured manner. When the risk analysis process has been completed, it is necessary to compare the estimated risks against risk criteria established by the organization. The risk criteria may include associated costs and benefits, legal requirements, socioeconomic and environmental factors, concerns of stakeholders, etc. Risk evaluation therefore, is used to make decisions about the significance of risks to the organization and whether each specific risk should be accepted or treated. Risk treatment is the process of selecting and implementing measures to modify the risk.

20.   The Committee of Sponsoring Organizations of the Treadway Commission (COSO) published an Enterprise Risk Management (ERM) standard in 2004. The COSO ERM cube is well known to risk management practitioners and it provides a framework for undertaking ERM. It has gained considerable influence because it is linked to the Sarbanes–Oxley requirements for companies listed in the United States. In 2009 the ISO 31000 Risk Management Principles and Guidelines was published. ISO 31000 is intended to be a family of standards relating to risk management, codified by the International Organization for Standardization. The purpose of ISO 31000:2009 is to provide principles and generic guidelines on risk management. ISO 31000 was published in 2009 as an internationally agreed standard for the implementation of risk management principles.

Enterprise Risk Management A framework of methods and processes used by organizations to manage their risks and take opportunities related to the attainment of their objectives

COSO ERM framework The COSO (Committee of Sponsoring Organizations of the Treadway Commission) Enterprise Risk Management-Integrated Framework published in 2004 defines ERM as a process, effected by an entity's board of directors, management and other personnel, applied in strategy setting and across the enterprise, designed to identify potential events that may affect the entity, and manage risk to be within its risk appetite, to provide reasonable assurance regarding the achievement of entity objectives

Sarbanes–Oxley Act A law defining acceptable accounting practices including audit and control of financial information

12.4 SOLE TRADERS

21.   The sole trader is the simplest form of business organization – one person in business on his own. The legal requirements for setting up such a business are minimal, but the owner is fully liable for any debts incurred in running the business, since the owner literally is the business. Ownership and control are combined. All profits made by the sole trader are subject to income tax rather than the corporation tax levied on company profits. Apart from the need to maintain accounts for controlling the business and for dealing with the Inland Revenue, there are no formal accounts to be published. The main advantages of operating as a sole trader are:

- easy to start
- complete autonomy to run the business as the individual wishes
- the profits of the business belong to the trader
- various business expenses are allowable against income tax
- no public disclosure of accounts (except to Inland Revenue).

The main disadvantages are as follows:

- the sole trader is entirely responsible for the debts of the business
- the individual as owner and manager has to be responsible for all aspects of the business (marketing, product development, sales, finance, etc.).

12.5 PARTNERSHIPS

22.   A partnership is a type of business entity in which partners (owners) share with each other the profits or losses of the business. Partnerships are often favoured over other business forms for taxation purposes. However, owners of a partnership may be exposed to greater personal liability than they would as shareholders of a corporation. The legalities required to set up a partnership are minimal, although it is advisable to have a formal Partnership agreement drawn up by a solicitor. Such an agreement can specify the rights and obligations of individual partners, and can make provision for changes brought about by death or retirement of partners. As with a sole trader, the members of a partnership are owners of its property and liable for its contracts. Therefore they are fully responsible for meeting their debts to third parties. Partners are not automatically entitled to a salary for the services they provide for the partnership, but are entitled to their proper share of the profits of the business. However, many agreements do allow for salaried partners. United Kingdom partnership law refers to the rules under which partnerships are governed in the United Kingdom. The principal sources of law are the Partnership Act 1890 and the Limited Partnership Act 1907. Most professional persons, and especially accountants and solicitors, maintain partnership as their form of business in order to preserve the principle of individual professional accountability towards the client. The main advantages of partnership are:

- few formalities required for starting up

- sharing of partners' knowledge and skills

- sharing of management of business

- no obligation to publish accounts (except for Inland Revenue purposes)

- sharing of profits (or losses!) of business.

The disadvantages are primarily these:

- each partner is liable for the debts of the partnership, even if caused by the actions of other partners

- risk that the partners may not be able to work together at a personal level

- the death or bankruptcy of one partner will automatically dissolve the partnership, unless otherwise provided for in a partnership agreement.

12.6 COOPERATIVE ENTERPRISES

23.   Small groups of people, who wish to set up business along explicitly democratic lines and with the benefit of limited liability, can choose to establish a cooperative. This kind of business has been a feature of British commercial life for well over a hundred years. They are different because they are jointly owned and operated democratically by their members – and it is the members who are the beneficiaries of the activities of the business. The main advantages of cooperative enterprise are that it:

Cooperative Business organizations owned and operated by a group of individuals for their mutual benefit

- provides opportunity for genuine pooling of capital between a group of people

- encourages active collaboration between all sections of the workforce

- enables decisions to be made democratically

– provides rewards on an equitable basis among those involved

– provides limited liability (if registered).

The disadvantages are mainly:

– less likelihood of a level of profitability and growth that could be achieved by a limited company

– as with partnerships, relationships can deteriorate, especially when some members are seen to be making a smaller contribution than the rest

– democratic decision-making can lead to lengthy discussions before action is taken

– members who are not truly dedicated to the democratic ethos of the business may find themselves at odds with the openness of communication and decision-making.

12.7 THEORY OF THE FIRM AND THE TRIPLE BOTTOM LINE

24.   The theory of the firm consists of a number of economic theories which describe the nature of the firm (company or corporation), including its existence, its behaviour and its relationship with the market. The traditional 'theory of the firm' assumes that profit maximization is the goal of the commercial organization. More recent analyses suggest that sales maximization or market share, combined with satisfactory profits, may be the main purpose of large industrial corporations. Furthermore, whilst traditional views recognized only the shareholder as the focus of organizational goals, more recently, organizations have considered society as a key stakeholder. Organizations exist in a wider environment, where they typically compete with other organizations for revenue. If the costs of doing business are less than the amount customers are willing to pay for the organization's goods and services, the organization makes profit which may be retained or distributed to shareholders.

25.   Amongst the performance measurements for organizations is the triple bottom line. The triple bottom line (or 'TBL', '3BL', or 'People, Planet, Profit') captures an extended range of values and criteria for measuring organizational success; economic, environmental and social. The concept of TBL demands that a company's responsibility be to 'stakeholders' rather than shareholders. In this case, 'stakeholders' refers to anyone who is influenced, either directly or indirectly, by the actions of the organization. People (Human Capital) pertains to fair and beneficial business practices towards labour and the community and region in which a corporation conducts its business; Planet (Natural Capital) refers to sustainable environmental practices and Profit (not limited to the internal profit made by a company or organization) is the bottom line shared by all commerce – the economic benefit enjoyed by the host society. The triple bottom line idea proposes that an organization's license to operate in society comes not just from satisfying stakeholders through improved profits (the economic bottom line), but by also improving its environmental and social performance. As such, it encompasses environmental responsibility, social awareness and economic profitability. We revisit the concept of TBL when we discuss ethics and corporate social responsibility in Chapter 17.

CONCLUSION

26.   In Part I we explored management and organizational theory, discussing how organizations should be managed. Whilst in Chapter 2 we stated, in broad terms, what is meant by the term 'organization', we did not explore types of organization in practice. That was the focus of this chapter. Different types of company can exist in law and each have different advantages

and disadvantages and rules within which they must comply. In this chapter we explored the main types of organization (limited companies, sole traders, partnerships and cooperatives) and how they come into existence. We recognized that in some cases the owners and investors may not be employed by the company, typically in public limited companies. In such situations there is a need for mechanisms to ensure that the board, directors, managers and employees act in the best interests of the shareholders. We introduced the concept of corporate governance, explicit 'rules' and principles to guide the management of such companies by their directors. One key aspect of managing a company on behalf of shareholders is the management of risk – to assure assets are safeguarded and organizational goals attained. We highlighted the importance of risk management and introduced several risk standards and a generic risk management process. Finally, we recognized the importance of understanding company goals and introduced the theory of the firm and the triple bottom line.

QUESTIONS

1   After finishing your business studies, you and several friends decide to set up a consultancy company.
    Evaluate the types of business organization and select the one you believe is most suited to your venture. Explain your choice.

2   Review each of the main types of organization (limited companies, sole traders, partnerships and cooperatives) and discuss the role of corporate governance (rules and principles) in managing the company.

3   Explain how risk management enables good corporate governance.

4   Discuss why corporate governance is important for contemporary UK listed companies. Evaluate the role of governance codes in organizations.

5   Various codes of legislation which aim to ensure good corporate governance place obligations on the board to determine the nature and extent of significant risks. Such organizations should also maintain a sound risk management system. Why is this important?

6   Evaluate the IRM risk standard and risk process and explain how they might be used to help organizations fulfil their corporate governance obligations.

USEFUL WEBSITES

Institute of Business Ethics **www.ibe.org.uk**
The Management Standards Centre **http://www.management-standards.org**
Institute of Directors **http://www.iod.com**
The Uk Corporate Governance Code **http://www.frc.org.uk/documents/pagemanager/Corporate_**

Governance/UK%20Corp%20Gov%20Code%20June%202010.pdf
The Companies House website **http://www.companieshouse.gov.uk/index.shtml** Companies House is a registry of corporate information.

REFERENCES

IRM (2002) 'A Risk Management Standard', AIRMIC, ALARM, IRM, p. 1–14.
ISO/IEC (2002) 'GUIDE 73', Ed. 1. ISO/IEC.
Johnson, G., Scholes, K. and Whittington, R. (2006) 'Exploring Corporate Strategy Enhanced Media Edition', FT Prentice Hall.

Mallin, C. (2009) 'Corporate Governance', Ed. 3. Oxford University Press.
Stock, M., Copnell, T. and Wicks, C. (1999) 'The combined code: A practical guide', Gee Publishing Ltd.

CHAPTER 13
DEVELOPING AN ORGANIZATION CULTURE

Key Concepts

- Corporate culture
- Culture
- Organizational (corporate) culture

Learning Outcomes Having read this chapter, you should be able to:

- explain what is meant by organization culture
- discuss types of culture
- differentiate several dimensions of organization culture
- list factors that may be a source or manifestation of organization culture
- discuss culture change

1. Switzerland is home to six of the largest companies in Europe, one of which is Nestlé. Nestlé has a 145-year history and operations in virtually every country in the world their success is built, in part, on a recognition that their, 'principal assets are not office buildings, factories or even brands. Rather, it is the fact that we are a global organization comprised of many nationalities, religions and ethnic backgrounds all working together in one single unifying **corporate culture**'. The quotation is of interest to us in several ways. In this chapter we define **culture** and explore its impact upon organizations. This may, however, be difficult as several leading scholars believe culture to be extremely difficult to define and one of the most contentious concepts in business! If Nestlé attribute success to embracing diverse cultures then competitors may want to emulate this. Emulation may, however, prove either impossible or very difficult as some scholars see culture as something an organization 'is' rather than something it has. Nestlé see culture as a means to unify (integrate) employees, leading to cost efficiencies since employees are almost self regulated (self controlled) as opposed to being controlled through tight supervision and excessive bureaucracy. When culture is used as a unifying mechanism and when employees are more homogenous in their collective ways of thinking and behaving, we can say that a strong culture exists. Strong cultures are seen as efficient and more appropriate for stable environments but in a dynamic environment the organization may emphasize the importance of creativity. It has been argued that this is a more likely outcome from weaker, more heterogeneous cultures.

Corporate culture Defined by Bower as 'the way we do things around here'. Trice and Beyer elaborated this as: 'the system of . . . publicly and collectively accepted meanings operating for a given group at a given time'. Hofstede (1998) describes corporate culture as 'the psychological assets of an organization, which can be used to predict what will happen to its financial assets in five years time'. See also 'culture'

2. Culture has many functions (and dysfunctions) and deals with how things are done in a company (**practice**) therefore impacting upon many aspects of the organization, including its performance. It can help with motivation, recruitment, retention, sales and investment. In this chapter we start by explaining what we mean by and consider to be the main types of culture (national and organizational); we also identify how managers recognize culture in the work place. We then develop our concept of culture by considering leading thinkers' (Handy, Schein, Hofstede, and Trompenaars and Hampden-Turner) ideas on the matter. Having defined **organizational culture** we then consider its relationship with theories of motivation and leadership outlined in the first part of the book. Finally, we discuss the development of organizational culture, asking whether it is possible and why organizations might try to change their culture and how they might go about the task.

Culture Shared ways of thinking and behaving (uniformity)

Practice An accepted method or standardized activity

Organizational (corporate) culture A set of values, beliefs, goals, norms and rituals that members of an organization share

13.1 WHAT IS CULTURE?

3. There are many definitions and several types (levels) of culture. The two main types of culture, of interest to readers of this book, are national (country level) and organizational. Starting at the national level of culture, Hofstede (1984) provides a mechanistic definition when he famously refers to it as the collective programming of the mind; more recently, Kelly (2009) suggests that culture describes the shared ways of thinking and behaving (uniformity) within a group of people. Culture is always about something that is shared by a group but groups can be defined at different levels such as nations or organizations. However, members of a country or society can share things from an early and formative age whilst members' of organizations tend

Basic assumptions A term used by Schein to refer to the origins of values and cultural artefacts in organizations. Basic assumptions are shared and deeply embedded presuppositions about issues such as whether human beings do or should live for the moment (immediate gratification) or see their activities as a means to a future end or goal (deferred gratification)

to be adults when they work together. For this reason, definitions of organizational culture tend to be different. Schein (1996) notes the importance of culture which he refers to as – shared norms, values, and assumptions – in how organizations function. Huczynski and Buchanan (2010) define organizational culture as 'the collection of relatively uniform and enduring values, beliefs, customs, traditions and practices that are shared by an organization's members, learned by new recruits and transmitted from one generation of employees to the next'. The important point about culture is that whilst there may be striking differences between organizations, there is a shared understanding within them. The culture does not become established until this shared understanding achieves a dominance in the collective thinking of the members of the organization. Having said this, it also has to be accepted that within any single (dominant) culture, there are usually subcultures, which operate at a lower level of influence. For example, we may describe professional cultures such as that in the marketing or IT department, etc. At a simple level, many scholars define national culture in terms of shared values because psychologists believe these form in our early years whilst organizational culture is defined in terms of shared assumptions and practices (behaviour) because these may be shared and changed more easily than our thinking.

Figure 13.1 illustrates some important interrelationships that both produce and are deeply affected by the organization's culture.

FIGURE 13.1 Key interrelationships between culture and other aspects of an organization.

4.   The external environment, customers, competitors, suppliers and other external stake-holders will all exert some influence on what the organization chooses to do, and how it will do it. The social or socio-cultural factors in the macro environment typically include social values, attitudes and beliefs, demographic trends, lifestyle preferences and skills availability. When organizations operate internationally they need to understand how people in other countries may differ; the international Organization must operate in different countries where the inhabitants may differ from those of their home markets, see Chapter 15. As was noted earlier, the construct used to describe such differences is termed (national) culture and cul-tural differences can create problems within the business envi-ronment. Differences in culture (fit) may necessitate changes to business practices, management styles, products and services. Differences in societies arise through education, religion, lan-guage and social systems inculcating values and meanings that become shared by the country's people. Differences may also arise as a result of the country's location, physical environment, geography and climate. The environment is a source of challenge, shared by inhabitants who develop similar coping behaviours. The degree of difference between two countries impacts upon the extent of adap-tation required by an international organization. The organization therefore needs to have some awareness of the differences. To that end, a variety of frameworks exists to measure national culture (we will also highlight frameworks to distinguish organizational culture later in this chapter). Such frameworks (see for example Hofstede) typically decompose the com-plex construct of culture into several dimensions. Typically, dimensions at the national level are value based. The starting point in comparing different cultures concerns how to define culture and the cultural dimensions to study. There is no standard definition of culture and no universal set of cultural dimensions. There are potentially many ways that cultures can be different. Hofstede developed a model that identifies five primary dimensions to assist in differentiating national cultures: Power Distance (related to the problem of inequality – reflecting the degree to which a society accepts that organizational power is distributed unequally), Uncertainty Avoidance (related to the problem of dealing with the unknown and unfamiliar – some nations tolerate ambiguity more readily than others), Individualism–Collectivism (related to the problem of interpersonal ties – the tendency to take care of oneself and one's family versus the tendency to work together for the collective good) and Masculinity–Femininity (related to emotional gender roles). Later he added the fifth dimen-sion: Long- versus Short-Term Orientation (related to deferment of gratification). Despite arguments that suggest some aspects of culture cannot be measured or compared, or that the differences between countries is diminishing, the study and its findings have been widely embraced and continue to be used by many.

> **Cultural artefacts** Phenomena accessible to the senses, including architecture, myths, rituals, logos, type of personnel employed and so on, which signify the values in an organization's culture

5.   Some practitioners classify culture as strong or weak (see for example Peters and Water-man). A strong culture is one where thinking and behaving (shared attributes) is very similar amongst the group, i.e. it is homogeneous. A weak culture is the opposite. It has been argued that a strong culture is best in a predictable environment where the organizational goals are clear and unambiguous. In such cases there are efficiency gains from unity. However, such cultures may be disadvantaged in a turbulent environment where continuous change is required; where individuals need to challenge the status quo. A reasonable analogy is that of the lemmings – small rodents, usually found in or near the Arctic. Lemmings became notorious because of unsubstantiated myths that they commit mass suicide when they migrate – massive numbers of lemmings jumping off cliffs. Lemming suicide is a frequently used metaphor in reference to people who go along unquestioningly with popular opinion (collective way of thinking), with potentially dangerous or fatal consequences. In the case of organizations, employees may fail to challenge this thinking – thinking which could lead to lost revenue, etc. Hence a culture may be dysfunctional as well as functional. If it is dysfunctional it may need to be changed, a matter we address at the end of this chapter.

13.2 RECOGNIZING CULTURE

6.   When all has been said and done about the theoretical side of culture, the practical question remains: 'Where, and how, do managers come to recognize the dominant culture in their organization?' Where should they look, and what questions should they ask? As Figure 13.1 shows, there are several factors that are both a source of culture, and a manifestation of it. Examples of some of the ways in which managers learn about their culture are: **mission statements**, corporate aims, policy statements, organizational rituals (induction programmes for newcomers. Retirement parties/leaving speeches. Reward ceremonies for key sales staff etc.), organization logos, procedures/rules, management attitudes, organization structure, behaviour that is rewarded or punished, etc. Hofstede (1997) reminds us that a group's culture manifests itself in a variety of ways through symbols, heroes, rituals and values. **Symbols** are external signs of things that have a special meaning for those who share the culture. They may be pictures, objects, styles of dress or such things as particular words or gestures. Hofstede considers symbols to be the outer layer of culture, for which he uses the analogy of an onion – a multi-layered vegetable. Heroes represent the next layer. These are people (dead or alive) who are looked up to in the culture, and who serve as models for acceptable behaviour. Rituals, according to Hofstede, are collective activities considered as socially essential. Rituals include ways of greeting strangers, public and religious ceremonies, and also many business meetings. Symbols, heroes and rituals are visible, and essentially are the culture practices. What they do not show, but only imply, are the meanings attached to these practices. It is these meanings which lead us to the core of the 'onion', which is formed by the group's values.

Mission statement A mission statement is a statement of the overriding direction and purpose of an organization

Symbols Symbols are objects, events, acts or people which express more than their intrinsic content

Core values The principles that guide an organization's actions

7.   It is important that managers possess a cultural awareness of their organization since one of their tasks is to ensure that the values and assumptions around which the culture grows are passed on to their staff. Managers also need to be aware of the effect of the culture on their own work and their own values, since they may be in a position to bring about cultural changes. They experience at first hand the effects of technology, systems of work, people's reactions, the structure of jobs and decision-making channels and are thus able to see where obstacles are occurring which may need to be removed.

13.3 IDEAS ABOUT CULTURE

8.   Having defined organizational culture as a construct we now discuss it as a variable. Handy highlights some of the alternative types of culture favoured by many organizations. He identifies four main types of culture (Figure 13.2), which help to illustrate the point he makes earlier when commenting on the differences between organizations. Handy's model considerably simplifies the reality of organization culture which, more likely than not, is composed of elements of all four types. He himself admits that his typology is impressionistic and imprecise. Nevertheless, he raises some key aspects of culture, which are very significant, such as: how power and/or control is handled by the organization (centralized/decentralized); the type of power that is most respected in the organization; the preferred working methods (individualistic/collaborative/competitive); the interests best served by the dominant culture (leaders, key position holders, individuals or selected groups) and attitudes towards other stakeholders, such as customers, suppliers and shareholders.

FIGURE 13.2 Four types of culture in organizations (based on Handy).

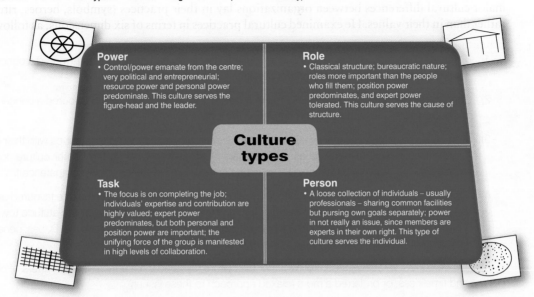

Power
• Control/power emanate from the centre; very political and entrepreneurial; resource power and personal power predominate. This culture serves the figure-head and the leader.

Role
• Classical structure; bureaucratic nature; roles more important than the people who fill them; position power predominates, and expert power tolerated. This culture serves the cause of structure.

Culture types

Task
• The focus is on completing the job; individuals' expertise and contribution are highly valued; expert power predominates, but both personal and position power are important; the unifying force of the group is manifested in high levels of collaboration.

Person
• A loose collection of individuals – usually professionals – sharing common facilities but pursing own goals separately; power in not really an issue, since members are experts in their own right. This type of culture serves the individual.

Source: Handy, C. (1976, 1993) *Understanding Organizations*. © Charles Handy, 1976, 1981, 1985, 1993, 1999. Reproduced with permission by permission of Penguin Books Ltd.

9.   Schein extends our understanding of culture when he suggests it is generated not only by sharing values and traditions, but even more by sharing the assumptions that emerge about the best way of handling problems. He describes espoused values, which may or may not be practised throughout the organization. We could say at this level that individuals may experience a certain amount of 'lip-service' being paid to selected values. Attention to customer care, for example, may be a value that is proclaimed in mission statements and departmental objectives, yet may be placed on one side when the organization is busy or when some other operational factor demands managers' attention. According to Schein's perception of culture, it is only as these second-tier values become absorbed into the organization's subconscious, and become implicit assumptions about behaviour, that they truly deserve to be termed the organization's culture. Thus, in this example, attention to customer care becomes so much a way of behaving that no one would compromise it, even when operational difficulties occurred.

10.   Hofstede sees values as broad tendencies to prefer certain things over others. Values, he argues, have a plus and a minus side, such as evil versus good, ugly versus beautiful and abnormal versus normal. Values are acquired very early in life, tend to become hidden in the person's unconscious and can only be inferred from the way the person acts. In trying to interpret people's values, it is important to distinguish between what they may think is desirable (what they think should apply to everyone), and what they personally desire (for themselves). Desirable things tend to have an absolute standard applied to them, which means they are seen to be either right or wrong, and are part of the group's ideology. Desired things are concerned more with practical matters, with people's wants and the standards applied are likely to be statistical, indicating the choices actually made by the majority. The culture that lies at the heart of Hofstede's onion is not a homogeneous collection of values, for it is itself made up of a number of different layers, including national aspects, regional, class and generation. In many modern societies these different subcultures are frequently in conflict with each other, and employers have to take such potential conflicts into account in their personnel/human resource policies. Issues concerning the effect of national cultural differences on employment are discussed in Chapter 15 as part of the examination of Hofstede's (1984) earlier research into how national differences were manifested in the workplace of a large multinational corporation, namely IBM.

11.   In subsequent research into the effects of culture on organizations, Hofstede found that the major cultural differences between organizations lay in their practices (symbols, heroes, rituals) rather than in their values. He examined cultural practices in terms of six dimensions, as follows:

1).   Process-orientation versus results orientation (whether the organization culture favoured a concern for means as opposed to a concern for results).

2).   Employee-orientation versus job orientation (whether the organization culture favoured a concern for people versus an emphasis on completing the job).

3).   Parochial versus professional [whether the individual employees identified themselves with their local organization or saw themselves as professionals hired for their skills; in the former culture, loyalty centred on the local organization, in the latter, it centred on professional pride (competence)].

4).   Open (social) system versus closed (social) system (whether the organization culture favoured an openness to newcomers and outsiders, or had an inward-looking, almost secretive attitude towards its members; on this dimension national cultural differences emerged, with the Danes generally favouring openness, whilst the Dutch preferred closed groups).

5).   Loose control versus tight control (whether the culture favoured strict adherence to matters of costs and timeliness, or preferred a more relaxed approach to these issues).

6).   Normative versus pragmatic approach to customers (whether the culture expected people to conform to rules in respect of customers, procedures and ethics, or to act flexibly in order to meet customers' wants or achieve targets).

12.   Broadly, the results showed that four of the above dimensions (1, 3, 5, 6) were closely related to the business or industry that the organizations represented. Thus, the key factors of task and markets were very influential in locating units along each dimension. Manufacturing operations and large office organizations, for example, showed a particular concern for processes, whilst research and development organizations and service units were more concerned with results. Those using traditional technology in their tasks tended to be parochial, whilst those employing high-tech equipment had a professional orientation. On the control dimension, pharmaceutical units and those engaged in the financial sector exercised strict controls, whereas units engaged in innovative activities favoured loose controls.

13.   Two other recent major contributors to thinking about organization cultures are Trompenaars and Hampden-Turner (2000). Their research into this field across job, company and national boundaries reached three main conclusions. These were (1) there is no 'one best way' of managing and organizing (a point recognized in contingency theory, see Chapter 10); (2) it is very important for managers to recognize and understand their own culture, and how cultural differences occur; and (3) cultural insights are vital in understanding the tension between local cultures and global issues in international companies. Most of their discussions were focused on national cultural differences, and are summarized later (see Chapter 15). However, their general comments about organization culture are worth mentioning here.

14.   They stress that culture is fundamentally a matter of shared meanings, which influence our priorities, our actions and our values. So, in work organizations the meanings that people assign to such concepts as 'the organization', together with its structure, practices and policies, are defined by their culture. There are no universal laws of organizing for optimum results. Instead there are only ways of assessing how people in different cultures make sense of their experiences. Throughout the second half of the twentieth century various solutions have been proposed to enable organizations to perform more effectively – management by objectives, total quality management, business process reengineering and performance management, to name but a few – but most of these ideas have been rooted firmly in North American and North-West European cultures. It has been shown that they do not work if merely transplanted from one national culture to another.

15.   In examining the impact of national cultures on organization culture, Trompenaars and colleague identified four types of corporate culture derived from two key dimensions: person-orientation versus task-orientation, and preference for an egalitarian versus an hierarchical structure. Using these two dimensions, they produced a typology of four alternative types of culture, as shown in Figure 13.3.

Power culture A form of culture that depends on a central power source that exerts influence throughout the organization

FIGURE 13.3   **Four corporate cultures.**

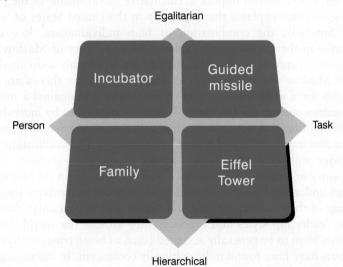

Source: Based on Trompenaars, F. & Hampden-Turner, C. (1997) *Riding the Waves of Culture*, 2nd Edition. Copyright © Nicholas Brealey Publishing. Reproduced with permission.

16.   Briefly the four types of culture can be summarized as follows:

- The family, where the dominant culture is one of paternalism, and where power is exercised through the members rather than over them. Nevertheless, there is no question that the leader knows best! This culture is similar to Handy's **power culture**.

- The incubator, by contrast, dislikes hierarchy and encourages equality. Relationships are spontaneous and creativity is highly respected. This type is close to Handy's **person culture**.

- The guided missile is a culture that thrives on successful teamwork in solving problems. Its people pride themselves on their professionalism. This culture is similar to Handy's **task culture**.

- The Eiffel Tower culture, as might be expected, is the one that embodies bureaucracy. The emphasis on task and roles within a defined hierarchy place this example is on a par with Handy's **role culture**.

Person culture A form of culture where the individual is the central focus and any structure exists to serve the individuals within it. Individuals have almost complete autonomy and any influence over them is likely to be on the basis of personal power

Task culture A form of culture which is task or job oriented and seeks to bring together the right resources and people and utilizes the unifying power of the group

17.   Of course, any typology is, of necessity, an over-simplification, and this is recognized by all the reputable writers on organization cultures and management. The useful aspect of a typology, however, is that it emphasizes the principal distinguishing features of alternative scenarios. It can also help managers to identify their own situation, and perhaps to become more sensitive to the alternatives that may be present in their customers, suppliers or other stakeholders.

Role culture A form of culture that is based on logic and rationality and relies on the strength of the functions of specialists in, for example, finance or production. The interactions between the specialists are controlled by procedures and rules

13.4 CROSS-CULTURAL MOTIVATION AND LEADERSHIP

18.   In Chapters 5 and 6 we discussed theories of motivation and in Chapters 7 and 8 considered leadership theories – all of which are culture bound. Employees and workers from countries with a high uncertainty avoidance may value and be motivated by job security. Workers from collectivist cultures (low individualism) are more likely to be motivated through group goals as opposed to individual reward. Employees of certain cultures do not like to openly compete with each other. Hofstede (1980:255) made reference to culture and motivation. He notes that high individualism implies a 'calculative involvement' of the Americans in organizations. He suggests this explains the popularity in the United States of 'expectancy' theories of motivation. Similarly, the combination of high individualism, low uncertainty avoidance and masculinity in the United States explains the popularity of Maslow's hierarchy of human needs – Maslow's supreme need, self actualization, is a highly individualistic motive. Hofstede suggests that Maslow's hierarchy and Hertzberg's two factor theory are culturally determined. He also argues for a motivational 'map of the world' and against a universal order of needs. Whereas countries such as the USA and UK may be motivated by individual success in the form of wealth, recognition and self actualization; other countries may determine success in terms of the collective and in the quality of human relationships. The implication is that no one motivational technique will achieve the same outcome in any given country. If we are to get people, from any country or culture, to do what we want them to do, in the best interest of the organization, we must understand their needs and goals in order to motivate them. This necessitates an understanding of their values, attitude and beliefs and in particular those in relation to work. Additionally, leadership styles and practices vary around the world. Certain leadership traits and behaviours seem to be generally accepted (such as being trustworthy) however certain styles and behaviours have been found to be culturally contingent. In discussing motivation theory we identified a relationship between culture and participation and similar relationships exist with other aspects of participation in leadership processes. Being a participative leader is more important in some countries as opposed to others. Once again, Hofstede's cultural dimensions provide a useful framework or model to study leader-subordinate relationships. Subordinates from high power distance countries are more likely to favour autocratic leadership whilst employees of lower power distance countries are more likely to prefer a consultative or participatory leadership style. An inappropriate style can be counterproductive in certain cultures.

13.5 DEVELOPING AN ORGANIZATION CULTURE

19.   Enid Mumford, a Professor at Manchester University and Senior Fellow of the Manchester Business School, and Geert Beekman (1994), a Dutch consultant, adopt a socio-technical approach to business change. They argue the 'organizational architect must always take account of the informal organization; the norms, values and behaviour patterns that employees collectively support and believe in'. They believe attitudes, norms and culture do not just 'happen' to an organization. 'They evolve over time, become an accepted way of behaving and are very difficult to change. Yet if they are dysfunctional or inappropriate for the future business mission and objectives of the organization, changing them must be an important part of the design and rebuilding task'. Some scholars take the view that culture is something an organization 'has' whilst others believe it is something the organization 'is'. Scholars of the latter school believe that managers cannot control culture in the way that many management writers advocate because it is so diffuse. Trice and Beyer (1993:12) also argue that cultures can be dysfunctional but suggest that 'there is less agreement on whether cultures can be deliberately changed' (p. 16). They differentiate between 'changing' and 'creating' cultures. Cultures change incrementally; they emerge and may be intentionally shaped. We discuss these two mechanisms in the two following and final paragraphs.

20.   Culture develops in response to organizational problems. The nature of the technology available, and the way it is implemented in the organization, will play a part in the development of culture and, of course, the organizational structures, mechanisms and procedures that are a major part of the organization's fabric. The latter analogy is illuminating because it helps to think of the culture as being woven in between all the other factors, linking them together and producing a whole tapestry. Depending on their relative power in a particular situation, the behaviour of stakeholders such as customers, suppliers, creditors (e.g. banks), and competitors may also influence the organization's culture. Competitors, in particular, can introduce changes into their marketing strategy and organization, which not only change their own culture, but also contribute to change in others, who may be forced to follow their lead in order to retain market share.

21.   Like any intentional change it is important to understand resistance to culture change as a part of the change process (see Chapter 24). Trice and Beyer (1993) emphasize the role of leadership in bringing about cultural change. It is what they pay attention to that focuses thoughts and actions of others. Schein (1997) also emphasizes the role of leaders, noting them to be a source of beliefs, values and assumptions – as role models they transmit and embed culture.

Amongst possible culture change tactics are (1) recruit like minded people; (2) socialize to instil and sustain ideologies; (3) cultural communications; (4) resource allocation methods; (5) criteria used to promote, reward and punish employees; (6) organization design and structure, systems and procedures; (7) design of buildings etc. and (8) formal statements of organizational philosophy, values, goals and mission (See for example the **Belief system (Formal)**). An example of intended culture change is TQM where employees are encouraged to put customers first and think and behave with continuous improvement and getting things right first time in mind. Embracing diversity is also associated with culture change.

> **Belief system (Formal)** The explicit set of organizational definitions that senior managers communicate formally and reinforce systematically to provide basic values, purpose and direction for the organization

CONCLUSION

22.   In this chapter we introduced and defined culture, noting it to have many functions but also arguing that it can be dysfunctional, ultimately impacting upon organizational performance. It is a very important but imprecise concept as it exists in many levels and is diffused throughout the organization. Culture is always about groups and the way they behave; in some cases we might also consider the way they think and their assumptions about the problems they face. Culture can be strong or weak and this is a measure of how similar thinking and behaviour is within the group. We noted that strong culture may be more appropriate in stable or predictable environments where efficiency is emphasized but that weak cultures may encourage the creativity and constant challenging attitude of employees needed to question their goals and ways of achieving them. Cultural differences encourage a contingency approach to management and cultural changes should reflect environmental changes. Culture change is difficult and incremental and relies heavily on organizational leaders.

QUESTIONS

1   Distinguish between national and organizational culture whilst considering the relationship between the two.

2   Discuss why organizations may seek to change organizational culture and identify the possible tactics they may use.

3   Explain what is meant by organizational culture then discuss the organizational culture at UPS. Why is culture such an important concept in business? You should discuss the functions and dysfunctions of organizational culture. In your opinion, is it better to have a strong or a weak organizational culture?

USEFUL WEBSITES

CIPD **www.cipd.co.uk/research/_visionandvalues.htm**
Vision and values: organizational culture and values as a source of competitive advantage

New Paradigm consulting **www.new-paradigm.co.uk/ Culture.htm** Organization Culture – Links & Articles
Geert Hofstede™ **www.geert-hofstede.com/** Hofstede's five Cultural Dimensions (national culture)

REFERENCES

Buchanan, D. and Huczynski, A. (2010) 'Organizational Behaviour', Ed. 7. Financial Times Press.

Hampden-Turner, C. M. and Trompenaars, F. (2000) 'Building Cross-Cultural Competence - How to create wealth from conflicting values', Wiley.

Handy, C. B. (1999) 'Understanding Organizations', Ed. 4. Penguin.

Hofstede, G. (1980) 'Motivation, leadership and organization: do American theories apply abroad?', Organizational Dynamics,summer, p. 42–43.

Hofstede, G. (1984) 'Cultures Consequences - abridged', Sage.

Hofstede, G. (1997) 'Cultures and Organizations', McGraw-Hill.

Hofstede, G. (1998) 'Attitudes, values and organizational culture: Disentangling the concepts', Organization Studies, 19 (3), p. 477–492.

Johnson, G., Scholes, K. and Whittington, R. (2006) 'Exploring Corporate Strategy Enhanced Media Edition', FT Prentice Hall.

Kelly, P. P. (2009) 'International Business and Management', Cengage Learning EMEA.

Knights, D. and Willmott, H. (2007) 'Introducing Organizational Behaviour and Management', Cengage Learning.

Mullins, L. (2005) 'Management and Organizational Behaviour', Ed. 7. FT Prentice Hall.

Mumford, E. and Beekman, G. J. (1994) 'Tools For Change & Progress', CSG Publications.

Peters, T. and Waterman, R. (1982) 'In Search of Excellence', Ed. 1995. Harper Collins Business.

Price, A. (2007) 'Human Resource Management in a Business Context', Ed. 3. Cengage Learning EMEA.

Schein, E. (1999) 'The Corporate Culture Survival Guide', Jossey Bass.

Schein, E. (1997) 'Organizational Culture and Leadership', Ed. 2. San Francisco: Jossey Bass.

Schein, E. (1996) 'Three cultures of management: The key to organizational learning', Sloan Management Review, 38 (1), p. 9.

Simons, R. (1995) 'Levers of Control', Harvard Business School Press.

Trice, H. M. and Beyer, J. M. (1993) 'The cultures of work organizations', Prentice Hall.

CHAPTER 14
WOMEN IN MANAGEMENT

Key Concepts

- Diversity
- Gender discrimination
- Glass ceiling
- Sex discrimination

Learning Outcomes Having read this chapter, you should be able to:

- discuss attitudes to the role of women at work
- identify how women may be discriminated against in the workplace
- distinguish gender-based role differences in the workplace
- discuss the organization consequences of discriminatory behaviours
- explain, with reference to social identity theory, stereotyping, generalizing, perception and attribution theory why some employees may be treated differently from others

1.   Globalization, amongst other factors, is changing the nature of the workplace and as a result managers must constantly ask how they can make best (and fairest) use of human resources to meet organizational goals. Today's workforce is older, more racially diverse, more female and more varied. Within such environments the management aim remains to maximize benefits and minimize costs and to enable all workers to achieve their full potential. Despite this there is still much progress to be made, especially in relation to the appointment of women and ethnic minorities to middle and senior management roles. This chapter examines some of the key issues involved in the employment of women as managers in the workplace against a backdrop of several **diversity management** challenges. The solution to these issues lies principally in bringing about cultural change (see previous chapter) in organizations in respect of most of the practices referred to elsewhere throughout this book, for there is hardly any aspect of management practice which could not benefit from a greater involvement by women and other non-white males. Organizations do not just face the problem of managing sex discrimination but discrimination of many types. Collectively, the contemporary problems of organizations centre on **diversity** in a more general sense. There is no question that today's workforce is more diverse. As with any social construct there are many definitions of diversity. It has been described as the heterogeneity of attitudes, perspectives and backgrounds amongst group members; valuing, respecting and appreciating the differences (such as age, culture, education, ethnicity, experience, **gender**, race, religion and sexual orientation, amongst others) that make people unique or, more simply, as all the ways in which we differ.

2.   Two general approaches to defining workforce diversity seem to dominate: the first, the narrow view, defines workforce diversity only as a term related to equal employment opportunity; the second argues that workforce diversity is a broader concept that includes all the ways in which people can be different. The narrow view typically adopts categories of race, colour, religion, sex and national origin whilst a broader definition makes use of additional categories such as teaching, education, sexual orientation and differences in values, abilities, organizational function, tenure and personality. Taking a broader view, diversity management initiatives attempt to maximize the potential of all employees in direct benefit to the organization. Consequently, the best employees are recruited, resulting in greater profits and job security.

3.   In this chapter we first draw on **social identity** to explain how we come to label groups and how people identify with them. We then consider how people from diverse groups perceive themselves and others and the implications of such thinking on their behaviour towards each other. Drawing on people **perception** theories, we discuss problems in generalization and stereotyping. Next we focus on the specific problem of sex discrimination and consider the initiatives employed to encourage equal opportunity and manage diversity within organizations.

Managing diversity The management of diversity goes beyond equal opportunity and embodies the belief that people should be valued for their differences and variety. Diversity is perceived to enrich an organization's human capital. Whereas equal opportunity focuses on various disadvantaged groups, the management of diversity is about individuals

Diversity All the ways in which we differ

Gender All human societies divide themselves into two social categories called 'female' and 'male' (this does not exclude other categories). Each category is defined on the basis of varying cultural assumptions about the attributes, beliefs and behaviours expected from males and females. The gender of any individual depends on a complex combination of genetic, body, social, psychological and social elements, none of which is free from possible ambiguity or anomaly.
Traditionally, sexual differences have been used to justify male-dominated societies in which women have been given inferior and secondary roles in their working lives

Social identity Part of the self-concept which comes from our membership of groups

Social perception The process of interpreting information about another person

14.1 THEORETICAL BACKGROUND

4.   Belonging to groups affects the way we think about and see ourselves (who we are) and the way others think about and see us. Such thinking impacts upon behaviour, the way we behave and the way others behave in relation to ourselves and the groups to which we may belong. How we view ourselves (self concept) is determined in part by the groups to which we belong (social identity). Thus, social identity defines the person and appropriate behaviours for them. This typically happens through social comparison – individuals not only compare themselves with other individuals with whom they interact, but they also compare their own group with similar, but distinct, out-groups. We all see ourselves as members of various social groupings, which are distinguishable and hence different from other social groupings. According to social identity theory (SIT), people tend to classify themselves and others into various social categories, such as organizational membership, religious affiliation, gender and age cohort. As these examples suggest, people may be classified in various categories, and different individuals may utilize different categorization schemas. Categories are defined by typical characteristics abstracted from the members; the consequence is that by identifying with certain groupings but not others, we come to see the world in terms of us and them. Whilst group membership may have its benefits (self esteem, privilege) it can also be a source of conflict and may, through generalizations and stereotypes determine inappropriate (discriminatory) behavioural responses.

> **Stereotypes** Stereotypes are formed when we ascribe generalizations to people based on their group identities and the tendencies of the whole group rather than seeing a person as an individual

5.   Two people can observe the same thing but perceive it in quite different ways – why should this be so? An answer to this question may be found in the perception process. Through our senses (especially sight) the brain receives incoming raw data from the outside world (stimuli). We are not able to pay attention to everything so we filter out less relevant or important information through perceptual filters; this allows us to focus on what we see is important (selective attention); we concentrate on the matters of particular interest and importance to us. Individual predispositions control what we see. Following selective attention, we organize the filtered incoming stimuli in systematic and meaningful ways; we classify or group similar stimuli together. During this activity (top-down processing) we may fill in the gaps of incomplete or ambiguous information (see the principle of closure). We make sense of a situation and then respond through our actions; our perceptions (the meanings we attach to incoming information) shape our actions. Such activities are susceptible to problems (see stereotyping to be discussed later). Classification or categorization helps us make sense of the world; for example, we categorize people as male or female, black or white – such categories are social constructs which we learn and what we learn is often culture bound. We classify people that resemble each other (the similarity principle); for example the person(s) may be of a similar ethnic origin. A related concept is the proximity principal where we assume people are similar just because they are near to each other – possibly living or working in the same location. One of the problems with 'closure' is that we may take incomplete information about someone or event and then draw inferences from it (see the problem of generalization). For example, we might only know a person's country of origin or gender but may then assign traits to them based on our learned knowledge of people from that country i.e. once we know or assume a person's apparent group membership (categorization) we may then attribute a range of qualities to them based on stereotypes and generalizations. In some cases such generalizations may prove convenient in other cases they could be wrong.

6.   Bias in person perception may take place during perceptual organization when we group together people who seem to us to share a similar characteristics – stereotyping. Stereotypes are over-generalizations which enable us to shortcut the evaluation process and make predictions about an individual's behaviour. The way we are categorized and the generalizations made

about the group we are associated with may result in others treating us more or less favourably. White women and racioethnic minorities have historically been excluded from the middle and upper levels of many organizations and while some improvement has been made in upward mobility, it is well documented that institutional racism and sexism persist in the workplace (to be explored in more detail later). Throughout life we become conditioned to thinking in ways that generalize and stereotype others. Such thinking may result in behaviours categorized as prejudice, privileged or oppressive. Such thoughts and the behavioural consequences have significant implications for the organization. Although usually rooted in some truth, stereotypes often do more harm than good. Stereotypes arise when we act as if all members of a group share the same characteristics. There are many indicators of group membership such as race, age, gender that may be used by the observer. In some cases the assumed characteristics are respected (positive stereotype) and in other cases may be disrespected (negative stereotype).

Sexism The belief or attitude that one gender or sex is inferior to or less valuable than the other

Prejudice Prejudice is an attitude, usually with negative feelings, that involves a pre-judgement about the members of a group

7.   Social identity theory, stereotyping, generalizing, perception and attribution theory explain why some people may be treated differently (discriminatory behaviour) from others. In some cases certain groups may be discriminated against. Prejudice and other discriminatory behaviours have consequences in the organization. If people feel that they are not being treated fairly, their motivation and performance is likely to be affected; people may leave the organization or be absent from work. This will impact upon productivity. In the face of gender discrimination, women have to find coping strategies.

Gender discrimination Many countries, including all members of the EU, have sex discrimination and equal pay legislation. However, informal psychological and organizational barriers continue to bar the progress of women. The processes of occupational segregation and sex-typing of jobs continue so that women tend to be concentrated at the base of most organizational hierarchies in jobs which are less prestigious and lower paid than those favoured by men

14.2 GENDER DIFFERENCES AT WORK

8.   Numerous studies show a continuing problem for women who aspire to senior management positions. In business, women earn less than men; they are promoted more slowly and work in less prestigious firms. These disparities exist even when men and women hold equivalent qualifications. Fiona Wilson is Professor of Organizational Behaviour in the Department of Business and Management, University of Glasgow. She believes that every prestigious or highly-paid occupation in Britain is dominated by men, both numerically and in terms of who wields power (Wilson, 2002). Wilson notes that women in the UK hold just one in five of all management positions. Studies on the relationship between gender, and the likelihood that a candidate will be recommended for hiring, find an advantage in favour of men. Sex stereotyping of women remains evident at work. Although women make up the majority of the local authority workforce, they tend to be concentrated in lower grades and are underrepresented at senior management level. The phenomenon of overrating men and underrating women job candidates appears to be widespread. Women fare worse than men in salary, promotion and ability to reach the top, regardless of the occupation. The gender pay gap emerges very quickly in the working lives of women and men, well before maternity and childcare responsibilities have an impact upon women's lives. Managers are reluctant to employ young married women who they fear may start a family. They give preference to older married women whose child-rearing responsibilities are completed. Despite this there has been some progress towards equality in the last 25 years as more women have entered the professions, and entry-level salaries are closer to parity than they were, but that progress is not uniform.

9.   Wilson seeks to explain why these inequalities persist. She suggests the first explanation is to be found in how commitment is viewed. The professions and management appear to accept the long-hours culture as the norm, together with the common practice of taking work home. Willingness to do this is seen as a major indicator of ambition and commitment, a problem for those wishing to balance home/life commitments. Cultures that encourage long hours are arguably institutionally discriminating against those with family commitments. A second explanation relates to gender schemas – concept of maleness and femaleness influences one's perceptions and behaviour. It would appear that our conceptions of what characteristics different jobs require are shaped by our conceptions of the people who carry them out. If a job is held predominantly by women, it is a feminine job, needs feminine characteristics and will be of less value. If it is a job predominantly held by men, we see it as masculine, emphasize masculine characteristics and value it more highly. Another explanation of the persistence of inequalities at work may be found in the home. Families can be damaging to the careers of women, but less so for men. Despite claims that marriages are becoming more symmetrical, and domestic tasks are being shared more equally, surveys persistently reveal that women still take the major share of housework and childcare–even when both partners work.

10.   Men and women come to terms with the existence of inequalities in many different and often contradictory ways. Men and women want to believe they live in a 'just world'. The majority of professionals advance the idea that the position of women is improving in the profession they represent. However, the statistics do not support this (Wilson, 2002). Alternatively, they will deny that inequality exists – gender inequalities can be covered by a 'cloak of equality'. Some women will identify that there are difficulties and inequalities in the profession. They may note that the work culture is masculine and find that they cannot work within or influence masculine work cultures so they leave. 'There are no signs of progression towards a more family-friendly environment, which might include flexible working arrangements such as job sharing, so individuals do not even broach the issue because of fear that raising the possibility might lead to them being seen as less committed. Some women believe they should put their families before their careers. Others choose to be career-centred, with domestic activities as a secondary activity', Wilson (2002). Based on her evidence Wilson finds it difficult to produce a positive conclusion about increased equality of opportunity for women. Unless men and women acknowledge the fact that we live in an unequal society and wish to see that glass ceiling well and truly broken, little is likely to change.

> **Glass ceiling** Expression used to denote a subtle barrier to women's promotion to senior posts in an organization, and usually implying that it is kept in place by men's innate prejudice against women in senior management positions

14.3 BREAKING THROUGH THE GLASS CEILING

11.   There have been numerous research studies into possible differences between men and women in aspects of workplace behaviour such as motivation, attitudes to work, ability to motivate teams and in work performance generally. The overall results demonstrate clearly that on these points there are no major differences between the sexes. What, therefore, can be done by organizations and by individuals to allow women to make a full contribution to work activities? The difficulties faced by women, in attempting to break into what has been, and still is, mainly a man's world, has been referred to as 'the glass ceiling', an analogy which attempts to describe the subtly transparent barrier that prevents women from gaining access to the more senior roles in their organizations. Given the nature of the male dominance over the workplace, what can organizations do to achieve greater fairness for women and a better balance of the sexes in managerial roles?

12.   Pichler, Simpson and Stroh (2008) comment on the consistent stream of research into the invisible barriers that have prevented women from reaching the upper echelons of management.

Research on sex stereotypes suggests that gender bias is an invisible barrier – the so-called glass ceiling – preventing women from breaking into the highest levels of management in business organizations. Recent studies on the lack of women in senior management and the gender pay gap indicate that women are disproportionately underrepresented in senior management and are paid less than men when they do reach the top. Stereotyping occurs when individuals are judged not on their unique characteristics or merits, but on generalized characteristics associated with the group to which they belong. For instance, sex stereotypes have consistently been found to portray men and women as opposites, with men perceived as masculine and achievement-oriented and women as being nurturing and facilitative. Applied to employment-related decisions, such portrayals can lead to biased evaluations of women's performance and qualifications. Sex stereotypes have been found to be disadvantageous to women in selection, placement and promotion decisions, especially for managerial jobs. The sex type of a job is determined by two factors: the gendered characteristics believed to be required for that job and the proportion of men (or women) occupying the job. Stereotypes also describe how men and women should be – that is, what behaviours are (and are not) appropriate, based on one's gender. When women demonstrate masculine behaviour or succeed at male-typed tasks, they meet with opposition and are not accepted, ultimately resulting in biased performance evaluations. Sex bias stemming from such stereotypes has contributed to the glass ceiling. More specifically, when a woman exhibits stereotypically feminine behaviour, she is considered a poor fit for most managerial jobs, and when a woman exhibits stereotypically masculine behaviour, she is typically perceived as being unnecessarily aggressive and hostile.

13.   Managers should be aware of the glass ceiling problem and attempt to remedy its causes. Meyerson and Fletcher (2000) outline three approaches to the management of gender diversity in organizations: (1) training women to be successful in a male-dominated world of management – providing women with the knowledge and skills needed to make it into senior management; (2) supporting women through organizational policies and practices (such as employer sponsored childcare) targeted at facilitating their inclusion in the workplace. Adopting women-friendly policies also can translate into a competitive advantage for organizations when there is a competitive market for talent, especially when the skills women bring to the workplace are valuable and difficult to imitate, and (3) valuing gender diversity. As Meyerson and Fletcher (2000) note, valuing gender diversity often involves sensitivity or diversity training. This type of training could be used to explain **sex discrimination** and associated biases. Although these three approaches to gender diversity management can help support the inclusion of women in the workplace, as well as their advancement into senior management, even in combination they may not be enough to remove the invisible barriers that form the glass ceiling. As Meyerson and Fletcher (2000) noted, the exclusion of women from senior management is related to biases entrenched in institutionalized organizational systems, such as performance appraisals; therefore, these systems must also be changed. Removing gender bias from such organizational systems as selection decisions and performance evaluation is essential to increasing gender diversity in organizations, especially at the highest levels of management. The continued problem is recognized by Buchanan and Huczynski (2010) who discuss 'jobs for the boys' noting that women are still poorly represented in management roles.

14.   Not only are there strong business arguments against discriminatory behaviours but there are also legal imperatives. Certain **legislation** is in force in the UK which provides a legal framework for implementing equal opportunities in society. Listed below are a few of the Acts which deal with harassment and discrimination: The Equal Pay Act 1970 (EPA) (amended 1983); The Sex Discrimination Act (SDA) 1975 (amended 1986); The

Sex discrimination Discriminatory or disparate treatment of an individual because of his or her sex

Gender legislation It is often illegal for a company to make employment decisions based on someone's sex or more appropriately, gender (i.e. male or female). If a man is promoted over a woman the woman who did not get the promotion may have a claim for sex discrimination

Employment Equality (Sexual Orientation) Regulations 2003; Disability Discrimination Act (DDA) 1995; The Disability Discrimination Act 1995 (Amendment) Regulations 2003; Disability Discrimination Act 2005; Race Relations Act 1976 and Race Relations (Amendment) Act 2000; Race Regulations 2003; The Employment equality (Religion or Belief) Regulations 2003; Employment Equality (Age) Regulations 2006 and the Human Rights Act 1998. Larger organizations typically create an Equal opportunity policy – a written statement of commitment to fair, non-discriminatory human resource management.

15.   On a more practical level, there are several possible actions that can be taken at an organizational level to provide a fairer framework of working conditions. These are more likely to succeed (i.e. to be fully accepted by both sexes) if they are open both to men and women, thus avoiding possible charges either of favouring men or of patronizing women. Possible steps that may be taken include:

- increasing part-time opportunities

- permitting flexible working hours

- making job-sharing available

- enhancing training opportunities for potential managers

- providing personal development opportunities in form of secondments, special projects and other opportunities to undertake new challenges and extend experience in managerial roles

- developing awareness training for senior management towards the benefits of women managers

- introducing career breaks

- providing, or paying for, crèche facilities for employees with family responsibilities

- ensuring that individuals' accrued rights (e.g. to pensions, holidays, etc.) are not disadvantaged. merely because the job-holder is a part-time employee or has had gaps in their service with the organization.

Although many of the above steps focus on practical aspects of employment conditions, they are nevertheless sending powerful messages to the members of the organization as a whole. Effectively, attention to the above implies cultural change within the organization. The clear implication here is that, if women are to make greater progress in obtaining managerial posts, work must be restructured to allow for greater flexibility of working – including part-time work for managers, agreed career breaks, improved arrangements for the reintroduction of women managers into the management hierarchy following a break, and other facilitating measures.

CONCLUSION

16.   In this chapter we considered the importance of treating employees fairly, focusing on sex discrimination in particular. We explained causes of the discriminatory behaviour with a reference to SIT, perception, stereotyping and other cognitive processes. Such theories help explain why minorities in the workplace (e.g. women) may operate under a glass ceiling which details their career progression and opportunities. Ideas at the strategic and tactical level were suggested to help organizations overcome such problems and embrace diversity. Ultimately, however, the problems highlighted are seen as cultural problems. As was noted in the previous chapter, culture change is far from simple and can take many years to accomplish.

QUESTIONS

1   Explain why sex discrimination remains a significant business problem despite management efforts (over the past 10 to 20 years) to overcome it.

2   Why is it important for organizations to embrace diversity and pursue equal opportunity – what is the business/social case? In your answer you should present arguments for and against diversity within organizations.

3   Identify how women may be discriminated against in the workplace and then discuss the organizational consequences of such discriminatory behaviour. What is the glass ceiling problem and what are the main approaches to the management of gender diversity in organizations? Finally, list five possible actions that can be taken at an organizational level to provide a fairer framework of working conditions.

USEFUL WEBSITES

Chartered Management Institute: **www.managers.org.uk/ practical-support/management-community/ professional-networks/women-management** Women in Management (WiM) Network. WiM Network is a national organization addressing the key issues affecting women managers today

Discrimination – In England: **www.adviceguide.org.uk/index/ your_rights/discrimination.htm** Information on discrimination because of age, disability, race, religion or belief, sex and sexuality; when is discrimination lawful or unlawful; taking action; discrimination in providing goods, services...

Discrimination at work: **www.direct.gov.uk/en/Employment/ ResolvingWorkplaceDisputes/DiscriminationAtWork/ index.htm** An introduction to what discrimination is, the types of discrimination

EHRC: **www.equalityhumanrights.com/** Promote equality in the areas of disability, gender and race

Catalyst: **www.catalyst.org/home** Catalyst is a non-profit membership organization working globally with businesses and the professions to build inclusive workplaces and expand opportunities for women and business

REFERENCES

Buchanan, D. and Huczynski, A. (2010) 'Organizational Behaviour', Ed. 7. Financial Times Press.

Meyerson, D. E. and Fletcher, J. (2000) 'A modest manifesto for shattering the glass ceiling', Harvard Business Review, 78(1), p. 127–136.

Nelson, D. L. and Quick, J. C. (2009) 'ORGB', Ed. 1. South Western.

Pichler, S., Simpson, P. A. and Stroh, L. K. (2008) 'The glass ceiling in human resources: Exploring the link between women's representation in management and the practices of strategic human resource management and employee involvement', Human Resource Management, 47 (3), p. 463–479.

Price, A. (2007) 'Human Resource Management in a Business Context', Ed. 3. Cengage Learning EMEA.

Wilson, F. M. (2002) 'Management and the Professions: How Cracked is That Glass Ceiling?', Public Money & Management, 22 (1), p. 15–20.

CHAPTER 15
THE INTERNATIONAL CONTEXT OF MANAGEMENT

Key Concepts

- Global
- Globalization
- International organization
- Internationalization
- Multinational

Learning Outcomes   Having read this chapter, you should be able to:

- distinguish between types of international organization
- explain what is meant by globalization
- distinguish differences between the domestic and global business environment
- examine the impact of national culture on aspects of business and management

Global A form of international organizational design where foreign subsidiaries are modelled on the parent companies' domestic approach (replication) – standardization and centralization are emphasized in order to achieve integration

1.   In Chapter 10 we introduced the contingency approach and emphasized the role of the environment in determining styles of management. This chapter takes a closer look at the international and global environment as a context for management. International business is vast and a significant source of opportunity (and threat) for many organizations. It requires organizations to manage internationally, presenting significant challenges. Many now see the world as a single and growing market – in recent years we have witnessed growth in international trade and investment and resource flows of many types between countries. In an era when half of the world's biggest economic entities are multinational corporations (that is to say many of our larger international organizations now produce more than some countries); where labour is increasingly mobile across borders and ICT enables companies to overcome barriers in time, distance and language, the contemporary manager simply cannot afford to remain parochial, ethnocentric or not in constant pursuit of competitive advantage, (Kelly 2009). To do so, is to be disadvantaged. Consumers and investors not only buy and sell across country boundaries but also invest in other countries (see foreign direct investment (FDI)). Organizations undertake FDI for a variety of reasons such as setting up offices, manufacturing, operations and distribution facilities. Additionally, in some cases, trade takes place using electronic channels (see e-business/ commerce).

2.   At this point, we might ask why international business has grown so much over the past 10–20 years. There are many explanations for the growth of international business. The (social, political and economic) pursuit of 'free trade' has also eroded barriers and borders. This has been further enabled through the widescale adoption of ('open') Information and communication technologies (ICT) which enable trade, communication and collaboration – eroding barriers in time, space and language and integrating financial, political and legal systems. Liberalization has not only resulted in increased mobility of people as workers and migrants but also in the movement of capital, goods and services. Consumers want choice, quality and low-cost products sourced from around the world. E-commerce and the MNC now bring the world to the doorsteps of businesses and consumers everywhere. With the phenomenal growth of e-commerce, anyone can be open for business on an international level 24 hours a day, no matter where the business is physically located. In other words, one location can serve the business needs over the entire globe. Companies may now not only import and export more easily but can also establish their operations overseas.

3.   Why conduct business internationally? Companies operating outside their home country are able to diversify and therefore mitigate home risk, tap new markets enabling growth and associated scale advantages, reduce costs not just through scale but also by accessing low cost materials, labour and facilities – they can also engage local expertise and may be able to avoid trade restrictions. Furthermore, organizations may internationalize as a strategic response to or in order to attack foreign competition. However, domestic managers must also be aware of the international context as it can bring opportunity and threat to their organizations.

4.   Organizations now source, manufacture, market and conduct value-adding activities on an international scale. This poses new management challenges and necessitates the rise of the international manager or manager within an international organization who can acquire the requisite business knowledge and skills to enable the organization to perform in our ever-increasing globalized business environment. Not only is there a need to understand international business theory and practice, because international business activities are increasing, but there is also a need to understand domestic business since international organizations and their subsidiaries also have local challenges. The number, size, activity and importance of international organizations are of significant and growing importance. However, it is not just the multinational corporation that is embracing global opportunity; international business may

Domestic exporter A strategy characterized by heavy centralization of corporate activities in the home country of origin

now be conducted by small and medium enterprises. In some cases organizations may simply engage in import and export activities from home, enabled through the Internet, and, in other cases, the organization may establish operations around the globe. However, overseas invest-ment is not without risk. Organizations can behave in an unacceptable way when trading in a foreign country. They may fail to take account of cultural differences and needs (cross-cultural risk), may become exposed to many new and potentially damaging country-specific risks (politi-cal risk) including financial (or currency) risks and other commercial risks such as those associ-ated with outsourcing or partnership selection. Certain national differences may require managers to tailor approaches to country needs – this may necessitate adaptation of products, services or business practices. In some areas, international business and management requires specialized knowledge whilst in others a global and standard approach may be adopted wher-ever the organization is working or conducting business.

In this chapter we build on contingency theory by considering it in practice. We focus on the international business environment as a context for management and explore implications for organizations. In particular, we consider the practical issues associated with conducting business and managing relationships in and between countries.

15.1 GLOBALIZATION, INTERNATIONALIZATION AND INTERNATIONAL ORGANIZATIONS

5.   **Globalization**, the opposite of protectionism (policies reflect-ing the belief that domestic manufacturers and workers need to be safeguarded from foreign competition), refers to the growing interdependency between nations and organizations through inter-national trade and factor mobility (integration). Economic global-ization has significantly increased the competitive pressure on enterprises in many sectors.

Globalization Growth and integration to a global or worldwide scale

6.   We may classify organizations according to where they do business, at home (domestic) or overseas (international). Some international organizations are based in their home country and export or **import** goods to and from other countries whilst other companies locate operations in other countries. 'Multinational companies' are organizations that behave in their foreign markets as if they were local companies. Some scholars identify with the

Imports Goods and services produced in one country and bought in by another country

'multinational enterprise' (MNEs) – a company headquartered in one country but having opera-tions or subsidiaries in other countries. We may also classify MNEs as either (1) global organi-zations – an organization which trades internationally as if the world were a single and boundaryless entity; (2) multidomestic organizations – an organization that trades internation-ally as if the world were a collection of many different (country) entities or (3) transnational enterprises – an international organization that standardizes certain aspects of its activities and output whilst adapting other aspects to local differences.

7.   The pull for a global (universal and centralized) versus 'multi' (decentralized and differenti-ated) approach is influenced by globalization factors considered previously. However, decisions on international organizational issues are not only influenced by the nature of the environment and a company's products or services. It is people who make decisions and such decisions may also be a reflection of the bias of such people. Organizational preferences are determined by the nature of the offerings, cost and the preferences of key decision-makers in the company. For example Perlmutter (1969:11) identifies three primary attitudes among executives towards building a multinational enterprise: the ethnocentric (home country) attitude (home nationals are superior); polycentric (host country) host country cultures are different and geocentric

(world oriented), superiority is not equated with nationality. Such attitudes impact upon strategic decision making, human resource management (HRM), organizational structure and enterprise system strategies, discussed later.

8.   A further way of categorizing and understanding international organizations is based on an analysis of how the organization adds value. Value is essentially what something is worth, the amount customers are willing to pay for a product or service. Added-value is the difference between the amount customers are willing to pay for a product minus the costs of inputs and transformational activities used to create that product or service (offering). There are three main factors that influence the value equation: input costs (supply-side), transformation costs and the amount the buyer is willing to pay for products or services on the demand side (based on perceived product benefits) relative to competing products. Porter (1985) identified the 'value chain' as a means of analyzing an organization's strategically-relevant activities. Value Chain Analysis helps the organization identify core competencies and distinguish those activities driving competitive advantage. The chain consists of five primary activities and four support activities. The nine activity groups are as follows.

Primary activities:

1).   Inbound logistics: materials handling, warehousing, inventory control, transportation;

2).   Operations: machine operating, assembly, packaging, testing and maintenance;

3).   Outbound logistics: order processing, warehousing, transportation and distribution;

4).   Marketing and sales: advertising, promotion, selling, pricing, channel management;

5).   Service: installation, servicing, spare part management.

Support activities:

6).   Firm infrastructure: general management, planning, finance, legal, investor relations;

7).   Human resource management: recruitment, education, promotion, reward systems;

8).   Technology development: research and development, IT, product and process development;

9).   Procurement: purchasing raw materials, lease properties, supplier contract negotiations.

9.   A value chain is a chain of activities. Products pass through all primary activities of the chain in order and at each activity the product gains some value. The chain of activities gives the products more added value than the sum of added values of all activities. Thus the value chain presents a tool to decompose organizations into their parts and then focus attention on these decomposed activities. The idea of the value chain is based on the process view of organizations (discussed further in Chapter 21), the idea of seeing a manufacturing (or service) organization as a system, made up of subsystems, each with inputs, transformation processes and outputs was discussed in Chapter 9. The value chain concept has been extended beyond individual organizations. An organization's value chain is part of a larger system including the value chains of upstream suppliers and downstream channels and customers. Porter calls this series of value chains the value system. Other scholars may refer to this as a value network or supply chain. Linkages exist not only in a firm's value chain, but also between value chains. Multinational organizations have had the opportunity to benefit from the comparative advantage of different countries, be they technology-driven or factor-abundance driven, to reduce the total costs of production, particularly through the ever more popular method of fragmentation (slicing up the value chain) in which different parts (activities) of the production process are located in different countries.

10.   A company may offer its goods and services solely in its domestic market or wider in a global market. Clearly there is more opportunity associated with the latter but not all

organizations become multinational. The domestic organization, headquartered at home, must decide whether or not to become a multinational organization and if not, will decide whether or not to export its goods and services (from production facilities at home). Companies may benefit from becoming a MNC if: there is an OWNERSHIP ADVANTAGE – derived from organization-specific capabilities, competences or resources that give a competitive edge over rivals (for example knowledge capital can be transported at low cost to foreign production facilities). If an organization owns a resource that can generate revenue in another country then it makes sense to do so providing there are no extraordinary costs associated; LOCATION ADVANTAGE – is associated with specific countries; low skilled production processes may be fragmented and based in low wage countries for example. This advantage recognizes that scarce resources are not in existence everywhere and may only be found in certain countries, thus accessing them may provide an advantage over other countries, and INTERNATIONALIZATION ADVANTAGE – makes it more profitable for an organization to undertake foreign production itself, rather than licensing it to a foreign organization.

11. Some organizations are 'born global', others evolve over time. One model of internationalization suggests that in the first stage, new products are initially developed for sale in the domestic market. In the second stage, exports start to develop to foreign markets where consumers have the same preferences and incomes as at home. In the third stage, as the foreign markets start to grow, the firm might establish a subsidiary abroad, to produce closer to the destination markets, implying that exports to the markets will fall and finally, in the fourth stage, as the foreign subsidiaries master the production process they might begin to export their products back to the initial home market, creating re-import of the same product. Organizations may enter foreign countries and markets in a variety of ways. The multinational must choose

Internationalization The gradual process of taking organizational activities into other countries

Exports Goods and services produced by a firm in one country and then sent to another country

between non-equity (exporting, licensing or franchising) and equity (Greenfield investments, acquisitions or alliances) modes of entry. Multinationals must determine the desired level of ownership, i.e. in the case of equity entry, choosing between wholly or partially owned and must analyze the advantages and disadvantages of buying an existing foreign entity or establishing a foreign operation from scratch.

15.2 THE GLOBAL BUSINESS ENVIRONMENT

12. The business environment is divided into the external and internal environment. The internal environment consists of all resources and capabilities found within the organization which influence the organization's ability to act (to create outputs). The analysis of the business environment allows the organization and its employees to understand the context within which they operate and strategy is developed and implemented. It is important to note, however, that environments are not static but constantly changing. Understanding the global business environment and its economic, social and political influences is crucial to success in today's international business world. Since the comments of Emery and Trist, almost 50 years ago, we have witnessed great change in the environment of many industries and organizations.

13. One of the first challenges is to recognize the enormity of factors in the business environment and therefore decompose it into manageable parts. Environmental variables are factors that affect the organization, but are beyond the direct or positive control of the organization. The external environment may be divided into layers: the macro-environment is the wider environment of social, legal, economic, political and technological influences (forces). The macro environment contains the more general factors likely to affect organizations in a similar manner, whereas, at the industry level, the factors are of more specific concern to a specific set of

organizations. The micro-environment is the immediate (industry) environment including customers, competitors, suppliers and distributors. One of the main factors affecting most international organizations is the degree of competition faced. Greater influence is likely to come from the actions of competitors and the behaviour of customers or prospects. Markets change rapidly through the entrance of new competitors, technologies, legislation and evolving customer needs. Aside from considering the macro and industry (micro) external business environment, the organization must also analyze the internal environment; resources and capabilities.

14.   Making sense of the macro environment poses a significant challenge. However, there are diagnostic frameworks that help break it down into more manageable components (environmental variables) which can be investigated. PESTEL (see also PEST, SLEPT, STEP and PESTLE) analysis is a common technique for analyzing the general external environment of an organization in terms of the political, economic, socio-cultural, technological, environmental and legal aspects. Organizations undertake the process of continuously monitoring the environment so they can respond accordingly; in some cases the analysis of the external environment may be described as an external audit. From an international organizational perspective it is important to recognize that legal, economic and sociocultural factors exist within each country. Consequently, the environment of the international organization is more diverse and complex. Not all factors will influence the organization's industry and the analyst must identify the more important factors, understand the implications and then act accordingly – typically adapting the organizations strategy, structure, practices, systems, culture, products and services. We consider the environmental variables forming the international context next.

15.   Governments can grant access to markets and rescind such permission at any time. Governments formulate policy toward international trade and vary in the degree to which they may intervene in order to protect or help their domestic organizations competing at home or abroad. The policies individual countries adopt affect the size and probability of markets and may create unfair competition; acts of government create winners and losers in the marketplace. However, political behaviour can be a source of efficiency and market power, particularly in international contexts.

16.   The economic environment is described through a collection of dynamic variables that impact upon supply and demand and ultimately the organization. Economics is the branch of social science that studies the production, distribution and consumption of goods and services. Organizations analyze their economic environment because it can impact upon production costs, costs associated with the management of financial resources such as the cost of capital and associated with currency exchange rates and the spending power of consumers (demand). When trading with another country, products and services may be purchased with currency from a country which is foreign to the producer. To exchange one currency for another in international transactions, organizations rely on the foreign exchange market – a market in which currencies are bought and sold and their prices determined; one currency is converted into another at a specific exchange rate. However, the presence of foreign currency in international transactions exposes organizations to risk when there is a delay between the sale and payment. If the exchange rate of the foreign currency drops during this period then the value of any payment, relative to the organization's home country will fall (meaning of course that it will receive less money). The practice of insuring against potential losses that result from adverse changes in exchange rates is called currency hedging.

17.   The social or socio-cultural factors in the macro environment typically include social values, attitudes and beliefs, demographic trends, lifestyle preferences and skills availability. When organizations operate internationally they need to understand how people in other countries may differ; the international organization must operate in different countries where the inhabitants may differ from those within their home markets. The construct used to describe such differences is termed (national) culture and cultural differences can create problems within the business environment (refer back to Chapter 13). Differences in culture (fit) may necessitate changes to business practices, management styles, products and services – a matter we consider in the next section.

15.3 INTERNATIONAL AND CULTURAL DIFFERENCES IN MANAGING ORGANIZATIONS

18.   The universal application of various management theories has been researched and discussed by many scholars and practitioners. They ask whether a management theory that works well in one country might work equally well in another. Over thirty years ago, Ouchi documented studies (when the Japanese economy was flourishing) into the differing characteristics of Japanese and American organizations to see if selected practices from Japanese industry could be translated to the USA. His primary concern was with identifying aspects of practice that could be adapted. Ouchi proposed 'theory Z' as a means by which American companies could imitate certain features of the Japanese approach to managing people (This term is also considered in Chapter 6). In a similar vein, Hofstede (1980) argued that managers who have to operate in an unfamiliar culture may not benefit from training based on home-country theories as it is of very limited use and may even do more harm than good. Management is concerned with the effective utilization and coordination (leveraging) of resources and activities to achieve defined objectives with maximum efficiency. To that end there is a focus on getting things done with the aid of people and other resources. The scope of international management should include all aspects associated with the practice of managing business operations and strategy within and across countries. International management should take a supply chain and value system perspective, identifying how organizations can operate more effectively and efficiently, at a global level. There is a need to focus on how organizations use their assets such as information, people, knowledge, technology and finances to achieve their goals and compete in the global marketplace.

19.   In Chapter 13 we reported on Hofstede's landmark study into national culture. The degree of difference between two countries impacts upon the extent of adaptation required by an international Organization. The organization therefore needs to have some awareness of the differences. To that end, a variety of frameworks exist to measure national culture. Such frameworks (see for example Hofstede, 1984) typically decompose the complex construct of culture into several dimensions. These dimensions include individualism versus collectivism, power distance, uncertainty avoidance, masculinity versus femininity andlLong-term versus short-term orientation (refer back to Chapter 13). Hofstede found that, when comparing the results obtained from the forty countries (see Figure 15.1) against the criteria of the framework, it was possible, using the technique of statistical cluster analysis, to allocate them to eight 'cultural clusters', each of which had a particular profile of characteristics under the four dimensions. These clusters were labelled according to geographical area (Asian, Near Eastern, Germanic and Nordic) or language (Latin and Anglo) and can be summarized as in Figure 15.2.

20.   The most significant feature of Hofstede's research is that it draws attention to five crucial areas of human behaviour at work where there are likely to be substantial differences in cultural assumptions (see Chapter 13 above), and therefore quite different ways of approaching the management of people. In essence these five areas of difference can be re-stated as follows:

–   different attitudes towards the sharing of power and status, and what alternative structures, management styles and other manifestations to which these may lead

–   differences in the extent to which uncertainty is tolerated, and thus the degree of risk likely to be acceptable, especially in novel situations

–   differences in the value afforded to team work as opposed to individual effort and achievement, leading to alternative ways of structuring work and roles, and rewarding people

–   different attitudes towards 'success' and how it should be obtained, giving rise to different goals (for example, personal success or the common good), and different ways of achieving them (such as personal drive and assertiveness versus harmonious relationships and collaborative methods)

– differences in the extent to which a long-term rather than a short-term view is taken concerning business results, the use of resources, the pressures for change, and the setting aside of funds (investment) for future needs.

FIGURE 15.1 Culture Dimension Scores by Country.

Country	Ind	PD	UA	Mas
Argentina	46	49	86	56
Australia	90	36	51	61
Austria	55	11	70	79
Belgium	75	65	94	54
Brazil	38	69	76	49
Canada	80	39	48	52
Chile	23	63	86	28
Colombia	13	67	80	64
Denmark	74	18	23	16
Finland	63	33	59	26
France	71	68	86	43
Germany	67	35	65	66
Great Britain	89	35	35	66
Greece	35	60	112	57
Hong Kong	25	68	29	57
India	48	77	40	56
Iran	41	58	59	43
Ireland	70	28	35	68
Israel	54	13	81	47
Italy	76	50	75	70
Japan	46	54	92	95
Mexico	30	81	82	69
Netherlands	80	38	53	14
New Zealand	79	22	49	58
Norway	69	31	50	8
Pakistan	14	55	70	50
Peru	16	64	87	42
Philippines	32	94	44	64
Portugal	27	63	104	31
Singapore	20	74	8	48
South Africa	65	49	49	63
Spain	51	57	86	42
Sweden	71	31	29	5
Switzerland	68	34	58	70
Taiwan	17	58	69	45
Thailand	20	64	64	34
Turkey	37	66	85	45
USA	91	40	46	62
Venezuela	12	81	76	73
Yugoslavia	27	76	88	21

Sources: Based on 'Cultural clusters arising from Hofstede's research' adapted from *Cultures Consequences: International Differences in Work-related Values* by G. Hofstede, 1980, p. 336. Reproduced with permission of Dr G Hofstede.

FIGURE 15.2 Cultural clusters arising from Hofstede's research (adapted from Hofstede 1980, p. 336).

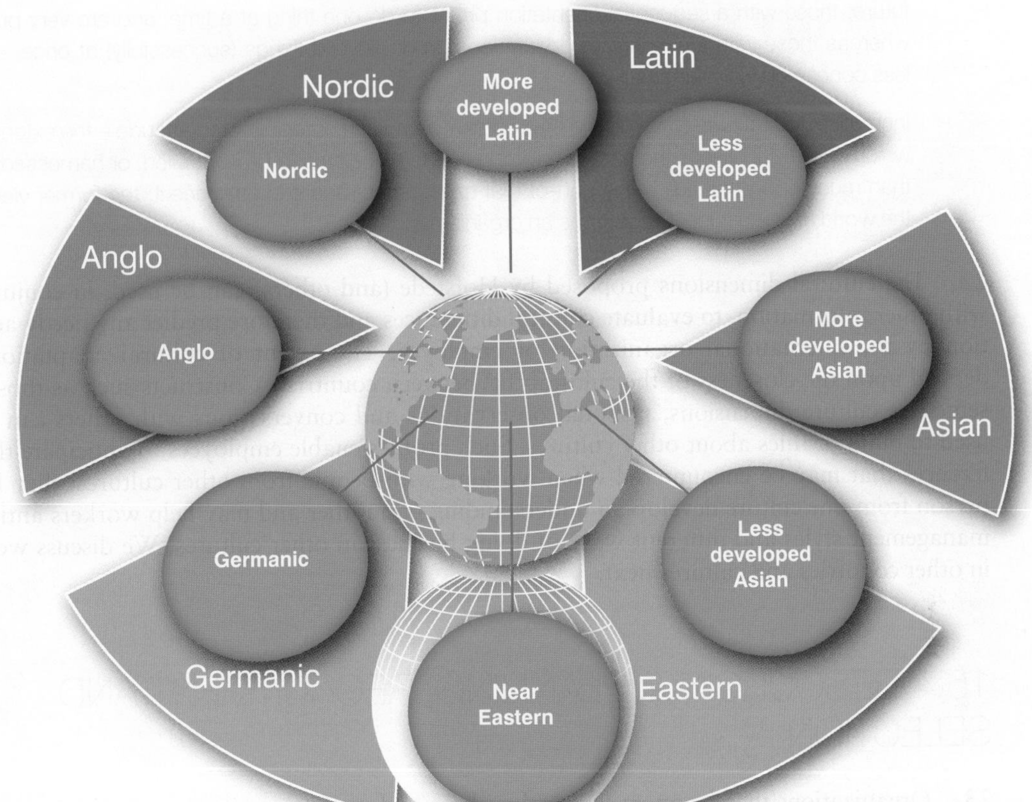

Adapted from Hofstefe, G. (1980) *Cultures Consequences: International Differences in Work-related Values*. p. 336. Copyright © Geert Hofstede BV. Reproduced with permission.

21. More recent studies of international cultural differences have been conducted by Trompenaars and Hampden-Turner (2000), who have grouped the major differences around six dimensions. Their dimensions are:

– Universalism versus particularism – the extent to which rules predominate over relationships, which asks the question 'is keeping to the rules more important than loyalty to others?' Universalists are concerned with consistency, equality and adherence to the rules, whereas particularists are less concerned with abstract rules, but take account of people's needs in particular circumstances.

– Communitarianism versus individualism – the extent to which the community's needs are placed before those of individuals, or, in the case of work situations, where the team effort is considered as more important than individual efforts.

– Diffuse versus specific – the extent to which interpersonal relations are seen as involving the whole person or merely the person as customer, supplier or other specific role; the former approach sees building relationships as central to business dealings, the latter focuses on the facts of the matter.

– Achievement versus ascription – the extent to which a person is judged by what they do (have achieved) or on the basis of who they are (age, gender, business connections); in an achievement culture, a new recruit is more likely to be asked what they studied and what degree they obtained, whereas in an ascriptive culture they are more likely to be asked where they went to university, and how much they enjoyed it.

- Sequential versus synchronic notions of time – the extent to which people view time in a linear fashion as one event after another, or as something that links the present with both the past and the future; those with a sequential orientation prefer to do one thing at a time, and are very punctual, whereas those with a synchronic orientation can do several things (successfully) at once, and are less concerned with punctuality.

- Inner-directed attitude towards the environment versus an outer-directed attitude – the extent to which an individual sees the natural environment as something to be controlled, or harnessed, rather than recognizing that the self is part of that environment and can embrace it; the former view sees the world as a machine, the latter as an organism.

22.   The cultural dimensions proposed by Hofstede (and others) can be used, in conjunction with other information, to evaluate cultural differences and therefore predict any needy adaptation by the international organization or employee. The extent of cultural adaptation will depend upon the closeness of the cultural 'fit' between countries. Constructs such as those presented as culture dimensions, personal observations and conversations with others can all be used to build profiles about other cultures. Such profiles enable employees to anticipate the differences that may be encountered when working with people from other cultures; they help a person from one culture develop an understanding of another and may help workers anticipate management styles and different ways of doing business in other cultures. We discuss working in other countries and cultures next.

15.4 RESOURCING: PLANNING, RECRUITMENT AND SELECTION

23.   Organizations that fragment their value chain and establish overseas operations must then resource them. Resourcing includes the activities responsible for filling positions within the organization (staffing, recruitment and selection). We will consider personnel management in more detail later (see Chapters 42–50). In this chapter about the international context of management we touch on issues briefly. Staffing is a major practice that MNEs have used to help coordinate and control their far-flung global operations. In companies functioning in a global environment, there is a need to distinguish between different types of employees. Traditionally, they are classified as one of three types: (1) Parent Country National (PCN) – the employee's nationality is the same as the organization's; (2) Host Country National (HCN) – the employee's nationality is the same as the location of the subsidiary and (3) Third Country National (TCN) – The employee's nationality is neither that of the organization nor that of the location of the subsidiary. Traditionally MNEs have sent PCNs or expatriates abroad to ensure that the policies and procedures of the home office were being carried out to the letter in foreign operations. As costs became prohibitive and career issues made these assignments less attractive, MNEs turn to TCNs and HCNs to satisfy international staffing needs. When individuals from the home country manage operations abroad, staffing is referred to as ethnocentric; under polycentric staffing, individuals from the host country manage operations and in the case of Geocentric staffing, the best-qualified individuals, regardless of nationality, manage operations.

15.5 INTERNATIONAL ASSIGNMENT PREPARATION

24.   Expatriates need an understanding of the host culture and require skills that will enable them to choose the 'right' combination of verbal and non-verbal behaviours to achieve a smooth and harmonious relationship with their hosts in the foreign culture. Typically they require skills, such as adaptation, cross-cultural communication and partnership, work transition, stress-management, relationship building and negotiation techniques. The management of international

assignments is a vast and complex subject, covering many different topics. It is therefore impossible within the scope of this section to do more than outline the important points to be considered. The main elements of international assignments include: resourcing, preparation, terms and conditions, remuneration, dual career problems and repatriation. International assignments incur substantial direct costs for the employer related to the relocation of the employee (and family), the provision of remuneration packages whilst abroad, repatriation costs and the recruitment and relocation of a replacement, if required. The costs of failure are also high and include damage done to relations with subsidiary staff, customers, suppliers and the local community. Some of the important implications of inadequate adjustment to international assignments are costly for both the organizations and individuals in terms of absenteeism; early return to the home country; and lower performance.

25. Hofstede (1997:207) discusses intercultural encounters. He suggests that the simplest form of intercultural encounter is between one foreign individual and a new cultural environment – 'The foreigner usually experiences some form of culture shock'. Acculturation refers to the changes that occur as a result of first-hand contact between individuals of differing cultural origins. It is a process whereby an individual is socialized into an unfamiliar or new culture. The greater the acculturation, the more the language, customs, identity, attitudes and behaviours of the predominant culture are adopted. However, many expatriates experience difficulty in fully acculturating; only adopting the values and behaviours they find appropriate and acceptable to their existing cultures. It is a question of willingness and readiness. Expatriates typically experience a new culture which is unfamiliar and strange. In the initial stage of confrontation with the new culture, the user experiences a culture shock. Then full or partial acculturation takes place, depending on factors such as former experience, length of stay, cultural distance between home and new culture, training and language competency amongst other factors. The greater the users' ability to acculturate, the less the impact of culture shock on them. The ability to acculturate and reduce the impact of the culture shock can be developed through an appropriate and effective cross-cultural training. Apart from that, training can also help the users to develop intercultural communication competence, which is needed to adapt better and perform well in the new environment. There are several key areas to explore when selecting and preparing expatriates for assignment: adaptiveness, listening skills, empathy, respect for others, self-management, self-awareness, time management and political awareness; self-awareness is key.

> **Culture shock** Psychological process affecting people living and working abroad that may affect their work performance

> **Cultural distance** Cultural distance aims to capture the overall difference in national culture between the home-country and affiliates overseas. As the cultural distance increases, the difficulties facing business processes overseas also increase

26. An important category of international operator is the international business traveller (IBT), also known popularly as globetrotter or frequent flier. IBTs are often a neglected resource, particularly in terms of skills and knowledge transfer. The international business traveller plays an important role in furthering the objectives of the internationalizing firm in areas such as sales, knowledge transfer, performance monitoring and control. During their frequent visits, IBTs are acquiring, collecting, assimilating, recording and transferring information and knowledge about foreign markets and operations. They are agents or carriers of articulated and tacit knowledge.

> **International operations** Process by which the firm makes and delivers its goods or services across national borders

15.6 DEVELOPING GLOBALLY MINDED MANAGERS

> **Multinational** The multinational (multidomestic) is a collection of national companies that manage their businesses with minimal direction from headquarters – decentralization is emphasized to achieve differentiation and a local response

27. Multinational corporations are still heavily influenced by the characteristics of their home country. However, as global competition increases, it is increasingly important for successful

companies to have a group of managers with a global perspective argues Treven (2006). Scholars have argued that the development of a cadre of managers with a global mindset is the only way in which organizations working across borders can create a common culture and deal effectively with the complexity inherent in international business. International assignments are used to develop such a mindset. Companies must identify managers with global potential and provide them various training and development opportunities. For example, having one or more international assignments, working on cross-national teams and projects, and learning other languages and cultures contribute to making a manager more globally minded. In addition, an organization should include not only parent country nationals but also host country nationals and third country nationals in this group.

15.7 INTERACTING AND WORKING PRODUCTIVELY WITH OTHERS – WORKING WITH OTHER CULTURES

Cross cultural Competence An individual's effectiveness in drawing on a set of knowledge, skills and personal attributes in order to work successfully with people from different national cultural backgrounds at home or abroad

28. Many international business failures have been ascribed to a lack of cross cultural competence (the ability of individuals to function effectively in another culture) on the part of business practitioners. A globally competent manager must learn about many foreign cultures, be skilful in working with people and be able to adapt to living in different cultures. We discussed national culture in Chapter 13 and earlier in this chapter we noted various benefits of internationalization. However, as Prof. Geert Hofstede, Maastricht University states, 'Culture is more often a source of conflict than of synergy. Cultural differences are a nuisance at best and often a disaster'. Globalization opens many opportunities for business, but it also creates major challenges. An important challenge is the understanding and appreciating of cultural values, practices and subtleties in different parts of the world. To be successful in dealing with people from other cultures, managers need knowledge about cultural differences and similarities amongst countries. They also need to understand the implications of the differences and the skills required to act and decide appropriately and in a culturally sensitive way. Cultural sensitivity and competence can help individuals and organizations to adapt and develop; interact and manage (AIM) to attain their goals. Cross cultural understanding (see cultural literacy) refers to the basic ability of business people to recognize, interpret and react correctly to people, incidences or situations that are open to misunderstanding due to cultural differences. The fundamental intention of cross cultural training is to equip the learner(s) with the appropriate skills to attain cross cultural understanding. People typically develop 'cross cultural knowledge and awareness' becoming familiar with cultural characteristics such as values, beliefs and behaviours. This may lead to an ability to read into situations, contexts and behaviours that are culturally rooted and be able to react to them appropriately (sensitivity). 'Cross cultural competence' is and should be the aim of all those dealing with multicultural clients, customers or colleagues. 'Competence' refers to an ability to work effectively across cultures. Cultural competence has been defined as a set of skills and attitudes that allow individuals to effectively and appropriately communicate with people who are different from themselves.

29. Many business practitioners and scholars argue that when doing business in another culture, it is important to understand the other culture's customs and manners (ways of behaving). A lack of understanding may result in embarrassing mistakes or offence. Such a knowledge (business etiquette) may help with negotiations, marketing and operations management. There is no question that one of the most important features of a global manager's job is to communicate effectively with people from other parts of the world. Negotiation is a process of communication, involving the exchange of information on parties' interests, positions and needs. Negotiations and decision-making are both intertwined and culture bound. Cross cultural negotiations may be a one-off occurrence (a sale) or a frequent occurrence (in alliances and joint ventures).

30.   In Chapter 8 we discussed groups and group behaviour. As organizations globalize their operations, it is likely that there will be increased frequency with which employees interact with people from different countries. Further, domestic populations are becoming more diverse, suggesting that domestic organizations will also need to learn how to manage more heterogeneous workgroups than they have managed previously. In addition, the trend towards using teams to coordinate and manage work in organizations is increasing the amount of time that employees spend with people outside their particular functional or product groups, thereby bringing them into contact with people who may have very different training, skills, functional background and even values. In this last section we consolidate previous work on diversity, perception, culture and working with others and turn our attention to specific problems associated with making diverse and multicultural groups work within the international organization. The international organization needs groups that perform, are motivated and productive, creative, dynamic and a source of sustainable competitive advantage. Research on heterogeneity in groups suggests that diversity offers both a great opportunity for organizations as well as an enormous challenge. Diversity appears to be a double-edged sword, increasing the opportunity for creativity as well as the likelihood that group members will be dissatisfied and fail to identify with the group. A group that is diverse could be expected to have members who may have had significantly different experiences and, therefore, significantly different perspectives on key issues or problems. However, such differences can create serious coordination and communication difficulties for groups. Research repeatedly suggests the presence of a systemic problem, namely, that groups and organizations will act systematically to push out individuals who are different from the majority, unless this tendency to drive out diversity is managed. This finding is a manifestation of the tendency of people to identify with particular groups and then define these groups as the in-group and all other groups as out-groups, and it is the outcome of natural social processes (refer back to SIT theory). In the context of organizations, such processes will tend to create homosocial reproduction resulting in the creation of very homogeneous groups that are not representative. This tendency to drive out diversity is an extremely serious and systematic force which organizations who value diversity will have to develop mechanisms to counteract. It is clear that there are many benefits associated with diversity; however, diversity also leads to serious affective costs.

> **International organization** Any organization that engages in international trade, investment or offers products or services outside their home country

CONCLUSION

31.   In this chapter we have described, and presented frameworks (PESTLE etc.) to analyze, the external (international) environment and commented on the concept of globalization. We presented arguments suggesting why domestic companies may internationalize and described this as a process. The international context is relevant to both domestic and international organizations. Building on systems theory we introduced the value chain as a framework to analyze organizations but also explored the concept of value chain fragmentation where organizations may 'separate' activities and then locate them around the world. The extent of internationalization and the way organizations see the world can be used to categorize companies – as domestic, domestic with an export department, global, multidomestic and transnational. Whatever the company type, globalization means that the internal workforce is likely to be diverse and employees are likely to come into contact with customers, suppliers, partners and subsidiary employees, etc. who are different. We therefore discussed practical implications of intercultural encounters and the need for organizations to get these right. Finally, we recognized that management styles are not universal and practices may need to be adapted when working in other countries.

> **International trade** The purchase, sale, or exchange of goods and services across national borders

QUESTIONS

1 Evaluate the impact of globalization on the domestic organization.

2 Discuss the importance of preparing employees for work overseas.

3 Select a company with which you are familiar and describe its value chain. Next, evaluate the primary and secondary activities and discuss whether the value chain could be fragmented, with responsibility for some activities given to operations overseas. In your answer you should present the arguments for and against value chain fragmentation.

4 Use the PESTLE framework to analyze the external environment at UPS.

5 How has globalization and Internet technology impacted upon UPS?

6 To what extent would you expect UPS to be a global organization (as opposed to a multi-domestic organization) – should it see the world as one marketplace or many different marketplaces?

7 Discuss the process of internationalization at UPS.

USEFUL WEBSITES

International Monetary Fund: **www.imf.org** The International Monetary Fund (IMF) is an organization of 185 countries, working to foster global monetary cooperation, secure financial stability, facilitate international trade, promote high employment and sustainable economic growth, and reduce poverty around the world.

UNESCO: **www.unesco.org/** United Nations Educational, Scientific and Cultural Organization – Topics include: Publications; Statistics; UNESCO partners; Information services

World Trade Organization: **www.gatt.org/** World Trade Organization official site

United Nations: **www.un.org/**

Geert Hofstede™ Cultural Dimensions: **www.geert-hofstede.com/** On each country page you will find the unique Hofstede graphs depicting the Dimension scores and other demographics for that country and culture – plus an explanation of how they uniquely apply to that country.

EUROPA: **europa.eu/pol/socio/index_en.htmeuropa.eu/ pol/socio/index_en.htm** EUROPA is the portal site of the European Union (europa.eu). It provides up-to-date coverage of European Union affairs and essential information on

European integration. Users can also consult all legislation currently in force or under discussion, access the websites of each of the EU institutions and find out about the policies administered by the European Union

World Trade Organization (WTO): **www.wto.org/**

European Union information service: **www.europa.eu.int**

UN Global Compact: **www.unglobalcompact.org/** The UN Global Compact is a strategic policy initiative for businesses that are committed to aligning their operations and strategies with ten universally accepted principles in the areas of human rights, labour, environment and anti-corruption. By doing so, business, as a primary agent driving globalization, can help ensure that markets, commerce, technology and finance advance in ways that benefit economies

OECD – Public Employment and Management: **www.oecd.org/** The work of the Directorate for Public Governance and Territorial Development on public sector employment and management supports productive managerial change and improved personnel policies in the public service, integrating them with budgetary and other reforms to improve the responsiveness of government and the efficient delivery of public services.

REFERENCES

Bartlett, C. and Ghoshal, S. (1992) 'What Is a Global Manager?', Harvard Business Review, September-October 1992, p. 124–132.

Hampden-Turner, C. M. and Trompenaars, F. (2000) 'Buildling Cross-Cultural Competence - How to create wealth from conflicting values', Wiley.

Hofstede, G. (1984) 'Cultures Consequences - abridged', Sage.

Hofstede, G. (1980) 'Motivation, leadership and organization: do American theories apply abroad?', Organizational Dynamics, summer, p. 42–63.

Hofstede, G. (1997) 'Cultures and Organizations', McGraw-Hill.

Hofstede, G. (2006) 'What did GLOBE really measure? Researchers' minds versus respondents' minds', Journal of International Business Studies, 37, p. 882–896.

Kelly, P. P. (2009) 'International Business and Management', Cengage Learning EMEA.

Ouchi, W. G. and Wilkins, A. L. (1983) 'Efficient Cultures: Exploring the relationship between culture and organizational performance', Administrative Science Quarterly, 28 (3), p. 468–481.

Perlmutter, H. (1969) 'The Tortuous Evolution of the Multinational Corporation', Columbia Journal of World Business, Jan/Feb 69, Vol. 4 Issue 1, p. 9–19.

Porter, M. E. and Millar, V. E. (1985) 'How information gives you a competitive advantage.', Harvard Business Review, July-August 63, p. 149–174.

Treven, S. (2006) 'Human Resources Management in the Global Environment', Journal of American Academy of Business, Mar 2006, Vol. 8 Issue 1, p. 120–125.

Section Eight
Management Planning

CASE STUDY

MANAGEMENT PLANNING

STRATEGIC OBJECTIVES AT MONTBLANC – A LUXURY GOODS MANUFACTURER IN RETAIL

In 1981 Prince Charles and Diana, the Princess of Wales, signed their marriage contract with a Montblanc pen. Montblanc (owned by Compagnie Financière Richemont S.A.) has been known for generations as a maker of sophisticated, high quality writing instruments. In 1906 a Hamburg banker, Alfred Nehemias, and a Berlin engineer, August Eberstein, decided to manufacture pens, laying the foundation for what would become Montblanc. In 1910 the name Montblanc was registered as a trademark. The name of the company was inspired by the 'MontBlanc' mountain, which is the highest mountain in Europe located in France; the mountain also forms the basis of the company's logo. For one hundred years the name Montblanc has stood for the art of writing, while the snow-covered peak of Mont Blanc has symbolized the high quality status of the brand with the distinctive white star. Montblanc's classic fountain pen, the Meisterstück first produced in 1924, has become a cult object.

Montblanc competes with such famous names as Cartier, Luis Vuitton, Tiffany and Gucci. For many years their strategy was one of increasing market share and product development. However, it was during the decade of the 1990s that Montblanc embarked on a strategy of geographic expansion. With a vision for global growth, Montblanc took its powerful marketing strategy to an entirely new level with the opening of its first boutique in Hong Kong. This was followed by shops in Paris and London, marking the beginning of the company's international expansion. By 1995, Montblanc had established several similar boutique shops in major markets in the United States. Over subsequent years, Montblanc opened hundreds of boutiques worldwide.

Around the same time, the company realized that it would need to diversify into other products to mitigate the growing impact of the digital age on the market for fine pens. Leather products, desk accessories and fine jewellery have all become part of its offering. But from the start, the company saw the watch business as a natural fit with the values of craftsmanship, precision and heritage it espoused in its pens. Having launched its handmade watches in 1997, Montblanc struggled for a long time to gain credibility from either industry insiders or consumers. In recent years, it has made an effort to redress this. Overall, the companies' diversified business strategy was characterized by a fast-expanding range of products as a result of new product developments. Montblanc re-wrote its business model again in 2006 by expanding into accessories.

In the past few years, the product range has been expanded further. Montblanc has thus become a purveyor of exclusive products which reflect the exacting demands made today for quality design, tradition and master craftsmanship. Montblanc is a truly international brand with operations in more than 70 countries. Montblanc sells its products exclusively through its international network of authorized retailers, jewellers and hundreds of Montblanc Boutiques worldwide. The strategy to differentiate into a host of luxury goods under the Montblanc brand seems to be paying off. Sales grew and as the company entered its second century, it had made a key transition, from pen manufacturer to purveyor of a range of luxury goods.

Montblanc products are enjoyed for their functional properties and craftsmanship, or as status accessories; they are timeless collectables and may be given as gifts or purchased by customers for themselves. Montblanc products are in high demand as regional consumers seek out bespoke and limited editions. Montblanc sells its products but at the same time, have always been an active promoter of culture and the arts. They are actively involved in charitable work through sponsorship and donations. Montblanc takes a long-term customer strategy. Ultimately, Montblanc's goal is to create customer relationships as long-lasting as its products. Those relationships hopefully will bring 'multiple sales over many years'.

Fundamentally, Montblanc's success has come from the teamwork, dedication, hard work and commitment of its employees; its strategies have frequently relied upon their creativity. Employees take pride in supporting the Montblanc brand name and selling its products. People make the difference at Montblanc where the Human Resource Department pursues a clearly defined policy based on the business strategy. The company offers equal opportunity employment; supports professional and developmental training and has a policy of filling vacancies primarily from within the company. The basis of remuneration is on the achievement of objectives. The key to Mont Blanc's success is its people and Montblanc's development is seen to be the responsibility of everyone in the company. Employees are expected to involve themselves in company decision making. These expectations are encouraged by a cooperative management style where management doors are open to suggestions and ideas that can contribute to the company's success. Leaders set an example by creating a trusting atmosphere through credibility, loyalty and their ability to listen. Clear objectives, short lines of communication, and the willingness to accept responsibility are the basis for their ability to adapt to changing market conditions and embrace new ideas.

In 1998, Montblanc opened the Montblanc Academy in Hamburg to provide training in international business management, luxury product knowledge, sales skills and in the Montblanc philosophy and values. The company regard the Montblanc Academy as the foundation for a learning organization. It underlines the importance of educating and training employees and franchise partners. The Montblanc Academy is built around the belief that the quality of service depends on well-trained people with the right attitude towards the company and its products.

Source: http://www.montblanc.com/

CHAPTER 16
STRATEGIC ASPECTS OF MANAGEMENT

Key Concepts

- Business Strategy
- Capabilities
- Competitive advantage
- Competitive strategy
- Resource-based view of strategy
- Strategic management process
- Strategy
- Sustained competitive advantage
- VRIO framework

Learning Outcomes Having read this chapter, you should be able to:

- review the significance of the external and internal environment for strategy formulation
- explain what (corporate and business) strategy is and how it is formed
- identify the generic corporate and business strategies
- discuss theories of strategy formulation

1.   Business is about creating value and the challenge for strategy is firstly to create value for customers and secondly to take, for the organization, some of that value in the form of profit. Value may be created through production (discussed in Chapters 38–41) or by commerce. There are a number of fundamental questions every company must answer such as: what do we do? Why are we here? What kind of company do we want to be? What is happening in the environment? What is our current strategy? What are our goals? In which markets and in which geographic areas will we compete? What products and services will we offer and to whom? What technologies will we employ? What capabilities and capacities will we require? What will we make by ourselves and what will we buy (outsource) from others? Finally, how will we compete? The answers to such questions may be provided through strategic problem-solving activities. Strategy, as explored in this chapter, is concerned with how the organization will achieve its aims and goals.

Capabilities What the organization can do

Strategy Strategy is the direction and scope of an organization over the long term, which achieves advantage in a changing environment through its configuration of resources and competences with the aim of fulfilling stakeholder expectations

Competitive strategy Competitive strategy is concerned with the basis on which a business unit might achieve competitive advantage in its market

Internal Analysis Identification of a firm's organizational strengths and weaknesses and of the resources and capabilities that are likely to be sources of competitive advantage

Competitive advantage Used interchangeably with 'distinctive competence' to mean relative superiority in skills and resources

The resource-based view of strategy The competitive advantage of an organization is strategy explained by the distinctiveness of its capabilities

16.1 WHAT IS STRATEGY AND HOW IS STRATEGY CREATED?

2.   Strategy is often defined as the match between what a company can do (organizational strengths and weaknesses) within the universe of what it might do (environmental opportunities and threats).

3.   Taking the latter point first, Michael Porter has written much on competitive strategy: techniques for analyzing industries and competitors. His five forces model (to be discussed later) of environmental threats can help us to evaluate the organization's external environment and consider positioning strategies. The essence of the model is that the structure of an industry determines the state of competition within that industry and sets the context for companies' conduct – their strategy. Most important, structural forces (which Porter called the five forces) determine the average profitability of the industry and have a strong corresponding impact on the profitability of individual corporate strategies. This analysis placed the spotlight on choosing the 'right industries' and, within them, the most attractive competitive positions. Although the model did not ignore the characteristics of individual companies, the emphasis was clearly on phenomena at the industry level.

4.   Having introduced the key aspects of the external environment, we now identify the key aspect of the internal environment – moving from outside to inside the company (see Internal Analysis). As opposed to positioning within an industry, some consider the roots of competitive advantage to lie inside the organization and that the adoption of new strategies may be constrained by the company's resources. The resource-based view (RBV) of the firm acknowledges the importance of company-specific resources and competencies, yet it does so in the context of the competitive environment. It sees capabilities and resources as the heart of a company's competitive position, subject to the interplay of three fundamental market forces: demand (does it meet customers' needs, and is it competitively superior?), scarcity (is it imitable or substitutable, and is it durable?) and appropriability (who owns the profits?).

5.   Strategy then, is the link between the organization (strengths and weaknesses) and its external environment (opportunities and threats). Strategy is essentially about making choices with regard to where and how to compete; there is therefore a critical need to establish competitive advantage. Competitive advantage stems from the resources and capabilities of the organization which act as the basis for strategy formulation.

6.   Over the past century scholars and practitioners have labelled many types of strategy and discussed alternative processes of strategy formation. It is common for scholars to distinguish between planned (intended) versus emergent strategies. The planning mode depicts the process as a highly ordered, neatly integrated one, with strategies spelled out on schedule by a purposeful organization; planning theory postulates that the strategy-maker 'formulates' from on high whilst the subordinates 'implement' lower down. Conversely, strategy may also be described as 'a pattern in a stream of decisions' (realized strategy). Emergent strategies are realized strategies that were never intended. In other words, the strategy-maker may formulate a strategy through a conscious process before he/she makes specific decisions (formulation), or a strategy may form gradually, perhaps unintentionally, as he/she makes decisions one by one (strategy formation).

> **Planning** The formalization of what is intended to happen at some time in the future; concerns actions taken prior to an event, typically formulating goals and objectives and then arranging for resources to be provided in order to achieve a desired outcome

7.   Strategies can be combined in three ways: (1) intended strategies which are realized; these may be called deliberate strategies; (2) intended strategies that are not realized, perhaps because of unrealistic expectations, misjudgements about the environment or changes in either during implementation; these may be called unrealized strategies and (3) realized strategies that were never intended, perhaps because no strategy was intended at the outset or perhaps because, as in (2), intended strategies were displaced along the way; these may be called emergent strategies.

8.   Strategy making under the planning view, typically includes:

1).   Environmental analysis;

2).   Objective setting;

3).   Distinctive competence selection or the choice of tools and competitive weapons with which to negotiate with the environment;

4).   Power distribution, or the determination of authority and influence relationships amongst organizational subunits;

5).   Resource allocation or the deployment of financial and physical resources to carry out a strategy and

6).   Monitoring and control of outcomes, or the comparison of intended and manifested strategy contents.

In some cases scholars suggest that the mission is determined first with analysis following – in reality the two activities are tightly intertwined. Analysis is followed by choice and then implementation which should lead to advantage.

9.   There are three basic levels of strategy within the large organization: corporate (defining scope-where to compete, the activities to perform and products to sell), business (how to compete and add value) and departmental. In this case the term corporate refers to the whole company and business corresponds with the division, strategic business unit or subsidiary of the multinational corporation. The corporate strategy considers industry attractiveness and the business strategy considers competitive advantage as sources of profitability. The departmental strategy may be a functional strategy such as the IT or marketing strategy or maybe a product or area-based strategy. Operational strategies are concerned with how specific parts of an

> **Business strategy** Describes how the organization competes within an industry or market

Strategic Management Process
A sequential set of analyses that can
increase the likelihood of a firm's
choosing a strategy that generates
competitive advantages

organization deliver the corporate and business level strategies effectively in terms of resources, processes and people.

10.   No matter what the level, strategy is about winning. It is the means (plans, actions and policies) by which organizations achieve their objectives. Strategy may be confined to the minds of senior managers or may be articulated in the vision, mission (statement of purpose), business model (statement of approach to revenue generation) or strategic plan (goals and the required resources and approach to goal attainment). Strategy is a device that unifies, constrains, coordinates and motivates the members of an organization.

16.2 STRATEGY DEVELOPMENT AND STRATEGIC MANAGEMENT

Mission statement A mission statement is
a statement of the overriding direction
and purpose of an organization

Sustained competitive advantage
A competitive advantage that lasts for a
long period of time; an advantage that is not
competed away through strategic imitation

11.   The development of the mission statement is a useful starting point for strategy development. It can be circulated and discussed, provides a sense of direction and focus and draws the organization together. The purpose of the mission statement is to communicate what the company stands for and where it is heading. It needs to reflect the basic values and beliefs of the organization and the elements of sustainable competitive advantage, be realistic and attainable, specific and flexible enough to guide behaviour in a dynamic environment. A mission statement answers the question, 'Why do we exist?' and articulates the company's purpose both for those in the organization and for the public; it identifies the reason for being and may define the organization's primary customers, the products and services they produce and the geographical location in which they operate. Effective mission statements generally have the following attributes and content: simple, declarative statements, easily articulated and remembered, realistic and can define not only what a company's business goals are, but also the methodologies it chooses to get there.

12.   Whilst the mission refers to the overriding purpose and communicates the answer to the question, 'what business are we in?' the vision describes strategic intent, where the organization wants to be in the future. A vision is a desired view of what the organization will be like in the future. The vision statement is a detailed description of how things will be when the organization eventually reaches its destination. In summary, the vision and mission of a company should be a driving force, setting the strategic direction of the business.

13.   General aims of the organization are communicated qualitatively in the organizational goals whilst objectives convey similar information in a more specific, measurable and often quantitative form (see next chapter). Specific objectives then translate the mission into more specific commitments of what will be done and when, if the objectives are to be accomplished. Whist the mission, vision and goals focus on what will be done, the business model and specific strategies may communicate how the organization will add value and compete. The explicit statements of purpose, values and mission statements serve to unify the members of an organization and the strength of this unification force will be, in part, governed by the way such statements were formed and are communicated (such statements are components of the organization's formal belief system and are linked strongly with culture and cultural development – particularly when they are shared).

16.3 STRATEGIES

14.   In the previous section we noted that, once the organization purpose and mission have been decided, the company must face choices about the markets within which to compete and the

means to do so. Strategic choices are concerned with decisions about the organization's future. Michael Porter described three general types of business strategy (options) that are commonly used by organizations (Generic Business Strategies). They are cost leadership, differentiation and market segmentation (or focus). An organization can develop cost leadership, product differentiation and business innovation strategies to confront its competitive forces.

Generic Business Another name for business-level strategies, which are cost leadership and product differentiation

15.   Competitive advantages exist in relation to rivals operating within an industry as factors that enable an organization to earn a higher rate of profit. Such advantages emerge from the actions of organizations (internal sources) or from changes in the external environment (external sources). With regard to external sources, an organization may be more capable or better equipped to exploit changes in customer demand, technology, political or economic factors. An external change may create opportunity for profit. Consequently, organizations must be able to identify and respond to opportunity. As markets become increasingly turbulent, so responsiveness to external change has become increasingly important as a source of competitive advantage. Companies that are more responsive may also have an advantage over their sluggish rivals. Responsiveness is enabled through resources (information) and capabilities (flexibility). Speed of response as a source of competitive advantage is termed time-based competition.

Product differentiation Refers to one way in which firms can maintain their competitive advantage; they differentiate their product, in ways that appeals to the customer, from all others on the market

16.   An organization may compete by offering customers what they want at the lowest price/cost or may differentiate their products and services in such a way that the customer is prepared to pay a premium price for them. Cost leadership requires the organization to find and exploit sources of cost advantage, typically selling a standard, no-frills product or service whilst differentiation necessitates the organization providing something unique and valuable to buyers. They represent two fundamentally (not mutually exclusive) different approaches to business strategy. A third source of competitive advantage is based on focus. Cost leadership and differentiation are industry-wide sources of competitive advantage whilst focus strategies seek out competitive advantages for particular market segments (see Niche Strategy).

Niche Strategy A firm reduces its scope of operations and focuses on narrow segments of a declining industry

16.4 OPERATIONAL EFFECTIVENESS AND STRATEGY

17.   Operational effectiveness and strategy are both essential to superior performance but they work in very different ways (Porter, 1996). Operational effectiveness (and efficiency) is about performing similar activities better (through operational improvements) than rivals perform them. Improvements can be made in productivity, quality or speed (see for example total quality management (TQM), continuous improvement, and benchmarking, time-based competition, outsourcing, partnering, reengineering and change management). Such initiatives change how organizations perform activities in order to eliminate inefficiencies, improve customer satisfaction, and achieve best practice. Some companies are able to get more out of their resources than others because they eliminate wasted effort, employ more advanced technology, motivate employees better or have greater insight into managing particular activities or sets of activities. Operational effectiveness refers to any number of practices that allow a company to better utilize its resources, resulting in differences in profitability among competitors because relative cost positions and levels of differentiation are directly affected.

18.   However, few companies have competed successfully on the basis of operational effectiveness over an extended period. One important reason for this is the speedy dissemination of best practices. Competitors can quickly imitate management techniques, new technologies, input improvements and superior ways of meeting customers' needs. The most generic solutions – those that can be used in multiple settings – diffuse most rapidly. The more benchmarking

companies do, the more they look alike. The more that rivals outsource activities to, often the same or similar companies, the more generic those activities become. When rivals invest in the same technologies or best practices, the resulting major productivity gains are captured by customers and equipment suppliers, not retained in superior profitability. As rivals imitate one another's improvements in quality, cycle times or supplier partnerships, strategies converge to the point where no one can win. Competition based on operational effectiveness alone is mutually destructive, halted only by limiting competition. This may lead to the simple approach, to buy up rivals. In such a case, the remaining companies in an industry are those that outlasted others, not companies with real advantage.

The principal distinctions between strategic and operational levels of planning are illustrated in simplified form in Figure 16.1.

FIGURE 16.1 **Differences between strategic and operational planning.**

19.   Figure 16.1 shows that the prime focus of strategy is effectiveness in the long term, which means making the best choices for the future, whereas operations are primarily concerned with the efficient use of resources in achieving short-term targets. Effectiveness is about doing the right thing; efficiency is about doing things right. Strategy is concerned with positioning the business in the market, establishing a reputation with customers, employees and other stakeholders. It is concerned with long-term growth and with the stewardship of resources. Those making strategy need to know they are in control of the business. Operational managers, by comparison, are concerned with the efficient delivery of goods and services. Their horizons are the present and the immediate future, as they attempt to make the best use of employee skills, operating procedures and technology in servicing their customers.

Strategy as Position A means of locating an organization in its environment (choice of niche). It can be considered in relation to competitors or simply with respect to markets or an environment at large. Strategy is creating situations where revenues may be generated and sustained.

16.5 POSITIONING STRATEGY

20.   Competitive strategy is about being different and strategic positioning means performing activities which differ from the activities of rivals or performing similar activities in different ways, (Porter, 1996). Strategy is the creation of a unique and valuable position, involving a different set of activities. The essence of

strategic positioning is to choose activities that differ from those of rivals. Positioning requires a tailored set of activities because it is always a function of differences on the supply side that is, of differences in activities.

21. Choosing a unique position, however, is not enough to guarantee a sustainable advantage. A valuable position will attract imitation by others. Positioning choices determine not only which activities a company will perform and how it will configure individual activities but also how activities relate to one another. Whilst operational effectiveness is about achieving excellence in individual activities, or functions, strategy is about combining (fitting together) activities. Imitators then find it more difficult to copy systems of related and interdependent activities. The whole matters more than any individual part. Competitive advantage grows out of the entire system of activities. The fit amongst activities substantially reduces cost or increases differentiation. Strategic fit amongst many activities is fundamental not only to competitive advantage but also to the sustainability of that advantage. It is harder for a rival to match an array of interlocked activities than it is merely to imitate a particular sales-force approach, match a technology or replicate a set of product features. Positions built on systems of activities are far more sustainable than those built on individual activities. The more a company's positioning rests on activity systems the more sustainable its advantage will be. Such systems, by their very nature, are usually difficult to untangle from outside the company and therefore hard to imitate.

22. Improving operational effectiveness ('how' work activities are undertaken) is a necessary part of management, but it is not strategy. Managers must clearly distinguish operational effectiveness from strategy (how the organization will compete and use its resources and scope: the 'what' and the 'where'). Both are essential, but the two agendas are different. The operational agenda involves continual improvement everywhere. There are no trade-offs. The operational agenda is the proper place for constant change, flexibility and relentless efforts to achieve best practice. In contrast, the strategic agenda is the right place for defining a unique position, making clear trade-offs and tightening fit. It involves the continual search for ways to reinforce and extend the company's position. A company must improve its operational effectiveness continually and strive to shift the productivity frontier. At the same time there needs to be ongoing effort to extend its uniqueness whilst strengthening the fit amongst its activities.

16.6 EVALUATING THE EXTERNAL ENVIRONMENT

23. At the macro level, we may use the PESTLE framework to analyze the external environment (refer back to Chapter 15). At the micro and industry level strategists typically make use of Porter's five forces framework. Collectively, the analysis helps the organization to understand threats and opportunities. Michael Porter, an engineer and economist, is concerned with the impact of the external environment on the firm. He sees five major influences (forces) on a firm's ability to compete (see Figure 16.2), comprising not only existing competitors in the industry, but also potential rivals (new entrants), the threat of substitute products, the bargaining power of buyers and the bargaining power of suppliers. These forces are represented schematically in Figure 16.2.

24. Porter's five forces can be utilized by firms in their formulation of strategy, and especially in their assessment of their strengths and weaknesses (see SWOT analysis, Chapter 17). Any analysis is most likely to begin with an examination of the firm's industry competitors. At a time of intense rivalry competitors are advertising strongly, offering incentives to buyers (interest free credit etc.) and devising ways of differentiating their products. Firms have to

Five forces framework Identifies the five most common threats faced by firms in their local competitive environments and the conditions under which these threats are more or less likely to be present; these forces are the threat of entry, of rivalry, of substitutes, of buyers and of suppliers

Rivalry The act of competing – a quest to secure an advantage over another

FIGURE 16.2 Outline of Porter's schema of competitive forces.

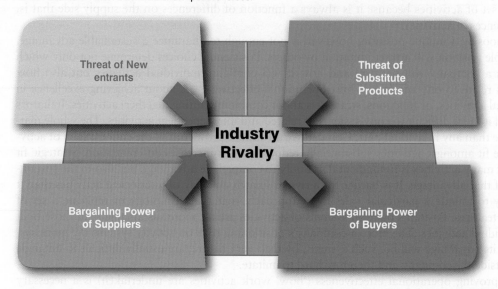

consider how they are going to respond to, or counter, these immediate sales threats from rivals. In such a case, suppliers are in a relatively weak position in relation to the firm, since their sales are dependent on the end product being sold. Buyers, conversely, are in a strong position in these circumstances and can thus drive a harder than usual bargain. Substitute products may be an issue. Given the intensity of the competition in this case, with low profit margins all round, new entrants to the industry are unlikely, as the costs of entering would be high and the returns low.

25.   Porter specifically considers the issue of entering new markets and lists seven major barriers to market entry, which can be summarized as follows:

Economies of scale, i.e. newcomers have to come in on a large scale or accept inevitable cost disadvantages. (This factor alone is likely to deter most would-be entrants, unless they can buy their way into the market by purchasing a firm already active in it.)

Product differentiation, i.e. newcomers has to find ways of overcoming existing brand loyalties in order to get their own product/brand accepted.

Capital requirements, i.e. the need to invest considerable sums of money in a new venture, much of which will be unrecoverable (e.g. start-up losses, advertising, research and development). (This is another huge disincentive to newcomers, unless they have cash surpluses from a cash cow business or some other possibility of raising the initial capital resources.)

Switching costs, i.e. the initial costs of machinery, equipment and other first-time resources required to enable the firm to switch into the new market.

Lack of access to distribution channels, i.e. the newcomer must work his way into existing distribution channels (e.g. dealer networks, wholesalers, etc.) or establish brand new ones. (See Chapter 34 for discussion of distribution channels.)

Cost disadvantages regardless of size, i.e. newcomers will always tend to have certain cost disadvantages compared with established firms, who will have gained experience in the market, may have access to proprietary technology, and favourable locations and may also benefit from government subsidies; new entrants may have none of these advantages.

Government policy, i.e. through licensing and legal regulation, governments can limit or even prevent newcomers from operating in the industry. (Typical licensed industries in the UK include road transport, oil exploration and retail alcohol sales.)

26. Porter's work on competitive advantage has been very influential. His ideas are not without their critics, however, and other commentators have pointed to the lack of reference to issues of the legality and ethics of the barriers described in Porter's list. Also in the schema of the five forces, there are no explicit references to other stakeholders in the firm's environment, especially the community at large, and employees. When Porter talks of buyers and suppliers he does so in terms of their power (or, by implication, lack of it) and avoids any issues regarding the obligations that firms might have in determining their strategy in the market-place.

27. Porter (2001) considers the consequences of the Internet, presenting arguments for the changing nature of competition and the resultant challenges for strategy formulation. The Internet has created new industries; however, its greatest impact has been to enable the reconfiguration of existing industries that had been constrained by high costs for communicating, gathering information or accomplishing transactions. Internet technology provides buyers with easier access to information about products and suppliers, thus strengthening buyer bargaining power. The Internet mitigates the need for such things as an established sales force or access to existing channels, reducing barriers to entry. Marketplaces automate corporate procurement by linking many buyers and suppliers electronically. The benefits to buyers include low transaction costs, easier access to price and product information, convenient purchase of associated services, and, sometimes, the ability to pool volume. The benefits to suppliers include lower selling costs, lower transaction costs, access to wider markets and the avoidance of powerful channels. By enabling new approaches to meeting needs and performing functions, it creates new substitutes. Because it is an open system, companies have more difficulty maintaining proprietary offerings, thus intensifying the rivalry among competitors. On the Internet, buyers can often switch suppliers with just a few mouse clicks, and new web technologies are systematically reducing switching costs even further. The use of the Internet also tends to expand the geographic market, bringing many more companies into competition with one another.

16.7 THE INTERNAL ENVIRONMENT – LEVERAGING RESOURCES AND CAPABILITIES

28. Scholars and practitioners alike strive continuously to perfect our knowledge of what makes some organizations perform better than others. Generally they focus upon the effects of industry and positioning (see above, e.g. Porter) but also consider organization factors (see **RBV**) on performance variability. Leverage reflects the extent to which resources are utilized in the organization. The idea of looking at organizations as a broader set of resources goes back to the seminal work of Penrose (1959). Wernerfelt (1984) argued that we can identify types of resources which can lead to high profits. He discussed resources and profitability; by a resource he meant anything which could be thought of as a strength or weakness of a given organization. More formally, an organization's resources at a given time could be defined as those (tangible and intangible) assets which are tied semi-permanently to the organization. Examples of resources are brand names, in-house knowledge of technology, employment of skilled personnel, trade contacts, machinery, efficient procedures, capital, etc. Wernerfelt posed the question: 'Under what circumstances will a resource lead to high returns over longer periods of time?' To analyze a resource for its potential for high returns, one has to look at the ways in which an organization with a strong position can influence the acquisition costs or the user revenues of an organization with a weaker position.

29. The resource-based (RBV) theory is the perspective on strategy stressing the importance of capabilities (sometimes known as core competences) in determining sustainable competitive advantage. The fundamental principle of the RBV is that the basis for organizational competitive advantage lies primarily in the application of the bundle of valuable resources at its disposal. The bundle of resources, under certain conditions, can assist the organization, sustaining above average returns. Such

Core competence Those capabilities fundamental to the organization's strategy and performance

resources must be valuable and must enable the achievement of goals. Which resources matter? Resources within the RBV are generally broken down into two fundamental categories: 1) tangible and 2) intangible resources. The central proposition of the RBV is that not all resources are of equal importance in contributing to organizational performance. The resource-based literature describes resources in terms of their value, rareness, inimitability and non-substitutability (VRIN).

VRIO Framework Four questions that must be asked about a resource or capability to determine its competitive potential: the questions of value, rarity, imitability and organization

30.   Organizational assets may be [intangible] assets that (see also **VRIO Framework**) can resist the imitation efforts of competitors. Organizational assets (e.g. culture, HRM policies and organization structure) contribute order, stability and quality to the organization. Some scholars suggest that without strong organizational assets, the organization will weaken productivity, deliver poor quality products and services and will have inferior human talent. Organizational assets may be difficult to duplicate. Although not legally protected by property rights, reputation is argued to be an important and sophisticated asset; reputation is built, not bought, suggesting that it is a non-tradable asset that may be far more difficult to duplicate than tangible assets.

31.   Capabilities, as ultimately reflected by the organization's know-how, are argued to be the principal source of organizational performance; the productivity and performance of any organization is solely dependent upon the know-how of its employees. Lastly, the ability to build and maintain relationships external to the organization is not only essential for competitive success; it is largely reflective of the knowledge-generating, knowledge-sharing and learning ability of the organization. In other words, building and maintaining external relationships is critical for the organization and largely consists of a 'collective', organization-wide effort of the know-how of a variety of employees and managers. Although intangible assets may be resistant to competitor duplication, capabilities are viewed as a 'superior' intangible resource.

16.8 CORPORATE STRATEGY

32.   For much of this chapter we have discussed business level strategy. The corporate level represents a whole company plan or pattern of decisions identifying where the company will compete (in terms of geography, product, and industry) and which resources will be used. Corporate level strategy tends to focus on matters such as vertical integration – the extension of the organization's activities into adjacent stages of productions i.e. those providing the organization's inputs or outputs; diversification – a strategy that takes the organization into both new markets and products or services (when a firm operates in multiple industries or markets simultaneously) and strategic alliances – where two or more organizations share resources and activities to pursue a strategy. Ansoff suggested a matrix of product-market alternatives, which has become widely used. In basic terms the matrix offered alternatives as shown in Figure 16.3.

Forward Vertical Integration A firm incorporates more stages of the value chain within its boundaries and those stages bring it closer to interacting directly with final customers

33.   What the matrix suggests is four growth strategies based on remaining with present products or markets, or moving into new products or markets. Firms choosing to stay in present markets with current products are presented with a strategy of market penetration (i.e. going for increased market share); those looking for new products in present markets will focus on developing appropriate new products or brands; those aiming to take existing products into new markets will concentrate on sustaining market development activities; and, finally, those firms which intend to develop new products in new markets will pursue a strategy of diversification. This last option is developed by Ansoff to include further alternatives such as horizontal diversification (i.e. sideways extension into same type of markets with related products), vertical integration and conglomerate diversification, which refers to new products in an unrelated technology and with a new type of market.

FIGURE 16.3 Ansoff's product-market growth strategies.

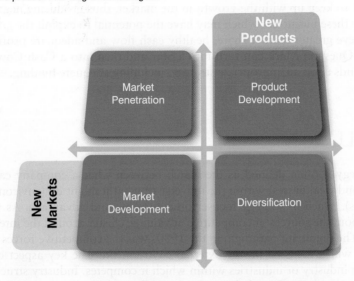

Source: *Corporate Strategy* (1965) H. Igor Ansoff. Reproduced by permission of the Ansoff Family Trust.

34. Another set of alternative strategies proposed is contained in the Boston Consulting Group's (BCG) matrix – named the 'portfolio framework' (see Figure 16.4). This matrix is based on three major variables: a firm's relative market share, the growth rate of its market(s) and the cash flows (negative or positive) generated by the firm's activities. The matrix yields four alternative outcomes for a firm, expressed somewhat idiosyncratically as Stars, Cash Cows, Dogs or Question Marks. Stars are businesses that have a high market share in an expanding market and could be profitable, but where there may be a negative cash flow because of the need to keep up investment to keep pace with market growth. Cash Cows are businesses which have a high share of a slow-growing market and which are usually very profitable and generate a positive cash flow. Dogs are businesses with a low share of a slow-growing market and may produce either a modest positive cash flow or an equally modest negative one. Question Marks are those

FIGURE 16.4 Outline of The Boston Matrix.

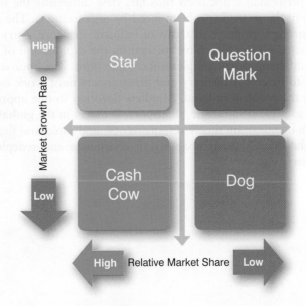

Source: The BCG Portfolio Matrix from the Product Portfolio Matrix (c) 1970, The Boston Consulting Group. Reproduced with permission.

businesses which have a low share of a fast-growing market and which require considerable investment to keep up with the growth in the market, thus producing negative cash flow. Yet it is precisely these businesses which may have the potential to exploit the growing market and go on to achieve greater market share, healthy cash flow and adequate profitability. Eventually a successful Question Mark can turn into a Star and then into a Cash Cow. However, this outcome depends upon an appropriate strategy, including adequate funding.

CONCLUSION

35.   Strategy is often defined as the match between what a company can do (organizational strengths and weaknesses) within the universe of what it might do (environmental opportunities and threats). Much of strategy focuses on competing and advantage. As was noted, dominant theories about the sources of competitive advantage cluster around the internal or external environment. The dominant paradigm in the 1980s was the competitive forces approach, developed by Porter, which focussed on the external environment. The key aspect of the firm's environment is the industry or industries within which it competes. Industry structure strongly influences the competitive rules of the game as well as the strategies available to firms. In the competitive forces model, five industry-level forces – entry barriers, threat of substitution, bargaining power of buyers and suppliers and rivalry amongst industry incumbents – determine the inherent profit potential of an industry. The approach can be used to help the firm find a position in an industry from which it can best defend itself against competitive forces or influence them in its favour. Such an approach is often referred to as a model of strategy emphasizing the exploitation of market power. Later, the 'resource-based perspective,' was proposed, with an internal focus, emphasizing firm specific-capabilities as the fundamental determinants of organizational performance. This perspective represents a strategy model emphasizing efficiency. The resource-based (RBV) approach sees organizations with superior systems and structures being profitable not because they engage in strategic investments that may deter entry and raise prices above long-run costs, but because they have markedly lower costs, or offer markedly higher quality or product performance. Organizations which are able to accumulate resources and capabilities that are rare, valuable, nonsubstitutable and difficult to imitate will achieve a competitive advantage.

36.   The different approaches to strategy and the attainment of superior and sustainable organizational performance discussed thus far, view differently the sources of wealth creation and the essence of the strategic problem faced by organizations. The competitive forces framework sees the strategic problem in terms of industry structure, entry deterrence and positioning. Resource-based perspectives have focused on the exploitation of firm-specific assets. Each approach asks different, often complementary questions. The approaches discussed are generally considered to be complementary and practitioners must work out which frameworks are appropriate for the problem in hand. Mindless devotion to one approach to the neglect of all others is likely to generate strategic blindspots. Winners in the global marketplace are organizations who can demonstrate timely responsiveness and rapid and flexible product innovation, coupled with the management capability to coordinate and redeploy internal and external competences effectively.

QUESTIONS

1 Explain how the RBV may complement the positioning view of strategy.

2 Review the significance of the external and internal environment for strategy formulation. You should use the Montblanc study to provide examples.

3 What is strategy and how has the strategy at Montblanc evolved? You should make use of the Ansoff and Boston matrix in your answer.

VIDEO CASES

Now take a look at the online video cases – visit the companion website to work through real world business problems associated with the concepts presented within this chapter.

1 Business Model – John Kearon of BrainJuicer

John Kearon, current Chairman and Chief Executive of BrainJuicer Group PLC (an online market research agency) gives an interview about their business model.

John explains how he represents a new company establishing itself in a well established business/industry. He discusses how he successfully achieved this despite entrenched competition. The case may be used as a vehicle to explore marketing (competing) and related concepts.

61 Introduction to Strategic Management

Introduction to Strategic Management through interviews with directors at RC2 which has been particularly successful in recent years. Turnover increased by 20 per cent in 2008 as the business introduced new product lines and expanded further into Europe. Sales growth in mainland Europe (excluding the UK) was 50 per cent.

89 Managerial planning and strategy

To formulate effective strategies, companies must be able to answer basic questions such as: what business are we in? How should we compete in this industry? And who are our competitors? Such questions are considered from the perspective of CEO, Hans Hickler, at DHL Express (USA) in this case. Specifically, consideration is given to:
SUSTAINABLE COMPETITIVE ADVANTAGE, CORPORATE, INDUSTRY AND FIRM LEVEL STRATEGIES, GROWTH STRATEGY AND INDUSTRY LEVEL STRATEGY.

96 Introduction to Strategic Management (SM) – a brief history of UPS

Under Michael Eskew's direction, UPS is expanding its emphasis on developing new lines of business that complement the company's core package operations. Driving this initiative, he oversees efforts to integrate technology into UPS's physical infrastructure – to create business opportunities for customers and help ensure the company's leadership position in the new age of global commerce. In this case, Eskew provides an overview of UPS's history (who they are), where the company is going and how it intends to get there.

98 Perspectives on strategy at Twitter

This case considers what is meant by strategy: as plan, strategy deals with how leaders try to establish direction for organizations, to set them on predetermined courses of action. As ploy, strategy takes us into the realm of direct competition, where organizations manoeuvre for advantage in a dynamic setting. As pattern, strategy focuses on action and consistency of behaviour. As position, strategy encourages us to look at organizations in context, specifically in their competitive environments and finally as perspective, strategy is considered as behaviour in a collective context, the pursuit of a common mission and helps us understand how patterns of behaviour become deeply ingrained within the organization. The different perspectives are used to discuss strategy in Twitter.

102 The internal environment – THE STARTING POINT FOR STRATEGY FORMULATION

Business success can be realized by focussing on the organization, rather than the external business environment. Aside from a need to be aware of the external environment, the manager must also know the internal business environment – managers need to understand the strengths and weaknesses of their organizations; they need to leverage resources. In order to do this they must know what they are and how they contribute to value creation and goal attainment.

REFERENCES

Barney, J. and Hesterly, W. (2009) 'Strategic Management and Competitive Advantage:International Edition', Ed. 3. Prentice Hall.

Barney, J. (1996) 'The Resource-based Theory of the Firm', Organization Science, Sep/Oct 96, Vol. 7 Issue 5, p. 469.

Day, G. S. and Wensley, R. (1988) 'Assessing Advantage: A Framework for Diagnosing Competitive Superiority', Journal of Marketing, Vol. 52, No. 2. (Apr., 1988), p. 1–20.

Grant, R. (1991) 'The Resource-Based Theory of Competitive Advantage: Implications for Strategy Formulation', California Management Review, Spring 91, Vol. 33 Issue 3, p. 114–135.

Grant, R. (2007) 'Contemporary Strategy Analysis', Ed. 6. Blackwell Publishing.

Johnson, G., Scholes, K. and Whittington, R. (2006) 'Exploring Corporate Strategy Enhanced Media Edition', FT Prentice Hall.

Mintzberg, H. (1987) 'The Strategy Concept I: Five Ps For Strategy', California Management Review, 30/1 (Fall 1987), p. 11–24.

Penrose, E. G. The Theory of the Growth of the Firm, Wiley New York, (1959).

Porter, M. E. and Millar, V. E. (1985) 'How information gives you a competitive advantage', Harvard Business Review, July-August 63, p. 149–174.

Porter, M. E. (1996) 'What Is Strategy?, Harvard Business Review, Vol. 74 Issue 6, p. 61–78.

Porter, M. E. (2001) 'Strategy and the Internet', Harvard Business Review, March 2001, p. 62–78.

Stalk, G. (1988) 'Time – The Next Source of Competitive Advantage', Harvard Business Review, Jul/Aug 88, Vol. 66 Issue 4, p. 41–51.

Wernerfelt, B. (1984) 'A Resource-based View of the Firm', Strategic Management Journal, Apr–Jun 84, Vol. 5 Issue 2, p. 171–180.

CHAPTER 17
OBJECTIVES, POLICIES AND ORGANIZATIONAL ETHICS

Key Concepts

- Business ethics
- Business model
- Business plan
- Corporate social responsibility
- Objectives
- Policy
- SWOT analysis

Learning Outcomes
Having read this chapter, you should be able to:

- discuss the role of corporate objectives in strategy and management planning
- review the role of policy in strategy implementation
- identify and discuss the application of ethics to managerial decision making and business conduct
- explain what is meant by corporate social responsibility and the reasons organizations pursue CSR strategies
- appraise how organizations create business plans
- apply the SWOT framework to support strategy

Strategic management process
A sequential set of analyses that can increase the likelihood of a firm's choosing a strategy that generates competitive advantages

1. One way of looking at **strategic management** is from the perspective of corporate planning. This has been described variously as a technique, a style of management or a **process**. It is probably best to think of it as a process which enables an organization to identify the following:

– what it is there for, and its principal objectives

– its current strengths and weaknesses

– what opportunities and threats are posed by its external environment

– the basis of its long-term plans (resourcing etc.)

– the context of its short-term plans (annual budgets/rolling plans etc.)

– the key performance standards it seeks to achieve

– what rules of conduct/ethical principles it is prepared to support.

Objectives Objectives are statements of specific outcomes that are to be achieved

Business plan A document that summarizes how an entrepreneur will organize a firm to exploit an opportunity, along with the economic implications of exploiting that opportunity

Corporate governance The system used to control and direct a company's operations

2. Planning, as was noted in the introduction to this section, involves decisions about ends (**objectives**) as well as means, and decisions about conduct as well as results. This chapter is about translating the organizational purpose into action and the associated need to define expectations of outcome and the behaviours used to attain such outcomes. There are many concepts and tools used to affect employee behaviour. There are informal mechanisms such as culture and more formal mechanisms such as objectives, policy and codes of conduct (ethics). Whilst the **business plan**, with the mission and objectives may define 'what' needs to be done, the aforementioned mechanisms guide 'how' employees and the organization will conduct themselves in attaining their goals and fulfilling their purpose. Mechanisms discussed in Chapter 12, such as **corporate governance**, help assure that the conduct of the organization is controlled and regulated. Further control mechanisms are discussed in the final chapters of this part of the book.

3. The chapter outlines the process of corporate planning, and aims to show the relationship between corporate objectives, policies and ethical statements and operating plans, as illustrated in diagrammatic form in Figure 17.1.

17.1 CORPORATE OBJECTIVES

4. Objectives, introduced in the previous chapter, are statements of specific outcomes that are to be achieved. They exist at many levels within the organization: corporate (goals of the organization) and strategic, tactical and operational. For simplicity we will assume strategic objectives to be similar to corporate objectives. Corporate objectives tend to be longer lasting and more general. Objectives tend to be more generalistic at the corporate level, becoming more specific toward the operational level. SMART objectives are objectives that are specific, measurable, attainable, realistic and time bounded.

FIGURE 17.1 An outline of corporate planning.

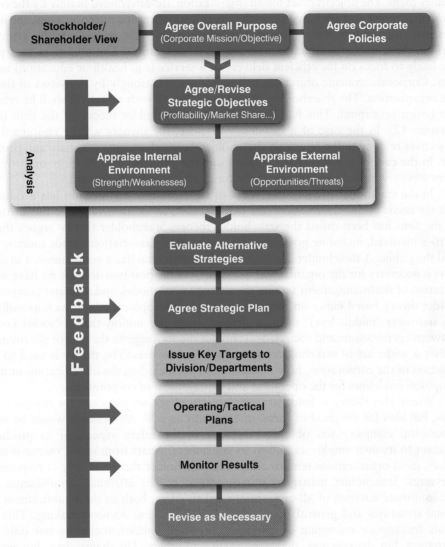

5.   A major part of corporate planning is the business of setting corporate objectives. Such objectives are usually of two kinds – those that state the overall objective or purpose of the organization – its mission – and those that set out the organization's long-term strategic aims. An example of an overall purpose for a business organization could be 'to grow a successful business for the benefit of customers, employees, shareholders, suppliers and the community in which the company operates'. A similar example for a public service could be 'to provide an efficient, responsive and considerate revenue collection service for the state'. Overall objectives tend to be stated in general terms, and are intended to be relatively permanent. The clarification and definition of key objectives is vital for any organization since objectives provide it with a sense of direction and a mission. The primary purpose of objectives is to align, coordinate, guide and motivate employee action. Refer back to Chapter 6 where we discussed the powerful role of goals (goal setting theory) in motivation.

6.   So far we have outlined what objectives are and why we have them. We now consider who creates them. The objectives set for an organization are determined mainly by the owners or senior management and are based upon the organization's prime purpose. Thus, the objectives of a business organization will be based around concepts such as profitability, growth, customer service, share-holder satisfaction and employee motivation. The objectives of a public service are likely to focus on the efficient delivery of a service (e.g. health or education) to the community. Corporate/strategic objectives will be influenced strongly by the views of the directors of the organization. The shareholders may decide that all such objectives shall be related firmly to the return on capital. This has been called the shareholder theory of the firm (refer back to Chapter 12). In the case of a business enterprise, the owners will be concerned with setting objectives relating to the return on shareholders' capital, earning per share and profit, for example. In the case of a state-owned corporation, the emphasis will be more on providing an efficient service within the limitations of the funds allocated by Parliament.

7.   In the traditional (shareholder) view of the firm, the organization has a fiduciary duty to put the needs of the shareholders (the owners) first, to increase value for them. Another theory of the firm has been called the stakeholder theory. Stakeholder theory argues there are other parties involved, including governmental bodies, trade associations, trade unions, communities and the public. A stakeholder is a member of a group who has a vested interest in or whose support is necessary for the organization to exist. Over the past two decades we have seen a gradual rejection of the 'management serving the shareowners' model, and a greater acceptance of stakeholder theory based either on broad theories of philosophical ethics, such as utilitarianism, or on narrower 'middle-level' theories derived from the notion that a 'social contract' exists between corporations and society. Stakeholder theory suggests the role of the organization is to satisfy a wider set of stakeholders, not simply the owners. The theory is used to interpret the function of the corporation, how things should be, including the identification of moral or philosophical guidelines for the operation and management of corporations.

8.   Where this theory is held, strategic objectives are set not only for the good of the business, but also for the good of these other groups as well. An example would be where a pharmaceutical company sets objectives relating to the safety aspects of its products, both in relation to its own employees and to its consumers. Apart from small, owner-managed, enterprises, most organizations tend to adopt the stakeholder theory, if only in response to external pressures. Stakeholder management requires, as its key attribute, simultaneous attention to the legitimate interests of all appropriate stakeholders, both in the establishment of organizational structures and general policies and in case-by-case decision making. This requirement holds for anyone managing or affecting corporate policies, including not only professional managers, but shareowners, the government and others. The theory does, however, not imply that all stakeholders (however they may be identified) should be equally involved in all processes and decisions.

17.2 POLICIES

9.   Once an organization has established its corporate objectives, it can begin to say in what manner it intends these to be achieved. Policy statements are made to indicate to those concerned just what the organization will, and will not, do in pursuance of its overall purpose and objectives – it frames the objectives. Such statements are one expression of the organization's culture and belief system. Policies are not the same as objectives or plans, even though they are frequently confused with them. Objectives state an aim or goal, i.e. they are ends; plans provide a framework within which action can take place to attain objectives, i.e. they are means; policies, on the other hand, are neither ends nor means, they are statements of conduct – principles designed to influence decisions and actions. Policies cause managers to take action in a certain

way; they are not actions in themselves. Policies both reflect and contribute to the organization culture. Examples of different kinds of policies are as follows:

- All overseas travel must be requested using the official company 'travel authorization form', signed by the appropriate department manager (travel policy).

- Job applicants or existing members of staff are treated fairly in an environment which is free from any form of discrimination, on the grounds of gender, race, ethnic or national origin, nationality or colour, marital status, civil partnership, disability, part-time, caring responsibilities, gender reassignment, sexual orientation, religion or belief, age, membership or non membership of a trade union or spent convictions (equality and diversity policy).

- Everyone has a responsibility to ensure they take reasonable care of their own health and safety and the safety of others. It is essential that managers and their people seek to work in ways where safe behaviour is seen as normal and unsafe acts are not acceptable (health and safety).

- Customer care will be provided in a professional manner across the company by well trained and knowledgeable staff.

- It is our policy to achieve for all our operations, best practice in our standards of business integrity. This includes a commitment to maintaining the highest standards of corporate governance and ethics.

10. Some of the above policies state what the organization will do and some state what it will positively not do. Some policies relate to marketing issues, others relate much more to ethical and philosophical issues. The variety can be considerable, but the intention is the same: to guide the organization's managers in the conduct of its affairs. Policies are typically disseminated through official written documents. They are formal and seek to assure consistency and standardization, to guide employee behaviour. To that end, they are essentially aspects of a bureaucratic system of management (see Chapter 4).

11. **Policy** documents typically contain standard components including a purpose statement (why the organization is issuing the policy, and what the desired effect or outcome of the policy should be); an applicability and scope statement (describing who the policy affects and which actions are impacted by the policy); an effective date; a responsibilities section (indicating which parties and organizations are responsible for carrying out individual policy statements) and policy statements which indicate the specific regulations, requirements or modifications to organizational behaviour that the policy is creating. Some policies may contain additional sections, including a background section that may point out the reasons and intent (motivating factors) that led to the creation of the policy. This information is often helpful when policies must be evaluated or used in ambiguous situations. Finally, definitions, for terms and concepts may also be found in the policy document. Typically accompanying the creation of policies is the need to establish new roles and responsibilities and allocate resources to assure action and policy conformance.

> **Policy** A guiding principle designed to influence decisions, actions, etc.

17.3 ETHICS

12. When seeking to fulfil objectives, aside from considering policy, employees might ask, 'what is acceptable business practice?' they may answer with a view from the organization, their own or a range of stakeholder perspectives. Ethics (see also morals and morality) considers what is right and wrong and **business ethics** concerns the accepted principles (beliefs and values) of right or

> **Business ethics** The accepted principles (beliefs and values) of right or wrong governing the conduct of business people

wrong governing the conduct of business people. Ethical principles can be used by individuals to make choices which guide their behaviour. Unethical behaviour can cost a company its reputation and its customers and therefore revenues and hard cash; it can also result in a loss of investors and may lead to a reduction in share price. Furthermore, employees do not like working for unethical companies and suppliers and other value-system players do not like to do business with such companies. If loss of revenue were not incentive enough, corporate wrong doings may be dealt with in the courts with directors, employees or the organization receiving punishment. It is no longer sufficient for organizations to simply follow a profit only goal and recognize investors as the only stakeholders who matter.

13.   The principal aspects of a business likely to produce moral dilemmas include:

-    the way certain activities or decisions are reported in the annual accounts

-    the gaining of sales contracts in highly competitive markets, where inducements or trade offs may be suggested (bribery and corruption)

-    the acquisition of competitors' plans, designs and other critical information by underhand means (industrial espionage)

-    the deliberate suppression of facts that might compromise the safety or effectiveness of a product.

14.   Other ethical issues may arise from the exploitation of women or child labour either directly, or by suppliers. Multinational enterprises, in particular, may have to confront local practices involving vulnerable groups working long hours for low wages. There are also many environmental matters that can be directly influenced for good or worse by business corporations. The world is increasingly endangered by pollution, destruction of rainforests and other ecosystems and the problem of global warming. The boards of large enterprises can contribute positively to alleviating such problems by minimizing pollution, reducing waste and developing eco-friendly methods of production. In some cases they are encouraged to act positively by national laws and international agreements, but where no such laws or agreements exist, the responsibility for creating a healthier environment lies with the leaders of such enterprises and the ethical standards they adhere to.

15.   Over time, a variety of general principles have been proposed to describe what is meant by ethical behaviour. Individuals should keep promises (fidelity), be fair (justice), not harm others, put right any wrong caused (reparation), show gratitude to others and improve the lives of one's self and others (beneficence). Other principles include fiduciary obligations (not putting self-interest above the overall interests of the organization), reliability (fulfilling promises), transparency (open and honest), dignity (respect others), fairness (not taking bribes or colluding with others), citizenship (respecting the law and the environment), responsiveness and respecting property. When people and organizations adhere to a moral code, they are said to have integrity. As integrity is eroded, unethical and illegal behaviour follows.

16.   Managing the organization ethically may mean following laws and regulations, ensuring equal opportunity or dealing with social responsibility issues. In many cases it is about ensuring ethical decision-making and resultant action. In order to do this, the organization must ensure employees understand ethical and moral values and can use this understanding to make sense of business problems. In considering options for action, the organization needs its employees to show good ethical judgement, being able to evaluate different options and determine which are more acceptable, based on the moral values and beliefs of the decision-makers and the organization as a whole.

Code of ethics A set of ethical behaviour rules developed by organizations or by professional societies.

17.   The organization may create and adopt a number of statements to communicate the corporation's view on the subject of ethics. A code of ethics is a written document that states explicitly what constitutes acceptable and unacceptable behaviour for all employees in the organization. Common issues in business ethics to be included are accountability (transparency and reporting),

business conduct (compliance with the law, competitive conduct, corruption and bribery, conflicts of interest), community involvement (community economic development and employment of locals), corporate governance (investor rights), environment (policy, code of conduct and management systems to protect the environment), human rights (health and safety, child labour, forced labour, freedom of association, working hours, wages and benefits), consumer protection (marketing, product quality and safety, consumer privacy) and labour (workplace/employee) relations.

18.   The existence of a code of practice in ethics, supported by senior management and made a natural feature of a company's culture, will enable better distinctions to be made between what is acceptable business practice and what is sharp practice. It has often been said that leadership by example is the most effective way to improve business ethics. Leaders must therefore be honest and trustworthy with high integrity. To be perceived as an ethical leader, it is not enough to just be an ethical person. An executive ethical leader must also find ways to focus the organization's attention on ethics and values and to infuse the organization with principles that will guide the actions of all employees.

17.4 CORPORATE SOCIAL RESPONSIBILITY (CSR)

19.   One important area for policy development we shall now consider is that of 'social responsibility'. Being 'socially responsible' implies playing more than just an economic role in society. Corporate social responsibility (CSR) is a concept whereby organizations consider the interests of society by taking responsibility for the impact of their activities on customers, suppliers, employees, shareholders, communities and the environment in every aspect of their operations and decision-making; it is about good business citizenship.

Corporate social responsibility A concept whereby organizations consider the interests of society by taking responsibility for the impact of their activities on all stakeholders, including the environment

20.   Central to the CSR approach is that the organization should use resources responsibly (sustainable, no waste, to produce the goods and services for society in a profitable manner) and should comply with relevant laws and regulations. In addition to the moral issue, there are many arguments in favour of CSR. A CSR programme can be seen as an aid to recruitment and retention, particularly within the competitive graduate student market. Reputations and brands that take time and resources to build up can be ruined in hours through unethical decisions manifest in incidents such as corruption scandals or environmental accidents. These events can also draw unwanted attention from regulators, courts, governments and media. Building an ethical culture of 'doing the right thing' can offset these risks. Furthermore, by taking voluntary action, organizations can persuade governments and the wider public that they are taking issues such as health and safety, employee relations or the environment seriously, and so avoid intervention.

21.   What does it mean for a corporation to be socially responsible? The main components are legal – they obey the law; ethical – they do the right thing (see previous section); efficiency and profitable – they use resources efficiently and finally such companies show good judgement, they are charitable and philanthropic. Four key arguments have been offered to encourage organizations to act in a socially responsible manner: (1) MORAL OBLIGATION – companies have a duty to be good citizens and to 'do the right thing'; they should achieve commercial success in ways that honour ethical values and respect people, communities, and the natural environment; (2) SUSTAINABILITY – emphasizes the environment by meeting the needs of the present without compromising the ability of future generations to meet their own needs; (3) LICENSE TO OPERATE – every company needs tacit or explicit permission from governments, communities and numerous other stakeholders to do business, and (4) REPUTATION – through this argument, attempts are made to justify CSR initiatives on the grounds they will improve a company's image, strengthen its brand, boost morale and even raise the value of its stock.

17.5 BUSINESS PLANS

22.   In Figure 17.1 we outlined corporate planning and have, so far, discussed the definition of overall organization purpose with reference to the shareholder and stakeholder view and policies to assure employees behave in a desirable manner to attain goals. In the previous chapter we also discussed the corporate mission and strategic management. Business planning – the theme of this section – follows on from the setting of the organization's key objectives and policies. Plans essentially state how the organization intends to move forward over a given period, usually between one and five years. At the head of such planning the strategic or corporate plan is created which identifies the direction the organization is to take over the next two to five years, or in some cases up to ten years, and the resources to be deployed to ensure that the plan is implemented. The resources are generally expressed in financial terms sufficient to cover anticipated expenditure on people, buildings, machinery, etc. Because of the number of variables at work in the external environment, most business organizations tend to work on a rolling three to five year plan basis, in which only the next year's budgets are expressed in detailed terms, and the remaining years are set out in flexible terms, allowing for a range of unexpected contingencies.

23.   In order to decide which product-market, competitive and other strategies to adopt, business organizations have to consider two major questions: (1) what is the organization's current performance, especially in terms of its major strengths and weaknesses? And (2) what factors in

SWOT analysis Summarizes the key issues from the business environment and the strategic capability of an organization both of which are most likely to impact upon strategy development

the external environment might affect the organization's proposed plans for the future? One way of assessing the evidence for these two questions is to conduct what has been called a 'SWOT analysis'. This is essentially a review of the organization's major internal strengths and weaknesses, together with an assessment of those opportunities and threats in the external environment which are likely to make an impact on strategic choices. In the following paragraphs we want to build upon the discussion on analyzing the environment presented in the previous chapter. Evaluating a firm's environment is an essential activity in the planning process (see Figure 17.1), following which, alternative strategies can be considered, choices made and articulated in the agreed plan – a document that summarizes how a firm will be organized to exploit opportunity.

24.   A SWOT analysis summarizes the key issues from the business environment and the strategic capability of an organization both of which are most likely to impact upon strategy and the development of plans to attain corporate objectives. A simple SWOT analysis based on a typical UK supermarket chain is illustrated in Figure 17.2. Current internal performance is usually assessed in terms of key performance ratios, such as sales turnover, net profit, output per head and other ratios (see Chapter 28). In a SWOT analysis, however, managers will be encouraged to make qualitative judgements about performance, based on their assessment of customer satisfaction (e.g. as in the supermarket example above), and other key issues such as employee motivation, workflow processes, impact of on-the-job learning and other non-quantifiable elements in the total performance of the organization.

25.   The appraisal of the external environment follows a similar approach, except that here the two headings employed are opportunities and threats. In this case, the organization's planners are assessing the likely impact on organizational objectives of technological, economic, political and social trends (see the PESTLE framework introduced in Chapter 15), together with the activities of competitors (see Porter's five forces framework). Taking the last-mentioned factor first – the competition – this is always a potential threat to a supermarket chain, which is operating in a highly competitive marketplace, and is vulnerable to price-cutting and novel in-store developments which it might find hard to match. To take another example, supposing a firm has been first in the field with a mass-production light-weight battery car for urban use, what opportunities does this lead give them and what threats might be posed by other manufacturers?

FIGURE 17.2 SWOT analysis for a major supermarket chain.

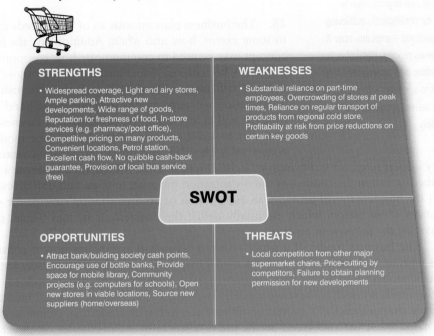

One opportunity might be to offer competitors the possibility of producing the vehicle under licence; another might be to seek some joint production and marketing facility. A major threat could be the manufacture of cheaper varieties of such a car by overseas competitors with lower labour costs and/or the benefits of improved production technology. Another example, taking economic trends into consideration, could be the opportunities and threats posed by an organization's dependence on oil. In this situation there might be no opportunities other than seeking alternative forms of energy, whereas the threats could be fundamental to the future existence, let alone growth, of the organization.

26.   The next step following a SWOT analysis is to develop a list of alternative corporate strategies which will form the basis for the final corporate plan. Such strategies, outlined in the previous chapter, point the direction in which an organization is to move over the medium to long term. Tactical and operational plans can then be created and will be heavily influenced by the overall plan. Examples of operational plans include marketing, production and human resource plans. This leads us on to one of the final stages of corporate planning: the issue of key targets in a year-on-year format to the various departments and divisions of the organization. Some targets may be expressed in budget form, indicating, for example, sales revenue, direct and indirect costs and trading profit. Others may be expressed in alternative measures of performance, such as output per employee, percentage utilization of machines, percentage increase in market share or costs as a percentage of sales. Once targets have been set, they are monitored and revised as necessary. If revisions are made, the whole plan is rolled forward as a consequence. Thus the long-term perspective is maintained, but the entire plan is kept up-to-date.

27.   The value of the business plan has been called into question, particularly in smaller entrepreneurial firms. On the one hand it can be argued that they help provide focus, communicate goals, and intentions (therefore motivate action) and force managers to be explicit about assumptions (which can be critically analyzed by others) yet on the other hand they may stifle creativity, provide an illusion of control and take time and company resources to complete. Business plans are also considered later in Chapter 52.

17.6 BUSINESS MODELS

Business model The organization's essential logic for consistently achieving its principle objectives – explains how it consistently makes money, highlights the distinctive activities and approaches that enable the firm to succeed – to attract customers and deliver products and services profitably

28. The business plan informs us of what needs to be done and, to some extent, how and when. Additionally, the business model concept may be used to communicate how corporate and strategic goals may be achieved. Most business models show how the organization will meet customer needs (value proposition); how the organization will earn money (revenue model) and how the organization will compete and be structured. A business model refers primarily to value creation whereas a revenue model is primarily concerned with value appropriation. Leading writers on strategy vary in their reference to business models. Thompson and Martin (2005) devote a whole chapter to the concept in the context of the organization purpose, mission and objectives. They suggest that the business model provides an explanation of an organization's recipe for success, and it contains those factors which essentially define the business. It is, they argue, the vehicle for delivering the purpose or mission.

29. The business model of a profit-oriented organization explains how it consistently generates revenue and profit. The business model may be described more precisely with attention to specific model components. The components of a business model may include (1) pricing model (e.g. no-frills service); (2) revenue model; (3) channel model (the traditional bricks 'n' mortar as a single channel, clicks 'n' mortar combining the web with traditional channels, clicks only as a .com and other variants based on the use or absence of intermediaries i.e. direct-to-customer), (4) commerce process model (e.g. auction); (5) organizational form (stand-alone business unit, integrated internet capability) and (6) value proposition (less value and very low cost, more value at the same cost, much more value at greater cost).

CONCLUSION

30. Business planning at the corporate/strategic level is a continuing process by which the long-term objectives of an organization may be formulated, and subsequently attained, by means of long-term strategic actions designed to make their impact on the organization as a whole. Corporate planning also involves deciding the policies, or code of conduct, of the organization in pursuit of its objectives. Thus business aims and ethical considerations are brought together. The typical planning process adopts a contingency perspective and is based upon analysis of the environment. However, the process is not entirely mechanical and rational/economic and there is plenty of scope for choices to be made that are influenced by the values and beliefs of managers and other stakeholders.

QUESTIONS

1   Review the role of policy in strategy implementation.

2   Explain what is meant by corporate social responsibility and the reasons organizations pursue CSR strategies.

3   Summarize the key issues from the Montblanc business environment and present a SWOT analysis

4   Evaluate the Montblanc business model.

USEFUL WEBSITES

The Centre for Ethics and Business: **cba.lmu.edu/ academicprograms/centers/ethicsandbusiness.htm** Provides an environment for discussing issues related to the necessity, difficulty, costs and rewards of conducting business ethically

Institute of Business Ethics: **www.ibe.org.uk/** Raise public awareness of the importance of doing business ethically

VIDEO CASES

Now take a look at the online video cases – visit the companion website to work through real world business problems associated with the concepts presented within this chapter.

2 CSR – energy with a large carbon footprint

As oil prices continue to reach record highs, the search for new sources of energy has led the world to Alberta, Canada and its vast oil sands. Canada finds itself caught between fuelling the world's oil-hungry economy and ecological devastation (the future of northern Alberta's aspen and pine woods, its rivers and animals are in doubt) and soaring greenhouse gas produced emissions by exploiting the tar sands. A decade ago, a fairly minor and barely profitable sand oil industry was prevalent alongside the vast landscape of forests and lakes around Fort McMurray and the Athabasca River. This area is now pitted with hundreds of square kilometres of toxic waste ponds, mines that are 300ft deep, hundreds of miles of pipes and burgeoning petrochemical works.

Shell, Chevron, Exxon, Total, Occidental, Imperial and most other oil majors had (by 2008) invested over $100bn Canadian dollars (£50bn) in the 1,160 square mile (3,000 square kilometre) 'bitumen belt', referred to as the 'new Kuwait'. Conventional oil production involves drilling into rock to find reservoirs. Since the oil is in liquid form, it is relatively easy to force to the surface. However, extraction from oil sands is more difficult, and results in a much larger carbon footprint. The greater energy needed to produce a barrel of

oil from the sands results in three times more greenhouse gas emissions than that produced from a barrel of conventional oil. Greater energy is required firstly because the oil has to be dug out and then separated from the sand, and secondly because it is low grade and must be heavily refined.

30 Corporate ethics: winning back public trust

Why business ethics and corporate social responsibility matter. A focus on the role of trust in business. Why should the international organization worry about how business is conducted, ethics, integrity and doing the right thing? In recent times we have witnessed environmental issues gaining prominence, financial mismanagement, the use of child labour and exploitation of workers, unsafe work practices, excessive surveillance, breaches of privacy, intellectual property theft and many other events leading to the erosion of confidence in corporations. Whereas unethical behaviour may result in a loss of confidence, trust and business, ethical and responsible behaviour can

78 The external environment – leading change: a conversation with Ron Williams

Considers the EXTERNAL MACRO ENVIRONMENT and the INDUSTRY (MICRO) ENVIRONMENT for the health insurance industry. Enables students to practice PESTLE, Five Forces and SWOT analysis.

90 Strategic objectives at Montblanc

Strategies are means to ends-the ends are defined in terms of vision, mission and objectives; they define the purpose and direction for the organization and are discussed in this case study. The business model describes the strategy of how the organization will achieve its purpose. Whilst profit maximization will be a goal at the heart of many commercial organizations, other objectives exist and will be explored in brief. This case study focuses on a single organization. Montblanc has been known for generations as a maker of sophisticated, high quality writing instruments. In the past few years, the product range has been expanded to include exquisite writing accessories, luxury leather goods and belts, jewellery, eyewear and watches. Montblanc has developed into what has been termed a lifestyle brand, encompassing a range of products associated with a well-to-do manner of living. The company has changed dramatically from what it was.

94 Strategic objectives – the purpose of business

One common view of business makes a sharp distinction between making money and doing good in society. This is a 'limited and distorted' perspective, according to John Browne. Business that focuses just on money doesn't invest in the future – in its employees, new ideas, markets or products – and won't be around for long. Any successful business is part of society, says Browne, 'and exists to meet society's needs'.

99 Perspectives on strategy – turning AOL around

Charts the downfall of AOL and the attempts to turn it around by a new CEO in 2009. Focuses on strategy and the mission. What the new CEO did in the first 100 days.

102 The internal environment – THE STARTING POINT FOR STRATEGY FORMULATION

Business success can be realized by focussing on the organization, rather than the external business environment. Aside from a need to be aware of the external environment, the manager must also know the internal business environment – managers need to understand the strengths ad weaknesses of their organizations; they need to leverage resources. In order to do this they must know what they are and how they contribute to value creation and goal attainment.

REFERENCES

Barney, J. and Hesterly, W. (2009) 'Strategic Management and Competitive Advantage:International Edition', Ed. 3. Prentice Hall.

Fisher, C. and Lovell, A. (2009) 'Business Ethics and Values: Individual, Corporate and International Perspectives', Ed. 3. FT Prentice Hall – Pearson education Limited, Harlow England.

Grayson, D. (2001) 'Everybody's Business', Financial Times/ Dorling Kindersley.

Johnson, G., Scholes, K. and Whittington, R. (2006) 'Exploring Corporate Strategy Enhanced Media Edition', FT Prentice Hall.

Rees, W. and Porter, C. (2008) 'Skills of Management', Ed. 6. Cengage Learning EMEA.

Thompson, J. L. and Martin, F. (2005) 'Strategic Management', Ed. 5. Cengage Learning EMEA.

CHAPTER 18
PERFORMANCE STANDARDS IN MANAGEMENT

1. In the previous chapter we discussed corporate and strategic planning. What is needed now are mechanisms to ensure that strategy cascades down the organization and leads to action. Johnson, Scholes and Whittington (2006) discuss converting strategy into action and the relationship between overall business strategy and strategies in resource areas such as people, information and technology. They discuss strategy and people and the ways in which human resource activities can help enable the strategy. In particular they recognize the important role of goal setting and performance management (p. 449). The importance of people as a source of sustainable competitive advantage (refer back to RBV) is widely acknowledged. A conscious effort must be made to link the corporate/strategic plan with individual performance. Aguinis (2009) argues that the mere presence of a strategic plan does not guarantee that this information will be used effectively as part of the performance management system.

2. Once organizational strategies and objectives have been defined, unit level managers, in conjunction with senior management, create unit level objectives and plans which ultimately influence team and individual performance expectations and job descriptions; the behaviour, results and developmental plans of all employees must be aligned with the vision, mission, goals and strategies of the organization and the unit for which they work.

18.1 PERFORMANCE MANAGEMENT

Performance Management Any system for improving management effectiveness by means of standard-setting, appraisal and evaluation; combines informal day-to-day aspects with formal appraisal interviews and goal-setting

3. **Performance management** is a continuous process of identifying, measuring and developing the performance of individuals and teams and aligning performance with the strategic goals of the organization, Aguinis (2009). It ensures that employee activities and outputs are congruent with the organization's goals. Performance management systems usually measure both employee behaviours and the outcomes of such behaviour. We will consider the measurement of results and behaviours towards the end of this brief chapter.

4. The performance management system has several purposes: it may be used to help senior management achieve strategic business objectives, encourage behaviours consistent with the attainment of organizational goals; make decisions about employee compensation (interlinked with the reward system); it is a communication device to set goals, provide feedback and drive action, identifying training needs, etc.

18.2 PERFORMANCE MANAGEMENT SYSTEMS AND PROCESS

5. Performance management systems should be congruent with strategy and provide information that allows for the identification of effective and ineffective performance; the measures of performance should be valid, consistent and reliable and the system perceived as fair by all participants. A good system is operated transparently and in a consistent manner. The performance management system is typically integrated with other HR systems such as training (Chapter 44); performance appraisal and compensation systems (Chapter 45); competency development (Chapter 46) and may also be used in conjunction with wider aspects of human resource management. Not only does the system provide information for these dependent systems but the performance management system itself is dependent on job evaluation (Chapter 48) and the corporate or strategic planning process (see previous chapter).

6. The performance management process is made of several key activities: planning (determining what needs to be done, objectives and required behaviours/competences), execution (employee undertakes the work), assessment (evaluating the extent to which the desired behaviours have been displayed and results achieved), review (appraisal) and is a continuous process. It is dependent on both strategic goals (and those cascaded downward as departmental and individual objectives) and the specific job in question-the key components identified through job analysis. Job analysis is used to identify the knowledge, skills and abilities required for a particular job/role. These are typically represented in the form of a job description.

Job analysis The process of job analysis is that of gathering and analyzing job-related information. This includes details about tasks to be performed as part of a job and the personal qualities required to do so. Job analysis can provide information for a variety of purposes including: determining training needs, development criteria, appropriate pay and productivity improvements. For resourcing purposes, job analysis can generate job and personnel specifications.

18.3 IMPLEMENTATION – MEASURING RESULTS AND BEHAVIOURS

7. In measuring employee results, the organization typically identifies the areas where an employee is accountable, then sets objectives (measurable outcomes) and performance standards (acceptable performance). An emphasis on objectives and standards should allow employees to translate organizational goals into individual goals. This is a key aspiration of management by objectives (MBO) discussed next in more detail. A behavioural approach to measuring performance includes the assessment of competences – measurable clusters of knowledge, skills and abilities; we explore the competency approach in the final part of this chapter.

Performance standard An expected level of performance against which actual performance can be compared

Management by objectives (MBO) An approach to management which aims to integrate the organization's objectives with those of individuals; it involves the reduction of overall objectives into unit and individual objectives; in the UK the approach is associated with John Humble. (See also Key Result Area)

18.4 MEASURING RESULTS – MANAGEMENT BY OBJECTIVES (MBO)

8. Accountabilities are determined from the job description and are based on the requirements of the individual's job. For example, where the jobholder manages a team there may be team-building, coaching or supervisory accountabilities. After the accountabilities have been identified, the next stage is to determine the specific objectives. Typically these will be specific, measurable, achievable, results based and time specific (SMART, see previous chapter). For example, the jobholder may have an objective to deliver team training sessions throughout the year. Having developed objectives, the next step is to define performance standards. When managing performance, we need to determine how well the objectives were achieved (quality), how much was produced (quantity) and whether deadlines were met; ideally standards will include an action, the desired result, a due date and some type of quality or quantity indicator. They describe satisfactory performance. Standards should be specific and measurable, meaningful, realistic and achievable and will be reviewed regularly.

9. MBO is a means of integrating organizational goals, such as profit and growth, with the needs of individual managers to contribute to the organization and to their own self-development. A system of management by objectives, therefore, seeks to achieve a sense of common purpose and common direction amongst the management of an organization in the fulfilment of business results. The most important features of MBO are as follows: it focuses on results (system outputs) rather than on activity (system processes); it develops logically from the corporate planning process by translating corporate and departmental objectives into individual managerial objectives and it seeks to improve management performance.

10. The link between corporate objectives and the strategic plan was shown in the previous chapter (Figure 17.1). The link between the strategic plan and a system of MBO, together with the respective time-spans, can be shown as in Figure 18.1. The diagram demonstrates how objectives at the front-line of the organization's operations flow logically from the overall strategic plan for the organization. In systems terms the MBO activities are a key part of the conversion processes of the organization. Linked as it is with the strategic plan of the organization, MBO can only be operated successfully with senior management approval and support. The Key Results referred to in Figure 18.1 are derived from an analysis of the individual manager's job, in which key result areas are identified and key tasks drawn up from them. These are worked out by agreement between the individual manager and his or her line manager. The resulting job description, unlike one that merely describes job activities, sets out the job in terms of its most vital, and potentially most productive, responsibilities. These are the responsibilities that produce the biggest returns for the job, and usually there are no more than eight or nine of these for a managerial position.

Key Result Area Term used especially in management by objectives; refers to those areas of a person's job that make the biggest impact on end results. (See also Management by Objectives)

FIGURE 18.1 The link between the strategic plan and a system of MBO.

11. It is from the key tasks that the short-term targets are developed (see Performance targets). These targets serve as the focus for immediate and short-term priorities in the job. Figure 18.2 sets out the format of a typical MBO-type of job description and gives some examples of the kind of information one could expect to find in it. Note that each key task has one or more performance standards against which it can be measured over a period of time (usually one year). These standards should express satisfactory performance and not necessarily ideal performance. They are usually expressed in terms of end-results and qualified in some

Performance targets Performance targets relate to the outputs of an organization (or part of an organization), such as product quality, prices or profit.

FIGURE 18.2 An MBO-type job description.

Job Title: Branch Manager (Retail Chain)   *Date:* Jan 2000

Reporting to: Area Manager

Own staff: 65 Full-time (incl. 12 Section Managers)
45 Part-time

Scope of Job: Annual Branch Revenue £x
Average Sales per sq. ft. £x

Overall Purpose of Job:
To achieve Revenue targets in accordance with Area budget
by providing and maintaining an attractive and reliable retail
service that meets customer needs in the locality.

Key Result Areas:

Key Tasks:	*Performance Standards*	*Control Data*
Prepare and gain acceptance for Branch revenue targets as contribution to Area budget	Target accepted without major amendments	Area Budget
Set recruitment levels and standards for guidance of subordinate managers etc. etc.	(a) Branch fully staffed throughout year	Weekly staff report
	(b) Staff turnover not to exceed 20% per annum	Area Personnel Figures

---

way, e.g. in respect of time, quality and quantity. The column for control data ensures that consideration is given to the evidence against which performance can be checked.

12.   One of the most attractive elements of MBO for senior management has been its emphasis on setting standards and specifying results for all managers at the operating level of the business. The performance standards, which are set as a measure of the degree of achievement of key tasks, are expressed in terms of quantity, where this is practical, or in terms of some agreed judgement of what could be reasonably expected, i.e. some qualitative measure. Examples of the two broad categories of measurement are as follows. (1) quantitative e.g. increase sales of product X by 20% in 12 months and (2) qualitative e.g. vacancies for branch manager posts to be filled by internal promotion.

13.   MBO allows for two types of review – Performance Review and Potential Review. The performance review is concerned with the individual managers' results in the key areas of their present job; the potential review is concerned with managers' anticipated abilities to succeed in their next job. This assumes, of course, that the organization concerned has a management development plan into which such a potential review can fit as part of management succession planning. For further information on the subject of management development, see Chapter 46. The principal stages of an MBO system can now be summarized, as shown in Figure 18.3.

FIGURE 18.3 **The MBO cycle.**

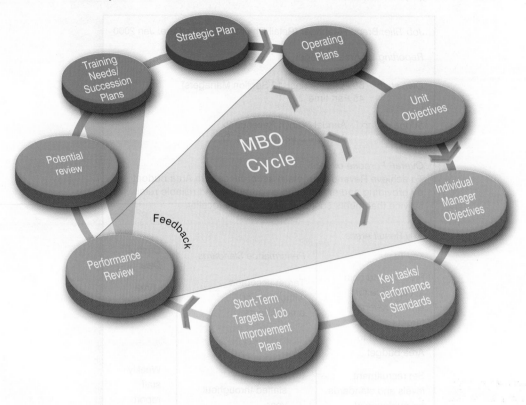

14.   The cycle of events demonstrates the links between the organization's strategic plan, the objectives and key tasks of individual managers, and the vital review of performance which provides important feedback for other parts of the system. The performance review provides feedback to the operating system (plans and objectives), and to the training and development system (training needs and succession plans). The potential review feeds back to the training and development system.

15.   Evaluating the MBO approach, Mullins (2010) acknowledges the MBO system is attractive with much to recommend it and that it has been adopted in a wide range of organizational settings. However, he questions its relevance today. MBO appears to have suffered a decline in popularity as it is difficult to specify and measure targets for some important aspects of work. Consequently, these areas may become neglected. Despite this, many present day methods are very similar to MBO in their approach and results. When results may be difficult to measure, the organization can measure behaviour as an alternative, a matter to which we next turn our attention.

18.5 MEASURING BEHAVIOURS – COMPETENCY MODELS OF MANAGEMENT

Competence Work related knowledge, skill or ability held by an individual

16.   A behavioural approach to measuring performance includes the assessment of competencies. A **competence** is an ability to perform activities within an occupation or function to the standards expected in employment. Indicators are used to confirm whether the competency is present or not. Whilst there has been some argument, even confusion, about the meaning that should be

ascribed to the word 'competence', it is generally agreed that it is concerned with a person's performance of a task. Thus, as a concept, it is closely related to the idea of 'skill', or, more precisely, 'skill at' performing some task. The expression 'competent', however, is more likely to be employed in a holistic way – to imply an individual's overall **capability** to undertake certain work rather than just their ability to perform certain aspects of their work to an acceptable standard. A term often used to describe the detailed aspects of an individual's job performance is 'competency' (i.e. this person has shown competency in so and so), and what is looked for in individuals is a range of 'competencies'. An indicator is a behaviour that, if displayed, suggests that the competency is present. Typically there may be several indicators for any given competency. **Core competences** can be evaluated comparatively (with reference to other employees) or absolutely (using rating scales etc.). Performance information is typically gathered by managers and their employees throughout the year and presented on appraisal forms. We will discuss performance appraisal in more detail in Chapter 45. The primary purpose of this chapter was to focus on strategy implementation through people.

> **Capability** The capacity for a team of resources to perform some task or activity

> **Core competence** Those capabilities fundamental to the organization's strategy and performance

18.6 EVALUATING PERFORMANCE MANAGEMENT

17.   Aguinis (2009:4) lists the many advantages associated with the implementation of a performance management system: motivation and self-esteem is increased (refer back to motivation theory), managers get to know their employees better, expectations are clearly articulated and managed; resultant actions (for example reward management) are deemed to be fairer; the organization's goals are clearly articulated in a manner relevant to the employee and such advantages not only aim to improve organizational performance but also aim to improve loyalty and commitment by employees.

18.   The benefits of the performance management system do not always materialize and it is possible to implement such systems badly resulting in negative consequences. When implemented inappropriately there is a danger of upsetting employees who may then leave the organization or become dissatisfied and demotivated. Important relationships with managers and others can be damaged and resources may be wasted whilst creating and maintaining the performance management system.

CONCLUSION

19.   This chapter builds on the previous chapter concerning corporate and strategic planning. In this chapter we highlighted mechanisms to ensure that strategy cascades down the organization and leads to action. In particular we focussed on the performance management system as a tool to align every manager and employee with the organization's goals thus ensuring effective and efficient behaviours and ultimately helping to assure that organizational goals are attained.

QUESTIONS

1   An organization is presently reviewing its systems for turning strategy into action. It has asked you to compare measuring results with behaviours as a part of the performance management process and to determine which method you prefer. You should explain your answer and consider different organizations and contexts (e.g. small with large organizations; bureaucratic with entrepreneurial,organizations operating within a turbulent environment compared with a more stable environment etc.).

2   Present an overview of the Montblanc strategy and then evaluate mechanisms that might be used to ensure that strategy cascaded down the organization leads to action.

USEFUL WEBSITES

People Management magazine: **www.peoplemanagement. co.uk/pm/subjects/performance-management/**
Performance management – This site is the online magazine for the CIPD
HRM Guide: **www.hrmguide.co.uk/performance/**
UK Performance Management Articles

CIPD: **www.cipd.co.uk/subjects/perfmangmt/general/ perfman.htm**
Performance management: an overview
Local Government Improvement and Development:
    www.idea.gov.uk/idk/core/page.do?pageId=76209
Performance management resources

VIDEO CASES

Now take a look at the online video cases – visit the companion website to work through real world business problems associated with the concepts presented within this chapter

100 Performance management
Human Resource Management (HRM): Discusses the purpose, process and content of performance management systems.

REFERENCES

Aguinis, H. (2009) 'Performance Management: International Edition', Ed. 2. Pearson Higher Education.
Johnson, G., Scholes, K. and Whittington, R. (2006) 'Exploring Corporate Strategy Enhanced Media Edition', FT Prentice Hall.

Mullins, L. (2010) 'Management and Organizational Behaviour', Ed. 9. Financial Times Press.

CHAPTER 19
DECISION-MAKING IN ORGANIZATIONS

Key Concepts

- Classical decision theory
- Decision
- Decision making

Learning Outcomes   Having read this chapter, you should be able to:

- examine how decisions may be made within organizations
- list the main types of decision made within organizations
- name three decision making tools

Decision making The process of making choices from among several options

1.   This book looks at management theory and practice. In some ways it is really about the art and science of management. Management may be described as science, art and craft. It is worth exploring such notions before turning our attention to decision making. One of the enduring questions in the field of management is whether it is an art or a science. An art is a 'skill in conducting any human activity' and science is 'any skill or technique that reflects a precise application of facts or a principle'. Management as a science would indicate that, in practice, managers use a specific body of knowledge (established tools, techniques and know-how) to guide their behaviours; management as an art requires no specific body of knowledge, only skill. Practising managers who believe in management as a science are likely to believe that there are ideal managerial practices for certain situations. When faced with a managerial problem, such a manager will expect that there is a rational and objective way to determine the correct course of action. They are likely to follow general principles and theories. Many early management researchers discussed in the first part of this book subscribed to the vision of managers as scientists. The scientific management movement, pioneered by Taylor, the Gilbreths and others, was the primary driver of this perspective. Managers considering management as an art (e.g. Mintzberg and Drucker) are likely to rely on their own knowledge of a situation, experiences and judgment, rather than generic rules, to determine a course of action. Today, much of the management research conducted in academic institutions blends the notion of management as an art and as a science.

Decisions Commitment of resources

2.   Decision-making is an accepted part of everyday human life. As individuals we may make decisions (choices/commitment of resources) on the spur of the moment or after much thought and deliberation, or at some point between these two extremes. Our decisions may be influenced by emotions, by reasoning or by a combination of both. As members of groups we may find ourselves making decisions on a group basis, where our own views and feelings have to be tested and argued with the other members. In organizations, people with managerial roles are expected, among other things, to make decisions as an important part of their responsibilities. Indeed Mintzberg felt that decision-making was possibly the most important of all of the managerial activities. Decisions can lead a company to success or failure.

3.   In this chapter we are concerned with managerial decision-making. That is to say we are concerned with behaviour that is designed to cause things to happen, or not to happen, as the case may be. Whilst it may be affected by feelings and interpersonal relationships, managerial decision-making tends to be rational in its approach. Considerable time and effort may be spent in assessing problems, developing alternative solutions and evaluating their consequences before arriving at an agreed decision. Certain types of decision-making can be made easier and faster by means of special techniques, some of which are briefly referred to later in the chapter.

19.1 DECISION PROCESSES: A THEORETICAL MODEL

Classical decision theory decision
A theory which assumes that decision-makers are objective, have complete information and consider all possible alternatives and their consequences before selecting the optimal solution

4.   An analysis of the way decisions are made in organizations results in the sequence of events shown in Figure 19.1.
This sequence indicates a rational (scientific) approach that can be applied to the business of reaching decisions in organizations (see also Classical decision theory). It commences by seeking to ask the right questions, continues by encouraging creative answers, and concludes by ensuring that the chosen solution is monitored and evaluated. There are several important issues raised by a model such as the one we have described. These can be summarized as follows:

–   The technical quality of the decision, i.e. doing the right thing has to be distinguished from the acceptability of the decision by the parties involved, i.e. doing things right.

FIGURE 19.1 **Decision model.**

- Both the development of alternatives and the selection of an optimum solution will be limited considerably by the organization's objectives and policies, and by the attitudes of managers and other employees.

- The assessment of the possible consequences of proposed solutions is a step that is frequently given insufficient attention.

- The model makes no allowance for the time factor. Clearly, however, it favours decision-making for the future rather than decision-making for immediate problems.

5.   We have already been introduced to this decision making model when discussing strategic planning. Strategic planning is effectively about decision making. The model will recur, slightly modified, in many functional aspects of business like choosing an information system (see the systems development lifecycle), creating a marketing plan and many other situations requiring choices.
6.   Whilst widely applied, the rational model, depicted in Figure 19.1, has a number of inherent weaknesses. For example, it is rarely possible to consider all alternatives since there are too many and some alternatives will not have occurred to the decision maker. It may be impractical to consider all consequences and accurate information may not be available; furthermore generated or purchased information has a cost. Consequently decisions are often made on incomplete, insufficient and only partially accurate information. Individual decision makers may lack the mental capacity to store and process all the information relevant to a decision and frequently lack the ability to perform the mental calculations required.
7.   Each decision made by an individual or group is affected by a number of factors. These include individual personality, group relationships, organizational power relationships and political behaviour, external environmental pressures, organization strategic considerations and information availability (or lack of). Bounded rationality refers to individuals making decisions by constructing simplified models which extract the essential features from problems without capturing all their complexity. With turbulent environments there is greater uncertainty and a lack of information available for decision-making. Consequently rational decision-making may be seen as more

Intuitive decision makers Cognitive style that describes people who approach a problem with multiple methods in an unstructured manner, using trial and error to find a solution

Semi structured decisions Decisions where only part of the problem has a clear-cut answer provided by an accepted procedure

Unstructured decisions Unstructured decisions tend to involve complex situations, where the rules governing the decision are complicated or unknown. Such decisions tend to be made infrequently and rely heavily on the experience, judgement and knowledge of the decision maker

Decision support system (DSS) A computer-based information system that combines models and data in an attempt to solve semi-structured problems with extensive user involvement

Structured decisions Decisions that are repetitive, routine and have a definite procedure for handling them

Strategic decision making Determining the long-term objectives, resources and policies of an organization

Decision tree A diagram showing the sequence of events, decisions and consequent actions that occur in a decision making process

appropriate in a stable environment whereas intuitive and subjective decision-making may dominate in turbulent environments.

19.2 TYPES OF DECISIONS

8.   Decisions can range from those of a vital, once-for-all nature to those of a routine and relatively trivial nature. They can be immediate in their effect or they can be delayed. Decisions may be classified or categorized in many ways such as by the organizational level and the degree of structure to the decision i.e. repetitive, routine and require judgments. Some decisions are semi structured – in such cases, only part of the problem has a clear-cut answer provided by an accepted procedure. Decisions (selecting the right action from a series of choices) can be structured (decision rules are known) or unstructured (not known – highly uncertain/ambiguous situations) and may be made/taken at a variety of levels (operational/tactical/strategic) within the organization. In the case of structured decision making the organization may formulate decision/business rules specifying what action is required in a given situation. Operational decisions tend to be structured, frequent with more certainty, often relying on data/information from within the organization. Strategic decisions on the other hand are unstructured, made less frequently and may use more information sourced form outside the organization. Routine decisions are made according to established procedures and rules whereas adaptive decisions require human judgement (management as art).

19.3 DECISION-MAKING TOOLS

9.   Figure 19.1 showed the key steps that can be identified in the (rational) decision-making process. In recent years several techniques have been developed to aid the processes of problem-definition, of devising solution options and of evaluating their possible consequences. Since the majority of decisions have to be made in conditions of relative risk and uncertainty, any techniques which can help sensitize users to future possibilities and likely outcomes are worth having. Spreadsheets, models, historic data (databases) and related technologies can be used to support decision making and in some cases may even make the decision according to programmable rules (see Decision support system). For example when you make a loan or credit request it is likely that technology will play a major role in determining the outcome. The chief benefits of such technologies are that they assist with the analysis of problems and the development of solutions. They do this quickly and without error. They are, however, limited primarily to structured decisions (for strategic decision making see business intelligence software).

10.   Another useful tool for management decision-makers is the decision tree. This is basically a conceptual map of possible decisions and outcomes in a particular situation. It is useful in cases when a manager is required to make decisions where earlier decisions will affect subsequent decisions. A simple decision tree is shown in Figure 19.2.

FIGURE 19.2 **R & D decision tree.**

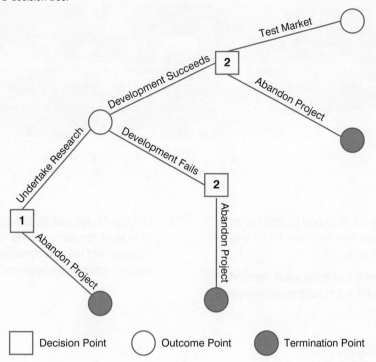

11.   Such a diagram focuses attention on outcomes or consequences as well as decisions. It is customarily built on three key features of decision-making: (i) a decision point, (ii) one or more outcomes, and (iii) a termination point. Outcomes can be further elaborated in terms of their probability and their anticipated pay off. It is also possible to add a time dimension to the whole diagram, so that in Figure 19.2 the period from decision point 1 to decision point 2 could be one year. These additional features all help to make the use of decision trees a valuable exercise for managers.

CONCLUSION

12.   Decision making is a very important aspect of management. There are many types of decision and many ways of making decisions. The scientific school makes used of the rational decision making process, supported by a range of technologies to improve the quality and speed of decision making. However, such an approach has limitations as the decision may be constrained through a lack of time, information or the abilities of decision makers. Furthermore, decisions may be coloured by decision maker values and politics. Whilst scientific management has more to offer when making structured and repetitive decisions, managerial judgement is more preferable for strategic decisions made in the face of considerable uncertainty. Consequently we may view decision making as much about management as an art as well as a science.

QUESTIONS

1 Management may be described as science, art or craft. Briefly discuss how decisions are likely to be made under each approach.

2 List and describe the typical stages of decision-making as portrayed in a rational decision-making approach.

3 Discuss the applicability of rational decision-making to strategic decision-making. Do you expect management science of management-as-art to feature most in such decisions? Explain your answer.

USEFUL WEBSITES

Management library: **managementhelp.org/prsn_prd/ decision.htm**
Resources in relation to decision making

Decision making: **www.decisionmaking.org/ decisionmakingbooklet.pdf**
Article on decision making and the homepage of the site has a range of other decision making materials

VIDEO CASES

Now take a look at the online video cases – visit the companion website to work through real world business problems associated with the concepts presented within this chapter.

39 Managerial decision making – when values take over rational economical thought
This case describes a challenging strategic decision about downsizing in Southwest Airlines. On the one hand, the company must reduce costs (after all, it is a low cost airline) and is presented an opportunity to do so as a result of the success of its e-commerce initiatives whilst on the other hand, the company is committed to provide its employees with a stable work environment and has a culture of job security and treating employees well.

111 Managerial decision making – rational decision-making within organizations
This case study can be used to investigate rational decision making within organizations. The case makes use of a film clip where a business owner is interviewed and discusses an office relocation decision. Students are encouraged to apply the rational decision making process and discuss how the decision was made. Key decision making concepts are explored and types of decision considered. Case study activities include problem definition, determining and weighting decision criteria and evaluating alternatives.

REFERENCES

Browne, N. and Keeley, S. (2007) 'Asking the Right Questions – A Guide to Critical Thinking', Ed. 8. Prentice Hall.

French, S., Maule, J. and Papamichail, N. (2009) 'Decision Behaviour, Analysis and Support', Cambridge.

Janis, I. L. (1989) 'Crucial Decisions', Free Press.

van Aken, J., Berends, H. and van der Bij, H. (2007) 'Problem solving in Organizations – A Methodological Handbook for Business Students', Cambridge, Cambridge University Press.

CHAPTER 20
HUMAN RESOURCE
PLANNING

Key Concepts

- Employee resourcing
- Human resource management
- Human resource planning (HRP)
- Human resource strategy

Learning Outcomes Having read this chapter, you should be able to:

- explain what is meant by HRM
- discuss the purpose and methods of HR planning
- assess why human resource planning is essentially a corporate activity

Human resource planning (HRP) A process which anticipates and maps out the consequences of business strategy on an organization's human resource requirements. This is reflected in planning of skill and competence needs as well as total headcounts

1.   Contemporary organizations have a need for talented employees. Human resource planning (HRP), like any other form of planning, is a means to an end. In this case the end is to secure the human resources of the organization in order to achieve corporate objectives. In organizations that have adopted a corporate planning or strategic approach to HRP, an overall assessment will have been made of the current strengths and weaknesses of the employee situation. This assessment will have led, where necessary, to a number of long-term proposals for HRP aimed at securing sufficient numbers and categories of suitable employees to undertake the task of producing the organization's goods or services to the standards expected by the end-users. Even organizations that rarely plan far ahead usually have to make some assessment of their present employee situation, so as to ensure that an appropriate range of skills is available for all the mainstream activities of the organization. This chapter assumes that a systematic and planned view of HRP is the norm.

2.   Whatever the nature of the organization, if it is of a size where changes in the workforce will have a significant effect on business results, then it will need some kind of human resource planning activity. In this book human resource planning is defined as:

'a rational approach to the effective recruitment, retention and deployment of people within an organization, including, when necessary, arrangements for dismissing staff.'

HRP is, therefore, concerned with the flow of people through and sometimes out of the organization. HR planning is used to ensure the organization has the appropriate number of suitably skilled people in the right places and at the right times. It is, however, not a mere numbers game. On the contrary, effective HRP is considerably more concerned with the optimum deployment of people's knowledge and skills, i.e. quality is even more important than quantity.

3.   Before moving on to look at the various stages of HRP, it is worth considering the questions which such planning aims to answer. These can be summarized as follows:

–   What kind of people does the organization require and in what numbers?

–   Over what time-span are these people required?

–   How many of them are employed by the organization currently?

–   How can the organization meet any shortfall in requirements from internal sources?

–   How can the organization meet the shortfall from external sources?

–   What changes are taking place in the external labour market which might affect the supply of human resources?

In responding to these questions, HRP is essentially concerned with four major activities:

1).   analyzing the existing human resource situation.

2).   forecasting future demands for people.

3).   assessing the external labour market and forecasting the supply situation.

4).   establishing and implementing human resource plans.

Human resource management A philosophy of people management based on the belief that human resources are uniquely important to sustained business success. An organization gains competitive advantage by using its people effectively, drawing on their expertise and ingenuity to meet clearly defined objectives. HRM is aimed at recruiting capable, flexible and committed people, managing and rewarding their performance and developing key competencies. See also 'Hard HRM', 'Soft HRM'

4.   HRP is typically coordinated by the human resource management (HRM) function which aims to improve the

productive contribution of individuals – it is about people and their ability to be economically productive, to enhance organizational performance. The goal of HRM is to help an organization meet strategic goals by attracting and retaining employees and managing them effectively. HRM is therefore concerned with the strategic management of human resources to achieve a competitive advantage.

20.1 THE HUMAN RESOURCE PLANNING PROCESS

5.   Human resource planning can only make sense when seen in relation to business objectives. The basic demand for people springs from the organization's need to supply goods or services to its customers. In this sense, HRP is a resourcing activity. However, it is also a fact that these resources in themselves have a vital influence on organizational objectives. For example, a firm may be unable to pursue its expansion plans in a new market because it is unable to find enough suitably trained personnel to carry them through. So, information arising from the HRP process produces feedback which may cause other business plans to be cancelled or amended. In its simplest form, human resource planning can be depicted as shown in Figure 20.1.

Employee resourcing Resourcing is the process by which people are identified and allocated to perform necessary work. Resourcing has two strategic imperatives: first, minimizing employee costs and maximizing employee value to the organization; secondly, obtaining the correct behavioural mix of attitude and commitment in the workforce

FIGURE 20.1 Personnel decisions and human resource requirements.

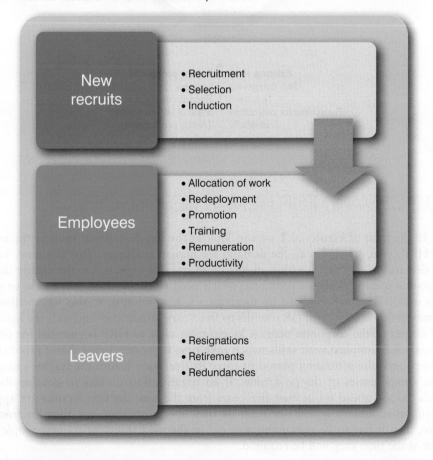

6.   Even this simple model of the process indicates the ramifications of human resource planning, and emphasizes its qualitative aspects. HRP is clearly not just concerned with numbers. Plans for training, redeployment, promotion and productivity all indicate the importance of getting the right people in the right jobs, as well as in the right numbers.

7.   Figure 20.1 shows the flow of people through the organization, and identifies some of the key actions that need to be taken at the operational level. This is the kind of model that almost every organization can utilize. However, larger or more complex organizations need a more strategic approach at the outset. Such an approach would incorporate the four major activities mentioned earlier in paragraph 4, but would link them into the overall business planning activity of the organization. Thus, a more appropriate and comprehensive model for this situation would be as shown in Figure 20.2.

FIGURE 20.2 **The human resource planning cycle.**

20.2 DEMAND FOR HUMAN RESOURCES

8.   In the light of Figure 20.2 we can look at the key features of each of the major stages of the HRP cycle, starting with the demand for human resources. This is a more or less continuing demand in any organization. It has its short-term aspects, i.e. the clearly defined requirements for specific skills, or positions, which need to be filled in the context of existing plans. This usually means periods of up to about six–nine months. It also has medium-term (six to 18 months) and long-term (18 months to five years) aspects, in line with the market and financial targets of the corporate plan. A longer-term view of HRP is essential for ensuring the organization is supplied with skills which take time to be developed. Most professional jobs, for example, require a training period of three to five years before the trainee can claim even the basic competencies of the profession. If an organization decides to develop its own staff, it needs to look ahead for at least five years from the time the first recruits are appointed. If the organization decides it will not train its own specialists, but buy them in from the marketplace, then it has to be reasonably assured of the availability of trained people in the labour force at the time they will be required.

20.3 SUPPLY OF LABOUR

9.   This leads us on to the question of the supply of labour, which is the next major stage in the cycle of events. Any analysis of the supply of labour must commence with the existing state of the organization's personnel. Answers need to be sought to such questions as:

–   What categories of staff do we have?

–   What are the numbers in each category?

–   What about age and sex distribution within the categories?

–   What skills and qualifications exist?

–   How many staff are suitable for promotion or re-deployment?

–   How successful are we in recruiting particular categories of staff?

10.   These are important questions for both immediate and future needs. If, for example, a contraction of the business was planned, it might be an advantage to have an ageing workforce. Equally, if expansion was planned in the same business, an ageing workforce would be a definite disadvantage, and the organization would need to draw heavily on the national labour market.

11.   When considering the existing supply of human resources available to the organization, we are not just considering the numbers and categories at a particular point in time. We are also considering (1) the organization's ability to continue to attract suitable recruits into its various operations, and (2) the rate at which employees are leaving the organization. Can the organization count on filling vacant posts satisfactorily when it goes into the market-place? Are some posts more difficult to fill than others, and can anything be done about this? What about leavers? Why are they moving out – retirements? seeking better opportunities elsewhere? pregnancy? dismissal? redundancy? Some organizations rely on a high fallout rate of employees to enable fresh recruits to be brought in at regular intervals. Other organizations expect a considerable degree of stability among their workforce, and build this expectation into their planning assumptions.

12.   The analysis of the existing supply of human resources must also take into account the potentialities of existing staff to undertake other roles in the organization. There are considerable variations in the policies of organizations concerning career development. Some offer no real prospects for increased variety or responsibility at work. Others claim career development as the high-spot of their reputation as employers. Clearly firms that take the latter view can call on far greater internal resources for meeting change than those in the former category. Increasingly, nowadays, organizations are seeking job flexibility across all job categories – manual, clerical technical, etc. – and are insisting on a multi-skilled workforce. This **strategy** serves the interests of organizations who wish to 'grow their own' flexible workforce. Having considered its existing supply of human resources, an organization will know the shortfall in its requirements for the future. If we assume that the organization cannot meet its future needs internally, then it must look to the external labour market. There are a number of important issues here. For example:

> **Human resource strategy** Overall plan for staffing, developing and rewarding employees and outsourced human resources tied to business objectives

–   What is the overall employment situation likely to be in the course of the next five years?

–   How is this situation likely to affect our local labour market?

–   What is the likely competition for personnel?

–   Are there any trends in the educational sector which might affect our recruitment plans?

–   Are there factors in our corporate plans which might speed up the voluntary leaving rate?

13.   The answers to these questions will indicate the likely prospects of meeting future person-nel needs from external sources. Skilled labour is usually a scarce resource in most advanced industrialized nations, but the situation has changed with relatively large-scale unemployment, and even a surplus of some skills. These changes do not happen overnight. Thus, firms that are planning ahead for their requirements can offset some of the worst affects of acute shortages or surpluses of labour arising from economic changes over which they have no control. Another example of the need to recruit externally is when changes in technology or production processes bring about changes in the number and types of employees required. Improved technology can lead to redundancies and/or monotonous/routine jobs for machine operators on the one hand, whilst leading to more jobs for skilled maintenance technicians on the other.

14.   Once the organization has assessed its supply position in relation to its requirements, it can then draw up plans to meet these requirements. Since people are probably the most volatile resource available to the organization, the best plans will be those which have the greatest flexi-bility. Most human resource plans are developed on a rolling five year basis, which means that forecasts for next year and the succeeding years in the cycle are updated every year in the light of this year's out-turn. Detailed plans for securing sufficient and suitable employees for current needs are devised for a one-year period, in line with current budgets. Less detailed plans are laid for the five year period, but at least major contingencies are prepared for in line with the organi-zation's corporate strategy.

15.   Whether long- or short-term, the plans for securing the workforce will usually include con-sideration of the following:

20.3.1 Recruitment

How do we ensure our anticipated needs for replenishing or adding to our workforce? By increasing traineeships and apprenticeships? Or by recruiting trained and experienced people? How much provision should be made for recruiting part-timers and contract staff? What steps should be taken to promote the organization in schools, colleges and universities? What use, if any, should we make of recruitment consultants? What improvements could be made to our selection procedures?

20.3.2 Training and Development

What job and professional training should be provided to prepare new and existing staff to fulfil their roles satisfactorily? Should we concentrate on in-company or in-service training, or should we send people on external courses? What special programmes need to be established to deal with re-training, or updating? How can induction procedures be improved? How best can multi-skilling be encouraged by means of workplace training?

20.3.3 Promotion, Redeployment and Career Planning

How can internal procedures be improved so as to facilitate the movement of staff to jobs where they can exercise greater, or different, responsibilities? What new succession plans need to be drawn up for key management and supervisory roles? How well is training linked to career devel-opment? How can job interest/career challenge be maintained in a flatter organization structure?

20.3.4 Pay and Productivity

What steps must be taken to ensure that pay and incentives are sufficient to attract, retain and encourage our workforce? What are the cost limits on pay? How can we make best use of high-cost groups of key employees? In what ways can labour costs be paid for out of improved output per employee, or other productivity indicators? How best can pay be related to performance?

20.3.5 Retirements and Redundancy

What provision should be made for those reaching retirement age? What inducements may be needed to encourage older employees to consider opting for early retirement? What arrangements should be made for dealing with planned redundancies? How should retirements and redundancies be phased over the course of the year? What are the estimated costs of these plans?

16. Human resource planning is essentially a corporate activity. It cuts across all the divisional and departmental boundaries of an organization. It is an activity which claims the attention of all managers. It is not the preserve of any one group of specialist managers (e.g. personnel), even though such specialists may well play a key coordinating role in the implementation and review of HR plans. So, as we turn to the final stage of the HRP cycle – the review – we can see this as a responsibility in which all managers share. Major reviews of progress will usually take place once a year, when revisions may be made to the subsequent years of the five-year planning cycle. There will also be reviews carried out half-yearly, or quarterly, by the specialist coordinators in the organization. The principal vehicle of the monitoring process will be budget statements, probably expressed in terms of headcounts, or wage and salary costs.

17. Human resource planning review activities are important for generating feedback information. This information tells the organization not only how well it is achieving its HR plans, but also points the way to necessary changes that must be made at one or more points in the cycle. Some changes need only be made at the tactical level, ie to amend next year's operational plans. Other amendments may have to be made at the highest strategic level, i.e. to plans for five, or even ten years ahead. Thus, the cycle of events depicted in Figure 20.2 comes full circle.

CONCLUSION

18. Human resource manangement is viewed as strategically important due to attributes which are difficult to imitate thus ensuring any derived competitive advantage is sustainable. As companies move into the war for talent and as individuals with specialized knowledge, skills and expertise are recognized as the scarce strategic resource, HR professionals must become key players in the design, development and delivery of a company's strategy. The HRM role can be both strategic and operational. It is strategic in that the continued availability of human capital must be assured in order for the strategy to be met. However, it must also be operational via the administration of certain HR practices such as resourcing, training and development and performance management (see later chapters).

QUESTIONS

1   Assess why human resource planning is essentially a corporate activity.

2   Define and discuss the HRM and HRP concepts commenting on the goals of each.

3   Why are human resources now viewed as strategically important?

USEFUL WEBSITES

HRM Guide: **www.hrmguide.co.uk/hrm/chap7/ch7-links3.htm**
Human Resource Planning
CIPD: **www.cipd.co.uk/subjects/hrpract/general/successplan.htm**
Succession planning factsheet

Institute for Employment Studies: **www.employment-studies.co.uk/consult/index.php?id=rap&tab=work**
IES helps employers make effective, practical and sustainable resourcing decisions to be sure their workforce is 'fit for purpose' both in the short and longer term.

VIDEO CASES

Now take a look at the online video cases – visit the companion website to work through real world business problems associated with the concepts presented within this chapter.

114 HRM strategy
Human resource management is closely identified with business strategy and focused upon within this case study. The concern with meeting business objectives in a strategic fashion is discussed, along with a need for HR to be proactive, long-term and able to support competitiveness. In particular, the case focuses on the war for talent and the challenge of managing costs; acquiring, developing and retaining talent and creating a skilled, committed and

motivated workforce, able to attain present and future corporate objectives.

139 HRM strategy
This case study makes use of three short film clips to develop student's conceptions of what HRM strategy is. The first film clip focuses on strategic planning and its relationship with HRM planning; the second film clip recognizes resourcing to be an important component of the HR professional's work, along with a set of systems and activities used to ensure strategic goals are met. Finally the last film clip focuses on employee (talent) retention.

REFERENCES

Bratton, J. and Gold, J. (2007) 'Human Resource Management Theory and Practice', Ed. 4. Palgrave Macmillan.
Leopold, J. and Harris, L. (2009) 'The Strategic Managing of Human Resources', Ed. 2. Financial Times Press.
Lepak, D. and Gowan, M. (2009) 'Human Resource Management International Edition', Upper Saddle River, Pearson Education.

Price, A. (2007) 'Human Resource Management in a Business Context', Ed. 3. Cengage Learning EMEA.
Torrington, D., Hall, L., Taylor, S. and Atkinson, C. (2009) 'Fundamentals of Human Resource Management: Managing People at Work', Ed. 1. Financial Times Press.

CHAPTER 21
WORK STRUCTURING, JOB DESIGN AND BUSINESS PROCESS RE-ENGINEERING

Key Concepts

- Business process reengineering (BPR)
- Division of labour
- Job design
- Job enlargement
- Job enrichment
- Job satisfaction
- Job simplification

Learning Outcomes   Having read this chapter, you should be able to:

- discuss the strengths and weaknesses of early ideas on the design of work
- identify the main approaches to the design of work
- evaluate the factors likely to influence job/work design
- list job characteristics thought critical to job satisfaction
- list the main benefits of job enrichment
- evaluate the business process reengineering approach

1.   This section of the book has been about management planning. In Chapters 16 and 17 we considered organizational purpose, mission and strategy along with goals and objectives. In Chapter 18 we considered mechanisms such as performance management systems to translate strategy into action, translating corporate objectives into managerial and team-based objectives at the operational level. Accomplishment of strategic goals is dependent upon human resources and in Chapter 20 we discussed human resource planning. In the final chapter of this section we focus on the design of work (jobs). Organizational strategies should fit with the various parts of work within an organization.

Job The set of tasks an individual performs

Job design Involves determining the specific job tasks and responsibilities, the work environment and the methods by which the tasks will be carried out to meet the goals of operations

Division of labour An approach to job design that involves dividing a task down into relatively small parts, each of which is accomplished by a single person

2.   The contemporary organization needs people to work willingly, effectively and productively to achieve organizational goals and contribute to organizational success. No one can do all of the work of the organization and there is therefore a need to differentiate work and consider how work should be designed to meet organizational goals. Jobs are interdependent and must be designed to make a contribution to the organization's overall mission and goals. As we will see in this chapter however, there are numerous approaches to designing jobs. An approach to job design that involves dividing a task into relatively small parts, each of which is accomplished by a single person is known as the division of labour. Job design involves determining the specific job tasks and responsibilities, the work environment and the methods by which the tasks will be carried out to meet operational goals. According to Daft (2009:518) job design is the application of motivational theories to the structure of work in order to improve productivity and satisfaction.

3.   The emphasis of this chapter is upon work and how that work is organized and designed. Work may be described in terms of labour, activities, jobs and tasks. Such terms are often used interchangeably. Job design requires knowledge of classical management theory (scientific management) and human relations theories (motivation) in particular – refer back to part 1 of the book. The scope of this chapter is more oriented towards the design of work at the level of the individual and small team and we give consideration to work design principles with this in mind. In the next chapter we turn our attention to design at the organizational level. Thus, this chapter is more about differentiation and the next about integration. This chapter examines some of the key issues involved in designing work for people, and outlines several important approaches which have been adopted in the search for the best ways of combining people's needs and aspirations with the constraints and opportunities offered by technology and work processes.

21.1 TRADITIONAL WORK DESIGN AND JOB SIMPLIFICATION

4.   One of the major legacies of 'Scientific Management' (see Chapter 3) is that work has generally been designed around technology and technical processes, rather than attempting to fit the latter around the needs and preferences of employees and their managers. Thus, the most important criteria for designing work have tended to include the following:

-    maximizing the degree of job/task specialization

-    minimizing the time required to do a specific job/task

–   minimizing the level of skill required to perform the job/task.

–   minimizing the learning/training time in the job

–   maximizing the use of machines and technology

–   minimizing the individual worker's discretion over how the job/task should be done.

5.   **Job simplification** (job engineering), drawing on the principles of scientific management, is an approach to job design based on a minimization of the range of tasks into the smallest convenient size to make the job efficient and cost effective. Job simplification typically reduces the number of tasks completed by an employee and as a consequence the employee requires less training and can master the task quickly.

> **Job simplification** An approach to job design based on a minimization of the range of tasks into the smallest convenient size to make the job efficient and cost effective

21.2 CONSEQUENCES, CRITICISMS AND IMPLICATIONS

6.   Despite the theoretical arguments in favour of simplifying industrial jobs, it is clear that Britain and many other industrial nations have experienced far fewer benefits than expected. Indeed Daft (2009:518) suggests that as a motivational technique, job simplification has failed. People dislike routine and boring jobs and react in a number of negative ways including sabotage, absenteeism, high labour turnover, lateness and poor attention to quality. Studies into motivation and job satisfaction (see Chapters 5, 6) have demonstrated clearly that employees at all levels seek some degree of self-control and self-direction at work.

7.   Numerous management scholars have argued that job simplification, the fragmentation of work tasks and various principles of scientific management lead to the deskilling of work and demotivation of employees. Consequently, the twentieth century was characterized by two contradictory trends in work design. The first half of the century placed greater emphasis on scientific management and job simplification without full regard to the needs of the employee. The second half of the century witnessed a reaction against Taylorism, adopting more people-oriented approaches, with emphasis on the quality of working life.

8.   In the latter part of the twentieth century two key debates ensued: deskilling and upskilling. Deskilling was arguably a consequence of scientific management principles (the separation of task conception from task execution, standardization, predictability, control and efficiency) and the adoption of technology. Organizations that seek to provide customers with a uniform, standardized product or service ultimately limit the discretion employees have when undertaking work tasks.

> **Quality of working life** An individual's overall assessment of satisfaction with their job, working conditions, pay, colleagues, management style, organization culture, work-life balance, training, development and career opportunities

9.   However, various criticisms were levelled at the deskilling thesis. Aside from its treatment of employees as passive, it ignores alternative management strategies. Furthermore, it fails to recognize the potential for hybrid approaches which draw upon classical and human relations theories. Japanization, a term that first came into vogue in the mid-1980s, describes the attempts of Western firms to make practical use of 'Japanese' ideas and practices. Team working and lean production, however, emphasized aspects of both schools of thinking i.e. scientific management and human relations. Additionally, workers can be upskilled when they participate as a group in job redesign and may then be de-skilled when they perform the job themselves.

10.   Aside from the critique of the deskilling thesis, some management scholars have argued an up skilling position as a result of technology adoption. They argue that the increasing use of

technology and need for flexibility requires higher levels of skill amongst employees. Technology may replace jobs involving boring repetitive work, enabling employees to focus on more interesting work. Consequently, many scholars now agree that some work may become de-skilled as a result of the application of job simplification whilst other work may become upskilled in the face of new technology.

11.   Jobs may vary according to whether they are transformational (directly creating products and services) or transactional. Jobs also vary in the amount of tacit knowledge or judgement required. It may therefore be helpful to categorize jobs when considering the different approaches to design. For example, jobs may be categorized according to the range of work, which may involve performing a small number of tasks (narrow) through to a wide range of tasks. Jobs may require little or large amounts of discretion. They may be specialized or general. If we redesign jobs to adapt technology to meet the motivational needs of employees, then it is important to know which elements of their work employees find demotivating. A range of factors have been shown to make work boring such as carrying out uninteresting, undemanding, repetitive or meaningless tasks (e.g. form-filling). Boredom may also arise from the lack of any sense of completion of the task i.e. the belief that however much work is achieved in a day; there is always more to come.

21.3 APPROACHES TO JOB DESIGN

12.   So far we have evaluated traditional approaches to work design (job simplification) and commented on the resultant shift towards the adoption of human relation theories of work design. The tasks to be undertaken in an organization need to be combined into specific jobs that make sense for people to undertake. Job design must take account of a variety of contextual factors (concerns and drivers) such as those shown in Figure 21.1.

13.   We can draw upon a variety of studies to suggest the crucial characteristics required in order that a job may satisfy human needs. Studies suggest that employees require a degree of autonomy over the way tasks are to be achieved; individuals need to be responsible for their own work, and for the resources they use (e.g. equipment); an element of variety should be present in the job, so as to permit variations in task, pace and method; task repetition should be reduced to a minimum; arrangements need to be made to provide feedback on job performance; wherever practicable, the job should enable the completion of an entire item; there should be some degree of social contact available to the job-holder; learning opportunities should be built into the job, so as to provide an element of challenge, as well as the opportunity to extend individual repertoire of knowledge and skills; roles should be clear so that job-holders and others know what is expected from the job and every job should have some definite goals for which to aim.

Job enlargement The horizontal increasing of job responsibility, i.e. by the addition of tasks of a similar nature to be distinguished from job enrichment

14.   There are three main approaches to achieving increased job satisfaction at work through task restructuring. These are (1) job enrichment, (2) job enlargement and (3) autonomous work groups. Each of these approaches embodies several, if not all, of the characteristics referred to in the previous paragraph. There are, of course, other methods of enhancing employee job satisfaction, for example by improving consultation or permitting participation in decision-making, but here we concentrate on the three principal approaches. The different methods of job design are not necessarily separate approaches. They are interrelated and there is some overlapping between them. We discuss each in turn and then consider business processes as structured and organized work.

Autonomous work groups A work team with delegated responsibility for a defined part of an organization's activities with the freedom to organize its own resources, pace of work and allocate responsibilities within the group

FIGURE 21.1 Determinants of job design.

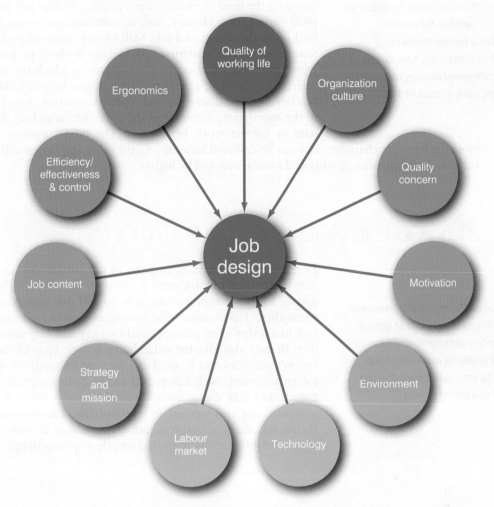

21.4 JOB ENRICHMENT

15.   The term 'job enrichment' is usually applied to the vertical extension of job responsibilities. It implies taking tasks from those both senior and junior to the job-holder in order to enable a job-holder to have more responsibility than before. Herzberg (see Chapter 5) saw job enrichment in terms of building motivators into a job. His view was that opportunities for achievement, rec-

Job enrichment The process of vertically increasing the responsibilities of a job, by the addition of motivators, e.g. more discretion, improved job interest, etc.

ognition and responsibility need to be included in a person's job. For individual employees the main benefits of job enrichment are felt in terms of increased job satisfaction resulting from increased intrinsic rewards in the job (see Expectancy Theory, Chapter 6). Organizations tend to benefit by a reduction in overhead costs caused by absenteeism, lateness, lack of attention to quality and other negative features of poor morale. One of the difficulties associated with job enrichment is that it will lead to changes throughout a job hierarchy. Some job-holders may find their jobs are threatened by a job enrichment programme. Supervisors, in particular, may find that many of their duties have been handed down to members of their team. Any attempt at job enrichment must take account of such consequential changes on the overall structure of jobs.

Job characteristics model A model of job enrichment based on the need to incorporate a number of core job dimensions (Skill variety, Task identity, Task significance, Autonomy and Feedback) into the design of a job

16.   The job characteristics model is a model of job enrichment based on the need to incorporate a number of core job dimensions (skill variety, task identity, task significance, autonomy and feedback) into the design of a job. Skill variety concerns performing a number of diverse activities; task identity is about performing the whole job; task significance is the degree to which the job is perceived as important, autonomy is the degree to which the worker has freedom and discretion and feedback – output that is returned to the appropriate members of the organization to help them evaluate or correct work behaviours. The model assumes that the more the five core characteristics can be designed into the job, the more employees will be motivated and performance, quality and satisfaction will be higher.

21.5 JOB ENLARGEMENT AND ROTATION

Job rotation The moving of a person from one job or task to another in an attempt to add variety and help remove boredom. It may also give the individual a holistic view of the organization's activities and be used as a form of training

17.   Job enlargement, in contrast to job enrichment, is the horizontal extension of jobs, extra tasks of the same level as before are added. To put it another way, it is 'to add one undemanding job to another!' Job rotation – the moving of a person from one job or task to another in an attempt to add variety and help remove boredom (It may also give the individual a holistic view of the organization's activities and be used as a form of training) – is a form of job enlargement. Such a step does increase job variety to a certain extent, and may create more meaningful tasks. What it does not achieve is any real increase in responsibility. The approach nevertheless has many supporters, not least because it often works in practice to bring about improved morale or productivity.

21.6 AUTONOMOUS WORK GROUPS

18.   A work team with delegated responsibility for a defined part of an organization's activities, with the freedom to organize its own resources, pace of work and allocate responsibilities within the group is often termed an autonomous work group. The idea behind autonomous work groups is that job satisfaction and hence employee morale can be enhanced if employees work together in a group to achieve their production goals. An autonomous group is a self-organized work group which is held responsible for the rate and quality of its output. This approach to work design resulted from the efforts of the socio-technical systems theorists from the Tavistock Institute (see Chapter 9). The first reported autonomous work groups were those established in the British coalmining industry under the 'composite longwall method'. Subsequent experiments in Norway and Sweden, especially the work at the Volvo car plant, have shown that such groups can improve quality and reduce overheads as well as providing greater job satisfaction for the employees concerned.

Job satisfaction An attitude or internal state which is associated with the working environment and working experiences. In recent years it has been closely associated with improved job design and work organization and the quality of working life

21.7 DIFFICULTIES IN WORK DESIGN

19.   Individual jobs are essentially a collection of tasks. These tasks are generated primarily by the needs of the organization, as made explicit by line managers who are confronted by a number of different pressures from marketing, financial and personnel (HR) colleagues. To a manager at the operational end of the business, every job represents some sort of compromise between conflicting pressures, arising mainly from the following: the

- need to meet the customer's specification
- need to meet financial targets
- operating requirements of the machinery involved
- nature of the production process
- requirements for stocking materials
- delivery arrangements, and
- the motivational needs of employees.

20.   In the light of the above pressures, it is not surprising that job redesign is rarely considered by the majority of firms, on account of the complexity of the problems at precisely the point where the product is being manufactured (or the service delivered), and where disruptions have an immediate effect. The approach likely to be taken by a typical production manager, for example, is to focus on the technical specification of the product, and how it is to be met within the cost, time and quality constraints imposed by senior management. Thus work is organized primarily to achieve accuracy, reliability, uninterrupted workflow and consistency of quality and the containment of costs. Only after these considerations have been met is the manager likely to consider employee needs. The extent to which he or she may defer to demands for increased job satisfaction will depend as much on the relative bargaining power of the employees as on any magnanimity on the manager's part!

21.8 BUSINESS PROCESSES

21.   As was noted at the outset, work is activity (a collection of tasks) directed at making or doing something. In the case of the organization, work activities transform inputs into outputs (products and services) for the benefit of customers, adding value along the way. A collection of related work tasks and activities is typically labelled as a business process. Such processes may be operational, management or supportive. Well-designed processes are both effective and efficient and contribute to organizational capabilities.

Business process A specific ordering of work activities across time and place, with a beginning, an end, and clearly identified inputs and output

22.   At the outset of the 1990s, the late Michael Hammer, a former professor of computer science at the Massachusetts Institute of Technology (MIT), known as one of the founders of the management theory of business process reengineering (BPR), challenged what he termed the 'centuries-old' notions about work. He argued that for many organizations, their job designs, workflows, control mechanisms and organizational structures came of age in a different competitive environment and before the advent of the

Business process reengineering (BPR) The redesign of business processes in an effort to reduce costs, increase efficiency and effectiveness and improve quality. BPR is characterized as radical rather than incremental in its approach to change and broad rather than narrow in its organization impact

computer. Such organizations were geared toward efficiency and control. According to Hammer, commenting on 20th century organizations, rules of work design are based on assumptions about technology, people and organizational goals that no longer hold. He suggested that business processes and structures were outmoded and obsolete and had not kept pace with the changes in technology and business objectives. Companies had typically organized work as a sequence of separate tasks and employed complex mechanisms to track its progress. Conventional process structures emphasized differentiation but as a result were fragmented and piecemeal, and they lacked the integration necessary to maintain quality and service.

23.   Also commenting on the 1990s, Tom Davenport – an American academic and author specializing in business process innovation – suggested the contemporary business world is abound with references to the concept of process – a noun denoting how work is done, (Davenport 1994). He starts by asking what is meant by the term 'process', defining it as a structured set of activities designed to produce a specified output for a particular customer or market. It has a beginning, an end and clearly identified inputs and outputs. A process is therefore a structure for action, for how work is done. Processes are therefore the structure by which an organization does what is necessary to produce value for its customers. Typical business processes include product development, receiving orders, marketing services, selling products, delivering services, distributing products, invoicing for services and accounting for money received. Processes are used to manage the flow of goods, products and services, information and money. They organize work as flows of related activities. Business process design considers the challenge of how to do things in the best way – effectively and efficiently i.e. do the right things right.

21.9 BUSINESS PROCESS RE-ENGINEERING (BPR)

24.   Organizations should seek to improve business processes continuously in order to enhance the organization's performance and benefit its interested parties. There are two fundamental ways to conduct process improvement: a) breakthrough projects which either lead to revision and improvement of existing processes or the implementation of new processes (typical of BPR); and b) small-step ongoing improvement activities conducted within existing processes by people (typical of TQM). In the 1970s and 1980s, organizations generally turned to continuous process improvement programmes whilst, later, in the 1990s, the same organizations turned to more radical process change approaches.

25.   The need for BPR was essentially born out of the lack of alignment between traditional organizations and the new environment of the 1990's in which they operated. This environment was more turbulent and required flexibility, innovation, adaptation and efficiency. Hammer (1990) argued that reengineering enabled companies to break away from the old rules about how they organize and conduct business. Reengineering requires looking at the fundamental processes of the business from a cross-functional perspective. At the heart of reengineering is the notion of discontinuous thinking – of recognizing and breaking away from the outdated roles and fundamental assumptions that underlie operations.

26.   Reengineering need not be haphazard and Hammer (1990) suggested several guiding principles. He argued a need to organize around outcomes, not tasks. In most organizations, those who do the work are distinguished from those who monitor the work and make decisions about it. Instead, he suggests the people who do the work should make the decisions and the process itself can have built-in controls. In rethinking a key business process, such as ordering, a company employing the BPR approach has to put its existing arrangements mentally to one side, and then question everything about the process – for example, how the customer orders, what it is he wants, why he wants it that way, who deals with the customer, how, and in what order. The idea is to go back to basic principles and completely rethink the process in question. The re-engineering process tends to lead to the following changes in the way work is undertaken:

- several jobs or tasks becoming combined with related jobs/tasks

- workers become more involved in decision-making (i.e. empowerment increases)

- a reduction in the number of checks and controls insisted on during the process

- the minimization of reconciliations (e.g. of orders) between customers and suppliers

- a single person as point of contact with the customer ('empowered' customer service representatives).

Important changes are likely to occur in structural forms and employee behaviour, as a result of introducing BPR. These include the following:

- Work structures move away from functional departments (see next chapter) towards process teams.

- Employees are empowered to act in ways that were previously controlled by rules.

- 'Empowerment' implies willingness, and an ability, to accept greater responsibility for work outcomes.

- Preparation for work implies a greater emphasis on education (i.e. to understand the 'why' of the job) rather than on training (which is usually directed at the 'how' of the job).

- The focus for performance and payment shifts from activities to results (expressed in terms of the value created for the customer).

- A culture change will occur in which the typical employee will see the customer as more important than the boss.

- Organizational structures are likely to become flatter and less hierarchical.

27.   Information technology (IT) plays an important role in the reengineering concept. The role of information technology (IT) in BPR is crucial as the horizontal approach necessitates information flows across departments and processes. Empowered employees require access to company information. It is considered a major enabler for new forms of working and collaborating within an organization and across organizational borders. Technological innovations throughout the 1990's, especially in the form of database and internet technologies, led to the creation of enterprise resource planning systems and broader enterprise wide systems. Such systems enable empowered employees by making data and information immediately available.

21.10 A CRITIQUE OF BPR

28.   Whilst there are many examples of companies having achieved dramatic performance improvements by moving toward a more horizontal structure, there are also failures. Research conducted by Stalk and Black (1994) found that much of what people label the 'Horizontal Organization' or 'Organizing Around Processes' is not. What really happens is the modification of traditional structures to make process management easier. Stalk and Black (1994) also found that different processes have fundamentally different characteristics – and they thrive in different structures and that 'one size does not fit all'. Critics claim that BPR dehumanizes the workplace, increases managerial control, and is or has been used to justify downsizing. The most frequent critique against BPR concerned the strict focus on efficiency and technology and the disregard for people within organizations subject to reengineering initiatives. Reengineering treated the people inside companies as if they were just interchangeable parts to be reengineered. But no one wants to 'be reengineered'. Other criticisms and problems associated with BPR include

implementation of generic (best-practice) processes that did not fit specific company needs and that many organizations simply perform BPR as a one-off project with limited strategy alignment and long-term perspective. The goal of process management is not to replace vertical structures with horizontal ones. Rather, it is to intertwine and reinforce the best aspects of both – strong functional expertise and flexible, responsive processes. The new organization must deliver both and more (Stalk and Black, 1994). We revisit BPR later in Chapter 24.

21.11 BUSINESS PROCESS MANAGEMENT (BPM)

29.   Business Process Management (BPM) can be considered as a successor to the BPR wave of the 1990s. BPM is intended to align business processes with strategic objectives and customers' needs but also requires a change in a company's emphasis from functional to process orientation. BPM has been defined as a systematic, structured approach to analyze, improve, control and manage processes with the aim of improving the quality of products and services. BPM differs from business process reengineering in that it does not aim at one-off revolutionary changes to business processes, but at their continuous evolution. The activities which constitute business process management can be grouped into three categories: design, execution and monitoring. Whereas TQM emphasized continuous improvement in a traditional (vertical) structure and BPR advocated transformational change within the horizontal organization, BPM embraces both types of change but within a more horizontal design. The term Business Process Management as a field of study is still in its infancy, yet the interest in BPM has grown steadily over recent years, Hung (2006); principles of Business Process Management include:

- a holistic view (BPM addresses the interdependence of strategy, people, processes and technology in achieving business objectives)

- strategic imperative

- enabled by information technology

- corporate-wide impact, BPM affects every aspect of an organization, from its structure (organized around processes) to its management (process leaders versus functional heads) and

- emphasizes cross-functional process management.

CONCLUSION

30.   Designing and redesigning jobs is not easy. Changes in one part of a job hierarchy are bound to bring about changes elsewhere. Change may be welcome in one group, but not in another. This is likely to cause tensions between groups. Individuals may initially welcome change, but then feel less enthusiastic if related job conditions (pay, re-training, etc.) do not meet their needs. Supervisory staff may feel particularly threatened by any form of job redesign, but will expect to benefit ultimately. However, when work can be redesigned effectively, the rewards are twofold. For individuals, there is the opportunity to find personally challenging and satisfying work. For firms, there is the opportunity to achieve lower costs, better quality and improved productivity through a more effective match between the needs of people and the requirements of technology. The approach to work structuring and job design embodied in some aspects of Business Process Re-engineering focuses on key business processes rather than on tasks and operational structures in designing work. This may lead to job losses for some, but also to more interesting and challenging jobs for others. Organizations employing BPR may enjoy reduced costs of production and improved customer relations.

QUESTIONS

1   Evaluate theories of motivation and their contribution to job design.

2   Select a job with which you are familiar and redesign it with the approaches discussed in mind. Explain what you may change and why.

3   List and describe the various approaches to work design.

4   Why should managers be concerned with job design? Why are they unlikely to give it the full attention it may deserve?

5   How might technology affect the organization of work?

6   Why, despite criticisms, is job simplification so popular amongst job designers?

7   Evaluate job simplification as an approach to job design.

8   Discuss the impact of human relations theories on work design, listing and describing three main approaches to achieving increased job satisfaction.

9   What is a business process? You should provide examples to support your answer.

10 Contrast two methods used by organizations to improve their business processes.

USEFUL WEBSITES

EDUCAUSE: **www.educause.edu/node/645/tid/ 17023?time=1286377022**
Business Process Reengineering – Resources

BPM: **www.bpm.com/**
Articles, news, research and white papers on Business Process Management and workflow

VIDEO CASES

Now take a look at the online video cases – visit the companion website to work through real world business problems associated with the concepts presented within this chapter.

43 Work Design – flexibility and the contemporary workplace
Explores alternative work arrangements. Considers technology and work organization.

REFERENCES

Buchanan, D. and Huczynski, A. (2010) 'Organizational Behaviour', Ed. 7. Financial Times Press.

Daft, R. L. (2009) 'New Era of Management', Ed. 9. South-Western, Div of Thomson Learning; International ed

Davenport, T. (1994) 'Managing in the New World of Process', Public Productivity & Management Review, Vol. 18 no 2, Winter 1994, p. 133–147.

Hammer, M. (1990) 'Reengineering Work: Don't Automate, Obliterate', Harvard Business Review, Jul/Aug 90, Vol. 68 Issue 4, p. 104–112.

Hammer, M. (2001) 'The Superefficient Company', Harvard Business Review, Sep 2001, Vol. 79 Issue 8, p. 82–91.

Hammer, M. (2007) 'The Process Audit', Harvard Business Review, Apr 2007, Vol. 85 Issue 4, p. 111–123.

Hung, R. (2006) 'Business Process Management as Competitive Advantage: a Review and Empirical Study', Total Quality Management, Vol. 17, No. 1, p. 21–40.

Laguna, M. and Marklund, J. (2005) 'Business Process Modeling, Simulation and Design', Prentice Hall.

Magal, S. and Word, J. (2009) 'Essentials of Business Processes and Information Systems', Wiley.

Mullins, L. (2010) 'Management and Organizational Behaviour', Ed. 9. Financial Times Press.

Stalk, G. and Black, J. (1994) 'The myth of the horizontal organization', Canadian Business Review, Winter 94, Vol. 21 Issue 4, p. 26–30.

Section Nine
Organizing for Management

CASE STUDY

ORGANISING FOR MANAGEMENT

STRUCTURE OF POLICING IN LONDON

London is a vibrant, successful city, the seat of Government and a cultural and financial world leader. It has a diverse population of over seven and a half million, rising by 40,000 a year, presenting the Police with a huge challenge, from street crime to sophisticated criminal networks and escalating technology-related crime.

The Metropolitan Police Service (MPS) is London's biggest employer – a large organisation with a £3.6 billion gross budget, more than 50,000 employees and an enormous responsibility to deliver good policing services. The MPS aims to satisfy an increasing body of stakeholders, particularly the Government, the Mayor and the people of London, whilst engaging in a growing number of partnerships to reduce crime and increase public reassurance. Objectives include reducing crime and catching criminals; making communities safer; saving lives and reducing harm (protecting the public); preventing violent extremism and engaging communities in fighting crime. The MPS mission focuses on making London the safest major city in the world. They must do this in a climate of tightening financial resources and an ongoing need to ensure value for money to taxpayers. They must therefore continually look to improve the way they do business in delivering effective and efficient policing whilst making their services accessible.

The MPS is famed around the world and has a unique place in the history of policing. It is by far the largest of the police services that operate in the UK. Founded by Sir Robert Peel in 1829, the original establishment of 1,000 officers policed a seven-mile radius from Charing Cross and a population of less than 2 million. Today, the Metropolitan Police Service employs more than 33,000 officers together with about 14,200 police staff, 270 traffic wardens and 4,700 Police Community Support Officers (PCSOs). The MPS is also being supported by more than 2,500 volunteer police officers in the Metropolitan Special Constabulary (MSC) and its Employer Supported Policing (ESP) programme. The Metropolitan Police Services covers an area of 620 square miles.

The head of the Metropolitan Police Service traditionally holds the rank of Commissioner. Next in the leadership structure is the Deputy Commissioner. There are five Assistant Commissioners: responsible for (1) Territorial Policing, (2) the Specialist Crime Directorate; (3) Specialist Operations and for (4) Central Operations and (5) Olympics. Additionally, the leadership team (senior managers) includes a Director for each of the following: Human Resources, Resources, Public Affairs and Internal Communication and a Director of Information. Collectively they make up the Management Board of the Metropolitan Police Service.

The Metropolitan Police Service is a large organisation with a complex command structure that reflects the diverse range of tasks it is expected to undertake. It is made up of many different departments. Each department has a different focus, but they all work together towards the vision of making London the safest major city in the world.

The rank structure of Metropolitan Police officers is as follows (starting at the top): Commissioner > Deputy Commissioner > Assistant Commissioner > Deputy Assistant Commissioner > Commander > Chief Superintendent > Superintendent > Chief Inspector > Inspector > Sergeant > Constable. The prefix detective is given to officers who have been assigned to investigative work after completing the appropriate selection and training. Detective ranks parallel uniformed ranks and range from Detective Constable to Detective Chief Superintendent.

The MPS (operations) structure is geared around the -five responsibilities of the assistant commissioners (see above). The day to day policing of London is the responsibility of 33 borough operational command units. Collectively these form London's local police (Territorial Policing). In addition to policing London's streets, the Met has various specialist units dedicated to reducing all aspects of serious and specialist crime. The intention of the Specialist Crime Directorate is to investigate serious and organised crime in London, and work with communities and partners to prevent harm to Londoners. They deal with crimes including murder; fatal and non-fatal shootings; armed robberies; drug trafficking; people smuggling, life threatening kidnaps; child abuse and paedophilia; organised

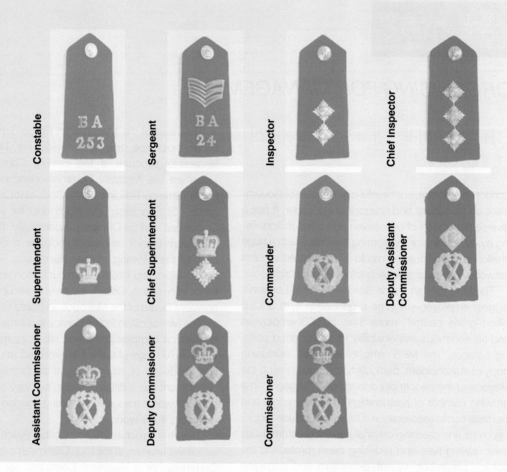

prostitution, people trafficking and extreme pornography; computer crime and fraud; rape and serious sexual offences. The Met has various specialist units that work across the capital or which fulfil a national role. A number of these are grouped into a section of the organisation known as Specialist Operations. Specialist Operations is divided into three sections known as commands. Within these three commands, there are seven units whose roles are to help keep safe people who live in, work in and visit London. The three commands are: (1) Counter Terrorism Command which aims to protect London and the UK from the threat of terrorism; (2) Protection Command provides armed personal protection services for ministers, high level government figures, visiting heads of government and Royalty Protection provides protection of the monarch and other members of the royal family; and (3) Protective Security Command which provides additional security and counter-terrorism coordination for London, as well as financial, resources and HR support for the Specialist Operations business group. Central Operations consists of a number of specialist units that provide a broad range of policing functions. These units

effectively provide an integrated, collaborative and community focussed service to London.

An organisation the size of the Metropolitan Police Service could not function without various management, administration and support functions. For this reason the Met has thousands of staff, including police officers as well as civilians, who work behind the scenes to ensure that the front line units can do their job. Their functions include recruitment, training, personnel management, provision of information technology, publicity and communications. Some functions, such as vehicle maintenance and aspects of information technology and telecommunications, have been contracted out to the private sector.

The work of the Metropolitan Police Service (MPS) is scrutinised by the Metropolitan Police Authority (MPA) who hold the MPS accountable for the business plan, its delivery and resources used. In planning terms the Service has a major challenge in managing police officer numbers against future funding levels given the lengthy recruitment and borough based training process.

Source: www.met.police.uk

CHAPTER 22
ORGANIZATION STRUCTURES

Key Concepts

- Contingency approach to organization structure
- Design (structure) purpose
- Functional structure
- Organizational design
- Organizational structure
- Product structure
- Structure
- Tall hierarchical structure

Learning Outcomes   Having read this chapter, you should be able to:

- define and discuss the nature of organization design
- identify factors likely to determine the design of organizations
- explain the basic parts of organizations
- evaluate common organization designs (structural forms)
- compare centralization and decentralization
- discuss organization levels in different contexts

22.1 INTRODUCTION

1. As was discussed in the previous chapter, not all employees perform the same work activities, nor should they if efficiency gains are to be made from specialization. There are many work tasks to be carried out in any organization and consequently the work must be divided up and allocated. Employees performing similar work are often grouped together in order to manage interdependencies and work activity. Once work has been allocated and differentiated there is then a need to integrate the various parts of the organization, ensuring they pull together to achieve corporate goals. The overall pattern of structural components and configurations used to manage the total organization is termed the organization design.

2. A number of fundamental design questions may be proposed for managers of organizations: should jobs be broken down into narrow areas of work (specialization) or do we, for flexibility, require generalists? Should there be a tall or flat hierarchy i.e. how many levels of management do we need? How should jobs and therefore people be grouped together (by function, geography or product)? How should employee groups be differentiated and integrated? Within this chapter we seek answers to such questions and consider aspects of organizational design and structure, noting Duncan (1972) who suggested that organizational structure is more than boxes on a chart; it is a pattern of interactions and co-ordination linking technology, tasks and human components of the organization to ensure the organization accomplishes its purpose.

Organizational design The design of an organization patterns its formal structure and culture. It allocates purpose and power to departments and individuals. It lays down guidelines for authoritarian or participative management by its rigidity or flexibility, its hierarchical or non-hierarchical structure

3. The study of organization design and structure (the words will be used interchangeably throughout this chapter) has been a major source of interest for classical theorists (see Chapter 3), the inspiration for Weber's theory of bureaucracy (Chapter 4), and a key element in the work of the theorists of complex organization – the contingency school (Chapter 10). This chapter summarizes the structural issues facing modern organizations and identifies the most important practical options available to senior management.

4. In the opening part of the chapter we explore what organizational design means and ask what is its purpose? We then consider elements of structure (the building blocks) before discussing how they may be configured. We outline the common designs to be found within organizations before concluding with a discussion of the determinants of structure.

22.2 DESIGN PURPOSE

5. An organization is a group of people who work together. The group share a unifying purpose i.e. they have common goals. As companies (organizations) grow they need to arrange and cluster workers together according to the business-related activities they undertake i.e. they need to decompose the group into smaller, more manageable groups. One of the most challenging tasks of a business may be organizing the people who perform its work. A business may start small but as the business grows, the amount and type of work performed increases, and more people are needed to perform various tasks. In order to avoid duplication and ensure all necessary work is undertaken, companies typically allocate work to individuals (see previous chapter) and group the individuals who perform similar work. Through this division of work, individuals can become specialists at a particular job (and therefore more efficient). However, no one person will typically transform all of the raw materials into the finished product or create and deliver the complete service to the customer. Consequently, the outputs of one person's work may form the inputs of another i.e. different individuals and parts of the organization become dependent upon each other. Because there are many people – often in different locations – working towards a common objective, there must be a plan showing how the work will be organized. The plan for the systematic arrangement of work is the formal organization structure.

6. An organization structure describes the way in which the interrelated groups of an organization are constructed – the way in which employees are formally divided into groups for co-ordination and control. The primary purpose of design is to divide and allocate work and then coordinate and control that work so that goals are met. An appropriate design might yield benefits such as efficiency and scale, the ability to access specialized and location-embedded resources, enhanced innovation through operations across markets and the creation of operational flexibility with which to respond to factors outside a firm's control. The design can impact upon performance through employee motivation, commitment and loyalty and has the ability to link interdependent activities. The design may also impact upon the sharing of resources, including information and knowledge.

22.3 ELEMENTS OF STRUCTURE

7. Structure is a complex term and there are many aspects to it. We introduced some of the elements of structure in Chapters 3 and 4 when we discussed specialization, centralization, formalization and standardization as dimensions of bureaucracy. Organization structure (also termed design) comprises functions, relationships, responsibilities, authorities and communication of individuals within each part of the company. In this section we explore the dimensions, tools and elements of organizational structure before considering how such dimensions and elements may be configured in overall organizational designs.

8. Tools used to add structure include:

Organizational chart – a plan of formal relations which the company intends should prevail within it.

Job definitions – the task requirements of a particular job in the organization.

Span of control – the number of subordinates who report directly to a single manager or supervisor.

Authority – the right to guide or direct the actions of others.

Responsibility – an obligation placed on a person, who occupies a certain position in the organization structure, to perform a task, function or assignment.

Accountability – responsibility for some activity.

Centralization The degree to which the authority to make certain decisions is located at the top of the management hierarchy

Design (structure) purpose The primary purposes of design are to divide and allocate work and then coordinate and control that work so that goals are met

Organizational structure The way in which the interrelated groups of an organization are constructed

Authority The right to make particular decisions and to exercise control over resources

9. Aside from considering the aforementioned elements of structure there are other constructs, tools and frameworks that may be utilized during the design process. Mintzberg, at the strategic level, identified five basic parts of an organizational structure (Figure 22.1), summarized as follows: A 'strategic apex' comprising the chief executive and directors; then, proceeding down the operational line, a 'middle line' of operational management, followed by the 'operating core' of those directly involved in supplying the firm's goods and services; on either side of the operational line (traditionally called 'the line' in classical thinking) are (i) the 'techno-structure' comprising functional specialists and advisors, and (ii) the 'support staff', who provide corporate services (and who in classical terms would be seen as 'staff' employees).

FIGURE 22.1 **The basic parts of organizations – Mintzberg's model.**

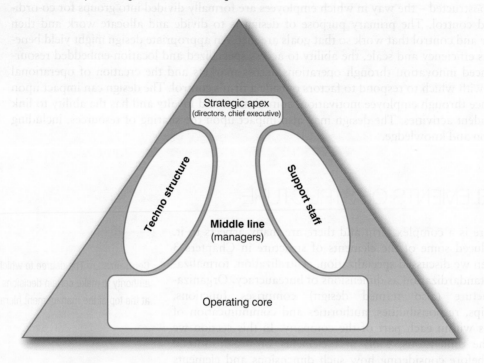

Source: Adapted from Mintzberg, H. (1983) 'Structural configurations' *Structure in Fives: Designing Effective Organizations*. pp 11, 280–281. Copyright © Pearson Education, Inc. Upper Saddle River, NJ. Used with permission.

10. Mintzberg's model looks, on the surface, as though it is the hierarchical model we associate with bureaucracy, but he uses it flexibly to develop five different configurations of structure. These configurations reduce the separate influences of key organizational features into manageable concepts that can be used in the study of organizations. In Mintzberg's own words 'In each structural configuration, a different one of the coordinating mechanisms is dominant, a different part of the organization plays the most important role, and a different type of decentralization is used.' The five configurations are as follows:

> **Machine bureaucracy** A type of organization which possesses all the bureaucratic characteristics. The important decisions are made at the top, while at the bottom, standardized procedures are used to exercise control

Simple Structure (basically no structure)

Machine bureaucracy (dominated by technical/specialist priorities)

Professional bureaucracy (dominated by skills of core staff)

Divisionalized form (dominated by products/outputs)

Adhocracy (shared dominance of core staff and support services).

> **Adhocracy** A type of organization design which is temporary, adaptive and creative, in contrast with bureaucracy which tends to be permanent, rule-driven and inflexible

11. Mintzberg analyzed each configuration in terms of the organization's prime coordinating mechanism, its key part, the main design parameters and certain contingency factors. The analysis can be summarized as shown in Figure 22.2. By reviewing the implications of the five-configuration model, an organization's senior management can consider the alternatives open to them, identify those parts of the organization that are most likely to be affected by them and design the appropriate parameters. They can consider these aspects of organization design against the contingency factors (e.g. size, age of

FIGURE 22.2   Structural configurations (Mintzberg).

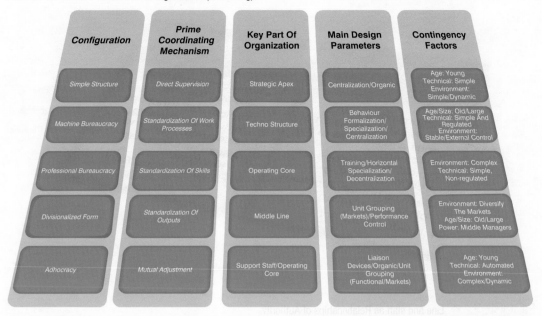

Configuration	Prime Coordinating Mechanism	Key Part Of Organization	Main Design Parameters	Contingency Factors
Simple Structure	Direct Supervision	Strategic Apex	Centralization/Organic	Age: Young Technical: Simple Environment: Simple/Dynamic
Machine Bureaucracy	Standardization Of Work Processes	Techno Structure	Behaviour Formalization/ Specialization/ Centralization	Age/Size: Old/Large Technical: Simple And Regulated Environment: Stable/External Control
Professional Bureaucracy	Standardization Of Skills	Operating Core	Training/Horizontal Specialization/ Decentralization	Environment: Complex Technical: Simple, Non-regulated
Divisionalized Form	Standardization Of Outputs	Middle Line	Unit Grouping (Markets)/Performance Control	Environment: Diversify The Markets Age/Size: Old/Large Power: Middle Managers
Adhocracy	Mutual Adjustment	Support Staff/Operating Core	Liaison Devices/Organic/Unit Grouping (Functional/Markets)	Age: Young Technical: Automated Environment: Complex/Dynamic

business, state of external environment) that typify their organization. The Aston Group (Chapter 10) had shown earlier, for example, that organizational growth tended to lead to greater specialization, more standardization (i.e. of procedures, methods, personnel practices) and more formalization (i.e. written rules etc.), but less centralization. What Mintzberg's ideas about configuration demonstrate is that particular sets of mechanisms and design features lead to identifiable forms of organization structure – the configuration (discussed in more detail later).

12. When establishing the structure, designers typically start by defining larger groups, then decomposing them into smaller units. Departmentalization is a process of grouping together employees who share a common supervisor and resources, who are jointly responsible for performance and who tend to identify and collaborate with each other. The organizational chart usually shows the departments within an organization. The chart also shows relationships between departmental staff in the organization which can be line (direct relationship between superior and subordinate); lateral (relationship between different departments on the same hierarchical level), staff and functional. At a high level, designers distinguish between different categories of employee. For example Staff employees are workers who are in advisory positions and who use their specialized expertise to support the efforts of line employees. The terms 'line' and 'staff' are usually understood in two senses: firstly, as functions contributing to organization objectives (Figure 22.3), and, secondly, as relationships of authority (Figure 22.4). Taking these meanings in order, we can summarize the most frequent views that have been expressed about 'line' and 'staff'. In terms of relationships of authority, 'line' and 'staff' can be more effectively distinguished if 'staff' is sub-divided into service and functional as shown in Figure 22.4.

13. Organization structure is as much about power and authority as it is about grouping activities and deploying key roles. The inevitable push towards specialization in all but the smallest of organizations leads to the diffusion of authority and accountability. The

Line relationship The links, as shown on an organizational chart, that exist between managers and staff whom they oversee directly

Staff relationship A link between workers in advisory positions and line employees – staff employees use their specialized expertise to support the efforts of line employees who may chose to act on the advice given

FIGURE 22.3 Line and staff as functions.

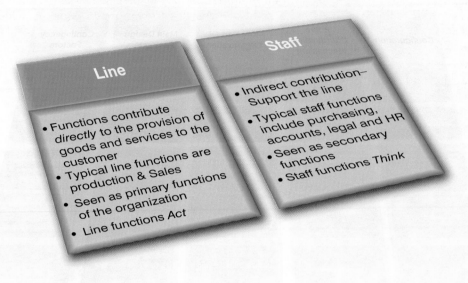

FIGURE 22.4 Line and staff as Relationships of Authority.

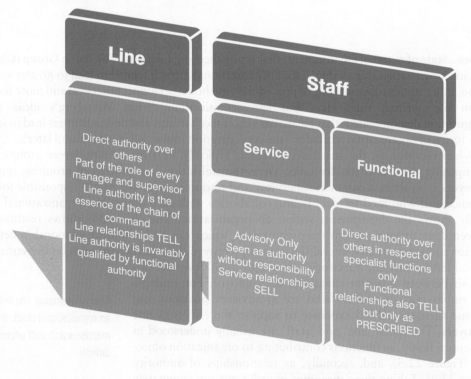

need to structure activities develops logically into the need to allocate appropriate amounts of authority to those responsible for undertaking those activities. Thus, every organization, regardless of size, has to consider what degree of authority to delegate from the centre, or the top. Only the small entrepreneurial organization can effectively retain authority at the centre. Most organizations have to decide how, and how much, to delegate to managers and others throughout the job hierarchy.

14. The concept of centralization, as it is being considered here, is not referring to the physical dispersal of an organization, but to the dispersal of the authority to commit the organization's

resources. The physical deployment of an organization may or may not reflect genuine power sharing. In our definition, therefore, a highly decentralized organization is one in which the authority to commit people, money and materials is widely diffused throughout every level of the structure. Conversely, a highly centralized organization is one where little authority is exercised outside a key group of senior managers. In practice, some functions are more easily decentralized than others. So, even highly decentralized organizations tend to reserve certain key functions to the centre. As well as planning and research, it is usually the finance and personnel functions that are least decentralized, because of the need to maintain procedural consistency and legal and other standards.

15. The advantages of decentralization are chiefly, it:

- prevents senior management overload

- speeds up operational decisions by enabling line units to take local actions

- enables local management to be flexible in their approach to decisions in the light of local conditions, and thus be more adaptable in situations of rapid change

- focuses attention on important cost and profit centres within the total organization, which sharpens management awareness of cost-effectiveness as well as revenue targets

- can contribute to staff (increased responsibility).

16. The main disadvantages of decentralization are that it:

- requires an adequate control and communication system if major errors of judgement are to be avoided on the part of operational management

- requires greater coordination by senior management to ensure that individual units in the organization are not working against the interests of the whole

- can lead to inconsistency of treatment of customers, clients or the public, especially in service industries

- may encourage parochial attitudes in subsidiary units

- does require a plentiful supply of capable and well-motivated managers, able to respond to the increased responsibility which decentralization brings about.

17. On balance, there are clear advantages and disadvantages associated with centralization which may suit some strategies but not others. Organizations vary in the extent of decentralization which may be viewed more as a grey scale than a binary choice. It is worth recalling at this point the University of Aston study's conclusion (see Chapter 10) that large size tends to lead to less centralization, but relatively more specialization, more rules and more procedures (formalization).

18. Organizations can be tall or flat in relation to their total size and number of management levels. The main features of a tall organization are shown in Figure 22.5.

> **Tall hierarchical structure** An organization that has narrow spans of control and a relatively large number of levels of authority

Tall (traditional/hierarchical) organization structures tend to have many authority levels with narrow spans of control. The advantages of tall structures arise mainly from their ability to sustain a very high degree of specialization of functions and roles. They can also provide ample career and promotion opportunities for employees. Their principal disadvantages are connected with long lines of communication and decision-making. Thus tall structures seem to go hand in hand with formality and standardization, which may discourage initiative and risk-taking at operational levels. Flat organizations tend to have few authority levels and a wide span of control. In recent times, as flatter structures become more common, there have been major efforts

FIGURE 22.5 **Chart of a tall organization structure.**

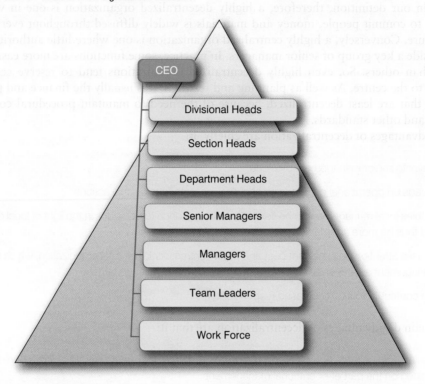

to delegate authority throughout the system by empowering workforce teams in a way not thought possible or desirable some years ago. A flat organization is less likely to provide career development opportunities than a taller structure. On the other hand, a flat organization has fewer problems of communication and coordination, does encourage delegation by the managers involved and can motivate rank-and-file employees to take greater responsibility for their output. See Figure 22.6

FIGURE 22.6 **Chart of a flat organization structure.**

19. The major factors in determining the number of levels for any one organization are likely to be the size of the operation; nature of operation, especially in relation to the complexity of production and the dominant management style. As a general rule, the smaller the organization, the more likely it is to have no more than three or four levels, and the larger it is, the more likely it is to have seven or eight levels (though many contemporary medium to large organizations will aim for five management levels). Factors such as the technology employed can offset the influence of size alone.

20. Two other concepts important to organization structure are authority and responsibility. Authority is the legitimate power to act in certain ways; it emanates from the top, and can be delegated to subordinates. Relatively few people in an organization are endowed with authority. Line authority is the authority that every manager exercises in respect of his or her own subordinates. Thus specialist managers, such as chief accountants and personnel managers, exercise line authority over their own staff. In this role they are not different from so-called line managers, such as production managers and sales managers. Line authority, then, is not dependent on line functions. It is the central feature of the total chain of command throughout the entire organization structure. Staff authority, is derived from the staff function, and this does relate it to the advisory and service functions of the internal structure of an organization. However, because of the very interdependence of all the key functions in a modern organization, one must distinguish between those aspects of the staff function that merely provide services (e.g. costing, recruitment, market research, etc.), and those that provide key standards of performance for all other sections of the organization (e.g. setting and monitoring company accounting procedures, installing and controlling industrial relations procedures, etc.).

21. Responsibility is the obligation to perform certain functions on behalf of the organization; responsibility may range from the very specific to the very broad; it is commonly called accountability; unlike authority it cannot be delegated. Every job-holder has some level of responsibility for their work. Both of the above concepts can be distinguished from power, which is the ability to implement actions, regardless of considerations of formal authority or responsibility.

22.4 COMMON STRUCTURES – ORGANIZATION DESIGNS

22. Organizations face choices when designing the formal organization. The formal organization is the collection of work groups that has been consciously designed by senior management to maximize efficiency and achieve organizational goals as opposed to the informal organization – the network of relationships that establish themselves spontaneously between members of an organization on the basis of their common interests and friendships. The formal organization is the planners' conception of how the intended consequences of the organization may best be achieved. The organizational design or **structure** must be a solution to many problems. When grouping activities and people the designer must consider how much to take account of specialization (how narrow the work will be); whether the organization should be tall or flat (span of control) and how to group people (by specialism, product or area). Degrees of control must also be determined along with centralization and formalization and the mechanisms to be used for **integration**.

Structure The structure of an organization is the way in which employees are formally divided into groups for co-ordination and control

23. Perhaps the first major design challenge – typically considered by senior managers and supported by HR professionals – concerns the manner in which employees are grouped together (by area, function/specialism, product or process worked on). Arguments for the alternative grouping approaches typically consider the type of knowledge that is most important when adding value and undertaking the organization's primary activities – is it more important to know about the area worked in or the product created?

Integration The required level to which units in an organization are linked together, and their respective degree of independence (Integrative mechanisms include rules and procedures and direct managerial control)

Arguments may also be made in relation to organizational strategy and the source of sustainable competitive advantage.

24. There are a number of alternative ways of deploying the intangible webs of relationships that make up an organization structure. The most common forms of structure that have been 'designed' are as follows:

Functional organization – based on groupings of business functions such as production, marketing, finance, personnel.

Product-based organization – based on individual products, or product ranges, where each grouping carries its own functional specialisms.

Geographical organization (**Area Structure**) – centred around appropriate geographical features, e.g. regions, nations, subcontinents.

Divisionalized structure – usually based on products, or geography, or both and with certain key functions such as planning and finance reserved for headquarters.

Matrix structures – based on a combination of functional organization with project-based structures, and thereby combining vertical and lateral lines of communication and authority.

Process organization.

> **Area Structure** The organization is structured according to geographical areas

These structures are considered in the following paragraphs, commencing with functional organization.

25. In a functional organization structure, tasks are linked together on the basis of common functions. Thus, all production activities, or all financial activities, are grouped together in a single function which undertakes all the tasks required of that function. A typical chart of a functional organization is as shown in Figure 22.7. The main advantages of functional organization are that by grouping people together on the basis of their technical and specialist expertise, the organization can facilitate both their utilization and their coordination in the service of the whole enterprise. Functional grouping also provides better opportunities for promotion and career development.

FIGURE 22.7 Functional organization structure.

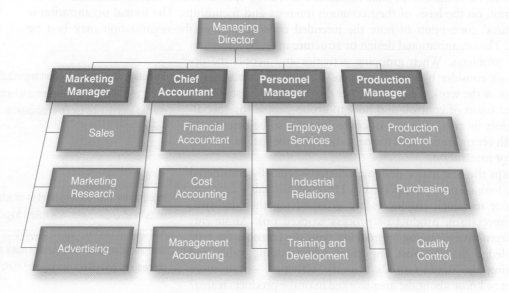

The disadvantages are primarily the growth of sectional interests which may conflict with the needs of the organization as a whole, and the difficulties of adapting this form of organization to meet issues such as product diversification or geographical dispersement. Functional structures are probably best suited to relatively stable environments.

Functional structure The organization is structured according to functional areas such as finance, marketing and HR

26. Another frequent form of grouping is by product. This is a popular structural form in large organizations having a wide range of products or services. In the National Health Service, for example, the key groups of employees – medical, nursing, para-medical and hotel services – are dispersed according to the service they provide, e.g. maternity, orthopaedic, surgical, psychiatric and

Product Structure The organization is structured according to related products or services

other services. By comparison, a large pharmaceutical company could be organized as shown in Figure 22.8. The advantages of a product organization as shown are that it enables diversification to take place, it can cope better with problems of technological change by grouping people with expertise and their specialized equipment in one major unit. The main disadvantage is that each general manager may promote their own product group to the detriment of other parts of the company. In this situation senior management must exercise careful controls, without, at the same time, removing the motivation to produce results within the product managers.

27. Another familiar form of organization structure is the one grouped on a geographical basis. This is usually adopted where the realities of a national or international network of activities make some kind of regional structure essential for decision-making and control. An example of this form of organization is shown in Figure 22.9. As in a product organization, the geographi-cally-based organization tends to produce decentralized activities, which may cause additional control problems for senior management. Hence it is usual with such structures to find groups of senior functional managers at headquarters in order to provide direction and guidance to line managers in the regions or product groups.

28. With increasing complexity and size, many companies are opting for a mixed structure, which may combine the benefits of two or more of functional, product and geographical forms of

FIGURE 22.8 Example of a product-based structure.

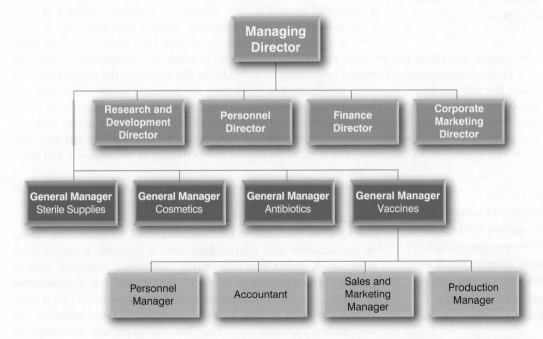

FIGURE 22.9 Geographically based structure for a road transport company.

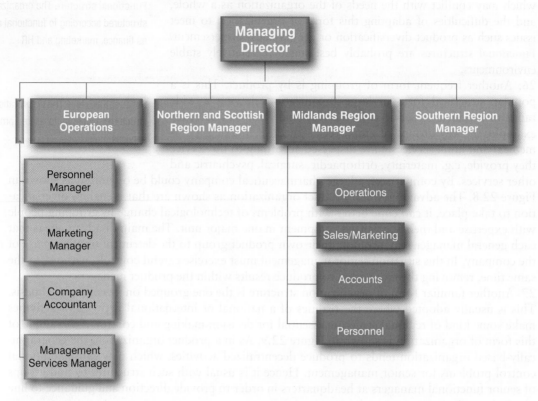

Divisional structure A design whereby an organization is split into a number of self-contained business units, each of which operates as a profit centre

organization. Two such mixed structures will be looked at briefly: divisionalized structures and matrix structures. In the case of a divisionalized structure, the organization is divided up into divisions on the basis of products or geography, and each division is operated in a functional form, but with certain key functions retained at company headquarters (e.g. planning, finance and personnel policy). This is a common organizational form for highly diversified firms operating in more than one country. Figure 22.10 shows an example of a divisionalized structure in a British pharmaceutical company, operating worldwide. In this example, the regions act very much like self-standing companies, producing and marketing the products developed by the parent company. Research and development activities and key corporate standards are controlled worldwide via the functional divisions, whilst the headquarters division provides group policy in key areas such as finance and personnel. A balance can therefore be maintained between necessary corporate control from the centre and desired divisional independence at the regional and functional levels.

29. Matrix structures are organizational forms which have evolved as a result of coordination problems in highly complex industries such as aircraft manufacture, where functional and product types of structure have not been able to meet organizational demands for a variety of key activities and relationships arising from the required work processes. A matrix structure usually combines a functional form of structure with a project or product-based structure, as demonstrated in Figure 22.8. The main feature of a matrix structure is that it combines lateral with vertical lines of communication and authority (see also matrix management). This has the important advantage of

Matrix Management A system of management operating in a horizontal as well as vertical organization structure, where, typically, a manager reports to two superiors – one a departmental/line manager and the other a functional/project manager

FIGURE 22.10 Divisionalized structure.

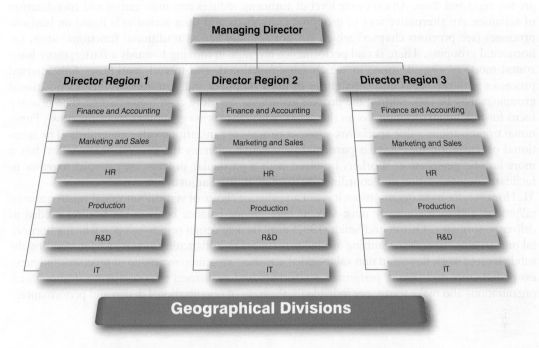

Managing Director

Director Region 1 | Director Region 2 | Director Region 3

Finance and Accounting | Finance and Accounting | Finance and Accounting

Marketing and Sales | Marketing and Sales | Marketing and Sales

HR | HR | HR

Production | Production | Production

R&D | R&D | R&D

IT | IT | IT

Geographical Divisions

combining the relative stability and efficiency of a hierarchical structure with the flexibility and informality of an organic form of structure. However, like all organizational form, matrix structures do have their disadvantages. The most important are the potential conflicts that can arise concerning the allocation of resources and the division of authority; the relative dilution of functional management responsibilities throughout the organization; and the possibility of divided loyalties. See Figure 22.11 30. The vertical/functional hierarchy (see previous designs) has been at the core of business since the industrial revolution. There are, however, many associated problems: the vertical design fosters fragmented tasks, overspecialization, empires, and turf wars, delays in decision-making and

FIGURE 22.11 Typical matrix structure (engineering industry).

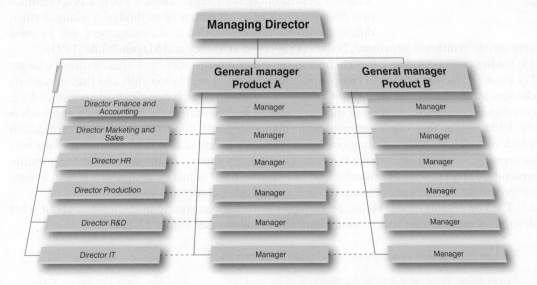

Managing Director

General manager Product A | General manager Product B

Director Finance and Accounting | Manager | Manager

Director Marketing and Sales | Manager | Manager

Director HR | Manager | Manager

Director Production | Manager | Manager

Director R&D | Manager | Manager

Director IT | Manager | Manager

other negatives that inhibit responsiveness. There is general agreement that vertical structures are too rigid and slow. An excessive level of authority reduces communication and coordination of activities. An alternative way of grouping individuals and their activities is based on business processes (see previous chapter) which cut horizontally across traditional functional areas i.e. horizontal grouping. There is real performance leverage in moving towards a flatter, more horizontal mode of organization, in which cross-functional, end-to-end workflows link internal processes with the needs and capabilities of both suppliers and customers. Whereas functional groupings may be task centred the process groupings are more customer-oriented. The primary focus for functional groupings is on the 'what' whereas process groupings focus on 'how'. Functional organizations value specialists whereas process organizations value generalists. The functional organization may have a parochial perspective whereas the process organization has a more holistic perspective. Workers involved with a particular process are grouped together to facilitate communication and coordination through mutual adjustment.

31. However, for most organizations it is not an either/or choice of vertical/functional versus horizontal/process and each company must seek its own unique balance between the features needed to deliver performance. Ostroff and Smith (1992) distil the key design principles upon which a horizontal organization depends: organizing around process not task; flattening hierarchy by minimizing the subdivision of work flows and non value-added activities; assigning ownership of processes and process performance and linking performance objectives and evaluation to customer satisfaction. Such organizations also make teams, not individuals, the basis of organizational design and performance.

22.5 DETERMINANTS OF DESIGN – KEY ORGANIZATIONAL VARIABLES

32. So far we have highlighted the common types of structure and listed the elements of structure that can be configured to create unique designs. The search for a good design is continual. But what makes a good design – what rules might designers draw upon when configuring the organization's structural variables? In Chapters 9 and 10 we advocated the need to ensure the structure 'fits' the strategy and therefore, an appropriate design might enable the achievement of strategies such as cost leadership, **differentiation** and focus.

Differentiation The degree to which the tasks and the work of individuals, groups and units are divided up within an organization

33. Designing the organization involves configuring necessary structures, processes, practices and policies and allocating resources to achieve a desired business strategy. 'There is not one best organization design, or style of management or method of working. Rather, different patterns of organization and management will be most appropriate in different situations', Nadler (1980) cited in Mabey and Mayon-White (1993).

34. Nadler points out that 'often changes in the environment necessitate organizational change. For example, factors related to competition, technology or regulation shift and thus necessitate changes in organizational strategy'. Contingency theory research has clearly demonstrated the correlation between structure and the environment and central to the contingency approach is the basic notion that organizational performance depends upon taking management action which is consistent with the situation. It is now widely accepted that there is no single best way to organize, structure or manage the firm. Contingency theory, in the context of organization structure, argues that an organization, to be effective, must adjust its design/structure in a manner consistent with its environment, technology and other contextual factors.

35. The key organizational issues, or variables featuring recurrently in discussions about what determines organization structures are basically as follows (see Figure 22.12):

Purpose/goals (the fundamental aims and goals of the group)

People (those who make up the organization).

FIGURE 22.12 Major variables in establishing organization structure.

Tasks (those basic activities required to achieve organizational aims and goals).

Technology (the technical aspects of the internal environment).

Culture (the dominant values guiding the organization).

External Environment (the external market, technological and social conditions affecting the organization's activities).

36. Environmental determinism theory states that internal organizational responses are wholly or mainly shaped, influenced or determined by external environmental factors. Externally, the contemporary turbulent environment calls for flexible, adaptable and responsive structures; historically, a more predictable environment favoured the bureaucratic approach. Environmental variables include: cultural, social, technological, educational, legal, political, economic, ecological and demographic factors. Specific environmental variables might include customers/clients, suppliers (including labour), competitors, technology and socio-political factors.

37. When undertaking any enterprise, the design of a suitable structure must begin with some idea of what the organization is there for, and where it intends to go. In other words, the prime purpose, or raison d'etre, of the group plays a key role in directing the members towards the kind of structure required. In making this step the group must take account of the external environment, and the nature of that environment in terms of change or stability. The next step is to identify the key tasks that must be accomplished if the group is to succeed in its purpose. This leads on to a consideration of people, especially the skills and talents of current members, and the identification of any gaps in their portfolio of skills and knowledge, which may have to be bridged by training, or the employment of newcomers. The question of technology will also have to be addressed. What production systems are already in operation, or planned? What equipment will be necessary? What are the demands of new software systems on people and work processes? How well do existing staff cope with new technology? Lastly, there is one other important variable, which must be taken into account, and that is the organization's culture (or

value system). Given the dynamic nature of organizations, it is likely that there will be pressures to adapt the structure somewhere in the organization, even if not overall. Thus structuring and re-structuring is a continual process in the life of many organizations.

CONCLUSION

38. This chapter focused on how to (organize) make efficient and effective use of human resources in order to attain goals through design and structure. We identified the purpose of design – to divide up organizational activities, allocate resources, tasks and goals and to coordinate and control activities so that goals can be achieved. An appropriate design might yield benefits such as efficiency, access to specialized and location-embedded resources, enhanced innovation and the creation of operational flexibility; the design can impact upon performance through employee motivation, commitment and loyalty and has the ability to link interdependent activities.

39. Mintzberg identified five basic parts of an organizational structure: strategic apex, middle line, operating core, technostructure and support staff. This presents a broad framework to guide thoughts at the start of the design process. Departmentalization is a process of grouping employees together. Such employees can then be assigned line, functional or lateral relationships with one another. Employees are often grouped together by area, function/specialism, product, customer group or process. Arguments stating why organizational parts should be configured in particular ways were presented through contingency theory. However, ultimately design is determined by decision-makers who make choices based on their predispositions (experience, values and beliefs).

40. The tools used to structure organizations include: organizational charts, job definitions, span of control, authority, responsibility and accountability descriptions. A key concept in contemporary design is decentralization, where specific delegation is given to sub-units or groups within an organization such that they enjoy a measure of autonomy or independence.

QUESTIONS

1   Consider any of the case studies presented throughout this book and create an organizational chart for the company in focus. You should consider a range of options and explain your preferred choice. There are a number of software products that can be used to create organizational charts. Microsoft Visio and PowerPoint are common tools. Most often, a rectangle represents a person, position or department on a chart. In a hierarchical organizational chart, the Chief Officer or President is represented by the top rectangle. The level underneath the chief officer contains senior managers or executives, and each succeeding level includes the subordinates of the line above.

2   With reference to the Metropolitan police case study, discuss the unifying purpose that binds the police service together and creates a need for both generalist and specialists.

3   Create an organizational chart from the information presented within the case study. Would you describe this as a tall or flat hierarchy? Is this a functional/service or geographic design or some hybrid of the three?

4   Evaluate the hierarchy and discuss whether there may be a case for delayering within the typical police force structure. Evaluate the advantages and disadvantages of a tall structure.

USEFUL WEBSITES

Organizational Structure Net: **organizationalstructure.net/**
This site is dedicated to the enhancement and awareness of organizational structure.

REFERENCES

Buchanan, D. and Huczynski, A. (2010) 'Organizational Behaviour', Ed. 7. Financial Times Press.

Duncan, R. (1972) 'Characteristics of Organizational Environments and Perceived Environmental Uncertainty', Administrative Science Quarterly, 17 (3), p. 313–327.

Hellriegel, D. and Slocum, J. W. (1973) 'Organizational design: A contingency approach A model for organic management design', Business Horizons, Volume 16, Issue 2, April 1973, p. 59–68.

Mabey, C. and Mayon-White, B. (1993) 'Managing Change', The Open University.

Mullins, L. (2010) 'Management and Organizational Behaviour', Ed. 9. Financial Times Press.

Ostroff, F., Smith, D. (1992), 'The horizontal organization', McKinsey Quarterly, 1992 Issue 1, pp. 148–168.

Price, A. (2007) 'Human Resource Management in a Business Context', Ed. 3. Cengage Learning EMEA.

Pugh, D. S. (1997) 'Organization Theory', Ed. 4. Penguin.

CHAPTER 23
DELEGATION AND EMPOWERMENT

Key Concepts

- Authority
- Delegation
- Empowerment
- Power
- Responsibility
- Span of control

Learning Outcomes Having read this chapter, you should be able to:

- evaluate when and why to delegate, empower and engage employees within the organization
- discuss good practice (how to) in delegating and empowering employees
- evaluate arguments for and against greater empowerment and engagement in contemporary organizations

23.1 INTRODUCTION

1. In this part of the book we continue to examine how management theory is translated into practice. Over the past two chapters we have focused on the application of scientific management, motivation, group work and contingency theory to the practice of organization and work design. Central to the design of work is the attainment of organizational goals through people and technology. One of the key challenges for management is therefore to get the most out of their human resources within the context of their organization. Completing work requires discretion and access to resources both of which rely upon power and authority. Power, however, is distributed by management to varying degrees.

Power The ability of individuals or groups to persuade, induce or coerce others into following certain courses of action

2. Throughout the book we have described and reviewed Taylorism, noting its impact upon job design (fragmented, repetitive, specialized and tightly controlled). This approach to job design was ignorant of the social aspects of work and the legacy of Taylorism contains many drawbacks such as those described in the previous chapter (dissatisfaction, demotivation, poor productivity and quality and a reduced ability to adapt to changing requirements). Attempts to address these problems involved organizing work along more human-centred lines. In response, practitioners set out to enrich work and increase employee involvement. Work redesign focused on the functional aspects of the work performed, autonomy and the level of meaning that people derive from work (completeness of task and ability to see the sense in what they do).

Authority The right to make particular decisions and to exercise control over resources

3. As we saw in the previous chapter, one of the central issues of organization design is the question of how to create the best balance between control from the centre and delegation throughout the rest of the system. This chapter examines some of the factors surrounding power distribution and delegation, including questions of span of control, empowerment and employee engagement. In the previous chapter, delegation was considered in organization-structure terms, especially in terms of centralization versus decentralization. This was taken to mean the degree to which the authority to commit resources was diffused throughout the organization by means of the formal allocation of roles within a structure. This chapter considers key concepts associated with power and employee engagement. We discuss delegation at the more personal level as the transfer of authority between one individual and another, i.e. as a management issue rather than an organizational one. We then progress to consider how management thinking has evolved in this area.

Delegation A distinct type of power sharing process that occurs when a manager gives subordinates the responsibility and authority for making certain decisions previously made by the manager

Span of control A measure of the number of employees who report to one supervisor or manager

23.2 CONCEPTS: AUTHORITY, POWER, EMPOWERMENT AND ENGAGEMENT

4. Discussion about delegation and empowerment are centred upon issues of authority, responsibility/accountability, and power. It is worthwhile reminding ourselves what these different concepts mean. The distinctions that are usually made between them are as follows:

Responsibility An obligation placed on a person who occupies a certain position in the organization structure to perform a task, function or assignment

Authority is a right conferred on some members of an organization to act in a certain way over others (this term was also considered in Chapter 4).

It can be regarded as a defined amount of power granted by the organization to selected members (legitimate power).

Accountability This is the ultimate responsibility which managers cannot delegate. While managers may delegate authority, they remain accountable for the decisions and actions of their subordinates

Responsibility is an obligation placed upon a person who occupies a certain position in the organization structure to perform a task, function or assignment. Another word for responsibility is '**accountability**', which in some respects is a more helpful term, since it implies that one person is accountable to another for a given task. In fulfilling their responsibilities, a person may delegate (i.e. hand down) some of their own authority to act, but they cannot pass off their responsibility (accountability). This is why there is always an element of risk attached to delegation, for if things go wrong, the delegator cannot blame the person to whom he or she assigned certain tasks. The delegator alone is accountable.

Power is the ability of individuals or groups to persuade, induce or coerce others into following certain courses of action.

5. Delegation is a distinct type of power-sharing process. It occurs when a manager gives subordinates responsibility and authority for making certain decisions previously made by the manager and involves the assignment of new and different tasks or responsibilities to a subordinate. Sometimes delegation involves the additional authority and discretion associated with tasks and assignments already performed by the subordinate. The extent to which a subordinate must check with the boss before taking action is another aspect of delegation. Once again, the benefits derived from delegation will be dependent upon situational factors that may include improved decision quality and enhanced subordinate commitment. Through delegation, work can be made more interesting, challenging and meaningful (enriched). However, delegation may have negative consequences should the subordinate not desire additional responsibility or lack the necessary skills or resources to discharge responsibilities. From the manager's perspective, delegation is a time management tool and a means to develop subordinates. In the process of delegating tasks with their commensurate authority, it is important to ensure that the amount of authority is defined, or prescribed, in an unequivocal way. The principal options open to a manager, ranging from tight to loose control, are shown in Figure 23.1.

6. Delegation does not come easily to most managers. It takes time, effort and confidence in one's team members to explain what is wanted and then let them go away and do it, whilst trusting that they will not disappoint. Insecure managers are less likely than confident individuals to take the risk of giving their staff greater freedom to act. An insecure person will tend to

FIGURE 23.1 Delegation – the main options.

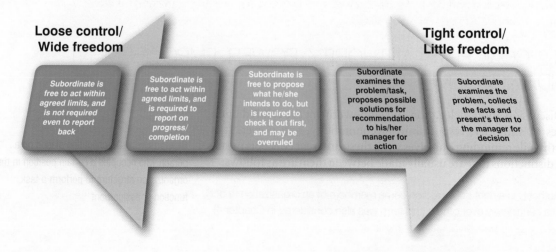

**Loose control/
Wide freedom**

**Tight control/
Little freedom**

Subordinate is free to act within agreed limits, and is not required even to report back

Subordinate is free to act within agreed limits, and is required to report on progress/completion

Subordinate is free to propose what he/she intends to do, but is required to check it out first, and may be overruled

Subordinate examines the problem/task, proposes possible solutions for recommendation to his/her manager for action

Subordinate examines the problem, collects the facts and present's them to the manager for decision

delegate at the lower end of Figure 23.1. However, there are ways in which delegation can be made 'safer' for managers. After all, even confident and experienced managers will not want to take unnecessary risks. Good delegation practice, in situations where either the manager is new, or the team is newly formed, is likely to include the following principles:

- ensure that the objective to be achieved is made clear
- indicate the standard of performance that is required (what, when, etc.)
- decide what level of authority to grant
- allocate adequate resources (staff, equipment, expenses, etc.)
- ensure that clear reporting arrangements are made
- encourage subordinate to request further help if needed
- inform subordinate that early mistakes will be used as learning opportunities
- ensure that the task is completed according to agreed standards
- thank the individual for their efforts.

We will revisit delegation in Chapter 27, with time management and personal effectiveness.

7. One of the major questions which has to be faced when considering the practical aspects of delegation is how many subordinates, or team members, can be managed effectively by any one manager or supervisor. This is the classical management issue of the so-called 'span of control', i.e. the number of employees reporting directly to one person. In practice spans can vary between one and forty or more subordinates directly supervised, although the most likely range is between three and twenty. Smaller spans tend to be found among managerial, professional and technical groups. Here factors such as cost, the complexity of work and the need to deal adequately with the problems of people, who may themselves be managers of others, require a closer involvement by superiors in the total operation of their units. Towards the bottom end of the organizational hierarchy, where routine tasks are being carried out by employees who have no subordinates themselves, it is practicable to have much larger spans.

8. The whole question of spans of control (refer to Chapter 3) is linked to senior management views about the number of levels they should have in their organization. If a flat organization is preferred, then larger spans are an inevitable consequence, especially for middle managers. If a tall structure is preferred, then spans can be smaller. Any final decision has to be a compromise between these opposing consequences. Other important influences on the size of the spans in an organization or unit include: (1) similarity of functions; (2) geographic contiguity – together or dispersed; (3) complexity of functions – in a range from simple repetitive to highly complex and varied; (4) direction and control – from minimum supervision and training to constant close supervision; (5) coordination – from minimum relation to others to extensive mutual non-recurring relationships and (6) planning – from minimum scope and complexity to extensive effort in areas and policies not chartered. Managers may also consider the costliness of possible mistakes by individuals in the unit and the degree of hazard or danger associated with the work.

9. 'Empowerment' was defined earlier as an approach to managing people which permits employees to exercise greater decision-making on day-to-day matters in their work. Empowerment involves the perception by members of an organization that they have the opportunity to determine their work roles, accomplish meaningful work and influence important events. Employees may be involved in determining what and how things should be done. Empowerment describes a situation where employees are allowed greater freedom, autonomy and self-control over their work, and the responsibility for decision-making. It is more than simple delegation and must be seen through the eyes of the employee, asking whether they feel empowered and not powerless. Consequently employee empowerment includes giving employees training and the tools necessary to undertake their tasks. Examined under these headings, empowerment can be seen as an umbrella term,

covering a number of human resource management activities referred to elsewhere in this book, such as job design, job enrichment, employee participation and business process re-engineering.

10. Robbins, Campbell and Judge (2010:62) ask what the major job attitudes are. They consider the more important ones to include job satisfaction, job involvement, organizational commitments and employee engagement. We discussed job satisfaction in the previous chapter. Related to job satisfaction is job involvement – the degree to which a person identifies with a job, actively participates in it and considers performance important to self-worth. Psychological empowerment is a related concept describing employee's beliefs in the degree to which they influence their work environment and the perceived autonomy of their work. A relatively new concept is employee engagement. This concept describes an individual's involvement and satisfaction with, and enthusiasm for, the work they do. Buchanan and Huczynski (2010:286) suggest that engagement means more than just motivation or job satisfaction. Engaged employees are open to new ideas, willing to change, have a customer focus and are confident in their ability.

> **Employee engagement** Refers to the individual's involvement and satisfaction with as well as enthusiasm for work

23.3 ARGUMENTS: WHY EMPOWER?

11. The reasons for delegation are mainly practical, but some are idealistic. From an idealistic position we may consider delegation a 'good thing' for individual growth, contributing to staff morale, helping to enrich jobs and humanizing work. Practical reasons include:

- senior managers can be relieved of less important or less immediate responsibilities
- enables decisions to be taken nearer to the point of impact, and without delay
- develops and encourages managers to cope with responsibility
- may motivate employees

Most organizations find the need to delegate forced upon them by circumstances, especially the pressures on managers to concentrate on environmental issues rather than on internal problems. However, the best practice is to be found in organizations that use delegation positively as an important employee motivator as well as a means of facilitating effective decision-making throughout the enterprise.

12. Today many employees are much less willing to tolerate bureaucratic control. The main reasons for introducing empowerment include those described in paragraph 11 but also tend to include quality, productivity, flexibility and cost reduction. Benefits include stronger commitment, great persistence and creativity and higher job satisfaction. Cascio and Aguinis (2010) suggest that the empowered worker is no passing fad. They argue that there is constant pressure to do more with less and a steady emphasis on empowerment. Drivers for empowerment may include:

> **Empowerment** A climate whereby employees are allowed greater freedom, autonomy and self-control over their work and the responsibility for decision-making

- requirement to be more responsive to the marketplace
- reduction in number of levels in structures – so-called de-layering (see BPR)
- need for lateral collaboration and communication among work teams with minimal supervision
- allows senior management to concentrate on longer-term (strategic) issues
- need to make best use of all available resources (especially human resources)

- pressure to meet the higher expectations of a better-educated workforce

- the development of 'learning organizations'.

13. Studies have shown (see Harter, Schmidt and Hayes 2002) that high levels of engagement are associated with high levels of customer satisfaction, productivity, profits and low levels of employee turnover; organizations reporting high levels of employee engagement are more likely to attract and retain high performing employees.

23.4 EMPOWERMENT: PREREQUISITES, TECHNIQUES AND PRACTICES

14. Buchanan and Huczynski (2010) suggest empowerment works best where there is uncertainty in the production process and employees have to deal with variable demands and ambiguity (routine jobs are unaffected by empowerment). Empowerment itself can bring more uncertainty at the organizational level; consequently, there is a requirement for a supportive organizational culture and work environment. If empowerment initiatives (described next) are to have a good chance of success then there are certain prerequisites or foundations required within the organization. At the individual level, employees must be able and willing to act autonomously, see Nelson and Quick (2009). Job redesign, a decentralized and less formal organization structure, a culture that fosters experimentation and not blame, are amongst the factors and conditions enabling empowerment in organizations. The main constraints on empowerment include traditional work and status delineations, hierarchical structures, management resistance and the organization culture (refer back to Chapter 13).

15. As seen in the previous chapter, techniques for improving motivation and performance through empowerment and engagement fall into two broad categories: individual job enrichment and self managing or autonomous teamwork. Involvement and employment practices include information sharing and communication, which encourage commitment and engagement; quality circles and team meetings can be used to involve employees in decision-making; similarly, total quality management and business process management may be used to inculcate a continuous improvement and customer focused culture where employees will seek out weaknesses and areas for improvement in every aspect of the organization. Other practices include developing the attitudes of employees through training and coaching where management values, behaviours and attitudes are developed. Finally employees may not only share in the decision-making aspects of running the company but may also be offered financial participation, through profit share and share option schemes. Empowerment techniques may be applied in a variety of circumstances or ways such as: to extend people's knowledge/skills, to provide discretion over tasks (when, how, design); to involve employees in policy-making, and help bring about organizational change.

CONCLUSION

16. In this chapter we discussed various forms of employee involvement (participation) and engagement. In turbulent environments and where work is surrounded by uncertainty, employees typically require greater freedom, autonomy and self control over their work and responsibility for decision-making. We discussed delegation as the process of allocating authority and responsibility to others throughout the various levels of the organization. Whereas managers occasionally used delegation throughout the 20th century, in the 21st century empowerment and engagement became the norm. As environments became more dynamic and turbulent, empowerment and engagement (more than simple delegation) became a necessity in many organizations.

QUESTIONS

1   Compare and contrast the related concepts of delegation, empowerment and employee engagement.

2   Contrast three companies with which you are familiar and discuss the extent of empowerment you might expect to witness within the organizations. Explain your expectations.

3   Whilst visiting a company, a manager informs you of her intent to further empower employees in her department. She would like your advice on the

techniques and practices associated with empowerment. You should list and describe five common approaches. You should also discuss the prerequisites for enabling empowerment strategies.

4   Evaluate when and why more responsibility and power may be delegated downwards in the police structure.

5   What are the general arguments for empowering employees within contemporary organizations?

USEFUL WEBSITES

IPA: www.ipa-involve.com/employee-engagement/
Employee engagement

REFERENCES

Buchanan, D. and Huczynski, A. (2010) 'Organizational Behaviour', Ed. 7. Financial Times Press.

Cascio, W. and Aguinis, H. (2010) 'Applied Psychology in Human Resource Management International Edition', Ed. 7. Pearson.

Fincham, R. and Rhodes, P. (2005) 'Principles of Organizational Behaviour', Ed. 4. Oxford University Press.

Harter, J. K., Schmidt, F. L., and Hayes, T. L. (2002) 'Business-Unit-Level Relationship Between Employee Satisfaction, Employee Engagement, and Business Outcomes: A Meta-Analysis', Journal of Applied Psychology, Volume 87, Issue 2, p. 268–279.

Martin, J. and Fellenz, M. (2010) 'Organizational Behaviour and Management 4e', Ed. 4. Cengage Learning EMEA.

Mullins, L. (2010) 'Management and Organizational Behaviour', Ed. 9. Financial Times Press.

Nelson, D. L. and Quick, J. C. (2009) 'ORGB', Ed. 1. South Western.

Robbins, S., Campbell, T. and Judge, T. (2010) 'Organizational Behaviour', Financial Times Prentice Hall.

Schein, E. (1999) 'Empowerment, coercive persuasion and organizational learning: do they connect?', The Learning Organization, 6 (4), p. 163.

CHAPTER 24
MANAGING CHANGE: KEY CONCEPTS

Key Concepts

- Change model
- Continuous change
- Episodic change
- Force-field analysis
- Organizational change
- Readiness for change
- Resistance to change

Learning Outcomes   Having read this chapter, you should be able to:

- describe the main theoretical foundations of change management
- explain the planned and the emergent approach to change
- discuss the common change management models
- understand resistance to change

1. Change is fundamental in order to guarantee long-term success within an organization. Senior and Swailes (2010) suggest those of us who work in organizations, sometime or another, get caught up in the need for change. In our previous discussions about contingency theory we noted that the organization must align itself with its environment. We only have to look briefly at today's environment to note constant change. Most contemporary management scholars and practitioners agree that the amount, pace, unpredictability and impact of change are greater than ever before. New products, processes and services have appeared at an ever increasing rate. Local markets have become global markets and industries have been opened up to competition.

2. Within organizations we have observed restructuring, delayering, fragmentation, outsourcing, culture change programmes, business process reengineering, the implementation of enterprise systems, empowerment strategies, the development of competences and capabilities, new business models and the introduction of new products and services. Yet perhaps the major organizational changes observed over the past twenty years may be better known for their failure than their success. Changes can take longer to implement than planned (time problems); may not live up to expectations (quality problems) or may cost more to implement than was budgeted (cost overrun problems). There is little doubt then that managing change is very difficult and risky. Change management requires an interdisciplinary perspective and an understanding of organization, strategy, change, systems, psychological and sociological theories.

Organizational change The alteration of organizational components (such as the mission, strategy, goals, structure, processes, systems, technology and people) to improve the effectiveness or efficiency of the organization

3. Before attempting to change something, managers must understand what it is they intend to change. They must also be aware of intervention strategies, alternative solutions and how to overcome resistance to change. We start by defining change and exploring what it is that can and usually is changed within organizations. Several change types are identified and the need for change discussed. In recognition of the absence of a single universal change theory we explore a number of related theories used in change management. A variety of change models are discussed. In the next chapter we consider the role of the change agent and the challenges associated with implementing change, particularly in the face of resistance and the context of complexities associated with contemporary organizations.

Resistance to change The desire not to pursue change

Change model An abstract representation describing the content or process of changes

24.1 UNDERSTANDING CHANGE

4. To change something implies altering it, varying or modifying it in some way. Organizations change, or adapt, what they want to achieve and how they wish to achieve it. Some organizations change mainly in response to external circumstances (reactive change); others change principally because they have decided to change (proactive change). Some organizations are conservative in outlook, seeking little in the way of change, others are entrepreneurial in outlook, ever seeking new opportunities and new challenges. Some organizations are constructed (even constricted!) so that change, i.e. adaptation, is a slow and difficult process; others are designed with an in-built flexibility, enabling adaptation to take place regularly and relatively easily.

5. Change is a process which is rarely contained by functional or specialist boundaries. Change in one part of an organization invariably affects people and processes in another part (refer back to systems theory). As Figure 24.1 illustrates, organizational change can influence, and be

FIGURE 24.1   Organizational change and key organizational features.

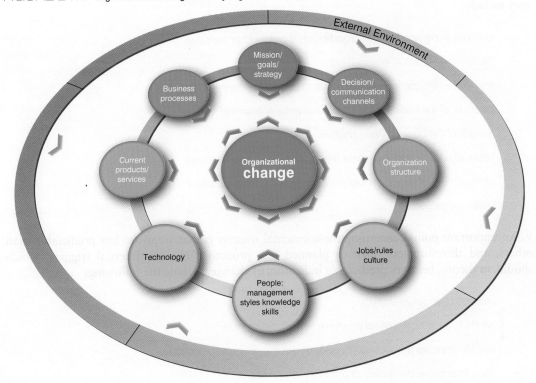

influenced by, several important features of organizational life – the organizational mission and strategy, its structure, products and processes, its people and culture, and the nature of the technology employed. These features of the organization are themselves affected by the nature of the external environment.

6. It is true that a successful organization's practices and behaviours, having worked for decades, can cease to be right. The realities (environment) faced by each organization change quite dramatically though assumptions about them may not. Whereas reality may change, the theory of the business (assumptions about the environment, the mission and the core competencies needed) may not change with it – in some organizations. Planned change is usually triggered by the failure of people to create continuously adaptive organizations. Thus, organizational change routinely occurs in the context of failure of some sort. Drucker (1994) suggests each organization should challenge every product frequently, every service, every policy, every distribution channel with the question, if we were not in it already, would we be going into it now? Without this self-challenging approach, an organization will be overtaken by events.

7. Organizational change concerns the alteration of organizational components (such as the mission, strategy, goals, structure, processes, systems, technology and people) to improve the effectiveness or efficiency of the organization. Change may take place in any part and at any level of the organization. When we think of organizational change, we may think of significant changes aimed at making the organization more effective such as mergers, acquisitions, buyouts, downsizing, restructuring, the launch of new products and the outsourcing of major organizational activities. Examples of smaller (efficiency based) changes include: departmental reorganizations, the implementation of new technologies and systems. The primary needs for change derive from the need for alignment between the organizations' internal and external environments.

8. Change can be triggered by any number of external and internal factors. External triggers may include:

- changes in demand for the organization's products or services

- threatening tactics of competitors

- arrival of a newcomer with a competing product or service

- takeover of the business by a more powerful enterprise

- merger of the business with another

- failure of a key supplier to meet the organization's requirements

- development of new technologies now available for application

- political changes.

9. An important point concerning these external triggers is that some are less predictable than others, and therefore less open to planned (i.e. proactive) change. Internal triggers, which should, in theory, be more predictable indicators of change, include the following:

- planned changes in strategy

- efforts to introduce cultural changes

- need to improve productive efficiency/make better use of resources

- need to improve the quality of products or services

- need to respond to the development of new products/services

- need to improve standards/systems for dealing with suppliers

- need to deploy people (the human resources) where they are most effective.

Trigger of change Any disorganizing pressure indicating that current systems, procedures, rules, organization structures and processes are no longer effective

Readiness for change A predisposition to welcome and embrace change.

Continuous Change Organizational changes that tend to be ongoing, evolving and cumulative

Episodic change Organizational changes that tend to be infrequent, discontinuous and intentional

10. In facing up to these internal triggers of change, management must plan how best to respond to them. Some changes will have been announced well beforehand, and in these cases planning is proactive. Some changes will, however, be brought about by a crisis of some kind (e.g. the failure of a new product or supplier or even a key manager). In these latter cases, it may be impossible to plan in any detail, but only to respond reactively and urgently. Where key individuals or products are concerned, however, well-organized enterprises will usually have a fallback position in the shape of a 'contingency plan'. This may not be the ideal response, but at least it will prevent a crisis from turning into a tragedy of major proportions. Having looked inside and outside the organization, it must ask if they are still in the right business and doing the right things or whether there is a need for change. If a need for change is identified, the organization must also consider how ready it is for such change. This will mean examining culture and then determining whether they are locked into particular ways of doing things.

11. There are many types of change such as discontinuous versus continuous and revolutionary versus evolutionary. The phrase episodic change is used to group together organizational changes that tend to be infrequent, discontinuous and intentional. Such changes arise as a result of the organization's inability to respond

adequately to external environmental changes. Change may be planned or unplanned – planned change is a deliberate, conscious decision to improve the organization in some manner. Furthermore, change may take place at a variety of levels. At the total system level, the emphasis is on organizational purpose, mission, strategy, structure of culture. In some cases there will be a need for significant (transformational) and in other cases less significant (transactional) change.

24.2 BUILDING THE NEED FOR CHANGE

12. In many cases, the need for change will derive from an evaluation of organizational outputs (products and services), where the organization operates, what it does (primary activities) and how it performs such activities (work). Some people may consider the current way of working to be ineffective or inefficient or may consider that such ways of working will become ineffective or inefficient in the future. The need for change is the pressure for change in the situation – sometimes the pressure is high (typically a problem of ineffectiveness), other times lower (a problem of inefficiency). This need can be viewed as a 'real need', demonstrated by data and facts, or a 'perceived need' seen by change participants. The need for change will often be based upon the analysis of internal and external data or the perspectives of the various stakeholders, the concerns of senior managers and change leaders in particular.

13. The need for change may arise from a crisis, commanding a reactive approach or from proactive thinking. In some cases it will result from new opportunities to do things differently and in other cases will be driven by threat, the failures of some existing system or approach to work. It is important to make such distinctions as they will impact upon the ease with which the argument for change can be based; the need for change being clearer in the case of a crisis. Once a need for change has been identified by a change initiator, it will then become important to direct the organization's attention to change (change awareness) and gain support for it. In many cases there is likely to be confusion and disagreement over the need for change, what needs changing, when and how to bring about change.

24.3 CHANGE MODELS

14. A variety of models exist to help managers develop a sense of what needs to change in their organization; such models enable the organization to be analyzed and consider the organization's strategy, how it fits with the changing environment and how the various components of the organization also fit with the strategy and the environment. We develop an appreciation of what to change, through the use of models of organizational analysis such as the McKinsey 7S model, the Nadler and Tushman congruence framework and the Burke-Litwin model.

15. The organizational system (diamond) model proposed in the 1960s by the late Dr. Harold Leavitt, a long-time business professor at Stanford University, is made of four major components: task (the organization's purpose), people (those who carry out the task), technology (tools and computers etc.) and structure. The

> **7S model** A model for organizational analysis and dynamics including components: strategy, structure, systems, style, staff, shared values and skills

components are interdependent and a change in any one of the components will result in change amongst the other three, he argues. The Leavitt model adopts a systems theory perspective but does not incorporate open systems theory, i.e. takes no account of the external environment.

16. A decade later, Nadler and Tushman developed their model (refer back to Figure 10.3 General model of contingency theory). Recognizing the organization is influenced by its environment, their model took account of both systems and open system theory. Nadler and Tushman divided their model into inputs, process and outputs. Their (transformation or internal) process

contained similar components to the model proposed by Leavitt. Inputs came from the environment including organizational history and current strategy which help define how people in the organization behave. Nadler and Tushman also argued a need for the transformational process components to be congruent or 'fit' with each other. Nadler and Tushman did however recognize that such congruence may present advantages and disadvantages. In the short-term, a system with high congruence is an effective and performing system. However, such a system may be resistant to change. Their model suggests there is no one best way to organize. Rather, the most effective way of organizing is determined by the nature of the strategy as well as the work, the individuals who are members of the organization, and the informal processes and structures (including culture) which have emerged over time. One criticism of this model is that a system which is highly congruent may in fact be resistant to change as it develops ways of insulating itself from outside influences.

17. One way of thinking about organizational components and their alignment with the environment can be found in the McKinsey 7S model explained by Peters and Waterman (1982:10). The components of this model include strategy, structure, systems, style, staff, shared values and skills. The underlying thesis of the model is that organizational effectiveness is a function of the degree of 'fit' achieved amongst these factors and the environment. When organizations experience change, the degree of 'fit' is affected, and the challenge of change management is to make changes so that high levels of 'fit' can be achieved amongst the seven elements. Changes to one of the components can affect all the other components. The strengths of the 7S model are its description of organizational variables which convey obvious importance – strategy, structure, systems, etc. – and its recognition of the importance of the interrelationships amongst all of these seven variables, or dimensions. The 7S model, on the other hand, does not contain any external environment or performance variables. The model is a description of these seven important elements and shows that they interact to create organizational patterns but there is no explanation of how these seven dimensions are affected by the external environment. Nor do we know how each dimension affects the other or what specific performance indices may be involved.

18. More recently Burke and Litwin (1992) presented a complex model of organizational performance and change. Their model conforms to the open system way of thinking, with the external environment represented as an input. The authors go beyond description and suggest causal linkages that hypothesize how performance is affected and how effective change occurs. Change is depicted in terms of both process and content, with particular emphasis on transformational compared with transactional factors. Transformational change occurs as a response to the external environment and directly affects organizational mission and strategy, the organization's leadership and culture. In turn, the transactional factors are affected – structure systems, management practices and climate. These transformational and transactional factors together affect motivation, which, in turn, affects performance. Through their model, Burke and Litwin attempt to provide a causal framework that encompasses both the what and the how – what organizational dimensions are key to successful change and how these dimensions should be linked causally to achieve the change goals. Burke and Litwin incorporated dimensions from earlier models, in one form or another, to develop their model. Interestingly, both the 7S and the Burke and Litwin models were informed by consulting practice.

> **Transformational change** A fundamental change impacting upon the whole organization (the leader, mission, strategy and culture)

24.4 GENERIC CHANGE MODEL

19. Figure 24.2 (taken from Kelly, 2009) also shows the environment as a driver for change – a source of opportunity and threat, mediated through individuals who then see a need to change

FIGURE 24.2 Generic change model (Kelly 2009).

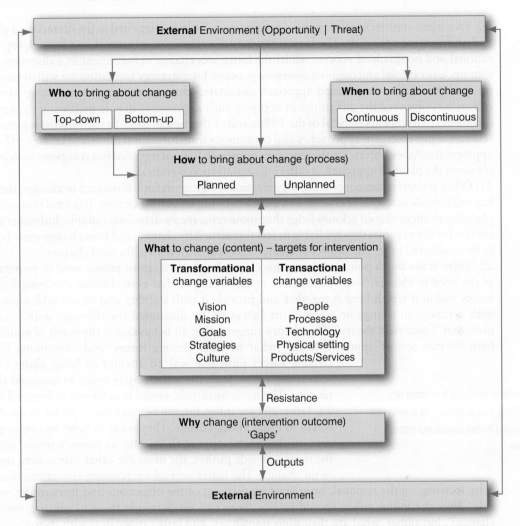

aspects within the organization. In some cases the change initiators are the senior managers (top down change) and in other cases may be managers, professionals or employees from lower levels within the organization (bottom-up change). Change may also be initiated by external consultants or other employees. Change may occur as a 'one-off' activity or may be viewed as a constant process of alignment and pursuit for efficiency. In some cases the change will be formally planned, typically using rational tools and techniques and in other cases will simply emerge from the day-to-day activities and decisions of the organizational members. As we said earlier, there are many aspects of the organization that can be changed – some more fundamental than others. Change managers differentiate between major or transformational change or less major transactional change. Examples of transformational and transactional targets for intervention are shown in the figure. Change is initiated for a reason – there is a need for the change. In some cases the need is more obvious than other cases. In the case of the model shown in Figure 24.2 we could have shown the 'Why change' box directly beneath the environment. We have shown it further down the model to emphasize a need to demonstrate the need for change in order to overcome resistance, particularly emanating from the recipients of change.

Transactional change Changes to components of the organization such as the structure, systems and processes

24.5 HOW TO CHANGE AND RESISTANCE TO CHANGE

20. Two main approaches to change management have been suggested in the literature: a planned and an emergent approach. The former tends to see change management as a formal, top-down, rational and pre-planned process whilst the latter sees change management as a disordered, bottom-up, less rational and ongoing emergent process. Like strategy formation we will observe that, up until the 1980s, the planned approach dominated change management thinking. However, researchers observed the difficulties in applying such approaches in ever increasing dynamic and turbulent environments (typical of the 1990s and of the present day). In such environments, many scholars argue emergent approaches and continuous transformation models of change to be more appropriate. As with strategy, the emergent approach has not replaced but competes with or complements the planned approach in differing organizational contexts.

21. Other general issues concerning organizational change include resistance to change, the use of key individuals as agents of change and the costs of implementing change. It is vital that managers planning changes should acknowledge that some resistance will be unavoidable. Individuals at every level in the organization are liable to feel threatened by change, and thus change must be 'sold' to those affected by it. The subject of change agents is dealt with in the next chapter.

22. There is not much point in 'change for change's sake', and most people need to be persuaded of the need to change. Some people fear it. The reality is that every human grouping has some forces within it which keep it together and provide it with stability and others which provide it with a reason to change or adapt. Kurt Lewin neatly illustrated the dilemma with his classic notion of 'Force-field theory'. This theory suggests that all behaviour is the result of equilibrium between two sets of opposing forces (what he calls 'driving forces' and 'restraining forces').

Force-field analysis A process of identifying and analyzing the driving and restraining forces associated with a change

Driving forces push one way to attempt to bring about change; restraining forces push the other way in order to maintain the status quo. The basic force-field model is as shown in Figure 24.3.

23. Generally speaking, human beings tend to prefer to use driving forces to bring about change. They want to 'win' by exerting pressure on those who oppose them, but, as Lewin's model suggests, the more one side pushes, the more the other side resists, resulting in no change. The better way of overcoming resistance, therefore, is by focusing on the removal, or at least weakening, of the objections and fears of the resisting side. Thus the initial policy should be not 'how can we persuade them of our arguments for change?', but rather 'what are their objections/fears, and how can we deal with them?'

24. Lewin developed a three-stage approach to changing behaviour, which was later adapted by Edgar Schein. This comprises the following three steps:

Unfreezing existing behaviour (gaining acceptance for change).

Changing behaviour (adopting new attitudes, modifying behaviour).

Refreezing new behaviour (reinforce new patterns of thinking/working).

The unfreezing stage is aimed at getting people to see that change is not only necessary but desirable. The change stage is mainly a question of identifying what needs to be changed in people's attitudes, values and actions, and then helping them to acquire ownership of the changes. The role of a change agent (i.e. a person who is responsible for helping groups and individuals to accept new ideas and practices) is crucial at this stage. The refreezing stage is aimed at consolidating and reinforcing the changed behaviour by various support mechanisms (encouragement, promotion, participative management style, more consultation, etc.).

25. The management of innovation and change is a challenge to every person in an organization. For management it is particularly important to develop positive attitudes towards change and to support these by means of appropriate learning and action. In a highly competitive marketplace, made even more complex by the activities of governments and pressure groups of all kinds, firms must adapt or cease to trade.

FIGURE 24.3 **Force-field theory.**

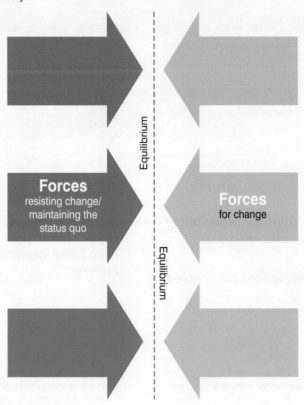

26. Finally, in this introduction to change, the question of costs must be briefly addressed. All change will incur some direct costs (e.g. equipment costs, relocation costs, recruitment costs, new system or equipment costs and possible redundancy payments). There will also be indirect costs, such as communicating the changes to employees, providing appropriate training and temporarily redeploying key managers and staff on change projects. However when considering costs (and benefits) it is important for an organization to consider what might be the costs of not introducing proposed changes.

CONCLUSION

27. Organizational change concerns the alteration of organizational components (such as the mission, strategy, goals, structure, processes, systems, technology and people) to improve the effectiveness or efficiency of the organization. Change may take place in any part and at any level of the organization. When we think of organizational change, we may think of significant changes aimed at making the organization more effective or smaller (efficiency based) changes such as departmental reorganizations, the implementation of new technologies and systems. The primary needs for change derive from the need for alignment between the organizations' internal and external environments. Diagnosis (Through models such as the McKinsey 7S model, the Nadler and Tushman congruence framework and the Burke–Litwin model) is used to motivate and determine what to change. Having established the need for change, change initiators then consider whether the organization is in fact ready for change. Lewin concluded that the change process needs to follow a three-step procedure: unfreezing, moving and refreezing. Many change agents use force-field analysis as an analytical tool to understand the dynamics of change.

QUESTIONS

1   Discuss the need for change in organizations, listing possible reasons (with examples) why change occurs.

2   Comment on how and why managers build the need for change.

3   Discuss how managers overcome resistance to change commenting on force-field analysis and Lewin's three stage approach to changing behaviour.

VIDEO CASES

Now take a look at the online video cases – visit the companion website to work through real world business problems associated with the concepts presented within this chapter.

17 Making Australia's Telstra Nimble

Performance relates to organizational purpose (mission); reflects achievements relative to the resources used by the organization (how well the organization manages its resources) and must be considered within the environment in which the organization does its work (adaptability). Organizational performance must integrate the concepts of 'effectiveness' and 'efficiency'. That is, the organization must be able to meet its goals (effectiveness) and to do so with an acceptable outlay of resources (efficiency). The organization must be able to develop and implement strategies which will ensure performance over extended periods of time. In summary, the performance of organizations can be considered in three broad areas: performance in activities which support the mission (effectiveness), performance in relation to the resources available (efficiency) and performance in relation to long-term viability or sustainability (ongoing relevance). However, it is worth remembering that organizational performance is a broad construct and may include productivity (quantity and effort), employee satisfaction (the extent to which workers are satisfied with their work and conditions), client or customer satisfaction and quality dimensions. This case examines change at Telstra, an Australian telecommunications and media company, formerly state-owned, triggered by poor performance.

37 Organization change: using technology to change practice

Organizational change is essential to guarantee long-term success within an organization. Most contemporary management scholars and practitioners agree that the amount, pace, unpredictability and impact of change are greater than ever before. Changes can take longer to implement than planned (time problems); may not live up to expectations (quality problems) or may cost more to implement than was budgeted (cost overrun problems). Perhaps more worrying, is the fact that, in relation to the three aforementioned change initiatives, failures occurred despite there being a great deal of information, advice and assistance available. There is little doubt then that managing change is both very difficult and risky. Change management requires an interdisciplinary perspective and an understanding of organization, strategy, change, psychological and sociological theories. Before attempting to change something, managers must understand what it is they intend to change. They need to understand organizations, organizational behaviour, technology, operations, marketing and finance. Managers also need the ability to lead the organization, coordinate, motivate and control people and other resources. They must also be aware of intervention strategies, alternative solutions and how to overcome resistance to change. This case explores a real organizational change initiative whereby, at Lloyds, technology was used to improve outdated manual processes.

91 Strategic change management – styles and roles

This case is concerned with the management tasks and processes involved in changing strategies. Practitioners must recognize that simply designing a new strategy, business process, structure or system will not necessarily result in change taking place. Other factors must be considered in order to make change happen. Making change happen requires the organization to diagnose problems, create solutions, overcome inertia and resistance to change. Through this case, students should recognize that not all strategic change happens in a top-down manner (where senior managers decide strategy, plan how it will be implemented and then effect the required change). Strategies often emerge from lower down in the organization. Considers the role people play in managing strategic change and how

they do it – styles of managing change; Mark King discusses the innovation in managerial techniques that transformed TaylorMade Adidas Golf Co.

REFERENCES

Burke, W. W. (2008) 'Organization Change – Theory and Practice', Ed. 2. Sage.

Burke, W. W. and Litwin, G. H. (1992) 'A Causal Model of Organizational Performance and Change', Journal of Management, Sep 92, Vol. 18 Issue 3, p. 523–545.

Burnes, B. (2004) 'Managing Change', Ed. 4. FT Prentice Hall.

Carnall, C. (2007) 'Managing Change in Organizations', Ed. 5. FT Prentice Hall.

Drucker, P. (1994) 'The Theory of the Business', Harvard Business Review, Sep/Oct 94, Vol. 72 Issue 5, p. 95–104.

Kelly, P. P. (2009) 'International Business and Management', Cengage Learning EMEA.

Peters, T. and Waterman, R. (1982) 'In Search of Excellence', Ed. 1995. Harper Collins Business.

Senior, B. and Swailes, S. (2010) 'Organizational Change', Ed. 4. Pearson.

Weick, K. E. and Quinn, R. E. (1999) 'Organizational change and development', Annual Review of Psychology, Vol. 50 Issue 1, p. 361–386.

CHAPTER 25
IMPLEMENTING CHANGE

Drake, R. W. (1994) *Organizational Change*, Basic Paper 9, FT Pitman.

Carnall, C. A. (1995) *Managing Change in Organizations*, 3rd ed., FT Prentice Hall.

Plunkett, H. (1998) *Managing Change*, 3rd ed., FT Prentice Hall.

Kennedy, C. (2002) *The Next Big Idea: Managing in the Digital Economy*, Random House.

Kotter, J. P. and Cohen, D. S. (2002) *The Heart of Change: Real-Life Stories of How People Change Their Organizations*, Harvard Business School Press.

Stacey, R. D. (2002) 'The Theory of the Development in the Management Sciences', *Journal of Management Studies*, Vol. 41, No. 4, pp. 623–15.

Key Concepts

- Change agent
- Organization development

Learning Outcomes   Having read this chapter, you should be able to:

- understand the role of leaders, managers and change agents in the change process
- critically compare and contrast the planned and emergent approaches to implementing change
- review the application of organization development (OD) theory to implement change within organizations
- discuss typical difficulties associated with implementing change

1. Understanding the triggers that lead people to think changes are needed, and what happens when managers try to make changes, is essential given the volatile world that we live in (Senior and Swailes, 2010). Change is about replacement – one system for another, one process for another, one strategy or mission for another. In the previous chapter we discussed what is meant by change and distinguished types of change such as radical (transformational) and less major change (continuous improvement, transactional). Generally, change scholars and practitioners associate 'planned' approaches with radical change and 'emergent' approaches with less major change. Planned approaches are more likely to make use of the change models, tools and techniques discussed thus far.

2. We have organized this chapter around two dominant approaches to change implementation: the planned and the emergent. There are many prescriptions for the planned approach and we start by describing a generic change process. Many change management scholars suggest the planned approach to change is closely associated with the practice of organizational development (Carnall, 2007). Despite this approach originating during the middle of the twentieth century it has evolved to present an integrated framework of theories and practices capable of solving or helping to solve most of the important problems confronting the human side of organizations. OD represents an enormously influential mode of thinking about and practice in the change management field; it is about planned change, getting individuals, teams and organizations to function better. We therefore describe this approach immediately after describing the generic change process. Whilst linear models and plans have the merit of simplicity they are not without criticism. Recognizing criticisms of the planned approach (that it is impossible to plan in a constantly changing world), in the final part of this chapter we briefly describe emergent approaches to change.

Change implementers The person who puts the change plan into practice and takes steps to assure the change vision is realized – make change happen

3. This chapter is essentially about the action side of change – making it happen. Williams, Woodward and Dobson (2002) raise the following practical questions relating to the implementation of change: do we need external consultants for the implementation process? How do we motivate people to implement change? What kinds of leadership are best when implementing change? How can we help staff cope with the stress of change? And how do we get individuals to adopt mental sets compatible with the changes being introduced? In addition we might have further questions such as: should change be a top down or bottom-up approach, planned or emergent? What tools and techniques may be appropriate? We will consider a number of these questions throughout this chapter.

25.1 PLANNED APPROACHES TO CHANGE

4. Models of planned organization change depict the process in a linear, step by step fashion. Many models are based upon the work of Lewin, introduced in the previous chapter. It makes sense to view a change intervention as a sequence of unfreeze, transition, refreeze. Models are also broadly based on rational decision making (refer to Chapter 19). We have outlined a generic 'planned' approach to change (change process) in Figure 25.1.

5. Working around the model, a number of circumstances may trigger change such as performance problems and new opportunity or threat – competition will drive organizations and individuals to innovate and change. Performance feedback and benchmarking is used to identify areas in need of attention. Such triggers will create forces for change. The forces act upon the status quo, however there will also be forces for stability. There then follows an initial analysis or diagnosis phase. A range of tools and techniques may be applied. We have already discussed tools such as PESTLE, SWOT and attitude surveys. Additionally, organizational and industry data may be gathered, analyzed and presented to define the change problem.

FIGURE 25.1   Change process.

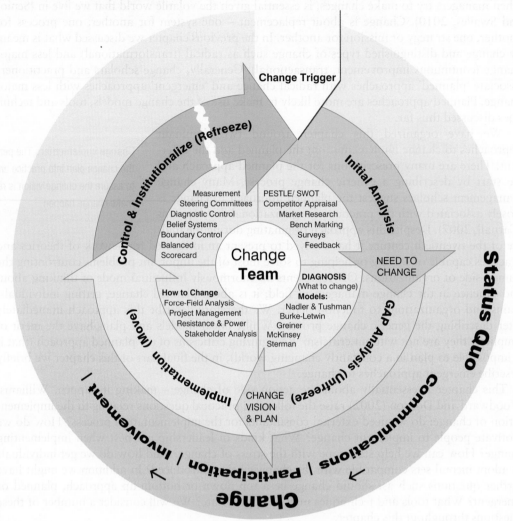

6. Having analyzed and diagnosed the present ('as-is') situation, organizations must decide where they want to be in the future (vision) and how to get there i.e. what to change. In determining what to change they typically take account of contingency and systems theory as depicted in various change models such as the ones presented by Nadler and Tushman or Burke and Letwin. Aside from a need to determine the desirable future situation (vision), they must establish and communicate the need for change and overcome prechange problems, the organization must then execute the things that will bring about the change.

7. Implementing the change involves translating the change vision into specific actions undertaken by employees. The plan outlines targets and dates and considers contingencies. Programme and project management tools and techniques are typically adopted to ensure the change plan is executed as intended.

8. Change requires decision-making and resource allocation and is therefore dependent on the will of the organization's power holders. Successful change managers build a change team, develop detailed communication plans and understand how to manage the change transition.

Change agents and the change team (see centre of Figure 25.1) specify who does what, when and how and may manage planned change through the use of project management tools and techniques. There is a need to mobilize commitment to change (through joint diagnosis and the development of a shared vision and fostering consensus), reduce resistance, communicate and manage the change. We have previously mentioned the need to educate and communicate with others so that they can see the need and logic for the change. There is also a need to get others involved and participating and to allocate resources, training or time to support the change. Change agents attempt to create willingness for change by making people aware of the pressures for change.

Change agent Any person seeking to promote, further, support, sponsor, initiate, implement or help to deliver change within the organization

9. Aside from considering the forces for change, the organization will seek to understand people's fears and concerns that may bring about resistance to change. Openness helps people to understand the need for change. There is a need to gain support (see coalition building) from people and as a consequence, many organizations develop an involvement strategy. Communication and involvement are essential to gain people's understanding of the need for change and to develop their commitment to such change. Successful change requires attention to many areas but it is generally thought there is a need to establish a sense of urgency; create a guiding coalition; develop a vision and strategy; communicate this with others; empower action; generate short-term wins; consolidate gains and produce more change and anchor new approaches in the culture – see Kotter (2007) Eight Steps To Transforming Your Organization.

Coalition building The forming of partnerships to increase pressures for or against change

10. Finally, measures are critical components of the control system which guide the change and integrate the initiatives and efforts of various parties. There are many ways to control change projects and care must be taken in selecting the methods of control and the variables to measure; noting the belief that what gets measured gets managed. Typically, a change champion will fight for the change and senior executives will act as sponsors, fostering commitment to the change and helping to make it happen. In larger change initiatives, it is common to establish a steering and a design and implementation team. The steering team provide advice to the champion regarding the direction of the change in light of other events and priorities in the organization. The steering team plays an advisory and navigational function for the change project and is the major policy determining group. The design and implementation team focuses on the tasks that must be accomplished and deals with the stakeholders who have primary responsibility for implementation. Typically, the design and implementation team will often have a change project manager who tracks the change efforts and the team's progress towards change targets.

25.2 ORGANIZATION DEVELOPMENT (OD)

11. As was highlighted in the introduction to this chapter, the planned approach to change is closely associated with the practice of organizational development, Burnes (2004). In the USA at least, OD has become a profession with its own regulatory bodies, to which OD practitioners must belong, with its own recognized qualifications, a host of approved tools and techniques and its own ethical code of practice. Organization development is a generic term which embraces a wide range of planned intervention strategies which are aimed at the development of individuals,

Organization Development A systematic process aimed at improving organizational effectiveness and adaptiveness on the basis of behavioural science knowledge; typical stages in an OD programme include analysis, diagnosis, action plans and review, an external third party assists the process. (See also change agent.)

groups and the organization as a total system. More specifically, it is a strategy and systematic process for improving organizational effectiveness by means of behavioural science approaches, involving the application of diagnostic and problem-solving skills (typically by an external consultant) in collaboration with the organization's management. OD is a methodology or technique used to effect change and managed from the top. Furthermore, it is an organization-wide process that takes essentially a systems view of the organization and utilizes the techniques and approaches of the behavioural sciences.

12. OD is utilized when senior management recognize that the key components of the organizational system are not working harmoniously together. In other words, when the complex mix of objectives, people and structure is failing to produce the fruits of organizational activity, then is the time to consider revitalizing the entire enterprise. This situation could be due to rapid expansion of the business, or radical changes in markets or technology, or to internal social pressures for change.

25.3 OD PROGRAMMES: THE KEY STAGES

13. There is no one best way of introducing and designing an OD programme. Nevertheless, certain patterns of treatment have developed over recent years, and the following sequence of events would not be untypical:

PRELIMINARY STAGE. The senior management team discuss the scope and implications of OD with the external third party (the 'change agent'). This will include discussion about the aims of a possible programme and the means by which it might be achieved. It will also define the nature of the relationships between the third party and the organization's management, i.e. whether the third party is to play the role of an expert, a catalyst for new ideas, educator or some other agreed role.

If agreement is reached about the idea of commencing an OD programme, the next stage is ANALYSIS AND DIAGNOSIS. This is the stage where the third party usually takes the initiative by designing appropriate methods for obtaining relevant information (e.g. interviews, surveys, etc.) and by proposing a strategy for implementation with the full backing of the management team. Examples of the kind of questions which may be put to management staff, in particular, are shown in Figure 25.2. The information obtained should clarify the problems facing the organization, and build up a picture of staff attitudes and opinions, as well as supplying some important suggestions as to how the problems might be solved. On the basis of the information received, the management team, aided by the third party, agree their diagnosis of the situation.

The third stage is AGREEMENT ABOUT AIMS OF THE PROGRAMME. The management team, in close collaboration with the third party, agree the aims and objectives of the programme. These aims could be to improve profitability, secure a share of a new market, improve staff motivation or other desired improvement. To these ends, specific objectives would be required, such as 'to achieve the restructuring of the company along matrix lines over a period of eighteen months' and 'to obtain the full commitment of all management staff to an open and democratic style of leadership' or 'to reduce substantially the number of customer complaints about after-sales service'. With aims and objectives firmly established, the next stage can be initiated – action plans.

ACTION PLANNING. Now comes the moment for planning the content and the sequence of the activities (discussed later) designed to achieve the aims of the programme.

EVALUATION AND REVIEW. Once the plans have been translated into action, they should be monitored at frequent intervals by the management team and their third party colleague. Difficulties and misunderstandings are bound to occur, and these must be registered as soon as possible and dealt with just as quickly. If a particular activity is having adverse results, it will have to be amended or even dropped from the programme. From time to time, more substantial reviews of progress towards the aims and objectives of the exercise will be required, and this often leads on to a further and final stage as follows.

REVISED AIMS AND PLANS. In the light of a major review, it is possible that some important revisions of aims may be necessary, for which a further sequence of plans will be required. At the end of the programme, the third party leaves the scene and the management team get on with the task of running a more successful business.

FIGURE 25.2 Part of an Organizational Diagnosis questionnaire.

KEY TASKS

(a) List the four most important tasks in your Department/Section:

1 ....

2 ....

3 ....

4 ....

(b) How do you know how well are doing in relation to your most important key task?

☐ FORMAL FEEDBACK (Committees, reports, etc)

☐ INFORMAL FEEDBACK (calls, notes, gossip, etc)

☐ OTHER MEANS ....

(c) How long is it before you know how well you are doing in relation to this key task?

☐ IMMEDIATELY   ☐ FEW WEEKS

☐ FEW MONTHS   ☐ YEARS

☐ NEVER

(d) If a wrong decision about the key task was to be made today, when would its effects be noticeable?

☐ ALMOST   ☐ AFTER A
    IMMEDIATELY   FEW WEEKS

☐ MONTHS   ☐ YEARS

☐ NEVER

STRUCTURE-ENVIRONMENT

(a) How appropriate is the structure of your organization in terms of fulfilling its purpose?

☐ VERY APPROPRIATE   ☐ QUITE APPROPRIATE

☐ NOT VERY   ☐ NOT SURE
    APPROPRIATE

If you don't think it appropriate, why? ....

....

(b) How is your organization basically divided? (Tick all that apply)

☐ PRODUCT   ☐ REGION

☐ MARKET   ☐ BUSINESS FUNCTION

☐ MANAGERIAL   ☐ TECHNICAL

☐ NOT SURE

(c) What are the three most important outside pressures to which your organization must respond?

1 ....

2 ....

3 ....

14. The success of any OD programme depends largely upon the part played by the change agent. The change agent must be a good relationship builder able to establish credibility and gain trust and respect in order to obtain the commitment required. The roles required by the third party range from the highly directive, leader type of role to a non-directive counselling

role. In the first mentioned role, the third party will tend to prescribe what is best for clients; at the other extreme they will tend to reflect issues and problems back to clients without offering any judgement. In between these extremes are several other possible roles, as indicated in Figure 25.3.

FIGURE 25.3 **Range of roles for third party.**

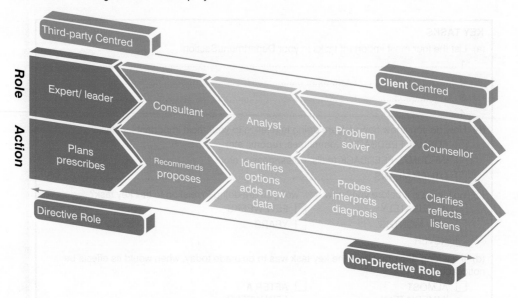

15. The desirable qualities, values and abilities required of change agents include the ability to listen diagnostically, and to apply rational approaches to problems and situations; they should be able to handle conflict openly and constructively. They also require good communication skills such as interviewing and presentation skills and the ability to establish and maintain comfortable relationships with a wide cross-section of people.

25.4 MAJOR APPROACHES IN OD

16. This part of the chapter considers the means by which OD programmes are carried out. Most of the activities in a programme can be classified in three ways: those aimed at,

1). changing people's behaviour,

2). changing organization structures, and

3). problem-analysis.

17. Examples of typical activities for each of these three classifications are briefly described below.
Activities designed to change behaviour at work include the following:

– coaching and counselling to help individuals, and usually on a one-to-one basis

– team-building to improve team relationships and task effectiveness

- inter-group activities, to improve the level of collaboration between interdependent groups

- training and development to improve key areas of employee knowledge and skill, and involving a range of participative learning methods.

Activities aimed at changing structures include:

- role analysis – i.e. focusing on what is expected of people rather than on their present job description, and devising new configurations of jobs and tasks

- job re-design/job enrichment – reassessing current jobs in terms of their range and type of tasks, reallocating tasks and redefining jobs, including vertical job enlargement.

Activities aimed primarily at problem-analysis include:

- diagnostic activities utilizing questionnaires (see Figure 25.4), surveys, interviews and group meetings

- planning and objectives-setting activities, designed to improve planning and decision-making skills

- **process consultation**, where the third party helps clients to see and understand the human processes that are taking place around him (e.g. leadership issues, communication flows, competition between individuals or groups, power struggles, etc.)

- business process re-engineering – examining key business processes from a questioning point of view (see Chapter 21).

Process consultation An approach to organization development in which the role of the consultant is to facilitate understanding of how to explore problems and find workable solutions

FIGURE 25.4 **Part of an employee opinion questionnaire.**

	Strongly agree	Partly agree	Neither agree nor disagree	Slightly disagree	Strongly disagree	Score
Employees in this organization know what it's objectives and aims are	1	2	3	4	5	
The organization structure helps us achieve our objectives and aims	1	2	3	4	5	
Communications in the organization are clear	1	2	3	4	5	
Relations between managers and their staff are usually harmonious	1	2	3	4	5	
People in this organization have a good team spirit	1	2	3	4	5	
People are always encouraged to try out new ideas in the organization	1	2	3	4	5	

25.5 BENEFITS OF ORGANIZATION DEVELOPMENT

18. The most significant benefits of an OD programme are indicated below. The relative importance and relevance of any one benefit obviously depends upon the needs of the organization at the commencement of the programme. However, in general terms, the benefits of OD can be summarized as follows:

- – it enables an organization to adapt to change with the full commitment of employees

- – it can lead to structures that facilitate employee cooperation and the achievement of tasks

- – it releases latent energy and creativity in the organization

- – it can improve understanding of organizational objectives by employees

- – it can improve decision-making processes and skills

- – it provides opportunities for management development in the context of real organizational problems

- – it may stimulate more creative approaches to problem-solving throughout the organization

- – it usually increases the ability of management groups to work as teams.

25.6 DIFFICULTIES IN IMPLEMENTING CHANGE

19. Kotter (2007) identifies eight typical mistakes made by senior management in relation to organizational change: They,

1). allow too much complacency

2). fail to create a sufficiently powerful guiding coalition

3). underestimate the power of vision (the sense of an end-goal)

4). greatly under-communicate the vision to be attained

5). permit obstacles to stand in the way of the vision

6). fail to create short-term wins

7). declare victory too soon

8). neglect to anchor changes in the organization's culture.

20. The result of such errors is to reduce the positive effects of new strategies or schemes, producing fewer outcomes over a longer than expected period with greater costs than forecast. Kotter's answer to the above problems is to establish an eight-stage process of creating major changes, as follows:

1). create, and sustain, a sense of urgency about the future

2). create and empower a leadership team (a 'guiding coalition')

3). develop an end-goal (a 'vision') and a strategy for achieving it

4). constantly communicate the new vision and set out what changes in behaviour are required

5). empower employees to help change happen by removing obstacles

6). generate benefits in the short-term so that people can see tangible improvements

7). consolidate short gains and produce more change by continuing the actions

8). embed the new approaches in the organization's culture ('anchoring') so as to avoid eventual regression into previous practices.

25.7 EMERGENT APPROACHES

21. Supporters of emergent change tend to be united more by their disbelief in planned change than by a commonly agreed alternative. Nevertheless, there does seem to be some agreement regarding the main view of what constitutes emergent change. It is a continuous process of experimentation and adaptation, aimed at matching an organization's capabilities to the demands of a dynamic and uncertain environment and such change is typically achieved through many small to medium sized incremental changes. Over time these can lead to a major reconfiguration and transformation of an organization. Change is a multilevel, cross organization process that unfolds in an iterative and disordered fashion, over a period of years and is comprised of a series of interlocking projects.

22. Proponents of the emergent approach believe change is a political-social process and not an analytical-rational one. The role of managers is not to plan or implement change but to create or cultivate an organizational structure and climate which encourages and sustains experimentation, learning and risk taking and to develop a workforce that will take responsibility for identifying the need for change and implementing it. Managers are expected to become facilitators and have responsibility for developing a collective vision or common purpose that gives direction to their organization. The key organizational activities which allow these elements to operate successfully are information gathering – about the external environment and internal objectives and capabilities; communication – the transmission, analysis and discussion of information; and learning – the ability to develop new skills, identify appropriate responses and derive knowledge from their own and others' past and present actions.

23. The emergent approach is founded on the assumption that organizations operate in a dynamic environment where they have to transform themselves continuously in order to survive. The rationale for the continuous transformation model is that the environment in which organizations operate is changing, and will continue to change rapidly and unpredictably. Only by continuous transformation will organizations keep aligned with their environment and thus survive. Similarly, when the pace of environmental change is so rapid and complex it is not possible for a small number of senior managers to identify, plan and implement the necessary organizational response. There is a need for a bottom-up response. Organizations wishing to create a climate for change must enable a bottom-up approach by empowering employees (see Chapter 23). There is a need for openness, broad participation and the sharing of information, particularly about the external environment, benchmarking and measurements about targets. Managers need to encourage experimentation and occasionally diverging views. Organizations seeking such an approach will also have a strong customer focus, a strategy of continuous learning and will be oriented toward the environment.

CONCLUSION

24. We have described two dominant approaches to change: planned and emergent. With foundations laid by Kurt Lewin the planned approach, reflected in the organization and development movement in particular, dominated management for much of the twentieth century. However, planned change has faced increasing levels of criticism due to the changing organizational

THE HENLEY COLLEGE LIBRARY

context, i.e. from predictable to turbulent environments. In such environments, change must be a continuous process and in many cases it is difficult to determine what must be done and then create a sophisticated plan to achieve it. The emergent approach tends to see changes driven from the bottom up rather than from the top down and stresses change as an open-ended and continuous process of adaptation to changing conditions and circumstances.

Visioning Mental process in which images of the desired future (goals, objectives, outcomes) are made explicit motivators for action

25. Diagnosis (through change models), problem information (from surveys, observations and data analysis), gap analysis and visioning are used to motivate and determine what to change. Having established the need for change, change initiators then consider whether the organization is in fact ready for change. Lewin concluded that the change process needs to follow a three-step procedure: unfreezing, moving and refreezing. Many change agents use force-field analysis as an analytical tool to understand the dynamics of change. It is used in conjunction with stakeholder analysis.

26. Various people are responsible for making change happen; leaders need to be persuasive and political and overcome resistance. They must monitor the environment, identify and establish the need for change and provide clear direction for organizational change effort. They must also communicate that need and initiate activities. Managers can identify opportunities, promote ethical behaviour and develop capabilities within the organization in order to keep it aligned with its environment. The success of implementing change is associated with those who facilitate the change process. Change leaders need to understand why people react to change as they do – they should consider those on the receiving end. Change recipients may be concerned about how the change will impact upon their relationships with others (the people they currently work with), their ability to do what is being asked of them and their future needs.

QUESTIONS

1   Discuss what is meant by planned and emergent approaches to change.

2   Identify and described the typical stages/steps and activities in a planned approach to change.

3   Why do supporters of the emergent approach not like the planned approach?

USEFUL WEBSITES

IFAL: **http://www.ifal.org.uk/** Action learning involves working on real problems, focusing on learning and actually implementing solutions. It is a form of learning by doing
CIPD: **www.cipd.co.uk/subjects/corpstrtgy/changemmt/** Change management resources

Local Government Improvement and Development: **www.idea.gov.uk/idk/core/page.do?pageId=5829768** Information and downloads
Institute for employment studies: **www.employment-studies.co.uk/consult/index.php?id=org&tab=work** OD, change and organizational effectiveness

VIDEO CASES

Now take a look at the online video cases – visit the companion website to work through real world business problems associated with the concepts presented within this chapter.

37 Organization change: using technology to change practice
Organizational change is essential to guarantee long-term success within an organization. Most contemporary management scholars and practitioners agree that the amount, pace, unpredictability and impact of change are greater than ever before. Changes can take longer to implement than planned (time problems); may not live up to expectations (quality problems) or may cost more to implement than was budgeted (cost overrun problems). Perhaps more worrying, is the fact that, in relation to the three aforementioned change initiatives, failures occurred despite there being a great deal of

information, advice and assistance available. There is little doubt then that managing change is both very difficult and risky. Change management requires an interdisciplinary perspective and an understanding of organization, strategy, change, psychological and sociological theories. Before attempting to change something, managers must understand what it is they intend to change. They need to understand organizations, organizational behaviour, technology, operations, marketing and finance. Managers also need the ability to lead the organization, coordinate, motivate and control people and other resources. They must also be aware of intervention strategies, alternative solutions and how to overcome resistance to change. This case explores a real organizational change initiative whereby, at Lloyds, technology was used to improve outdated manual processes.

REFERENCES

Buchanan, D. and Huczynski, A. (2010) 'Organizational Behaviour', Ed. 7. Financial Times Press.
Burnes, B. (2004) 'Managing Change', Ed. 4. FT Prentice Hall.
Carnall, C. (2007) 'Managing Change in Organizations', Ed. 5. FT Prentice Hall.
Cawsey, T. and Deszca, G. (2007) 'Toolkit for Organizational Change', Sage Publications.

Kotter, J. (2007) 'Leading Change', Harvard Business Review, Jan 2007, Vol. 85 Issue 1, p. 96–103.
Senior, B. and Swailes, S. (2010) 'Organizational Change', Ed. 4. Pearson.
Williams, A., Woodward, S. and Dobson, P. (2002) 'Managing change successfully : using theory and experience to implement change', Thomson.

CHAPTER 26
COMMUNICATION IN ORGANIZATIONS

Key Concepts

- Communication
- Formal communication
- Informal communication
- Lateral communication
- Vertical communication

Learning Outcomes   Having read this chapter, you should be able to:

- identify the main functions of communication
- describe the communication process and distinguish between formal and informal communication
- contrast different lines of (downward, upward and lateral) communication within organizations
- review common barriers to communication within the context of organizations
- evaluate the use of committees within organizations

1. The communication that takes place in an organization is an important influence in the success of that organization, Clampitt (2010). Philip Clampitt, a Business Professor at the University of Wisconsin, defines communication as the transmission or reception of signals through some channels that humans interpret, based on a probabilistic system that is deeply influenced by context. We transmit by talking, writing, texting, illustrating and touching. We receive by listening, reading, watching or feeling. Signals can be verbal, non-verbal or visual and we use an ever-changing array of channels, including face-to-face, mobile phones and e-mails to send messages and information to others.

2. Communication is central to understanding organizational behaviour. Communication serves many functions within the organization: control, motivation, emotional expression and information dissemination. Communication is related to employee satisfaction (see Chapter 6 and 21) and in Chapter 13 we discussed its role in developing organizational culture. Managers help develop culture through communication. They must communicate values, the mission and organizational purpose, goals and the expected way of doing things. They tell stories, issue rewards and sanction punishments. Communication also plays a major role in strategy (Chapter 16), performance management (Chapter 18) and decision-making in particular. In the previous two chapters we discussed change management and recognized the need to communicate with employees and convince them of the need to make change. This communication not only helped remove barriers to change but also helped motivate the change itself. Interpersonal communication is important in building and sustaining relationships at work.

3. Managers must understand how they can make the communication process and enabling technologies work for them. In order to do this they must understand the importance of communication, how communication takes place, how technology may enable communication, and must understand the barriers to communication if they are to become competent communicators, able to persuade and motivate others and build trusting relationships. Such matters and related theories, tools and techniques will be explored in this chapter.

Communication The activity of conveying information

Channel richness The amount of information that can be transmitted during a communication episode

Feedback (in the context of interpersonal communication) The processes through which the transmitter of a message detects whether and how that message has been received and decoded

Communications Essentially the process by which views and information are exchanged between individuals or groups; usually refers to the system of communication in use, but can also mean personal skills of communication

26.1 COMMUNICATION PROCESS

4. The transmission (exchange or sharing) of information between people and systems defines the communication process, see Figure 26.1. The transmitter and receiver are entities (people or electronic devices) and the message (the content of communication – ideas, facts, opinions and feelings) may be communicated verbally or non-verbally through a variety of channels such as face-to-face, telephone, email, text or video conference. Feedback is used to detect how the message has been received. Communications may be formal or informal, verbal or non-verbal, written, electronic, synchronous or asynchronous. Furthermore, communication may be enabled by technology, discussed later. Skills associated with communication include report-writing, chairing meetings, interviewing and telephone selling.

5. Formal communication involves presenting information in a structured and consistent manner. Such information is normally

Asynchronous communication The sending and receiving of messages in which there is a time delay between the sending and receiving; as opposed to synchronous communication

FIGURE 26.1 **Communication process.**

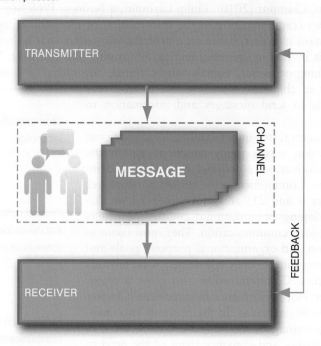

created for a specific purpose, making it likely to be more comprehensive, accurate and relevant than information transmitted using information communication. An example of formal communication is an accounting statement. Despite this, there are always unofficial, or informal, methods of communication within organizations, usually described as the 'grapevine', which refers to information passed on by individuals with no authority, and which gives rise to rumour and gossip. Sometimes such informal communication represents strongly felt opinions from amongst the workforce, and may eventually be recognized as legitimate, and be placed in the formal communication chain. This chapter is primarily concerned with formal communications only.

26.2 THE FLOW OF COMMUNICATIONS IN ORGANIZATIONS

6. The communications network of most organizations consists of vertical lines of communication providing upwards and downwards means of transmitting information, with a few integrating mechanisms such as committees built across these lines. Some organizations also provide lateral lines of communication, which are seen as having equal importance with the vertical. Mechanistic (bureaucratic) organizations tend to adopt vertical lines of communication and interaction, whereas organic organizations tend to adopt lateral lines. The greatest tendency in most organizations is for communication to be thought of in terms of vertical interaction. In particular, management communicates policies, plans, information and instructions downwards, and employees

communicate ideas, suggestions, comments and complaints upwards. The downwards communication is achieved by means of the management chain, whilst the upwards communication is achieved by work-group meetings, by joint consultation machinery and by grievance procedures. The flow of information across the organization (lateral communication) is used for coordinating the efforts of more than one department or section, and this may be done by means of interdepartmental meetings or committees (and cross functional information systems/business processes). This is a rational and controlled approach to the problem of integration.

> **Vertical communication** Communication flows up and down the management hierarchy

> **Lateral communication** Communication within an organization which exist between individuals in different departments or sections, especially between individuals on the same level

7. Research work carried out on groups at work suggests that, for simple problems, the quickest and most accurate results will be obtained by means of centralized (leader-dominated) channels of communication. Conversely, for complex problems, the most acceptable results are likely to come from decentralized communication channels, where there is greater encouragement to share facts, views and feelings. The most frequent channel-alternatives that have been tested are shown in Figure 26.2. The wheel represents the most centralized communication channel with its obvious leader or coordinator at the centre of relationships. By contrast, the circle and, especially, the all-channel networks rely on decentralized channels with shared leadership. The chain and 'Y' networks are basically hierarchical and not decentralized. Organic organizations would show a preference for all-channel networks, mechanistic organizations would tend to use the chain, the 'Y' and the wheel.

FIGURE 26.2 Communication networks.

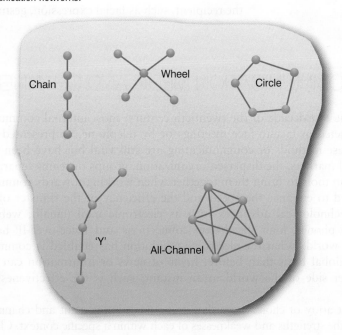

26.3 THE CONTENT AND FORM OF COMMUNICATION

8. Earlier we stated that the content of communication may typically be classified as ideas, facts, opinions and feelings. Whether information is supplied in written, electronic or audio-visual forms, its essential purpose is to convey some message. In a work organization the message is

usually factual, supplying information about internal policies and procedures, reporting on issues or providing details of meetings. Typical examples of such communications range from formal statements of new policies, minutes of joint employee-management meetings, reports to senior management, health-and-safety notices and staff vacancies. Some communications are intended to promote questions and discussion, perhaps prior to some new management initiative or the annual round of negotiations with trade unions. Others are aimed specifically at consultation, in order to obtain employees' viewpoints and opinions about proposed changes. Generally, the content of communications is open to public view, at least so far as the organizations' employees are concerned. There will also be communications that are restricted in their circulation and are not intended for the public domain. These may include discussion papers circulated to board members or senior staff, reports received from external consultants, draft budget documents and negotiating strategies prior to pay and salary negotiations.

9. This brings us on to the form in which communications are sent. Many of these have not changed much over the past decades. Internal memos, letters, formal reports, minutes of meetings, statements of accounts, invoices, bulletins and a variety of notices are still the principal form of formal communications, and have been unaffected by changes in technology. And, of course, we must not overlook the countless conversations that take place between individuals as they grapple with problems and situations at work. Written forms of communication tend to be more considered than face-to-face forms, and have a permanence that is lacking in the latter, which are usually spontaneous. Written forms are less susceptible to misinterpretation and, being visible, are less easy to deny, or qualify, than oral communications. This is one reason why written minutes of meetings are so important, because they attempt to capture the spoken words and put them on record. Written forms, of course, take longer to prepare, and are only as good as the powers of expression of the writer. Oral communication, whilst transient, nevertheless has the advantage of enabling the communicator to see the immediate non-verbal reactions of the recipient, such as facial expression, gestures and body posture.

Non-verbal communication Gestures and facial expressions which convey meaning within a particular linguistic context

26.4 COMMUNICATION MEDIA AND CHANNELS

10. Until the last decade of the twentieth century, most internal communications would have been conducted in face-to-face meetings or by telephone, or presented in hard copy written format. These methods of communicating are still vital but have been enhanced by technology. Virtual markets, the dispersed organization, groups or teams separated in time and space depend upon tools to bring them together when working towards common goals. Technology may be used to enhance the speed and the efficiency of the transfer of information/message content. Technological advances such as electronic mail (email), web pages and intranets and mobile phones, high speed data connections and voice-over-IP have changed lifestyles around the world. What the electronic revolution has enabled is communication on a faster and more global basis than before. Items of news or information can be sent to colleagues on the other side of the world in an instant; such is the effectiveness of the Internet. See Figure 26.3

11. The vast array of choices regarding communication content and channel demands employees understand the strengths and weaknesses of each within a specific context. Clampitt (2010:98) offers a model for selecting appropriate communication technologies. He suggests that we consider our objectives as the sender of a message (e.g. to educate, motivate, persuade, inform and impress); the attributes of the message (length, timing, formality, complexity); the channel (e-mail, phone, face-to-face, text message) and the characteristics of the receiver (location, occupation, access and age).

FIGURE 26.3 **Communication tools.**

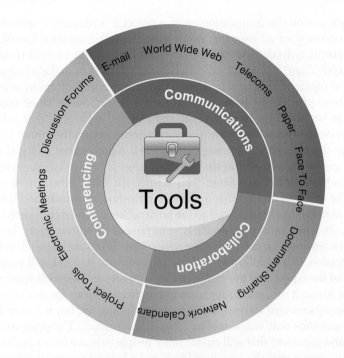

12. 'Dissemination' means the transmission of information useful in reaching decisions, making changes or taking specific action and is available to those who can most benefit from it. Traditionally, managers would receive information in the form of written reports, reports generated by the user of a Management Information System or verbal briefings. Reports may be generated and disseminated periodically (such as monthly budget reports), by exception (when targets were met or not met) or on demand i.e. ad hoc reports for specific one-off decisions. The problem with the periodic report is information-overload; however, exception reports can help reduce such problems. Technology also affects the traditional ways of delivering information (the salesman, the mail-shot, the advertising boarding), i.e. there is a separation between information and its carrier. Traditionally there was a trade-off between the richness of information (amount, quality and interactivity) and the reach (number of people involved in the information exchange): typically, the richer the information the smaller the reach. New technologies mean that information exchange is open and virtually cost-free.

26.5 COMMUNICATION SKILLS

13. The quality of communications in any organization is as good as the people who contribute to the process. It takes skill to write a good report or lead an effective meeting. It takes skill to sell services over the telephone or interview prospective staff. Sometimes there is tendency to assume that these skills are present in everybody, and that people just need a little practice to improve them. Most business enterprises soon discover that this attitude is not enough – staff need to be trained to develop appropriate skills. Fortunately, any communication skill that is improved is likely to remain with the individual for the rest of his life, because communication is a need we can exercise in every interpersonal relationship we encounter. There are three areas of communication where skills are particularly called for: report writing, chairing meetings and giving presentations. We shall examine key points relating to each of these.

26.6 REPORT WRITING

14. In a work organization the commissioning of a report is a frequent response to dealing with a problem that has occurred, or an issue that needs to be faced. Asking for a formal report gives those concerned the opportunity to delegate the essential fact finding and analysis to another member of staff (or external consultant) before they themselves are required to make a judgement on the matter. The first skill of report writing is to understand what sources of information and data are worth consulting in order to provide the basic material for the report. Some of the required information will be available in written form from internal and external sources. Other information must be gleaned from interviews with appropriate personnel. Some information may be available via the Internet. Whatever the outcome, one thing is sure – the report writer will end up with far more information than can be utilized within the report. A process of distillation must take place before any kind of summary material can emerge. This is often the most difficult part of writing a report because it forces the writer to decide what to include in the final document and what to leave out.

15. Once the raw material has been refined to the point where it can be considered suitable for inclusion in the report, the writer must then decide how to present the information. At this stage, meeting the needs of the readers must be the foremost requirement. What are these? The first need surely is for clarity of expression, closely followed by logic of argument. Readers will want to be able to see readily the thrust of the report and the evidence that supports it. They will want to know what the implications of the research are, and to see some alternative solutions for dealing with them. Report writers are not usually expected to come up with one right answer, but it is very helpful if they can point to possible scenarios that will stimulate ideas in the readers. The point of most reports is to provide evidence and argument that will enable other people to make better decisions.

16. Experience has shown that the headings likely to be helpful to report writers when considering how to set out their findings are as follows:

Title of report

Date of report

Terms of reference

(as given by the person/group requesting the report)

Executive summary

(a one or two page summary of key points in cases where the report is
lengthy or complicated)

Contents page

(in cases where the report is lengthy)

Introduction

(setting the scene; spelling out aims, purpose and scope; explaining
the methodology, outlining the report structure)

Main findings

(reporting the main facts)

Implications of the findings

(may be combined with Findings)

Conclusions drawn

(in the light of findings and implications)

Recommendations or proposals

Appendices

(supplementary or illustrative material to support main findings)

A clear, well-argued report will be received far better than one that is over-complicated and badly expressed, however relevant its content. Employees who can write good reports are well sought after in work organizations from chief executives down to junior managers.

26.7 CHAIRING MEETINGS

17. All managers are called upon to chair meetings at some time or another. Senior managers, in particular, may find that most of their time is taken up in this way but even junior managers will be called upon to conduct meetings of their own team. Learning how best to manage a meeting is an important skill, and one that can be improved by training and subsequent experience. Of course there are always exceptional individuals who consistently have the capacity to bring out the best in a group, but these are a minority. Most managers have to work at chairing a meeting and there are a few important guidelines that, if followed carefully, will enable them to do so relatively successfully. Pointers for formal committees are referred to later, but for less formal management meetings, helpful guidelines are likely to include the following:

Ensure there is an agenda (typically circulated in advance)

Be as well briefed as possible beforehand

Bring relevant reports/documents (may be circulated in advance)

Explain purpose of the meeting

Set out any procedures to be followed

Where possible, take account of personality and experience of group members

Encourage participation/questions/ideas when appropriate

Summarize progress as appropriate

Record minutes of the meeting

Ensure list of action points where appropriate

26.8 COMMITTEES IN ORGANIZATIONS

18. Committees abound in practically every kind of organization. They are an integral part of the operation of every public sector organization, and are almost as popular in the private sector. What are committees? The first thing that can be said about them is that they are formal groups with a chairperson, an agenda and rules of conduct. Committees invariably have a specific task or set of tasks to achieve. These tasks are frequently, although not always, associated with decision-making. Some committees meet regularly, e.g. monthly senior officers' committee in a public authority or a quarterly planning committee in a manufacturing company. Others meet for ad hoc purposes only, e.g. committees of enquiry set up by Parliament or steering committees set up to monitor short-term projects.

As was stated above, committees are formal groups. The formality of a committee is expressed by the following features:

A Chairperson who is responsible for ensuring (a) that the committee is conducted in accordance with the rules, and (b) that it is supplied with the necessary resources, particularly with the written information it requires to carry out its work effectively.

A Secretary, who is responsible for taking the minutes of meetings, sending out the agenda and other papers, and generally acting as the administrative link with the members.

An agenda, which sets out the agreed subject-matter of the meeting. Part of the Chairperson's job before the meeting is to approve the agenda, over which he or she usually has the final word. The agenda enables committee members to know what is to be discussed, and in what order, and this enables them in turn to prepare adequately before the meeting.

The minutes of the meeting, which are the official record of what has taken place. They serve to remind members of important issues or decisions debated at the time.

Committee Papers and Reports, which provide the committee with the quality of information to enable it to make well-informed decisions or proposals.

Rules of procedure, which are designed to promote the smooth-running of a committee and to ensure that consistency and fair play are maintained. Such rules include procedures for speaking in a debate, proposing motions, voting, adding emergency items to the agenda and other issues relating to the operation of the committee as a communication medium. The rules enable both sides in an argument to state their case, they help to minimize the effect of bullying tactics, and they ensure that a proper record of the proceedings is kept.

In the light of all this formality, what are the benefits and disadvantages of committees? The advantages can be summarized as follows:

Advantages

Decisions or proposals are based on a group assessment of facts and ideas, and not just on one powerful individual's preferences.

Committees can encourage the pooling of special know-how and talents possessed by individual members.

Committees are very useful for achieving coordination and collaboration between work groups.

Committees act as a useful focal point for information and action within organizations.

The main disadvantages are as follows:

Disadvantages

Decision-making is an altogether slower process when dominated by committees. It is also true that committee decisions may often represent compromise solutions rather than optimum solutions.

Managers may be tempted to hide behind committee decisions, where these have proved unpopular, and thus abdicate their personal responsibility.

Committees sometimes have a tendency to get bogged down in procedural matters, which reduces the time available for the discussion of substantive issues.

Committees do not exist between meetings, and thus cannot act quickly and flexibly to meet sudden changes in a situation.

On balance, committees are probably best suited to large-scale bureaucracies and organizations which have a high degree of public accountability. Smaller-scale enterprises, on the other hand, would probably benefit more from the greater flexibility obtainable from less formal processes of decision-making, such as informal management meetings and temporary project groups.

26.9 GIVING PRESENTATIONS

19. Most managers are called upon from time to time to make a presentation to their colleagues or more senior employees. Presentations are widely used in selling situations, and in management planning exercises; they are also used when formally introducing major reports or when introducing new ideas or proposals to colleagues. There are three key elements in any presentation:

- preparation

- content

- delivery.

20. Preparation is a vital prerequisite for any presentation. The person making the presentation needs to consider the content of a talk and its delivery. So far as content is concerned, this is primarily a question of considering what to include and what to leave out, taking into account the needs and prior knowledge of the audience. Senior management groups, for example, are mainly interested in the salient features of an idea or proposal, together with a summary of its principal benefits and disadvantages. Operational levels of management generally require more detailed information and will respond to a more technical approach than their senior counterparts. The question of how to deliver the presentation again depends largely on the nature of the audience and culture of the organization. Some groups will not be satisfied with anything less than a brilliant display of wit and ingenuity, others will be quite satisfied with a low-key, but extremely relevant, demonstration. One point that is always helpful, whatever the audience, is the use of visual aids. There is hardly a presentation that does not benefit enormously from visual illustration. Visual aids that are most frequently employed include PowerPoint, flipcharts, films and models or physical examples of an item. A code of good practice in the making of presentations could be as follows:

> Consider the venue, your audience and their needs.
> Assemble your facts and ideas in the light of the above and the complexity of the material.
> Develop sufficient and suitable visual aids.
> Consider what other information should be made available (drawings, specifications, reports, etc.).
> Tell your audience what you are going to tell them, tell them, and then tell them again!
> Be enthusiastic (unless this would be inappropriate, e.g. the announcement of a redundancy plan).
> Be natural, i.e. if you are a quiet person, then be quietly enthusiastic.
> Maintain eye contact with your audience.
> Be prepared for questions both during and at the end of your presentation.

26.10 NON-VERBAL COMMUNICATION

21. In face-to-face meetings, presentations and group work it is also possible to convey meaning (communicate) through non-verbal communication – gestures and facial expressions are elements of communication that do not involve words but do convey meaning within a particular linguistic context. When communicating face-to-face, we can use our own gestures, facial

expressions and tone to deliver a message and we can also use the gestures, facial expressions and tone of the recipient as feedback. Consequently, non-verbal communication can either enable or hinder the communication process dependent on whether the non-verbal communication is accurately interpreted. Amongst the forms of non-verbal communication to be considered are:

- Kinesics: body language, including winking, head nodding, hand gestures and arm movements.

- Facial and eye behaviour: which give clues about truthfulness, can enhance reflective listening, showing the message sender that you are listening.

- Paralanguage: variations in speech such as pitch, tone, loudness, tempo, also act as communication cues.

- Proxemics: when either person varies the physical distance that separates the two

It is important to note that non-verbal communication is culture-bound, a matter we turn to in the next section.

26.11 BARRIERS TO COMMUNICATION

22. Many managers and employees must now communicate in the global marketplace. Similarly, the workplace is becoming increasingly diverse and heterogeneous, presenting communication challenges. The aspects of the communication content and context that can impair effective communication in the workplace are referred to as barriers to communication. There are many barriers to communication. Aside from culture and language, there are also geographical and time barriers, language and technology barriers, legal constraints, gender and power differences to consider. All may impair communications. In many cases the receivers understanding may not be the same as the speaker's meaning. Schein comments on integration and the need for communication. We need to communicate what is important and what needs attention. Communication is highly important because without it, sharing is problematic and without sharing there is no collective experience. Organization culture and structure impacts upon the free flow of information within the organization. The communications climate is one dimension of organizational culture. This is the prevailing atmosphere in which ideas and information are exchanged. It may be described as more open, promoting collaborative working, or closed, where information tends to be withheld unless it is to the advantage of the sender; in such environments the atmosphere of secrecy and distrust can make working life very unpleasant. Hofstede (1997) also identified communications climate as a dimension of organizational culture, describing closed communication climates as secretive and relating it to the time taken for new employees to feel at home in the organization.

Communication climate in an organisation The prevailing atmosphere, open or closed, in which ideas and information are exchanged

23. There are numerous barriers to communication, and some of the most important ones are discussed briefly below:

- Individual bias and selectivity, i.e. we hear or read what we want to hear or see. People are often unaware of their bias until it is brought to their attention. Much of the bias is to do with cultural background and personal value-systems (see perception).

- Status differences, i.e. subordinates may well read more than was intended into a manager's message. By contrast, managers may listen less carefully to information passed up the line by subordinates. People at all levels may be reserved about passing information upwards, in case they incur criticism. One of the reasons for the relative failure of the 'open door' policy of communication adopted by many managers is that it relies on subordinates overcoming both their natural reserve and the status barriers of the organization.

- Fear and other emotional overtones can cloud the communication message. If a person has bad news to pass on, which is almost certain to upset the recipient, they will tend to avoid the whole truth and be content to pass on part of the message only. This issue of emotional barriers is particularly relevant in the handling of grievances. Angry people do not make good listeners, and thus any manager dealing with a deeply felt grievance must allow for a period of 'cooling off' before expecting to make any headway with a solution. Indeed, it is now recognized that it is precisely in the area of the emotions that human beings appear to be worst at sharing, i.e. communicating. Not surprisingly, this is an area of attention in organization development programmes, especially in relation to how conflict can be handled in a team.

- Lack of trust is another important barrier to effective communication. If we are not sure of someone, we tend to hold back in our communication with that person. This mistrust may arise because of doubts about the recipient's motives or his ability to grasp what is being said.

- Verbal difficulties are a frequent source of confusion and misunderstanding. These may arise because of the sheer lack of fluency on the part of the sender, or because of the use of jargon (specific application of words in technical and professional contexts), or perhaps because of pitching the message at too high a level of understanding. In terms of written words, the barriers are usually those associated with long-windedness, i.e. a failure to get to the point quickly and concisely.

- Other important barriers to communication include information overload (where a person is overloaded with memos, reports, letters, telephone messages, etc.), inadequate machinery for communication (committees, briefing groups, joint consultation meetings, etc.) and sheer lack of practice in the skills of communicating.

Overcoming, or at least reducing the effects of, barriers to communication mainly consists of finding answers to the issues raised in the paragraph above.

26.12 ETHICAL ISSUES

24. We discussed ethics in Chapter 17. Every communication decision has an ethical dimensional to it, Clampitt (2010:47). Choosing to disclose information, motives or feelings to others inevitably involves an ethical element. Company directors, managers and employees must make ethical judgements in choosing what, when and how to communicate. Managers may face many ethical dilemmas. For example, should they keep information secret or communicate with others? What should a manager or employee do when they disagree with organizational policy, procedure, practice or decision? Should they share their concerns and engage in constructive debate and dialogue or remain quiet through fear of possible retaliation? Should they blow the whistle and communicate with the media about corporate abuses or safety hazards? Should we engage in rumour and gossip which could have a disastrous effect on organizations and people? Ethical communicators must consider what is fair, right and wrong. However, many ethical challenges are complex, with no clear-cut solution.

CONCLUSION

25. Communication affects organizational performance and is central to an understanding of organizational behaviour. Effective communication is required to ensure that the goals, feedback and other management messages to employees are received as intended. Trust and clarity help ensure efficiency and effectiveness. Through effective communication, managers can develop productive employees. Effective communication requires an understanding of the communication process, an ability to select the correct channel, deliver the right message in the right form, in the right place and at the right time. This chapter has explored a number of concepts, tools and techniques to assist with these issues.

QUESTIONS

1   What channels should managers use to discuss an employee's performance problem?

2   Describe the communication process and distinguish between formal and informal communication.

3   Identify and describe important barriers to communication. Why should we focus on such barriers?

USEFUL WEBSITES

Article: **www.roxbury.net/images/pdfs/mc4ch1sample.pdf**
The Communication Process
CIPD: **http://www.cipd.co.uk/subjects/empreltns/comconslt/** Communication and consultation resources
Article by Gerard M Blair: **www.see.ed.ac.uk/~gerard/Management/art7.html?** Explanation of aspects of communication as a management skill

Newcastle University: **lorien.ncl.ac.uk/ming/Dept/Tips/present/comms.htm** Communication Skills – making oral presentations

VIDEO CASES

Now take a look at the online video cases – visit the companion website to work through real world business problems associated with the concepts presented within this chapter.

31 Communication in Alcan Packaging
Alcan Packaging represents one of four Alcan groups. With 29 000 people employed across 130 sites, in 31 countries, there are communication challenges – discussed in this case.

85 Managing communication – organization wide
This case can be used to explore managing communication, a topic in the principles of management curriculum (managing organization-wide communication, improving transmission and getting the message out).

104 Communication – unified
Communications, decision making and negotiation are three of the most important aspects of managerial activity. Whilst they are closely interlinked and are difficult to consider in isolation, we focus primarily on (electronic) communications within this case study. New (unified) forms of communication and technology are critically evaluated with regard to their business benefits and application in support of the communication process.

107 Managing communication – informal communication channels
Informal (personal) communications are discussed and evaluated in terms of gossip, both at the organizational and team levels.

REFERENCES

Andre, R. (2008) 'Organizational Behavior: An Introduction to Your Life in Organizations', Prentice Hall.
Buchanan, D. and Huczynski, A. (2010) 'Organizational Behaviour', Ed. 7. Financial Times Press.
Cameron, S. (2007) 'The Business Student's Handbook: Skills for Study & Employment, 4/E', Ed. 4. Prentice Hall.
Clampitt, P. G. (2010) 'Communicating for Managerial Effectiveness:Problems | Strategies | Solutions', Ed. 4.

Hofstede, G. (1997) 'Cultures and Organizations', McGraw-Hill.
Nelson, D. L. and Quick, J. C. (2009) 'ORGB', Ed. 1. South Western.
Price, G. and Maier, P. (2007) 'Effective Study Skills: Essential skills for academic and career success', Prentice
Robbins, S., Campbell, T. and Judge, T. (2010) 'Organizational Behaviour', Financial Times Prentice Hall.

CHAPTER 27
TIME MANAGEMENT AND PERSONAL EFFECTIVENESS

Key Concepts

- Role
- Time management

Learning Outcomes   Having read this chapter, you should be able to:

- discuss the importance of time management by individuals at work
- discuss the main factors affecting time management
- identify factors that might lead to the ineffective or inefficient use of time
- explain why it is important for a manager to understand their role if they are to be effective

1. So far in this section on organizing, we have been considering organizational and group issues. Ultimately, however, the effectiveness of organizations comes down to the effectiveness of individuals, which is the concern of this chapter. The management of time is an issue which is fundamental to job performance.

2. In the 1970s, Mintzberg conducted a study into how managers actually spend their time. He concluded that if managers want to be more effective, they must recognize what their job really is and then use the resources at hand to support rather than hamper their own nature. Understanding their jobs as well as understanding themselves takes both introspection and objectivity on the managers' part. Following the study he set out to break away from Fayol's words and introduce a more supportable, and what he believed to be a more useful, description of managerial work. The manager's job can be described in terms of various 'roles', or organized sets of behaviours identified with a position. That is to say, the manager's effectiveness is significantly influenced by their insight into their own work. Performance depends upon how well the manager understands and responds to the pressures and dilemmas of the job. Thus managers who can be reflective about their work are likely to be effective at their jobs.

Role A set of actions and activities that a person in a particular position is supposed to perform, based on the expectations of both the individual and surrounding people

3. The point made by Mintzberg is widely supported. Rees and Porter (2008) similarly argue the first essential requirement for an effective manager is to define their job carefully and accurately. They note that effectiveness depends upon the accomplishment of appropriate objectives rather than just being busy. Careful identification of the job is also a necessary foundation for effective time management. Much of the subject matter of this chapter overlaps with those dealing with such issues as leadership, delegation and communication. The interest in time management as a topic of attention in its own right has drawn together these other issues. The main factors affecting a person's use of time are set out in Figure 27.1.

Time management Refers to a range of skills, tools and techniques used to manage time when accomplishing specific tasks, projects and goals

These factors and the key issues arising from them form the subject of the remainder of the chapter. The principal issues of time management can be grouped under three headings – those related to the:

Delegation A distinct type of power sharing process that occurs when a manager gives subordinates the responsibility and authority for making certain decisions previously made by the manager

–   nature of the job

–   personality and attributes of the job-holder, and

–   people who make up the job-holder's role-set.

27.1 NATURE OF THE JOB

4. The nature of a person's job is fundamental to the amount of control over time that is both desirable and necessary. For example, a person whose job involves regular contacts with others is always going to be under greater pressure from interruptions than someone whose work is of a solitary nature. Similarly, a person who is employed in a new and developing job is more likely to suffer from conflicting priorities and unpredictable events than someone working in an established position, where predictability and routine are the order of the day.

5. An important issue for any job-holder is the identification of the priorities in the job. In cases where management by objectives (see Chapter 18) or some form of target-setting is practised, then individuals will have had experience of identifying and working towards priorities, or key result areas, in the job. However, by far the great majority of managerial and professional employees do not work under such systems, and are therefore unused to a systematic approach to prioritizing key tasks. A useful method is to encourage individuals to identify (a) the tasks

FIGURE 27.1 Main factors affecting time management.

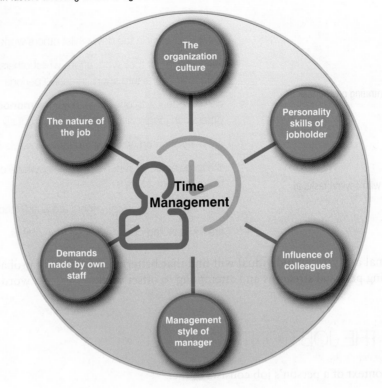

they alone are responsible for, and (b) the tasks that either require the greatest effort, or produce the greatest return (see Pareto effect). Once individuals have identified what they see as their key tasks or responsibilities, they can discuss these with their immediate boss. It is not enough, however, just to consider job priorities. It is also important to consider what the individual job-holder has to do in order to fulfil them. Some jobs call for administrative skills and a sound knowledge of organization procedures, others demand social skills and sensitivity to people-needs, and yet others require technical and specialist knowledge and the ability to apply it. Individuals, therefore, need to examine the processes associated with their jobs.

Pareto law A general law found to operate in many situations that indicates that 20 per cent of something causes 80 per cent of something else, e.g. 20% of effort in one area gains 80% of the results

6. A well-tried method of obtaining information about job processes is that of keeping a detailed time-diary, in which the individual records his or her work activities every day for a week or a month, for example. The simplest form is one listing the day in half-hour intervals alongside which are spaces for the job-holder to record what has happened, e.g. writing letters, conducting a meeting, travelling to a client, conducting an interview, answering the telephone, etc. Job-holders are frequently surprised at how little time they have to themselves at work, as well as at the number of interruptions they accept.

27.2 PERSONAL ATTRIBUTES OF THE JOB-HOLDER

7. A person's ability to make best use of their time depends, to a considerable extent, on their personality and inclinations. For example, a naturally assertive person will be better equipped to deal with people who trespass on their time than someone who is naturally rather inoffensive.

There are other important differences in personal attributes and styles, for example, some people:

Monochronic Concentrating on one task at a time

Polychronic Dealing with several tasks at once

– work best early in the day, whilst others work best later in the day

– like to pace out their work effort, whilst others prefer to concentrate their efforts into short, intensive periods

– can only deal with one issue at a time (**monochromic**), whereas others can juggle with several simultaneously (**polychronic**)

– are task-oriented whereas others are people-oriented

– like to delegate as much as possible, where others prefer to keep tasks to themselves

– are tidy and methodical, others are untidy and disorganized

– are more skilled or experienced than others.

In the final analysis, an individual will find that better use of time will probably come about by developing personal strengths and attempting to offset weaknesses, in a word self-discipline.

27.3 THE JOB CONTEXT

8. The context of a person's job consists of the:

– members of his or her role-set (boss, own staff, colleagues, etc.)

– physical surroundings (office, location of others, etc.), and

– culture of the organization (the dominant values that prevail).

Role set The collection of persons most immediately affected by the focal person's role performance, who depend upon the focal person for their own role performance and who therefore have a stake in it

The implications of these three job context factors will be considered briefly.

9. The people who work alongside an individual – their role set (see Figure 27.2) – are always an important influence on that person's use of time. An interfering boss, for example, can be very disrupting. By contrast, a boss who is an effective delegator can be a positive source of help in identifying job priorities. Subordinates' abilities to work effectively on their own, rather than seeking advice from their manager all the time, can enable the latter to work on personal tasks without undue interruptions. Colleagues can be a frequent cause of wasted time, especially when they call into your office at a time when they themselves are less busy, or want a short break from what they are working on. Senior or experienced members of any group will find that they are regularly sought out by junior members wishing to clarify a point or discuss an immediate problem. All these activities have their benefits, but at the cost of any one individual's time.

10. In these lean days of continuous job improvement and just-in-time methods of supplying line units (see Chapter 38), each person in an office, factory or workplace is being encouraged to regard workmates and colleagues as 'customers'. This adds extra pressure on people to deliver their particular service on time as well as deliver it effectively to their role-set. A basic role-set for a manager in touch with both external customers/clients, and internal 'customers' is shown in Figure 27.2.

FIGURE 27.2   Role set for customer service manager.

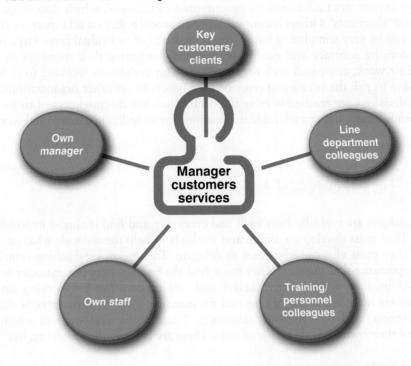

Given the prime importance of the external customer or client to the organization as a whole, it is likely that the manager in this case will often have to respond reactively, and sometimes even immediately, to customers who are directed towards him or her. It is well-nigh impossible for such a job-holder to fob off this kind of interruption to planned activities. Some customers will be referred by the line departments, and again the same considerations will tend to apply. In this example, the manager's best tactic would be to ensure that his or her own manager and staff respect the demands of the outside world and thus will adapt their expectations of the role-holder's priorities accordingly. The reference to training and personnel staff is made because customer complaints usually point to some deficiency in training or personnel, or both, and this normally requires the Customer Services Manager to alert the former concerning possible shortfalls amongst the staff.

11. Physical surroundings may help or hinder a person's efforts to make better use of his or her time. Clearly, if you do not have an office, then there are no real physical barriers that you can erect between you and all those who, however well-intentioned, wish to interrupt your work. Those who do have an office of their own can always shut the door, even at the risk of a certain amount of unpopularity. Whilst an 'open door' policy for staff communication is generally recommended, there are still occasions when it would be better to suspend this policy temporarily in the interests of personal work efficiency. The location of furniture and equipment can also affect the use of time. For example, if the photocopier and the computer terminal are on different floors to your office, or are at the opposite end of the building, then a good deal of time can be wasted walking to and from these machines. Currently, one of the most persuasive arguments for introducing computerized work-stations (see Chapter 30) is one of time-saving.

12. Another major physical influence on an individual's work pattern is that of travelling. The location of colleagues, customers and suppliers invariably means that an individual has to spend some time in travelling between appointments. This time can often be completely wasted, unless, for example, the individual travels by train or has a chauffeur-driven car, in which case it is possible to carry out work tasks whilst travelling.

13. The final aspect of the job context that we shall consider is the organization culture. Some cultures favour strict adherence to procedures and protocol, which discourages informal contacts and 'short cuts'. Others encourage an open access policy on all aspects of communications, which can be very stimulating but also very wasteful of individual time. Organizations that set great store by accuracy and quality are implicitly requiring their members to take more time over their work, compared with organizations who are always working to tight deadlines and thus have to risk the occasional error or inaccuracy. In yet other organizations, the speed with which decisions are reached is more important than the thoroughness of those decisions. Such an attitude clearly has considerable implications for an individual's personal work standards.

27.4 TIME MANAGEMENT

14. Managers are typically busy each and every day and find it almost impossible to do everything. They must develop an ability and methods to help them decide what to do and when to do it. They must also consider what to delegate. This means establishing priorities in terms of task importance and urgency. They must find the balance between manager-imposed, system-imposed (routine administrative tasks) and self-imposed work. Working on the wrong or unnecessary tasks is a waste of time and the manager must identify the right things to work on (effectiveness) and how to work efficiently. There are several ways in which managers can improve their own and others' use of time. These are broadly the following, by:

- personal priority and action planning, to-do lists

- target-setting

- work sequencing

- negotiation with key members of their role set

- delegating tasks to own team members

- developing appropriate skills (e.g. faster reading, writing, handling meetings and being assertive)

- developing an appropriate strategy for self-development.

15. Personal priority and action planning entails sitting down with one's manager, and subsequently one's work-team, in order to agree job priorities, and in particular those things that the others will look to you for completing. Prioritizing implies having a clear idea of the principal responsibilities of the job. It may lead to people setting targets for their own staff and for themselves, perhaps along the lines of those indicated earlier in Chapter 18. Managers always do well to consider the '80-20' Rule – that is identifying the 80% of their activities that are only likely to produce 20% of the required outcomes, and focusing on the 20% of the job that delivers 80% of the results. Time allocated to work by individuals tends to follow the sheer volume of activities involved in it rather than to be geared to their relative importance. Personal planning in management jobs also requires some time being set aside for reflection – a period in which further priorities and alternative actions can be thought about before being suggested to superiors or own staff.

16. One aspect of time management requires us to deal with time-wasters at work. Whilst a high level of interaction between people at work can normally be considered as a healthy phenomenon, there are nevertheless potential disadvantages for any one individual's personal effectiveness. These arise from the following:

- prolonged, or unnecessary, meetings with colleagues

- interruptions from own staff, colleagues or boss (however well-intentioned)

> - idle conversations (in the sense of casual chit-chat)
>
> - unnecessary memos and other paperwork.

17. A further problem is that of time lost due to travelling between jobs. It is not easy to overcome such lost opportunities for effective working, but some ways will be discussed later. There are other simple measures the manager may consider such as maintaining a clear desk so that things can be found when needed; controlling distractions and interruptions from e-mail or the telephone; doing things right first time and limiting time spent procrastinating.

27.5 DELEGATION

18. Delegation as an issue in management was considered earlier (Chapter 23). In the context of this chapter one or two points bear repeating. The art of successful delegation does not come easily to managers, and many have all too often done something themselves instead of delegating it because 'I could do it quicker myself'. It does indeed take time, effort, and confidence (in oneself as well as in one's team members) to delegate properly. It is necessary to explain what is wanted, answer any questions the staff may have, supply them with any resources they need (especially time!), before letting them go away and carry out what is required. An insecure manager will tend to delegate less readily than a confident manager. However, delegation can be made 'safer' for all managers if they take a few simple precautions.

19. Good practice in delegating includes ensuring the following:

> - Clear objectives/expected outcomes are set.
>
> - Standards of performance are established (i.e. what constitutes successful completion of the task, including reference to the timescale).
>
> - Appropriate authority is granted (i.e. the extent of empowerment).
>
> - Adequate resources are allocated (staff, equipment, expenses and time).
>
> - Clear reporting arrangements are made.
>
> - Team members are encouraged to seek help when needed.
>
> - Team members are informed that early mistakes will be used as learning opportunities.
>
> - The task is completed according to the agreed standards.
>
> - Those concerned are thanked for their efforts.

20. The first step is to explain what is required of the employee concerned, both in terms of what is to be achieved and to what standard. Unless the person concerned is extremely inexperienced or the task truly warrants it, the manager should not normally explain in detail how the job should be done. It will be enough to give general guidance initially and then be available to assist if necessary. This gives the subordinate an opportunity to learn from the experience. Part of the help that the manager must supply is to define the limits of the person's authority to commit the organization's resources (e.g. people, materials and money). Any authority delegated can only be within the authority of the manager himself. The next stage is for the manager to devise a simple control procedure for ensuring that progress is being made and that any difficulties are identified and dealt with. Part of this control procedure will embrace an opportunity for counselling, or coaching, the employee. In some cases special training may be required as part of the resourcing involved. In order that the delegation is seen to be taken seriously, the manager should ensure that the task is completed, or the responsibility fulfilled, to an acceptable

standard. If a task is delegated, but then forgotten by the manager, the credibility of the process comes into question. Finally, the employee should be thanked.

27.6 ASSERTIVENESS

Assertiveness The capacity to express our ideas, opinions or feelings openly and directly without putting down ourselves or others

21. **Assertiveness** can contribute to the better use of managers' time by enabling them to deal more effectively with interruptions. Assertion is the ability to express ideas, opinions or feelings openly and directly without putting down ourselves or others. Recently, attention has been given not only to identifying assertive rights, but also to training people in assertiveness. Assertive rights are based on the fundamental notion that each individual adult is the ultimate judge of his or her own behaviour. It implies taking personal responsibility for one's actions.

22. The right to say 'no' is difficult for most people to accept. They feel that they ought not to say 'no' because it is uncooperative, selfish, etc. Assertiveness training attempts to emphasize the importance for individual rights of the capacity to say 'no' without feeling guilty about it, and points out that in saying 'no' we are rejecting the request not the person. Making better use of one's personal rights can enable managers to fend off many of the interruptions inflicted on them by others, and thus create more space for themselves at work. Similar considerations apply to the right not to feel obliged to take responsibility for other people's problems. In this case managers can learn by assertiveness training to improve their ability to tactfully, but firmly, pass back to colleagues, team members and even superiors, problems which are the latter's responsibility.

23. Saying 'no!' to people is difficult for many managers, especially if the person applying the pressure is their manager. Some senior managers are inclined to forget that their own managers have pressing or important problems of their own to confront. They seem unaware that they are invading their team member's space, and see only their own problem. Refusing to be drawn into someone else's problem is not easy at first, especially when the problem is brought suddenly into one's work as an interruption, and you are being asked to respond right away. The important point about assertiveness is that the space-invasion problems you personally are facing, are likely to be experienced by your own staff and colleagues at some time or another. So, learning how to deal with others also enables you to see how they might deal with you in similar circumstances!

24. Possible assertive responses to one's manager, depending on the nature of the issue, could include the following:

- I am in the middle of this work you gave me earlier, and would have to leave it to deal with the question you have just put to me. Do you want me to change my priority, in which case I will have to put this work to one side?

- To be honest with you, it would be very inconvenient to take time out at the moment to deal with your request. I would prefer to look at it later, if that is alright by you.

- I am in the middle of a meeting with some of my own staff at this moment, but will be free to talk to you in about an hour's time.

- I am in some difficulty with your request to turn my attention to X, do you mind if I complete what I am finishing off at the moment?

27.7 PERSONAL COMMUNICATIONS SKILLS

25. A manager's use of time can be made more productive if personal communication skills are improved. Earlier we mentioned three particular aspects: faster reading, report writing and handling meetings. We shall look at these very briefly in turn.

Reading skills – being selective in reading is probably as important as being able to read faster. Managers need to be able to identify what is:

- – essential reading

- – essential and urgent

- – essential but not immediate

- – of marginal use/interest.

If a manager has to do a lot of reading in his or her job, then there are specific courses aimed at improving a person's speed in reading.

Report writing – one of the key tasks of every manager is to present ideas, impressions and proposals in writing. A knowledge of the basic strategy involved in drawing up a report will help a manager to make better use of the time incurred (see previous chapter).

Handling meetings – many managers find themselves at a meeting of one kind or another several times a day. To use the time spent on meetings more effectively a number of simple questions can be asked:

- – Is a meeting necessary to deal with this issue? (i.e. could a telephone call, fax or a memo suffice?)

- – What is the purpose the meeting?

- – How can we prepare for this meeting?

- – How can we ensure that the meeting is going to be worthwhile to those attending?

- – How long should the meeting last?

- – Who should be invited to attend?

- – How will action points be captured and dealt with?

CONCLUSION

26. Managers are typically busy each and every day and find it almost impossible to do everything. The management of time is therefore an issue which is fundamental to job performance. Managers wanting to be more effective must recognize what their job really is. That is to say, the manager's effectiveness is significantly influenced by their insight into their own work. The manager's job can be described in terms of various 'roles', or organized sets of behaviours identified with a position. Performance depends upon how well the manager understands and responds to the pressures and dilemmas of the job. Thus managers who can be reflective about their work are likely to be effective at their jobs. They must develop ability and methods to help them decide what to do and when to do it. They must also consider what to delegate. Assertiveness can contribute to the better use of managers' time by enabling managers to deal more effectively with interruptions. Assertion is the ability to express ideas, opinions or feelings openly and directly without putting down ourselves or others. Finally, a manager's use of time can be made more productive if personal communication skills are improved.

QUESTIONS

1   Explain why it is important for a manager to understand their role if they are to be effective.

2   Evaluate how the nature of the job, personal attributes of the job holder and the job content

impact upon the control a person may have over time.

3   Evaluate methods used by managers to manage their time.

USEFUL WEBSITES

The Association for Project Management (APM) **www.apm.org.uk/** Articles, resources, etc.

Project Management Institute in the United Kingdom **www.pmi.org.uk/** Active in promoting project management to industry and government organizations and publishes a bimonthly newsletter for members

Mind Tools **www.mindtools.com/pages/main/ newMN_HTE.htm** Time Management articles and tools

Time Management **www.timemanagement.com/** Section for managers: project management tools, effective meetings, etc.

Personal Time Management Guide **www.time-management-guide.com/** Time Management articles and tools

REFERENCES

Mintzberg, H. (1975) 'The manager's job: folklore and fact', Harvard Business Review, Jul/Aug 75, Vol. 53 Issue 4,

Rees, W. and Porter, C. (2008) 'Skills of Management', Ed. 6. Cengage Learning EMEA.

Section Ten
Control in
Management

CASE STUDY

CONTROL IN MANAGEMENT

'QUALITY WAY' AT HYUNDAI

Hyundai Motor UK Ltd sells through a network of dealers with dealerships across the UK. Globally, Hyundai has the world's largest manufacturing plant in its home country, Korea, and Hyundai Motor Group is one of the world's largest automotive manufacturers. Hyundai is a group of companies founded in South Korea. The name Hyundai was chosen for its meaning which in English translates to 'modern'. The Hyundai Motor Company (1967), with approximately 75 000 employees is a division of the Hyundai KIA Automotive Group. The Hyundai logo, a slanted, stylized 'H', is said to be symbolic of two people (the company and customer) shaking hands.

The Hyundai logo is symbolic of the company's desire to expand. The oval shape (in which the slanted letter 'H' appears) represents the company's global expansion. To stimulate economic growth, the South Korean government formulated a detailed plan for the development and manufacture of Korean cars by 1975. Production at Hyundai began that year with the release of the Pony. With the eventual goal to export automobiles to the United States, Hyundai released the Pony for testing, certification and approval in Europe. Exports of the Pony soon followed. For the next few years, Hyundai applied the knowledge gained from the Pony and set to work on two new projects. One was to be known as the Excel.

Hyundai used the Excel to enter the United States market in 1986; it sold for under $5000. Forbes magazine named it one of the top ten products of the year. That year, Hyundai set a record of selling the most cars in its first year of business in the United States compared with any other car brand (126 000 vehicles). Initially well received, the Excel developed embarrassing quality problems, and the company found itself the subject of adverse media attention. The Excel's faults soon became obvious; cost-cutting measures caused reliability to suffer. With an increasingly poor reputation for quality, Hyundai sales tumbled. At one point, Hyundai became the butt of many jokes. By 1998, Hyundai's name was so tainted in the US that its market share fell to 0.4%, and the company was on the verge of pulling out altogether. The situation was similar around the world. During the 80s and 90s, the focus was on Hyundai Automotives growth and producing as many cars as possible. Product quality and customer satisfaction suffered.

The leader of the Hyundai-Kia Automotive Group was changed in 1999 after the Asian financial crisis and government mandated breakup of the Hyundai Group. Previously led by the founder's brother the founder's son Mong-Koo Chung took over. He had performed well managing Hyundai's after-sale service and dealerships. When he took over he became the catalyst of an extreme turnaround for the company. From his experience working with dealerships and angry Hyundai customers, Mong-Koo knew well the damage to the Hyundai reputation and the high cost of warranty repairs. When Mong-Koo began broadcasting his intention to turn Hyundai into a top-five automaker, few outside the company took him seriously. Hyundai, like many family-controlled Korean companies, was ultra-hierarchical and slow to change. Managers rarely cooperated with one another and division heads ran their operations as personal fiefdoms. 'When a problem occurred, each division would blame other divisions.'

Instead of pulling out of the US, the parent company of Hyundai began investing heavily in the quality, design, manufacturing and long-term research of its vehicles. Mong-Koo's first step was to replace members of senior management with engineers. He formulated a strategy to challenge Toyota for quality. Extensive work with consultants, J.D. Powers, and benchmarking of the world's best automotive companies followed. He also sent teams to America to study weather, road conditions, and driver habits. Quality control staff increased tenfold to 1000 and they reported directly to him. Employees were encouraged and rewarded for their involvement.

Mong-Koo Chung earned a reputation for an obsession with quality. His zero defect policy led the Sonata model to be rated the most reliable car in America for 2004 with only two problems per 100 vehicles. (In 1998, Hyundai ranked among the worst in terms of initial defects.) Hyundai went from laughing-stock of the American auto market back in the 1980s, to seventh best-selling brand in the US, and fifth largest car maker in the world.

It achieved the turnaround through a focus on quality. In the US, the company was determined to win back car buyers with a focus on quality design and manufacturing, and with 'America's best warranty'. The ten year, 100 thousand mile guarantee the company implemented, was 'an incredible clarifier for the engineering team', forcing them to design systems for 'infinite life' (Krafcik, 2009). Hyundai's 'top down, hier-archical management approach' proved critical, too. Chairman Mong Koo combines 'Bill Gates, Barack Obama and the Pope', and 'when he says we must do something, the company aligns well around that goal'.

Hyundai engineers focused on the customer plac-ing cars at early stages in the hands of real drivers, and using feedback to improve designs. Also, Hyundai chose to design and build cars where it sold them. Quality remains of paramount importance to Hyundai worldwide. The Hyundai Corporate Message from the Chairman and CEO stated, 'In 2010, Hyundai Motor will continue in its endeavour to become a leading global company through increased worldwide produc-tion and sales. To do so, we will accelerate our com-petitive edge in product quality . . . and invest further in the development of innovative products, . . . since its establishment, Hyundai has placed customer satisfac-tion as its highest priority'.

It is Hyundai Motor Company's philosophy that adhering to the highest quality is its most important promise to its customers. This promise is kept through a policy labelled 'Quality Way', that aims for the devel-opment and production of zero defect vehicles. This has resulted in the company taking top honours in recent J.D. Power studies, beating rivals in the overall brand ranking; the J.D. Power Vehicle Dependability Study (VDS) focuses on problems experienced by original owners of three-year-old vehicles. The study is used extensively by the world's auto manufacturers to help design and build better vehicles (it provides insights into the long-term reliability of today's new vehicles) and by consumers to help make more-informed choices for both new and used vehicles.

In pursuit of quality, the company launched The Global Quality Initiative (known as GQ 3355 program) in 2008. Hyundai Motor Company wants to provide owners with top quality vehicles that are free from defects and troubles. GQ stands for Global Quality initi-ative; 3.3 stands for Hyundai's goal to improve the Ini-tial Quality to be ranked in the top three automotive manufacturers by the year 2011 and 5.5 stands for Hyundai's goal to improve the perceived quality to be ranked in the top five automotive manufacturers by the year 2013 i.e. 3rd place in global standing for actual quality within three years and 5th place in global stand-ing for perceived quality awareness within five years.

Sources:
1 Krafcik, J., (2009) MIT World Lecture: 'Great Leaps, Persistence, and Innovation: The Evolving Story of Hyundai', delivered April 8, 2009 available at http://mitworld.mit.edu/video/665
2 Hyundai-Motor.com
3 http://www.thehyway.com/Hyundai_History.htm

CHAPTER 28
CONTROLLING
PERFORMANCE

Key Concepts

- Budget
- Control
- Controlled performance
- Cybernetic system
- Diagnostic control system
- Formal management controls
- Informal management controls

Learning Outcomes Having read this chapter, you should be able to:

- distinguish the concepts of coordination and control
- explain the nature and importance of control
- with reference to contingency theory and strategic (managerial) choice explain how and why control strategies vary between organizations
- contrast common techniques for control

1.   Once the planning, organizing and motivating activities are under way, these activities must be monitored and measured, i.e. controlled. The primary aim of the control function of management is to measure performance against aims, objectives and standards with a view to enabling corrective actions to be taken, where necessary, to keep plans on course. Control is essentially a question of developing feedback systems throughout the organization. It was noted in the introduction to Organizing for Management that, if planning represented the route map for the journey, then organizing represented the means by which one could arrive at the chosen destination. We can now add that controlling ensures travellers know how well they are progressing along the route, the accuracy of their map and what deviations, if any, they need to make to stay on course.

> **Control** Ensuring plans are properly executed; assuring the organization functions as planned

2.   The chapter starts by contrasting coordination and control as integrative processes. We move on to discuss what should be controlled within the organization. Next, we consider aspects of 'controlling' as the final step in the management process. In this section we describe the control process and control systems generally. Finally, we turn our attention to control methods and strategies, focussing on performance in particular. This chapter should be considered in conjunction with the next two chapters where we focus on quality and quality control and the role of information systems in supporting the management process – to include coordination and control. This section completes part two of the book, management in practice.

28.1 COORDINATION AND CONTROL

3.   For any large complex organization a central and continuing concern is the problem of ensuring that its constituent parts act in accordance with overall policy, purpose and goals. The division of labour (the design process discussed in previous chapters) creates dependencies. Dependency concerns the extent to which an individual or unit's outcomes are controlled directly by or are contingent upon, the actions of another individual or unit. Dependencies typically cause problems that are overcome through coordination mechanisms. The specialization of subunits, which allows the organization to undertake complicated tasks, requires a system of integration to bind them into an operational whole. Integration processes include coordination and control. The integration of subunits into large organizations depends mainly on the manipulation of the two processes.

4.   Henri Fayol identified organizing, commanding, co-ordinating and controlling as key managerial activities. The need for coordination is dependent upon the extent of interdependence amongst the organization's groups. A given group may rely on mutual assistance, support, cooperation, or interaction amongst constituent members within its group, between other groups in the organization or with various partner organizations. In some cases they simply cannot exist or survive without each other (interdependent). Interdependence drives a need for cooperation and communication within and between the parts of the organization. Coordination, then, is the process of linking and integrating the functions and activities of different groups, units or divisions; it is about assuring that segments of the organization are operating in compatible ways i.e. one of the roles of management is to bring organizational parts together and cause them to work efficiently as a united entity.

5.   Groups and individuals may be dependent upon one another in differing ways. Tasks may be worked on jointly and simultaneous or work may be passed back and forth, between entities. As dependency increases, the amount of coordination increases. Typical mechanisms (to coordinate work and workflow) include: departmentalization, centralization or decentralization, through the hierarchy of formal authority, formalization (written policies, practices, rules, procedures, instructions, job descriptions and communications), standardization, mutual adjustment, liaison, line and staff roles, informal networks, and workflow systems. In summary,

coordination is seen as a response to problems caused by dependencies. Communication (see Chapter 26) and information (discussed in Chapter 30) are integral to all of the coordination mechanisms discussed.

6.   Whilst the concept of control has many meanings, for our purposes it refers to the management function of monitoring activities to ensure that they are accomplished as intended. Occasionally this may mean correcting deviations or reviewing plans, targets and goals. From an employee perspective the purpose of control is to minimize idiosyncratic behaviour and to hold individuals or groups to articulated policy, thus making performance predictable. Control is seen as a process which brings about adherence to a goal or target through the exercise of power or authority. Coordination, on the other hand, is seen more as an enabling process which provides the appropriate linkage between different task units within the organization. The two integration processes described provide very different solutions for the problem of binding subunits into the larger organization. Control is a more direct intervention into the operations of the company. Assuring organizational parts work together productively is a matter of coordination; Control systems, on the other hand, seek to assure organizational goals are attained; proactively ensure problems are kept away and drive corrective and adaptive responses reactively, keeping the organization on course. We focus on control for the rest of this chapter and the next two chapters.

28.2 WHAT SHOULD BE CONTROLLED?

7.   Controls may be applied to many aspects of organization: assuring strategy implementation and the attainment of goals; the management of finances and use of financial resources; the management of risk, protection of assets; the behaviour of employees in terms of performance and goal attainment; operations management in terms of transformational processes, inventory and quality and organizational change, including the management of projects. In this chapter we focus on controlling performance, primarily through methods to implement strategic and operational plans and the control of employees. We focus on quality management and control in the next chapter. Having considered what should be controlled, we conclude this chapter with an explanation of various control approaches i.e. how organizations effect control.

Controlled performance Setting standards, measuring performance, comparing actual with standard and taking corrective action if necessary

8.   Having developed the mission, goals and strategy, the organization must ensure appropriate action. It must translate the strategy into a comprehensive set of performance measures that provide the framework for a strategic measurement and management system. Additionally, managers need to keep track of the organization's financial and other resources. A primary goal of most commercial organizations will be profit maximization and many organizations, profit or not-for-profit, must consider the management of costs. To achieve such goals, managers need financial controls. Traditional financial measures include ratio and budget analysis,both of which are considered later in this chapter. Popular financial ratios include liquidity, leverage, activity and profitability. Budgets are a financial control used for planning and controlling. As a planning tool, they manage resource allocation; as controls they provide managers with quantitative standards against which to measure and compare resource expenditure. Deviations may then be acted upon.

9.   At the operational level, organizations typically seek to control raw materials (inputs), inventory, transformational resources and processes and outputs. Taking a manufacturing organization as an example, its inventory can be described as: raw materials and purchased items, work in progress (partly-finished goods/sub-assemblies, etc.) and finished goods. In many traditional organizations (with the exception of lean manufacturers), the inventory figure was the largest current asset, and a key factor in the ultimate profit situation. The reasons for maintaining inventory levels are chiefly as follows: (1) raw materials – to take advantage of bulk-buying, smooth out irregularities in supply and ensure internal supply to production; (2) work in

progress – to act as a buffer between production processes and (3) finished goods – to ensure availability of goods to meet and smooth out fluctuations in demand. The two basic questions of inventory control are: (1) how much to order to replenish stocks? And (2) when to order? Before these questions can be answered, organizations have to consider the costs involved. The two basic costs of inventory items are (i) ordering costs, i.e. wages, administration and transport costs, etc. and (ii) carrying, or holding costs, i.e. interest on money invested in stock, storage costs, insurance costs, etc. It is these two types of costs that inventory control aims to minimize in the light of the required inventory levels. Inventory control is an important feature of purchasing activities, and is referred to in more detail in Chapter 38.

28.3 CONTROLLING

10.   Having identified the purpose of control and what should be controlled we now turn our attention to control methods and controlling as an action. It is important for managers to recognize and anticipate that things do not always go as planned. Controlling is the final step in the management process. Managers must monitor whether goals established as part of the planning process are being accomplished efficiently and effectively. Appropriate controls can help managers look for specific performance gaps and areas for improvement.

11.   The organization assumes that everything is working to plan until a disaster arises. Information-as-control helps prevent surprise and disaster, providing early warning of a potential performance problem. Information and communication are critical elements of most control systems. Such elements support the decision making process, enabling the diagnosis and structuring of business problems, the identification, selection and implementation of solutions. Business information collected and analyzed from one part of the organization and communicated and reported to others may drive responsive action. In such cases that action will involve the selection and application of coordination and in other cases controlling mechanisms. Information systems also play an important role in coordination and control. Consequently it is important that they provide timely and accurate information to support adaptive action and decision making.

12.   Communication processes (discussed in Chapter 26) help to provide a sense of unity and purpose within the organization; the communication climate of the organization plays a crucial role in encouraging employees to become involved in the organization's activities. Organizations which are structured such that employees have easy access to management through an open and supportive communication climate tend to outperform those with more closed communication climates. The implication is that management needs to provide mechanisms for ensuring that there is a continual, free exchange of information between managers and employees. Employees must feel they have access to management and that their opinions and thoughts will be taken seriously, without fear of negative repercussions.

Behavioural control A form of control based on direct personal supervision which is responsive to the particular needs of the tasks, the abilities of the manager and the norms of the organization

13.   The organizational control system itself consists primarily of a process for monitoring and evaluating performance; the process of control is basically a process of monitoring something. An effective control system ensures that activities are completed in ways that lead to the attainment of the organization's goals. In controlling the work of people and of technologies, there are two phenomena which are typically observed, monitored and measured: behaviour and the outputs which result from behaviour. Thus, many control systems can be regarded as based essentially on the monitoring and evaluation of one or the other, and these will be referred to as being behaviour Behavioural control and output control. Controls may also be applied to inputs – see

Output control A form of control that is based on the measurement of outputs and the results achieved. This form of control serves the needs of the organization as a whole and is used when there is a need for quantifiable and simple measures of organizational performance

recruitment, selections, induction and socialisation in the case of people and raw materials or other transformational resources in operations.

14.   According to the cybernetic hypothesis, the feedback loop is the fundamental building block for action. Inputs or outputs are analyzed and tested against a standard; if the comparison reveals a discrepancy, an error signal is generated, and the system takes some action via the effector to reduce the discrepancy. Feedback loops are used in organizations to enable adaptive responses and continuous improvement. A key issue concerns what to measure – given the cliché what gets measured gets managed. Thus, the basic elements of control are as follows:

- Establish standards of performance.

- Measure performance.

- Compare actual results against standards.

- Take corrective action where required.

This sequence of events can be demonstrated diagrammatically in a simplified form, as in Figure 28.1, which shows how each element is linked to form a continuous process ending either in the achievement of targets or the modification of plans as a result of feedback (see Figure 28.2).

15.   Several comments can be made about Figure 28.1. Firstly, standards of performance (see Chapter 18) need to be verifiable and clearly stated, for example in units of production or sales volumes. Where standards are qualitative rather than quantitative, it is preferable for them to be expressed in terms of end-results rather than of methods. Budgets are a particularly useful vehicle for the expression of quantifiable results, and will be looked at more closely later in the chapter. Secondly, the measurement of performance depends heavily on the relevance, adequacy and timeliness of information. The supply of such information comes from a variety of sources within the organization. For example, the accounting department, is responsible for the regular production of operating statements, expenditure analyses, profit forecasts, cash flow statements and other relevant control information. Thirdly, when comparing actual against target performance, most organizations only require action to be taken when the deviation against standards is significant. Otherwise no action is taken and no upward referral is recommended. This is sometimes called the 'management by exception' principle. Fourthly, control is not just a matter of identifying progress, it is also a matter of putting right what may have gone wrong. Hence the importance of directing part of the control process to the implementation of appropriate corrective action.

FIGURE 28.1 **The control sequence.**

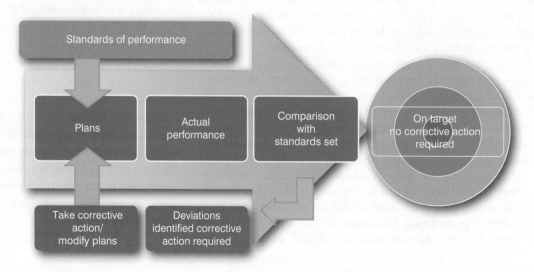

FIGURE 28.2 Feedback in the control system.

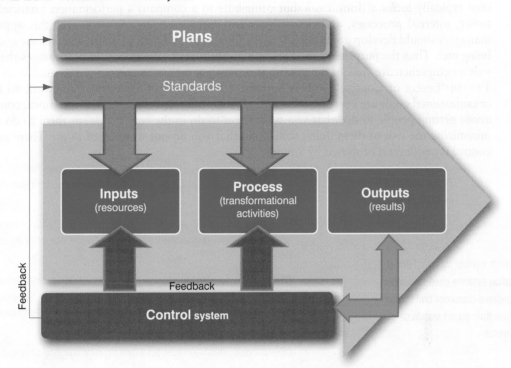

16. The information necessary to carry out the control function effectively is produced from a variety of sources and often in a variety of forms. The raw data is the basic facts and figures of operational life, such as output figures, hours worked, invoice values, part numbers, etc. This data may be stored on manual or computer systems. The data itself may not have great meaning. Taken together and assembled into relevant groupings, it becomes information, which is basically data that has been analyzed, summarized and interpreted for the benefit of the potential user, in this case a manager. A variety of computer based information systems are useful to management concerned with control at the tactical level. These will be discussed in the final chapter of this section.

17. The application of a management information system (MIS) to key management functions, assists control in a variety of ways, as the following examples suggest. In marketing/sales, information may be used to clarify current order position, identify profitability of particular products, identify selling costs, produce customer analyses and provide analysis of markets. In HR/personnel management, information is used to provide wage and salary analyses, identify sickness absence trends, analyze manpower statistics and for the production of labour turnover reports. Finally, MIS outputs can be used in Management Accounting to enable the production of operating and budget statements, analyses of costs/expenditure, etc. investment appraisal analysis, profit forecasts and cash flow projections/statements. In Chapter 30 we present a more thorough explanation of the role of information systems within organizations.

28.4 CONTROL METHODS AND STRATEGIES

18. Strategic control seeks to ensure progress in executing the corporate plan. The balanced scorecard approach (Kaplan and Norton, 1996) is a way to evaluate organizational performance and assure strategy is converted into action. Many organizations now realize that no single

type of measure can provide insight into all the critical areas of the business. The balanced score-card typically looks at four areas that contribute to a company's performance: financial, customer, internal processes, and people/innovation/growth assets. According to this approach, managers should develop goals in each of the four areas and then measure whether the goals are being met. Thus the purpose of the balanced scorecard is to develop a set of measures that provide a comprehensive view of the organization.

19. In 'Levers of Control', Robert Simons (1995) proposes a control framework to assure organizational goals are correct and achieved (effectively and efficiently). For Simons, control is about getting people to do what you want them to do in the way you want them to do it and minimizing the risk of them doing something that you do not want them to do. There are five control types (levers) proposed by Simons:

- Belief systems (values, vision, mission and purpose) motivate and direct the search for new opportunities.

- Boundary systems (formal rules, prescriptions, codes of conduct and operational guidelines) set the limits for opportunity-seeking behaviour.

- **Diagnostic control systems** – motivate, monitor and reward achievement of specific goals. Diagnostic control is essentially feedback control, reliant on data and information describing performance and is used to coordinate and correct.

- Interactive systems enable adaptation, renewal and change.

- Internal control systems are used to safeguard assets and assure the integrity and accuracy of accounting information.

Diagnostic control system Formal information systems used to monitor organizational outcomes and correct deviations from preset standards of performance

Financial control In financial control the role of the centre is confined to setting financial targets, allocating resources, appraising performance and intervening to avert or correct poor performance

Tight Control Severe limitations applied to an individuals freedom

Formal Management Controls A firm's budgeting and reporting activities that keep people higher up in a firm's organizational chart informed about the actions taken by people lower down in the organizational chart

Informal Management Controls Include a firm's culture and the willingness of employees to monitor each others' behaviour

20. Aside from the internal control systems, which also focus on the protection of financial resources and assets, Simon's control levers focus on people. Similarly, Don Hellriegel and John Slocum (1973) describe six management control strategies to exercise control over individuals on the basis of power. They describe control through organization structure, policies and rules, recruitment and training, rewards and punishment, budgets and machinery. We will consider financial controls and budgetary control later in the chapter.

21. The fact that there are a number of strategies for controlling people and organizations presents a problem for managers who must make choices; they must determine how to achieve control within their organizations. Such choices reflect the organizational culture (see Chapter 13) – organizations may be described on a continuum from loose to tight control. However, recall contingency theory and the need for the internal aspects of the organization to fit with the external environment. Ouchi suggests the control approach will be determined by the environment. Likewise, Pugh noted that internal context will determine aspects of control; company size in particular. As an organization increases in size, it increases in differentiation, which creates a control problem of integrating the differentiated subunits.

22. Ouchi and Wilkins (1983) also considered the problem of how to control employees, suggesting two broad organizational control strategies: traditional/formal (bureaucratic) and informal ('clan' or 'cultural') control. Bureaucracy is used to control employee behaviour through standardization, formalization,

specialization and centralization. Clan or culture as control is essentially based on peer pressure and the observation of 'the way things are done around here'. Ouchi and Wilkins proposed a general theory of clan control, based on goal congruence – the idea being that if both the employee and employer are pursuing common goals or at least not mutually exclusive goals, the employee will naturally act in the best interest of the organization, thus removing the costly requirement for 'close monitoring' typical of bureaucracy. Under clan control, the employee is committed to the organization and this becomes a source of motivation to cooperate. Ouchi and Wilkins discuss a variety of determinants and consequences of control mechanism. Clan control is argued to be more adaptive, processing information rapidly and requiring less supervision. They argue that clan control should be preferred when goal congruence and uncertainty is high. In contrast, they describe bureaucratic control, legitimate authority rules and close monitoring argued to make organizations more efficient in stable environments where goals may be incongruent.

23.   In Chapter 10, when we discussed contingency theory we also noted the role of managers in determining organizational arrangements i.e. they make choices based on their values, attitudes and beliefs. We have previously noted that managers vary in their attitude towards people as employees. Managers may consider employees generally to be responsible (Theory Y) or not to be trusted (Theory X). People who subscribe to Theory X believe that individuals will pursue their own goals, unless controlled, and that their goals will be incongruent with the organizational goals. Subscribers to Theory Y, on the other hand, treat people as responsible beings who, if treated as such, will strive for the good of their work organization.

24.   The amount and type of control adopted within organizations varies considerably. One explanation for this finding is given by Pugh (1997) who discusses the 'organizers' and 'behaviouralists', with the former believing in greater and the latter in less control within organizations. Organizers believe 'more and better control is necessary for efficiency' whilst behaviouralists believe that 'the continuing attempt to increase control over behaviour is self-defeating', that 'increased efficiency does not necessarily occur with increased control'. Pugh indicates that behaviouralists' beliefs are aligned with environmental turbulence and the organizers are more prevalent in predictable environments where bureaucracy is favoured.

25.   Controls may also need to be adjusted for cultural differences. As was mentioned in a previous chapter, national cultures vary in their tolerance of ambiguity and acceptance of how power is distributed within society and organizations. This has implications for the type of control to be selected in a given situation. Organizations may thus vary in the degree of control they seek to assert (organizers pushing for more control) and the way they seek to control – formally or informally. They may also vary according to who is controlling (specialists, the management team, supervisors, clan-control or self-regulation) and how control is achieved at the formal level (instructions, physical and technical controls).

28.5 FINANCIAL CONTROL

28.5.1 Budgets

26.   In this final part we turn our attention to financial control through budgets and ratios. A budget is a statement, usually expressed in financial terms, of the desired performance of an organization in the pursuit of its objectives over a specified period. It is an action plan for the immediate future, representing the operational and tactical end of the corporate planning chain. Budgetary control takes the targets of desired performance as its standards, then collates information systematically which relates to actual performance (usually on a monthly or four-weekly period basis) and identifies the variances between target and actual performance. Thus, whereas budgets in themselves are primarily tools of planning, the process of budgetary

control is both a planning device and a control device. The primary aims of a budgetary control system are to:

– establish short-term business plans,

– determine progress towards the achievement of short-term plans,

– ensure coordination between key areas of the organization,

– delegate measurable responsibilities to managers, without loss of control, and

– provide a controlled flexibility for meeting change in the short-term.

27.   The steps by which a budgetary control system is constructed are basically as follows:

1). Forecasts for key aspects of the business are prepared. These are statements of probable sales, costs and other relevant financial and quantitative data.

Budget A financial plan to manage the spending and saving of money

2). A sales budget is prepared based on an analysis of past sales and a forecast of future sales in the light of a number of assumptions about market trends. The resulting **budget** is an estimate of sales for a given budget period.

3). A production budget is prepared on the basis of the sales budget. This involves an assessment of the productive capacity of the enterprise in the light of the estimates of sales, and a consequential adjustment of either, or both, to ensure a reasonable balance between demand and potential supply. Production budgets will include output targets, and cost estimates relating to labour and materials.

4). A capital expenditure budget is drawn up to cover estimated expenditure on capital items (fixed assets) during the budget period.

5). A cash budget is prepared by the accountant to ensure that the organization has sufficient cash to meet the ongoing needs of the business. This budget reduces the organization's transactions to movements of cash and indicates shortfalls or excesses of cash at particular periods of time.

6). Departmental budgets are drawn up in the wake of the sales and production budgets.

7). Finally, the budgets are collected into one master budget, which is effectively a statement of budgeted profit and loss together with a projected balance sheet.

8). Production of period budget statements, which inform management about their performance against budget in the immediately preceding period and indicate any variances.

9). Action by management, as appropriate.

28.   In developing a system such as the one above, a number of good practice points need to be considered. These are as follows:

– Budgets should be sufficiently detailed to set clear targets for the managers responsible for carrying them out, but should not be so complex that they defeat their purpose of providing planning and control aids at the operating levels of the enterprise.

– Budgets should not be rigidly adhered to if conditions change significantly, but should permit reasonable flexibility. They are a means to an end, not an end in themselves.

– The responsibility for a particular budget should be clearly defined.

– Budgets should show variances between actual and budgeted performance (ideally in quantitative as well as financial terms, whenever possible).

– Managers responsible for carrying out budgets should participate in their formulation.

28.6 BREAK-EVEN ANALYSIS

29.   Not all control information is expressed in statements and computer printouts. Some useful information can be made available in chart form, such as a 'break-even chart'. This is a chart which shows how costs and profits vary with the volume of production. The name is taken from the point on the chart where the total costs line crosses the sales revenue line i.e. at the point where neither a loss nor a profit is being made. An example of a simple break-even chart appears as Figure 28.3. In the example given, total costs (i.e. total fixed costs plus variable costs) range from £20 000 to about £38 000. Total revenue ranges from nil to about £55 000. The break even point is achieved when a sales volume of about £32 000 is reached. Sales in excess of this figure begin to produce a profit.

FIGURE 28.3   Simple break-even chart.

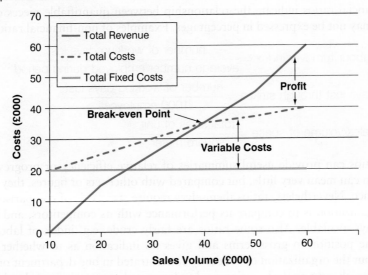

30.   Break-even charts are useful for their indication of the effects of marginal changes in sales volume or costs on profit figures. They are also useful for converting profit targets into production targets or sales targets. The major criticism of such charts is that they assume linear relationships between costs and output, and sales and revenue, whereas this is not always true. The straight lines on the charts may be over-simplified, therefore, and would need to be treated with some caution. Like many other information sources, break-even analysis should preferably be used as one of several devices for obtaining an accurate picture of the business.

> **Break-even analysis** The technique of comparing revenues and costs at increasing levels of output in order to establish the point at which revenue exceeds cost, that is the point at which it 'breaks-even'

28.6.1 Ratios

31.   A key feature of all planning and control activities is the analysis of performance data. We have mentioned budgets and break-even charts above, but another useful form of analysis is by the use of financial (and other) ratios. Financial ratios are relationships that exist between accounting figures, usually expressed in percentage terms. Such ratios can be grouped under a number of different categories, such as assessment of profitability, for example. Examples of typical financial ratios are as follows:

- Return on capital employed $= \dfrac{\text{net profit before tax}}{\text{net capital employed}} \times 100$

- Net profit margin $= \dfrac{\text{net profit}}{\text{sales}} \times 100$

The above are tests of profitability. Other ratios include tests of liquidity, cost ratios and stock exchange tests. Examples of each of these in turn are:

- Current ratio (liquidity) $= \dfrac{\text{current assets}}{\text{current liabilities}}$

(N.B. this should usually be a 2: 1 ratio.)

- Selling/distribution costs to sales $= \dfrac{\text{selling and distributing cost}}{\text{sales}} \times 100$

- Earnings per share = profit (after tax) in pence per share.

- Price – earnings ratio $= \dfrac{\text{market (stock exchange) price per share}}{\text{earnings per share}}$

Non-financial ratios indicate the relationship between quantifiable pieces of information, and may or may not be expressed in percentages. Examples of non-financial ratios are:

- Labour turnover index $= \dfrac{\text{number of working days lost}}{\text{average number employed during period}} \times 100$

- Days lost through strikes $= \dfrac{\text{number of working days lost}}{1000 \text{ employees}}$

- Sales/volume of space $= \dfrac{\text{total sales of unit}}{\text{square meter}}$

32. Ratios can provide useful summaries of relative efficiency or progress. Single figures on their own can mean very little, but compared with other sets of figures, they can take on greater significance. Nevertheless, ratios themselves require standards of comparison (see benchmarks) if an organization is to compare its performance with its competitors, and these standards are not always available. Also some ratios are fairly crude, e.g. index of labour turnover, which shows the position in gross terms and gives no indication as to whether turnover is spread throughout the organization or is heavily concentrated in one department or in one occupation. As with break-even analysis, ratios need to be treated cautiously, and should preferably be used in conjunction with other forms of performance analysis.

CONCLUSION

33. No amount of planning and organizing will assure that goals are attained. Control is therefore the essential final step in the management process to ensure that things proceed as planned or that unrealistic plans and targets are revised, where appropriate. As the final step in the management process, controlling provides the critical link back to planning. There are many purposes for control such as assuring goals are attained, employees empowered and motivated and organizational resources protected. There are also many business aspects that can be controlled, from plans, through behaviour to the raw materials and transformational resources of the organization. This chapter has emphasized the control of employee behaviour and their performance in relation to organizational goals but made reference to other targets for control. A key aspect of control is to enable the organization to function as planned, to minimize disruption, enable coordination and integration and help the organization to adapt to its environment.

QUESTIONS

1 Select two case studies from this book that focus on particular organizations or two organizations with which you are familiar. With reference to contingency theory and strategic (managerial) choice, explain how and why control strategies may vary between the organizations. You should state whether you would expect an emphasis on formal or informal control and explain why. You should also comment on control as a dimension of organizational culture and consider whether you might expect tight or loose control in each of the organizations.

2 Discuss the purpose of control in organizations, identifying what should or may be controlled.

3 What were the main targets of control at Hyundai?

4 Explain how feedback loops could be used in Hyundai to improve quality.

5 Finally, discuss the role of culture as control. What is a quality culture and how could the development of such a culture help Hyundai?

REFERENCES

Hellriegel, D. and Slocum, J W. (1973) 'Organizational design: A contingency approach. A model for organic management design', Business Horizons, Volume 16, Issue 2, April 1973, p. 59–68.

Kaplan, R. S. and Norton, D. P. (1996) 'The Balanced Scorecard', HBS Press.

Kaplan, R. S. and Norton, D. P. (2004) 'The strategy map: guide to aligning intangible assets', Strategy & Leadership, 32 [5], p. 10–17.

Klein, H. J. (1989) 'An Integrated Control Theory of Work Motivation', Academy of Management Review, 14 (2), p. 150–172.

Ouchi, W. G. and Wilkins, A. L. (1983) 'Efficient Cultures: Exploring the relationship between culture and organizational performance', Administrative Science Quarterly, 28 (3), p. 468–481.

Pugh, D. S. (1997) 'Organization Theory', Ed. 4. Penguin.

Robbins, S., De Cenzo, D. A. and Coulter, M. (2011) 'Fundamentals of Management', Ed. 7. Pearson Higher.

Simons, R. (2000) 'Performance Measurement & Control Systems for Implementing Strategy', Prentice Hall, New.

Simons, R. (1995) 'Levers of Control', Harvard Business School Press.

CHAPTER 29
QUALITY STANDARDS AND MANAGEMENT

Key Concepts

- Quality assurance
- Quality management
- Quality management system (QMS)
- Quality standard
- Total Quality Management (TQM)
- Value perspective

Learning Outcomes Having read this chapter, you should be able to:

- review what is meant by quality and quality management
- define the key concepts associated with quality
- discuss the importance of quality to contemporary organizations
- Identify key quality standards and frameworks and discuss their benefits
- list the eight quality management principles defined in ISO 9000

1.   Customers, wherever they are, want satisfaction. If they are buying a product they obviously want it to be fit for its purpose, safe, reliable, probably durable too and they are influenced by price. For example, most people want a car, but not everyone wants a top-of-the-range or an expensive executive model. They are quite happy with a standard middle-range vehicle, but they want it to be reliable, safe and economical. In the past many manufacturers were unable even to guarantee these three features. Nowadays, all manufacturers have to provide these, and many other standard features, in order to maintain their sales against the competition. In the case of a service, people are looking for factors such as availability, reliability, effectiveness (fitness for purpose) and courtesy. They may also be influenced by price. In summary we are discussing quality – from the customer's perspective.

2.   The subject of quality has been referred to throughout this book and in the previous chapter where we focussed on control, and is further mentioned in the chapters on Marketing and Production in part three. The concept of quality is omnipresent throughout management theory and practice. Indeed quality is a matter of concern for everybody from the board of directors down to the humblest employee. We therefore start this chapter by explaining key terms and concepts associated with quality and consider why quality is so important (rationale) to every organization today. Evans (2011) argues that many quality principles are based on management theories that are familiar to students and we will make links with strategy, organization design, leadership, marketing, production, organization behaviour, culture, decision making, information systems, business processes and continuous improvement. From the outset we recognize quality to be a complex construct, used to describe inputs (raw materials), processes and transformational resources and outputs. It is relevant to value creation through the organization's value chain and its value system. It is a stakeholder perception and may therefore be defined in many ways. Having considered what is meant by the term quality and why it is so important, we then focus on the management of quality in organizations, considering basic principles and methods and then quality standards.

> **Quality** Degree to which a set of inherent characteristics fulfils requirements

> **Quality standard** A framework for achieving a recognized level of quality within an organization. Achievement of a quality standard demonstrates that an organization has met the requirements laid out by a certifying body

29.1 QUALITY AND MANAGEMENT – KEY CONCEPTS AND RATIONALE

3.   What is 'quality'? It is difficult to find agreement on this, since much depends on the perspective of those concerned. For example, an engineer will tend to see quality in terms of how well the product or component fulfils its purpose, an accountant might judge the product in terms of its cost-effectiveness, whilst a customer may judge it in terms of its reliability. The point is, however, that 'quality' is seen as something good and worth having, whatever one's perspective. Most definitions of quality emphasize the degree to which something such as a product or service, or part there-of, fulfils requirements. Whilst the scope of quality is vast, there is one useful way of distinguishing between different sorts of quality, and that is to separate out the quality of the original design (the intention) from the quality of the conformance to that design (the implementation).

> **Value perspective** A quality perspective that holds that quality must be judged, in part, by how well the characteristics of a particular product or service align with the needs of a specific user. Value is often described in terms of quality and cost i.e. value = higher quality for lower cost (price)

4.   Much of traditional quality control has been directed towards the latter, i.e. to ensure that the production process delivered components or finished goods which conformed to their specification (or within close tolerances). This has been described as the internal view of quality, and

has been a feature of western production systems for decades. In contrast to this approach, the emphasis today is more on the former perspective, i.e. to focus on the original design, of which the customer ordered or expressed a preference for. This has been described as the external view of quality, and has been typified in recent years as the Japanese approach to quality.

5.   Another distinction drawn between the approaches to quality lies in the different attitudes towards specifications. In traditional quality control systems, based on the internal view, there is an underlying assumption that there will always be faulty parts, components, etc. and that allowance (tolerances) must be made in the production process. This viewpoint is not accepted in a total quality control approach, based on the external view, which expects that every part or component will be fit for its purpose, that everything will be 'right first time'. Such an approach places considerable responsibility on suppliers to provide exactly the right specifications. If, as in total quality systems, every person or unit in a production process is seen as a supplier of goods (or services) to others, then there is a clear pressure on all concerned to ensure they pass on a perfect product or service to their colleagues (who are, in effect, their customers).

6.   There are many reasons why organizations pursue and seek to manage quality. Quality may be associated both with organizational effectiveness, delivering what customers want, and efficiency through continuous improvement, a reduction in error and associated costs. The pursuit of quality and excellence is a strategy, enabling differentiation (see competitiveness) and impacts upon the organization (operations and tactics). Operational effectiveness (and efficiency) is about performing similar activities better (through operational improvements) than rivals perform them. Improvements can be made in productivity, quality or speed. Such initiatives change how organizations perform activities in order to eliminate inefficiencies, improve customer satisfaction and achieve best practice. Some companies are able to get more out of their resources than others because they eliminate wasted effort, employ more advanced technology, motivate employees better or have greater insight into managing particular activities or sets of activities.

Quality management Refers to systematic policies, methods and procedures used to ensure that goods and services are produced with appropriate levels of quality to meet the needs of customers

7.   Quality management refers to systematic policies, methods and procedures used to ensure that goods and services are produced with appropriate levels of quality to meet the needs of customers. Quality management may be viewed as a proactive or reactive approach. In some organizations it means continuously improving the product or service and aiming for the prevention of errors whilst others may rely on inspection to correct mistakes and/or to reject faulty components. Many organizations adopt frameworks for achieving a recognized level of quality. Achievement of a quality standard (discussed towards the end of this chapter) demonstrates that an organization has met the requirements laid out by a certifying body. In many cases they adopt a systematic approach to proactively managing quality, based on documented standards and operating procedures. The best known quality management systems are those based on the ISO9000 series of quality standards. See also Six Sigma – an approach to improvement and quality management that originated in the Motorola Company, originally based on traditional statistical process control, it is now a far broader 'philosophy of improvement' that recommends a particular approach to measuring, improving and managing quality and operations performance generally; the Malcolm Baldrige National Quality Award envisioned as a standard of excellence to help US organizations achieve world-class quality; and lean manufacturing systems and techniques of production enabling companies to reduce waste, leading to greater flexibility in production processes and products.

8.   To summarize, quality and its management is a company and value system wide concept that ripples through almost every aspect of the organization and its activities. When managing quality it is essential to adopt a system wide and holistic approach. We have used the value chain in Figure 29.1 to indicate the scope of quality and the important stakeholders. Quality goals are articulated through the corporate strategy. Through leadership an appropriate quality culture will be developed to ensure a customer and continuous improvement orientation by all employees. At the functional level (see part three), operations may set specifications for products and services and manage

FIGURE 29.1 **The scope of quality.**

operations to assure the products and services delivered meet such specifications; marketing will manage communications with customers to ensure expectations are met and the customer is satisfied. The quality of outputs is affected by the quality of the inputs and transformational resources. Thus suppliers and partners also play a key role in assuring quality.

29.2 BASIC PRINCIPLES AND METHODS

9.   Having considered what is meant by quality and quality management and why organizations strive to improve quality, we now briefly turn our attention to the practical aspects of quality i.e. how quality is managed – the main principles, methods, tools and techniques. We present only a brief explanation of quality principles and methods as the matter is revisited in part three when we consider production and marketing in more detail. We start by tracing the history of quality management and consider the significant influencers of the approach.

10.   The greatest influences on the total quality approach to management have been exercised by Deming, Juran and Ishikawa. The late William Edwards Deming and Joseph Juran, both Americans, applied and developed earlier techniques such as statistical process control (see Chapter 38) to the post-war industries of Japan. They showed that, by paying attention to the continuous improvement of production processes and gaining employee commitment to the idea of quality at every stage of production, it was possible to achieve consistently high standards of finished goods at a price the customer was more than willing to pay in order to secure reliability and acceptable performance. Juran argued for a proactive approach, that it is essential to look further ahead in order to prevent problems occurring in the first place. In essence, he was urging managements to stop trying to cure the symptoms of production problems, and concentrate instead on identifying and tackling their underlying causes.

11.   Deming is arguably the godfather of Japanese industrial success witnessed in the second half of the twentieth century. In the immediate post-war period, after Japan had suffered great devastation of its industries, Deming persuaded the Japanese Union of Scientists and Engineers (JUSE) to try his approach of looking at products from the customer's point of view, and then

meeting customer requirements in close collaboration with suppliers. A further key point in Deming's approach was to gain both managerial and employee commitment to engage in a process in which quality was paramount. Thus the total quality approach was born – an approach based not just on statistical process control but on a positive attitude towards quality at every level in the organization.

12.   Deming's initial work led him to promote Fourteen Points for Total Quality Control. These give considerable insight into his arguments for a total quality approach, and can be summarized as follows:

–   Create and publish a statement of the company's mission (aims and objectives).

–   Everyone from senior management down must aim to continuously improve customer satisfaction.

–   Provide the means to improve customer satisfaction.

–   Introduce participatory leadership style in order to achieve employee cooperation.

–   Develop climate of trust between management and employees, and between groups.

–   Develop an across-the-board approach to cooperation and teamwork.

–   Ensure adequate training both of employees and suppliers (so they know what is expected).

–   Continuously aim to improve the production system.

–   Eliminate numerical quotas for production in favour of instituting methods for improvement.

–   Use inspection first and foremost for improvement rather than for detecting and correcting errors.

–   Award business to suppliers on the basis of consistent quality and reliability of their product.

–   Remove barriers to workmanship by providing adequate training and equipment.

–   Encourage education and self-improvement at every level.

–   Create a climate where quality improvement is embedded in the organization's culture.

13.   In view of the above statements it is not surprising that Deming's approach emphasizes senior management commitment, the development of a longer-term rather than short-term view towards quality, the need for management to persist in the face of initial setbacks on the road to total quality, the encouragement of developing quality at source and a ban on emphasizing output at the expense of quality. Deming's approach tends to lead to a three-tier system of quality management with (1) senior management responsible for the quality of the aims, objectives and fundamental strategy of the organization; (2) middle management responsible for the implementation of those aims and objectives in accordance with the overall policy towards quality; and (3) the work group responsible for results within a continuous programme of improvements to production processes.

14.   The Japanese influence on quality came especially from Professor Ishikawa, who in the early 1960s introduced the idea of Quality Circles (see Chapter 40). This idea arose from his interest in the training of supervisors in the quality process, where he realized that if the work groups themselves participated in the process it would provide a means of securing quality standards at the workplace, and provide a system for giving feedback to supervisors and managers on quality problems. The strongly participative nature of Quality Circles aids the process of gaining every employee's commitment to quality. However, such groups are not intended to be ends in themselves but are an integral part of a total quality control approach. In a quality approach, especially where 'just-in-time' (JIT) systems are being implemented (see Chapter 38), an important lesson for Quality Circles is that their output is not passed on to the next process group until it is asked for. They in turn are not required to accept components, parts, etc. from their 'suppliers' until they are ready for them. Thus, each work group has to learn to react to the

needs of their 'customers'. This idea of everyone being a supplier and a customer of someone else in the organization is a key feature of a total quality approach.

15. In summary, **Total Quality Management (TQM)** – dominant in the 1970s and 1980s – is an integrated management philosophy and set of practices that emphasizes, amongst other things, continuous improvement, meeting customers' requirements, reducing rework, long- range thinking, increased employee involvement and teamwork, process redesign, competitive bench-

> **Total Quality Management (TQM)** A quality approach that emphasises a continuous process of improvement, through the involvement of people

marking, team-based problem-solving, constant measurement of results and closer relationships with suppliers. TQM may produce value, through a variety of benefits such as: the improved understanding of customers' needs; improved customer satisfaction; improved internal communication; better problem-solving; greater employee commitment and motivation; stronger relationships with suppliers; fewer errors; and reduced waste. Despite TQM and related philosophies emerging in the 1980's the tools and techniques remain useful for contemporary organizations.

16. As was noted earlier in this book, TQM was followed by BPR in the 1990s. BPR was used to radically change traditional organizations and align them with the new demands of the 21st century. However, once realigned with their environments, radical change occurs less frequently in such organizations. They then return effort and focus on continuous (incremental) improvement. Whilst many companies continue to adopt many of the principles of TQM, Business Process Management (BPM) has emerged to continually align business processes with strategic objectives and customers' needs. BPM requires a change in a company's emphasis from functional to process orientation. BPM may be defined as a systematic, structured approach to analyze, improve, control and manage processes with the aim of improving the quality of products and services. BPM differs from business process reengineering in that it does not aim at one-off revolutionary changes to business processes, but at their continuous evolution. Whereas TQM emphasized continuous improvement in a traditional (vertical) structure and BPR advocated transformational change within the horizontal organization, BPM embraces both types of change but within a more horizontal design. The roots of Business Process Management can be traced back to the 1980s and that of TQM philosophy, and in the 1990s of Business Process Reengineering (BPR). The primary principles of Business Process Management include:

- a holistic view
- strategic imperative
- enabled by information technology, and
- emphasizes cross-functional process management.

The role of information systems and technology is considered in the next chapter and Chapter 41. We now consider quality standards, what they are, their role and their benefits to organizations.

29.3 QUALITY STANDARDS

17. Quality improvement has been defined as actions taken throughout the organization to increase the effectiveness and efficiency of activities and processes, resulting in added benefits to both the organization and its customers. Quality improvement is achieved by improving processes. The continual improvement of the organization is considered within a number of quality standards. The International Organization for Standardization widely known as ISO, is an international-standard-setting body composed of representatives from various national standards

organizations. The organization disseminates worldwide proprietary industrial and commercial standards. ISO 9000 is a family of standards for quality management systems.

18.   The ISO 9000 family is amongst ISO's most widely known standards. ISO 9000 standards are implemented by approximately one million organizations in 175 countries. ISO 9000 has become an international reference for quality management requirements in business-to-business dealings. The ISO 9000 family is primarily concerned with 'quality management'. This means what the organization does to fulfil:

- the customer's quality requirements, and
- applicable regulatory requirements, whilst aiming to
- enhance customer satisfaction, and
- achieve continuous improvement of its performance in pursuit of these objectives.

19.   In adopting the standards organizations are required, amongst other things, to establish a set of procedures that cover all key processes in the business; monitor processes to ensure they are effective; keep adequate records; check outputs for defects, with appropriate and corrective action where necessary; regularly review processes and the quality system itself for effectiveness; and facilitate continual improvement. Developing a quality management system and meeting requirements of the standard can take months or years to do. Organizations may simply comply with the spirit of the standards as best practice or may elect to be audited by an independent and accredited certification body (not ISO). A company or organization that has been independently audited and certified to be in conformance with ISO 9001 may publicly state that it is 'ISO 9001 certified' or 'ISO 9001 registered'. ISO 9000 certification may be a requirement for doing business with certain other companies in the supply chain.

20.   Written procedures, instructions, forms or records (formalization) help ensure that everyone is not just 'doing his or her own thing', and that the organization goes about its business in an orderly and structured way. This means that time, money and other resources are utilized efficiently. To be efficient and effective, the organization can manage its way of doing things by systemizing it. This ensures that nothing important is left out and that everyone is clear about who is responsible for doing what, when, how, why and where. Large organizations, or ones with complicated processes, may not function well without management systems. ISO's management system standards make this good management practice available to organizations of all sizes, in all sectors, everywhere in the world. To keep customers satisfied, the organization needs to meet their requirements. The ISO 9001:2008 standard provides a tried and tested framework for taking a systematic approach to managing the organization's processes so that it consistently turns out products that satisfy customers' expectations. ISO 9001 is a useful basis for organizations to be able to demonstrate that they are managing their business so as to achieve consistent (good!) quality goods and services.

21.   As stated earlier, ISO 9001 can be used as a supply chain tool to ensure that suppliers understand what is expected from them, and are capable of providing a consistent, conforming product. Suppliers often refer to being 'ISO 9000 certified', or having an 'ISO 9000-compliant QMS'. This will normally mean that they are claiming to have a QMS meeting the requirements of ISO 9001. One objective of ISO 9001 is to provide a set of requirements that, if implemented effectively, will provide an organization with confidence that its suppliers can consistently provide goods and services that meet the needs and expectations of the organisaion and comply with applicable regulations. The requirements cover a wide range of topics, including senior management commitment to quality, customer focus, adequacy of resources, employee competence, process management, quality planning, product design, review of incoming orders,

Quality management System (QMS) A systematic approach to proactively managing quality based on documented standards and operating procedures. The best known QMSs are those based on the ISO9000 series of quality standards

purchasing, monitoring and measurement of processes and products, calibration of measuring equipment, processes to resolve customer complaints, corrective/preventive actions and a requirement to drive continual improvement of the QMS. ISO 9001 does not, however, specify requirements for the goods or services you, as a procuring company, are purchasing. That is up to the buyer to define by making clear the needs and expectations for the product.

22.   ISO 9001:2008 provides a set of standardized requirements for a quality management system, regardless of what the user organization does, its size or whether it is in the private, or public sector. It is the only standard in the family against which organizations can be certified. The other standards in the family cover specific aspects such as fundamentals and vocabulary, performance improvements, documentation, training, and financial and economic aspects. The quality management system standards of the ISO 9000:2008 and ISO 9000:2000 series are based on eight quality management principles. These principles can be used by senior management as a framework to guide their organizations towards improved performance. The eight quality management principles are defined in ISO 9000:2005, Quality Management Systems Fundamentals and Vocabulary, and in ISO 9004:2000, Quality Management Systems Guidelines for Performance Improvements:

- Principle 1: Customer focus – organizations depend on their customers and therefore should understand current and future customer needs, should meet customer requirements and strive to exceed customer expectations.

- Principle 2: Leadership – leaders establish unity of purpose and direction of the organization. They should create and maintain the internal environment in which people can become fully involved in achieving the organizations objectives (refer back to Chapter 7).

- Principle 3: Involvement of people – people at all levels are the essence of an organization and their full involvement enables their abilities to be used for the organization's benefit (see Chapter 23).

- Principle 4: Process approach – a desired result is achieved more efficiently when activities and related resources are managed as a process (see Chapter 21).

- Principle 5: System approach to management – identifying, understanding and managing interrelated processes as a system contributes to the organization's effectiveness and efficiency in achieving its objectives (see Chapter 9).

- Principle 6: Continual improvement – continual improvement of the organization's overall performance should be a permanent objective of the organization (see Chapters 10, 13 and 18).

- Principle 7: Factual approach to decision making – effective decisions are based on the analysis of data and information (see Chapters 19 and 30).

- Principle 8: Mutually beneficial supplier relationships – an organization and its suppliers are interdependent and a mutually beneficial relationship enhances the ability of both to create value (see Chapter 38).

23.   On the face of it, it may appear that the standards promote bureaucracy and to some extent they do. However, it is important to distinguish bureaucracy from red tape. The latter has rules for rules sake whilst the former has its focus on efficiency. As was mentioned earlier in the book, bureaucracy should be viewed as a continuum and not all bad. We also recognized that formalization and standardization were two key dimensions of bureaucracy. The requirements for a quality system have been standardized – but many organizations like to think of themselves as unique. So how does ISO 9001:2008 allow for diversity? The answer is that ISO 9001:2008 lays down the requirements a quality system must meet, but does not dictate how they should be met in any particular organization. This leaves great scope and flexibility for implementation in different business sectors and business cultures, as well as in different national cultures.

CONCLUSION

24.   Quality is an extremely important omnipresent strategic, tactical and operational management concept, associated both with differentiation and cost reduction strategies. It focuses on effectiveness and efficiency. Quality management typically begins with a consideration of customers, be they internal employees, other businesses or members of the public. Their wants and needs must be translated into specifications of one kind or another. These specifications need to be developed and tested. Resources and operational plans have to be drawn up. Then production (or delivery, if a service) can begin. The process of production (or delivery of a service) must be assessed and monitored at every stage in order to see where improvements could be made and ensure that the outputs meet customer needs. Once the customer has received the goods or service, procedures need to be in place to deal with after-sales problems or queries, and to assess the level of customer satisfaction. Then the quality process can begin all over again – in a total quality management system it is a cyclical process which never stops. Organizations may use standards to help them develop their quality management systems. Certification of compliance with a standard such as ISO 9001:2008 can bring many benefits and may help a company win business.

QUESTIONS

1 Evaluate why quality is fundamental to business operations – in your answer you should define the concept of quality and quality management, discuss its goal and business benefits.

2 Briefly discuss the role of culture in quality management.

3 Discuss the ultimate purpose of quality systems within organizations.

4 Identify and describe two fundamentally different strategies used to bring about improvement within organizations.

5 Discuss the importance of quality in Hyundai. Evaluate how the adoption of the eight quality management principles of ISO 9000 might help Hyundai achieve its goals.

USEFUL WEBSITES

International Organization for Standardization: **www.iso.org/iso/home.htm**
ISO (International Organization for Standardization) is the world's largest developer and publisher of International Standards. Management system refers to what the organization does to manage its processes, or activities, so that its products or services meet the objectives it has set itself, such as: satisfying the customer's quality requirements, complying with regulations or meeting environmental objectives. Management system standards provide a model to follow in

setting up and operating a management system. This model incorporates the features on which experts in the field have reached a consensus as being the international state of the art. The ISO 9000 family addresses 'Quality management'. This means what the organization does to fulfil: the customer's quality requirements, and applicable regulatory requirements, while aiming to enhance customer satisfaction, and achieve continual improvement of its performance in pursuit of these objectives.

VIDEO CASES

Now take a look at the online video cases – visit the companion website to work through real world business problems associated with the concepts presented within this chapter.

54 Managing quality inside a frozen pizza factory
Investigates how quality is managed in the production of frozen pizza.

95 Managing quality and performance – The Evolving Story of Hyundai
Hyundai entered the United States market in 1986 with a solitary model, the Hyundai Excel. That year, Hyundai set a record of selling the most cars in its first year of business in the United States compared with any other car brand (126 000 vehicles). Initially well received, the Excel's faults soon became obvious; cost-cutting measures caused reliability to

suffer. With an increasingly poor reputation for quality, Hyundai sales tumbled. At one point, Hyundai became the butt of many jokes. In response, the parent company of Hyundai began investing heavily in the quality, design, manufacturing and long-term research of its vehicles. In this case, John Krafcik, acting President and CEO.

105 Managing quality – Beyond Six Sigma at GE
A case used to discuss why quality is fundamental to business operations and organizations generally; discusses the General Electric and alternative organization's quality philosophy. The case is used to identify what is meant by quality philosophy with reference to various quality principles, to explore quality tools and explain what is meant by Six Sigma.

106 Managing quality and performance
A case to highlight why quality is fundamental to organizations. Discusses the organization's quality philosophy and is used to identify what is meant by quality with reference to various quality principles.

129 Quality Improvement Methods – An Introduction
Quality is consistent conformance to customer expectations. Quality, particularly when it is associated with competitive advantage, is a significant concern for most organizations.

When quality is managed, the costs of waste, reworked, complaints and returns are reduced and customer satisfaction enhanced and, in many cases, improvements in quality translate into improvements in profit. In the case of not-for-profit organizations, quality improvements ensure the efficient use of resources and improvements in service. This case considers the use of quality improvement methods by a not-for-profit organization that has learned from the quality improvements made in profit organizations.

REFERENCES

Barnes, D. (2008) 'Operations Management An International Perspective', Cengage Learning EMEA.

Bozarth, C. and Handfield, R. (2006) 'Introduction to Operations and Supply Chain Management with Advanced Decision Support Tools', Prentice Hall.

Collier, D. and Evans, J. (2009) 'OM', Ed. 1. Cengage Learning.

Evans, J. (2011) 'Quality Management, Organization, and Strategy', Ed. 6. South Western.

Goetsch, D. L. and Davis, S. (2010) 'Quality Management for Organizational Excellence: Introduction to Total Quality', Ed. 6. Pearson Higher Education.

Slack, N., Chambers, S. and Johnston, R. (2007) 'Operations Management', Ed. 5. Financial Times Press.

Summers, D. (2010) 'Quality', Ed. 5. Prentice Hall.

Summers, D. (2009) 'Quality Management', Ed. 2. Pearson Higher Education.

CHAPTER 30
THE ROLE OF INFORMATION TECHNOLOGY

Key Concepts

- Business information system
- Digital organization
- Enterprise system
- Information
- Information system
- Information technology

Learning Outcomes Having read this chapter, you should be able to:

- differentiate between the concepts of data, information and knowledge resources
- identify the role of information resources within the organization
- discuss how information resources can be used to deliver value and help the organization compete
- explain the roles of technology, people, structure, culture and processes in knowledge management
- identify the various types of information system
- identify ways the use of the Internet and Internet (Net) technologies can help the organization compete, create wealth and add value
- explain what is meant by e-commerce and e-business

30.1 INFORMATION RESOURCES: DATA, INFORMATION AND KNOWLEDGE

1.   Quality, as well as the management functions of coordination and control (Chapter 28), decision-making (Chapter 19), planning (Chapter 16) and performance management (Chapter 18), indeed all the major business functions (especially marketing, operations and finance to be discussed in part 3) and associated processes benefit from information systems (IS) and information technology (IT). Like quality, IS/IT is omnipresent and enables strategy, tactics and operations. It is extremely important, enabling organizations to be more effective and efficient, to differentiate products and services whilst reducing costs. It therefore helps them to compete and offer value for money whilst enhancing customer satisfaction. Through the use of IS/IT, companies can reach and break into markets world-wide, operate 24/7, enable and empower employees, share knowledge, integrate work activities, improve the quality of working life, enable time compression and time-based advantages, improve communication and enable team work – especially over time and space.

Information system (IS) A set of people, procedures and resources that collects, transform and disseminates information in an organization – accepts data resources as input and processes them into information products as output

2.   Clearly then, IT matters to the organization as pointed out by Reynolds (2010). He believes that future business managers need to understand how information technology can be applied to improve the organization. Similarly Cetindamar, Phaal and Probert (2010), argue that technology is a fundamental part of every organization: when managed correctly it can deliver a decisive advantage over competitors. The authors focus in particular on developing operational efficiency and productivity – a matter we address in Chapter 41. A goal of today's organization is having 'the right information, in the right place, in the right format, at the right time – at the right cost'. Additionally, exploiting an organization's proprietary information as a strategic asset remains a significant contemporary challenge.

Information technology The hardware and software that are used to store, retrieve and manipulate information

Information Data that has been processed (sorted, summarized, manipulated, filtered) so that it is meaningful to people

3.   In this chapter we focus on information system resources (hardware, software, communication technologies, data and people) and information resources (data, information and knowledge). Systems theory (see Chapter 9) is used to unite such resources. We will consider the hardware, software and processes and communication technologies that enable the capture of such resources, transfer and use in transformational activities. Various IT resources considered in this part of the book enable the free flow of information throughout the organization in support of commerce, planning, decision-making, control and coordination. Finally we consider the role of Internet technologies as the 'glue' and 'conduit' for bundling resources together, making them available for work and value adding activities. We will argue that information system resources are strategically important resources, enabling and informing strategy, creating capabilities and competences when bundled with other resources.

Data Raw facts

Knowledge What people understand as a result of what they have been taught or have experienced. Knowledge may then be applied to solve problems

4.   Data can be regarded as raw facts representing events occurring in organizations (such as business transactions) or the physical environment – objective measurements of the attributes (characteristics) of entities, such as people, places, things and events. The price of a product or service, the date of a customer order, contact details or an employee's date of birth are all examples of data. Data may be generated during business or may be collected from external sources. Sometimes the data refers to attributes of a person. In such cases the company may be obliged

to protect it according to various privacy or financial operating laws. We can classify data in a number of ways, for example, data may be structured or unstructured. People use both types of data every day. Examples of 'unstructured data' may include audio, video and unstructured text such as the body of an email or word processor document. Data that resides in fixed fields within a record or file (relational databases and spreadsheets) are examples of structured data. Structured data is managed by technology that allows for querying and reporting against predetermined data types and understood relationships. Data structure is a way of storing data in a computer so that it can be used efficiently.

5. Data may be stored in paper-based (manual) or computer based systems. A spreadsheet may be considered a simple database but its use is limited when considering many business problems. In many ways, the spreadsheet, for all its mathematical processing functionality, is little more than an electronic list. A Database is a system or programme in which structured data is stored. Databases may exist within or be external to the organization. There are many types of database such as the Marketing databases; databases support the major business operations of the organization. Transaction processing systems (TPS) are computerized systems that perform and record the daily routine transactions necessary to conduct the business (basic business transactions include purchasing, orders for goods and services, billing and payroll – banks, for example, handle millions of deposits and withdrawals each day); these systems serve the operational level of the organization. The records of such systems are typically stored within relational databases.

Database A system or programme in which structured data is stored

6. Data may be collected through manual or electronic means. For example, data can be captured using a keyboard, mouse, scanner, optical character or voice recognition. Once stored (see Figure 30.1 Information system), queries and other programs may be used to access or edit the data.

7. Total sales of a product in a particular location during a particular time period or a strategic summary of strengths and weaknesses represents examples of information. The words information and data are used interchangeably in many contexts. This may lead to confusion, however, since they are not synonyms. Information is the summarization of data. Data that has been processed (sorted, summarized, manipulated or filtered) so that it is meaningful to people is normally considered to be information. Information may be used to reduce uncertainty and may therefore be used to improve decision-making. Information may be communicated by formal (structured) or informal (e.g. casual conversation) means.

FIGURE 30.1 Information system.

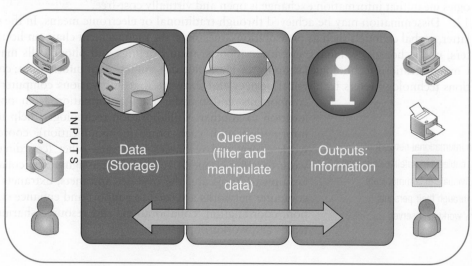

Information can add value to products and services and information flows can improve the quality of decision making, collaboration, planning, coordination and control and internal operations. The importance of information has been brought into sharp focus by advances in information and communication technology, especially the explosion in the use of the Internet, to be discussed later in the chapter, which has opened new windows of opportunity for accessing and disseminating information.

8.   Information reports are typically generated through queries, gathering and manipulating the data required to create the report. Reports may then be communicated and disseminated in many ways. Information (the output) is created (the process) from data (the input) when it is required. In many cases, therefore, there is no need to store information. Whereas data is typically the focus of the Transaction Processing System (TPS), information is at the heart of the Management Information System (MIS). The TPS serves the needs of operations (primary activities in the value chain) and stakeholders in the supply chain whereas the MIS serves the needs of managers, typically involved in tactical decision making.

9.   Management information systems (MISs) are systems designed to provide past, present and future routine information appropriate for planning, organizing and controlling the operation's functional areas in an organization. These systems provide feedback on organizational activities and help to support managerial decision making. Information is of more value when it is available to the right people, in the right form and at the time they need it.

10.   Thus far, we have not only revealed the relationship between data and information but also indentified information as an output of the information system. This output must be disseminated if managers and workers are to improve decision making, planning, control and coordination. 'Dissemination' means the transmission of information, whether orally, in writing or by electronic means. The purpose of a dissemination activity is to assure that information/knowledge is useful in reaching decisions, making changes or taking specific action and is available to those who can most benefit from it. Traditionally, managers would receive information in the form of reports generated by the MIS. Reports may be generated and disseminated periodically (such as monthly budget reports), by exception (when targets were met or not met), on demand i.e. ad hoc reports for specific one-off decisions and push reports (reports sent to recipients who may not have requested them).

11.   The problem with the periodic report is information-overload; however, exception reports can help reduce such problems. Technology also affects the traditional ways of delivering information (the salesman, the mail-shot, the advertising boarding) – i.e. there is a separation between information and its carrier. Traditionally there was a trade-off between the richness of information (amount, quality and interactivity) and the reach (number of people involved in the information exchange): typically, the richer the information the smaller the reach. New technologies mean that information exchange is open and virtually cost-free.

12.   Dissemination may be achieved through traditional or electronic means. In the case of the latter, verbal channels such as presentations, meetings, the management chain, in-house newsletters, notice boards, seminars, employee reports, team briefings and phone calls may be used. Communications technologies support the electronic dissemination of information; communications technology refers to physical devices and software that link various computer hardware components and transfer data/ information from one physical location to another. Collaboration technologies help us to share information with each other (communication), coordinate our work efforts and resources with each other (coordination), and work together cooperatively on joint assignments (collaboration). Groupware tools and the Internet, intranets, extranets and other computer networks are used to support and enhance communication, coordination, collaboration, and resource sharing amongst teams and workgroups.

Internet An international network of computers, cables and satellite links that enables individuals to communicate worldwide through their personal computer or workplace server

13. Technology (telecommunications and software applications) can overcome geographic barriers, enabling the capture of information about business transactions from remote locations; time barriers – providing information to remote locations immediately after it is requested (see virtual organisation); overcome cost barriers, reducing the cost of more traditional means of communication and can support linkages for competitive advantage (overcome structural barriers). Bill Gates of Microsoft argues that information flow is the major differentiator for every business – the lifeblood of your company. Like the blood circulatory or nervous system in the body, an organization needs information flows to link up its parts and create the whole.

> **Telecommunications** The exchange of information in any form (e.g. voice, data, text and images) over networks

14. Knowledge and information are closely related and, as was the case with data and information concepts, on occasions the two terms are used interchangeably. Many see knowledge as the understanding, awareness or familiarity acquired through education or experience. Others see knowledge as applying experience to problem solving. The source of knowledge as education or experience has led many to divide the concept in two classes: it may be about 'Knowing-that' (explicit) or 'Know-how' (tacit). Explicit knowledge is 'knowledge and understanding which is codified, expressed and available to anyone'; the knowledge that deals with objective, rational and technical knowledge (data, policies, procedures, software, documents, etc.). Tacit knowledge (also termed 'sticky' knowledge), on the other hand, is mainly intangible knowledge that is typically intuitive and not recorded since it is part of the human mind; the knowledge that is usually in the domain of subjective, cognitive and experiential learning. It is highly personal and hard to formalize. Thus, explicit knowledge is more easily confused with information; tacit knowledge with skills, abilities and competencies.

15. A system that facilitates knowledge management by ensuring knowledge flow from those who know to those who need to know throughout the organization is termed a knowledge management system (KMS). Once knowledge can be captured, the issue of where and how to store it arises. There are two knowledge management models (one for tacit and one for explicit knowledge) – the knowledge network and knowledge repository model (hybrid models also exist). In some cases databases may be used to simplify the task of identifying where knowledge exists (more likely when the knowledge is tacit), and in other cases the databases may be used to actually store knowledge (more likely when the knowledge is explicit). Technology is crucial to the success of the knowledge management system. Knowledge management systems are developed using three sets of technologies: communication, collaboration and storage. Communication technologies allow users to access the knowledge they need and to communicate with each other – especially with experts (e-mail, the Internet, corporate intranets and other web-based tools provide communication capabilities.). Collaboration technologies provide the means to perform group work. Groups can work together on common documents at the same time (synchronous) or at different times (asynchronous); in the same place, or in differing locations.

30.2 COMPETING WITH INFORMATION RESOURCES

16. Porter and Millar (1985) in their landmark article – how information gives you competitive advantage, discuss the impact of information and technology on the business we do and the way in which we do it. They review the impact upon internal operations (processes to create products – see the value chain) and relationships with other organizations (suppliers, customers, rivals, etc. – see the value system). Porter and Millar also examine how such resources alter industry structures, support cost or differentiation strategies and spawn entirely new businesses (competition).

17.   Internal operations are conceptualized as the value chain (linked business activities), which exists in a wider system – the value system (to include supplier and channel value chains). Value is measured by the 'amount that buyers are willing to pay for a product or service' and 'a business is profitable if the value it creates exceeds the cost of performing the value activities'. According to Porter and Millar (1985:151), 'to gain competitive advantage over its rivals, a company must either perform these activities at a lower-cost or perform them in a way that leads to differentiation and a premium price (more value)'. Information resources and technology may therefore enable the organization strategy by reducing cost or enabling it to add value and do things differently.

18.   However, whilst in the 1980s, companies tended to develop their own (differentiated) systems, they are now more likely to acquire systems off-the-shelf. Such systems are therefore available to competitors and may, therefore, be less likely to provide a sustainable competitive advantage. The challenge to companies is to source cost effective solutions. Organizations pursuing a differentiation strategy must also find systems that are difficult to imitate if a sustainable advantage is to be created.

19.   Information resources and technology may determine industry structure (see five forces, Chapter 16), competitive advantage (lower costs/enhanced differentiation) and new business. IT can increase buyer-power (making product information more readily available, enabling comparisons to be made between suppliers); raise or lower barriers-to-entry (dependent on the needs and cost technology investments); make it easier to create substitute products and increase rivalry. Throughout the 1980s and 1990s we have witnessed many examples of technology-driven product substitutions. The video gave way to the DVD and the record to the CD and then the MP3. Aside from the threat of losing market share to a new product, organizations face the threat of new organizations entering their market. Technology may lower the cost of entry to a given industry.

20.   Knowledge resources are most often associated with sustainable competitive advantage. The 'knowledge-based view' focuses upon knowledge as the most strategically important of resources; it is an outgrowth of the RBV. Under the'"knowledge-based-view of the firm', knowledge is seen as the resource upon which organizations base their competitive strategies.

21.   Organizations may need to develop their infrastructure before seeking to implement specific knowledge management initiatives. Three key infrastructures, technical, structural and cultural, enable the creation, sharing and use of knowledge. In order to leverage infrastructure, KM processes must also be present in order to store, transform and transport knowledge throughout the organization. These processes enable the organization to capture, bring together and transfer knowledge in an efficient manner. Many scholars have identified processes associated with knowledge management. Three common knowledge processes are: knowledge generation, knowledge codification and knowledge transfer/realization. Knowledge generation includes all processes involved in the acquisition and development of knowledge. Knowledge codification involves the conversion of knowledge into accessible and applicable formats. Knowledge transfer includes the movement of knowledge from its point of generation or codified form to the point of use.

30.3 TYPES OF BIS

Business information system Specific information system used to support business

22.   At this point we might ask, 'What is a business information system?' An information system is a system designed to produce information that can be used to support the activities of managers and other workers; or interrelated components working together to collect, process, store and disseminate information to support decision making, coordination and control in an organization. Similarly it is (1) a set of people, procedures and resources that collects, transforms and disseminates information in an

organization. (2) A system that accepts data resources as input and processes them into information products as output.

23. At the highest level we might distinguish two types of information system: formal and informal. Formal systems rest on accepted and fixed definitions of data and procedures, operating with predefined rules whilst informal systems are unstructured i.e. 'office gossip networks' that use unstated rules of behaviour. With informal systems there is no agreement on what constitutes information or on how it will be stored and processed. In many ways, the use of the terms 'formal' and 'informal' is consistent with the way such terms have been used previously within this book. It is common to subdivide the formal system into (1) manual (i.e. paper and pencil) and (2) computer based systems. Computer Based Information Systems (CBIS) rely on computer hardware and software technology (the technical foundation) to process and disseminate information.

24. We may describe system parts in terms of a particular resource type (hardware, software, data) or as a collection of resources bound through some sub-goal; for example we might discuss the part of a system responsible for interfacing with other systems or the part responsible for processing bookings rather than payments. Parts are related in as much as they may share data inputs or the outputs of one part become the inputs of another. Parts may also come together in order to fulfil some higher order goal (see Holism). As an example, consider a hotel management system. One part of the system will manage the reservation process and allocate rooms; another may take and process payments and yet another may allocate goods and services to guests enabling them to charge a restaurant meal to their room. However, the charging of services to a room is dependent upon the guest being registered in the system and a room having been allocated. Similarly, invoice generation is dependent upon customer details having been entered.

25. Classifying computer based information systems is not unlike classifying cars. Cars have a series of common components no matter what the make or model: wheels, engine, fuel, steering and seats. In some cases a car may be placed in more than one category and in some cases it is difficult to categorize. Information systems also have common components: inputs, processes and outputs and sometimes storage. They tend to be categorized according to their use, the user and purpose.

26. A functional business system is a system designed to support a specific activity of the organization. Business applications have traditionally served the functional areas of an organization, such as: production; inventory; purchasing; accounting; human resources; inbound and outbound logistics and marketing and sales; a selection of functional systems are described below:

Functional business system A system designed to support a specific primary activity of the organization

- Accounting Information Systems are used to record and report business transactions, the flow of funds through an organization, and produce financial statements. This provides information for the planning and control of business operations, as well as for legal and historical record-keeping.

- Sales & Marketing Systems are used to record customer information; process sales orders; manage product pricing information; provide sales forecast information and manage market research and analysis information; track competitor data; support telemarketing and may include a geographical information system.

- Inventory Systems are used for stock control and may link with the sales order processing (SOP) or supplier information systems.

- Production and Manufacturing Systems include production control, computer aided manufacturing and Workflow management systems.

- Packaging & Distribution Systems include logistical planning and customer database-labelling systems.

- HR Systems include payroll database, skills, training and development, employee record and payroll systems.

- Purchasing Systems include product pricing information, market research and analysis information and supplier information systems.

Functional systems serve the specific and local needs of parts of the organization and are developed using specific programming languages. Typically they have their own database(s), data structures, operating systems and other idiosyncrasies.

30.4 NET TECHNOLOGIES

27.   The key to understanding the Internet is the concept of connectivity. The Internet is simply a global network of interlinked computers, operating on a standard protocol which allows data to be transferred between otherwise incompatible machines. The word itself simply means a 'network of networks'. The Internet can be a powerful source of competitive advantage in global markets and companies develop Internet based strategies to support overall business development.

Digital organization An organization where nearly all significant business processes and relationships with customers, suppliers and employees are digitally enabled and key corporate assets are managed through digital means

28.   In this section we explore the opportunities presented by the Internet and web technologies before discussing what is meant by e-commerce and by e-business. The digital organization is, an 'organization where nearly all significant business processes and relationships with customers, suppliers and employees are digitally enabled, and key corporate assets are managed through digital means'. According to Laudon and Laudon (2002:17) 'the world's largest and most widely used network is the Internet', which 'is creating a new universal technology platform'. They claim that it is reshaping the way information systems are used in business life. The Internet, the primary technology for the digital firm, offers many new possibilities for doing business. Organizations that use the Internet for communication, coordination and the management of the organization are considered to be conducting business electronically and the term e-business is used to describe such technology use. The Internet and other networks have made it possible for businesses to replace manual and paper-based processes with the electronic flow of information. Net technologies manifest in the form of the Inter, Intra and Extra-nets.

Intranet Internal, in-company Internet networks for routine communications, fostering group communications, providing uniform computer applications, distributing the latest software or informing colleagues of marketing developments and new product launches

29.   An intranet is a network inside an organization that uses Internet technologies (such as web browsers and servers, TCP/IP network protocols, HTML hypermedia document publishing and databases and so on) to provide an Internet-like environment within the organization for information sharing, communications, collaboration and the support of business processes. Intranets can significantly improve communications and collaboration within an organization. Examples include: using an Intranet browser and PC to send and receive e-mail and to communicate with others within your organization, and externally through the Internet and extranets and using Intranet groupware features to improve team and project collaboration with services such as discussion groups, chat rooms and audio and videoconferencing. The comparative ease, attractiveness and lower cost of publishing and accessing multimedia business information internally via intranet web sites have been one of the primary reasons for the explosive growth in the use of intranets in business. Intranet software browsers, servers and search engines can help companies and individuals navigate and locate the business information required. Enterprise information portals are a growing trend in the

design and deployment of intranets in business. An enterprise information portal (EIP) is a web-based interface and integration of intranet and other technologies that gives all intranet users and selected extranet users' access to a variety of internal and external business applications and services. Business benefits of enterprise information portals include providing easy access to key corporate intranet website resources. A company's intranet can also be accessed through the intranets of customers, suppliers and other business partners via extranet links.

30.   Extranets are network links that use internet technologies to interconnect the intranet of a business with the Intranets of its customers, suppliers or other business partners. Extranets enable a company to offer new kinds of interactive web-enabled services to their business partners. Thus, extranets are another way that a business can build and strengthen strategic relationships with customers and suppliers; they enable and improve business collaboration with customers and other business partners and facilitate an online, interactive product development, marketing and customer-focused process that may bring better designed products to market more rapidly.

31.   In summary we have outlined the 'net technologies': the Internet, which connects everyone; extranets, which connect companies to one another; and intranets, which connect individuals within companies. The Internet and Internet-like networks inside the enterprise (intranets), between an enterprise and its trading partners (extranets), and other types of networks are now the primary information technology infrastructure of many organizations. The internetworked e-business enterprise enables managers, business professionals, teams and workgroups to electronically exchange data and information with other end users, customers, suppliers and business partners anywhere in the world.

E-business applications rely on telecommunications networks that include the Internet, intranets, extranets and other types of networks. Electronic business applications of an internetworked enterprise can conceptually be grouped into three major categories. These categories include:

> **E-business** Using Internet technologies as the platform for internal business operations, electronic commerce and enterprise collaboration

- Electronic commerce (applications supporting the buying and selling of products, services, and information over the Internet and extranets e.g. web retailing).

- Internal business systems (applications of an internetworked e-business enterprise support a company's internal business processes and operations e.g. **CRM**, ERP, etc.).

> **Customer relationship management (CRM)** Uses technology-enhanced customer interaction to shape appropriate marketing offers designed to nurture ongoing relationships with individual customers within an organization's target markets

- Enterprise communications and collaboration (applications support communication, coordination, and collaboration amongst the members of business teams and workgroups. Examples include e-mail).

30.5 COMPETING WITH NET TECHNOLOGY: E-COMMERCE AND E-BUSINESS

32.   Many see e-commerce as simply buying and selling using the Internet; for some, e-commerce is more than electronic financial transactions, extending it to all electronically mediated transactions between organizations, and any third party with which it deals. Others have defined e-commerce with a broad scope, as the exchange of information across electronic networks, at any stage in the supply chain, whether within an organization, between businesses, between businesses and consumers, or between the public and private sector, whether paid or unpaid. E-business, on the other hand, is the transformation of key business

> **E-commerce** All electronically mediated information exchanges between an organization and its external stakeholders (see sell-side and buy-side e-commerce)

processes through the use of Internet technologies; the buy-side, e-commerce transactions with suppliers and the sell-side e-commerce transactions with customers can also be considered key business processes. Thus e-business is seen as a larger concept embracing e-commerce plus the internal (process) aspects of the digital organization.

33.   Whilst the Internet presents new opportunities it also intensifies competition and shifts power to buyers. Porter (2001) considers the consequences of the Internet, presenting arguments for the changing nature of competition and the resultant challenges for strategy formulation. The Internet has created new industries; however, its greatest impact has been to enable the reconfiguration of existing industries previously constrained by high costs for communicating, gathering information or accomplishing transactions. Internet technology provides buyers with easier access to information about products and suppliers, thus strengthening buyer bargaining power. The Internet mitigates the need for such things as an established sales force or access to existing channels, reducing barriers to entry (see disintermediation). Marketplaces automate corporate procurement by linking many buyers and suppliers electronically. The benefits to buyers include low transaction costs, easier access to price and product information, convenient purchase of associated services and, sometimes, the ability to pool volume. The benefits to suppliers include lower selling costs, lower transaction costs, access to wider markets and the avoidance of powerful channels.

34.   By enabling new approaches to meeting needs and performing functions, it creates new substitutes. As an open system, companies have more difficulty maintaining proprietary offerings, thus the rivalry amongst competitors is intensified. On the Internet, buyers can often switch suppliers with just a few mouse clicks, and new web technologies are systematically reducing switching costs even further. The use of the Internet also expands the geographic market, bringing many more companies into competition with one another. A number of businesses are able to increase revenue through network effects which can create demand-side economies of scale and raise barriers to entry. However, the openness of the Internet makes it difficult for a single company to capture the benefits of a network effect. On-line companies have found it more difficult to build Internet brands, perhaps because of the lack of physical presence and direct human contact. Despite advertising, product discounts and purchasing incentives, most dot-com brands have not approached the power of established brands, achieving only a modest impact on loyalty and barriers to entry. Whilst partnering is a well-established strategy, the use of Internet technology has made it much more widespread. In e-commerce, complements (products that are used in tandem with another industry's product) have proliferated as companies seek to offer broader arrays of products, services and information.

35.   Internet technologies tend to reduce variable costs and tilt cost structures towards fixed cost, creating much greater pressure for companies to engage in destructive price competition. In general, new Internet technologies erode profitability by shifting power to customers. The great paradox of the Internet is that its very benefits – making information widely available; reducing the difficulty of purchasing, marketing and distribution; allowing buyers and sellers to find and transact business with one another more easily – also make it more difficult for companies to capture those benefits as profits. Much of the value, however, is absorbed by customers and may not result in expected wealth creation for the business. The Internet is an enabling technology – a powerful set of tools which rarely offers a direct competitive advantage. Internet technology, itself is not as a source of advantage because it is readily available to all. Competitive advantages arise from traditional strengths fortified through Internet technology, by tying a company's activities together in a more distinctive system (Porter 2001).

CONCLUSION

36.   Information resources include data, information and knowledge. Data refers to raw facts and information is the summarization of data. Technology and information/knowledge

represent 'hard' and 'soft' resources available to the organization. Unlike most resources which deplete when used, information and knowledge can be shared, and actually grow through application. It is now widely accepted that winning strategies are more often grounded in the accumulation and creative exploitation of intangibles that are more difficult to replicate. Computer-based Information Systems are used to support all roles at all levels of the organization. They improve information access and (in the case of integrated systems) the flow of information within the whole organization. Traditionally, the business functions acquired and developed computer-based Information Systems to help them meet their localized goals. A functional business information system is used to support a specific organizational activity. Businesses compete in two worlds: a physical and a virtual world. The latter has given rise to the world of electronic commerce (EC) and e-business (EB), a new focus of value creation. Much of the value created by e-business is due to the more effective use of information. Managers must now focus upon how their companies create value in both worlds alike. The effectiveness and efficiency of organizational information systems can be enhanced significantly by a move to Internet technologies. Internet technologies enable EC and EB. The web provides the connective tissue for information flow within and between organizations anytime – anyplace. Interoperability of web services permits the creation of enterprise-wide information-system architectures linking all the corporate core business systems to the firm's web site. Information systems extend far beyond the boundaries of the organization to encompass vendors, customers and even competitors. The Internet has both created new industries and enabled the reconfiguration of existing industries. Whilst the Internet presents new opportunities it also intensifies competition. The Internet is an enabling technology – a powerful set of tools which rarely offers a direct competitive advantage. Internet technology, itself is not as a source of advantage because it is readily available to all. Competitive advantages arise from traditional strengths fortified through Internet technology – by tying a company's activities together in a more distinctive system.

QUESTIONS

1   What is a business information system? What is information technology? What is hardware? In your answer you should list examples of hardware components.

2   Summarize the main purposes of information systems in organizations and list the main uses of Business Information Systems

3   Evaluate the business benefits associated with barcode technology, other forms of scanners and related input technologies.

4   The words data and information are used frequently in business. Define and distinguish the two concepts and explain what constitutes a database.

5   Explain how organizations compete with information resources, systems and technology. Which of the information resources (data, information and knowledge) do you believe is most important to strategy and competitive advantage? Explain your answer.

6   Explain what is meant by e-commerce, e-business and the digital organization.

USEFUL WEBSITES

British Computer Society – Project Management:
www.bcs.org/BCS/Products/Publications/Books/ BySeries/textbooks/ProjectManagement/

Project Management for IT-Related Projects – Textbook for the ISEB Foundation Certificate in IS Project Information Commissioner: **www.dataprotection.gov.uk**
Forrester research: **www.forrester.com**
The Gartner group: **www.gartner.com**

VIDEO CASES

Now take a look at the online video cases – visit the companion website to work through real world business problems associated with the concepts presented within this chapter.

27 Tesco: use of IT and information systems – Introduction to MIS
The case investigates Tesco's use of IT/IS.

29 Databases and the edge for FreshDirect
This case focuses on the use (importance) of corporate databases (and their data/information), particularly in support of primary activities, the organizational goals and generating revenue/advantage.

48 Doing Business Online
Considers how small businesses can adjust their strategies to earn more money on the web – focus is on extension selling

and creating a secure environment to allay fear and build trust.

70 Business hardware scanners in the supply chain
This case considers the use of input devices into business information systems – in particular the bar code scanner is reviewed. A collection of videos are used to determine what a barcode is and how such technologies are used by organizations to make operators more productive.

77 Introduction to MIS Improving information management
Considers what businesses believe are their information management challenges; acts as an introduction to business information systems course.

REFERENCES

Aksoy, P. and DeNardis, L. (2007) 'Information Technology in Theory', Cengage Learning.

Cetindamar, D., Phaal, R. and Probert, D. (2010) 'Technology Management – Activities and Tools', Palgrave

Chaffey, D. and Wood, S. (2005) 'Business Information Management', FT Prentice Hall.

Chaffey, D. (2007) 'E-Business and E-Commerce Management', Ed. 3. FT Prentice Hall.

Hawryszkiewycz, I. (2009) 'Knowledge Management Organizing Knowledge Based Enterprises', Ed. 1. Palgrave Macmillan.

Kelly, P. P. (2009) 'International Business and Management', Cengage Learning EMEA.

Laudon, K. C. and Laudon, J. P. (2002) 'Management Information Systems: Managing The Digital Firm', Ed. 7.

Oz, E. and Jones, A. (2008) 'Management Information Systems', Ed. 1. Cengage Learning EMEA.

Porter, M. E. and Millar, V. E. (1985) 'How information gives you a competitive advantage.', Harvard Business Review, July-August 63, p. 149–174.

Porter, M. E. (2001) 'Strategy and the Internet', Harvard Business Review, March 2001, p. 62–78.

Reynolds, G. (2010) 'Information Technology for Managers', Ed. 1. Course Technology Cengage Learning.

PART III

FUNCTIONAL MANAGEMENT – MARKETING, PRODUCTION, PERSONNEL AND FINANCIAL

There are four sections to the final part of this book: marketing, production, personnel and financial management.

MARKETING MANAGEMENT

Marketing is the one function of management which has to be more concerned with what is going on outside the organization than with what is happening internally. Marketing activities are conducted mainly across the external boundaries of the organizational system, and they are undertaken by managers of all kinds, not only by marketing specialists. The idea of the 'marketing concept' is taken up in Chapter 31, and is compared with other approaches to marketing. The other chapters in the section deal with those aspects of marketing which are the most frequent topics of examination for non-marketing specialists. These are: the marketing mix, market research, the organization of a marketing department and consumer protection. The marketing mix is considered in the section case study about WOW toys. The case

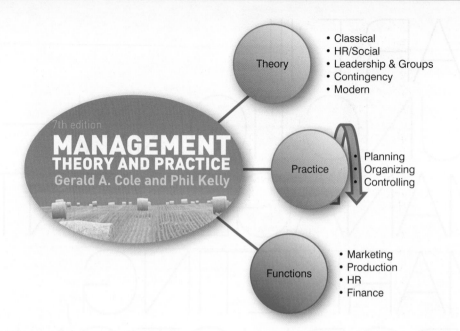

study discusses toys as products and can be used to highlight the close integration between marketing and operations (production) next.

PRODUCTION MANAGEMENT

The production function of an organization exists in order to make available the goods or services required by the customer. Production management, in particular, is concerned with the provision of goods. It is the central part of the manufacturing process. Its responsibility is to plan, resource and control the processes involved in converting raw materials and components into the finished goods required to satisfy the needs and wants of the organization's existing and potential customers. In order to help relate theory to practice we start the section with a case study on the manufacture of Easter Eggs.

In a market-oriented organization, production begins with the customer in the market-place (this is also highlighted in the WOW Toys case). An idea for a new product is generated, or assessed in marketing terms, by the market research section. If the idea seems viable, it will be brought to the attention of the Research and Development (R&D) section, where any necessary research, design and development work can be carried out. The next stage forward is for early prototypes to be produced. If the prototypes are satisfactory, then the pre-production stage can commence. This stage aims to simulate, as far as possible, the actual conditions on the production line. Thus, at this stage, the customer's needs are being set against the cost of materials and labour, the manufacturing capacity of the production department and issues such as quality levels. In the case of a firm manufacturing industrial goods, it is likely that at this stage, if not earlier, samples of the new product will be sent to the customer for testing and approval. If the pre-production runs have been successful, then the product can move forward again, this time to the manufacturing stage. There are several key elements in the production process, and this section looks at those elements most relevant for business and management students. Chapter 38 sets out the main features of a production planning and control system, Chapter 39 briefly outlines the principal methods of production available to organizations, Chapter 40 examines some of the leading aids to production, such as Work Study, whilst Chapter 41 summarises key aspects of new technology in manufacturing.

PERSONNEL MANAGEMENT

This section on HR starts with a case study about Google in the UK. The case emphasizes people as the critical resource for organizations. It also identifies the contemporary role of the HR function within organizations. There are nine chapters in this section on Human Resource Management. The emphasis throughout is on the activities of specialists in HR. Chapter 42 introduces the Personnel Management (HR) function. Chapter 43 deals with recruitment and selection. Chapter 44 focuses on employee development. Chapters 45 and 46 examine key aspects of performance appraisal, grievances, disciplinary matters and management development. Chapter 47 outlines the topic of workplace stress and summarizes some of the ways in which this can be avoided or at least minimized. Chapter 48 briefly outlines key aspects of job evaluation, whilst Chapters 49 and 50 deal with the legal consequences of employment, firstly at the collective level and secondly at an individual level.

FINANCIAL ASPECTS OF MANAGEMENT

The final section of this book focuses mainly on the needs of small and medium-sized enterprises for adequate financial controls. The basics of financial reporting and control, required as part of general management, are described. Chapter 51 considers the company accounts and financial statements and Chapter 52 explores financial planning and control. Both chapters refer to a case study about Streetcar Limited, a UK based car club.

Section Eleven
Marketing Management

CASE STUDY

MARKETING MANAGEMENT

WOW TOYS

Award winning WOW Toys was formed in 1997 by toy maker Nadim Ednan-Laperouse, a graduate of Industrial Design, and is based in Fulham, London. The company designs and supplies multi-functional toys that do not need batteries for children aged 0–5 years. WOW would never dream of using PVC plastic but instead chose to make use high of grade materials that are very strong so their toys are durable and don't break. Particularly conscious of safety, there are no small parts in their toys and they don't use any toxic materials. All of their toys are regularly tested by a certified independent testing house to high global safety standards. WOW toys stimulate learning through long lasting creative play with exciting features to discover which help develop and feed young imaginations. From basic motor skills to more advanced social interactive role-play, the toys provide children with a fun way to make sense of the world around them and assist with early development.

WOW Toys' is devoted to product development. All WOW toys are designed in their London workshop. The design process can take up to one year and starts with the generation of ideas through customer research ('with WOW fans like Mums or Grandparents'). Following this, the WOW design team sketch lots of ideas and then ask shop keepers and customers what they think. Feedback is then used to develop the design concept. A product designer then builds a working model which is then used to create a prototype. This prototype model is used to make moulds at the factory. While this is happening a one-off colour model is produced at a cost of about £10 000. Children then play with it to check its right! Company designers spend a lot of time watching children play with their toys (and they admit to playing with the toys themselves!) to understand how play patterns and development change over the years. Plastic test samples are then made and at this point the toys go through rigorous independent safety testing. Finally the toy is ready to be manufactured and boxed.

When creating their toys, designers will not only make use of customer research and product testing but will draw upon knowledge they have accumulated. For example, bright colours, sounds and chunky shapes provide visual, auditory and tactile stimulation; removable mix and match figures and animals are perfect for little hands to grip and for developing hand/eye co-ordination. Knobs to turn or buttons to push help develop fine motor skills; and introducing themes from real life and fantasy, WOW toys help stimulate imaginative play.

Nadim launched WOW toys at the 1997 London Toy Fair also used by international toy giants. The companies' strong and clever designs soon caught the attention of a number of influential UK retailers. Since then WOW has expanded and grown and is now available in over 900 UK retailers and 40 countries around the world.

Toy News, a monthly trade magazine for the toy business, writer Ronnie Dungan (2010) recently argued that building a brand that is known for design innovation in a licence-led, pre-school market takes time. But Wow Toys is finally beginning to see its long-game pay off. Dungan comments on two ways to succeed in the preschool market: (1) licensing (pay a royalty to an inventor) and (2) appealing to aspirational parents with a home grown quality product. Evaluating each option, Dungan recognizes the latter approach to be dependent upon research and development and is therefore both resource and time hungry. Despite this, building a brand that is trusted by parents and recognized and enjoyed by children (the strategy of wow toys) has many benefits (particularly in terms of sales).

Suppliers must develop solutions to increase distribution through a range of channels and like many other manufacturers of goods relying on repeat purchases, must develop strategies to encourage first-time buyers. Suppliers may operate a direct to consumer business model (typically making use of the Internet and e-commerce) or may offer their products through intermediaries with access to retail outlets. In many cases a multi channel strategy is pursued. With the indirect model you are heavily reliant upon the intermediary (retailer) to market your product. Nadim has therefore taken steps to support intermediaries,

'We put a big shop-fit display into 20 stores . . . A mix of Indies, garden centres and other stores and we tracked them on EPOS and there was a phenomenal increase of between 200–300 per cent. It's amazing what can be achieved when you go that extra mile. . . It's all about in-store presentation – at WOW Toys, we're very confident that the track we are following is what the public wants. The difficulty though, is in getting the retailer to see that. That is the big job in marketing'. The firm is experimenting with a TV campaign in the UK for the first time this year and is also looking at some distribution into the nursery sector, too. In addition, four new staff have been added so far this year, and the range will be a third bigger in 2011. All in all, WOW Toys is on the upward curve, (Dungan, 2010).

Dungan (2010) states that innovation-in-design is the cornerstone of WOW's success. Nadim states that, 'When we are able to do our own form of innovation, we know a toy will sell for ten years and we usu-ally get payback in year one. So we get nine years of stability, which is why we're able to plan ahead'. But market conditions don't make it easy for innovators in the toy market. Retailers are still very rigid when it comes to pricing, he claims. Nadim gets frustrated with the 'short-sighted' toy business whereby retailers 'still want products to be £9.99'. This is the same price as it was ten years ago, he notes. This presents challenges for Nadim and his company as production costs have doubled in price during the same period. He believes that short-sightedness stifles innovation and argues that real innovation only takes place in the toy market when the price allows it to.

Sources:
1 http://www.wowtoys.com
2 Dungan, R. (2010), 'SUPPLIER FOCUS: Wow Toys', Toy News, Friday, 16th July 2010, available from www.toynews-online.biz/features/254/SUPPLIER-FOCUS-Wow-Toys

CHAPTER 31
THE MARKETING CONCEPT, COMPETITIVENESS AND THE GLOBAL DIMENSION

Key Concepts

- Competitive dynamics
- Diamond of competitive advantage
- Global strategy
- Internationalization
- Marketing
- Marketing concept
- Marketing orientation

Learning Outcomes   Having read this chapter, you should be able to:

- outline the marketing concept
- evaluate alternative generic competitive strategies
- discuss the impact of globalization on marketing
- explain the internationalization process

Marketing The processes associated with the transfer of goods from and the relationships between producer and consumer – it is also concerned with anticipating the customers' future needs and wants – marketing involves researching, promoting, selling and distributing products or services

Marketing concept The philosophy that an organization should try to provide products that satisfy customers' needs through a coordinated set of activities that also allows the organization to achieve its goals

1.   **Marketing** is the one function of management which has to be more concerned with what is going on outside the organization than with what is happening internally. Marketing activities are conducted mainly across the external boundaries of the organizational system, and they are undertaken by managers of all functions, not only by marketing specialists. The idea of the 'Marketing concept' is introduced in this chapter. Managers frequently pose questions such as how might we communicate with customers; what is the role and value of the brand; how do I identify markets and then enter them; what products should we offer and what should be the content of the business and product portfolio and, how do we price offerings. We address such issues in this part of the book. The other chapters in the section deal with those aspects of marketing which are the most frequent topics of examination for non-marketing specialists. These are: the marketing mix, market research, the organization of a marketing department and consumer protection.

2.   Every business or public organization has its market, that is to say the group of existing and potential buyers (prospects) or users of its goods and services. A market may consist of a mere handful of people, or it may consist of millions. Clearly, relationships with the market are an important ingredient of corporate planning and policy-making. Organizations have developed several different ways of regarding their existing and potential customers. The most notable options are as follows:

-   Production orientation – in this situation, the organization concentrates its attention on production efficiency, distribution and cost in order to attract customers to its products. This works well when demand is well ahead of supply, and where lower costs will encourage people to buy. Engineering firms tend to favour this orientation.

-   Product orientation – in this case the organization stands or falls by the quality of its products. The thinking behind this orientation is that customers buy products or services rather than solutions to problems. Examples of product orientation are to be found in education, the arts and journalism, where the inference is often that the supplier knows best what the customer needs.

-   Sales orientation – here the dominant concept is that people will not buy until they are persuaded to buy by positive selling. Thus the focus of attention is more on the skills of selling, than on the needs of the buyer. Several life-insurance companies have adopted this approach over the years.

-   Market orientation – a market-oriented organization is one which focuses on the needs of its customers. Its primary concern is to identify customer needs and wants so that these may be met with the highest level of customer satisfaction. In this situation production responds to the demands of marketing rather than the other way round. This approach to marketing is called the 'marketing concept' and its perspective is radically different from the approaches of production, product and sales-oriented organizations. Examples of market-oriented attitudes can be found in supermarket chains, a number of travel agency operations and in motor-car manufacturing (e.g. 'everything we do is driven by you').

3.   Few business organizations have total control over their markets. On the contrary, most businesses find they are in fierce competition with others wanting to serve the same group of buyers. In recent times competition has become more widespread, as foreign competitors join domestic competitors in offering similar goods or services to the same market. Lower trade barriers, better worldwide transport systems and access to the Internet mean that new competitors can enter markets previously the preserve of just one or two key players. Suddenly, the world seems a smaller place, and major firms decide on their marketing strategies in a

global context, both in terms of markets and suppliers. Thus 'globalization' and 'competitiveness', especially in terms of competitive advantage, become increasingly important concepts to modern companies.

> **Global** A form of international organizational design where foreign subsidiaries are modelled on the parent companies' domestic approach (replication) – standardization and centralization are emphasized in order to achieve integration

31.1 MARKETING AND THE MARKETING CONCEPT

4. Baines Fill and Page (2008) recognize the concept of marketing has changed over the years. Marketing is the management process responsible for identifying, anticipating and satisfying customer requirements profitably. The marketing concept is the philosophy that an organization should try to provide products that satisfy cus-

> **Globalization** Growth and integration to a global or worldwide scale

tomers' needs through a coordinated set of activities that also allow the organization to achieve its goals. It takes the view that the most important stakeholders in the organization are the customers. This does not necessarily mean that the customer is always right, but it does mean that the customer forms the starting point for the organization's corporate strategy. Organizations adopting the marketing concept also tend to see marketing as a very diffuse activity, shared by many and not just the preserve of a specialist group called marketing and sales. This is a very important consideration, for, as we shall see shortly in the discussion of the marketing mix, there are certain key issues, such as pricing, which have to be considered and agreed on a shared basis.

5. Reference was made earlier to customer needs and wants. How do customer needs and wants differ? One way of distinguishing between them is to define needs as basic physical and psychological drives arising from being human (e.g. need for food, clothing, self-esteem, etc.), and to define wants as specific desires directed towards fulfilling the basic needs. A need for food, for example, could be transformed into a specific desire (want) for curried chicken, or for bread and cheese or countless other variations of food. The point is that human beings have relatively few needs, but can generate an enormous number of wants. Not surprisingly, therefore, most marketing efforts concentrate predominantly on satisfying people's wants. In addition to this, some marketing is directed specifically at creating or changing people's wants.

6. The marketing role in an organization is carried out by numerous individuals. In the first place all those senior managers, and their advisers, contributing to the organization's corporate plan, are fulfilling, among other things, a marketing role by examining the marketplace and assessing the organization's ability to meet current and future demands on its resources. Many middle managers also carry out a marketing role when dealing with issues relating to their public. Finally, there is the marketing department. Their staff are specifically charged with marketing duties – assessing customer wants, gathering market intelligence, obtaining customer reactions and organizing sales and distribution. The other chapters in this section concentrate mainly on the activities of these marketing specialists, but before considering detailed aspects of marketing, it will be helpful to look briefly at the twin issues of competitiveness and globalization, since they are of such significance within modern marketing practice.

31.2 COMPETITIVENESS

7. When customers have a choice, the organization must compete for their business. With this in mind we might ask how companies compete. As was noted in Chapter 16 (see five forces), Porter's analysis of the competitive situation facing firms showed that current competitors were not the only competitive forces at work in the external environment. Suppliers and buyers also made an impact on the competitive situation, as did the actions of potential newcomers and the possibility of substitute products. Competitiveness, according to Porter and others, is primarily about delivering enhanced value to customers.

8.   Competitive advantages exist in relation to rivals operating within an industry as factors that enable an organization to earn a higher rate of profit. Such advantages emerge from the actions of organizations (internal sources) or from changes in the external environment (external sources). With regard to external sources, an organization may be more capable or better equipped to exploit changes in customer demand, technology, political or economic factors. An external change may create opportunity for profit. Consequently, organizations must be able to identify and respond to opportunity. As markets become increasingly turbulent, so responsiveness to external change has become increasingly important as a source of competitive advantage.

Generic routes to competitive advantage
Cost leadership, differentiation and focus; not mutually exclusive

9.   There are two fundamental, internal sources of competitive advantage(See generic routes to competitive advantage): cost and differentiation. An organization may compete by offering customers what they want at the lowest price/cost or may differentiate their products and services in such a way that the customer is prepared to pay a premium price for them. Cost leadership requires the organization to find and exploit sources of cost advantage, typically selling a standard, no-frills product or service whilst differentiation necessitates the organization providing something unique and valuable to buyers. They represent two fundamentally different approaches to business strategy and two of the three generic strategies referred to by Porter. A third source of competitive advantage is based on focus. Cost leadership and differentiation are industry-wide sources of competitive advantage whilst focus strategies seek out competitive advantages for particular market segments.

10.   Cost leadership may be achieved in many ways such as through efficient manufacturing processes (see Chapters 38–41) whilst differentiation is dependent upon creativity and marketing abilities (see later chapters in this section). Exploiting new technologies and business processes may improve production techniques and thus increase efficiency. Cost advantages may also be obtained through a reduction in input costs. This may come from access to raw materials and location advantages (global sourcing). One form of location advantage may be a reduction in labour costs. Differentiation is about understanding customers and how the organization can meet customer needs. The organization differentiates itself from competitors when it provides something unique and valuable to those customers; for example the product may perform better or be of higher quality. In return, customers are prepared to pay the organization a premium price.

11.   Differentiation may manifest itself in product or service features and in any of the possible interactions between the organization and the customer in selling, delivering and providing associated customer services in relation to the product or service offered. Differentiation is based much more on an understanding of customers and their needs. Establishing differentiation advantage requires creativity. As with cost advantages, the value chain provides a useful framework for analyzing opportunities to gain differentiation advantage. The value chain enables the organization to analyze how value is created for customers and focus on those activities which can be used to achieve differentiation. The essence of differentiation advantage is to increase the perceived value of offerings to customers. Differentiation is only effective if it is communicated to customers.

12.   Differentiation advantages tend to be more sustainable than cost-based advantages. This is because cost-based advantages are much more vulnerable to change as a result of external forces. Advantages based on low labour costs, technology or business processes can disappear quickly.

13.   Whilst we have presented two core generic strategies, they are not presented as an either/or choice and organizations tend not to consider differentiation strategy in isolation to cost based strategies. All organizations must consider efficiency goals. Interestingly, however, differentiation adds costs. Differentiation costs include higher quality raw materials and other inputs, specialized production machinery and skilled employees. Organizations which differentiate are likely to spend more on packaging, marketing and sales channels. In pursuit of differentiation strategies, organizations will still seek out cost efficiencies as a prerequisite of profitability.

14.   Companies that are more responsive may also have an advantage over their sluggish rivals. Responsiveness is enabled through resources (information) and capabilities (flexibility). Speed of response as a source of competitive advantage is termed time-based competition. Technological improvements in communications, and business process improvements, coupled with

manufacturing technologies, have enabled organizations to be both flexible and responsive, reducing cycle times drastically.

15.   Once established, competitive advantage is subject to erosion by competition. The durability of the advantage is related to the ability of competitors to either imitate or substitute factors leading to advantage. Imitation necessitates competitor identification and diagnosis of the source of competitive advantage and must be both able and motivated to acquire or develop the resources and capabilities necessary for imitating the advantage. Organizations seek out sustainable competitive advantages where barriers exist to imitation. For example they may secure exclusive access to key raw materials, develop proprietary standards, act in secrecy or take steps to persuade rivals that imitation will be unprofitable. In some cases there may be a first mover advantage whereby the initial occupant may gain access to resources and capabilities that a follower cannot match, for example through a patent or copyright.

31.3 GLOBALIZATION AND INTERNATIONAL MARKETING

16.   As mentioned earlier, the tendency for firms to operate in a global market, both for sales and supplies, has accelerated over the past decade (globalization was discussed in Chapter 15). It is no longer unusual for major manufacturing firms to be investing in substantial operations overseas, whilst maintaining similar facilities in their domestic market. Adopting a global approach to marketing strategy provides two distinct ways in which firms can gain a competitive advantage, or at least offset a domestic disadvantage. These are (1) a global firm can spread activities among nations to serve the world, and this not only enables business expansion but also helps to offset poor returns in domestic or other select markets; and (2) a global firm can coordinate dispersed activities, for example where marketing, distribution and after-sales are located in the buyers' nation, but manufacturing and supply can be located anywhere. Global presence makes available to the firm's managers five value-creation opportunities: (1) to adapt to local market differences, (2) to exploit economies of global scale, (3) to exploit economies of global scope, (4) to unleash optimal locations for activities and resources, and (5) to maximize knowledge transfer across locations.

> **Value creation** Performing activities that increase the value of goods or services to consumers

17.   Porter believes that competitive industries, when compared internationally, are those that improve and innovate by investing in such activities as R&D, learning, modern facilities and training. He acknowledges that this innovatory behaviour is conditioned by other key factors in determining national advantage, which are set out in a 'diamond' system (see Diamond of competitive advantage) as shown in Figure 31.1.

Apart from firms' own strategic choices, including the structure of their organization, the local competitive situation has to be taken into account. These aspects are themselves affected by conditions in the national economy – supply of labour, skills, adequate transport and communications infrastructure – together with the availability of sufficient capital in firms to sustain innovation. The demand situation is critical, since this is the national marketplace. However, Porter considers that conditions in the home market need to be sufficiently promising to enable a firm to be able to study what customers really want before launching out into other nations, even

> **Diamond of competitive advantage** Configuration of four sets of attributes (factor conditions, demand conditions, supporting industries and inter firm rivalry) which, in Porter's theory, determine a nation's competitive advantage.

> **Internationalization** The gradual process of taking organizational activities into other countries

though their needs may not be exactly the same. Finally, the existence of key suppliers and related industries is an important factor in the ability of a national industry to compete globally.

18.   Companies must simultaneously capture global-scale efficiency, respond to national markets and cultivate a worldwide learning capability for driving continuous innovation across borders. Internationalization is the gradual process of taking organizational activities into other

FIGURE 31.1 Determinants of national advantage.

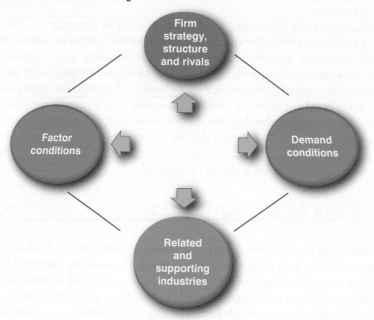

Source: Adapted from 'The Competitive Advantage of Nations' by Michael Porter. *Harvard Business Review*, Mar/Apr 1980, pp. 73–93, copyright © Harvard Business Publishing, 1980. Reproduced with permission.

Multidomestic Organization An organization that trades internationally as if the world were a collection of many different (country) entities

Global strategy Assumes a single market and offers a standard product(s) to meet customer needs wherever they are located

countries. Such companies may then be described as global, **multidomestic** or transnational in their orientation. The global organization trades internationally as if the world were a single and boundaryless entity whilst the multidomestic organization trades internationally as if the world were a collection of many different (country) entities. Transnational enterprises (TNE) operate a balanced combination of the multidomestic and **global strategies**. There are several alternatives open to companies wishing to globalize their operations, as follows:

–   By exporting their goods and services to foreign countries, which is the easiest option.

–   By entering into joint ventures with companies in the target nation through licensing agreements or joint ownership, for example.

–   By direct investment in new plant and manufacturing facilities in the foreign country. Worldwide operations will imply that the organization's marketing mix (see following chapters) will have to be adapted to meet conditions in the foreign countries in which the firm is operating. It will also be necessary to have an appropriate marketing organization to support its overseas activities, ranging from an export sales department (at the very least) through an international division to the establishment of a full international subsidiary company.

International marketing involves the organization making one or more marketing mix decisions across national boundaries.

CONCLUSION

19.   This chapter sets the scene for the marketing section of the book. We defined marketing and the marketing concept and then contrasted marketing from a domestic and global standpoint. We went on to recognize that when customers have a choice, the organization must compete for their business. With this in mind we outlined how companies compete.

QUESTIONS

1   Organizations have developed several different ways of regarding their existing and potential customers. Evaluate the most notable options.

2   Explain what is meant by a) product orientation, b) sales orientation, c) production orientation and d)

a market orientation. Which one of these best describes the orientation at WOW toys?

3   With reference to general competitive strategies explain how WOW toys compete.

USEFUL WEBSITES

European Marketing Academy: **www.emac-online.org**
   European Marketing Academy – a website that provides a society for persons professionally concerned with or interested in marketing theory and research

Michael Porter: **www.isc.hbs.edu/** Based at Harvard Business School, the Institute studies competition and its implications for company strategy; the competitiveness of nations, regions and cities; and solutions to social problems.

American Marketing Association Site:
   www.marketingpower.com/Pages/default.aspx
   Provides a 5-step overview to marketing planning

Academy of Marketing: **www.academyofmarketing.org/**
   Academy of Marketing (UK) – a Learned Society catering for the needs of marketing researchers, educators and professionals

Chartered Institute of Marketing: **www.cim.co.uk** A leading international body for marketing and business development.

Knowledge Wharton: **http://knowledge.wharton.upenn.edu/**
   Leading business school publishes a bi-weekly online magazine that often includes articles on marketing

A. T. Kearney Globalization Index: **www.atkearney.com/index.php/Publications/globalization-index.html**

VIDEO CASES

Now take a look at the online video cases – visit the companion website to work through real world business problems associated with the concepts presented within this chapter.

3 India's Design Boom: The Rise and Rise of Indian Design (fragmentation of the value chain)

Economic globalization has significantly increased the competitive pressure on enterprises in many sectors. This comes as a result of, amongst other factors, the emergence of new, lower-cost producers, fast-changing demand patterns, increased market fragmentation and shortened product life cycles. In such an environment, innovation (either in terms of business processes or of final products and services) becomes crucial for the long-term competitiveness and survival of enterprises.

Multinational organizations have had the opportunity to benefit from the comparative advantage of different countries, (be

they technology driven or factor abundance driven), to reduce the total costs of production, particularly through the ever more popular method of fragmentation (slicing up the value chain) in which different parts (activities) of the production process are located in different countries. In this case, an Indian design company provides the context to consider country level competitive advantage, multinational outsourcing strategy and global environmental change.

12 Being Global: Globalization and Globality

This case is primarily concerned with the changing global environment and competition from developing economies. Concepts of globalization and globality are contrasted. The sources of success for the new global challengers from rapidly developing economies is analyzed and the necessary response from incumbents determined.

REFERENCES

Baines, P., Fill, C. and Page, K. (2008) 'Marketing', Oxford University Press.

Barney, J. and Hesterly, W. (2009) 'Strategic Management and Competitive Advantage: International Edition', Ed. 3. Prentice Hall.

Conklin, D W. (2010) 'The Global Environment of Business – New Paradigms for International Management', SAGE Publications.

Dibb, S., Simkin, L., Pride, W. M. and Ferrell, O.C. (2006) 'Marketing: Concepts and Strategies', Ed. 5. Houghton Mifflin International Inc.

Harrison, A. (2009) 'Business Environment in a Global Context', Oxford University Press.

Kelly, P. P. (2009) 'International Business and Management', Cengage Learning EMEA.

Morrison, J. (2009) 'International Business: Challenges in a Changing World', Palgrave Macmillan Ltd.

CHAPTER 32
THE MARKETING MIX: PRODUCT AND PRICE

Key Concepts

- Marketing mix
- Marketing plan
- Price variable
- Product development
- Product life cycle

Learning Outcomes   Having read this chapter, you should be able to:

- specify the key elements of the marketing mix
- discuss what is meant by branding and explain how packaging and labelling can contribute to a brand's success
- understand how the management of products and services changes over the different stages of the lifecycle and explain the process by which new products are developed and adopted by markets
- understand how to price product and services

Marketing mix The tactical 'toolkit' of the marketing programme; product, place/distribution, promotion, price and people variables that an organization can control in order to appeal to the target market and facilitate satisfying exchange

1. Once a company determines its target market and establishes a position within that market, it is ready to begin its marketing. The tools used for this are the controllable variables of the marketing mix (Barringer and Ireland, 2010); the variables are used by the organization to satisfy customers in the target markets. The mix is effectively the tactical 'toolkit' of the marketing programme; product, place/distribution, promotion, price (and people) variables, as illustrated in Figure 32.1. Baines, Fill and Page (2008) deem it to be the list of items a marketing manager should consider when devising plans for marketing products, including product decisions, place (distribution) decisions, pricing decisions and promotion decisions. Later the mix was extended to include process, and people decisions to account for the lack of physical nature in service products. When marketing their products, firms need to create a successful mix of: the right product, sold at the right price, in the right place and using the most suitable promotion. Optimizing the marketing mix is the primary responsibility of marketing. By offering the product with the right combination of the four Ps, marketers can improve their results and marketing effectiveness. The marketing mix is probably the most famous marketing term and its elements are the basic components of a marketing plan. The offer made to the customer can be altered by varying the mix elements. Each aspect of the marketing mix is described in this section of the book, starting in this chapter with the product and price.

Marketing plan The written arrangements for specifying, implementing and controlling an organization's marketing activities and marketing mixes

FIGURE 32.1 The marketing mix

32.1 PRODUCT

2. Any discussion about the marketing mix must begin with the product. The 'product', in this context, means anything that is offered to a market for its use or consumption. The product can be a physical object or a service of some kind. New product or service development is an essential part of business. The marketer must assess what constitutes its product from the customer's

perspective. Product decisions include determining the brand name, functionality, level of quality, warranty, accessories and ancillary services. Product design can be thought of as the characteristics or features (including quality) of a product or service that determine its ability to meet the needs of the user. In contrast the product development process is the overall process of strategy, organization, concept generation, product and marketing plan creation and evaluation and commercialization of a new product. In order to reach a final design of a product or service, the design activity must pass through several stages. Stages are not, however, necessarily followed in a linear fashion.

Brand A name, term, design, symbol or any other feature that identifies one seller's good or service as distinct from those of other sellers

Product development A strategy of increasing sales by improving present products or developing new products for current markets

3.   Whilst there are many ways to describe the product development process, the first phase of a product development effort is typically termed the concept development phase. Here a company identifies ideas for new or revised products and services. Ideas for new products or services can come from many different sources inside and outside the organization. New ideas may come from customers, competitors, front office staff or the research and development department. The second (screening and planning) phase of a product development effort begins to address the feasibility of a product or service. Organizations will assess the ability of an operation to produce a product or service (feasibility), the acceptability of the product or service (will customers want it?) and the associated risks. Having created a feasible, acceptable and viable product or service concept, the next stage is to create a preliminary design. The company invests heavily in the development effort and builds and evaluates prototypes (design and development phase). Preliminary designs are evaluated and improved upon. In the fourth phase of a product development effort (commercial preparation phase) the organization invests heavily in the operations and supply chain resources (infrastructure) needed to support the new product or service. The final phase of a product development effort is termed the launch phase. For physical products, this usually means 'filling up' the supply chain with products. For services, it can mean making the service broadly available to the target market-place. Once a product has been designed, operational managers must make important decisions concerning processes for producing those goods or services. The choice of production process is discussed in Chapters 38–39.

4.   Once designed and developed, branding is used to help customers differentiate between the various offerings in a market. Buyers use information from a variety of sources in order to evaluate the product they may wish to purchase. The design, performance and quality of the product itself provide intrinsic cues (signals) whereas brand names present extrinsic cues. Companies may choose from several branding strategies: (1) all branding may occur at the organizational level-corporate brand (see for example Disney or Virgin). A corporate brand increases the attractiveness of the entire company, building trust, loyalty and even commitment amongst stakeholders. Through a corporate brand, a consistent appearance is maintained. This approach is common amongst related product lines but may be problematic as product variety and market diversity increases; (2) when products or customer expectations vary, an alternative branding approach, house branding, may be adopted. In such cases, the company name may be used in conjunction with the product name and (3) finally in some cases it may be beneficial to engage in separate branding.

Branding The process of creating and developing successful brands

5.   Packaging is an important factor in the presentation of a product to the market. It has both a functional and communication role. Similarly, labels deliver information about product use and help promote the brand. Not only does packaging provide protection for the product, but it can also reinforce the brand image and the point-of-sale attraction to the buyer. The protective aspect of packaging is vital in respect of certain items. Some goods may not need

Packaging The development of a product's container and label, complete with graphic design

such protection, but other considerations apply, such as the appearance of the goods on the shelf, or the possibility of seeing the contents through the packaging. Other aspects of packaging may emphasize the convenience of the pack, as for example in cigarette packets which may be opened and reopened several times, or beer cans, which can be opened safely by pulling a ring.

6.   Some products are sold with a very strong emphasis on after-sales service, warranties, guarantees, technical advice and similar benefits. Mail-order firms invariably have an arrangement whereby, if customers are not satisfied with the goods received, they may return them at the firm's expense without any questions being raised. Car retailers sell vehicles with various kinds of warranties concerning replacement of faulty parts at the supplier's expense. In recent years the growth of 'consumerism' or consumer protection lobbies has led to many organizations taking action to improve the service to the customer after the sale has been concluded.

7.   Since most, if not all, of the organization's revenue is going to be obtained from the sale of its products, it is clearly important that the range and quality of the product mix is frequently evaluated and amended. Organizations need to develop and maintain a competitive combination of products and/or services – a product portfolio. Portfolios will vary in terms of the number of product lines, the age structure of products and the number of variations of the total products. The marketer must ensure a sufficiently large number of products exist in order to generate sufficient cash flow to finance new product development or penetration and expansion strategies. In order to maintain a balanced portfolio, new products are developed continually and introduced into markets.

Product portfolio The variety of products manufactured or supplied by an organization

8.   The process of managing groups of brands and product lines is called portfolio planning. The business portfolio is the collection of businesses and products that make up the company. The best business portfolio is one that fits company strengths and helps exploit the most attractive opportunities. The company must (1) analyze its current business portfolio and decide which businesses should receive more or less investment, and (2) develop growth strategies for adding new products and businesses to the portfolio, whilst at the same time deciding when products and businesses should no longer be retained.

The Boston Matrix Also called The BCG Matrix, the Growth-Share Matrix and Portfolio Analysis

9.   The The Boston Matrix is a well known tool for the marketing manager – it is an approach to product portfolio planning (see product portfolio analysis). The matrix analyzes the success of a company's products or services by looking at the percentage of sales they have in the market and how fast the sales are growing. It has two controlling aspects, namely relative market share plotted on the X-axis and market growth, plotted on the Y-axis. Typically each axis is divided in two with a low and high category thus making a 2X2 matrix, see Figure 32.2. Market share is the percentage of the total market serviced by the company, measured either in revenue terms or unit volume terms. Market growth is used as a measure of a market's attractiveness. Markets experiencing high growth reflect expansion of the total market share available, with plenty of opportunity for all to make money. By contrast, competition in low growth markets is often bitter and whilst a company may enjoy high market share in the short term, given a few months or years, the situation might be very different; this makes low growth markets less attractive.

product portfolio analysis a strategic planning tool that takes a product's market growth rate and its relative market share into consideration in determining a marketing strategy

10.   Having considered relative share and growth rates, the organization may consider one of four possible strategies: (1) build Share: the company can invest to increase market share; (2) hold: the company invests just enough to remain in its present position; (3) harvest: the company reduces the amount of investment in order to maximize the short-term cash flows and profits; and (4) Divest: the company can divest – in order to use the resources elsewhere. Thus, product management includes the introduction of new products, marketing of existing products and the elimination of others. Resources and the marketing system may not cope with the introduction of too many products over a short space of time.

FIGURE 32.2 **The boston Matrix**

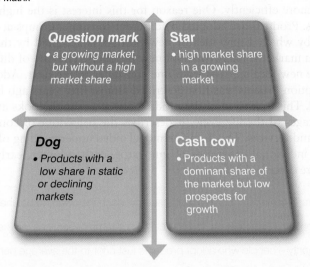

Question mark
- a growing market, but without a high market share

Star
- high market share in a growing market

Dog
- Products with a low share in static or declining markets

Cash cow
- Products with a dominant share of the market but low prospects for growth

Source: The Boston Consulting Group (1970) *Product Portfolio Matrix*. Copyright © The Boston Consulting Group. Reproduced with permission.

11. Emphasis on the make-up of the product is not only vital because of the need to sell benefits to potential customers, but also to take account of another key factor, the 'Product life cycle'. Studies have shown that most products pass through a series of stages – their life cycle – from the time they are introduced until the time they are withdrawn. A product will typically pass through five major stages in its life. These are shown in Figure 32.3.

Product life cycle The four major stages through which products move: introduction, growth, maturity and decline

The consequences of these stages of the product life cycle are as follows:

- Introduction: costs are high (because they include the development costs), sales and profits are low. Few competitors. Price relatively high.

- Growth: sales rise rapidly. Profits at peak level. Price softens. Increasing competition. Unit costs decline. Mass market appears.

- Maturity: sales continue to rise, but more slowly. Profits level off. Competition at its peak. Prices soften further. Mass market.

- Saturation: sales stagnate. Profits shrink. Measures taken against remaining competition. Prices fiercely competitive. Mass market begins to evaporate.

- Decline: sales decline permanently. Profits low or even zero. Product is withdrawn from the market.

FIGURE 32.3 **Product life cycle**

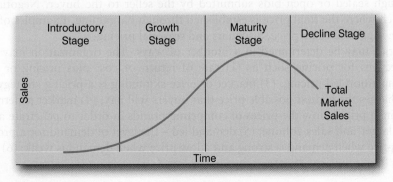

Introductory Stage | Growth Stage | Maturity Stage | Decline Stage

Sales

Total Market Sales

Time

12.   Marketing managers within organizations have long been concerned with how to launch new products more efficiently. One reason for this interest is the high failure rate of new consumer products. Products are adopted by different consumer groups at different times. Diffusion is the process by which a new idea or new product is accepted by the market; the extent and pace at which a market is likely to adopt new products. The rate of diffusion refers to the speed with which the new idea spreads from one consumer to the next. Adoption is similar to diffusion. The Adoption Process was first described almost fifty years ago but remains an important marketing tool. This extension of the product life cycle simply looks at who adopts products at the different stages of the life cycle. It describes the behaviour of consumers as they purchase new products and services. The diffusion model aided understanding of the consumption of new products. The individual categories of innovator, early adopter, early majority, late majority and laggards are described below:

- Innovators – the first people to adopt a new product; they want to be ahead, and be the first to own.

- Early adopters – amongst the first to get hold of items or services, are key opinion leaders.

- Early majority – people who adopt products just prior to the average person.

- Late majority – tend to purchase the product later than the average person, sceptical but eventually adopt because of economic necessity or social pressure.

- Laggards – the last people to adopt, suspicious of new products and oriented towards the past.

Various scholars and practitioners argue the marketer should focus on one group of customers at a time, using each group as a base for marketing to the next group. The most difficult step is making the transition between early adopters and early majority (the chasm). If a successful organization can create a 'bandwagon' effect then momentum builds and the product becomes a de facto standard.

32.2 PRICE

Price variable The aspect of the marketing mix that relates to activities associated with establishing pricing policies and determining product prices

13.   Of the marketing mix variables, many managers regard pricing decisions (Price variable) to be the most difficult decisions. After all, the price often determines the attractiveness of a company's offer. In this section we explain the importance of pricing decisions and the factors which influence the final price. Product pricing is important because it may be used by the buyer to judge quality, attractiveness and general value (cues). Pricing may be used as a competitive strategy and will interact with distribution. In short, proper pricing of goods and services can be a key to success for the organization.

14.   The marketing manager may select from several alternative pricing methods and strategies. Administered pricing is a method in which the seller determines the price for a product and the customer pays the specified price. An alternative is bid pricing where the determination of prices is through sealed or open bids submitted by the seller to the buyer. Negotiated pricing is an approach where the final price is established through bargaining. Examples of pricing decisions include: suggested retail price, discounts and seasonal pricing.

15.   Price may be determined in a number of ways. The organization may consider a range of objectives for pricing such as (1) rate of return or cost plus pricing or mark-up pricing; (2) competition-led pricing; (3) market or price-skimming is a pricing strategy whereby a company charges the highest possible price that buyers will pay; (4) market penetration – a strategy of setting a price below the prices of competing brands in order to penetrate a market and produce a larger unit sales volume; (5) demand led – the level of demand for a product, resulting in a high price when demand is strong and a low price when demand is weak; (6) premium pricing,

(7) pricing an item in the product line low, with the intention of selling a higher-priced item in the line (bait pricing), (8) pricing together two or more complementary products and selling them for a single price (bundle pricing) and (9) early cash recovery.

16.   The marketing manager may have less influence over pricing of some products than others. Commodities and commoditized products have an established market price – the mechanisms of supply and demand dictates that price when products are undifferentiated. A variety of factors influence price setting. Costs determine a product's lower-price limit. The attractiveness of a product to the target customers determines the theoretical price ceiling in a given market. However, the purchasing power of customers, itself influenced by income distribution, exchange rates and inflation will drive price down. Furthermore, additional costs must be accounted for when selling in another country.

17.   Few products stand still in terms of their costs. Labour costs increase from year to year; material costs and energy costs may be subject to less regular, but sharper, increases; interest rates may be extremely variable, and hence the cost of financing products fluctuates. Many costs can be offset by productivity savings. Therefore, the costs which are the most crucial are those which represent sudden and substantial increases, which cannot be absorbed by improving productivity. In this situation, price increases are practically inevitable, and the question is 'by how much should we increase them?'. In certain situations, it may be possible to gain a temporary advantage over competitors by raising prices by the lowest possible margin, and offering some other advantage such as improved after-sales service or credit terms.

18.   Competitor activity has an important bearing on pricing decisions. The most obvious example is when a competitor raises or lowers prices. Assuming your product offers no particular advantages over a rival and the rival drops their price, you may be forced to follow suit; however, price wars are often destructive. If, on the other hand there are other advantages to be offered in your marketing mix, there may be no pressure at all to reduce your price. If a competitor raises their price, perhaps because of rising costs, it may be possible to hold yours steady, provided rising costs can be contained. Pricing is a very flexible element in the marketing mix and enables firms to react swiftly to competitive behaviour.

19.   Payment terms also reflect important decisions for the marketing manager. The organization desires payment as quickly as possible due to the impact upon cash flows and subsequent non or late payment risks. Payment methods regulate the way goods or services are exchanged. Alternatives include payment in advance, deposits, letters of credit and payment against documents (invoices). Companies may manage payment risks through the use of terms and conditions (transferring liabilities, identifying preferred currency), guarantees and insurance. Companies may also conduct customer risk assessment and credit risk assessment before making offers.

CONCLUSION

20.   Products (including services) must be developed and launched in order to generate revenue for the organization. They then pass through various stages as reflected in the product lifecycle. Organizations rarely rely on a single product and the process of managing groups of brands and product lines is called portfolio planning. We introduced the Boston matrix to help consider management of the portfolio. Products must compete with similar rival offerings and brands help customers to differentiate between offerings. Packaging and labelling can help contribute to the success of a product/brand. Before a product is offered, the organization must determine the offer price. This is important because price determines profitability and revenue generation. Price, costs, quality and value are interconnected. There are a variety of pricing policies and strategies and the marketing manager must consider many factors when setting price. Whilst competitor pricing must be considered, price wars can devastate companies and there are ways to avoid them.

QUESTIONS

1   What is the product life cycle?

2   What are the two main strategies for new product introduction?

3   New products and services have to offer benefits that meet customer needs. How might companies identify customer needs? Identify sources of new product ideas.

4   An effective development process for products or services should be divided into a number of key

stages. Define what is meant by product development process and brainstorm and describe the key stages.

5   Explain and evaluate the product development process at WOW toys.

6   Discuss how The Boston Matrix might help the marketing manager at WOW toys.

USEFUL WEBSITES

IDSA: **www.idsa.org** The Industrial Designers Society of America (IDSA) is the world's oldest, largest, member-driven society for product design, industrial design, interaction design, human factors, ergonomics, design research, design management, universal design and related design fields

Product Development and Management Association: **www.pdma.org/** A comprehensive glossary of new product development terms

VIDEO CASES

Now take a look at the online video cases – visit the companion website to work through real world business problems associated with the concepts presented within this chapter.

13 Finally here: Your personal jetpack – a focus on product development and operations

There is a need for the organization to design the products and services and offerings generally sought after by customers; the collection of people, knowledge, technology and systems within an organization that has primary responsibility for producing and providing the organization's products or services is referred to as operations. New product or service development is an essential part of business. A process

represents a way of doing something such as designing or producing products and services. Through this case we consider such processes.

59 Developing products at WOW Toys

Toy maker Nadim Ednan-Laperouse talks about the value of new product development, and how it has benefited his business.

Subjects covered in brief:

The lifecycle of products and services.

Developing ideas.

Matching products and services to market needs.

The project development process.

REFERENCES

Baines, P., Fill, C. and Page, K. (2008) 'Marketing', Oxford University Press.

Barringer, B. R. and Ireland, D. (2010) 'Entrepreneurship: Successfully Launching New Ventures: Global Edition', Ed. 3. Pearson Higher Education.

Muhlbacher, H., Leihs, H. and Dahringer, L. (2006) 'International Marketing', Ed. 3. Thomson Learning EMEA.

CHAPTER 33
THE MARKETING MIX: PROMOTION

Key Concepts

- Customer relationship management (CRM)
- Marketing communication
- Promotion
- Promotional mix
- Relationship marketing

Learning Outcomes   Having read this chapter, you should be able to:

- understand the role, purpose and aims of promotion in the marketing mix
- discuss and evaluate the principal methods of promotion
- explain what is meant by relationship marketing
- discuss the technologies used to enable marketing

1.   Every product needs to be promoted, that is to say it needs to be drawn to the attention of the marketplace, and its benefits identified. Promotion is another ingredient of the marketing mix that is concerned with decisions about marketing communications. Many definitions have been offered for the marketing term of promotion. It has been defined as all types of marketing communication; one of the four Ps in the marketing mix and the use of communications to persuade individuals, groups or organizations to purchase products and services. Marketing communication is the transmission of persuasive information about goods, services or an idea, aimed at key stakeholders and consumers within the target market segment. Marketing communication aims to raise product visibility and awareness and, at the same time, differentiate the company's products and services from its competitors.

2.   Within the marketing function, the term promotional mix is often discussed. This refers to the specific combination of communication tools an organization uses to promote a product, including: advertising, personal selling, publicity and public relations, sales promotion; and direct marketing. Furthermore, some marketing practitioners and scholars distinguish between online and offline promotional tools. The scope of marketing communications is vast. In his book Essentials of Marketing Communications, Jim Blythe (2006) discusses print media advertising, active media, TV, radio and cinema, outdoor advertising, public relations and corporate image, branding, packaging and merchandising, managing exhibitions and trade events, direct and database marketing, sales promotion, personal selling and sales management and twenty-first century marketing communications. In addition Kotler *et al* (2008) add building customer relationships and more recently, De Pelsmacker, Geuens and Van Den Bergh (2010), in their book on marketing communications, add sponsorship and coverage of e-communication, including e-marketing, mobile marketing and interactive television. They also comment on integrated communications and ethical issues in marketing communications. In this chapter we touch on many of these issues but limit ourselves to an overview of the key concepts, tools and techniques.

3.   When discussing promotion, many marketing textbooks start with an overview of the communications process. Communication is concerned with a sharing of meaning through the transmission of information. Many organizations will typically develop a central 'promotional' or brand-related message to be communicated to stakeholders (mainly prospects and customers but others included); for example 'I'm lovin' it' is a trademark of McDonald's Corporation and its affiliates. Communication was covered in Chapter 26 (refer back to Figure 26.1). Such textbooks may also discuss culture (Chapter 15) and the role of Internet technologies (Chapter 30). We start by considering the various tools of marketing communications and will then consider relationship management and the specific role of technology and its application in marketing (the Internet, databases and customer relationship management).

Promotion Communication with individuals, groups or organizations in order to facilitate exchanges by informing and persuading audiences to accept a company's products

Marketing communication The diffusion of persuasive information about a product aimed at key stakeholders and consumers within the target market segment

Market segment A market segment is a group of customers who have similar needs that are different from customer needs in other parts of the market

Promotional mix The combination of five key communication tools: advertising, sales promotions, public relations, direct marketing and personal selling

Advertising A paid-for form of non-personal communication that is transmitted through mass media (television, radio, newspapers, magazines, direct mail, outdoor displays and the Internet)

Personal selling The task of informing and convincing customers to purchase through personal communication

Publicity Non-personal communication in news-story form about an organization and/or its products that is transmitted through a mass medium at no charge

Sales promotion An activity or material that acts as a direct inducement by offering added value to or incentive for the product to resellers, sales people or consumers

Direct marketing The use of non-personal media, the Internet or telesales to introduce products to customers, who then purchase the products by mail, telephone or the Internet

Sponsorship The financial or material support of an event, activity, person, organization or product by an unrelated organization or donor

33.1 TOOLS OF MARKETING COMMUNICATIONS

4. In this section we outline the main promotional tools of advertising, personal selling, sales promotion, public relations and direct marketing, before discussing relationship management and marketing technologies: the Internet and CRM systems.

33.1.1 Tools – Advertising

5. Advertising is the process of communicating persuasive information about a product to target markets by means of the written and spoken word, and by visual material. By definition the process excludes personal selling. The principal media of advertising are as follows:

- the press – newspapers, magazines, journals
- commercial television
- direct mail
- commercial radio
- outdoor – hoardings, transport advertisements, and
- Internet and the World Wide Web.

6. Whatever the medium a number of questions must be decided about an organization's advertising effort. These are basically as follows:

- How much should be spent on advertising?
- What message do we want to put across?
- What are the best media for our purposes?
- When should we time our advertisements?
- How can we monitor advertising effectiveness?

7. Decisions about advertising expenditure will usually be made in conjunction with assessments about the position of the product in its life cycle and with consideration to the product adoption process (see previous chapter). If the product is at the introductory stage, a considerable amount of resources will be invested in advertising. Conversely, if the product is in decline, little or no expenditure on advertising will be endorsed. Some organizations decide to adopt a 'percentage-of-sales' approach, where advertising expenditure is related to sales revenue. Another approach is to base expenditure on what the competition is spending. Various organizations provide regular information on media expenditure for subscribers, and alternative sources provide information on other key facts such as competitor market share. The sales-task approach to advertising expenditure can be particularly useful in situations where it is possible to state clearly defined objectives for advertising, e.g. 'to increase awareness of product X in Y market from present levels to (say) 70%.' This approach has the merit of allocating advertising expenditure to specific targets, but relies heavily on the organization's ability to define its objectives realistically.

8.   Probably the most important aspect of any advertising campaign is the decision about what to say to prospective customers, and how to say it. This is the message which aims to make people aware of and desire the product and favourably inclined towards it. The entire process is the fundamental one of turning customer needs into customer wants. Advertising aims to achieve one or more of the following:

– increase customer familiarity with a product

– inform customers about specific features or the key benefits of a product

– establish the credibility of a product

– encourage potential customers to buy the product

– maintain loyalty of existing customers.

9.   In setting out to achieve such aims, advertisers must abide by a series of laws and codes of practice. Most countries exert some degree of state control over the content and form of advertising. Issues such as obscenity, blasphemy, racial prejudice and sheer misrepresentation figure high on the list of prescriptions.

10.   What is the best way of putting a message across? This is an important question at this stage. The content and the form of the advertisement have been dealt with, and now the key point is to get the message over to the customers. The choice of media depends upon the organization's requirements in terms of the:

– extent of coverage sought to reach customers

– characteristics of the target market

– characteristics of the product

– customer access to the advertising media (e.g. will they have broadband?)

– frequency of exposure to the message

– effectiveness of the advertisement

– timing of the advertisement

– costs involved.

11.   This brings us to the question of how do organizations assess the effectiveness of their advertising? There are two main ways of looking at the question of advertising effectiveness – the first is to consider the results of the advertising in achieving target improvements in specific tasks, e.g. increasing brand awareness in a specific market; the second is to consider the impact of advertising on sales generally. It is extremely difficult to assess the impact of advertising on sales as a whole, because so many other factors, internal and external, are at work in the marketing process of an organization. It is easier to assess the impact of specific advertising campaigns on sales in specific product areas.

33.1.2 Tools – Personal Selling

12.   However vivid the message transmitted by advertising, there is little substitute for the final face-to-face meeting between the buyer and the seller or his representative – this is more true of specialist products but less true in the case of commodities or commoditized products. Advertising creates the interest and the desire, but personal selling clinches the deal. In industrial markets, personal selling plays an even more extensive role. For the moment, let us consider the

basic sales process. This is generally understood to encompass five immediate aims, plus a fol-low-up, as shown in Figure 33.1.

FIGURE 33.1   Personal selling.

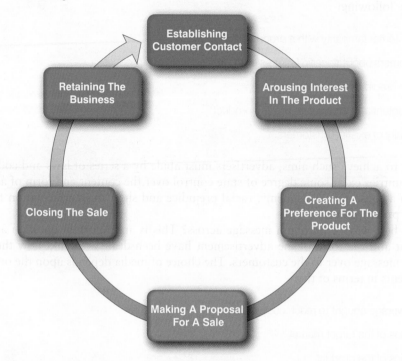

13.   So far as consumer markets, and especially mass markets, are concerned, advertising must play a vital role in the first three stages of the process. After that, advertising becomes rapidly less important, and personal selling takes over. By comparison, advertising plays a much less im-portant role in industrial markets, where even the first stage is dominated by personal selling. Personal selling is the most expensive form of promotion and ranges from the mere taking of an order in a shop or a sales office, to the creation of new sales in a highly competitive market. Companies which utilize an aggressive sales policy, based on personal selling, are said to be adopting a **push strategy**. The tasks of a sales representative, except in the routine order-taking role, include other duties than making sales. These other duties can comprise:

Push strategy Information is just 'pushed' by the seller toward the buyer

 – after-sales servicing (dealing with technical queries, delivery matters),

 – gathering information (feedback on customer reactions, competitor activities),

 – communicating regular information to buyers (new catalogues), and

 – prospecting (looking out for new selling opportunities).

14.   In order to fulfil these duties a sales representative needs to have relevant information about:

 – his or her own organization (policies, resources available, organization structure),

 – the products on offer (goods, services, ranges),

 – sales and profit targets,

– customers (size, type, location),

– sales plan for his/her area,

– promotional material (brochures, catalogues), and

– techniques of selling (creating interest, dealing with objections, closing a sale).

15.   Whilst many organizations still see the primary role of the sales representative as that of generating sales, there is an increasing trend which sees the representative in a wider marketing role, which emphasizes the profit responsibility of the position. If sales are pursued regardless of costs, other factors, such as reputation and the value of the sales volume obtained, can be severely reduced, e.g. if costs have been excessive and/or the organization's image has been tarnished by over-zealous representatives. If, on the other hand, representatives are trained to put themselves in their customers' shoes, i.e. develop a market-oriented approach, they are less likely to put immediate sales gains before the prospect of much larger market opportunities in the future. This, of course, assumes that they are rewarded on this basis as well. In a sales-oriented approach the sales representative is focusing on his or her needs as a seller. By comparison, a market-oriented approach to selling concentrates on the needs of the buyer.

16.   We should note that personal selling is costly. There are direct costs of wages, commissions, royalties, bonuses, etc. to pay as well as infrastructure costs including rent for retail outlets, utilities, etc. Such costs may be relatively low for some highly differentiated products but when competing more on price, such costs may need to be reduced or eliminated. For this reason, many organizations have turned to e-commerce which we discuss later.

33.1.3 Tools – Sales Promotion

17.   Sales promotion activities are a form of advertising designed to stimulate sales mainly by the use of incentives; they refer to communication tools that seek to encourage people to buy now rather than at some point in the future. Sales promotion activities tend to be organized and funded by the organization's own resources. They can take a number of different forms, as, for example:

– coupons,

– twin-pack bargains (two for the price of one 'BOGOF'),

– temporary price reductions and special discounts,

– point-of-sale demonstrations,

– frequent user incentives and loyalty cards,

– money refunds,

– consumer competitions, and

– free merchandise.

18.   Reference was made earlier to 'push' and 'pull' strategies. Sales promotion falls into the first category. It aims to push sales by offering various incentives at, or associated with, the point-of-sale. Its use is most frequent in the field of consumer products. The objectives of a promotion directed at consumers could be to:

– draw attention to a new product or line,

– encourage sales of slow-moving items,

- stimulate off-peak sales of selected items,

- achieve higher levels of customer acceptance/usage of a product or product-line, and

- persuade dealers/retailers to devote increased shelf space to an organization's products.

33.1.4 Tools – Publicity and Public Relations

19.   Publicity is news about the organization or its products, reported in the press and other media, without charge to the organization. Publicity differs from the other promotional devices mentioned in this chapter in that it often does not cost the organization any money! Of course, although the publicity itself may be free, there are obvious costs in setting up a publicity programme, but, pound for pound, these are considerably lower than for advertising, for example. Publicity usually comes under the heading of public relations, which is concerned with the mutual understanding between an organization and its public; managing and controlling the process of using publicity effectively. It is the planned and sustained effort to establish and maintain goodwill and understanding between an organization and its target publics.

20.   Sponsorship is a marketing communications activity, whereby one party permits another an opportunity to exploit an association with a target audience in return for funds, services or resources. Sponsorship events in the arts and sports are becoming an increasingly popular form of publicity. Again, although the publicity itself is free, the costs of sponsorship are not. Nevertheless, such activities can contribute significantly to an organization's public image.

33.1.5 Tools – Direct Marketing

21.   Direct marketing refers to the use of non-personal media, the Internet or telesales to introduce products to customers, who then purchase the products by mail, telephone or the Internet. Common direct marketing approaches include: direct mail, telemarketing, door-to-door personal selling,and the Internet. New technologies may enable direct marketing. For example advances in automated call centres may enable telemarketing. Direct marketing may be used to avoid dependence on intermediaries and may also enable the organization to focus marketing communications on specific segments and targeted customers.

33.2 RELATIONSHIP MANAGEMENT AND MARKETING TECHNOLOGIES: THE INTERNET AND CRM SYSTEMS

22.   Baines, Fill and Page (2008) suggest that the basic (traditional) marketing approach is presented around the marketing mix (4Ps) concept. However, they recognize that some practitioners and scholars consider this to be both an outdated and inappropriate explanation of how marketing works. Marketing may also be regarded in terms of interactions with individuals (prospects and customers). Traditional marketing places emphasis on the marketing mix and individual transactions whereas relationship marketing focuses on winning and retaining customers. Similarly, Dibb *et a*l (2006) discuss the 'relationship marketing era' as the current period, in which the focus is not only on expediting the single transaction but on developing ongoing relationships with customers. Relationship marketing requires a different philosophy in the organization

Relationship marketing Places emphasis on the interaction between buyers and sellers, and is concerned with winning and keeping customers by maintaining links between marketing, quality and customer service and is reliant upon database technologies to support customer acquisition, retention and continued selling activities.

23.   Organizations are now critically dependent upon marketing technologies to enable their marketing processes and activities (communication in particular). Technology facilitates the collection, analysis and dissemination of information for marketing purposes worldwide. Not only does technology make such processes faster but it also allows achievement at lower cost. Earlier in the book we touched on the role of Internet technologies in communication. Technologies of particular interest include those associated with e- business and e-commerce, database technologies and electronic communication tools. In this final section we focus on technology in more detail, considering technologies, processes and philosophies associated with winning and retaining customers; such approaches seek to build a sustainable long-term business (relationship) with customers.

24.   The Internet is both a communication and a transaction vehicle and can thus be discussed in terms of all of the marketing mix variables. Consequently it impacts upon marketing and may be used to build a brand image, provide product support, win business and interact with prospects and customers. Transaction capabilities can have both revenue generation and cost reduction potential. The dissemination of information via the Internet can also reduce costs, replacing expensive alternative and less efficient communication channels. Some organizations use the Web primarily as a communication tool whilst others use it to reach and sell to (transact) consumers who may be inaccessible.

25.   In some cases, the organization will use the Internet to communicate with domestic audiences only whilst in other cases the international audience will be targeted. The Internet impacts upon the marketing mix in a variety of ways. It enables the adaptation of price to the level of the individual user but transparency makes comparative pricing possible at low cost for the consumer. Consequently, the buyer power is increased and there is a tendency for the standardization of prices online. Web-based technologies lower barriers to entry and increase rivalry through the transparency of product-pricing. Distribution channels are affected through the process of disintermediation as the Internet makes direct contact between end-users and producers more feasible (see next chapter). However, problems of information overload drive reintermediation. The Internet will also impact upon product management. Small companies offering specialized niche products should be able to find customers more easily. The Internet also enables the customization of marketing communications to the level of the individual. It offers an efficient medium for conducting worldwide market research (see online surveys, web visitor tracking, advertising measurement, customer identification systems and e-mail) and the understanding of consumers (see Chapter 35).

26.   Customer relationship management (CRM) is the entire process of maximizing the value proposition to the customer through all interactions, both online and traditional. Effective CRM advocates one-to-one relationships and participation of customers in related business decisions. CRM may be described as a broad management approach or philosophy that emphasizes the financial value of developing long-term relationships with and detailed knowledge of customers. For example, through the use of information systems databases, it is assumed that customers can be 'captured' so that customized goods and services may be targeted appropriately to them. However, the term is generally taken to mean more than simply the application of technology but includes the corporate (customer-oriented) culture, beliefs and goals.

Customer relationship management (CRM) The entire process of maximizing the value proposition to the customer through all interactions, both online and traditional. Effective CRM advocates one-to-one relationships and participation of customers in related business decisions

27.   The aim of CRM technology is to provide an interface between the customer and the employee – to replace or facilitate direct interaction. Ideal CRM systems support multichannel communications, needs of customers (product information, order placement, post sales support)

and the core needs of employees (placing orders received by phone, fax, email or face-to-face and to answer a customer's questions). Databases lie at the heart of such systems.

28. There are three phases of CRM: customer (a) acquisition, (b) retention and (c) extension. Each is discussed in more detail in these final sections.

33.2.1 Customer Acquisition Management

29. The aim of Customer Acquisition Management (CAM) is to gain leads which generate new sales. With e-commerce such leads will normally be processed using digital channels. Customers may be attracted to digital channels using either off or online methods (search engines, links, banners and e-mail). With time, organizations may seek to collect more information, allowing a customer profile to be drawn. Thus we may see the first step as customer identification (using cookies and logon screens) from which a customer profile can be built (customer differentiation) allowing the organization to segment customers. Relationships are enhanced using interaction and personalization.

33.2.2 Customer Retention and Customer Extension

30. Companies typically want to keep customers so they continue buying from them. This is a challenge for organizations as today's customers are more empowered, impatient, with short attention spans, facing lots of choice and able to switch easily from one supplier to another. In many industries, profitability is seen to be dependent on loyalty and loyalty on satisfaction (Chapter 37). With reduced loyalty and satisfaction comes the threat of defection; worse still, dissatisfied customers may actually deter other prospects and customers from doing business with the organization. Consequently it is important for companies to identify, measure and track loyalty drivers and implement plans to make improvements. In e-commerce, a range of tools to generate repeat visits are used. One method is to regularly update content.

31. Personalization and mass customization can be used to tailor information. Whilst the two concepts are similar, personalization aims to tailor content to an individual's needs whilst mass customization tailors content to a group with similar interests. Such techniques take advantage of the dynamic possibilities of web content. Users, preferences are stored in and content is taken from a database. Customers generate revenue for companies from one-off or continued purchases. Continued purchases (referred to as extension selling) may be of the same or different (cross sales) products and services. The combined revenue attributable to a customer during their relationship with a company is termed the lifetime customer value (LCV). Customer extension is about activities to deepen the relationship with customers through increased interaction and product transactions.

CONCLUSION

32. The primary role of promotion is to communicate with a range of stakeholders with the aim of directly or indirectly facilitating exchanges. Promotion is often referred to as marketing communications. To gain maximum benefit from promotional efforts, marketers must make every effort to plan, implement, coordinate and control (manage) communications properly. An important purpose of promotion is to influence and encourage prospects and customers to access or adopt goods and services. The major promotional methods include advertising, personal selling, public relations and sales promotion and may include sponsorship, direct

marketing and the use of Internet technologies such as the World Wide Web. The basic (traditional) marketing approach is presented around the marketing mix (4Ps) concept. However, some practitioners and scholars consider this to be both an outdated and inappropriate explanation of how marketing works. Marketing may also be regarded in terms of interactions with individuals (prospects and customers). Traditional marketing places emphasis on the marketing mix and individual transactions whereas relationship marketing focuses on winning and retaining customers. Relationship marketing requires a differing philosophy within the organization and is reliant upon database technologies to support customer acquisition, retention and continued selling activities.

QUESTIONS

1   Identify and describe the main promotional tools of marketing communications.

2   Critically compare traditional with relationship marketing.

3   Explain what is meant by customer relationship management (CRM) and discuss the three phases of CRM.

4   Evaluate the role of technology in supporting CRM.

USEFUL WEBSITES

Brand Channel: **www.brandchannel.com** Valuable source for information about brands and branding strategies

Adage: **www.adage.com** Online sources for advertising and media news

Interbrand: **www.interbrand.com/** Interbrand is a web link that brings together a diverse range of insightful thinkers to discuss, create and design branding strategies.

Warc: **www.warc.com** Provide data on trends and forecasts of advertising expenditure for all major economies, which are used by media researchers worldwide

Brand Republic: **www.brandrepublic.com/** Latest news for marketing, advertising, media and PR

eMarketer Inc: **www.emarketer.com/** Market research on e-business and online marketing

Direct Marketing Association: **www.dma.org.uk/content/home.asp** Regulation, news and information on direct marketing

Institute of Sales Promotion: **www.isp.org.uk/** Information on sales promotion industry and various items such as award winning campaigns.

All About Branding: **www.AllAboutBranding.com** For brands design and creation

Brand Strategy Insider: **www.brandingstrategyinsider.com/** A website dedicated to helping marketing oriented leaders and professionals build strong brands

REFERENCES

Baines, P., Fill, C. and Page, K. (2008) 'Marketing', Oxford University Press.

Blythe, J. (2006) 'Essentials of Marketing Communications', Ed. 3. Financial Times Press.

De Pelsmacker, P., Geuens, M. and Van Den Bergh, J. (2010) 'Marketing Communications: A European Perspective', Ed. 4. Financial Times Press.

Dibb, S., Simkin, L., Pride, W. M.and Ferrell, O.C. (2006) 'Marketing: Concepts and Strategies', Ed. 5. Houghton Mifflin International Inc.

Kotler, P., Armstrong, G., Wong, V.and Saunders, J. (2008) 'Principles of Marketing – European Edition', Ed. 5. Financial Times Press.

CHAPTER 34
THE MARKETING MIX: DISTRIBUTION

Key Concepts

- Distribution channel
- Place or distribution

Learning Outcomes   Having read this chapter, you should be able to:

- explain the purpose of distribution as a variable in the marketing mix

- define what a channel of distribution is (including functions) and key considerations in channel strategy and decision-making

- discuss the types and roles of intermediaries

- explain the importance of supply chain management

Place or distribution Is essentially about how you can place the optimum amount of goods and/or services before the maximum number of members of your target market, at times and locations which optimize the marketing outcome, i.e. sales

1. Having looked at three major elements in the marketing mix – product, price and promotion – we can now turn to the fourth and last element: place/distribution. The organization must make the product available (distribute) to potential customers. Place or distribution is essentially about how to place the optimum amount of goods and/or services before the maximum number of members of your target market, at times and locations which optimize the marketing outcome, i.e. sales. In this chapter we focus on the aspect of the marketing mix that deals with making products available in the quantities desired, to as many customers as possible and keeping the total inventory, transport and storage costs as low as possible. The distribution system exists for two prime reasons, (1) to establish and maintain customer relationships and (2) to distribute goods and services.

2. In a society that expects everything to be right here, right now, 24 hours per day and 365 days per year, the marketing mix variable of place has evolved considerably. Compare for example, developments in banking – how we now manage our money (ATMs and Internet banking); how we buy tickets for entertainment, shows or travel and how we buy food (fast-food restaurants, drink and snack dispensing machines). Distribution channels are important because they enable sales and therefore revenue generation and permit the company to deliver offerings that meet customer expectations. Distribution activities help the organization add value – however, distribution may be costly. Consequently, the marketing manager must make many trade-offs when deciding upon the best channel strategy.

Logistics The management of both inbound and outbound materials, parts, supplies and finished goods

3. Distribution ranges from production and manufacturing to logistics, warehousing and the final delivery of goods to the customer. In this chapter we first consider and evaluate distribution channels before discussing logistics and supply chain management. Finally, briefly, we evaluate the impact of Internet technologies on distribution. As with all marketing mix decisions, distribution and channels are also dependent upon the target market. We will discuss market segmentation and its relationship with all of the marketing mix variables in Chapter 36.

Supply chain A network of manufacturers and service providers that work together to convert and move goods from the raw materials stage through to the end user. These manufacturers and service providers are linked together through physical flows, information flows and monetary flows

34.1 MARKETING (DISTRIBUTION) CHANNELS

Distribution channel Interlinked stages and organizations involved in the process of bringing a product or service to the consumer or industrial user

4. Distribution channel (or marketing channel) refers to a group of individuals and organizations that direct the flow of products from producers to customers. In general, there are two ways to distribute goods; the organization may deal with the customer either directly (integrated) or indirectly (through the use of intermediaries) with the customer. Direct channel structure is where the product goes directly from the producer to the final customer. In contrast, the indirect channel structure is where the product goes from the producer through an intermediary, or series of intermediaries, such as a wholesaler, retailer, franchisee, agent or broker to the final customer. However, it is quite common for an organization to operate both distribution methods simultaneously. A hybrid channel structure is where some products go directly

Direct channel structure Distribution channels in which products are sold directly from producers to users

Intermediary Brings together buyers and sellers

from producer to customers and others go through intermediaries. The three options are shown in Figure 34.1.

FIGURE 34.1 Channels of distribution.

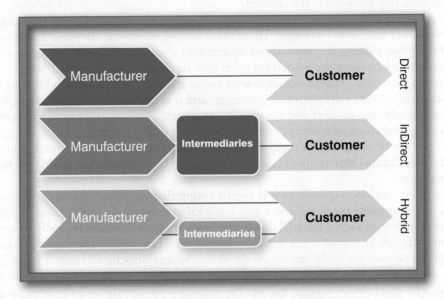

5.   Marketing channels can be classified generally as channels for consumer products and services, or channels for industrial, business to business products and services. We may also categorize channels according to length. Channel length refers to the number of intermediaries a product passes through before it reaches the final consumer.

6.   Channel functions have evolved considerably. They may be required to distribute products and services, manage customer relationships including undertaking research, promote, price and assemble the product, negotiate the sale, manage credit arrangements and provide financing and service options. When determining the channel strategy it is important to consider who will perform such functions; it is also important to consider whether the channel needs to provide access to exclusive, selective or mass markets.

7.   In an integrated distribution system the organization's own employees generate sales, administer orders and deliver products or services. In the case of indirect channels, two fundamental types of intermediary are encountered: agents and merchants – the agent operates in the name of the organization and does not purchase the products being distributed; merchants (distributors and wholesalers) typically buy, handle and sell the goods and services on their own account (see also franchisees and retailers). The benefits of intermediaries include improved efficiency, accessibility and the provision of specialist services. There are however disadvantages, a loss of control (and power) and cost in particular.

8.   Retailing means all transactions in which the buyer intends to consume the product through personal, family or household use. It is all the activities related directly to the sale of goods and services to the ultimate end consumer for personal and non-business use. This is also called the retail trade. Retailers are intermediaries that purchase products and resell them to final consumers. They are a business purchasing products for the purpose of reselling them to ultimate consumers – the general public – often from a shop or store. The primary purpose of a retailer is to provide customers with access to products. They do this conveniently, i.e. they enable speedy access and an easy way for consumers to obtain products. Examples of retailers include departmental stores, convenience stores, supermarkets, speciality shops, etc.

9.   Intermediaries (middlemen) may perform a variety of functions such as the physical handling of products (from import through assembly and inventory to delivery); product promotion,

sales and customer acquisition; the development and management of business relationships and may also assume certain business risks. The distribution of power between the organization and its intermediaries varies from one country to another and from one product market to another. Power relationships impact upon the organization's ability to control the implementation of marketing mix decisions in the channel.

10.   Accepting there to be a range of channel options we might ask, how then does the organization select its channel strategy? Three main factors, economic coverage and control, are considered when making decisions about distribution channels. From an economic standpoint it is important to consider the associated costs and revenues to be generated with each channel in order to maximize profit; associated with revenue is the issue of availability and being able to reach large numbers of customers (coverage) and it is important to retain as much control as is necessary over the product and the way it is marketed. This control factor will normally be balanced against cost and coverage considerations. For example a desire for coverage may necessitate the use of intermediaries and therefore a reduction in control. As with many managerial decisions, channel management is often a balancing act, optimizing variables to meet organizational goals.

11.   When considering options it is worth noting that the direct channel requires capital (and has an opportunity cost), resources and knowledge to establish and operate. Furthermore, customers may shun such a channel due to the low variety of products typically offered by a single manufacturer. In contrast, the indirect channel structure allows the manufacturer/provider to focus on production whilst relying on the skills and infrastructure of one or more intermediaries for distribution. This has the benefit of reach and allows the manufacturer to do what they do best. The main disadvantages include the reduction of control and the need to share profits. Hybrid approaches also increase reach whilst providing greater control and allowing for the optimization of margins whilst developing direct relationships with customers and prospects. Such approaches are prone to conflict however.

12.   The use of multiple channels creates the possibility of channel conflict and cannibalization. Channel conflict is where one channel member perceives another channel member to be acting in a way that prevents the first member from achieving its distribution activities. There may be price differences etc. A further source of channel conflict comes from the sharing of control between the producer and the intermediary. In some cases the distribution structure may also create conflict with customers who may not understand which channel they should use. Channel cannibalization means the decrease in sales through an existing channel due to the introduction of a new channel. This may be a particular problem when an established physical channel operated by an intermediary suddenly has to compete with a new online and direct channel offered by the manufacturer. Compare, for example, the physical travel agent with the online cheap fares website.

Channel cannibalization The decrease in sales through an existing channel due to the introduction of a new channel

Supply chain All of the activities related to the acceptance of an order from a customer and its fulfilment. In its extended format, it also includes connections with suppliers, customers and other business partners

Supply chain management The management of all activities that facilitate the fulfillment of a customer order for a manufactured good to achieve satisfied customers at reasonable cost

34.2 SUPPLY CHAIN MANAGEMENT AND LOGISTICS

13.   Dibb *et al* (2006:411) note that an important function of the marketing channel is the joint efforts of all channel members to create a supply chain. They note that the key tasks in supply chain management include planning and coordinating of marketing channel partnerships; sourcing necessary resources, goods

and services to support the supply chain; facilitating delivery; and relationship building in order to nurture ongoing customer relationships.

14.   The supply chain is a network of manufacturers and service providers working together to convert and move goods from the raw materials stage through to the end user. These manufacturers and service providers are linked together through physical, information and monetary flows. Supply chain management (SCM) involves the active management of supply chain activities and relationships in order to maximize customer value and achieve a sustainable competitive advantage. It represents a mindful effort by an organization or group of organizations to develop and run supply chains in the most effective and efficient way possible. Internationalization, globalization, increasing competition, EC and relationship management has increased the importance of SCM to managers working within organizations. Major SCM activities include: running overseas plants or coordinating international activities, selection of transformation processes; forecasting; capacity planning; inventory management; planning and control, purchasing and logistics.

15.   The management of the physical flow of products from the point of origin as raw materials to end users as finished products is termed logistics. Logistics is that part of the supply chain process that plans, implements and controls the efficient, effective flow and storage of goods, services, and related information, from the point of origin to the point of consumption' in order to meet customer requirements. Logistics covers a wide range of business activities such as: transportation, warehousing, material handling, packaging and inventory management.

16.   Logistical operations impact upon costs, flexibility and delivery performance and are critical to many organizations. Transportation modes include the roads, water, air, rail and pipeline. Each has its own advantages and disadvantages. Road transport is flexible but costly, water transport is typically slow but cheap and air transport is both the quickest and most expensive. Many organizations adopt a multimodal system i.e. they seek to exploit the strengths of multiple transportation modes through physical, information, and monetary flows that are as seamless as possible. The logistics strategy is a functional strategy ensuring an organization's logistic choices – transportation, warehousing, information systems and even form of ownership are consistent with its overall business strategy and support the performance dimensions most valued by targeted customers. As logistics becomes more globalized and information-intensive, more organizations are outsourcing the logistics function to specialists, most notably third-party logistics providers (3PLs).

17.   Transportation systems represent just one part of the physical flow of goods and materials – the other is warehousing; any operation that stores, repackages, stages, sorts or centralizes goods or materials. Organizations use warehousing to reduce transportation costs, improve operational flexibility, shorten customer lead times and lower inventory costs. The organization must identify where its customers are located and in what quantity; they need to consider export volumes, the value density of their products and whether or not customers require rapid delivery. Such factors will influence distribution channel, transportation and storage decisions.

34.3 INTERNET, DISTRIBUTION AND SCM

18.   Having described traditional approaches to supply chain management we now turn to how e-commerce can be used to make enhancements. Supply chain management incorporates both e-procurement, upstream activities and sell side e-commerce, downstream activities; it involves the coordination of or supply activities of an organization from its suppliers and delivery of its products to its customers. The objectives of supply chain management (SCM) include (1) maximize efficiency and effectiveness of the total supply chain for all players and (2) maximize the opportunity for customer purchase by ensuring adequate stock levels at all stages of the process. Internet and associated technologies are vital to SCM since managing relationships with customers, suppliers and intermediaries is based on the flow of information and the transactions between these parties. Organizations seek to enhance the supply chain in order to

provide a superior value proposition (quality, service, price and fulfilment times), which they do by emphasizing cost reduction, increased efficiency and consequently increased profitability. Not only can we conceive the supply chain as an opportunity to increase profits, it may also be viewed as a sequence of events intended to satisfy customers. Typically, it will involve procurement, manufacture, and distribution together with associated transport, storage and information technology.

19.   The 1960s and 1970s were typified by a focus on the management of finished goods (stock management, warehousing, order processing and delivery) using manual (paper-based) information systems. The just-in-time philosophy (JIT) was the philosophy of the 1970s and 1980s. Efficiency was seen to derive from flexibility; holding limited stock whilst ensuring customer orders were met in a timely manner. Under supply and oversupply can impact significantly upon an organization's profitability. In the 1980s and 1990s we witnessed much closer integration between the supplier, customer and intermediaries. During this period, the Internet became an enabling technology, especially for smaller players who could now globally source raw materials and therefore improve competitiveness. During this period, new integrated information systems such as the SAP enterprise resource planning system (see Chapter 41) helped manage the entire supply chain.

20.   Technology enabled the introduction of faster, more responsive and flexible ordering, manufacturing and distribution systems. Early supply chain thinking was manufacturing-led whereby the first consideration was product development, followed by market identification (push supply chain). An alternative approach focuses on customer needs and starts with analysis of their requirements. This latter approach relies on greater communication within the supply chain (pull supply chain).

21.   Marketing is about identifying, anticipating and satisfying customer requirements profitably; it includes the creation, distribution, promotion and pricing of goods, services and ideas. Traditional marketing-communications-media included TV, print and radio that were pushed towards customers with no or limited interactivity. Customer needs were either assumed, addressed collectively en-mass or determined using costly and time-consuming market research questionnaires and face-to-face interviews. E-marketing refers to the use of any technology to achieve marketing objectives. Digital media (Internet, interactive TV and wireless mobile communications) have all impacted upon marketing activities. Internet-based marketing may include the use of web sites, banner advertising and direct e-mail to win new customers and build relationships with existing customers. New media is considered to be more interactive (two way) – the customer usually initiates contact, seeking information (pull); it allows low-cost and timely intelligence (market research) gathering; allows greater individualization (personalization); can be integrated with and complement other channels and can extend reach.

Disintermediation The process of doing away with 'middlemen' from business transactions

22.   Distribution channels are affected through the process of disintermediation (the elimination of intermediaries; removing the layers of intermediaries between sellers and buyers) as the Internet makes direct contact between end-users and producers more feasible. As more information about products and services becomes instantly available to customers, and as information-goods are transmitted over the Internet, traditional intermediary businesses and information brokers are circumvented (disintermediated) and the guiding logic behind some traditional industries begins to disintegrate. At the same time, new ways of creating value are opened up by the new forms of connecting buyers and sellers in existing markets (reintermediation).

CONCLUSION

23.   Distribution or place is the marketing mix variable referring to activities which aim to make products available to customers when and where they want to purchase them. Activities are organized within distribution channels which may be direct, indirect or hybrid. In the case

of the direct channel, the manufacturer distributes products and services to the end consumer. In the case of the indirect channel, the manufacturer makes use of intermediaries as a link between themselves and the ultimate consumer. Each channel has differing advantages and disadvantages, particularly in terms of economics, coverage and control. The distribution channel is responsible for many functions and their joint efforts may be captured under the general banner of supply chain management. This latter concept promotes the coordination of all business entities engaged in the activities of providing customers with the products or services demanded. Internet technologies have impacted upon the supply chain to enable both e-procurement, upstream and e-commerce downstream. Such technologies reduce transaction costs and enable two-way communication with consumers. They also enable manufacturers to adopt direct channels or hybrid models that can lead to channel conflict and cannibalization.

QUESTIONS

1   Explain the purpose of the distribution variable in the marketing mix.

2   Explain how Internet technologies have enabled marketing, particularly distribution. You should discuss supply chain management, channels and disintermediation in your answer. You should also contrast e-marketing with traditional marketing.

USEFUL WEBSITES

Institute of Supply Chain Management: **www.ism.ws/** ISM is a not-for-profit association that provides opportunities for the promotion of the profession and the expansion of professional skills and knowledge

Electronic Retailing Association: **www.retailing.org/** ERA serves as the cohesive voice for multi-channel marketers

British Retailing Association: **www.brc.org.uk/** The British Retail Consortium (BRC) is the lead trade association representing the whole range of retailers, from the large multiples and department stores through to independents, selling a wide selection of products through centre of town, out of town, rural and virtual stores

National Retailing Federation: **www.nrf.com/** The world's largest retail trade association, with membership that comprises all retail formats and channels

VIDEO CASES

Now take a look at the online video cases – visit the companion website to work through real world business problems associated with the concepts presented within this chapter.

16 The Welly Boot Box: starting up

This case documents the challenges of starting up a new (simple) company with a single product. However, it enables the exploration of many start-up related business issues and theories such as the business plan, the value chain and value configuration, the fragmentation of the value chain and outsourcing production to low-labour cost countries (globalization), disintermediation and the use of the web as a sales channel. Additionally, marketing concepts are considered, particularly the use of PR as a means to promote sales in a cost efficient manner. Case-study users may pick and mix their preferred concepts for discussion and activity.

REFERENCES

Arnold, D. (2000) 'Seven Rules of International Distribution', Harvard Business Review, Nov/Dec 2000, Vol. 78 Issue 6, p. 131–137.

Baines, P., Fill, C. and Page, K. (2008) 'Marketing', Oxford University Press.

Bozarth, C. and Handfield, R. (2006) 'Introduction to Operations and Supply Chain Management with Advanced Decision Support Tools', Prentice Hall.

Collier, D. and Evans, J. (2009) 'OM', Ed. 1. Cengage Learning.

Dibb, S., Simkin, L., Pride, W. M. and Ferrell, O.C. (2006) 'Marketing: Concepts and Strategies', Ed. 5. Houghton Mifflin International Inc.

Johnson, G., Scholes, K. and Whittington, R. (2006) 'Exploring Corporate Strategy Enhanced Media Edition', FT Prentice Hall.

Muhlbacher, H., Leihs, H. and Dahringer, L. (2006) 'International Marketing', Ed. 3. Thomson Learning EMEA.

CHAPTER 35
MARKETING RESEARCH

Key Concepts

- Marketing intelligence
- Marketing research

Learning Outcomes   Having read this chapter, you should be able to:

- identify what is meant by, and the purpose of, marketing research
- list the steps typically included in the marketing research process
- evaluate how technology may enable market research
- discuss the purpose of a marketing audit

1.   Why is it we find some advertisements highly influential and some products really useful? Earlier we recognized the role of marketing in determining what to make and sell. This requires an understanding of the needs of customers. Customer requirements may be assessed through market research – the systematic gathering, recording, analysis and interpretation of data on problems relating to the marketing of goods and services.

Marketing research The process of gathering, interpreting and disseminating information to help solve specific marketing problems or take advantage of marketing opportunities

2.   Marketing research is fundamentally about the acquisition and analysis of information required for the making of marketing decisions. The two basic areas in which the information is sought are (a) markets (existing and potential), and (b) marketing tactics and methods. The former is oriented towards what is happening outside the organization, in the marketplace. The second is oriented towards the way in which the organization is responding internally to its customers, present and future. Information is utilized to improve the quality of marketing decisions; minimizing risks by ensuring such decisions are well informed.

3.   This chapter considers marketing research in general. First we outline the marketing research (MR) process and discuss how such studies are initiated. The MR process is similar to the research process many readers will have completed as a part of their academic studies, for research projects, dissertations, etc. We then introduce the concept of marketing intelligence, information about buyer needs and competitor activities compiled, analyzed, or disseminated in an effort to provide insight and assistance in decision-making. As research is based upon data collection, storage, analysis and dissemination we then consider briefly how database and internet technologies enable the MR process. Both marketing research and intelligence are used to guide decisions associated with the marketing mix. However, the organization must also evaluate continually the efforts of the marketing department. We finish this brief chapter with a method of evaluating the organization's total marketing effort – the marketing audit.

Marketing intelligence Information about buyer needs and competitor activities compiled, analyzed and/or disseminated in an effort to provide insight and assistance in decision-making

Marketing audit A systematic examination of the marketing function's objectives, strategies, programmes organization and performance

35.1 MARKETING RESEARCH PROCESS

4.   We have explained the purpose of MR and now outline how organizations go about the task. It is useful to distinguish between research output users and research suppliers. The user is typically a marketing manager and the supplier may be a specialist colleague in the same department (in-house) or may be from an external company (agency). As a significant amount of work is involved, it is normal to establish and fund research projects that have specific goals and timescales. The requirements for such projects, normally encapsulated within a brief, must then be communicated with the supplier. The supplier then responds with a proposal explaining how the research goals will be met within the specified timescales.

5.   The use of In-house resources or agencies to conduct MR are each associated with differing advantages and disadvantages. Agencies may be cheaper and allow the client to remain anonymous. However there are also disadvantages. Sometimes the agency cannot achieve the depth of knowledge of the client's problem, product or market, to thoroughly research it. Whether an external agency is commissioned or employees from the organization are used to do the work, both will then conduct the study.

6.   A marketing research study (process) usually includes the following steps:

-   Problem definition and specification of information required (goals and objectives) – PURPOSE.*

-   Design of study/project, with particular reference to data collection methods (surveys etc.).

-   instrumentation (questionnaires etc.) and sample design (of target population) – POPULATION.

-   Field work (utilizing questionnaires, structured interviews, consumer panels to collect data).

-   Data analysis and processing (using statistical and OR techniques) – PROCEDURE.

-   Presentation of report – PUBLICATION.

7.   As was noted earlier, marketing operates on the external boundaries of the organization. Its main object of attention is the customer (or marketplace), and it is the customer's response, or non-response, that gives rise to most of the problems to which marketing research is applied. A typical problem could be that of a falling market share for one or more of the organization's product lines. In order to clarify the problem and place it in perspective, a number of questions need to be asked. For example, 'Is the market expanding, declining or stable?'; 'What is the situation for competitors?'; 'Is the threat from UK competitors, or from overseas?'; 'What advantages, if any, are enjoyed by competitive products?'; 'What is the organization's reputation with its existing customers?'. Some of these questions can be answered by analyzing secondary data and others by analyzing primary data.

8.   The data which form the raw material of marketing research can be placed under two categories: primary and secondary. Primary data is gathered directly from the persons concerned, be they customers, wholesalers or even competitors. Such data is usually collected by means of **Market surveys** and other formalized methods. Secondary data refers to information available from published sources externally, and from company records. The use of secondary material is cheaper than developing primary data, but may be less relevant or up-to-date.

Market surveys Structured questionnaires submitted to potential customers, often to gauge potential demand

9.   Sources of secondary data are twofold: firstly, internal information from sales budgets, field sales reports and others; and secondly, external information from government statistics, trade, banking and other reports, the press and marketing research agencies. The last-mentioned – marketing research agencies – play a significant role in the whole area of marketing research. They are employed not only by firms with no market research specialists of their own, but also by firms with large market research departments. Some agencies offer a comprehensive marketing research service, some offer a range of specialized services and others offer what is basically an information-selling service. Some well-known agencies include ACNielsen, which provides regular data on sales, brand shares and prices, etc. in the retail trade, Gallup, which specializes in opinion research, and others which are involved in television audience measurement. Television and readership surveys in Britain are conducted under the umbrella of two national bodies – JICTAR (Joint Industry Committee for Television Advertising Research), which meters a representative sample of television sets throughout the nation, and JICNARS (Joint Industry Committee for National Readership Surveys), which conducts, and reports on, 30 000 interviews annually, covering over 100 different publications.

10.   Primary data is most frequently collected by means of surveys, based on questionnaires or interviews. These surveys are invariably undertaken by specialist research organizations, since the construction and administration of questionnaires is a highly-skilled operation. Interviews are generally conducted in a structured form, so as to ensure consistency between interviewers.

*Bradley (2010:36) discusses the marketing research mix as a means to structure research programmes. He comments on 4P's (like the marketing mix) of purpose, population, procedure and publication. We have mapped these, against our steps above. A similar process is described by Baines, Fill and Page (2008:143).

The agencies use trained interviewers, briefed about the objectives of each assignment. Both the questionnaires and the structured interviews tend to concentrate on what the customer likes and dislikes, rather than why. This last question is handled by means of a number of behavioural techniques, which form part of what has been called motivational research. The techniques include in-depth, and less-structured, interviews, discussion groups, role-playing and psychological tests. Motivation research is one of the newer aspects of marketing research, and since it concentrates on motives and attitudes, it relies heavily on the expertize of psychologists for the design of and interpretation of its surveys.

11. Finally, we should note the need for researchers to conform to the professional codes of conduct and the relevant data protection laws. Marketing research should be carried out in an objective, transparent, unobtrusive, confidential and honest manner. Key principles can be found in various marketing codes of conduct.

35.2 MARKETING INTELLIGENCE

12. Marketing intelligence means information about buyer needs and competitor activities compiled, analyzed, and/or disseminated in an effort to provide insight and assistance in decision-making. Aside from collecting data and intelligence about customers and prospects it is also important to collect data and intelligence about rivals. Competitive intelligence is the organized, professional, systematic collection of information, typically through informal mechanisms, used for the achievement of strategic and tactical organizational goals. Intelligence about competitors can be obtained from their websites and marketing communications, products, annual reports, from trade shows and conferences and from customers and suppliers of competitors. Such data and intelligence is often stored in marketing information systems.

Marketing information systems A system incorporating ad hoc and continuous market and marketing research surveys, together with secondary data and internal data sources, for the purpose of decision making by marketers

35.3 TECHNOLOGY AND MARKETING RESEARCH

13. The Internet and database technologies enable data collection, storage and analysis. They enhance reach, increase the richness of the study and may be conducted not only faster but cheaper. Online surveys are now commonplace and allow the respondent to complete them at a place and time convenient to themselves. Responses can be sent electronically, automatically entered, reducing error, and analyzed. The use of electronic surveys makes data capture simpler and therefore enables the collection of larger volumes of data either in the form of more questions to the respondent or the inclusion of more respondents in the sample. However, this can make analysis more problematic. Advances in data mining technology can help. Data mining is the process of finding trends, patterns and connections in data in order to inform and improve competitive performance. This involves searching organizational databases in order to uncover hidden patterns or relationships in groups of data. Data mining software attempts to represent information in new ways so that previously unseen patterns or trends can be identified. Another way of thinking about data mining is as knowledge discovery using a sophisticated blend of techniques from traditional statistics, artificial intelligence and computer graphics. Analysis is then used to compile the research report. Internet technologies may also enable the dissemination of findings.

35.4 THE MARKETING AUDIT

14. So far we have been concerned mainly with the market research aspects of marketing research. The other prime interest of marketing research, as was noted in paragraph 1 in this chapter, is the way in which the organization responds to the demands of the market-place. The most important method of evaluating the organization's total marketing effort is by employing a marketing audit. This is an independent examination of an organization's marketing objectives, marketing activities and marketing environment, with the primary aims of assessing present effectiveness and of recommending future action.

15. The audit may be carried out regularly and undertaken by the organization's employees or by external consultants. The requirements of the task call for objectivity, independence and suitable experience. The advantage of such an audit lies in its ability to produce a critical assessment of the organization's marketing strengths and weaknesses, whilst at the same time weighing up the threats and opportunities posed by the external environment – it is a diagnostic tool. This critical assessment is valuable to the organization's corporate planning process as well as to its marketing planning. The main disadvantages are those of time and cost. It takes a considerable amount of time to conduct an audit covering the points mentioned above, and this time is expensive in labour costs.

CONCLUSION

16. Marketing research is fundamentally about the acquisition and analysis of information required for the making of marketing decisions – to shape the marketing mix variables. The process used to conduct marketing research usually includes the following steps: problem definition and specification of research purpose; design of study/project, with particular reference to data collection methods, instrumentation and sample design; field work to collect data; analysis and the creation and presentation of a report. The Internet and database technologies enable the whole process.

QUESTIONS

1   Identify what is meant by, and the purpose of, marketing research.

2   List and describe the steps typically included in the marketing research process.

USEFUL WEBSITES

OECD: **www.oecd.org/home/** OECD: Organization for Economic Co-operation and Development. The organization provides a setting where governments compare policy experiences, seek answers to common problems, identify good practice and coordinate domestic and international policies

The World Bank: **publications.worldbank.org/ecommerce/ publications.worldbank.org/ecommerce/** The World Bank publications section is a vital source of financial and technical assistance to developing countries around the world

MRS (The Market Research Society): **www.mrs.org.uk/** To represent and communicate good practice in research to the business community

CIA World Fact book: **www.cia.gov/library/publications/the-world-factbook/index.html** For information on countries

The World Trade Organization: **www.wto.org/** The World Trade Organization (WTO) deals with the rules of trade between nations at a global or near-global

Fortune Global 500: **www.pathfinder.com/fortune/ global500/** Fortune Global 500 contains the annual ranking of America's largest corporations

International Monetary Fund: **www.imf.org/external/ index.htm** For information on countries

Country Reports: **www.countryreports.org/** Country Reports provides useful country information for students and educators

Research info: **www.researchinfo.com/** For information on the market research industry

VIDEO CASES

Now take a look at the online video cases – visit the companion website to work through real world business problems associated with the concepts presented within this chapter.

1 Business Model – John Kearon of BrainJuicer

John Kearon, current Chairman and Chief Executive of BrainJuicer Group PLC (an online market research agency)

gives an interview about their business model. John explains how he represents a new company establishing itself in a well established business/ industry. He discusses how he successfully achieved this despite entrenched competition. The case may be used as a vehicle to explore marketing (competing) and related concepts.

REFERENCES

Baines, P., Fill, C. and Page, K. (2008) 'Marketing', Oxford University Press.

Bradley, N. (2010) 'Marketing Research: tools and techniques', Ed. 2. Oxford University Press.

Dibb, S., Simkin, L., Pride, W. M. and Ferrell, O.C. (2006) 'Marketing: Concepts and Strategies', Ed. 5. Houghton Mifflin International Inc.

CHAPTER 36
MARKETING ORGANIZATION

Key Concepts

- Marketing objective
- Marketing strategy
- Organizing by function
- Segmentation

Learning Outcomes   Having read this chapter, you should be able to:

- define marketing strategy
- review the marketing strategy formulation process
- discuss the principal objectives of the marketing department
- review the major structural alternatives that are available to a marketing department

1.   Earlier in the book we noted that organizing means determining activities and allocating responsibilities for the achievement of plans; coordinating activities and responsibilities into an appropriate structure. In this chapter we consider organizing the marketing function. We start with the strategic role of marketing and consider the formulation of marketing strategies and their relationship with corporate strategy. Next we consider the principal objectives of a marketing department and discuss the major structural alternatives that are available. Finally, we evaluate the differing perspectives between the marketing and other departments within the organization.

36.1 PLANS: MARKETING STRATEGY, SEGMENTATION AND THE MARKETING MIX REVISITED

2.   Marketing can be described in operational/tactical and strategic terms. Operationally it is concerned with achieving target market share through the tactical use of the marketing mix. Strategically, it seeks to ensure corporate goals are achieved through a balanced portfolio of products. In the case of profit-oriented companies, the end goal of strategy is to make a profit. We discussed strategy and the strategy formulation process in Chapter 16 and build on that knowledge here. Strategies are about the allocation of people, resources and capital to achieve long-term goals. As with the corporate strategy, the marketing strategy may be formally developed as a plan or may emerge as a result of managerial decision-making. West, Ford and Ibrahim (2010) suggested the essentials of marketing strategy are: (1) understanding the external environment; (2) establishing the organizational purpose and objectives; and (3) assessing the internal environment in terms of resources and capabilities.

Marketing strategy A plan indicating the opportunities to pursue, specific target markets to address, the types of competitive advantages that are to be developed and exploited and maintenance of an appropriate marketing mix that will satisfy those people in the target market(s)

3.   West, Ford and Ibrahim (2010) present a marketing strategy blueprint comprising four key phases. In the first phase, the organization establishes where it is now through the use of analytical tools such as PESTLE, SWOT and the five forces analysis (all of which have been described previously in this book). The output of the analysis is essentially an audit of the internal and external environment. This acts as the input to phase 2; in this next stage the organization determines where it wants to be. Objectives are set, markets are segmented and targeted and a positioning strategy determined. This is the strategy and forms the input to phase 3 which focuses on implementation. The strategy is translated into the marketing mix. Finally phase 4 concerns control, measurement and evaluation, to assess and assure success.

4.   Strategic marketing goals and objectives include (a) niche-focus on a small part of a segment where customers' special needs can be met through a strongly differentiated product offering; (b) hold (defend) – normally the strategy of the market leader; (c) harvest – a goal typically employed in mature markets which involves a reduction in investment and costs (particularly of marketing communications) whilst maximizing revenues; (d) divest – market withdrawal when experiencing negative cash flows and (e) growth. There are different forms of growth such as by focusing on familiar activities and product markets; by vertical integration and undertaking activities up or downstream or through diversification.

Segmentation The process of grouping customers in heterogeneous markets into smaller, more similar or homogeneous segments – customers are aggregated into groups with similar needs and buying characteristics

5.   Marketing strategies have evolved over the past three decades: starting with an emphasis on the marketing mix as a tool to achieve corporate goals, later other concepts such as segmentation (to be discussed later) and positioning were added. Utilizing the

concept of segmentation and positioning, marketing strategy was defined as a means that identifies the target markets towards which activities are to be directed, types of competitive advantages to be developed and exploited. For many organizations, the marketing strategy is seen as a functional strategy developed by the marketing department to help them meet their goals. In other organizations the marketing concept permeates the whole organization. In summary, the marketing strategy is used to select target markets and determine how to compete; the marketing mix describes one set of variables that can be manipulated to provide an advantage.

> **Marketing concept** The philosophy that an organization should try to provide products that satisfy customers' needs through a coordinated set of activities that also allows the organization to achieve its goals

6. Market segmentation is the division of a market into different groups of customers with distinctly similar needs and product/service requirements (Baines, Fill and Page 2008). The purpose of market segmentation is to leverage scarce resources: to ensure that the elements of the marketing mix are designed to meet particular needs of different customers. Market segmentation is related to product differentiation, i.e. companies adapt to different offerings and variations of offerings to satisfy segments. There are a number of ways to segment the market and the process of segmentation is discussed by a number of the authors cited in this chapter. The approach used for the consumer market is likely to differ from that of the business market as different variables (Segmentation variables or bases) may be used to group customers. Segments should be distinct, accessible and profitable. The organization must decide which segments to serve, i.e. determine its target markets.

> **Market segmentation approach** Designing product and service offerings around consumer demand

> **Segmentation variables or bases** The dimensions or characteristics of individuals, groups or businesses that are used for dividing a total market into segments

7. Having assessed the attractiveness of potential markets and the organization's competitive position in the markets under consideration, the organization decides which markets should be served. The Ansoff Growth matrix is a tool to help organizations determine their product and market growth strategy. Portfolio analysis enables organizations to analyze market attractiveness and competitive position simultaneously and includes consideration of both opportunities and threats. The Product/Market Grid has two dimensions: products and markets. Four options may be considered such as product market penetration, geographic expansion, product market development and diversification. Market penetration (sell more of the same products or services in current markets) involves increasing market share of an existing product, or promoting a new product, through strategies such as bundling, extensive advertising, lower prices or volume discounts. It is a marketing strategy used by an organization to increase the sales of a product within an existing market, through the employment of more aggressive marketing tactics. Geographic expansion is a marketing strategy that seeks to expand operations to new geographic areas – sell more of the same products or services in new markets. Selling new products or services in current markets is a marketing strategy termed product development and finally, the most risky type of strategy is diversification – selling new products or services in new markets. Ansoff's Product/Market Grid is a model proven to be very useful in business unit strategy processes for determining business growth opportunities.

8. Ultimately the organization will seek out sources of (sustainable) competitive advantage through positioning and the advantages it can gain from its own bundles of resources. We have previously discussed generic strategies such as cost leadership, differentiation and focus. In terms of positioning, the organization may aim to be the market leader, a challenger with aspirations of leadership or simply a follower, content to survive. Alternatively, the organization may become a niche player.

9. So far in this chapter we have considered the key activities associated with developing a marketing strategy, considering analysis, goals and action. Organizations typically develop marketing plans through a series of sequential activities in order to coordinate and manage

intentions. The marketing plan will typically contain an executive summary, list of objectives, background information on products and markets, marketing analysis, strategies, goals and details of the marketing program (a marketing mix for each target market segment is developed), an implementation plan along with other supporting documentation. It then needs a structure to allocate roles and responsibilities.

36.2 ALLOCATING RESPONSIBILITIES – MARKETING STRUCTURES

10.   The key objectives of the marketing department will typically be to contribute to the organization's corporate aims in respect of profitability, growth and social responsibility by (a) proposing, and seeking acceptance for improvements in the organization's marketing policies; (b) seeking out and identifying advantageous marketing opportunities; (c) preparing, in conjunction with other departments, suitable marketing strategies to meet opportunities identified; (d) selling and distributing the organization's products; (e) developing new products in the marketplace; (f) designing and implementing approved marketing plans; (g) acquiring sufficient and suitable information, both internal and external, concerning the organization's products, and their impact upon customers, competitors, suppliers and others in the marketplace; (h) ensuring the organization's products are brought to the attention of existing and potential customers by means of suitable advertising and promotional methods; and (i) promoting a reputable image for the organization in the marketplace.

11.   The stages of development of the marketing organization associated with the developing organization are shown in Figures 36.1. At first, in small and new companies, there is no specific marketing section or department. The Sales Manager is responsible for advertising and promotion as well as selling. Stage two introduces the first formal recognition of marketing as such, but

FIGURE 36.1   **Marketing structures stages 1–4.**

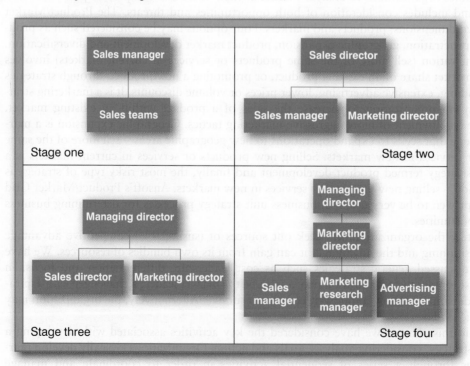

places the Marketing Manager under the direction of the Sales Director. At this stage, marketing is seen as an important provider of information to support the organization's sales effort. The marketing section will probably be concerned with advertising, sales promotion, product development and marketing research. By stage three, marketing has moved up to a position of equality with sales. This situation probably produces the maximum amount of conflict between sales and marketing, as the former concentrate on their preoccupation with current sales and the latter concentrate on long-term market developments. Since marketing will see the sales effort as part of the total marketing mix, there will be a strong desire to tell sales what to do and why! The resolution of this built-in conflict has been achieved, in many companies, by giving predominance to marketing. Stage four presents a functional view of the marketing department. The separate specializms of sales, research and advertising/promotions each have their own manager.

12. This is a common form of structure for a marketing department. Organizations frequently add other specialist sections, such as customer services and product development. The main advantage of this type of structure is its relative simplicity, whereby identifiable divisions of labour can be made without causing unwanted overlap or competition between sections. The main disadvantage of a functional structure (See organizing by function) is its inability to cope with multiple products or markets, because of difficulties in allocating priorities amongst the specialist sections. In order to cope with the increased diversity of decision-making required in these circumstances, several companies have introduced a matrix-type of structure, incorporating a number of operational roles, as in Figure 36.2.

> **Organizing by function** A way of structuring a marketing department in which personnel directing marketing research, product development, distribution, sales, advertising and customer relations report to the topevel marketing executive

13. This structure allocates specific responsibility for individual products/product groups and for specific markets, whilst retaining all the key functional posts. As in every matrix structure, the operational roles have reporting responsibilities to functional managers as well as to their immediate line managers. So, for example, a Brand Manager's freedom to act is not only prescribed by his immediate Product Group Manager, but also by any one of the functional managers, in respect of his own speciality. Thus, advertising programmes for a brand would have to be agreed not only by the Product Group Manager, but also by the Advertising Manager.

FIGURE 36.2 Matrix organization in marketing.

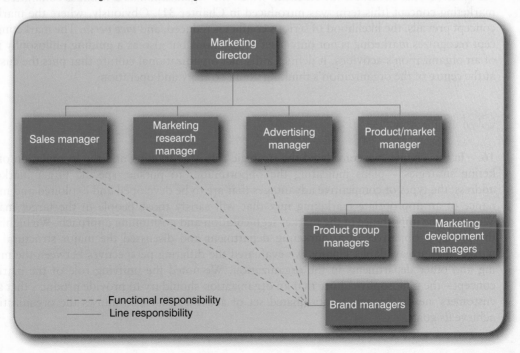

14.   In very large organizations, where a divisionalized structure may have developed because of product or geographical reasons, for example, a decision has to be made about splitting the marketing activities between the divisions and corporate headquarters. Here the underlying values of the organization's senior management come into operation. If the philosophy is to decentralize, in the way described in Chapter 22, that is to say by delegating authority to the (local) sub-units, then it is likely that little or no role will be available for a corporate marketing department. If, however, divisionalization is seen as a way of delegating part, but only part, of the organization's marketing effort, then a definite marketing role at corporate level will be established. A corporate role could just be confined to the provision of specialist services, such as marketing research and specialist advertising advice. Alternatively, there could be a strong corporate role, giving employees concerned the right to direct key functional aspects of marketing in the divisions, e.g. in terms of product design, corporate image and marketing control information systems.

36.3 THE MARKETING DEPARTMENT IN THE ORGANIZATION

Marketing objective A statement of what is to be accomplished through marketing activities – the results expected from marketing efforts

15.   Earlier we listed typical marketing objectives and indicated the contributive nature of the marketing department's efforts to corporate aims. Other departments, too, make their contribution to these overall aims. If the organization's strategy has been worked out in a thorough and collaborative way, there should exist a mutual understanding of roles between departments. This will affect the manner in which problems of misunderstanding and conflict are handled. However, there is no practical way in which it is possible to avoid all such misunderstandings and conflict. In any organization it is natural for each sub-division to have its own perspective concerning the ultimate goals of the organization, and the best way of achieving them. The degree of conflict which may occur depends largely on the way in which departmental or functional objectives have been drawn up, and whether suitable conflict-resolution mechanisms exist (e.g. regular meetings between common interest groups, inter-departmental committees, etc.). Also, in the context of marketing vis-à-vis the others, a vital element is the extent to which the organization as a whole is committed to the marketing concept (this term was introduced in Chapter 31). Obviously, where the marketing concept prevails, the likelihood of serious conflict is reduced, and *vice versa*. The marketing concept recognizes marketing is not only a set of functions but also as a guiding philosophy for all of an organization's activities. It defines a distinct organizational culture that puts the customer at the centre of the organization's thinking about strategy and operation.

CONCLUSION

16.   In this chapter we considered the strategic role of marketing and the formulation of marketing strategies – plans indicating the opportunities to pursue, specific target markets to address, the types of competitive advantages that are to be developed and exploited and maintenance of an appropriate marketing mix that will satisfy those people in the target markets. We noted the importance of the market segmentation and positioning approach. We highlighted the principal objectives of a marketing department and discussed the major structural alternatives that are available. Finally, we evaluated the differing perspectives between the marketing and other departments in the organization. We noted the unifying role of the marketing concept – the philosophy/culture that an organization should try to provide products that satisfy customers' needs through a coordinated set of activities that also allows the organization to achieve its goals.

QUESTIONS

1   Discuss what is meant by marketing strategy and explain the marketing strategy formulation process.

2   Discuss the contribution of the marketing department to the overall organization commenting on key objectives, roles and responsibilities.

USEFUL WEBSITES

Euromonitor: **www.euromonitor.com** Euromonitor International is a global market research company specializing in industries, countries and consumers

MOSAIC – Experian: **www.business-strategies.co.uk/** Marketing Information Services – Providing a detailed understanding and analysis of consumers, markets and economies in the UK and around the world, past, present and future. Consumer profiling and market segmentation services provide a deep and rich understanding of consumers and local markets

Chartered Institute of Marketing (CIM): **www.cim.co.uk/** Organization for professional marketers

REFERENCES

Baines, P., Fill, C. and Page, K. (2008) 'Marketing', Oxford University Press.

Blythe, J. and Megicks, P. (2010) 'Marketing Planning: Strategy, Environment and Context', Financial Times Press.

Kotler, P., Armstrong, G., Wong, V. and Saunders, J. (2008) 'Principles of Marketing – European Edition', Ed. 5. Financial Times Press.

West, D., Ford, J. and Ibrahim, E. (2010) 'Strategic Marketing – Creating Competitive Advantage', Ed. 2. Oxford University Press.

CHAPTER 37
CUSTOMER SERVICES AND CONSUMER PROTECTION

Key Concepts

- Customer satisfaction
- Customer service

Learning Outcomes   Having read this chapter, you should be able to:

- define and evaluate the requirements for customer satisfaction and customer service
- list common methods to protect consumer interests

1.   Commercial organizations spend a great deal of effort assessing the needs and wants of their customers, and yet, as we saw in Chapter 31, there are a variety of possible orientations towards customers. Not all firms are 'market oriented' to the extent that they put the customers' needs and wants before all else. Even if firms were completely market oriented, they would still make errors of judgement from time to time. Therefore, even in the best-regulated circles, the customer may sometimes be badly treated. Over recent years consumers have become more vocal in reacting to shoddy products or poor service. As a result there are now government, as well as private consumer organizations whose purpose is to stand up for consumers' rights. The word 'consumerism' has been coined to describe the activities of pressure groups in this area, and the term 'consumer protection' used to describe the efforts made by government and other bodies to provide rules and codes of conduct for relations between commercial organizations, public services and customers or users.

2.   A consumer may be defined as 'any person (including a corporate body) who buys goods and services for money.' A 'user', in this context, describes someone who uses a public service of some kind (e.g. a national health service). Aside from companies wanting to protect customers in order to win business, in the UK, there are several means by which consumer interests may be protected. These involve the application of one or more of the following: The Law, codes of 'good practice' or various charters, standards and trade marks and independent consumer groups. Each of these will be examined briefly in this chapter, along with some of the leading public and private pressure groups which help ordinary citizens to obtain redress against unfair trading in goods and services. We start with arguments that are directly in the interests of organizations making an offer to market and consider their self-driven pursuit of customer satisfaction.

> **Customer satisfaction** When an exchange meets the needs and expectations of the buyer

37.1 CUSTOMER SATISFACTION AND CUSTOMER SERVICE

3.   Throughout this section of the book we have emphasized the role of marketing in satisfying the customer. This means meeting their expectations. The consequences of not meeting customer expectations may include: a reduction in sales and increase in the number of dissatisfied customers (churn); costs associated with managing defective goods and services, reputation risk and costs associated with defending cases brought against the company in court. Companies seek to satisfy customer wants through the application of the marketing mix, quality control and a set of activities collectively known as customer service. Not only do such measures seek to prevent dissatisfaction, they also seek to attract customers and win business, building sales.

> **Customer service** Customer satisfaction in terms of physical distribution, availability, promptness and quality

4.   Customer 'wants' may include fair prices, acceptable quality, dependability, safe products and services, availability and a timely response. Achieving this may require the organization to implement quality management systems and standards, maintain inventories, implement efficient order processes and fulfilment systems, make information available to consumers, replace faulty goods promptly and put right problems, manage complaints, issue warranties and guarantees.

5.   Despite this, companies should recognize that it may not be profitable to pursue very high levels of customer satisfaction. Significant costs may be associated with achieving such levels. In some cases the organization will have choices about the way it does business, its products and its marketing, whilst in other cases it may have no option but to comply with legislation. Additionally, the actions of competitors may provide pressure to act and perform in a particular manner.

37.2 CONSUMER PROTECTION LEGISLATION

6.   A number of laws and other forces influence marketing decisions and activities. Aside from a need to consider consumer protection laws, the company should also consider anti-competitive laws and regulations. The number of regulatory mechanisms and specific laws have grown significantly in recent years. Not only may they come from the home country but also from any country to which goods may be exported. Furthermore, companies may have to comply with European Union regulations. In this section we present a high-level overview, focusing more on the general obligations to protect consumers.

7.   Treating customers fairly is vital to winning and retaining customers. The following provides an overview of the consumer protection laws. Consumer protection is linked to the idea of 'consumer rights' (that consumers have various rights as consumers), and to the formation of consumer organizations which help consumers make better choices in the marketplace. Consumer is defined as someone who acquires goods or services for direct use or ownership rather than for resale or use in production and manufacturing. Consumer protection laws are a form of government regulation which aim to protect the interests of consumers. Generally, goods must fulfil three basic conditions, they must be: of merchantable quality, fit for the purpose and as described. Consumers need protection against being misled by false or inaccurate descriptions of goods on sale. The consumer's physical safety is considered in legislation' to minimize risks to consumers from potentially dangerous products. Furthermore, it has become increasingly important, too, that borrowers should not be exploited unknowingly.

8.   Common law rights are acquired as a result of custom and practice over many years. However, by far the greatest protection for consumers in Britain is provided by parliament, which in several important pieces of legislation has set up a framework in which the respective rights and duties of consumers and suppliers can be identified and clarified. The most important statutes concerning consumer affairs include the following: Sale of Goods Act, 1979, Trade Descriptions Act, 1968, Consumer Safety Act, 1978, Consumer Credit Act, 1974, Consumer Protection Act 1987,Unfair Contract Terms Act, 1977, Unfair Terms in Consumer Contracts Regulations 1999, Fair Trading Act, 1973, Supply of Goods and Services Act, 1982, Consumer Protection (Distance Selling) Regulations 2000, Electronic Commerce Regulations 2002, Enterprise Act 2002, General Product Safety Regulations 2005, and Consumer Protection from Unfair Trading Regulations 2008. The United Kingdom, as member state of the European Union (EU), is bound by the consumer protection directives of the EU.

9.   The Enterprise Act and the Consumer Protection from Unfair Trading Regulations are used to ensure businesses comply with consumer protection legislation. The regulations introduce new rules about consumer protection and the responsibility of businesses to trade fairly. It places a general duty on traders not to trade unfairly. The regulations also include a blacklist of 31 banned trading practices.

10.   One of the growing practices in modern legislation is to set up supervisory bodies, or 'watchdogs', to monitor the effects of the law in society. In the consumer rights arena the central watchdog is provided by the Office of Fair Trading, set up by the Fair Trading Act, 1973, to encourage voluntary codes of practice between sellers and their customers, and to provide a central reference point for doubtful cases and matters of principle.

11.   In England and Wales, a manufacturer has a common law duty of care to ensure that his products do not cause injury or damage to a person or to his property. Note that this duty does not extend to the quality or performance of the goods, but only to their causing injury or damage. In such a case, it is up to the complainant to show that the damage or injury was due to the manufacturer's negligence. Statutory duties are imposed on manufacturers by the Health and Safety at Work etc. Act, 1974. This act, amongst other duties, requires designers, manufacturers and importers to ensure, so far as practicable, that any article is safe when properly used.

37.3 CODES OF PRACTICE AND CHARTERS

12.   The Fair Trading Act, 1973, requires the Director General of Fair Trading to encourage trade associations to draw up codes of practice for fair trading (Its role was modified and its powers changed with the Enterprise Act 2002). Codes do not have the force of law in their own right, but are nevertheless very influential when a court is determining the rights and wrongs of a situation. Codes are less formal, more easily amended and less time-consuming to operate than legal provisions. Codes of practice have been developed by associations such as the Association of British Travel Agents (ABTA). There is no statutory requirement for airlines providing flight-only or other companies providing any accommodation-only holidays to give consumer protection in unforeseen difficult circumstances. ABTA looks after consumer protection from the tour operator end of the contract, which is, in turn, legally overseen by the Air Travel Organizers' Licensing (ATOL) scheme of the Civil Aviation Authority which came into effect in 1973. The ATOL regulations are the core of the consumer protection by which ABTA members must conform; all UK-bought package holidays including a flight have to abide by ATOL. UK tour operators have to be ATOL-licensed by the CAA.

13.   Since advertising and promotion play such a significant part in the marketing of consumer goods, it is not surprising that consumer protection applies to these activities. The Trade Descriptions Act, 1968, has already been mentioned, but another very important voluntary body operating in this field is the Advertising Standards Authority (ASA). The ASA is the self-regulatory organization (SRO) of the advertising industry in the United Kingdom. Its role is to regulate the content of advertisements, sales promotions and direct marketing in the UK.

37.4 STANDARDS AND TRADEMARKS

14.   All formal standards are developed with the views of consumers and a wide range of stakeholders incorporated. As a result, standards represent a consensus on current best practice. The BSI Group, also known as the British Standards Institution (or BSI), is a multinational business services provider whose principal activity is the production of standards and the supply of standards-related services – see also ISO introduced in Chapter 29. Standards are designed for voluntary use and do not impose any regulations. However, laws and regulations may refer to certain standards and make compliance with them compulsory.

15.   A trademark is a distinctive sign or indicator used by an organization to identify that the products or services originate from a unique source, and to distinguish its products or services from those of other entities. Trade marks were originally established to protect

> **Trademark** Legal designation indicating that the owner has exclusive use of a brand

manufacturers' products from being 'pirated' by their rivals. Once certain marks became well known, they also provided an advantage to consumers, who were able to associate particular trade marks with particular quality goods. Persons buying products bearing those names are entitled to expect the particular standards associated with them.

37.5 INDEPENDENT PRESSURE GROUPS AND PUBLICLY APPOINTED CONSUMER GROUPS

16.   There are a number of independent pressure groups in the United Kingdom working directly on behalf of consumers. These include:

- The Citizens' Advice Bureau which provides free advice for local citizens on a wide range of matters, including consumer affairs.

- The Consumers' Association, which now trades as Which?. This body carries out independent tests on a wide variety of consumer goods and services.

- Mediawatch-uk, formerly known as the National Viewers' and Listeners' Association, is a pressure group in the United Kingdom, which campaigns against the publication and broadcast of media content which it views as harmful and offensive, such as violence, profanity, sex and blasphemy.

17.   Publicly-appointed bodies representing consumers' interests are considerably more numerous than private groups. Local authorities have established services such as Trading Standards Departments and Consumer Advice Centres, for example. There are also several bodies established by statute to represent the views of users of public services. See also independent regulators such as Ofcom, Ofwat, Ofgas, etc.

CONCLUSION

18.   Treating customers fairly is vital to ensuring customers are both won and retained. In this chapter we have evaluated the need for organizations to satisfy customers through the application of the marketing mix, customer service and compliance with the law, standards and codes. We noted that it may not be profitable to attain 100% satisfaction levels and this may not be a suitable goal for some organizations. However, some aspects of satisfaction (consumer protection) are beyond the realm of organizational choice and there may be legal requirements that govern action. Since advertising and promotion play such a significant part in the marketing of consumer goods, it is not surprising that consumer protection applies to these activities.

QUESTIONS

1   Identify and discuss the common methods used to
    protect consumer interests.

USEFUL WEBSITES

The Trading Standards Institute: **www.tradingstandards.gov.
uk/** The Trading Standards Institute encourages honest
enterprise and business and helps safeguard the
economic, environmental, health and social well-being
of consumers

Consumer Protection Agency: **www.
consumerprotectionagency.co.uk/**

Consumer Direct: **http://consumerdirect.gov.uk/** Consumer
Direct is the government-funded telephone and online service
offering information and advice on consumer issues

Office of Fair Trading: **www.oft.gov.uk/advice_and_
resources-old/small_businesses/protection** Information
for businesses on the Consumer Protection from Unfair
Trading Regulations

REFERENCES

Baines, P., Fill, C. and Page, K. (2008) 'Marketing', Oxford
University Press.

Dibb, S., Simkin, L., Pride, W. M. and Ferrell, O.C. (2006)
'Marketing: Concepts and Strategies', Ed. 5. Houghton
Mifflin International Inc.

Section Twelve
Production Management

PRODUCTION MANAGEMENT

MANUFACTURING EASTER EGGS

The Easter Egg market is one of the most exciting confectionary markets, with new ranges and presentations attracting more consumers every year. It also poses many challenges for manufacturers who must cope with seasonal demand, pressure to reduce packaging and processes that account for nut allergies. They must be innovative and flexible but at the same time focus on efficiency and cost. Sales of Easter Eggs in the UK are worth around £200m a year, equivalent to something like 80m eggs. Several products are associated with the Easter Egg. Making up a large portion of the market are egg shells. These hollow eggs may be sold empty or filled with chocolate assortments. Eggs may also be filled or packaged with non-confectionery products such as toys.

It is possible to make an Easter Egg at home from chocolate and an egg mould. The egg is made by first heating water in a pan (hot but not boiling); a dish half filled with chocolate is then allowed to stand in the water and stirred with a wooden spoon until it has melted. The molten chocolate is then ladled in until it is about one third full. The mould is then tilted in all directions until the chocolate covers the entire mould. Excess chocolate is tipped back into the bowl. Finally, the mould is placed into a fridge until it completely solidifies. Commercially manufactured eggs follow a similar production process. There are a number of Easter Egg manufacturers such as Cadbury, Nestle and Kinnerton.

Cadbury, now part of Kraft Foods was founded in 1824 when John Cadbury opened a shop in Birmingham, selling cocoa and chocolate. Since then the firm has expanded business throughout the world. The company employs around 50 000 people to make and sell confectionery. It operates in over 60 countries. They first manufactured Easter Eggs in 1875. Progress in the chocolate Easter Egg market was slow until a method was found for making the chocolate flow into the moulds. The modern chocolate Easter Egg owes its progression to the two greatest developments in the history of chocolate – the Dutch invention of a press for separating cocoa butter from the cocoa bean in 1828 and the introduction of pure cocoa by Cadbury Brothers in 1866. The Cadbury process made large quantities of cocoa butter available and this was the secret of making moulded chocolate or indeed, any fine eating chocolate. The launch in 1905 of Cadbury's Dairy Milk Chocolate made a tremendous contribution to the Easter Egg market. The popularity of this new chocolate vastly increased sales of Easter Eggs and establish them as seasonal best sellers. Principles of chocolate Easter Egg manufacturing haven't changed greatly over the years. Cadbury has always been at the forefront of machine design and commissions and produces Easter Eggs using highly efficient computer-operated technology. Liquid chocolate is deposited in moulds that are then rotated to achieve a uniform thickness. The eggs are then cooled and the two halves of the egg joined to produce the Easter Egg.

Kinnerton, established in 1978, is also a major UK manufacturer of confectionery. The company manufactures more than 16 million Easter Eggs a year (2009), ranging in all different sizes and shapes. The manufacture of Easter Eggs can be broken down into stages and optional sub processes. Manufacturers must source raw materials (including packaging), manage inventory, produce the confectionery items, foil items, package and subsequently assemble 'bundled' gifts. They will typically make use of a warehouse to store packaging and work-in-progress items. A picking process is used to select component parts to ship either to the packaging facility or to the factory. The eggs are made in the following stages: (1) deposit molten chocolate into the (half) mould shell, (tip upside down to remove excess chocolate for recycling); (2) remove eggs from the mould; (3) (join halves) and wrap in foil; (4) place eggs and extras into tray, then carton. Manufacturers operations differ in relation to the mould. Kinnerton use two moulds – chocolate is deposited into the inside and the two moulds are fixed together using magnets and then the mould and content are spun using machinery to achieve an even thickness of chocolate. The key difference between Kinnerton and Cadbury's is that Kinnerton form the egg before the chocolate hardens i.e. at the beginning of the process, resulting in less waste. Cadbury's make two halves (from the same single mould) and then 'stick' them together later.

Manufacturers must cope with several important challenges when producing Easter Eggs. Easter is probably the biggest seasonable output that Kinnerton have making around 30–40 million eggs per year; this is a significant task since production typically takes place approximately six weeks prior to consumption. Half of all eggs are sold in the four days before Easter and Easter Eggs typically have a limited 25 week shelf. However, perishability or exposure to high temperatures is an issue. Production related challenges also exist in the form of waste and quality management: manufacturers may choose more or less expensive ingredients and may have high numbers of rejects that have to be thrown away. Aside from sell-by dates, the manufacturer must consider additional product Health and Safety issues. Nearly two children in every 100 suffer from a nut allergy in the UK, and for some, even a slight exposure to nuts can kill. This issue has greater salience when we recognize Easter Eggs as confectionary for kids. In 2007 Chocolate giant Cadbury recalled Easter Eggs because they had the wrong nut allergy labelling. In 1999 Kinnerton created a nut Segregated Zone in their factory. There are many factory regimes in place to keep nuts out of their segregated factory. They operate a segregated warehouse, they have two different mould washing units to ensure that nut moulds and trays etc. do not contaminate non-nut moulds and trays; they have separate colour-coded engineering tools (again to stop contamination); utilize different equipment for each process, have separate development kitchens, first aid rooms, changing rooms, engineering shops as well as separate mixing rooms, preparation areas and packing lines. They also control the air flow and movement of people in the factory.

Acting responsibly, manufacturers must also be conscious of the fact that consumers are tired of excess packaging. Chocolate industry bosses have responded to calls to be more environmentally aware, by reducing all that unnecessary packaging surrounding the product. In 2009 companies such as Nestlé and Cadbury made significant reductions to the packaging of their Easter Eggs. Nestle announced that it was dropping the plastic containers that hold eggs in position on leading brands – making a 30 per cent reduction. Cadbury's has increased the number of eggs it sells without boxes, and claims to have cut other eggs' carton sizes by 25 per cent. Aside from packaging, manufacturers must source raw materials ethically and responsibly. Thousands of children have been found working as slave labour on West African cocoa farms to help produce Easter chocolate for the UK.

Sources:

1   www.cadbury.com and www.cadbury.com.au/About-Chocolate/The-Story-of-Easter-and-Easter-Eggs.aspx
2   www.kinnerton.com/business.html

CHAPTER 38
PRODUCTION PLANNING AND CONTROL

Key Concepts

- Just-in-time (JIT)
- Production process
- Purchasing

Learning Outcomes   Having read this chapter, you should be able to:

- list the basic elements of a typical production planning and control system
- explain why purchasing is an important part of production management
- explain material requirements planning (MRP)
- discuss the use of just-in-time systems in production operations
- evaluate the need for inspection and quality control throughout the production process

1.   There is a close relationship between marketing and operations (production). In the previous section we focussed on marketing and commented on satisfying the customer through products. We described product development in Chapter 32 paragraph 3 and noted the various stages leading up to production. Those products need to be manufactured or created. The production function of an organization exists in order to make available the goods or services required by the customer. There are several key elements in the production process, and this chapter sets out the main features of a production system.

Production process The way that businesses create products and services

2.   Greasley (2009) divides the subject of operations management into two distinct parts: design and management. In the design part he considers manufacturing process types (to be discussed in the next chapter), process technology (see Chapter 41) and process and work design (refer back to Chapter 21). He then turns his attention to the management of operations. Areas covered include operations planning and control, lean operations (see lean production) and just-in-time, enterprise resource planning and supply chain management. Such matters form the basis of this chapter. Other topics typically associated with operations include the Internet (see e-commerce and e-procurement), quality management and business process management. As these subjects have already been covered, to some degree, in other chapters, we will not engage in a detailed discussion about them here.

Lean production A term commonly used to refer to just-in-time production

38.1 OPERATIONS, PRODUCTION AND MANUFACTURING

3.   Production deals with activities involved in creating a product and the production process (aka transformation process or manufacturing) refers to the way that businesses create products and services; the use of machines, tools and labour to make things for use or sale. A broad definition of operations includes all the activities necessary for the fulfilment of customer requests, (Slack, Chambers, and Johnston, 2007). They suggest the broad responsibilities of operations management include the wider, long-term, ethical and strategic activities involved in producing products and services (the core activities of a business).

4.   Meredith and Shafer (2011) argue that operations should be considered at the heart of every organization; organizations exist to create value and operations involve tasks that create value. Two key themes are central to operations: customer satisfaction and competitiveness. Both of these themes were considered in the previous section on marketing. Operational improvements can lead to enhanced customer satisfaction and a reduction in costs. This is important since consumers purchase their products from the provider who offers the most value for money.

5.   Meredith and Shafer (2011) advise that we take a systems perspective when considering production. You may recall that we discussed organizations as systems in Chapters 9 and 10. Indeed Figure 9.3 The basic cycle of the organizational system, can be used as a template for the production system and a structure for this chapter. A production system is defined in terms of the environment, a strategy, a set of inputs, the transformation process, the outputs and some mechanism for controlling the overall system. The system perspective, as noted in Chapter 9, focuses on how the individual components interact. This enables us to see the complete picture and the relationship between various system parts. Without considering these relationships, decision makers are prone to a problem called sub optimization. Sub optimization occurs when one part of the system is improved to the detriment of other parts of the system and perhaps the organization as a whole.

6.   Thus, the traditional way to think about operations is as a transformation process which takes a set of inputs and transforms them in some way to create outputs (goods or services – offerings) valued by the customer. Inputs include the raw materials and the transformation process describes how they may be altered, transported, stored and inspected. The outputs from a production

process are the services and products offered to the customer. The control aspect of the system seeks to ensure that the outputs meet requirements and to identify areas for improvement and change.

Purchasing The organizational function, often part of the operations function, that forms contracts with suppliers to buy in materials and services

7. Operations includes not only those activities associated with the production system but also a variety of other activities, (Meredith and Shafer, 2011). For example, purchasing or procurement activities are involved when obtaining the inputs needed for the system. Similarly, shipping and distribution are sometimes considered marketing activities and sometimes considered operational activities. Because of the important interdependencies of these activities, many organizations are attempting to manage these activities as one process, commonly referred to as supply chain management (see previous section).

Procurement The act of getting possession of something from a supplier

38.2 PRODUCTION ORGANIZATION AND STRATEGY

8. Given the importance and size of operations it is important to organize, plan, coordinate and manage the function so it makes a valued contribution to organizational goals. Strategy was discussed in Chapter 16 where we focussed on corporate strategy but also introduced business and functional strategies (levels of strategy). Collier and Evans (2009) suggest that the operations strategy describes how an organization will execute its chosen business strategies. The operations strategy is the overall direction and contribution of the operation's function to the business; the way in which market requirements and operational resource capabilities are reconciled within the operation (Slack, Chambers and Johnston, 2007). Similarly, but more broadly, the operations and supply chain strategy is a functional strategy that indicates how structural and infrastructural elements within the operations and supply chain areas will be acquired and developed to support the overall business strategy, (Bozarth and Handfield, 2006).

9. Operations may contribute to strategy through its impact on quality, speed, dependability (in meeting delivery times to a customer), flexibility and cost. Approaches to operations strategy have changed over time. Historically there may have been an emphasis on high volume and low cost. More recently an emphasis has been placed on flexibility, speed and reliability. To be successful, an operations strategy should support the competitive advantage being pursued by the business strategy. Operations management are responsible for the planning, scheduling and control of the activities that transform inputs into finished goods and services.

Scheduling A term used in planning and control to indicate the detailed timetable of what work should be done, when it should be done and where it should be done

10. In Chapter 16 (and Chapter 10) we commented on the relationship between strategy and structure. Before we proceed further, it is helpful to consider the likely organization structure of the production function in a manufacturing organization. The organization chart in Figure 38.1 illustrates the principal divisions of labour within the function and provides an example of the structural relationships between the different departments or subunits.

11. The organization chart in Figure 38.1 represents just one of several ways in which production could be organized. Much depends on the type of production, the relative standing of groups such as Quality Control, Purchasing and Maintenance, and the extent to which sophisticated computerized systems are in operation. In the example shown, quality control is shared amongst three subunits: Manufacturing (as shopfloor Inspection), Production Planning and Control (as quality control of processes, materials and purchased items), and Production Engineering (responsible for quality of design and with overall responsibility for quality control standards in production).

Maintenance The activity of caring for physical facilities so as to avoid or minimize the chance of those facilities failing

FIGURE 38.1 Organization of the production function – manufacturing industry.

Production Director			
Manufacturing Manager	**Manager: Production Planning and Control**	**Technical Manager**	**Maintenance Manager**
Manufacturing Assembly Product Processing Inspection	Production Scheduling Purchasing Stores/Inventory Materials Planning Works Orders Progressing Quality Control	Research Design Development Quality Control Work Study Value Analysis	Machinery Plant Equipment Buildings

12. In the example given, the production function has been divided into four subunits or departments. There could have been a greater degree of specialization, but this has been avoided here in order to emphasize the collaborative nature of many of the specializms to be found in production. Brief observations that can be made about the four subunit management positions are as follows:

– Manufacturing Manager – this person is responsible for the manufacturing and assembly processes, together with their associated product processes; this work is carried out in accordance with works orders and schedules submitted by Production Planning and Control; inspection has been included here, although it could have been located separately to provide an independent inspection service; the Manufacturing Manager has a responsibility for the recruitment, training, rewarding and retention of employees;

– Manager, Production Planning and Control – this role is responsible for providing the framework and the impetus for production;

– Technical Manager or Production Engineer – the latter title is the more popular of the two, in practice, although the former is probably a better description of the role. The role is the first major link between Marketing and Production, being involved at the earliest possible stages of transforming customer needs and wants into practical possibilities; and

– Maintenance Manager – this role has been given considerable status in this example; it could have been placed in a subordinate position to the Manufacturing Manager, where it is frequently to be found.

The important point to remember is that all the subunits are needed if the production function is to meet its aim of providing the quality of goods required by its customers, and to do so in a way that meets the profit, growth and other objectives of the organization.

38.3 PRODUCTION PLANNING

13. Thus far we have stated what is incorporated within operations and operations management; we have discussed the relationship between the operations strategy and the corporate and

business strategies and finally we have briefly discussed the organization and structure of operations. In the remaining paragraphs of this chapter we focus on operations activities and processes – the work they do. Planning and control is about matching customer demand to the operations capacity. As we know, demand is not always easily predicted however. There are a number of ways of dealing with unstable demand. One way is to produce the product or service in advance (see make-to-stock, a push strategy). A different way is referred to as make-to-order (a pull strategy). Make-to-stock (MTS) products require no customization. They are typically generic products and are produced in large enough volumes to justify keeping a finished goods inventory. Products customized only at the very end of the manufacturing process are termed assemble- or finish-to-order (ATO) products. Make-to-order (MTO) products are products that use standard components, but the final configuration of those components is customer-specific (e.g. a Dell computer). Finally, products that are designed and produced from the start to meet unusual customer needs or requirements are called engineer-to-order (ETO) products. They represent the highest level of customization. When customization occurs early in the supply chain, organizations have more flexibility to respond to customer needs but costs increase and lead times lengthen. When customization occurs late in the supply chain, flexibility is limited but lead times and cost may be less.

14.   Operations planning is concerned with taking actions, such as ensuring resources are in place, in anticipation of future events. The basic elements of a typical production planning and control system can be summarized as follows:

- Translate the customer's requirements, as defined by the final pre-production design and preliminary sales forecasts, into production instructions (works orders).

- Prepare production schedules and software programs (where applicable).

- Plan the supply of materials, parts, components, etc.

- Plan availability of machines, specify jobs, tools, etc.

- Allocate people/work-teams.

- Set production and quality targets.

- Maintain stock and purchasing records.

- Progress orders throughout the factory.

- Liaise with the marketing department.

- Raise final production documents (delivery notes, invoices, etc.).

15.   There are several important points arising from the above summary of a production planning and control system:

- The plans referred to are short-term plans for periods of from one week to one month. At the start of a new production process, these plans may be altered at frequent intervals.

- Production schedules are basically timetables, usually of a detailed nature. They specify the timetabled requirements for precise operations and jobs, and set out the sequence of priorities, including the setting up of appropriate software programs. The major aims of scheduling are to ensure, so far as possible, that the work is completed on time and within budgeted costs. Wide use is made of Gantt charts in production scheduling. These are particularly useful for the scheduling of relatively straightforward, routine projects.

- Plans for machines include the availability, capacity and loading of machines.

- Labour requirements are a vital part of the production process (numbers and types of employees required, pay and incentives, training and safety).

- All plans should set targets and will take into account considerations such as planned maintenance, product quality control and machine breakdowns.

- The progressing of orders through the production process is essentially a monitoring and reporting task, which also involves some 'chasing-up' of progress in situations where orders have fallen behind schedule. The main role of a progress chaser is to identify and report any deviations from schedule, and provide help in sorting out delays in production.

- Liaison with the marketing department is important to ensure that the productive effort is meeting the customer's needs, or where there are difficulties in production, ensuring that the customer is informed and/or is prepared to accept a slightly different standard or quality of product, for example.

- Finally, the outputs of the production system need to be accounted for, invoiced and delivered (to the customer or into stock). Thus the final step is to ensure the appropriate information systems are updated.

38.4 SOURCING STRATEGIES, PURCHASING (PROCUREMENT) AND INVENTORY MANAGEMENT

16.   Earlier we noted that the production system relied upon inputs (raw materials etc.). Each organization will consider whether or not to make or buy the raw materials and inputs. High-level, often strategic decisions regarding which products or services will be provided internally and which will be provided by external supply chain partners are referred to as sourcing (make-or-buy) decisions. Insourcing concerns the use of resources within the organization to provide products or services as opposed to outsourcing where supply chain partners provide products or services. Such decisions are not without consequences. Insourcing provides for greater control and opportunity for scale advantages but may require high levels of investment and a loss of access to superior products. Outsourcing may enhance flexibility, improve cash flow and allow access to state-of-the-art products and services but creates communication and coordination challenges, reduces control and introduces the possibility of selecting an ineffective supplier.

17.   Purchasing concerns the activities associated with identifying needs, locating and selecting suppliers, negotiating terms and following up to ensure supplier performance. Sourcing may take place within or outside the home country. Global sourcing is the process of identifying, evaluating negotiating and configuring supply across multiple geographies. When evaluating global sourcing opportunities, the organization should consider the purchase price, transportation costs, inventory carrying costs, cross-border taxes, tariffs and duty costs, supply performance and risks. Operations may also seek to ensure they only deal with ethical suppliers.

18.   Purchasing is an important aspect of production management. Purchasing costs, for example, often represent a substantial part of the total costs of production. At a time of extreme competitiveness in the marketplace, an efficient and cost-effective purchasing section can make all the difference between a competitively priced product and one that is comparatively more expensive. The primary responsibility of the purchasing/procurement department is to secure sufficient and suitable raw materials, components, other goods and services to ensure that the manufacturing process is fully supplied with all its materials, and to achieve this responsibility in a cost-effective and timely manner. To this end the purchasing department can usually be expected to be responsible for the following:

- Appraisal and selection of and maintaining good relationships with suppliers.

- Collation of up-to-date information on suppliers, prices, distribution methods, etc.

- Negotiating the purchase of goods and services at prices which represent the best value to the business in the long-term (i.e. not necessarily the lowest prices at a given time).

- Ensuring that suppliers are familiar with, and adhere to, relevant quality standards operated by the company.

- Maintenance of adequate stock/inventory levels.

19. The Purchasing Manager exercises responsibilities in close collaboration with other colleagues. For example, most purchasing decisions can only be taken after due agreement with financial, production or marketing colleagues. If a decision is made to proceed with a purchase, then the sequence of events (procurement process) could follow these lines:

- Purchasing receives a requisition from an appropriate authority.

- They then approach a selected supplier to negotiate quantity, quality, price and delivery of goods.

- The next stage will be to seek an alternative supplier if a satisfactory agreement cannot be reached, or to place an order with the supplier.

- Purchasing maintains records of orders made, orders fulfilled, delivery dates, invoices, etc.

- Purchasing arranges for the originating requisition to be met, either directly from the supplier or via stores, and amends its stock or delivery records as appropriate.

20. The negotiating skills required of those in the purchasing function are likely to be crucial elements in a company's ability to produce quality goods at a competitive price. In the purchase of material goods, issues of quantity, quality, price and delivery are crucial in several respects. These could be described as the key elements of the 'purchasing mix'. Each item of the mix is described below:

- QUANTITY. The quantity of goods to be ordered, and the time at which they need to be ordered, are major (inventory management) considerations. On the one hand insufficient quantities at a particular point in time will cause costly delays in production. On the other hand, the larger the quantity ordered, the more will have to go into stock as temporarily idle resources, also a costly business. The ideal to be aimed at is to find the optimum way of balancing the costs of insufficient stock against the costs of holding stock (e.g. tied-up capital, storage space, insurance costs, damage, deterioration, etc.). Techniques have been devised by operational research scientists to enable organizations to work out the **Economic Order Quantity (EOQ)** for individual stock items, and to aid them in setting optimum re-order levels (i.e. the levels at which stock needs to be replaced). In some cases, the decision about quantity (and indeed time) may be dictated by considerations of future supply, particularly where these may be threatened by economic or political pressures. Decisions may also be influenced by favourable trends in short-term prices.

  > **Economic order quantity (EOQ)** The order size that minimizes the total cost of ordering and carrying inventory

- QUALITY. The quality of the goods purchased needs to be suitable (a) for the manufacturing process, and (b) for the customer's wants. In seeking decisions about quality, the purchasing department have to work closely with both production and marketing employees to arrive at a suitable compromise. Inspection of goods received is vital to check that the supplier is fulfilling the order to the correct specification.

- PRICE. Purchasing should ideally aim for a price which gives the best value to the organization, taking quality, delivery and relative urgency into account. This may not always be the lowest price available, but the one which represents the best value over a period of time.

- DELIVERY. One of the factors which needs to be considered by the purchasing department in the appraisal and selection of suppliers is the reliability of deliveries. The lead time between an order and a delivery is an important aspect of stock control. Where lead times are certain, they can be allowed for in stock calculations. Where they are uncertain, it makes stock control much more difficult. Not only is stock affected by the delivery situation, so is production. The latter is particularly vulnerable to delays in deliveries for items which are used continuously, and for which minimum buffer stocks are held. Buffer stocks are reserve stocks held for emergency shortages.

21.   Several aspects of stock control have already been mentioned above, and these can be drawn together in a simplified graph of stock levels. Such graphs have a typically saw-tooth pattern, reflecting the outputs (usage) and the inputs (deliveries) to stock, as in Figure 38.2. The Figure indicates how usage reduces stocks over a period of time, and invariably absorbs some of the buffer stock, unless planned deliveries are made on time. The lead time, as shown, is the time taken between the order being made and delivery taking place. As soon as the delivery is made, stocks shoot up again, until further usage reduces them, and this produces the saw-tooth effect on the graph. Should planned deliveries not take place, and should usage continue, then eventually a 'stockout' situation will be reached, where, in the short-term, the goods in question will be out-of-stock.

FIGURE 38.2   Simple stock control graph

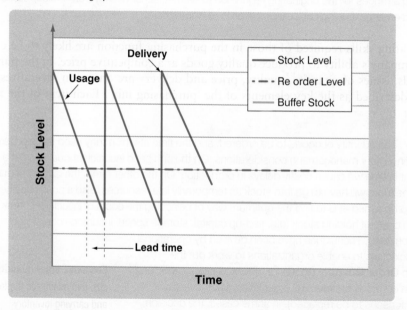

22.   Meredith and Shafer (2011:264) suggest organizations that are highly effective in supply chain management purchasing seem to follow three practices: (1) leverage their buying power- i.e. they typically centralize many aspects of procurement in order to gain benefits from scale and purchasing power; (2) they commit to a small number of dependable suppliers and (3) they will help suppliers reduce their total cost of production which is of mutual benefit.

38.5 ENTERPRISE RESOURCE PLANNING, MRP AND JIT

23.   In the previous paragraphs we discussed inventory management from the perspective of procurement. Inventory management can be considered part of materials management (the movement of materials within the organization) i.e. the acquiring of inventory (procurement), the movement of inventory (physical distribution) and decisions about how much to order and when. Inventory management systems calculate the volume and timing of demand items. As was

mentioned in the marketing section, inventory management is important because it affects both customer service and costs.

24. **Material requirements planning (MRP)** is an internal production process designed to ensure that materials (i.e. raw materials, components, sub-assemblies and parts) are available when required. The process is closely linked both to production planning and purchasing, which provide the context for MRP decisions. The starting point for MRP is the master schedule of production plans from which the process works backwards to develop both a timetable for deliveries and an optimum quantity of the required materials. By adopting MRP, manufacturing plants hope to achieve relatively low levels of stocks (inventory), a reduction in warehousing and associated costs and a faster turnaround time for finished goods. Once set up, the process lends itself to computerization, which in turn enables other functions such as ordering and purchasing to be linked (integrated) into the system. Such a system presupposes the existence of adequate production schedules, the support of a purchasing section and agreement about the quality aspects of materials. Scheduling is the allocation of a start and finish time to each order whilst taking into account the loading and sequencing policies employed (Greasley, 2009). Computer-based information systems such as enterprise resource planning (ERP) software provide great assistance not only to the operations manager but to many functions of the organization. We consider such systems in more detail in Chapter 41.

> **Material requirements planning (MRP)** A planning process (usually computerized) that integrates production, purchasing and inventory management of interrelated products

> **Master production schedule (MPS)** The important schedule that forms the main input to material requirements planning, it contains a statement of the volume and timing of the end products to be made

25. **Just-in-time (JIT)** systems represent a good step forward from MRP, since, unlike the latter, they aim to coordinate the supply of materials so they arrive just when they are needed – not before, not afterwards, but just in time! In theory, the system should lead to no stocks (buffer stocks/reserves) being held; in practice, it minimizes them (in contrast to MRP which aims to optimize stock levels). Like the rigorous approach to quality embodied in total quality control (see Chapter 29), JIT systems require total commitment from the workforce and its suppliers – there is no room for errors such as faulty components, delays in delivery, etc. The JIT approach is based on the twin assumptions of (1) uninterrupted production flows, and (2) fully acceptable quality of materials. It works best in a stable production environment, and, of course, relies heavily on the efficiency of suppliers and their dedication to total quality. The benefits claimed for JIT systems include cost savings through reduced inventories, reduction in manufacturing time, increased equipment utilisation, simplified planning and scheduling, improved quality and reduced scrap and wastage.

> **Just-in-time (JIT)** Methods of managing inventory (stock) whereby items are delivered when needed in the production process instead of being stored by the manufacturer

38.6 INSPECTION, MONITORING, CONTROLLING AND MAINTENANCE

26. Thus far we have described various aspects of operations, focussing on planning and materials management (the inputs) in particular. We described the production system, noting that inputs are then transformed, through manufacturing and operations, to outputs – the goods and services. Manufacturing processes are discussed in the next chapter; for now we move on to consider the next part of the production system – control. Operations control seeks to ensure that the actual behaviour of the operations (production) system conforms to that required. Of particular concern is the control of quality (refer back to Chapters 28–29). This control begins with inspection of raw materials, continues with inspection during production, and ends with a final inspection before delivery to the customer. The responsibility for checking quality on the

shop-floor is usually that of the inspection department, whose main task is to ensure adherence to the organization's quality standard. These standards are normally set with several objectives in mind:

- to turn out products which are satisfactory to the customer (quality, reliability, variety, etc.)

- to turn out products in a safe and socially responsible manner and

- to attain the above within agreed levels of inspection and quality control costs.

27. The cost of ensuring quality is twofold: direct costs, such as the wages and salaries of designers and inspectors, and indirect costs, such as the loss of orders, wastage and rectification costs. Some of these costs are directed towards preventing faults and errors, other are directed towards curing faults and errors. In inspection there are three main reasons for inspecting work:

- to accept or reject items

- to control the process of producing the items

- to improve the process itself, if necessary.

Process control systems These systems deal with the large volume of data generated by production processes

28. There are two main methods of dealing with these issues, and these are Process Control and Acceptance Sampling, which are examples of what has been called 'Statistical Quality Control'. Process Control consists of checking items as they progress through the production process, comparing them with the relevant standards, and taking any immediate corrective action to prevent further faults. Process Control may be expedited by the use of control charts, which can show, in graph form, actual performance against standard performance, and the amount of any deviation. Another form of process control is automatic process control, where sensing and other measuring devices are built into the machine concerned – to provide immediate information and immediate corrective action. Automatic inspection of this kind is more feasible than human inspection in cases where (a) accurate measurement is possible, (b) where continuous inspection is highly desirable and (c) where reliability of inspection is important. Objective measurement in inspection is called checking by variables, which contrasts with checking by attributes, which is a subjective method. Acceptance sampling consists of taking a random sample from a larger batch or lot of material to be inspected. The quality of the sample is assumed to reflect the overall quality of the lot (Greasley, 2009).

29. Having described the production system we finally turn our attention to maintenance – the activity of caring for physical facilities, systems and equipment (transformational resources) so as to avoid or minimize the chance of the system failing. Maintenance seeks to assure that production has the optimum availability of plant and machinery in the conduct of its operations, and that, if an unexpected breakdown occurs, it will be dealt with in the minimum possible time. There are several different kinds of maintenance, which may be preventive or corrective. The operations manager will adopt a planned programme of maintenance for each major piece of plant, building, system or machine. Planned maintenance means that routine servicing and overhaul arrangements are scheduled in advance and contingency plans drawn up for unexpected breakdowns. The effect of having planned maintenance is to minimize unforeseen faults or breakdowns. Thus maintenance can make an important contribution to containing machine running costs as well as ensuring optimum machine availability.

CONCLUSION

30.   There is a close relationship between marketing and operations (production) – the production function of an organization exists in order to make available the goods or services required by the customer. It is common to take a systems perspective when considering production. A production system is defined in terms of the environment, a strategy, a set of inputs, the transformation process, the outputs and some mechanism for controlling the overall system. Thus, the traditional way to think about operations is as a transformation process which takes a set of inputs and transforms them, in some way, to create outputs (goods or services – offerings) valued by the customer. Inputs include the raw materials and the transformation process describes how they may be altered, transported, stored and inspected. The outputs from a production process are the services and products offered to the customer. The control aspect of the system seeks to ensure that the outputs meet requirements and to identify areas for improvement and change. The operations and supply chain strategy is a functional strategy that indicates how structural and infrastructural elements within the operations and supply chain areas will be acquired and developed to support the overall business strategy. Operations may contribute to strategy through its impact on quality, speed, dependability (in meeting delivery times to a customer), flexibility and cost.

QUESTIONS

1   Describe what is meant by Make-to-stock and Make-to-order – what are the advantages and disadvantages of each?

2   Discuss operations management (production manufacturing) from a systems perspective. What are the benefits of reviewing operations in this way?

3   Evaluate how operations may contribute to strategy.

4   Discuss what is meant by operations planning then list and describe the basic elements of a typical production planning and control system.

5   Explain why purchasing is an important aspect of production management.

6   Identify and describe the key elements of the purchasing mix.

7   Discuss the importance of materials and stock control to production commenting on materials resource planning and just-in-time systems.

USEFUL WEBSITES

The association of Operations Management: **www.apics.org** Various OM resources/news
Institute for Operations Management: **www.iomnet.org.uk** OM in the UK
European Operations Management Association: **www.euroma-online.org** Information on publications etc.

Manufacturing Institute: **www.manufacturinginstitute.co.uk** News and events in the UK
Institute for Operations Research and Management Sciences: **www.informs.org** Resources, links, journals

VIDEO CASES

Now take a look at the online video cases – visit the companion website to work through real world business problems associated with the concepts presented within this chapter.

24 Costco operations
MANAGING PRODUCTION
LOGISTICS AND THE SUPPLY CHAIN

53 Lean LG
Investigates South Korean-based LG Electronics who build flat-panel televisions. The case (film) considers LG's hi-tech production plant and processes, focussing on lean operating systems in response to the demands of the external environment.

55 Managing capacity Nissan cuts production
Focus is on use of available resources for ongoing operations when demand fluctuates – short range (six to 24 month) capacity decisions.

65 Lean enterprise Boeing 737 manufacturing Lean Production System
Assembling a 737 is a complex job. Factory employees must take 367 000 parts, an equal number of bolts, rivets and other fasteners and 36 miles (58 kilometres) of electrical wire then put them all together to form an airplane. Production methods have evolved enormously since the first 737 was made in 1966. The main difference is that instead of the aircraft being assembled in one spot (static production bays – traditional manufacture) they are now on a moving assembly line similar to that used in car production. Since the late 1990s the company has continuously improved production, becoming a lean enterprise. This case can be used to show what a lean enterprise may look like.

54 Managing quality inside a frozen pizza factory
Investigates how quality is managed in the production of frozen pizza.

REFERENCES

Barnes, D. (2008) 'Operations Management An International Perspective', Cengage Learning EMEA.

Bozarth, C. and Handfield, R. (2006) 'Introduction to Operations and Supply Chain Management with Advanced Decision Support Tools', Prentice Hall.

Chapman, S. N. (2006) 'The Fundamentals of Production Planning and control', Pearson Prentice Hall.

Greasley, A. (2009) 'Operations Management', Ed. 2. Wiley.

Meredith, J. R. and Shafer, S. M. (2011) 'Operations Management', Ed. 4. John Wiley & Sons.

Slack, N., Chambers, S. and Johnston, R. (2007) 'Operations Management', Ed. 5. Financial Times Press.

CHAPTER 39
TYPES OF
PRODUCTION

Key Concepts

- Batch manufacturing
- Flow shop processes
- Jobbing processes
- Mass processes
- Production process

Learning Outcomes   Having read this chapter, you should be able to:

- distinguish between types of production and production systems
- explain jobbing production
- list the key characteristics of batch production
- list the key characteristics of mass production

1.   Primary activities and core organizational processes aim to produce the goods and services customers desire. Collectively, such activities add value; transforming materials into finished goods. In the previous chapter we described the production system and identified the transformational process as one part of the production system. This chapter builds upon previous chapters, focusing on the transformational processes. The chapter examines how the organization may undertake interrelated activities and processes associated with making and supplying goods and services. Several types of production process are described as alternatives for operations. Each is evaluated and strengths/weaknesses considered.

> **Production process** The way that businesses create products and services

39.1 PRODUCTION PROCESSES

2.   The way businesses create products and services is known as the production process. Ultimately, the objective of the production process is to create goods and services that meet customer requirements. The needs of customers will be met if a business can produce the correct number of products, in the shortest possible time, to the best quality and at low cost.

3.   Two sets of resources are needed – the transforming resources (the facilities, machinery, technology and people to carry out the transforming processes), and the raw material inputs (transformed resources). At each stage, value is added in the course of production. Adding value involves making a product more attractive to a consumer so they will pay more for it. Adding value is not restricted to operations, but may relate to all supply chain processes such as marketing, etc. which make the final product more desirable. There are several key types of production process – project, job shop, batch, assembly line and continuous flow. We consider the production processes in more detail next.

> **Job shop** A type of (flexible) manufacturing process used to make a wide variety of highly customized products in quantities as small as one

> **Batch manufacturing** A type of manufacturing process where items are moved through the different manufacturing steps in groups, or batches

39.2 JOBBING AND PROJECT-BASED PRODUCTION

4.   The essential feature of jobbing production is that it produces single articles or 'one-off' items. These products may be small, tailor-made components, huge pieces of equipment or large single items, such as a ship. Most products are made for a particular customer or to a particular order. Jobbing production is to be found in industries such as heavy engineering (e.g. production of electricity generating plant), shipbuilding and civil engineering (e.g. bridge construction). It is also to be found in most other industries, where it is employed to produce prototype models, spare parts, modifications to existing plant and countless other 'one-off', tailor-made pieces.

5.   Within jobbing production, because of the unique or individual nature of each article or item to be produced, planning is not easy and neither is control. Efficiency of operations has to give way to inventiveness and creativity. This can be illustrated by considering some of the key characteristics of jobbing production. These are as follows:

-   A wide variety of different operations to be performed under varying circumstances, i.e. no standardization.

-   Varying sequences of operations, also subject to varying circumstances.

- General-purpose machinery and equipment.
- Varied work layouts, depending on process and/or operation.
- Unpredictable demands on stores.
- Workforce with broad skill range.
- Adaptable and equally skilled supervision.

6.   Many of the above conditions make it extremely difficult to plan, integrate and control the types, sequence and timing of operations. It is difficult to avoid idle time for both employees and machines. Thus the entire manufacturing process tends to be relatively expensive compared with other forms of production. Against this can be weighed the advantages of producing an article or item which is made especially to the customer's own specification.

39.3 BATCH PRODUCTION

7.   Batch production is the production of standardized units, or parts, in small or large lots (batches). It represents a halfway position between jobbing production and mass production. The main distinction between batch and jobbing production lies in the standardized nature of the former. Unlike the varied operations and sequences of the unique 'one-off' products of jobbing production, the products of batch production are dealt with systematically in lots, or batches, only moving on to the next operation when each lot has been machined or processed in the current operation.

8.   Batches may be produced to order and forwarded direct to the customer, as in the production of subcomponents for another manufacturer, or they may be made for stock. One of the major problems associated with batch production is to determine the optimum size of batches, particularly where a generalized rather than specific demand for a product exists. If too many units are produced, stocks will lie idle or go to waste; if too few are produced, the item will go out of stock, and it may be difficult to fit in further batches in the short-term.

9.   The key characteristics of batch production are as follows:

- A standardized set of operations, carried out intermittently, as each batch moves from one operation to the next.
- General purpose machinery and plant, but grouped in batteries of the same type.
- Heavy shop-floor stores requirement.
- Narrower range of skills required.
- Emphasis on production planning and progressing.
- Relatively short **production runs**.

Production run Completion of all tasks is associated with a production order

These characteristics lead to a generally well controlled and efficient method of production, whose main disadvantage is the time-delay caused by the queuing effect of individual units waiting for the batch to be completed before moving on to the next operation. This problem can be overcome by changing to an assembly line operation which is a prominent feature of flow production, or mass production, as it is commonly called.

39.4 MASS AND CONTINUOUS PRODUCTION

10.   Mass production dates from the time of Henry Ford, who was the first man to adopt the principle of the production line, when he used this approach to produce a restricted range of motor cars constructed in a flow-line process. In a unit mass production system, a small range of products is produced in large quantities by 'flowing' uninterruptedly from one operation, or process, to the next, until completion. This type of production requires careful and lengthy planning of plant and processes. The capital costs are high on account of the specialized nature of the machines required for the production line. However, once the line has been established, control is relatively simple. Mass production systems are dependent on the high demand created by mass markets, for it is only by making the fullest use of the capital equipment involved that a manufacturing organization can achieve its target profit levels.

11.   The key features of mass production are as follows:

–   Rigid product specifications, previously tested.

–   Specialized machines and equipment, set out in a line formation.

–   Highly standardized methods, tools and materials.

–   Long production runs for individual products.

–   Narrow range of skills, and specified range of operations required by workforce at any one point in the line.

12.   In purely rational terms, mass production is the most efficient way of producing large quantities of articles or items. Control can be exercised to a sophisticated level because of the standardized nature of the entire process. Its greatest drawback is that it requires human beings to adapt themselves to the production process, and in most western countries, there has been a reaction against this requirement. Employees are seeking to counteract the tedium and monotony of the highly specialized work patterns in mass production by pressing for more integrated roles, requiring a wider range of skills and operations.

13.   Another form of mass production, usually called flow production or process production, can be seen in continuous process industries such as steel-making, paper-making and cement production. In such industries the products literally flow from one process to the next, but, unlike in the mass production of individual products, this process is continuous for weeks or months on end. In flow processes, the supply of raw materials has to be planned to the highest standards in order to avoid complete plant shutdown owing to unforeseen shortages. In these situations, shortages have a much more serious effect than in unit mass production. Fortunately, the control mechanisms and procedures for flow processes are usually so sophisticated that the processes become automatically self-regulating. Another important difference between this form of mass production and unit mass production is that the former invariably requires a lower labour force than the latter.

39.5 SELECTING THE PROCESS

14.   Having discussed types of production process we now consider how the organization determines the optimal process. Process selection is influenced by product variety and volume. Generally, a job shop process is used in support of differentiation strategies and flow shops are used to support cost based strategies. Other factors also influence process selection. Cost of labour,

Flow shop processes Organized around a fixed sequence of activities and process steps, such as an assembly line to produce a limited variety of similar goods or services

technology and facilities, energy and transportation may be considered. Furthermore, the stage of the product lifecycle may be taken into consideration. A job shop may be more appropriate early in the product's lifecycle but at maturity, when higher volumes are required, an assembly line may be more appropriate. Service processes vary also, with some devoted to producing knowledge-based or advice-based services, usually involving high customer contact and high customization, (such as management consultants) and those with a high number of transactions, often involving limited customization, for example call centres.

CONCLUSION

15.   This brief chapter has sought to describe the main features of the basic types of production systems – jobbing, batch and mass production. Jobbing production refers to the production of unique or 'one-off' items, made to order. These items may be small or large, and they are produced under the appropriate conditions at a given time, rather than conditions which are standardized. Both planning and control are difficult to achieve in this form of production. Batch production refers to the production of standardized units in batches, or lots. Only when a batch has completed one process can it be moved to the next. Batches may be produced to order, or for stock. Batch production can be relatively well planned and controlled, but queuing problems may arise when batches are ready to move on to the next operation. These problems can be overcome by utilizing assembly lines, i.e. moving over to a mass production method. Mass production refers to the production of vast quantities of product units in a flowline process, where each flows smoothly from one operation, or process, to the next until completion. Where the mass production of continuous processes is concerned, the method is called flow production or process production. Mass production methods call for detailed planning and sophisticated control procedures. There is very little scope for the exercise of skills by the workforce, and the flowline layout has been challenged in several quarters.

QUESTIONS

1   With reference to production processes distinguish between types of production and production systems.

2   Explain how the organization determines the optimal production process.

USEFUL WEBSITES

The Institute of Operations Management (IOM): **www.iomnet.org.uk/** OM learning resources
Technology & Operations Management: **www.sussex.ac.uk/ Users/dt31/TOMI/whatisom.html**

The portal provides information on a wide range of topics within the technology and operations management field, such as purchasing, product development, innovation management, manufacturing strategy, inventory control, logistics, quality and service operations

VIDEO CASES

Now take a look at the online video cases – visit the companion website to work through real world business problems associated with the concepts presented within this chapter.

51 Operations processes at the Cadbury's factory
What is an Easter egg? It is a chocolate egg, perhaps accompanied by some mini chocolate bars or truffles. Often it is a combination of these items with vividly-coloured, glossy card, a plastic box and shiny foil, all jumbled into one seductive whole. This case considers how Easter eggs are made at the Cadbury's factory in Bournville, Birmingham – the case focuses on operations and the production process.

54 Managing quality inside a frozen pizza factory
Investigates how quality is managed in the production of frozen pizza.

132 Process design and analysis at Dell
The challenges of the global external environment, through strategies, drive organizations to search out ways to reduce costs, deliver the products and services customers need and when they need them. This forces a focus on efficiency and effectiveness. In this case we focus on how work is organized

and performed within the organization. Our focus on how work is performed will be illuminated through an exploration of business processes. We identify what business processes are and how they are designed and managed. The success of any organization depends upon the performance of each of the three elements which comprise the organization: its products and services, i.e. its deliverables; business processes and the fabric which supports them, and people, i.e. its employees and suppliers (Jones, 1994). Processes are the essential link between customer or client requirements and the delivery of products or services. They are the means whereby the organization and its employees fulfil their purpose or 'mission'. Work activities transform inputs into outputs (products and services) for the benefit of customers, adding value along the way; a collection of related work tasks and activities is typically labelled as a business process. Such processes may be operational, management or supportive. Well-designed processes are both effective and efficient and contribute to organizational capabilities. Dell is a large sized international company through which issues of managing processes are presented for students to engage with.

REFERENCES

Collier, D. and Evans, J. (2009) 'OM', Ed. 1. Cengage Learning.
Kelly, P. P. (2009) 'International Business and Management', Cengage Learning EMEA.

Slack, N., Chambers, S. and Johnston, R. (2007) 'Operations Management', Ed. 5. Financial Times Press.

CHAPTER 40
AIDS TO PRODUCTION

Key Concepts

- Quality circles
- Value analysis
- Value engineering
- Work study

Learning Outcomes   Having read this chapter, you should be able to:

- list the reasons why work study techniques are utilized in production
- explain the 'method study' technique
- explain the 'work measurement' technique
- list the typical stages of value analysis
- evaluate quality circles

1. This chapter outlines the key features of three aids to production management – **work study**, **value analysis** or **value engineering** and **quality circles**. They may all have application elsewhere, but in the paragraphs which follow they are considered in terms of their contribution to production.

40.1 WORK STUDY

2. Work study was developed in American industry in the 1920s. The first known attempts to make a rational assessment of work and tasks were made by Taylor and the other 'scientific managers', whose ideas were described earlier, in Chapter 3. Since their time, work study has become an established part of the industrial scene. Work study has been defined as a term describing several techniques for examining work in all its contexts, in particular those factors affecting economy and efficiency, with a view to making improvements; the two most common techniques of work study are method study and work measurement. Explained more simply, work study means measuring the performance of jobs through two elements: method study and work measurement, (Greasley, 2009).

3. The two basic techniques are complementary to each other, and are rarely utilized in isolation from each other. The usual practice is for a method study of some kind to precede a work measurement activity. Each technique will be described in outline shortly. The reasons why work study techniques are utilized in production include the following; to:

- eliminate wasteful work
- improve working methods
- increase production
- achieve cost savings and
- improve productivity of workers and machines.

Work study A term describing several techniques for examining work in all its contexts, in particular those factors affecting economy and efficiency, with a view to making improvements; the two most common techniques of Work Study are Method Study and Work Measurement. (See also Method Study and Work Measurement)

Value analysis A term used to describe an analytical approach to the function and costs of every part of a product with a view to reducing costs whilst retaining the functional ability; sometimes known as value engineering

Value engineering An approach to cost reduction in product design that examines the purpose of a product or service, its basic functions and its secondary functions

Quality circles These are meetings of group of workers committed to continuous improvement in the quality and productivity of a given line of production

40.2 METHOD STUDY

4. This technique is itself composed of a collection of systematic techniques, all of which examine and record existing and proposed methods utilized in an operation or process, with a view to increasing efficiency. It could be said that method study attempts to answer the questions what? when? how? who? and where? in contrast to work measurement's emphasis, which asks how long? and when? The scope of method study, therefore, is considerably wider than that of work measurement.

5. Method study is used to aid solutions to a variety of production problems. These problems include those of workplace layout, materials handling, tool design, product design and process design for example. The basic approach of a method study is illustrated in a simplified diagram (Figure 40.1).

FIGURE 40.1 **Method Study: an outline.**

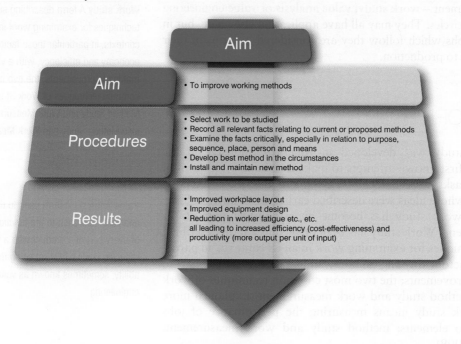

Aim	• To improve working methods
Procedures	• Select work to be studied • Record all relevant facts relating to current or proposed methods • Examine the facts critically, especially in relation to purpose, sequence, place, person and means • Develop best method in the circumstances • Install and maintain new method
Results	• Improved workplace layout • Improved equipment design • Reduction in worker fatigue etc., etc. all leading to increased efficiency (cost-effectiveness) and productivity (more output per unit of input)

Flowchart A pictorial summary that shows, with symbols and words, the steps, sequence and relationship of the various activities involved in the performance of a process

6. The procedures noted in the diagram are the vehicle for a rational analysis of working methods. Firstly, the target operation or process is selected. If a choice has to be made between priorities for attention, the likelihood is that the activity having the biggest impact upon costs will be selected, since if this can be improved, some real savings will be achieved. Secondly, a thorough examination of all the pertinent facts is made. Much of the data collected for a method study is presented in a **flowchart** form, which utilizes a standard set of symbols for all the basic activities and operations. The symbols are as shown in Figure 40.2.

FIGURE 40.2 **Flowchart symbols.**

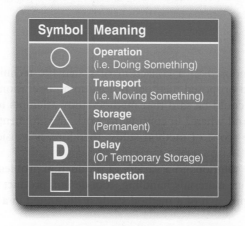

Symbol	Meaning
◯	**Operation** (i.e. Doing Something)
→	**Transport** (i.e. Moving Something)
△	**Storage** (Permanent)
D	**Delay** (Or Temporary Storage)
▢	**Inspection**

7. A simple flowchart records the activities in the order in which they occur, assigns the appropriate symbol to each activity, notes the elapsed time taken for each activity and adds any comments that may be useful. Thus the recording of facts for a method study is a very detailed business. The third step in the procedure is to examine critically the data obtained, even to the extent of questioning the very purpose of an activity. 'Is this activity necessary?' 'Is this the most economical sequence of events in the process?' 'What are the alternative ways of conducting this operation?' These and other questions can help the person conducting the study to produce a best method of working, taking all the circumstances into account. If this new method is approved, the final stages are implementation and subsequent maintenance and review.

40.3 WORK MEASUREMENT

8. This is a collection of techniques, particularly time study, aimed at establishing the time taken by a qualified worker to complete a specified job at a defined level of performance. As mentioned above, work measurement techniques set out to answer the questions How long? And when? They usually follow or overlap with a method study, and are employed not only to improve methods of working, but also to develop costing systems, production schedules and incentive schemes, as well as to establish machine capacities and manning levels.

> **Time study** A term used in work measurement to indicate the process of timing (usually with a stopwatch) and rating jobs, it involves observing times, adjusting or normalizing each observed time (rating) and averaging the adjusted times

Like method study, work measurement has a systematic set of procedures to be followed, and these are set out below. When work measurement is linked into a method study, it is introduced at the 'DEVELOP best method' stage, as shown in Figure 40.1. The basic steps in work measurement are as follows in Figure 40.3.

9. It can be seen from Figure 40.3 that the aim of work measurement is significantly different from that of method study. The latter aims to improve working methods; the former aims to

FIGURE 40.3 **Work Measurement: an outline.**

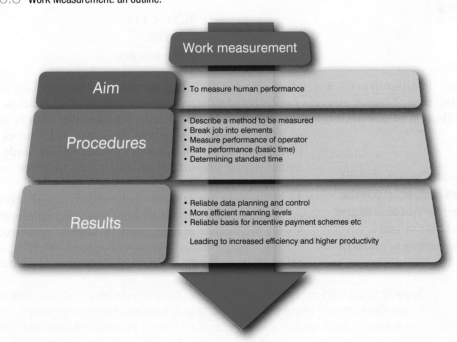

Work measurement

Aim
• To measure human performance

Procedures
• Describe a method to be measured
• Break job into elements
• Measure performance of operator
• Rate performance (basic time)
• Determining standard time

Results
• Reliable data planning and control
• More efficient manning levels
• Reliable basis for incentive payment schemes etc

Leading to increased efficiency and higher productivity

measure, or assess, the performance of people. In pursuing its aim, work measurement has to rely on the exercise of a greater degree of subjective judgement than is required for method study. In particular, the rating of performance and the determination of the standard time rely heavily on the judgement of the person conducting the measurement.

10.   The procedures of work measurement require the method (or job) to be described. This has usually been done as part of a method study. The point is, that if someone is to measure an operation, they must be clear what the operation is! Once the job or method of operation has been described, logically, from beginning to end, then it is broken down into very small elements based on time taken. These elements typically last no more than 30 seconds. Having broken the job down in this way, the person conducting the study then measures the performance of the employee concerned, generally using a stop-watch for the purpose. This is usually known as direct time study, in contrast to indirect time study (see below). Once sufficient numbers of elements have been timed, we can arrive at the elapsed or observed time, for the job.

11.   The next step in the procedure – rating – is that most vulnerable to mistakes or errors on the part of the investigator. The latter is required to 'rate' the employee, i.e. to decide how quickly (or slowly!) the employee is working compared with a standard. This is usually the standard rating of 100 in the British Standard 3138 (BS 3138:1992 provides definitions of terms related to the methodologies of management services, in particular with regard to work study) which is equivalent to the 'average rate at which qualified workers will naturally work at a job, provided they know and adhere to the specified method and provided they are motivated to apply themselves to their work.' Thus if an employee is adjudged to be working at a slower pace, he may be rated at, say, 80; by comparison an employee adjudged to be working at a faster pace than average may be rated at 115 for example. Clearly, if the person conducting the measurement is relatively inexperienced in work study and is unfamiliar with the job being rated, the probability of reaching a mistaken rating is quite high. Rating the job enables a basic time to be established, using the following formula:

$$\text{Basic Time} = \frac{(\text{Observed Time} \times \text{Rating})}{(\text{Standard Rating})}$$

12.   For example, if an employee's time for a particular element is observed to be 0.30 minutes, and is rated as 115, then his basic time will be as follows:

$$\text{Basic Time} = \frac{(0.30 \times 115)}{100}$$
$$= 0.345 \text{ minutes}$$

13.   In order to reach a standard time for the job, a number of allowances are added to the basic time. These allowances are designed to accommodate such contingencies as relaxation, collection of materials or tools, and unavoidable delays, for example. This is another area of work measurement where subjective judgements have to be made, and where the person conducting the study may come under strong pressure from employees to allow more, rather than less, time for these allowances.

Predetermined Motion–Time Systems (PMTS) A work measurement technique where standard elemental times obtained from published tables are used to construct a time estimate for a whole job

14.   Where indirect time study is carried out – that is where times are worked out on paper without observing employees – the following techniques are the most commonly employed: Synthetic Timing, Predetermined Motion Time Study (PMTS), and Analytical Estimating. Briefly these may be described as follows.

–   Synthetic timing is a technique for obtaining basic times for new jobs, which have not been time-studied previously and where it is impracticable (e.g. because of time constraints) to conduct direct time studies. In developing synthetic (or made-up) times, a job is broken down into elements, following a study of the drawings involved. Element times are assigned on the basis of past experience by utilizing records from previous studies. The key to synthetic timing, therefore, is the existence of adequate past records of earlier direct studies. It has proved to be a reliable and consistent method for many businesses.

– Predetermined Motion Time Study (PMTS) is a technique which, according to BS 3138:1992, is one in which 'times established for basic human motions (classified according to the nature of the motion and the conditions under which it is made) are used to build up the time for a job at a defined level of performance'. PMTS differs from synthetic timing in that it is concerned not with job elements but with the basic motions that underlie every job element. PMTS is concerned with the lowest common denominators of work carried out by human beings. The most important method, to date, of PMTS is known as Methods Time Measurement (MTM). This is based on a small number of basic hand, eye and other movements, for which universal times have been established for skilled workers.

– Analytical Estimating is a form of calculated guesswork. It is the most subjective technique employed in Work Measurement, and consequently the least reliable. It involves breaking a job into larger than usual elements and allocating basic times on the basis of the estimator's knowledge of the operations and skill in estimating times. This method tends to be used for one-off jobs.

40.4 VALUE ENGINEERING (VE) AND VALUE ANALYSIS (VA)

15.   Value engineering is an approach to cost reduction in product design that examines the purpose of a product or service, its basic functions and its secondary functions. It seeks to eliminate unnecessary features and functions that do not contribute to the value or performance of the product. Value analysis is a similar concept (concerned with cost reduction after the product or service has been introduced); it involves a systematic interdisciplinary examination of factors affecting the cost of a product or service, in order to devise means of achieving the specified purpose most economically at the required standard of quality and reliability. The stages of a value analysis are typically as follows:

– Select product to be studied.

– Determine function, design and cost of product (including components).

– Develop alternative designs for product in order to achieve same function at less cost

– Evaluate the alternative designs.

– Adopt optimum design, i.e. the one able to perform the required function reliably but at least cost.

– Implement design and review results.

16.   This process is usually carried out by a multi-disciplinary team composed of the following: value analyst/engineer, product designer, cost accountant, production representative and purchasing manager. Value analysis is applied most frequently in mass production or assembly line production processes, where large numbers of items are being produced, and where marginal cost savings can lead to substantial savings overall. Figure 40.4 provides an illustration of this point, indicating the effects, in terms of quantity savings, of unit savings of a few pence or even a fraction of a penny. Motorola used value engineering to reduce the number of parts in its mobile phones from thousands to hundreds with a drastic reduction in processing time and cost (Slack, Chambers and Johnston, 2007).

17.   The benefits of value analysis are that it encourages cost consciousness and the search for alternative designs and materials, etc. and also permits more competitive pricing. However, it does tend to require large-scale production to show it off to the greatest advantage, and must, to a certain extent, duplicate work carried out at the design stage of a product.

FIGURE 40.4 Value analysis: examples of cost savings.

	Cost per item	Best cost saving	%	Volume per annum	Total savings
Item a	£1.00	£0.15	15	50,000	£7,500
Item b	£0.25	£0.01	4	4 million	£40,000

40.5 QUALITY CIRCLES

18.   This chapter has essentially been about making improvements to operations-solving problems. In order to do this, the organization will often draw upon multidisciplinary problem-solving teams. Working in teams has always been an important feature of work organization and was discussed in Chapter 8. There are many kinds of teams in organizations but perhaps the best-known type of problem-solving team is the quality circle (Barnes, 2008). Quality circles are one practical manifestation of **Kaizen** (the principle of continuous improvement) that forms an integral part of the whole TQM philosophy (discussed in Chapter 29).

Kaizen Japanese term for continuous improvement

19.   Quality circles are small groups of about eight to ten employees, meeting together on a regular basis to discuss day-to-day issues such as quality, **productivity** and safety, with the object of (a) making improvements, and (b) organizing their implementation. The second object is significant, as it implies a degree of grass-roots decision-making which is new to most shop-floor situations. In the past employee involvement in initiating changes on the shop floor could only arise via formal productivity committees or via the firm's suggestion scheme. With quality circles, there is an attempt to delegate (refer back to delegation and empowerment discussed in Chapter 23) real power to ordinary employees not only to make suggestions regarding quality etc but also to implement those suggestions.

Productivity Economic measure of efficiency that summarizes the value of outputs relative to the value of inputs used to create them

20.   Typically, a quality circle will adopt the following approach to its task:

– Identify and clarify problems in the local work situation.

– Select a problem for solution (e.g. wastage rates).

– Set a realistic target for improvement (e.g. to reduce wastage rates by 15% over next 12 months).

– Establish a plan, together with a timetable, for achievement of the target.

– Propose plan to local management.

– Implement and test plan.

– Revise plan, where necessary, and monitor results.

21.   No one can know a process quite like the employees who operate it. Not only does participation improve operations problem-solving it also can motivate and lead to enhance productivity through problem ownership. The benefits of quality circles are:

– greater awareness of shop-floor problems by circle members

– greater confidence in tackling problems and generating solutions on the part of circle members

– improved productivity and/or quality and

– improved motivation on the shop-floor.

CONCLUSION

22. In this chapter we investigated how the organization can bring about improvements in operations. We focused on three aids to production management – work study, value engineering, and quality circles. Work study seeks to make improvements (typically reducing costs and time but also enhancing quality) through operational activities and people; value engineering and value analysis seek to make improvements (typically cost reduction) in products through the elimination of unnecessary features and functions and quality circles make use of empowered and multidisciplinary teams of employees to solve operational problems, bringing about improvements in productivity and quality, whilst reducing cost and waste.

QUESTIONS

1   Explain what is meant by the term work study and list the reasons why work study techniques are utilized in production.

2   Explain the purpose of the method study technique.

3   Discuss the work measurement technique.

4   Explain what quality circles are and discuss their purpose.

5   Discuss how quality circles approach tasks and problems.

USEFUL WEBSITES

The Chartered Quality Institute: **www.thecqi.org/** The chartered body for quality management professionals
Business Open Learning Archive (BOLA): **www.bola.biz/ operations/workstudy/index.html** Operations strategy, capacity, scheduling, quality management, JIT, safety and business process re-engineering

VIDEO CASES

Now take a look at the online video cases – visit the companion website to work through real world business problems associated with the concepts presented within this chapter.

129 Quality Improvement Methods an Introduction
Quality is consistent conformance to customer expectations. Quality, particularly when it is associated with competitive advantage, is a significant concern for most organizations. When quality is managed, the costs of waste, reworked, complaints and returns are reduced and customer satisfaction enhanced and, in many cases, improvements in quality translate into improvements in profit. In the case of not-for-profit organizations, quality improvements ensure the efficient use of resources and improvements in service. This case considers the use of quality improvement methods by a not-for-profit organization that has learned from the quality improvements made in profit organizations.

REFERENCES

Barnes, D. (2008) 'Operations Management An International Perspective', Cengage Learning EMEA.
British Standards,. (1992) 'Glossary of terms used in management services BS 3138:1992', Ed. 4. BSI.
Evans, J. and Collier, D. (2007) 'Operations Management Integrated Goods and Services Approach, International Edition', Ed. 2. South Western.

Greasley, A. (2009) 'Operations Management', Ed. 2. Wiley.
Handfield, R. and Nichols, E. (2002) 'Supply Chain Redesign: Transforming Supply Chains into Integrated Value Systems', Financial Times Press.
Slack, N., Chambers, S. and Johnston, R. (2007) 'Operations Management', Ed. 5. Financial Times Press.

CHAPTER 41
NEW TECHNOLOGY
IN MANUFACTURING

Key Concepts

- Automation
- Computer-aided design (CAD) software
- Computer-aided manufacturing (CAM) software
- Enterprise resource planning (ERP) systems
- Flexible manufacturing systems
- Robot

Learning Outcomes   Having read this chapter, you should be able to:

- review the use of ERP systems in manufacturing
- evaluate the role of technology in manufacturing
- distinguish CAD from CAM
- explain what is meant by CIM and what a flexible manufacturing system (FMS) is

Batching The process of producing large quantities of items as a group before being transferred to the next operation

1. In Chapter 39 we discussed types of production (job shops, batch and mass production) and in Chapter 40 discussed continuous improvement through aides to manufacture. Kalpakjian, Schmid and Kok (2010) also discuss the general types of production but additionally describe a wide range of specific manufacturing processes; methods to produce components for a product. For example, there are casting processes, bulk deformation, sheet metal forming, polymer processing, machining and finishing and joining processes. In this chapter we are concerned with the application of technology to the different operations processes (work) and the manufacturing organization holistically.

2. When considering the application of technology we may focus on the needs of management, knowledge and administrative workers or we may focus on the specific work tasks of those directly involved in creating goods. This chapter is therefore divided into two parts. The first considers new technology from a more general management and holistic business perspective and the second considers more specific technologies used to aid manufacturing tasks and methods.

3. When considering the application of technology to manufacturing it is useful to consider general trends. Kalpakjian, Schmid and Kok (2010) suggest that product variety and complexity continue to increase, product life cycles are becoming shorter, markets are becoming more global and market conditions fluctuate widely, customers are consistently demanding high-quality and low-cost products and on-time delivery. The goals in manufacturing view operations activities in a holistic systematic manner. Organizations seek to build quality into the product at each stage of its production, adopt the most flexible, economical and environmentally friendly methods, aim for high levels of productivity, eliminate waste, provide dependable and on-time deliveries and seek continuous improvement. Manufacturers apply IT to all aspects of production. The trends and goals set the context for the aspirations of manufacturing organizations. Before we consider the management perspective in detail we will briefly explore the evolution of operations.

41.1 THE EVOLUTION OF OPERATIONS

4. Throughout the 20th century, operations and manufacturing evolved with changes in technology, mobility and transport, customer requirements, corporate strategies and competitive pressures. Scientific management and Taylorism were dominant influences in the first half of the century. Some companies used their low labour costs to gain entry to various industries (for example industries with a high labour content such as textiles). As wage rates rose and technology became more significant, i.e. advantages and competitive edge eroded, companies shifted first to scale-based strategies (1950s) achieving high productivity and low costs by building the largest and most capital-intensive facilities that were technologically feasible; investment boosted workforce productivity – savings were achieved in the cost of production because the cost of initial investment could be spread across a greater number of producing units.

5. The search continued for ways to achieve even higher productivity and lower costs. In the mid-1960s, it led companies to a new source of competitive advantage – the focused factory. Seeing the problem not as 'How can we increase productivity?' but as 'How can we compete?' Scholars argued a need to consider the efficiency of the entire manufacturing organization, not only the efficiency of the direct labour and the workforce. A factory that focused on a narrow product mix for a particular market niche would outperform the conventional plant, which attempted a broader mission. Since its equipment, supporting systems and procedures concentrated on a limited task for one set of customers, its costs and especially its overheads were lower than those of the conventional plant. The focused factory did a better job because repetition and concentration in one area allowed its workforce and managers to become effective and experienced in the task required for success.

6.   Factory costs were very sensitive to the variety of goods a plant produced. Reduction of the product-line variety by half, for example, raised productivity by 30% and cuts costs by 17%. In manufacturing, costs fall into two categories: those that respond to volume or scale and those driven by variety. Scale-related costs decline as volume increases. Variety-related costs, on the other hand, reflect the costs of complexity in manufacturing: setup, materials handling, inventory and many of the overhead costs of a factory. In most cases, as variety increases, costs increase, usually at a rate of 20% to 35% per unit each time variety doubles. The sum of the scale- and variety-related costs represents the total cost of manufacturing.

7.   Traditional batch manufacturing has always had inherent limitations. Work in process levels are high and machine utilization is low. Jobs spend a high proportion of time waiting for something to happen to them, waiting for a machine to be set up, waiting to be moved or waiting for other jobs on the machine to be completed. Batch production often requires a mass of expediters or progress chasers in order to keep jobs flowing through the manufacturing facilities. It was recognized that some means of automatically routing jobs through the manufacturing system from one machine to the next was required and some way of greatly reducing the set-up time of jobs on a machine. These requirements were met with the aid of computer and numerical control techniques and this led to the development of the basic concept of a flexible manufacturing system (FMS), to be discussed later in this chapter. Among the options for competition are price (cost), quality, delivery, service and flexibility.

8.   In the late 1970s variety became a competitive weapon. Japanese companies exploited flexible manufacturing to the point that a new competitive thrust emerged – the variety war. The advantage of flexible manufacturing – a flexible factory enjoys more variety with lower total costs than traditional factories, which are still forced to make the trade-off between scale and variety. In a flexible factory system, variety-driven costs start lower and increase more slowly as variety grows. Scale costs remain unchanged. Thus the optimum cost point for a flexible factory occurs at a higher volume and with greater variety than for a traditional factory. The advent of just-in-time production (see previous chapters) brought with it a move to flexible factories (1970/80s), as leading Japanese companies sought both low cost and great variety in the market.

9.   Thus far we have discussed competing through price (cost), quality, service, flexibility and variability. Since the 1980s, companies have capitalized on 'time' as a critical source of competitive advantage. They managed structural changes to speed up operational processes. Such companies competed with flexible manufacturing and rapid-response systems, expanding variety and increasing innovation. A company that builds its strategy on this cycle is a more powerful competitor than one with a traditional strategy based on low wages, scale or focus. Older, cost-based strategies require managers to do whatever is necessary to drive down costs: move production to or source from a low-wage country; build new facilities or consolidate old plants to gain economies of scale; or focus operations down to the most economic subset of activities. These tactics reduce costs but at the expense of responsiveness.

41.2 MANAGEMENT PERSPECTIVE

10.   Being responsive, lean and efficient drives a need for improvements in decision-making, planning, control and coordination – all of which are enabled through information flows. In Chapter 15 paragraph 8 and in Chapter 30 paragraph 16 we described the value chain, citing the work of Porter (1985). Operations are typically conceived as the primary internal activities of the value chain. However, such activities rely upon raw materials, which may be sourced from upstream suppliers, and relationships downstream. The supply chain is a network of manufacturers and service providers that work together to convert and move goods from the raw materials stage through to the end user. These manufacturers and service providers are linked together through physical, information and monetary flows, see Figure 41.1. In this section we

FIGURE 41.1 Physical, information and monetary flows.

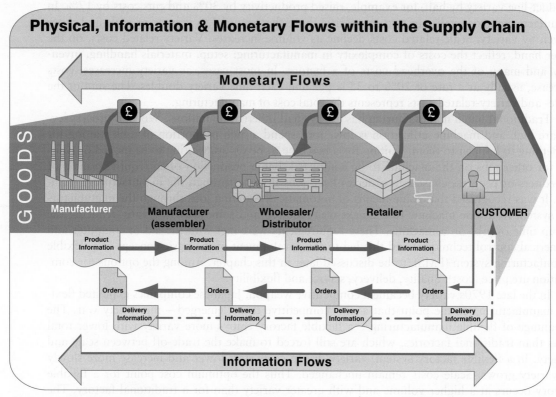

will focus on the information flows and how, through integrated systems, they can be managed efficiently to tie organizational parts together in a responsive manner.

41.2.1 Information Systems Technology Today: ES and ERP

11.When discussing information technology in Chapter 30 (paragraph 26) we noted that organizations historically developed functional business information systems to support different primary and secondary activities such as the manufacturing, order processing, accounting or HR systems. We noted that functional systems serve the specific and local needs of parts of the organization and are developed using specific programming languages. Typically they have their own databases, data structures, operating systems and other idiosyncrasies.

12.   In the 1980s, Porter discussed the role of information in providing competitive advantage and the use of IT spread throughout the value chain. IT not only affects how individual activities are performed but, through new information flows, it also greatly enhances a company's ability to exploit linkages between activities, both within and outside the company. Technology helps manage linkages between activities, allowing companies to coordinate their actions more closely with those of their buyers and suppliers. Information systems allow companies to coordinate value activities in far-flung geographic locations and create many new interrelationships amongst businesses.

13.   Whilst Porter and Millar (1985) noted the role of IT/IS in support of activities and linkages between such activities, the 1980s were characterized by a greater focus on the activities (a functional orientation), identifying ways in which systems could either replace or complement employee activity. Furthermore, the focus was much more intra-organizational rather than inter-organizational. The way IS/IT systems supported the functions of the traditional organization led to the creation of information islands or 'silos' within the organization. This in turn created

coordination and control problems and contributed to problems associated with responsiveness and adaptation to the environment. Not only was the organization fragmented but, through outsourcing and global competition, so too was the supply chain.

14. In the 1990s the BPR movement focussed on the linking of activities and company-wide processes through horizontal flows (process integration) – see Chapter 21 paragraph 21. Organizations became flatter, more global in scope and employees more autonomous. Such changes drove a need for systems to better support the linkages of activities undertaken by various functions. There was a need for systems to support cross-functional processes and inter organizational collaboration and deliver information widely throughout the organization. For example consider the relationship between the procurement, fulfilment and production intracompany processes. As noted by Magal and Word (2009) in the real world, the three key processes are tightly integrated. Consider what happens when a customer places an order for something out-of-stock. The fulfilment process is paused and the production process may be activated. Similarly, if raw material inventories are running low, the procurement process may also be activated. In a similar manner, contemporary organizations must tie together intercompany processes. Consequently, enterprise systems evolved throughout the 1990s to replace the functional systems emanating in the 1980s.

15. ERP systems are information systems that integrate all manufacturing and related applications for an entire enterprise; they are applications used by organizations to manage inventory, resources and business processes across departments in the enterprise. More recently, ERP is considered as business software for running every aspect of a company including managing orders, inventory, accounting and logistics. Well known ERP software providers include BAAN, Oracle, PeopleSoft and SAP. The advantages of an ERP system include the creation of a more uniform organization (does business the same worldwide); efficiency and customer driven; improved decision making and the creation of a process understanding and consequently better control throughout the organization. The system may also drive inventory and staff reduction or productivity improvements. Disadvantages and problems may also be encountered. Implementation is costly and takes considerable time; there is often a need for BPR.

> **Enterprise resource planning (ERP) systems** Large, integrated, computer-based business transaction processing and reporting systems. ERP systems pull together all of the classic business functions such as accounting, finance, sales and operations into a single, tightly integrated package that uses a common database

16. Møller (2005) presents a succinct overview of enterprise systems and how they have evolved. The concept of enterprise systems (ES) is often explained through the evolution of ERP and has evolved over the past 50 years. The fundamental structure of ERP has its origin in the 1950s and 1960s with the introduction of computers into business. The first applications automated manual tasks such as bookkeeping, invoicing and ordering. The early inventory control systems (ICS) and similar systems progressively became material requirements planning (MRP) systems. The development continued in the 1970s and 1980s with the evolution of MRP II. This development peaked in the early 1990s with the advent of the ERP systems often embodied in SAP R/3 along with the other major vendors. Although the ERP systems were influenced by the needs of accounting, planning and control, their philosophy is entrenched in manufacturing.

17. ERP is standardized software designed to integrate the internal value chain of an enterprise; based on an integrated database, the ERP consists of several modules each designed for specific business functions. ERP is a method for the effective planning and controlling of all the resources needed to take, make, ship and account for customer orders in a manufacturing, distribution or service company.

18. In the new millennium we have witnessed the growing scope of ERP systems which essentially started out as back-office systems but have taken on more front-end roles. We have also witnessed such systems operating in support of more senior managers with business intelligence systems complementing decision making. Advances in database and communication and collaboration (Internet) technologies and the evolution of open standards have all facilitated the evolution of information systems in the global organization. Today, it is often more appropriate to classify such systems as enterprise-wide systems (ES).

19.   An ES is an organization-wide information system that integrates key business processes so information can flow freely between different parts of the organization. Enterprise systems, considered by many to be the most important development in the corporate use of IT in the 1990s, presented a new model of corporate computing. In the form of ERP systems they allowed companies to replace their existing information systems, which were often incompatible with one another, with a single, integrated system. An ES streamlines a company's data flow and provides management with direct access to a wealth of real-time operating information. Unlike business information systems of the past, which were typically developed in-house and with a company's specific requirements in mind, enterprise systems (in the form of ERP systems) tend to be off-the-shelf solutions. They impose their own logic on a company's strategy, culture and organization, often forcing companies to change the way they do business. The popularity of ERP/ES is attributed to its potential to improve the profitability potential of an organization by reducing the time and costs of completing business activities.

41.3 MANUFACTURING PERSPECTIVE

Automation The use of control systems (such as numerical control) and information technologies (such as CAD, CAM and robotics) reducing the need for or enhancing human intervention and leading to enhanced productivity

20.   In this section we consider the manufacturing perspective on the application of technology. Whereas the managerial perspective emphasizes the strategic, tactical and holistic application of Information Systems technology to help managers and administrators in particular, this section focuses more on operational demands on technology.

41.3.1 Automation of Manufacturing Processes

Robot A programmable machine designed to handle materials or tools in the performance of a variety of tasks

21.   Key to manufacturing is automation and control, replacing or enabling manual labour. **Automation**, using computer based technology to speed up the performance of existing tasks, has been implemented in manufacturing processes, material handling, inspection, assembly and packaging at increasing rates, (Kalpakjian, Schmid and Kok 2010). Beginning with the numerical control of machines (a method of controlling the movements of machine components through coded instructions), automation seeks to reduce costs, increase flexibility and facilitate making different parts with less operator skill. Operations may be continuously monitored and material handling improved particularly through the use of industrial **robots** and automated guided vehicles. Levels of automation typically depend on the processes used, the products to be made and production volumes.

Computer-aided design (CAD) software Software that allows designers to design and 'build' production prototypes, 'test' them as a computer object under given parameters, compile parts and quantity lists, outline production and assembly procedures, and then transmit the final design direct to milling and rolling machines

41.3.2 CAD, CAM and CIM

Computer-aided manufacturing (CAM) software Software that uses a digital design such as that from a CAD system to directly control production machinery

22.   **Computer technology** is pervasive and exists at many levels. **Computer-aided design (CAD)** refers to the use of a computer-based system for translating engineering concepts into engineering designs by means of programs incorporating data on (i) design principles and (ii) key variables (e.g. product size, shape, etc.). CAD programs are capable of providing three-dimensional representations on a screen. These representations can be rotated through a number of different perspectives. This form of computer modelling is extremely useful in the design process, as it enables detailed changes to be made, and their effects measured, with speed and accuracy. Computer-aided

manufacture (CAM) is a general term which refers to any production system in which manufacturing plant and test equipment are controlled by computer. A CAM system can be expected to be faster, more consistent (and higher quality) and has the ability to achieve high production levels even when skilled craftsmen are in short supply.

23. **Computer integrated manufacturing (CIM)** integrates the software and hardware needed for computer graphics, computer-aided modelling and computer-aided design and manufacturing activities, from initial product concept through its production and distribution in the marketplace (Kalpakjian, Schmid and Kok, 2010). CIM typically involves the total operation of an organization. Such systems comprise various subsystems which are integrated into a whole. Typical subsystems include business planning and support, product design, manufacturing process planning, process automation and control and production monitoring systems. Typically the output of one subsystem service is the input for another. Such systems may be clustered according to whether they fulfil the planning or business execution role. Thus CIM is seen as a more holistic concept that may include CAD, CAM and various automation technologies.

24. Such technologies enable the organization to be more responsive, reduce inventory (and therefore cost) and gain better control of production. There are various elements to CIM such as industrial robots; automated materials handling, i.e. moving a part from one machine to another, and then to points of inspection, to inventory and finally to shipment; automated assembly systems; computer aided process planning; cellular manufacturing and flexible management systems. **Flexible manufacturing systems (FMS)** integrate all of the major elements of production into a highly automated system. Kalpakjian, Schmid and Kok (2010:1132) argue that CIM systems have become the most important means of improving productivity, responding to changing market demands and enhancing the control of manufacturing and management functions. The relationship between a number of these technologies is summarized in Figure 41.2.

Computer integrated manufacturing (CIM) A term used to describe the integration of computer-based monitoring and control of all aspects of a manufacturing process, often using a common database and communicating via some form of computer network

Flexible manufacturing systems Two or more computer controlled machines or robots linked by automated handling devices such as transfer machines, conveyors and transport systems. Computers direct the overall sequence of operations and route the work to the appropriate machine, select and load the proper tools, and control the operations performed by the machine

FIGURE 41.2 Hierarchy of manufacturing systems

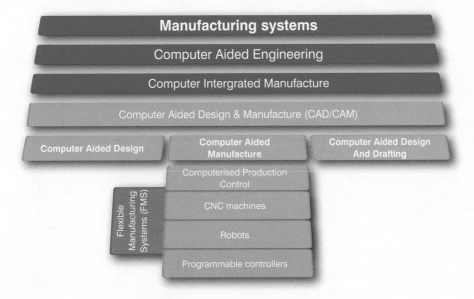

CONCLUSION

25. In this chapter we evaluated the role of technology in manufacturing, from the general and specific manufacturing standpoints. Initially focussing on information flows, we discussed the use of ERP systems in manufacturing. ERP systems and broader ES integrate the parts of the organization, its value and supply chain, to make the organization more responsive and efficient. In the second part we considered Computer integrated manufacturing. CIM systems have become the most important means of improving productivity, responding to changing market demands, and enhancing the control of manufacturing and management functions. Both sets of technologies represent efforts to integrate operations and processes in order to make manufacturers more effective and efficient.

QUESTIONS

1   Review the use of ERP and enterprise systems generally in manufacturing. In your answer you should contrast enterprise systems with functional systems, commenting on the advantages and disadvantages of enterprise systems such as ERP systems.

2   Evaluate the role of automation in manufacturing. In your answer you should comment on the application of technology at various stages of manufacturing and discuss benefits. You should also make reference to the Easter Egg case study to provide examples of automation in manufacturing.

USEFUL WEBSITES

British Automation and Robot Association: **www.bara.org.uk**

VIDEO CASES

Now take a look at the online video cases – visit the companion website to work through real world business problems associated with the concepts presented within this chapter.

25 Whirlpool Cleans Up Its Supply Chain
IOM STRATEGY
LOGISTICS AND THE SUPPLY CHAIN

52 Managing capacity
Sales of easter eggs in the UK are worth around £200m a year, equivalent to around 80m eggs. This case considers how

easter eggs are made – the case focuses on operations and the production process and the associated seasonal demand/ capacity issues and challenges.

54 Managing quality inside a frozen pizza factory
Investigates how quality is managed in the production of frozen pizza.

REFERENCES

Bozarth, C. and Handfield, R. (2006) 'Introduction to Operations and Supply Chain Management with Advanced Decision Support Tools', Prentice Hall.

Collier, D. and Evans, J. (2009) 'OM', Ed. 1. Cengage Learning.

Kalpakjian, S., Schmid, S. R. and Kok, C. (2010) 'Manufacturing, Engineering and Technology', Ed. 6. Prentice Hall.

Kelly, P P. (2009) 'International Business and Management', Cengage Learning EMEA.

Magal, S. and Word, J. (2009) 'Essentials of Business Processes and Information Systems', Wiley.

Møller, C. (2005) 'ERP II: a conceptual framework for next-generation enterprise systems?', Journal of Enterprise Information Management, Volume 18 Number 4, p. 483–497.

Monk, E. and Wagner, B. (2006) 'Concepts in Enterprise resource Planning', Ed. 2. Thomson Course Technology.

Porter, M. E. and Millar, V. E. (1985) 'How information gives you a competitive advantage.', Harvard Business Review, July-August 63, p. 149–174.

Sandoe, K., Corbitt, G. and Boykin, R. (2001) 'Enterprise Integration', Wiley.

Sumner, M. (2005) 'Enterprise Resource Planning', Pearson Prentice Hall.

Section Thirteen
Personnel
Management

PERSONNEL MANAGEMENT

MANAGING HUMAN RESOURCES – COMPETING FOR, RECRUITING AND RETAINING TALENT AT GOOGLE UK

Over a decade ago, 'a pair of idealistic lads in a garage set up a company (Google) that would change the way many of us live' (Usborne 2009). Google is now Fortune Magazine's fourth best place to work and the second (after Apple) most admired company (2010). It is known for having an informal corporate culture, operating under a philosophy where they believe work should be challenging and the challenge should be fun. The Independent newspaper recently took up an invitation to spend a day at Google London. They wanted to ascertain whether or not it really was the greatest place to work in the world? The reporter toured the offices and spoke with employees (Googlers). The UK Director of Operations stated that 'We look after our staff so that they want to come to work.' Having toured the office for a day the reporter departed, 'secretly wishing [he] were a Googler'.

Founders Larry Page and Sergey Brin named the search engine they built 'Google', a play on the word 'googol', the mathematical term for a 1 followed by 100 zeros. The name reflects the immense volume of information that exists, and the scope of Google's mission: to organize the world's information and make it universally accessible and useful. Google hosts and develops a number of Internet-based services and products, and generates profit primarily from advertising; the Google web search engine is the company's most popular service. Google runs over one million servers in data centres around the world, and processes over one billion search requests every day. Revenues typically exceed $20 Billion per year. Google's rapid growth has triggered a chain of products, acquisitions and partnerships beyond the company's core search engine. It has also created significant Human Resource Management (HRM) challenges.

Google has around 20 000 full-time employees worldwide and aims to attract and retain the smartest designers and engineers. Google claim to be 'inclusive in [their] hiring, and favour ability over experience'. With offices around the world and dozens of languages spoken by Google staffers the company is diverse. The result is a team that reflects the global audience Google serves. They aim to 'nurture an invigorating, positive environment by hiring talented people'.

At Google London, the company employs technical and administrative staff, including human resources, finance, legal, facilities, marketing, communications, business development and corporate development staff. Google's HR team (People Operations) work closely with management teams to attract, hire, develop and reward talented people. The HR function is committed to preserving Google's 'uncommon culture' as they continue to grow worldwide. Within the HR team they have specialists working on staffing, benefits, compensation, development, people programs and talent management.

Supporting the company's growth, Google Staffing is responsible for developing strategies to hire exceptionally talented people. 'Google is organized around the ability to attract and leverage the talent of exceptional technologists and business people. We have been lucky to recruit many creative, principled and hard-working stars.' Larry Page, Google Co-founder. Google's People Programs are geared to anticipate the demands and meet the requirements of the company's rapid expansion throughout the world. They aim to encourage talented people to explore career opportunities with the organization. This department helps Google's recruiting and HR processes work effectively, engage in ongoing dialogues with university students and professors. Providing information on their 'hiring' process, Google claim to take great care in how they attract and hire the very best talent – 'because at Google, people are our most important asset'. For candidates, the process begins with searching for a job opening that interests them. Following application, qualifications and experience are reviewed by Google recruiters to determine suitability.

Recruiters may then contact candidates to learn more about their background and answer candidate questions. A phone interview may then be conducted in order to determine whether a candidate should be brought in for interview. The interview process for technical positions evaluates core software engineering skills and for business and general positions evaluates problem solving and behavioural abilities. Several interviewers, drawn from both management and potential colleagues, are typically involved. The company recognize this to be a time consuming and costly approach but believe it to be a fair process, more likely to result in the selection of the right talented people. Following interviews, recruiters will decide if a candidate is suitable for the job opening and will then make a job offer. Recognizing the ongoing need to develop talented employees, Google's Learning and Leadership Development (LLD) team designs and implements innovative learning programs that support and develop employees.

HR Business Partners are on the front line of servicing and interacting with employees. They perform both operational and strategic roles in providing human resources expertise in employee relations, coaching/ development, compensation, conflict management, organizational development, and training – placing considerable focus on retention, scaling and culture issues. Google aims to guide employee actions and behaviour in order to encourage creativity and productivity. The founders believe that great, creative things are more likely to happen with the right company culture. There is an emphasis on team achievements and pride in individual accomplishments that contribute to overall success. As a motivation technique, Google uses a policy often called Innovation Time Off, where Google engineers are encouraged to spend twenty per cent of their work time on projects that interest them. Some of Google's newer services originated from these independent endeavours. As noted by Mediratta (2007), a software engineer at Google, 'It sounds obvious, but people work better when they're involved in something they're passionate about'.

The company lists reasons to work at Google. 'Appreciation is the best motivation, so we've created a fun and inspiring workspace you'll be glad to be a part of, including on-site doctor; massage and yoga; professional development opportunities; running trails; and plenty of snacks to get you through the day'. Google offers a variety of benefits, including a choice of medical programs, stock options, maternity and paternity leave and much more.

Sources:
1 www.google.com/intl/en/about.html
2 Usborne, Simon (Wednesday, 13 May 2009), 'Inside Google London', The Independent, www.independent.co.uk/life-style/gadgets-and-tech/features/inside-google-london-1683959.html Retrieved September 29, 2010
3 http://money.cnn.com/magazines/fortune/bestcompanies/2010/snapshots/4.html accessed 29 September 2010
4 Mediratta, Bharat (October 21, 2007), 'The Google Way: Give Engineers Room', The New York Times (The New York Times Company), http://www.nytimes.com/2007/10/21/jobs/21pre.html. Retrieved September 29, 2010

CHAPTER 42
HUMAN RESOURCE
MANAGEMENT

Key Concepts

- HR system
- Human resource management
- Human resource strategy
- Personnel management

Learning Outcomes Having read this chapter, you should be able to:

- explain the role of the HRM function and HR specialist (personnel)
- list the key areas of HR policy and practice
- discuss alternative structures for the HR function

Human Resource Management
A philosophy of people management based on the belief that human resources are uniquely important to sustained business success. An organization gains competitive advantage by using its people effectively, drawing on their expertise and ingenuity to meet clearly defined objectives. HRM is aimed at recruiting capable, flexible and committed people, managing and rewarding their performance and developing key competencies. See also 'Hard HRM', 'Soft HRM'

Personnel management The specialist management function which determines and implements policies and procedures which affect the stages of the employment cycle

1.   The effective management of Human Resources (HR) is a major determinant of success or failure in business. **Human Resource Management** (HRM) – Chapter 20 – aims to improve the productive contribution of individuals and teams; to enhance organizational performance. The goal of HRM is to help an organization meet strategic goals by attracting, and retaining employees and also to manage them effectively. HRM* is therefore concerned with the strategic management of human resources to achieve a (sustainable) competitive advantage. Managing people is part of the role of every manager or team leader responsible for the work of others. Managers often identify a need for new employees, leading to recruitment. In doing so they specify the work each employee will be required to do. Once employed they must guide, develop and motivate them (refer back to Chapters 4–8). In order to maximize the return on investment from the organization's Human Capital (HC) larger firms establish an HR function. HR specialists are typically used to support line managers, inculcate best HR practice, and ensure a fair, legal and consistent company wide approach. This chapter focuses on the general role of the HR function, what some companies may refer to as **personnel management**. Subsequent chapters will review specific HR practices in more detail.

42.1 THE ROLE OF HR

2.   The job of HR has been evolving since the 1950s, essentially from an administrative to a broader, more important strategy-enabling role. The contemporary HRM function may undertake a variety of activities, such as determining staffing needs and whether to use temporary staff or hire employees to fill these needs, recruiting and training the best employees, ensuring they are high performers, dealing with performance issues and ensuring HR practices conform to various regulations. Activities also include managing employee benefits and compensation, employee records and personnel policies. In many organizations, the HR function will seek to implement best practice in HRM.

3.   Bartlett and Ghoshal discuss the evolving role of HR and the implications for HR professionals (for a more recent discussion see Torrington *et al* 2009:ch1). In the 1980s the professional HR function was typically supportive and administrative. The role of HR staff was to ensure that recruitment, training, benefits administration and the like supported the well-defined strategic and operational agenda. When strategic priorities became more organizationally focused in the 1990s, human resource managers were increasingly included in the strategic conversation, often to help define and develop the company's core competencies – and almost always to align the organizational design and management skills to support those strategic assets (2002:37). Now, as companies move into the war for talent and as individuals with specialized knowledge, skills and expertize are recognized as the scarce strategic resource, HR professionals must become key players in the design, development and delivery of a company's strategy. The key HR activity in the evolving role of human resources suggested by Bartlett and Ghoshal

---

*Those specialists who focused on the management of employees tended to work for a business function labelled personnel management; however, more recently this term has been replaced by many organizations with HR and HRM. Some managers and professionals use the terms interchangeably whilst others have argued a difference in the terms. For many scholars and practitioners the main difference centres on the role of the specialists. Whereas personnel management may be argued to be more administrative, HRM is integrated within strategic planning (Bratton and Gold, 2007).

(2002:37) is building human capital as a core source of competitive advantage. This presents a central role for HR in strategy. Bartlett and Ghoshal outline three major strategic tasks which align the HR function with the strategic challenge of developing the company's HC for sustainable competitive advantage:

– Building (HR systems, processes and culture).

– Linking (developing social networks – vital to knowledge management).

– Bonding (creating a sense of identity and belonging).

42.2 STRATEGIC USE OF HR

4. According to Bartlett and Ghoshal (2002) skilled and motivated people are central to the operations of any company that wishes to flourish in the new age – 'In short, people are the key strategic resource, and strategy must be built on a human-resource foundation'. It is widely accepted that in order to compete in a rapidly changing environment, companies must improve their performance continually by reducing costs, innovating products and processes, and improving quality, productivity and speed to market. HR systems represent an opportunity to improve company performance. However, the HR contribution is not limited to making the organization more efficient but also more effective (Torrington *et al* 2009).

5. Whilst it can be argued that it is the workforce itself (when highly skilled and motivated) that constitutes a source of sustainable competitive advantage, HR practices, when viewed collectively as a (HR) system, can be unique and difficult to replicate and may therefore be a source of sustainable competitive advantage. An organization not only needs skilled people, these people must also be well managed. Whilst any given employee may be talented they may not necessarily apply that talent to perform. In short, competitive advantage is also dependent upon the employee choosing to engage in behaviour that will benefit the organization.

6. There are many practices that seek to influence behaviour. Sustainable competitive advantage is not just a function of isolated components but rather a combination of skills, behaviour and the supporting **HR system**. HR activities are thought to lead to the development of a skilled workforce and one that engages in functional behaviour for the organization; this results in higher operating performance, which translates into increased profitability.

HR system A set of distinct activities, functions, policies and processes that are directed at attracting, developing and maintaining the human resources of an organization

7. HRM thinking should consider the integration of HRM with business strategy, the development of distinctive corporate culture and the creation of a skilled, flexible and committed workforce which is adaptive to changing circumstances. The **human resources strategy** is the overall plan for staffing, developing and rewarding employees and outsourced human resources tied to business objectives. As with production and information technology we might ask how the HR strategy fits with the corporate strategy which we discussed in Chapter 16. There are a number of ways (relationships) in which the corporate strategy may fit with the

Human resource strategy Overall plan for staffing, developing and rewarding employees and outsourced human resources tied to business objectives

HR strategy. In some organizations strategies may be separate whilst in others the corporate strategy will dictate what should be in the HR strategy. Strategic HRM means directing people, processes and HR systems to achieve strategic objectives so that individual goals are tied to the business needs of the whole organization.

8. Thus far we have described what is essentially a one-way relationship, a monologue: the HR strategy is created to ensure the corporate goals are achievable. Contemporary organizations tend to adopt a dialogue whereby HR, as a functional strategy, may both be informed by and inform the corporate strategy. In this sense, HR may enable the creation of corporate

strategy, making the organization more effective. Some organizations have gone further still and may either take a holistic stance where the people of the organization are recognized as key to competitive advantage or HR may be used to drive organizational strategy. In addition to their important strategic role, in parallel, the HR function typically continues with more traditional administrative (operational) roles.

42.3 OPERATIONAL USE OF HR

9.   Personnel services (day-to-day HR activities) represent the operational or production aspect of personnel management. Personnel or HR services typically include the following:

- recruitment services (see Chapter 43)

- training services (see Chapter 44)

- appraisal procedures (see Chapter 45)

- employment services (i.e. conditions of service procedures – informing managers and employees, recording employee details, handling enquiries, etc.)

- pay and associated procedures

- employee relations (see Chapter 49) and

- safety, health and welfare services (e.g. organizing safety committees, maintaining safety records, provision of welfare and canteen facilities, etc.).

10.   Ultimately the role of HR (personnel) will be determined by the attitudes of the senior management of the organization. Where personnel is recognized as having a major part to play in the renewal and maturation processes of the organizational system, then the HR (director) will be given a key role in the corporate development of the organization. Where, in contrast, personnel is seen mainly as a provider of services to other managers, then the Personnel Manager will be given a routine administrative role.

42.4 HR POLICIES AND PRACTICES

11.   Policies, practices and procedures constitute elements of the formal HR system and are used to influence HR related decisions throughout the organization. Personnel or HR policies, like any other corporate policies, are not just the preserve of a particular group of managers. Such policies have to be agreed by the senior management team as a whole, and approved by the board. The role of the HR team is to draft HR policies and to argue the case for their acceptance. In many instances it will be the HR department which provides the initiative for the introduction of new policies and the revision or rejection of existing policies. Key areas of personnel policy and practice can include the following:

- recruitment and selection

- training

- pay and benefits (pensions, etc.)

- relations with trade unions or staff associations

- career development

– safety and health

– employment legislation.

12.   As in other policy areas, personnel policies are guidelines for behaviour, stating what the organization will do, or positively will not do, in relation to its employees and employee affairs. An example of a personnel policy may be as follows, 'every job vacancy shall be advertised within the organization before any external advertising takes place'. From policies come more specific HRM practices. These are the HRM activities that have a direct impact on employees, e.g., types of compensation, staffing methods, appraisal methods and forms of training and development. There are many choices amongst the array of possible practices. And because they influence the behaviours of individuals, they need to be selected systematically to be aligned with the other HRM activities. HR practices are discussed in the remaining chapters of this book.

42.5 ORGANIZING THE HUMAN RESOURCE FUNCTION

13.   HR functions may be organized in many ways. HR organization is dependent upon the degree of power exercised by the HR function within the company and the size of the HR function in particular. The function's power will be dependent upon its role in the corporate strategy and upon environmental factors such as the extent of employment law, occupational health and safety regulations and power of the trade unions. Flatter or international organizations may seek to decentralize or even outsource various HR practices and activities thus reducing the size of the HR function. The type of structure which may be found in an HR (personnel) department will be a reflection of the role it is expected to play in the organization. For example, in an organization where personnel is held to be of vital importance to the future of the organization as well as to its present, the personnel (HR) department is likely to be structured along the lines of the example shown in Figure 42.1. Some junior posts have been ignored in the interests of simplicity.

14.   In Figure 42.1, the senior Personnel Manager is shown as an executive director, to emphasize the board level role which is expected of personnel in this organization. The Personnel Services' Manager is responsible for recruitment and personnel administration, and would also have other responsibilities not indicated on the chart (e.g. welfare, canteen, office services, etc.). The Employee Relations Manager is responsible for industrial relations matters, including job

FIGURE 42.1   Personnel function with wide-ranging role.

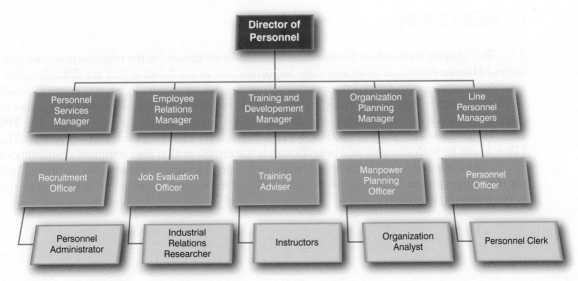

evaluation, job grading and industrial relations intelligence. The Training and Development Manager is responsible for all aspects of training, including job training, management development and related matters. The Organization Planning Manager is responsible for assessing manpower requirements, organization design projects, management succession planning and career planning.

15.   In an organization where little is expected of personnel apart from the provision of services, and where line managers are expected to bear the brunt of dealing with the personnel matters raised by their own employees, then the structure shown in Figure 42.2 is likely to be met. In this form of structure, the emphasis is entirely on the provision of services. Each of the jobs referred to is intended to pursue a routine, here-and-now path. There is no intention of including personnel in any strategic activity, nor in any corporate advice-giving, except for routine information.

16.   In between the two structures and approaches illustrated are many other options, as personnel departments grow or decrease in stature, as senior management attitudes to HR change, and as external conditions (especially legislation) make labour more, or less, important. Companies may also consider HR outsourcing an important part of maximizing their performance. Outsourcing can be defined as the delegation of one or more HR business processes to an external provider who then owns, manages and administers the selected HR processes, based on defined and measurable perfromance metrics.

FIGURE 42.2   Routine-oriented personnel department.

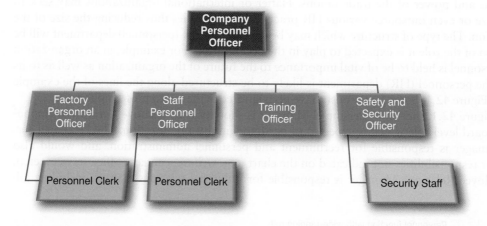

CONCLUSION

17.   This chapter focussed on human capital and its management in the organization – we considered Human Resources as strategically important due to attributes which are difficult to imitate, thus ensuring any derived competitive advantage is sustainable. In particular we focussed on the role of the specialist HR function in acquiring, developing and motivating HC in order to improve (productive) performance and develop a sustainable competitive advantage. The HR function develops and implements HR systems comprising the HR policies and practices. The HR role can be both strategic and operational. It is strategic in that the continued availability of HC must be assured in order for the strategy to be met. However, it must also be operational via the administration of certain HR practices such as resourcing, training and development and performance management.

QUESTIONS

1   (a) – List key activities associated with managing people in organizations – what activities must be undertaken when managing people?

(b) – In order to maximize the return on investment from the organization's human capital, larger firms establish a human resources (personnel) function. What is the role of the HR function in the organization? Of the activities listed in question 1, which do you believe require attention from an HR specialist and which should be undertaken by line management? In your answer, you should critically evaluate how the role of specialists has changed-starting with the industrial age, through scientific management to the intangible economy (from personnel to HRM).

2   Drawing from both the Google case study and your reading, evaluate the role of HR, discussing both the strategic and operational use.

USEFUL WEBSITES

Chartered Institute of Personnel Management **www.cipd.co.uk** International Labour Organization **www.ilo.org**

Institute for employment studies **www.employment-studies. co.uk/consult/index.php?id=hre&tab=work** Getting the most from your HR, L&D and OD functions

VIDEO CASES

Now take a look at the online video cases – visit the companion website to work through real world business problems associated with the concepts presented within this chapter.

121 Introducing HRM – This case introduces some of the essential elements of HRM and contrasts traditional views of personnel management with contemporary HRM. The specialist role of the HRM professional within organizations is considered, along with strategic challenges. Finally, various structures for the HRM function within the organization, including options for outsourcing, are considered. This is an introductory case study, aimed at sensitising students to the various activities involved in managing people; students need to consider which activities require specialist support.

REFERENCES

Bartlett, C. and Ghoshal, S. (2002) 'Building Competitive Advantage Through People', MIT Sloan Management Review, Winter 2002, Vol. 43 Issue 2, p. 34–41.

Bratton, J. and Gold, J. (2007) 'Human Resource Management Theory and Practice', Ed. 4. Palgrave Macmillan.

Leopold, J. and Harris, L. (2009) 'The Strategic Managing of Human Resources', Ed. 2. Financial Times Press.

Martin, J. (2010) 'Key Concepts in Human Resource Management', Sage.

Torrington, D., Hall, L., Taylor, S. and Atkinson, C. (2009) 'Fundamentals of Human Resource Management: Managing People at Work', Ed. 1. Financial Times Press.

CHAPTER 43
RECRUITMENT AND SELECTION

1. In Chapter 20 we discussed HR Planning, defining it as 'a rational approach to the effective recruitment, retention and deployment of people within an organization, including, when necessary, arrangements for dismissing staff'. HR planning identifies staffing needs and is therefore an input to the resourcing process. In other chapters we have noted the strategic importance of recruitment in securing talent for competitive advantage (see previous chapter) and as a means to develop organizational culture. The previous chapter also discussed the HR (people management) system. This chapter outlines the typical stages of the recruitment and selection process in organizations, and considers certain aspects of the process in greater detail. Some practitioners and scholars use the concept of resourcing to describe three main areas of HR activity: recruitment, selection and appointment (Martin, 2010). Others use this concept more broadly to include the process by which people are identified and allocated to perform necessary work.

2. It will be helpful to distinguish 'recruitment' from 'selection'. The aim of recruitment is to ensure that the organization's demand for employees is met by attracting potential employees (candidates) in a cost-effective and timely manner; recruitment focuses on the identification of a vacancy (job analysis), identifying where likely candidates may be found, advertising, documenting and initial sifting. This is followed by selection. The aim of selection is to identify, from those coming forward, the individuals most likely to fulfil the requirements of the organization. Selection methods include application forms and CVs, interviews, psychometric testing, assessment centres and references. In simple terms, recruitment is concerned with attracting applicants, and selection is concerned with screening those applicants and choosing the preferred ones. The final stage of the selection process should be identification of the chosen applicants for the jobs. Typically a job offer is made to the preferred applicant. If the job offer is accepted then the applicant is appointed. An outline of the resourcing process is shown in Figure 43.1.

Recruitment Locating, identifying and attracting capable applicants

Employee resourcing Resourcing is the process by which people are identified and allocated to perform necessary work. Resourcing has two strategic imperatives: firstminimizing employee costs and maximizing employee value to the organization; secondly, obtaininthe correct behavioural mix of attitude and commitment in the workforce

Job analysis The determination of the essential characteristics of a job in order to produce a job specification/description

Selection Screening job applicants to ensure the most appropriate candidates are hired

FIGURE 43.1 Resourcing process.

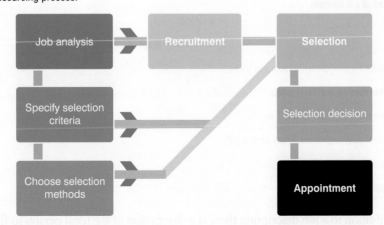

Application forms (blanks) Usually sent out to jobseekers who respond to some kind of job advertising. The form or blank is a template for the presentation of personal information that should be relevant to the job applied for. This ensures that all candidates provide the desired range of information in the same order of presentation to facilitate comparison and preparation of a short-list for further selection procedures

Psychometric tests Written tests that assess a person's aptitude and personality in a measured and structured way. Such tests are often used by employers as part of their recruitmentand selection processes

Person specification A list of the knowledge, experience and skills necessary for a person to be able to perform a particular job

Job description A statement of the overall purpose and scope of a job, together with details of its tasks and duties; the description is a product of job analysis

Activities may be performed by the manager owning the vacancy or HR or may be outsourced. Furthermore, they may be enabled by Internet and database technologies. We discuss each stage of the process in this chapter.

43.1 RECRUITMENT – ATTRACTING THE RIGHT PEOPLE

3.   In this stage of the resourcing process a pool of applicants is generated. Recruitment activities may be carried out by operational/line managers, HR or a combination of the two. Typically HR will take the lead, providing a service to the line manager in need of new staff. It is important that such activities are conducted in a non discriminatory and legal manner that sustains or enhances the good reputation of the organization. The key activities undertaken may include identification of a vacancy and the job analysis, identification of where likely candidates may be found, advertising, documentation (role and **person specification**, advert, application forms, standard letters, etc.) and initial sifting (short listing). Each are described in more detail before we consider the selection process.

43.1.1.1 *Job and Competency Analysis*

4.   Resourcing starts with the identification of a vacancy and an analysis of the job. Job analysis helps us understand what people do at work. Information about the job role and its associated tasks are used to derive a specification of the knowledge, skills and abilities and other characteristics that are essential or desirable for a person performing the job role. This information helps determine the attributes that are to be assessed in order to make a decision about the suitability of a particular job candidate/applicant. Thus the product of job analysis is a **job description**. The job description usually contains at least the following information about the job concerned:

- title of job

- grade/salary level of job

- title of immediate superior's job

- number of subordinates

- overall purpose of the job

- principal responsibilities of the job

- limits of authority

- location of job.

5.   In addition to a job description there is a description of the ideal person to fill the job. The 'candidate', or 'person(nel)' specification, as it is frequently called, is a summary of the knowledge, skills

and personal characteristics required of the job holder to carry out the job to an acceptable standard of performance. This is an extremely important feature of the recruitment process, because it sets down a standard by which candidates for interview may be tested. The personal specification (see Figure 43.2) typically identifies the physical characteristics of the person, their attainments, qualifications and experience, general intelligence, specific aptitudes and abilities, interests, disposition and motivation. Whereas a job analysis focuses on the work, competency analysis may be described as worker-oriented analysis. The competency-based approach involves the development of a list of abilities and competencies (competency specification) necessary to perform a given job successfully and against which the applicant's performance can be assessed. This approach may be used in conjunction with job analysis or as an alternative to it.

> **Competency-based approach** The development of a list of abilities and competencies necessary to perform successfully a given job, and against which the applicant's performance can be assessed

FIGURE 43.2 Person specification.

	Essential	Desirable
Formal Qualifications		
Knowledge		
Experience		
Skills - Manual - Social - Other		
Personality/Motivation		
Physical Requirements		
Interests		
Circumstances		

6.   Having analyzed the job, the recruiter must now develop a strategy to promote it. The job description may be used along with other company documentation to create the job advert. This advert must then be communicated with potential employees. The main approaches used to attract applicants include: advertising, websites, employee referrals, recruitment agencies and professional or educational associations. The choice of media will depend upon cost, time, equal opportunity and diversity legislation and regulations and the mobility of labour. Typically adverts contain a specification of requirements, including basic educational requirements and previous relevant experience. The advert should typically contain information to attract potential applicants but also enable them to make a self-selection decision. The basic principles of an effective job advertisement (i.e. one that attracts sufficient numbers of the right kind of candidates) can be summarized as follows:

–   Provide brief, but succinct, details about the position to be filled.

–   Provide similar details about the employing organization.

–   Provide details of all essential personal requirements.

–   Make reference to any desirable personal requirements.

–   State the main conditions of employment, especially the salary indicator for the position.

- State to whom the application or enquiry should be directed.

- Present the above information in an attractive form.

7.   If an external advertisement has hit the target segment correctly, then only relatively small numbers of applications will be forthcoming, and most of these will be strong candidates for interview, and the difficulty will be to decide who not to invite. If the advertisement has been drawn up rather loosely, or has deliberately sought to tap a large segment of the labour market, then large numbers of applications can be expected, many of whom will be quite unsuitable. Short-listing arrangements are necessary to select from the total number of applicants those who appear, from their application form, to be worthy of an interview. In drawing up a short-list, it is common practice to divide the applications into three groups as follows:

1   Very suitable – must be interviewed.

2   Quite suitable – call for interview if insufficient numbers in category (1), or send holding letter.

3   Not suitable – send polite refusal letter, thanking them for their interest in applying.

8.   Shortlisting may be a subjective exercise where the line manager or resourcing specialists simply trawl through the pack of received applications and chose the best few or may be accomplished objectively by scoring applicant information and its relevance to the job. The applicants with the highest scores are deemed suitable for interview. This latter approach lends itself to the application of technology, a matter we revisit later in the chapter. In parallel with the advertising and initial sifting activities, the organization will prepare for the next stage (selection) by specifying selection criteria and choosing selection methods. Such methods will be described next.

43.2 SELECTION

9.   The main outputs of recruitment include the outputs from job analysis: the job description and competency specification and the attributes that act as criteria for decision-making during selection. Selection is very much a two-way process – the candidate is assessing the organization, just as much as the organization is assessing the candidate. The main objective of selection, therefore, is to be able to make an acceptable offer to the candidate who appears, from the evidence obtained, to be the most suitable for the job in question. Selection is primarily about taking steps to assess whether or not the applicant will fit in with the organization, the department and team and the job itself.

Halo (or horn) effect The bias introduced when attributing all of the characteristics of a person to a single attribute, i.e. drawing a general impression or making a judgement about an individual on the basis of a single characteristic. When this is positive it is a 'halo' effect, when negative a 'horns' effect. The perception of a person is formulated on the basis of a single favourable or unfavourable trait or characteristic and tends to shut out other relevant characteristics of that person

10.   Selection or assessment methods are used to determine the suitability of applicants for particular jobs. Methods vary in the amount of subjectivity utilized by selectors and in some cases methods may be subject to bias. For example the bias introduced when attributing all of the characteristics of a person to a single attribute i.e. drawing a general impression or making a judgement about an individual on the basis of a single characteristic (such as the school they went to) is termed the halo or horns effect. When this is positive it is a 'halo' effect, when negative a 'horns' effect. The perception of a person is formulated on the basis of a single favourable or unfavourable trait or characteristic and tends to shut out other relevant characteristics of that person. Additionally, judging someone on the basis of one's perception of the group to which that person belongs is known as stereotyping. Selectors may be trained to overcome such bias. In addition,

Stereotyping Judging someone on the basis of one's perception of the group to which that person belongs

psychologists work to minimize bias from a range of selection methods that will be discussed next.

43.2.1 Selection Methods

11.   The first contact a job applicant typically has with an organization is usually through a curriculum vitae (CV) or an application form. These documents provide a summary of relevant biographical information such as education and previous job experience. Application forms are similar to CVs but are organization lead. An application form or a letter of application tells an organization whether or not an applicant is worthy of an interview or a test of some kind. Application forms vary considerably in the way they are set out. Some require prospective candidates to answer routine questions in a form that gives them no opportunity to discuss their motives for applying or to talk about themselves in a general way. Others are very open-ended in their format, and require applicants to expand at some length on themselves and on how they see the job. In between the two forms are several compromise versions, which aim to establish some kind of balance between closed and open questions. The answers to the closed questions supply the organization with routine information in a standardized form; the answers to the open questions provide a clue to the motives, personality and communication skills of the applicants.

12.   The selection interview is far and away the most common technique used for selection purposes. Unlike most other management techniques, it is employed as much by amateurs as by professionals. Few managers and supervisors carry out selection interviews regularly; many of them have received no formal training in the technique either, so it is not surprising to learn that research has shown that such interviews are frequently neither reliable nor valid. The measure of the reliability of an interview is the extent to which conclusions about candidates are shared by different interviewers; the measure of the validity of an interview is the extent to which it does measure what it is supposed to measure, i.e. the suitability of a particular candidate for a particular job. The main reasons why so many poor interviews are carried out are two-fold: (1) lack of training in interviewing technique, and (2) lack of adequate preparation for an interview.

13.   Much has been written about selection interviewing, but most of the points made can be condensed into the following guide to good practice (Figure 43.3). This highlights the sort of issues which busy managers need to know about if they are to make optimum use of their own, and the candidates', time in the short period available for the interview. There are a few points arising from the guide which ought to be stressed. The first is the question of preparation. As with so many tasks, the better the preparation, the better the final result. It is very important to be properly prepared before an interview. It enables the interviewer to feel confident in themselves about their key role in the process, and enables them to exploit to the full the information provided by the candidate. It also helps to minimize embarrassment caused by constant interruptions, inadequate accommodation and other practical difficulties.

14.   Questioning plays a vital role in a selection interview, as it is the primary means by which information is obtained from the candidate at the time. Questions have been categorized in a number of different ways. There may be closed and open questions. The major differences between them are as follows: (1) closed questions are questions which require a specific answer or a yes/no response. For example: 'how many people were you responsible for in your previous job?' (specific); (2) open questions are questions that require a person to reflect on, or elaborate upon, a particular point in their own way. An example of an open questions is, 'what is it that attracts you about this job?' Open questions invariably begin with what? or how? or why? It is usual to ask closed questions to check information which the candidate has already partly supplied on his application form, and to re-direct the interview if the candidate is talking too much and/or veering off the point. Open questions tend to be employed once the interview is underway, with the object of getting the candidate to demonstrate their knowledge and skills to the interviewer.

FIGURE 43.3 Selection interviewing – guide to good practice

Be Prepared	Obtain available information, eg job details, candidate specification & application form. Arrange interview room. Ensure no interruptions. Plan the interview
Welcome the Candidate	After initial courtesies, thank candidate for coming. Explain briefly what procedure you propose to adopt for the interview Commence by asking relatively easy and non-threatening question.
Encourage Candidate to talk	Ask open-ended questions. Prompt where necessary. Indicate that you are listening. Briefly develop points of interest raised by candidate.
Control the Interview	Direct your questions along the lines that will achieve your objectives. Tactfully, but firmly, clamp down on the over-talkactive candidate. Do not get too involved in particular issues just because of your own interests. Keep an eye on the time.
Supply Necessary Information	Briefly add to information already made available to candidate. Answer candidate's questions. Inform candidate of the next steps in the selection procedure.
Close Interview	Thank candidate for his/her responses to your questions. Exchange final courtesies.
Final Steps	Write up your notes about the candidate. Grade, or rank, him/her for suitability. Operate administrative procedures regarding notifications etc.

15. Interview questions may also be categorized as behavioural, competency or situational. Behavioural interviews or questions are based on key job requirements and ask interviewees to describe past experiences of performing such tasks; for example describe a recent project that involved you working as part of a team. Competency-based interviews or questions are similar to behavioural but focus on a specific competency such as team working, problem-solving or leadership, etc. Both behavioural and competency-based interviews and questions focus on past behaviour. Situational interviews or questions are used to evaluate how a candidate might respond to a future challenge. The candidate may be given a scenario and asked what they would do in that situation.

16.   Interviews may be conducted on a one-to-one basis, but a two-to-one situation is also widely favoured, and there is still a lot of support for panel interviews, especially in the public services. In a two-to-one situation, the two interviewers usually agree amongst themselves as to how they will share the questioning and information supplying during the interview. Frequently, in medium and large organizations, one of the two organization representatives is a personnel specialist, and the other is the (operational) 'client', seeking to fill the vacancy in question. The advantages of this type of interview are that whilst one interviewer is asking a question, or pursuing a point, the other can observe the candidate's reactions and make an independent evaluation of this response; and that each interviewer can specialize in his own areas of interest in the selection process, the 'client' concentrating on technical capability and the ability to fit into his team and the personnel member concentrating on the wider aspects of having such a person as an employee of the organization. The panel interview is an altogether different prospect for a candidate. In this case the individual candidate is faced by several interviewers. In the case of a panel interview, it is of greatest importance to decide who is going to ask which questions, and how the panel is to be chaired.

17.   In the final stage of the interview the candidate may be provided with any routine information about conditions of service and invited to ask questions for themselves. Taken as a whole, interviews are most useful for assessing the personal qualities of an individual. They help to answer questions such as 'is this candidate likely to be able to fit into our team or our environment?' and 'has this particular candidate any special personal characteristics which give them an advantage over rivals?' Interviews are not so useful for assessing technical ability or the value of past experience. This is one of the reasons why organizations may consider using psychological tests to supplement information gained during interviews.

43.2.2 Psychological Tests

18.   Psychological tests, or selection tests as they are often called, are standardized tests designed to provide a relatively objective measure of certain human characteristics by sampling human behaviour. Such tests tend to fall into four categories as follows:

–   intelligence

–   aptitude

–   attainment and

–   personality tests.

19.   Checks for validity are designed to ensure that any given test measures what it sets out to measure, e.g. an intelligence test should be able to measure intelligence, and a manual dexterity test should be able to measure manual dexterity. Checks for reliability are designed to ensure that tests produce consistent results in terms of what they set out to measure. Thus, if a test which is carried out on an individual at a particular point in time is repeated, the results should be similar. The different categories of tests are as follows:

–   Intelligence tests
    These tests are designed to measure thinking abilities. It is enough for our purposes to understand that general intelligence can be manifested by verbal, spatial or numerical ability, or a combination of these. Popular tests in use for personnel selection are often composed of several different sections, each of which aims to test candidates on the key ability areas to which we have just referred.

–   Aptitude tests
    These are basically tests of innate skills. They are widely used to obtain information about such skills as mechanical ability, clerical and numerical ability and manual dexterity.

– Attainment tests

These tests measure the depth of knowledge or grasp of skills which have been learned in the past – usually at school or college. Typical attainment tests are those which measure typing abilities, spelling ability and mental arithmetic, for example.

– Personality tests

Where they are employed in work situations, they usually take the form of personality inventories – lists of multiple choice questions in response to theoretical situations posed by the test designers – or of projection tests – where the candidate is required to describe a series of vague pictures or a series of inkblots. The aim of personality tests is to identify an individual's principal personality traits or dimensions, e.g. introverted or extroverted, sociable or isolated, etc.

20.   Psychological tests can provide useful additional or confirming information about a candidate for a position. They can supplement the information obtained from application forms and from interviews, and are particularly useful where objective information would be illuminating. Thus far we have described several assessment methods used in selection. Some organizations make use of assessment centres to provide information on candidates for jobs. They typically consist of multiple evaluations including job-related simulations, interviews and psychological tests. The strength of assessment centres is in the richness of the information they produce on candidates.

Assessment centres Centres used to provide information on candidates for jobs. They typically consist of multiple evaluations including job-related simulations, interviews and psychological tests

43.2.3 The use of Technology in Assessment

21.   Databases and the arrival of the Internet have provided an opportunity for organizations to process applications and conduct selection tests remotely. Multinationals, in particular, can benefit from 'e-testing' of new recruits, or promotion prospects, without having to incur all the costs involved in bringing individual candidates into a recruitment centre or personnel office. Using the Internet it is possible to create interactive application forms, provide richer information about the job to applicants and request applicant information in a standard format. Today it is quite common for larger organizations to receive application forms and a CV (and other bio data) electronically. Information provided by the applicant can then be manipulated by software and a score of fit with the job calculated automatically. Scores may then be used to shortlist candidates. The advantages and disadvantages of e-testing can be summarized as follows:

Bio data Scoreable information about a job applicant

Advantages	Disadvantages
– Reduction in costs of organizing tests.	– Lack of control over the test environment.
– Flexibility of timing of tests.	– Difficulty in ensuring consistency of treatment for all candidates.
– Faster scoring of tests as results.	– Possibility of candidates getting unauthorized help in responding to questions.
– Convenience and privacy for test.	– No immediate advice or support available to candidates who may be having difficulties.
	– understanding what they are being asked to do.
	– Possible lack of security of personal data.

43.2.4 Fairness in Selection

22. Earlier we discussed the need for assessment and selection to be reliable and valid. It should also be ethical and conform to legal requirements. Good practice in recruitment and selection can result in a more effective, better motivated workforce. Labour turnover and absence can be reduced and discrimination avoided on the grounds of race, sex, disability, sexual orientation and religion or belief. Getting recruitment and selection wrong may result in a variety of problems such as: high labour turnover, absenteeism, low morale, ineffective management and supervision, disciplinary problems, dismissals and possible unfair dismissal complaints. Individuals, who consider they have been discriminated against during recruitment and selection, on the grounds of their race, sex, disability, sexual orientation or religion or belief or refused employment on the grounds of membership or non-membership of a trade union, may make a claim to an employment tribunal. If the tribunal finds in the applicant's favour, it may award compensation or recommend some other course of action to reduce or stop the effect of any discrimination. Furthermore, it is a criminal offence to employ a person with no immigration authorization to work in the UK.

23. Bratton and Gold, 2007) discuss the legal context for the resourcing process, noting the importance of UK legislation and directives from the European Union. In particular they discuss the Data Protection Act (ensuring accuracy and protection of stored personal data, etc.), the Human Rights Act, Sex Discrimination Act (refer back to Chapter 14), the Race Relations Act, the Disability Discrimination Act, the Equal Pay Act and various other regulations. Collectively, this has made employment law in general something of a minefield. In general, it is the role of the HR Department to bring organizational resourcing practices in line with the provisions of the law.

24. The Equality Act (2010) replaces previous legislation (such as the Race Relations Act 1976 and the Disability Discrimination Act 1995) and ensures consistency in what is needed to make the workplace a fair environment and to comply with the law. The Act covers the same groups that were protected by existing equality legislation – age, disability, gender reassignment, race, religion or belief, sex, sexual orientation, marriage and civil partnership and pregnancy and maternity – but extends some protections to groups not previously covered, and also strengthens particular aspects of equality law.

25. Whilst it is advisable to seek legal guidance, the following checklist should help assure that recruitment and selection activities are performed in a legal and non-discriminatory manner:

  - Create and adopt a resourcing (recruitment and selection) policy.

  - Ensure interviewers are aware of the recruitment policy and are appropriately trained.

  - Create and adopt an effective equal opportunities policy and approach.

  - Use the person specification to avoid inadvertent discrimination.

  - Consider whether an existing employee could be trained to do the job.

  - Consider whether the work could be done by part-timers, job-sharers or home-based workers.

  - The application form should only ask for information that is relevant to the job.

  - Consider using a variety of methods to select the best candidate.

  - When carrying out interviews, ensure that 'open ended' questions are asked but do not ask questions which may be considered discriminatory.

  - Keep all notes, including any rough jottings made during the interview – be prepared to give reasons for rejection to unsuccessful candidates who make a request.

26. Approaches to recruitment vary worldwide. Variance may be determined by culture, law, Government policy and other factors. Mistakes may be avoided when working to a checklist of

recruitment activities, designed to minimize errors and thus avoid damaging the organization's image externally and HR/Personnel's reputation internally. A checklist helps to ensure a rational and logical approach to the recruitment of employees throughout the organization. Question to be considered:

- – Has the vacancy been agreed by the responsible manager?
- – Is there an up-to-date job description for the vacant position?
- – What are the conditions of employment (salary, hours, holidays, etc.) for the vacant position?
- – Has a candidate specification been prepared?
- – Has a notice of the vacancy been circulated internally?
- – Has a job advertisement been agreed?
- – Have details of the vacancy been forwarded to relevant agencies?
- – Do all potential candidates (internal or external) know where to apply and in what form?
- – What arrangements have been made for drawing up a shortlist of candidates?
- – Have the interviewing arrangements been agreed, and have shortlisted candidates been informed?
- – Have unsuitable candidates or candidates held in reserve, been informed of their position?
- – Have offer letters been agreed and despatched to successful candidates?
- – Have references been taken up, where necessary?
- – Have suitable rejection letters been sent to unsuccessful shortlisted candidates, thanking them for their attendance?
- – Have all replies to offer letters been accounted for?
- – Have the necessary procedures for placement, induction and follow-up of successful candidates been put into effect?

43.3 APPOINTMENT

27.   The final stage of the resourcing process should be the identification of the chosen applicants. Earlier we identified references as one form of selection method. Some organizations take up references prior to interview. However this can be time consuming and costly, particularly as the majority will never be utilized. For this reason, many organizations take up references once the applicant has been chosen. References are normally obtained from the current or previous employer and the job offer may be made subject to satisfactory references.

43.3.1 Job Offer and Contract of Employment

28.   Normally, the applicant is contacted with a formal offer of employment; a starting date is negotiated should this be accepted. The contract of employment is typically a written document that seeks to establish the basis of the working arrangements between employer and employee. A contract is only formed when an offer is made and accepted and a consideration has exchanged (Martin, 2010). It is important to note that a contract of employment does not have to be written to exist. It is also important to recognize the totality of a contract of employment will include things that are 'custom and practice' within the organization; elements from the law; and

agreements with trade unions. In addition to the formal contract of employment, managers should also be mindful of the psychological contract – the unspoken and unwritten expectation that both parties have in relation to the role and responsibilities of each other.

> **Psychological contract** An unwritten agreement that sets out what management expects from an employee and vice versa

43.3.2 Contingency Plans

29. In some cases, the preferred applicant may reject the job offer. In such cases, the organization may choose to offer the job to an applicant who narrowly missed out, may decide to repeat the recruitment process or withdraw the vacancy. When offering the job to the next preferred applicant, the organization should take steps to avoid that applicant perceiving they were 'second best'.

Of course there are many HR related activities that follow the resourcing process. There is a need to induct the new employee and embark upon various strategies to retain them. Such activities will be explored in the following chapters.

CONCLUSION

30. In this chapter we described the resourcing process in terms of recruitment, selection and appointment. Key recruitment activities include identification of a vacancy and the job analysis, identification of where likely candidates may be found, advertising, documentation and initial sifting. Many of the outputs from the recruitment sub process form inputs to the selection process which aims to identify, from those coming forward, the individual(s) most likely to fulfil the requirements of the organization. The cornerstone of effective selection is the job analysis which defines the assessment criteria. Selection processes are designed on the assumption that there are job relevant individual differences between people, which can be assessed. A range of selection methods were described and the need for fairness argued. The output of the selection process is the identification of the chosen applicants. A job offer is made and an employment contract issued and signed. At this point, other aspects of the HR system associated with induction and employee retention are employed.

QUESTIONS

1 Highlight the difference between recruitment and selection – what is the selection process really about?

2 Discuss the role of personality measurement in the recruitment process: should a candidate's personality trait/scores be used to select/deselect them? Do you believe that personality can be measured? How helpful is personality assessment in enabling a manager to make predictions about a potential employee's future job performance? How valuable is personality assessment in enabling a career guidance counsellor to advise clients effectively on suitable and unsuitable career options?

3 Identify and describe the two main human resource management processes used to attract qualified employees.

4 Identify and discuss, in sequence, the key activities involved in recruiting.

5 Discuss the purpose of the key activities involved in selecting workers and the devices used in selection.

6 The interview is a common method used to fill vacancies within the organization. With reference to the formal and informal, identify what is meant by the selection interview. You should also comment on the function of the interview.

7 Evaluate the importance of recruitment and selection to Google.

8 With reference to both the Google case study and your wider reading, distinguish the typical stages of the recruitment and selection process.

9 Evaluate the role of technology in recruitment and selection.

10 Discuss the importance of fairness in selection and list typical activities which may be performed to ensure that recruitment and selection is conducted in a legal and non-discriminatory manner.

USEFUL WEBSITES

ACAS website **www.acas.org.uk** – templates and checklists – see Hiring new staff
The Equalities and Human Rights Commission **www.equalityhumanrights.com**

DTI Factsheets **www.dti.org.uk/publications**
Assessment Centers **www.assessmentcenters.org** – resources for the use of assessment centres

VIDEO CASES

Now take a look at the online video cases – visit the companion website to work through real world business problems associated with the concepts presented within this chapter.

35 HR Selection in Carlson – selecting a CEO
Whereas recruitment is concerned with generating a candidate pool, selection is about evaluating and deciding upon an individual's suitability for a particular job.

44 Automated (web enabled) recruitment and selection
Examines the activities associated with recruitment and selection and how technology may enable these activities. Identified

are the advantages and disadvantages of approaches using technology and finally the whole approach to recruitment and selection is evaluated.

93 Managing human resources – recruiting and competing for talent
Human resource management is the process of identifying, developing and retaining the right people to form a qualified workforce. Resourcing includes the activities responsible for filling positions within the organization (staffing, recruitment and selection). In the associated case study we explore how

companies use recruitment and selection techniques to attract and hire qualified employees to fulfil those needs.

108 Selecting employees through interviews
This case considers employee selection (interviewing) both from the perspective of the candidate and the interviewer.

Employee selection is considered as a resourcing decision, based upon the perceptions and judgements of interviewers. We consider and evaluate the effectiveness of interviewing, and discuss interview objectives, methods, techniques and approaches.

REFERENCES

Arnold, J. and Randall, R M. (2010) 'Work Psychology: Understanding Human Behaviour in the Workplace', Ed. 5.

Bandura, A. and Wood, R. (1989) 'Social Cognitive Theory of Organizational Management', Academy of Management Review, 14 (3), p. 361–384.

Bratton, J. and Gold, J. (2007) 'Human Resource Management Theory and Practice', Ed. 4. Palgrave Macmillan.

Cascio, W. and Aguinis, H. (2010) 'Applied Psychology in Human Resource Management International Edition', Ed. 7. Pearson.

Martin, J. (2010) 'Key Concepts in Human Resource Management', Sage.

Woods, S. A. and West, M. A. (2010) 'The Psychology of Work and Organizations', South-Western, Cengage Learning.

CHAPTER 44
EMPLOYEE DEVELOPMENT AND TRAINING

Key Concepts

- Development
- Learning organization
- Training
- Training and development

Learning Outcomes   Having read this chapter, you should be able to:

- review the role of training and development activities within the organization
- review the key features of the training and development sub-system within the HR function
- distinguish the terms training, development, learning, competence and education
- discuss a systematic approach to training and describe the training and development process
- list the benefits of systematic training
- explain what is meant by the learning organization

1. In the previous chapter we discussed how employees may be carefully selected and appointed to fulfil certain roles within the organization. This HR sub-process alone does not guarantee such employees will perform well. The HR subsystems of training and development help ensure employees know what to do, why and also how to do it. New employees must be provided with the information required to function. They are typically inducted into the organization (see also orientation and on boarding) and may well be provided with initial training. The induction programme aims to make the employee feel welcome, provide them with the basic information they need to function effectively, enable the employee to understand the organization in a broad sense and therefore how their role contributes to organization's success and socialize the employee into the organizational culture and way of doing things.

2. You may recall from the previous chapter that job analysis defines the tasks (work) and competencies employees need to perform effectively. Organizations use this information to determine training needs. At a basic level, training and development are needed to ensure that (recruited) employees are able to do their jobs well. Training and development, therefore, are critical activities for ensuring the success of the company (Lepak and Gowan, 2009). However, it is not just new employees who require training and development. The changing environment results in change to products, equipment, facilities, procedures and the way work is done. Consequently, there is an ongoing need to ensure all employees are able to do their work well.

3. Human resources are the most dynamic of all the organization's resources. They need considerable attention from the organization's management, if they are to realize their full potential in their work and ensure the achievement of business strategy. This short chapter highlights the principal features of a training and development sub-system within the HR system. The main focus is on training, with development discussed further in Chapter 46. We start by defining key concepts before evaluating the strategic role of training and development. We then describe the training and development process, highlighting various methods.

Training Any intervention aimed at increasing an individual's knowledge or skills

Development Anything that helps a person to grow, in ability, skills, confidence, interpersonal skills, understanding, self-control and more

Training and development The design and delivery of workplace learning to improve performance

44.1 KEY CONCEPTS

4. A question frequently raised by examiners is 'what is the difference, if any, between "training" and "development"?' Another question which is sometimes asked is 'what is the difference between "education" and "training"?' Given the continuing interest in the implications of such concepts as the 'learning organization' and competence-based training (see below), it would also be useful to consider what is meant by the expressions 'learning' and 'competence'. We can thus compare the core meanings of each of these five concepts, as follows:

- **EDUCATION** – formal, typically more general, learning outside (and often before entering) the workplace.

- TRAINING – this usually implies preparation for an occupation or for specific skills; it is narrower in conception than either education or development; it is job-oriented rather than personal.

- DEVELOPMENT – this usually suggests a broader view of knowledge and skills acquisition than training; it is less job-oriented than career-oriented; it is concerned more with employee potential than with immediate skill; it sees employees as adaptable resources.

Education Formal learning outside (and often before entering) the workplace

Learning The development of knowledge

Competence Work related knowledge, skill or ability held by an individual

- **LEARNING** – this is the process of acquiring knowledge, understanding, skills and values in order to adapt to our environment; it underpins all of the above three; the amount, quality and rate of take-up of learning depends mainly on (a) the innate intelligence and motivation of the learner, (b) the skills of the teacher and (c) the conditions in which the learning takes place (especially the use of relevant learning aids).

- COMPETENCE – this refers primarily to a person's ability to demonstrate to others that they can perform a task, process or function to a predetermined standard; **competence** is all about putting learning into practice; it is about the difference between 'knowing how' and 'doing' to a satisfactory level; using predetermined standards in this way is called 'competence-based' training.

44.2 STRATEGY

5.   HR is likely to have a development strategy that fits with the overall HR strategy and this will fit with the business and corporate strategies. Yet the strategic approach of the organization may be reactive or proactive. As previously discussed, functional strategies may simply be created to assure business goals are met, or in some cases, may define those goals. For example in a reactive, needs-driven approach the purpose of the development strategy may simply be to identify and remedy skill deficiencies in relation to the organizational strategy. However, in a proactive approach, the purpose of the development strategy may be to develop abilities, competences and behaviours which may be the source of future competitiveness.

Learning organization An organization skilled at creating, acquiring, and transferring knowledge and at modifying its behaviour to reflect new knowledge and insights

6.   Learning, training and development may be considered at many levels within the organization. Strategically, the organization may focus on cultural issues, organizational learning and the learning organization; they may seek to align the development with corporate strategy. Of vital importance is the organizational and individual ability to learn – creating a learning climate. Contemporary organizations typically pursue entrepreneurial and innovative cultures in which learning is part of everyday work. Learning, training and development may also be considered at the group, team or individual level. There are a range of stakeholders to consider when addressing developmental needs. Senior managers act as sponsors of training and development, line managers are responsible for the performance of their teams, participants are influenced by their career aspirations and then there are facilitators and training providers to consider.

7.   There are many factors that will impact upon the development strategy. Development typically comes at a cost and the organization will expect a return on its investment. Measuring this is easier said than done however. One major factor associated with resourcing (see previous chapter) and impacting upon development is the external availability of individuals with required skills and competencies. When skilled employees are abundant, the organization has a greater choice of whether, and to what extent it wishes to develop employees internally. However, when skilled employees are in short supply, the organization is more likely to prioritize and invest in development.

44.3 TRAINING AND DEVELOPMENT

8.   The scope of training and development activities, as in most other activities in an organization, depends upon the policy and strategies of the organization. There are many organizations

in the commercial field that carry out the minimum of staff training and development, because, as a matter of policy, they prefer to recruit employees that are already trained or professionally qualified. The majority of organizations, however, do have a positive policy on training and development.

9.   A term frequently used to describe well-organized training (and development) is 'systematic training'. This can be illustrated diagramatically as a cycle of events (a four step training process), which is initiated by the organization's policy, and sustained by its training organization, as shown in Figure 44.1.

10.   Once the training organization has been set up, the first priority is to establish the training and development needs of the organization. This will involve the use of job descriptions, employee appraisal records and other data which may indicate such needs. The next step is to plan the training required to meet the needs identified. This entails such matters as setting budgets and timetables, and deciding on the objectives, content and methods of training to be employed. The implementation of plans is usually a joint affair between the training specialists and their line and functional colleagues. Having implemented the required training, it is important to evaluate the results, so far as possible, so that, if necessary, subsequent changes can be made to content and methods. Events then move on to the identification of new needs, which re-starts the cycle afresh. We consider each of the aforementioned stages in more detail later.

11.   The benefits of systematic training include:

–   the provision of a pool of skilled personnel for the organization

–   the improvement of existing skills

FIGURE 44.1 Systematic training: the basic cycle.

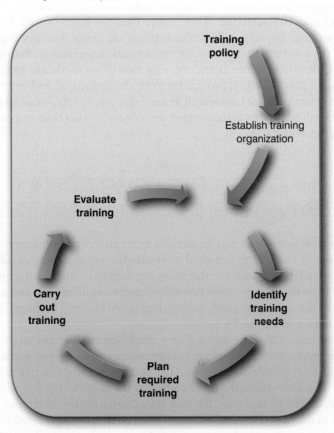

- an increase in the knowledge and experience of employees

- improvements in job performance with resulting improvement in productivity overall

- improved service to customers

- greater commitment of staff (i.e. Increased motivation)

- increased value of individual employees' knowledge and skills and

- personal growth opportunities for employees.

Organizations should also look at development from the employee's perspective. In previous chapters we have discussed the concept of the psychological contract and employees would typically expect to be developed during their time with an organization. It may be a tool for recruitment and retention or a reward for work undertaken.

12.   Whilst the systematic approach has its merits, rationality and efficiency, Torrington *et al* (2009: 418) suggest it has been less prominent of late. Apart from not having a focus on learning it is somewhat mechanical and sluggish in the face of continual change. Despite this, the model or a modified version, has applicability in today's environment and has not been abandoned by many organizations. The model can be adapted to enable individuals to identify their learning needs and to do so in partnership with the organization.

44.4 LEARNING, TRAINING AND DEVELOPMENT

13.   In paragraph 10 we described the traditional training and development process. Torrington *et al* (2009) prefer the term learning and development as opposed to training and development. They suggest there has been a considerable move in the way that individual development is understood and characterized. They argue that we have moved from identifying training needs to identifying learning needs, 'the implication being that development is owned by the learner with the need rather than by the trainer seeking to satisfy that need'. This has implications for who identifies the needs and the way that those needs are met. Contemporary organizations pursue a partnership approach between the individual and organization. A wide range of development methods are considered and we discuss, briefly, some of those later in this chapter. The partnership approach encourages employees to also take responsibility and ownership for their development.

44.5 TRAINING AND DEVELOPMENT PROCESS: (1) IDENTIFYING LEARNING AND TRAINING NEEDS

14.   Training/learning needs may be derived from analysis of the organization, task or individual. At the highest level, there is a need to ensure the organization's vision, mission, values and goals are accomplished. These are therefore key inputs to needs assessment. A training need is any shortfall in terms of employee knowledge, understanding, skill and attitudes against what is required by the job, or the demands of organizational change. In diagrammatic form this can be expressed as shown in Figure 44.2.

15.   Training needs may arise when a new employee commences work or when a current employee is underperforming. The two main approaches to analyzing needs are therefore (1) problem centred and (2) profile comparison. The former is more reactive and focuses on employee performance shortfalls whilst the latter considers the needs of the job with the capabilities of the individual appointed to that job. We will focus more on the latter but return to performance management in the next chapter. In the previous chapter we discussed job analysis and the outputs of this activity, the job descriptions and job specifications that define specific duties and

FIGURE 44.2 Training need.

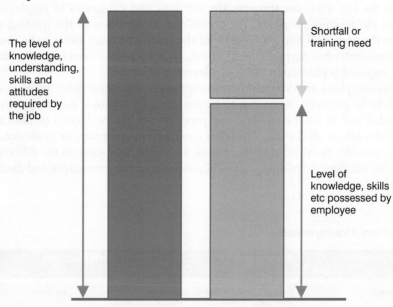

The level of knowledge, understanding, skills and attitudes required by the job

Shortfall or training need

Level of knowledge, skills etc possessed by employee

skills can be used to determine the training required. When training staff conduct a comprehensive training needs analysis in their organization, they will focus on four main sources for their information:

– organization-level data (mission, goals, products/ services offered)

– job-level data (job descriptions and person specifications)

– individual data (**performance appraisal** data) and

– competence standards (i.e. occupational standards – see Chapter 46 for an example).

16. The data obtained in this way enable individuals and the training staff to draw a comprehensive picture of the areas of current and potential shortfall in requirements. The collection of information for a training needs analysis is carried out by interviewing employees, managers and supervisors about their own or their subordinates' training and development needs; and through the analysis of existing records. One particularly important document which contributes to the analysis of training needs is the appraisal form. This is the record of an employee's job performance. Appraisal interviews, and the documentation which accompanies them, are the formal mechanisms by which organizations can assess or evaluate their human assets. In a well-managed organization, this formal appraisal merely rounds off, in a relatively standardized way, the frequent informal appraisals carried out regularly by the organization's managers as a normal part of their job. Amongst the objectives of the appraisal is to identify training and development needs and encourage and motivate employees.

44.6 TRAINING AND DEVELOPMENT PROCESS: (2,3) PLANNING TRAINING AND METHODS OF LEARNING AND DEVELOPMENT

17. Once training needs have been identified by means of the training needs analysis, the training staff can begin the tasks of determining training priorities, drawing up initial plans, costing

them and then submitting draft plans for approval by senior management. These draft plans spell out the key areas for training, the numbers and categories of employees concerned, the nature of the training proposed, the preliminary timetabling of the training programmes contained in the proposals and an estimate of the costs which are likely to be incurred. In the case of a learner-centred or partnership approach, once a learning need has been identified, the development required is phrased in terms of a learning objective.

18.   Training plans are designed to encompass the following: what training is to be provided, how it is to be provided, when it is to be provided, by whom it is to be provided, where it is to be provided and at what cost. Training programmes can be formal or informal, and can take place on-the-job or off-the-job. The latter can mean in-company, or in-service, training or it can refer to externally provided training. Figure 44.3 illustrates some of the different methods of on-the-job and off-the-job training, and indicates some of the advantages and disadvantages of each approach.

FIGURE 44.3 Summary of training methods.

On-the-job training methods	Advantages	Disadvantages
On-the-job instruction	Relevant; develops trainee -supervisor links	Noise, bustle and pressure of workplace
Coaching	Job-related; develops boss-subordinate relationship	Subject to work pressures; may be done piecemeal
Counselling	Employee needs help and Boss provides it	Counselling skills have to be developed
Delegation by boss	Increases scope of job; provides greater motivation	Employees may make mistakes or may fail to achieve task
Secondment	Increases experience of employees; creates new interest	Employee may not succeed in new position
Guided projects/action learning	Increases knowledge and skills in work situation, but under guidance	Finding suitable guides and mentors
Off the job training methods	**Advantages**	**Disadvantages**
(A) in-company		
Lectures/talks	Useful for factual information	One-way emphasis; little participation
Group discussions	Useful for generating ideas and solutions	Requires adequate leadership
Role-playing exercises	Useful for developing social skills	Requires careful organising; giving tactical feedback is not easy
Skills development exercises e.g.: manual operations, communication skills etc	A safe way to practice key skills	Careful organisation required
(B) External		
College courses (long)	Leads to qualification; comprehensive coverage of theory; wide range of teaching methods	Length of training time; not enough practical work
College courses (short)	Supplement in-company training; independent of internal politics	May not meet client needs precisely enough
Consultants/other training organisations	Clients needs given high priority; fills gaps in company provision; good range of teaching methods	Can be expensive; may rely heavily on packages

19.   It is important to note that learning need not be planned. Employees may also learn from their experiences (emergent learning). Learning from experiences or activity was emphasized by Kolb (see the learning cycle) and by Honey and Mumford who described four learning styles: activists, reflectors, theorists and pragmatists.

20.   In previous chapters we have noted how Internet technologies have enabled various HR subsystems. Internet technologies are used to enable e-learning which may be more cost efficient, more timely, more flexible and therefore better value for money. E-learning enables distant learning and learning at a time more convenient for the learner. Learning and training now involves a much wider range of activities which are typically blended to suit the needs of the learner. For many companies the resources placed in training and development represent a considerable investment in time, money and manpower. This investment needs to be evaluated from time to time to ensure, so far as possible, that it is being deployed wisely.

44.7 TRAINING AND DEVELOPMENT PROCESS: (4) EVALUATION OF TRAINING

21.   Torrington *et al* (2009:379) suggest there seems to be general agreement that training and development is a good thing, and that it increases productivity, but the question is 'how much'? The evaluation of training is part of the control process of training. Evaluation methods aim to obtain feedback about the results or outputs of training, and to use this feedback to assess the value of the training, with a view to improvement, where necessary. Like any other control process, training evaluation is firstly concerned with setting appropriate standards of training. These may take the form of policies, objectives, adherence to external standards and standards of trainer-training and qualifications. Clearly, the more precise the standards set, the easier it is to evaluate the success of training. This brings us on to the next key point, which is the collection of relevant feedback data about training. Evaluation can take place at a number of different levels, ranging from immediate to long-term results. Each level requires a different evaluation strategy, as indicated in Figure 44.4.

22.   Training-centred evaluation aims to assess the inputs to training, i.e. whether we are using the right tools for training. Reactions-centred evaluation, which is probably the most

FIGURE 44.4 Training and evaluation

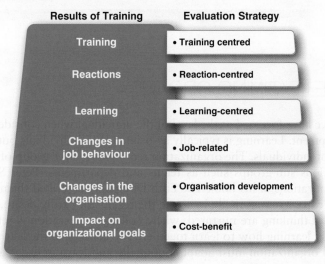

widely-used strategy for evaluation, seeks to obtain and assess the reactions of trainees to the learning experiences in which they have engaged. Learning-centred evaluation seeks to measure the degree of learning that has been achieved. This is usually achieved by testing trainees following the training, as in a driving test. Job-related evaluation is aimed at assessing the degree of behavioural change which has taken place on-the-job after returning from a period of training. It is, of course, a measure of learning, but learning which has been applied in the workplace. It is not an easy task to evaluate the degree to which learning has been applied, especially in cases where training in social skills, such as leadership, are concerned. Finally, there is the impact on organizational goals to be considered, i.e. what has training done for profitability or company image, for example? This is a favourite question asked by senior management, but is extremely difficult to evaluate on account of the many other variables which have an impact on these goals.

23.   It was said earlier that, where training standards are laid down precisely, it is easier to assess the value of the training. One of the ways in which organizations attempt to set clear standards is by establishing the overall purpose of a particular programme, and setting specific objectives for the kind of behaviour expected of trainees at the end of the training. It is obviously easier to set specific objectives for measurable features of behaviour, than it is for those features which are difficult to measure. A typical example of an attempt to set standards for a training programme is set out in Figure 44.5. In each case, the objective aims to describe behaviour (i.e. what the trainee is expected to do) at the end of the course.

FIGURE 44.5 **Training objectives**

Course:	Recruitment and selection for supervisors
Overall purpose:	To improve key skills needed in the recruetement and selection process, and to assist in the application of these skills in the workplace.
Objectives:	At the end of the course, a supervisor should be able to: 1. Describe the key stages in the recruitment and selection process, 2. Prepare unacceptable job descriptions and personnel specifications, 3. State the role of the personnel Department in recruitment and selection 4. Apply the seven-point plan as an assessment tool in an interview, 5. Conduct a systematic interview of a prospective employee, and 6. Complete correctly all the company's selectiondocuments, which apply to his/her role as a supervisor.

44.8 THE LEARNING ORGANIZATION

24.   So far we have focussed at the level of the individual when considering learning and training or development. Learning is typically associated with individuals but may also be associated with groups of individuals. The organization represents a large group of individuals and is comprized of various sub-groups such as teams and departments. Peter Senge, who popularized learning organizations in his book The Fifth Discipline, described them as places where people expand their capacity continually to create the results they truly desire, where new and expansive patterns of thinking are nurtured, where collective aspiration is set free and where people are continually learning how to learn together. The concept of the learning organization is that the successful organization must adapt continually and learn in order to respond to changes in the environment.

25.   According to Garvin (1993:80), a learning organization is an organization skilled at creating, acquiring, and transferring knowledge, and at modifying its behaviour to reflect new knowledge and insights. He suggests learning organizations are skilled at five main activities: systematic problem solving, experimentation with new approaches, learning from their own experience and past history, learning from the experiences and best practices of others and transferring knowledge quickly and efficiently throughout the organization. Systematic problem solving, the first activity, rests heavily on the philosophy and methods of the quality movement, an area discussed in Chapter 29. A learning organization is one which sees that learning, training and development are best achieved by collaborative efforts. Every employee from top to bottom is expected to reflect on present practices, suggest better ways of doing things, and collaborate with others to achieve improvements.

26.   Organizations may learn through two major mechanisms: the first is trial-and-error experimentation (learning by doing/experiential learning); the second mechanism is learning from the experience of others such as competitors and suppliers; training and development; external benchmarking; consultants, customers and suppliers; factory visits, trade shows, online databases, magazines and journals; mergers, acquisitions, strategic alliances, licensing and franchises. Organizations capture the experience of other organizations (see imitation) through the transfer of encoded experience in the form of technologies, codes, procedures or similar routines.

27.   Learning organizations are not built overnight, (Garvin 1993:91). The first step is to foster an environment that is conducive to learning. In addition Garvin recommends opening up boundaries which inhibit knowledge flows and the use of programmes or events designed with explicit learning goals in mind.

CONCLUSION

28.   The HR subsystems of training and development help ensure employees know what to do, why and how to do it. Training may be necessary at the start of or throughout work. A term frequently used to describe well-organized training (and development) is 'systematic training'. This can be portrayed as a cycle of events, a four step training process starting with needs assessment. Training needs derive from organizational goals, job descriptions and employee performance appraisals. To fill identified gaps, a development plan is created; training methods are selected, implemented and then evaluated. The evaluation of training is part of the control process of training. Evaluation methods aim to obtain feedback about the results or outputs of training, and to use this feedback to assess the value of the training, with a view to improvement, where necessary. More recently, the systematic approach has been adapted to

Performance appraisal The process of assessing the performance of an employee in his job; appraisal can be used for salary reviews, training needs analysis and job improvement plans, for example

embrace a partnership approach whereby individual employees take more responsibility for their continued development. Finally we discussed the learning organization and the need for a climate and culture that fosters a supportive approach to learning throughout the organization.

QUESTIONS

1   Discuss the meaning of human resource management, human resource planning, employee resourcing and human resource development. Is there any overlap in the meaning of these concepts? How do the concepts relate to each other?

2   Discuss the function and purpose of human resource development and expand on your definition of the concept, highlighting key principles.

3   Why is it important for employees and organizations to learn continuously?

4   Learning is typically associated with individuals but may also be associated with groups of individuals and the organization itself. Discuss how organizations may learn and identify what is meant by organizational learning and the learning organization.

5   Briefly discuss the meaning of learning and then brainstorm the benefits for individuals and organizations.

6   Two important methods of management development include mentoring and coaching

Explain the meaning of these two terms, discussing both how they differ and are similar. You should also comment on factors influencing the learning process i.e. what will make mentoring work?

7   Discuss the benefits of mentoring from the perspective of the mentor and the mentored; you should comment on knowledge management, developing talent and competitive advantage.

8   Compare the meanings of the following five concepts: training, development, learning, education and confidence.

9   With reference to the Google case study, identify and discuss the benefits of systematic training.

10 Discuss what is meant by the term training need and identify how such needs may arise or be determined.

11 Evaluate three on-the-job and three off the job training methods.

12 Identify and discuss the remaining stages of the training and development process.

USEFUL WEBSITES

Investors in People: **www.iipuk.co.uk**
Learning and Skills Council: **www.lsc.gov.uk**
UK Lifelong Learning: **www.lifelonglearning.co.uk**
Department: **www.dfes.gov.uk**
UK Department for Business, Innovation and Skills, BIS:
    www.bis.gov.uk

Institute for Employment Studies: **www.employment-studies.co.uk/consult/index.php?id=dev&tab=work**
    Developing your people
LearnDirect: **www.learndirect.co.uk**

VIDEO CASES

Now take a look at the online video cases – visit the companion website to work through real world business problems associated with the concepts presented within this chapter.

110 Human Resource Development (HRD) – Invest In Your People

The main focus of this case is training and development. It is now widely recognized (for many organizations) that the ability to recruit, develop and retain employees provides a significant and sustainable competitive advantage. For many organizations, it is simply not possible to buy in the required skills as and when needed. This case examines human resource development (HRD) from a number of perspectives. Organizations that consider people to be key to competitive advantage must recruit and develop talented employees, enhance their capabilities and motivation, whilst seeking to retain such resources. Organizations need people with appropriate skills, abilities and experience; such people may be brought in from the outside (recruitment and selection) or 'grown' by training and developing existing employees. The organization must provide opportunities for learning and development and personal growth. In summary, much of this case is about investing in human capital.

118 Organizational Learning

This case study explores organizational learning and learning within organizations through four short film clips. The film clips discuss the need to let people make mistakes and learn from these errors and the need to have a culture that permits mistakes, especially when the organization seeks to empower employees. Employees who take necessary risks are bound to make mistakes sometimes – what is important is that they do not make the same mistake again. Learning is the process of acquiring knowledge through experience which leads to an enduring change in behaviour. Ultimately, that behaviour should manifest in better organizational decision making, improved productivity, better performance, etc. An organization which encourages and facilitates the learning and development of people at all levels of the organization, values the learning and simultaneously transforms itself, is deemed a learning organization.

119 Learning on the job and Facilitating Learning

Managers must learn continually and develop their skills to cope with the changing and growing demands of the market place. This case study considers mentoring as a means to transfer knowledge and develop employees.

REFERENCES

Dessler, G. (2011) 'Human Resources Management', Ed. 12. Pearson Higher Education.

Garvin, D. (1993) 'Building a Learning Organization', Harvard Business Review, July-August 1993, p. 78–91.

Gomez-Mejia, L., Balkin, D. and Cardy, R. (2010) 'Managing Human Resources: Global Edition', Ed. 6. Pearson Higher Education.

Lepak, D. and Gowan, M. (2009) 'Human Resource Management International Edition', Pearson Education (Upper Saddle River, United States).

Mondy, R. (2009) 'Human Resource Management: International Edition', Ed. 11. Pearson Education.

Senge, P. M. (1996) 'Systems thinking', Executive Excellence, 13 (1), p. 15.

Senge, P. M. (1991) 'Learning Organizations', Executive Excellence, 8 (9), p. 7.

Torrington, D., Hall, L., Taylor, S. and Atkinson, C. (2009) 'Fundamentals of Human Resource Management: Managing People at Work', Ed. 1. Financial Times Press.

CHAPTER 45
PERFORMANCE APPRAISAL, DISCIPLINE AND GRIEVANCES

Key Concepts

- Disciplinary Procedure
- Grievance
- Performance appraisal
- Performance Management

Learning Outcomes Having read this chapter, you should be able to:

- clarify the nature and purpose of performance management and performance appraisal
- explain the appraisal process
- identify key elements of the appraisal form
- evaluate methods to measure individual performance at work
- recognize good practice in the design and execution of performance appraisals
- review disciplinary and grievance procedures

1. According to HRM philosophy, employees are an important business resource that must be managed carefully in order to maximize return on investment and achieve business objectives. In recent years, performance management and appraisal have become key features of an organization's drive towards achieving high performance and thus competitive advantage. Performance management has existed in the language of HR and people management since the 1980s. Since the early development of objective-setting (see Chapter 18), the underlying assumption of performance management is that individual performance can be raised through a focus on setting and monitoring goals and aligning development and reward to individual aspirations and potential to grow and develop new skills. Performance management assumes that by raising individual levels of performance, organizational performance will also improve. Thus HRM aligns people strategies with business strategies by designing performance assessment systems which identify, develop and reward talent to achieve business objectives.

Performance A continuous process for improving the performance of individuals by aligning actual performance with that desired (and with the strategic goals of the organization) through a variety of means such as standard-setting, appraisal and evaluation both informally, day-to-day, and formally/ systematically through appraisal interviews and goal-setting

2. Traditionally performance appraisal systems have provided a formalized process to review employee performance (Torrington *et al* 2009). They tend to be centrally designed, usually by the HR function, requiring each line manager to appraise the performance of their staff, usually each year. What is being appraised varies and may cover personality, behaviour or job performance, with measures being either quantitative or qualitative. Criteria such as the achievement of objectives, customer care, creativity, quality, flexibility, competence, productivity, teamwork may all feature in the process. Furthermore performance information may come from a variety of sources (different stakeholders and systems). Consequently every performance management system is different, with some being more effective than others.

Performance assessment One of the many people management techniques which 'classify and order individuals hierarchically' (Townley). Modern assessment is often focused on competences. See also 'Appraisals'

3. In this chapter we explore the process and methods used, commenting on sources of bias and problems of under or over-rating. Ultimately, the performance system aims to reward and improve employee behaviour. However, when managers fail to create the desirable employee behaviours or encounter problematic undesirable behaviours they may have to resort to disciplinary action. Finally, grievances are concerns, problems or complaints that employees raise with their employer (ACAS, 2009). We will therefore explore discipline and grievance practices towards the end of the chapter.

45.1 PERFORMANCE MANAGEMENT AND PERFORMANCE APPRAISAL

4. We have discussed performance management previously in this book. We discussed performance standards in Chapter 18 and controlling performance in Chapter 28. The CIPD (2009) tracked the evolution of performance management since the early 1990s from a heavily bureaucratized procedure focused on objective-setting or merit rating to a more wide-reaching and inclusive process, integrated with other related practices such as career management, talent management and development. In Chapter 18 we highlighted mechanisms to ensure that strategy cascades down the organization and leads to action. In particular we focussed on the performance management system as a tool to align every manager and employee with the organization's goals thus ensuring effective and efficient behaviours and ultimately helping to assure that organizational goals are attained. We discussed MBO as an early

Talent management A strategic and integrated approach to developing a skilled and competent workforce, involving targeted recruitment, development and retention

attempt to align individual with organizational goals but recognized a number of shortcomings associated with the approach (too mechanistic to deal with a fast-changing environment).

5.   In simple terms, performance management is the means by which many organizations make certain that managers ensure people know what they ought to be doing, have the skills to do it and complete it to an adequate standard. It establishes shared understanding about what is to be achieved. It is the system through which organizations set work goals, determine performance standards, assign and evaluate work, provide performance feedback, determine training and development needs and distribute rewards.

6.   Research has identified a number of underlying trends, such as the shift of ownership of performance management from HR to line managers – performance management is most usually designed by HR and delivered by line managers; performance management has evolved from a heavily bureaucratized procedure to a wider-reaching and inclusive process; it has acquired a much more central role in the strategic management process and has become a primary tool for managing the business. There is a surprising degree of agreement that performance appraisal (assessment), objective-setting, regular feedback, regular reviews and assessment of development needs are the cornerstones of performance management (CIPD, 2009).

Performance appraisal The process of assessing the performance of an employee in his job; appraisal can be used for salary reviews, training needs analysis and job improvement plans, for example

7.   Performance management is an ongoing or continuous process whilst performance appraisal is done at discrete time intervals. Performance appraisal is the systematic description of an employee's job-relevant strengths and weaknesses. Appraisal provides an analysis of a person's overall capabilities and potential, allowing informed decisions to be made in the process of engaging and managing (controlling) employees. Appraisals are used to ensure an individual's performance is contributing to business goals. There are several reasons why appraisals are carried out in organizations. These may be summarized as follows, to:

Appraisals Appraisals rate individuals on quasi-objective criteria or standards deemed to be relevant to performance. Traditional appraisals rated individuals on a list of qualities, primarily work-related attitudes and personality traits. See also 'Performance assessment'

–   identify an individual's current level of job performance

–   identify employee strengths and weaknesses

–   enable employees to improve their performance

–   provide a basis for rewarding employees in relation to their contribution to organization goals

–   motivate individuals

–   identify training and development needs

–   identify potential performance and

–   provide information for succession planning.

45.2 DEFINING AND MEASURING WORK PERFORMANCE

8.   In Chapter 18 we discussed the measurement of results and behaviour. Performance assessment and appraisal necessitates a definition for performance and a means to measure it. In order to make comparisons between employees and to make the assessment process more valid and reliable, a number of practitioners seek to measure underlying components (job performance factors/competencies) of work performance that are common to all work roles. For example, Bartram (2005) listed eight 'great' factors of job performance:

Leading and deciding – takes control and exercises leadership. Initiates action, gives direction and takes responsibility.

Supporting and cooperating – supports others and shows respect and positive regard for them in social situations; puts people first, working effectively with individuals and teams, clients, and staff; and behaves consistently with clear personal values that complement those of the organization.

Interacting and presenting – communicates and networks effectively; persuades and influences others successfully; and relates to others in a confident, relaxed manner.

Analyzing and interpreting – shows evidence of clear analytical thinking; gets to the heart of complex problems and issues; and applies own expertize effectively. Communicates well in writing.

Creating and conceptualizing – works well in situations requiring openness to new ideas and experiences; handles situations and problems with innovation and creativity; and thinks broadly and strategically.

Organising and executing – plans ahead and works in a systematic and organized way; follows directions and procedures; and focuses on customer satisfaction and delivers a quality service or product to the agreed standards.

Adapting and coping – adapts and responds well to change; manages pressure effectively and copes well with setbacks.

Enterprising and performing – focuses on results and achieving personal work objectives; shows an understanding of business, commerce, and finance; and seeks opportunities for self-development and career advancement.

9.   Other researchers and practitioners have generated similar lists, considering factors such as core task proficiency, demonstrated effort, teamwork and others. Our ability to define work performance is important because it impacts on how it is measured and assessed.

10.   Performance data may come from the judgements of the managers and other stakeholders coming into contact with the employee or from objective data such as production data, e.g. the total number of sales made or revenue generated etc. The most common form of performance data is still derived from managers' direct or indirect observation of employees in the workplace (Arnold and Randall, 2010). Aside from direct observation, recently there has been an upsurge in the use of electronic methods, common in call centre environments.

11.   Both objective and subjective assessment data have their strengths and weaknesses. Objective/production data may be seen as fair in that it is difficult to dispute it but such data often measures not only the performance of the employee concerned but also other factors outside of their control. It does not not measure behaviour but rather the outcomes of behaviour. Consequently, subjective data is often used. Despite this, many problems are typically reported when evaluating judgement as a performance assessment technique. Judgements are subject to bias often referred to as halos and horns (see Chapter 43, p. 10).

12.   A considerable amount of work has been done on judgemental biases in rating and the tendency for managers to be lenient or severe in their assessments. Many assessors avoid using the high and low extremes of rating scales (central tendency) treating everybody as average. This fails to discriminate, making the process meaningless. Further sources of bias will be discussed in more detail later.

45.3 APPRAISAL PROCESS

13.   Performance appraisal involves two distinct processes: (1) observation and (2) judgement, (Cascio and Aguinis, 2010). Observation processes include the perception and recall of specific behavioural events whilst judgement processes include the categorisation, integration and evaluation of information. When observing and judging their employees, managers must be aware of the work and personal requirements of a particular job (refer back to job analysis), the required performance standard and must then describe the job-relevant strengths and weaknesses of each employee.

14.   At its simplest, the appraisal process can be depicted as in Figure 45.1. Any systematic approach to performance appraisal will include the completion of an appropriate appraisal form. This preparatory stage will be followed by an interview, in which the manager discusses progress with the employee. The result of the interview is some form of agreed action. The action generally materializes in the shape of a personal development or job improvement plan, promotion to another job or to a salary increase, for example.

FIGURE 45.1   The appraisal process.

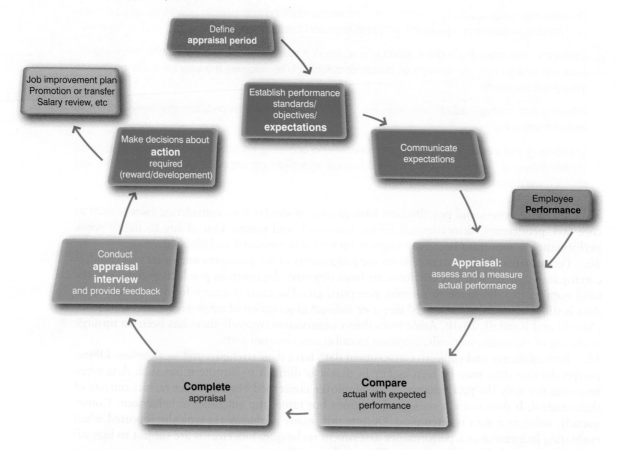

15.   One contentious issue concerning the appraisal process concerns who shall rate or make judgements or provide performance information about the employee's performance. Most appraisals are conducted by line managers on the employees who report to them, and so an element of formal authority is invariably present in the appraisal interview. However, in recent years, so-called 360° appraisals have been introduced by organizations that are keen to improve the appraisal process. A variety of stakeholders are consulted, so that appraisal becomes all-round rather than just top-down. In the following paragraphs we will describe the key stages of the appraisal process in more detail.

360° appraisal Performance assessment of a person by the key people or groups with whom they interact. May include external people or groups such as customers

45.4 APPRAISAL FORMS

16.   Aguinis (2009:Ch6), discussing the gathering of performance information, recognizes that an important component of the performance assessment stage is the use of appraisal forms–

instruments used to document and evaluate performance. Appraisal forms usually include a combination of the following components: (1) employee information–job title, department, key dates, etc.; (2) objectives, weighted in terms of importance (if a result approach has been adopted) and the extent to which they have been achieved; (3) competences and indicators (if a behavioural approach has been adopted); (4) major achievements and contributions; (5) developmental achievements i.e. the extent to which the employee has met developmental goals during the review period; (6) developmental needs; (7) stakeholder input; (8) employee comments and (9) signatures.

17.   There is no such thing as a universally correct appraisal form. However, generally desirable features include simplicity, relevancy, descriptiveness (include evidence and enable understanding by parties not present in the interview), adaptable, comprehensive, clearly defined competencies (where applicable), and has both a past and a future orientation.

18.   Appraisal criteria are generally either personality (behaviour) or results oriented. Within each of these orientations appraisers are still required to 'measure' individual performance. They do so by using one or more scales for rating performance. The principal options available are:

- Linear or Graphic Rating Scales, in which the appraiser is faced with a list of characteristics or job duties and is required to tick or circle an appropriate point on a numerical, alphabetical or other simple scale. See Figure 45.2.

- Behavioural Scales, in which the appraiser has a list of key job items against which are ranged a number of descriptors, or just two extreme statements of anticipated behaviour. Another scale, dealing with customer relations, could demonstrate a range of possible behaviour from the best, e.g. 'deals politely and efficiently with customers at all time', to the worst 'is barely civil to customers, is inefficient.'

- Results/Targets Set.

- Free Written Reports, in which appraisers write essay-type answers to a number of questions set on the appraisal document.

19.   Performance ratings may be intentionally or unintentionally distorted or inaccurate. It is important to understand how and why assessors may distort ratings. Assessors may provide inflated or deflated ratings. They may inflate ratings in order to maximize an employee's reward, encourage and motivate them or they may inflate ratings in order to avoid confrontation, make

FIGURE 45.2 **Linear rating scales.**

	Excellent				Non-existent
Initiative	A	B	C	D	E

	Excellent				Poor
Relationship with customers	A	B	C	D	E

	Low				High
Initiative	1	2	3	4	5

	Poor				Excellent
Relationship with customers	1	2	3	4	5

themselves look good or to get the employee promoted out of the managers team. In some cases, the assessor may deflate ratings in order to send a message to or shock the employee.

20.   Thus the rating process may be influenced by emotions, hidden agendas and politics. Distorted ratings are clearly damaging for the organization's performance management system and the HR professional will take steps to prevent conscious distortion of ratings. They will seek to train and make managers accountable for their ratings. It is important that assessors understand the company's reasons for implementing the performance management system, how to collect performance information, how to minimize rating errors, use the appraisal form and manage the process.

21.   After the form has been completed, there is usually a need to compute an overall performance score (Aguinis, 2009). This enables subsequent decisions based on performance. There are two main methods used to compute the overall performance score: judgemental and mechanical (objective/calculated). In the case of the former, the assessor will formulate an overall summary and in the case of the latter, category scores are simply added up; in many cases, category scores will be weighted to reflect the relative importance of each performance by dimension measured. Clearly the objective approach is more defensible and is less likely to be affected by assessor bias.

22.   Organizations must determine the period of time that should be included in the appraisal form-in many companies this will be a yearly activity; other companies may appraise employees more frequently, for example six-monthly or quarterly. Organizations will also specify the best time to complete the reviews and this will normally be linked to the company's financial reporting year or the calendar year. Having considered the appraisal documentation and the validity and reliability of the performance information it contains (see Figure 45.1 the appraisal process), we can now turn to the next stage in the process, the appraisal interview conducted by the job-holder's manager.

45.5 APPRAISAL STYLES, INTERVIEWS AND THE PROVISION OF FEEDBACK

23.   Undertaking the appraisal process will require at least one meeting between the subordinate and line manager. Meetings are required in order to discuss the performance system and set expectations, discuss self-appraisal, undertake the performance review itself, award and discuss rewards, discuss employee development needs and to set objectives for the following review period. Clearly some of these tasks may take place together under one meeting; however, a number of organizations prefer to separate out certain tasks and include them in a separate meeting.

24.   The appraisal interview is the formal face-to-face meeting between the job-holder and their manager at which the information on the appraisal form is discussed and after which certain key decisions are made concerning salary, promotion and training, for example. The manner in which managers approach an appraisal interview will be strongly influenced by their understanding of the purpose of the interview. Appraisal interviews can serve several purposes, to:

- evaluate the subordinate's recent performance

- formulate job improvement plans

- identify problems and/or examine possible opportunities related to the job

- improve communication between superior and subordinate

- provide feedback on job performance to the employee

- provide a rationale for salary reviews

- identify potential performance/possibilities for promotion or transfer and

- identify training and development needs.

25.   Amongst other things, performance appraisals serve as an employee development tool. Feedback is used to bring about improvements in present performance. However, feedback must be delivered in the appropriate manner if it is to be motivating and encourage desirable behaviours. In order to make appraisal interviews more effective, managers are encouraged to provide frequent performance feedback to employees and maintain comprehensive records of an employee's performance in their assigned roles. The manager should be trained in performance appraisal techniques and should understand the organization's performance management system. They should encourage employees to prepare for appraisal interviews. This will typically mean explaining the appraisal system, categories, process and encouraging the employee to engage in self appraisal prior to the meeting. During the appraisal interview, the manager should be specific, constructive and an active listener whilst encouraging subordinate participation. When setting goals for the next assessment period, the manager should be mindful of goal setting theory (refer back to Chapter 6) and the need for employees to generate their own goals.

26.   Basic approaches to the appraisal interview may be represented on a continuum of interviewer behaviour, ranging from a relatively autocratic style to one that is fully participative. The continuum may be described graphically as in Figure 45.3. The likely success of the varying styles, judging from research into appraisals, can be summarized as follows:

'TELLING' can be counterproductive. It has been found that praise has little effect one way or the other on employees. Criticism, however, has a negative effect on subsequent achievement. At least this approach does give the employee some idea of his or her progress.

'TELLING/SELLING'. Unless the manager is very persuasive, it is unlikely that the employee will accept the manager's version of what is required to be done.

'TELLING/LISTENING'. This approach has the merit of informing employees of their progress, but then goes further by actively involving them in the process of deciding what ought to be done, which is much more likely to produce a positive response.

FIGURE 45.3 **A continuum of appraisal interview styles (after Maier)**

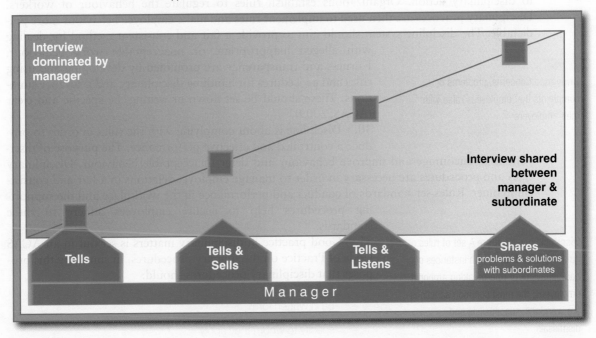

'SHARING'. This is generally considered to provide the best basis for an appraisal, owing to its joint problem-solving approach, in which the manager and his or her team member work together more or less as equals. This approach is closer to coaching than anything else.

27.   Despite the merit of the aforementioned goals and purpose of the appraisal process, the annual appraisal risks becoming an annual ritual rather than offering meaningful direction, (CIPD, 2009). Performance appraisal problems are likely to occur less frequently when:

- performance criteria are relevant to the job
- performance criteria are clearly understood
- appraisers and employees both understand the system
- appraisal occurs frequently
- performance ratings are collected from more than one source and
- appraisers are accountable for their ratings.

28.   Aside from rewarding results and desirable behaviours, one of the key roles of performance appraisal and management is to bring about the modification of employee behaviours. It is important therefore to specify desirable behaviours and to devise intervention strategies that target undesirable behaviours or seek to strengthen desirable behaviours. Various intervention strategies exist and include the use of rewards, training and development and feedback.

45.6 DISCIPLINARY AND GRIEVANCE PROCEDURES

29.   Whilst we will consider employee relations in Chapter 49, we will explore one of the important dimensions (discipline) in this section. When managers fail to create the desirable employee behaviours or encounter problematic undesirable behaviours they may have to resort to disciplinary action. Organizations establish rules to regulate the behaviour of workers. Disciplinary practices are then used to implement rules and make employee behaviour more predictable. The discipline system should aim to provide a fair and consistent method for dealing with alleged inappropriate or unacceptable work behaviour. Fairness and transparency are promoted by developing and using rules and procedures for handling disciplinary and grievance situations. These should be set down in writing, be specific and clear (ACAS, 2009).

Grievance Concerns, problems or complaints that employees raise with their employers

30.   Discipline is about complying with the rules in order to produce a controlled and effective performance. The purpose of discipline is to encourage and improve behaviour and deter unacceptable behaviour. Disciplinary rules and procedures are necessary in order to manage employee relations in a fair and consistent manner. Rules set standards of conduct and performance in the workplace and the supporting procedures help to ensure employees adhere to these standards.

Disciplinary procedure A set of rules or guidelines for dealing with instances of bad behaviour or rule-breaking amongst employees; the most common sanctions are warnings, suspensions and dismissals

31.   Good practice in disciplinary matters is set out in an ACAS Code of Practice on disciplinary procedures. In summary this proposes that disciplinary procedures should:

- be in written form
- specify to whom they apply

–   be non-discriminatory

–   be capable of dealing speedily with disciplinary matters

–   be confidential

–   indicate the forms of disciplinary action which may be taken (e.g. dismissal, suspension or warning)

–   specify the appropriate levels of authority for the exercise of disciplinary actions

–   provide for individuals to be informed of the nature of their alleged misconduct before any hearing

–   allow individuals to state their case and to be accompanied by a fellow employee (or union representative)

–   ensure that every case is properly investigated before any disciplinary action is taken

–   ensure that, except for gross misconduct, no employee is dismissed for a first breach of discipline

–   ensure that employees are informed of the reasons for any penalty they receive and

–   provide for a right of appeal against any disciplinary action, and specify the appeals procedure.

Source: ACAS (2001–2009) *Code of Practice, Disciplinary and Grievance Procedures*. © Crown Copyright.

32.   A model disciplinary procedure should aim to correct unsatisfactory behaviour, rather than to punish it. It should specify, as fully as possible, what constitutes 'misconduct' and what constitutes 'gross misconduct'. It should then state what the most likely penalty is for each of these categories. In cases of proven 'gross misconduct', this is most likely to be immediate (or summary) dismissal, or suspension, followed by dismissal. In cases of less serious misconduct, the most likely consequence is that a formal warning will be given. For repeated acts of misconduct, it is likely that the employee concerned will be dismissed. So far as appeals are concerned, a model procedure should aim to ensure that appeals are dealt with quickly, so that the employee involved can be informed of the final decision without undue delay. Because of the serious implications of disciplinary action, only senior managers are normally permitted to carry out suspensions, demotions or dismissals. Other managers are normally restricted to giving warnings of one kind or another.

45.7 GRIEVANCES

33.   A grievance, unlike a disciplinary matter, is first raised by the employee. The onus is on the employee to state the nature of the grievance and what, if anything, he or she wants done about it. In a work team where the manager or supervisor is in close touch with the members, issues that might lead to a grievance tend to be dealt with in the course of day-to-day problem-solving. Where, however, an issue is still not resolved satisfactorily from the employee's point of view, then a formal application may be made to raise the issue under the appropriate procedure.

34.   Grievances are concerns, problems or complaints that employees raise with their employer (ACAS, 2009). There is no legally binding process that either must follow when raising or handling a grievance at work. However, there are some principles which the employee and employer should observe (DirectGov, 2010). There is an ACAS (Advisory, Conciliation and Arbitration Service) Code of Practice on disciplinary and grievance procedures (the Code). It sets out principles employees and employers should follow to achieve a reasonable standard of behaviour in handling grievances.

35.   The ACAS statutory Code of Practice on discipline and grievance is issued under section 199 of the Trade Union and Labour Relations (Consolidation) Act 1992 and was laid before both Houses of Parliament in 2008. It came into effect by order of the Secretary of State in 2009

and replaces the Code issued in 2004. A failure to follow the Code does not, in itself, make a person or organization liable to proceedings. However, employment tribunals will take the Code into account when considering relevant cases. Tribunals will also be able to adjust any awards made in relevant cases by up to 25 per cent for unreasonable failure to comply with any provision of the Code. This means that if the tribunal feels that an employer has unreasonably failed to follow the guidance set out in the Code they can increase any award made by up to 25 per cent. Conversely, if they feel an employee has unreasonably failed to follow the guidance set out in the code they can reduce any award made by up to 25 per cent.

36.   Typical stages of a grievance process include:

- The employee informs the employer about the nature of the grievance.

- Employers arrange for a formal meeting to be held without unreasonable delay after a grievance is received.

- The employee should be allowed to be accompanied at the meeting. Following the meeting a decision is made on what action, if any, to take. Decisions should be communicated to the employee, in writing, without unreasonable delay and, where appropriate, should set out what action the employer intends to take to resolve the grievance.

- The employee is allowed to take the grievance further (appeal) if not resolved.

- The appeal should be dealt with impartially.

- The outcome of the appeal should be communicated to the employee in writing without unreasonable delay.

37.   When dealing with a grievance interview, a manager or supervisor is usually unable to prepare in advance for it. An employee, however, may have been storing up a particular grievance for weeks. In order, therefore, to help them cope with the demands of what is often an extremely emotional situation, many managers and supervisors are trained in the tactics of grievance interviewing. The fundamental point is that no hasty judgements or solutions should be made until all the facts of the case are clear, and all third parties have been consulted and, where appropriate, have agreed to the proposed solution. The key points to be noted can be summarized as in Figure 45.4

38.   Whether or not a grievance turns out to have any substance, after due investigation, it has still been a source of upset feelings for an employee. It is important, therefore, that managers and supervisors aim for a mutually beneficial result at the end of a grievance interview. The employee concerned should feel reassured that, either he or she has no problem, or, if they have, it is being tackled constructively by the immediate line manager. The manager or supervisor

FIGURE 45.4 **Planning a grievance interview.**

Objectives	1. **Obtain the facts** 2. **Arrive at an acceptable solution**
Strategy	Aim for a 'win-win' conclusion
Tactics	1. Listen carefully to the employees side of the story 2. Ask probing questions to elicit relevant facts and feelings 3. Summarise from time to time to ensure mutual understanding 4. Attempt to unravel cause(s) of grievance 5. Check facts obtained and meet any of the parties involved 6. Consider actions that could be taken and assess their consequences 7. Reply to the aggrieved employee and record actions taken

concerned should feel that the grievance has been handled correctly, and that both parties have 'won'. As with disciplinary cases, the ideal is that the outcome of a grievance includes appropriate learning by all those concerned.

CONCLUSION

39. In previous chapters we have commented on the strategic role of HRM. Indeed the adoption of a performance management system can be seen as an attempt to integrate HRM processes with strategy. An organization's goals (business strategy) are translated into sector and then departmental goals, manager and then employee goals respectively. At each stage, there will be an attempt to provide measurable performance indicators of the achievement of goals, (Bratton and Gold, 2007). The general opinion is that performance management is most useful when it aligns individual objectives with business goals and helps individuals to understand the contribution they are making and how their role fits into overall strategic business objectives. However, this does not mean that performance management is viewed simply as a vehicle for cascading objectives. Performance appraisal is the systematic description of an employee's job relevant strengths and weaknesses. Appraisal provides an analysis of a person's overall capabilities and potential, allowing informed decisions to be made in the process of engaging and managing (controlling) employees. Appraisals are used to ensure an individual's performance is contributing to business goals. In this chapter we described the appraisal, discipline and grievance processes as means to manage behaviour within organizations, ensuring it contributes to strategic goals.

QUESTIONS

1   What advice would you give to an organization eager to implement a new performance appraisal process that is rigorous, fair and objective?

2   Why do performance management (specifically appraisal) systems often fail?

3   What is the difference between performance management and performance appraisal?

4   Compare and contrast performance management with performance appraisal.

5   List the common reasons why appraisals are carried out in organizations.

6   Explain the appraisal process.

7   Identify the typical components of an appraisal form.

8   Outline the main purposes of the appraisal interview.

9   Discuss the different styles that may be adopted during an appraisal interview.

10 Identify what the manager can do in order to minimize the likelihood of performance appraisal problems.

USEFUL WEBSITES

Performance Management & Appraisal Help Center: **www.performance-appraisals.org/** Free resource centre's mandate is to offer you help in designing, implementing and making use of performance management and performance appraisal systems

Institute for employment studies: **www.employment-studies.co.uk/consult/index.php?id=rew&tab=work** Reward and performance management

ACAS: **www.acas.org.uk/index.aspx?articleid=651** Advisory booklet – Employee appraisal

ACAS: **www.acas.org.uk/CHttpHandler.ashx?id=1041** Disciplinary and grievance procedures

DirectGov: **www.direct.gov.uk/en/Employment/ResolvingWorkplaceDisputes/Grievanceprocedures/DG_10027992** Raising a grievance at work

CIPD Performance management: **www.cipd.co.uk/subjects/perfmangmt/general/** Practical advice, guidance, tools; Surveys, research, reports

VIDEO CASES

Now take a look at the online video cases – visit the companion website to work through real world business problems associated with the concepts presented within this chapter.
143 Performance feedback
Discusses the importance of providing timely and honest feedback to employees

100 Performance management
Human Resource Management (HRM): discusses the purpose, process and content of performance management systems

REFERENCES

ACAS (2009) 'Disciplinary and grievance procedures', TSO (The Stationery Office) and available from: Online www.tsoshop.co.uk © Crown Copyright 2009.

Aguinis, H. (2009) 'Performance Management: International Edition', Ed. 2. Pearson Higher Education.

Arnold, J. and Randall, R M. (2010) 'Work Psychology: Understanding Human Behaviour in the Workplace', Ed. 5. FT Prentice Hall.

Bartram, D. (2005) 'The Great Eight Competencies: A Criterion-Centric Approach to Validation', Journal of Applied Psychology, Volume 90, Issue 6, November 2005, p. 1185–1203.

Bratton, J. and Gold, J. (2007) 'Human Resource Management Theory and Practice', Ed. 4. Palgrave Macmillan.

Cascio, W. and Aguinis, H. (2010) 'Applied Psychology in Human Resource Management International Edition', Ed. 7. Pearson.

CIPD (2009) 'Performance management in action: current trends and practice', CIPD – Survey report November 2009 – www.cipd.co.uk.

CIPD (2009) 'Performance management: history and foundations', CIPD.

Torrington, D., Hall, L., Taylor, S. and Atkinson, C. (2009) 'Fundamentals of Human Resource Management: Managing People at Work', Ed. 1. Financial Times Press.

CHAPTER 46
DEVELOPING MANAGERIAL COMPETENCIES

Key Concepts

- Experiential learning
- Management development
- Succession planning

Learning Outcomes Having read this chapter, you should be able to:

- list the features/attributes of an effective (successful) manager
- discuss the role of managerial competencies in management development
- discuss how organizations may develop the capabilities of current or future managers (management development methods)

1.   Performance management systems are not restricted to a concern with outcomes and targets but may also be concerned with developing staff (managers in the context of this chapter). As was noted in the previous chapter, performance can be assessed through employee behaviour and we noted the role of competencies and competency frameworks which can provide a 'map' or inventory of the competencies (knowledge, skills, abilities and behaviours) that are needed in a job role; in this case a managerial role. Once a framework, standard or map has been identified or created, managers can be assessed against it in order to decide whether and what further training or development is required. Competency frameworks may also be used in other HR practices such as recruitment and selection (Chapter 43), employee development and training (Chapter 44) and performance management (Chapter 45).

2.   In Chapter 44 we introduced training and development. In the field of training and development, management development has become an important activity in its own right. It has developed its own techniques, practices and literature. This chapter reviews the subject of management development, its techniques and practices. We start by developing thoughts on what constitutes management (referring to the theory we introduced back in Chapter 2) and then ask what a competent manager should be able to do. Frameworks and standards of management competency can then act as targets for which to aim; development techniques and methods are selected and applied to develop the manager into a competent manager.

Management development A systematic process for ensuring that an organization meets its current and future needs for effective managers; typical features include manpower reviews, succession planning, performance appraisal and training

46.1 MANAGEMENT DEVELOPMENT

3.   Management development is a systematic process for ensuring that an organization meets its current and future needs for effective managers; typical features include manpower reviews (see HR Planning), succession planning, performance appraisal and training. See Figure 46.1.

Management Coordinated activities (forecasting, planning, deciding, organizing, commanding) to direct and control an organization

4.   Development is essentially a learning process undertaken over time. Some managers have a greater capacity than others to learn and apply their knowledge through skills and abilities. We might therefore describe a continuum from the novice, who learns facts and rules without criticism or discussion, to the expert, capable of producing a masterly performance. There are clearly a variety of stages in between. The novice develops further by incorporating lessons drawn from experience and with further development may reduce reliance on absolute rules, tending to experiment and learn through trial and error. This may lead to competence and eventually proficiency when intuition may play a greater role.

Succession planning A process through which senior-level openings are planned for and ultimately filled

5.   Prior to developing a manager we must have some idea about what constitutes a manager, what the managerial function should be and the knowledge skills and abilities (competencies) that are required for an effective managerial performance. In the next section we recap on what constitutes a manager before exploring the behaviours attributed to effective and efficient managers. Management development approaches vary according to whether we are dealing with the general or the specific, i.e. generic competencies employed in a range of situations and managerial roles or more technical skills associated with a specific job. The main emphasis of this chapter will be on generic competencies.

FIGURE 46.1 **Formal management development system**

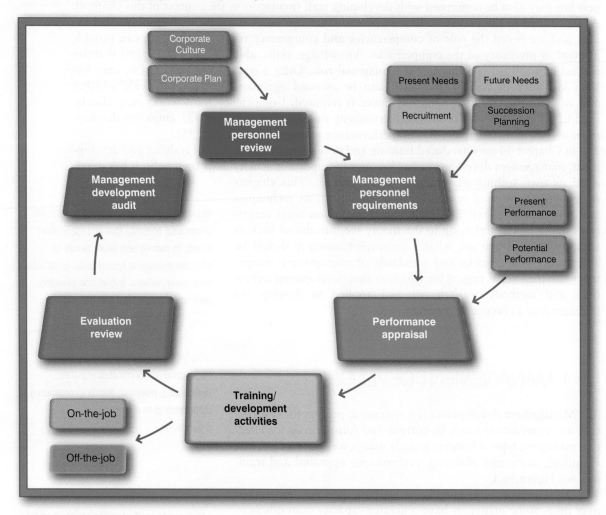

46.2 MANAGEMENT – KNOWLEDGE AND SKILLS

6. Management was discussed in Chapters 1 (see paragraph 2) and 2 (see paragraphs 2–8). Fayol saw the task of management to forecast and plan, to organize, to command, to coordinate and to control. Such a definition is always limited by its generality. It does inform us what managers need to know or do in order to be able to carry out the functions described. In recent years there has been an emphasis on examining what managers actually do in practice. This approach has led to other developments, where attempts have been made to identify specific areas of knowledge and skill in managerial positions. A useful example of this development is provided by Pedler *et al* (2001) in their list of attributes of 'successful' managers. Their list comprises the following features of an effective manager:

-   command of basic facts

-   relevant professional knowledge

-   continuing sensitivity to events

-   analytical, problem-solving, decision-making and judgement-making skills

- – social skills and abilities

- – emotional resilience

- – proactivity, i.e. the inclination to respond purposefully to events

- – creativity

- – mental agility

- – balanced learning habits and skills and

- – self-knowledge.

Pedler and colleagues raise several questions under each of their eleven features to enable managers to assess themselves at the start of a series of self-development exercises built around their list.

7. Taking various views about the nature of managerial jobs as a whole, four key elements can be discerned in terms of what managers might need to know or be able to do. These are as follows:

Managerial knowledge – what the manager needs to know about the organization, the job, and the procedures involved, etc.

Managerial skills – what problem-solving, social and other skills the manager needs to be able to practise

Managerial attitudes – what the manager is required to accept in terms of coping with stress, dealing with clients, etc.

Managerial style – the expectations that people have concerning the way the manager exercises leadership.

8. These four elements can be found in most management development programmes, whether for individuals or for groups. However, organizations and HR practitioners have continued their pursuit of a profile of a capable manager, searching for a list of the typical behaviours they demonstrate when accomplishing their business goals. Much of this work falls under the banner of managerial competency definition.

46.3 MANAGERIAL COMPETENCIES (KNOWLEDGE, SKILLS AND ABILITIES)

9. Competencies, in the general sense, have been discussed in several chapters of this book (see Chapter 18 paragraphs 7 and 16; Chapter 43 paragraph 5). Competencies can be used to define the behaviours needed at work to achieve business strategy. In recent years, information derived from the analysis of work performance has been utilized to create a taxonomy of either criterion related behaviours or standards of performance referred to as competencies. Competences are the patterns of behaviour required to perform the tasks and functions of a particular job. Managerial jobs are associated with a number of (managerial) competencies; each one defined and described by a range of indicators that enable assessment and measurement.

10. Managerial competencies are measurable clusters of knowledge, skills and abilities (KSAs) considered vital in determining how managers accomplish goals. Indicators are measured in order to determine the extent to which the manager possesses a competency. Each indicator is an observable behaviour that provides information about the relevant competency. In other words the competency is not measured directly, we measure indicators that tell us whether the

competency is present or not. An indicator is a behaviour that, if exhibited, suggests that the competency is present. Thus when describing a managerial competency, it is common to first define it and then describe the specific behavioural indicators that can be observed when a manager demonstrates the competency. It is also common to describe specific behaviours that are likely to occur when somebody does not demonstrate a competency and finally, suggestions for developing the particular competency may be documented.

11.   The Management Standards Centre (MSC), is the standards-setting body for National Occupational Standards (NOS) in management. The NOS for management and leadership are statements of best practice which outline the performance criteria, related skills, knowledge and understanding required to carry out various management and leadership functions effectively. The standards describe the activities/functions of management and leadership at various levels of responsibility and complexity. Therefore, they are relevant to anyone for whom management and leadership is, to a greater or lesser extent, part of their work. This applies to managers and leaders in all sizes and types of organization, and in all industries and sectors. The MSC argue the key purpose of management and leadership is to provide direction, gain commitment, facilitate change and achieve results through the efficient, creative and responsible deployment of people and other resources.

12.   The standards, designed to act as a benchmark of best practice, continue to provide a framework for the development of qualifications; they have also been designed to support a wide range of HRM and development purposes. The standards are proven benchmarks of best practice and have been developed based on extensive consultation with genuine managers doing real management jobs. They offer a practical resource to aid decisions in everything from day-to-day matters like recruitment and selection to long-term issues such as the recognition and development of future leaders. They draw together the outcomes, behaviours and knowledge required to deliver identified management functions into a coherent tool which can be used by individual managers and their employers. Managers can use the standards to identify and describe the skills they need, and evaluate the skills they already have; employers can use the standards to evaluate the skills already in the workforce, identify skills gaps and plan training and recruitment. They can also be used as an aid to recruitment, selection and employee development. An example of the logic and content of typical standards are given in Figures 46.2 and 46.3.

FIGURE 46.2   Management standards: key roles.

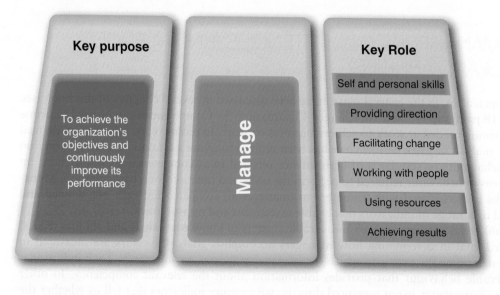

FIGURE 46.3 Management standards: units of competency.

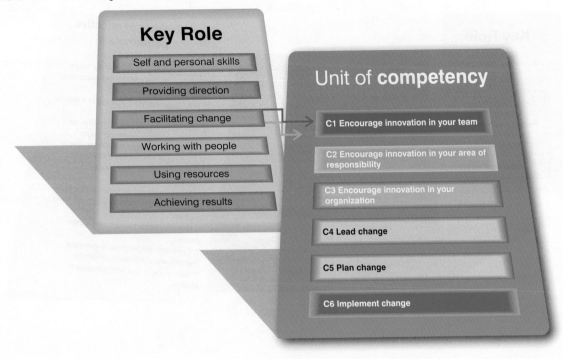

13. The initial logic identifies six key roles (competency clusters) that managers undertake in the workplace (i.e. using resources, managing self and personal skills, etc.) required to achieve the overall purpose. These functions are expressed in very general terms; units of competence are identified within each function. The standards also include behaviours that underpin effective performance. So, for example, the key function of facilitating change is broken down into six 'units of competence'. Figure 46.3 gives some examples of units of competence for this role, and Figure 46.4 shows the outcomes relevant to Unit C4 (Lead change).

14. We discussed change management in Chapter 24. The NOS for the competence of 'leading change' lists the main generic 'skills' that need to be applied in leading change. They list leadership, communicating, decision-making, motivating, delegating, negotiating, influencing, problem-solving, valuing and supporting others, setting objectives and prioritizing. The NOS also identifies outcomes of effective performance (see Figure 46.4). Examples of the behaviours which indicate the competence are (1) 'you articulate a vision that generates excitement, enthusiasm and commitment' and (2) 'you show sensitivity to stakeholders' needs and interests and manage these effectively'. There are eight such behaviours identified in the NOS unit. Also listed is what managers need to know and understand when leading change such as (1) the main models and methods for leading organizational change, and their strengths and weaknesses and (2) the relationship between transformational and transactional change.

15. Reading about change models in Chapter 24 paragraphs 14–19 and about transformational and transactional change in Chapter 24 paragraph 11 develops managerial ability in line with the MSC managerial competency framework! Moving forward offers the reader an opportunity to improve understanding of change and their own organization. The text helps readers to understand their organization's current position in the sector and market in which it operates, compared with its main competitors; current and emerging political, economic, social,

FIGURE 46.4   Management standards: Elements of performance.

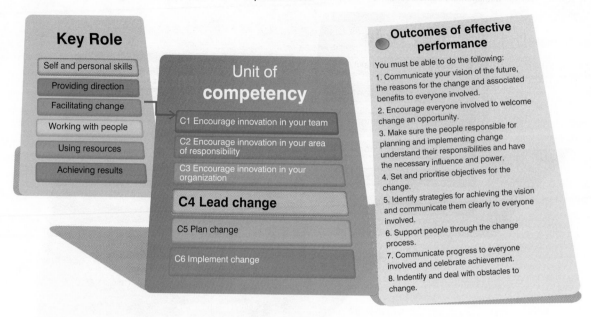

technological, environmental and legal developments in the sector; plus the organization's vision for the future, the reasons for change, the risks and expected benefits; those factors (for example, strategy, procedures, policies and structure) that need to be changed, and the associated priorities and reasons, the culture of the organization and the implications this has for the change process. Learning In this area might be aided by consulting Chapters 13, 16 and 26 for further knowledge.

16.   The complete set of National Occupational Standards for Management and Leadership are listed at the MSC web site. Individual units may be downloaded by clicking on the unit title. For example, clicking on C4 'Lead change' opens the unit. In summary, National Occupational Standards specify UK standards of performance which people are expected to achieve in their work, and the knowledge and skills they need to perform effectively; they set out the skills, knowledge and understanding required to perform competently in the workplace. The standards are used by a variety of individuals and organizations in different ways. Existing and future managers use the standards to expand their skills and knowledge of management and leadership, either through structured training courses, qualifications or as a stand alone reference indicating best practice for specific subject areas. Trainers use the standards to develop training courses and to teach accredited qualifications, whilst awarding bodies use the standards as the basis for a variety of Management and Leadership qualifications. NOS can be used to support any and all HRM and development activities.

17.   Competencies are also used in the framework for national-vocational qualifications (NVQs) and Scottish vocational qualifications (SVQs). Such frameworks provide qualifications based on required outcomes expected from the performance of a task in any work role, expressed as performance standards with criteria. These describe what competent people in a particular occupation are expected to be able to do. Having spent the past few paragraphs outlining managerial competencies and what managers should be able to do we must now turn our attention to the methods used to develop managers and make them competent in their current and future roles.

46.4 MANAGEMENT DEVELOPMENT METHODS

18. Management development methods include coaching, counselling, project work, mentors, action learning, secondments, development centres, formal training courses, etc. The various methods employed in management development can be placed into four main categories, as follows:

- Management education: qualification-bearing courses run by universities or public-sector colleges, for example MBA degrees, Diplomas in Management Studies, and various professional examinations, such as the Chartered Institute of Personnel and Development (CIPD); the level of work is regarded as post experience, and the emphasis is on acquiring knowledge and theory.

- Management training: internal and external courses, off-the-job and focusing on acquiring specific knowledge and relevant job skills; some experiential learning via course exercises.

- Experiential learning: 'learning by doing'; on-the-job experience usually with guidance from a more senior manager or colleague.

- Continuing professional development (CPD): activities designed to update knowledge and learn new skills flexibly, using one or more of the previous three methods; also used to enable individuals to upgrade their membership of a professional body (e.g. to obtain chartered manager/engineer etc. status); online personal profiling and assessment questionnaires increasingly available from a range of professional bodies.

19. The most widely used experiential methods are as follows: coaching/guided experience, delegation, projects, secondments/job rotation. In Figure 46.5, we examine each of these briefly, and highlight their key points and advantages.

FIGURE 46.5 Experiential methods in management development.

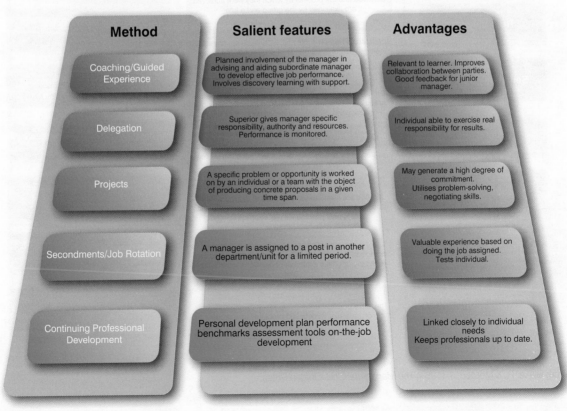

Method	Salient features	Advantages
Coaching/Guided Experience	Planned involvement of the manager in advising and aiding subordinate manager to develop effective job performance. Involves discovery learning with support.	Relevant to learner. Improves collaboration between parties. Good feedback for junior manager.
Delegation	Superior gives manager specific responsibility, authority and resources. Performance is monitored.	Individual able to exercise real responsibility for results.
Projects	A specific problem or opportunity is worked on by an individual or a team with the object of producing concrete proposals in a given time span.	May generate a high degree of commitment. Utilises problem-solving, negotiating skills.
Secondments/Job Rotation	A manager is assigned to a post in another department/unit for a limited period.	Valuable experience based on doing the job assigned. Tests individual.
Continuing Professional Development	Personal development plan performance benchmarks assessment tools on-the-job development	Linked closely to individual needs Keeps professionals up to date.

20.   The emphasis in these experiential approaches is on learning whilst doing the job. In some cases, off-the-job training will be required to enable the manager concerned to understand important concepts or to carry out initial practice in a 'safe' environment. Such off-the-job training, however, is only employed in a supporting role. Nevertheless, there are several well-tried methods for employing experiential learning in a 'safe' off-the-job environment. Some of the leading methods will be described below.

Experiential learning Learning from doing

21.   The majority of experiential methods used in management courses are directed at social skills development, e.g. leadership, influencing skills, negotiating, assertiveness, etc. A few are directed at cognitive skills development, e.g. problem-identification, problem-analysis, etc. Perceptive use of such methods by trainers can overcome many of the problems of lack of relevance to the job levelled at off-the-job training by its critics. The point here is that skills development in these particular areas extends the range of an individual's competence in their whole life, not just in his present job.

22.   Typical methods used in courses are described briefly in Figure 46.6.

FIGURE 46.6   Experiential methods (courses)

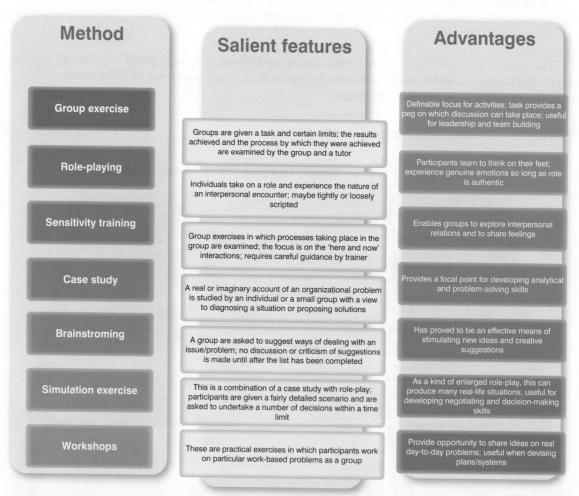

Method	Salient features	Advantages
Group exercise	Groups are given a task and certain limits; the results achieved and the process by which they were achieved are examined by the group and a tutor	Definable focus for activities; task provides a peg on which discussion can take place; useful for leadership and team building
Role-playing	Individuals take on a role and experience the nature of an interpersonal encounter; maybe tightly or loosely scripted	Participants learn to think on their feet; experience genuine emotions so long as role is authentic
Sensitivity training	Group exercises in which processes taking place in the group are examined; the focus is on the 'here and now' interactions; requires careful guidance by trainer	Enables groups to explore interpersonal relations and to share feelings
Case study	A real or imaginary account of an organizational problem is studied by an individual or a small group with a view to diagnosing a situation or proposing solutions	Provides a focal point for developing analytical and problem-solving skills
Brainstroming	A group are asked to suggest ways of dealing with an issue/problem; no discussion or criticism of suggestions is made until after the list has been completed	Has proved to be an effective means of stimulating new ideas and creative suggestions
Simulation exercise	This is a combination of a case study with role-play; participants are given a fairly detailed scenario and are asked to undertake a number of decisions within a time limit	As a kind of enlarged role-play, this can produce many real-life situations; useful for developing negotiating and decision-making skills
Workshops	These are practical exercises in which participants work on particular work-based problems as a group	Provide opportunity to share ideas on real day-to-day problems; useful when devising plans/systems

Source: Blake, R. & Mouton, J. (1964) *The Managerial Grid*. Dryden Press.

23.   Whilst it is by no means easy to measure the effects of management training courses and on-the-job development, the outcomes senior management might expect from 'successful' management development activities will include:

- individual managers performing at a fully satisfactory level

- improved performance from work teams as a result of better leadership

- pool of managers ready and able to take up promotion or stand in for absentees

- managers working collaboratively

- improved communication between managers and their staff and between managers and colleagues

- improved problem-solving capacity throughout the organization.

46.5 SUCCESSION PLANNING AND TALENT MANAGEMENT

24.   In the chapter introduction (paragraph 3) we noted that one of the key features of a structured management development system is a succession plan. This is basically a plan for identifying who is currently in post and who is available and qualified to take over in the event of retirement, voluntary leaving, dismissal or sickness, for example.

25.   We discussed resourcing as a HR practice in Chapter 43. Succession planning is really about hiring people from within the organization and is a process used to identify, assess and develop employees systematically to fill higher level (leadership) positions. Typically, senior managers, with support from HR, will identify future senior manager needs, particularly for key positions, and will specify the competencies required to function in the role. Management then turns its attention to creating candidates for these jobs. This means identifying potential and then providing candidates with the developmental experiences required. Finally, candidates will be assessed and selected to fill the key position.

26.   Succession planning is related to **talent management** which seeks to ensure the organization has a flow of people capable of meeting the need for talent at every level. Talent management seeks to maximize the contribution from all employees but can also be associated with the attraction, selection, retention, development and career management of those people identified as critical to the future success of the business (Martin, 2010).

> **Talent management** A strategic and integrated approach to developing a skilled and competent workforce, involving targeted recruitment, development and retention

46.6 MANAGEMENT DEVELOPMENT AND CORPORATE CULTURE

27.   The approach to management development in an organization will tend to reflect the dominant value-system of the senior management. They are the persons who, above all, are charged with building a management team and developing their successors. If the senior management is centralist and bureaucratic, then its view of management development is likely to produce a logically structured system such as that shown in Figure 46.1 above. In such a system, job descriptions, appraisal forms, succession charts and the like are vital items in the analysis of needs and in decisions about how they are to be met. Such a system would probably favour structured

efforts, both on and off-the-job to supply individual manager needs. Where senior management believes in delegation and devolution, then the emphasis in management development will be on self-development on-the-job. Where management is considered an elite group, then features such as 'accelerated promotion' and graduate trainee programmes tend to predominate. Such systems provide selective support for managerial development by concentrating on so-called 'high fliers', i.e. persons with outstanding potential.

CONCLUSION

28.   This chapter reviewed the subject of management development, its techniques and practices. We defined what constituted management and then discussed what a competent manager should be able to do. Managerial competencies are measurable clusters of knowledge, skills and abilities (KSAs) that are considered vital in determining how managers accomplish goals. Indicators are measured in order to determine the extent to which the manager possesses a competency. Each indicator is an observable behaviour providing information about the relevant competency. In other words the competency is not measured directly, we measure indicators that tell us whether the competency is present or not. An indicator is a behaviour that, if exhibited, suggests that the competency is present. Frameworks and standards of management competency were introduced and can be used as targets for which to aim; development techniques and methods such as coaching, counselling, project work, mentors, action learning, secondments, development centres, formal training courses, etc. were identified to develop the manager into a competent manager. Finally, we noted that one of the key features of a structured management development system is a succession plan (see also talent management). This refers to a plan for identifying who is currently in post and who is available and qualified to take over in the event of retirement, voluntary leaving, dismissal or sickness, for example.

QUESTIONS

1 Discuss the function and purpose of human resource development and expand on your definition of the concept, highlighting key principles.

2 Many organizations discuss problems of skill shortages, particularly in relation to information systems and technology skills. Discuss why organizations are likely to want to make sure the 'best people' stay with the organization.

3 Brainstorm ideas of what constitutes management and then create a definition. In your answer, you should make reference to the concept of effectiveness and efficiency and should discuss why a focus on only one of these concepts is unlikely to ensure success for the organization.

4 Identify and discuss the main functions associated with management (consider the work of Henri Fayol).

5 Which function do you believe is most important?

6 List the attributes (features) of successful (effective) managers.

7 Taking various views about the nature of managerial jobs as a whole, four key elements can be discerned in terms of what managers might need to know or be able to do. List briefly explain the four key elements.

8 Define managerial competence and explain how they are used within organizations.

9 Discuss the four main categories of management development method.

10 List and describe four experiential development methods; discuss the emphasis of experiential approaches and identify the typical skills they seek to develop.

USEFUL WEBSITES

CIPD Career management and development: **www.cipd.co.uk/ subjects/lrnanddev/careermand/?area=hs** Practical advice, guidance, tools; Surveys, research, reports and news

The Management Standards Centre: **www.management-standards.org/** Standard setting for Management – The MSC is the Government recognized standards setting body for the management and leadership areas

VIDEO CASES

Now take a look at the online video cases – visit the companion website to work through real world business problems associated with the concepts presented within this chapter.

113 Introduction to PoM – Management
Through its leaders and managers, organizations seek to do the right thing (effectiveness) as reflected in the organizational mission and goals and to do those things efficiently, thus keeping costs to a minimum. In doing so, the organization will

achieve its purpose. In this case study, we ask what management is, giving consideration to the types of manager and management functions.

122 Principles of Management – an Introduction
This case considers what is meant by management from the perspectives of commercial and not-for-profit organizations. Similarities and differences are considered and arguments from two people presented over three short film clips.

109 Human Resource Development and the retention of talented employees

It is now widely recognized (for many organizations) that the ability to recruit, develop and retain employees provides a significant and sustainable competitive advantage. For many organizations, it is simply not possible to buy in the required skills as and when needed. This case examines human resource development (HRD) from a number of perspectives. Organizations that consider people to be key to competitive advantage must recruit and develop talented employees and enhance their capabilities and motivation, whilst seeking to retain such resources. Organizations need people with appropriate skills, abilities and experience; such people may be brought in from the outside (recruitment and selection) or 'grown' by training and developing existing employees. The organization must provide opportunities for learning and development and personal growth. In summary, much of this case is about investing in human capital.

110 Human Resource Development (HRD) – Invest In Your People

The main focus of this case is training and development. It is now widely recognized (for many organizations) that the ability to recruit, develop and retain employees provides a significant and sustainable competitive advantage. For many organizations, it is simply not possible to buy in the required skills as and when needed. This case examines human resource development (HRD) from a number of perspectives. Organizations that consider people to be key to competitive advantage must recruit and develop talented employees, enhance their capabilities and motivation, whilst seeking to retain such resources. Organizations need people with appropriate skills, abilities and experience; such people may be brought in from the outside (recruitment and selection) or 'grown' by training and developing existing employees. The organization must provide opportunities for learning and development and personal growth. In summary, much of this case is about investing in human capital.

REFERENCES

Leopold, J. and Harris, L. (2009) 'The Strategic Managing of Human Resources', Ed. 2. Financial Times Press.

Martin, J. (2010) 'Key Concepts in Human Resource Management', Sage.

Mathis, R. L. and Jackson, J H. (2011) 'Human Resource Management', Ed. 13. South Western.

Mintzberg, H. (1975) 'The Manager's Job: folklore and fact', Harvard Business Review, Jul/Aug 75, Vol. 53 Issue 4.

Pedler, M., Burgoyne, T. and Boydell, T. (2001) 'A Manager's Guide to Self Development', Ed. 4. McGraw Hill.

Rees, W. and Porter, C. (2008) 'Skills of Management', Ed. 6. Cengage Learning EMEA.

Robbins, S. and Coulter, M. (2007) 'Management', Ed. 9. Pearson – Prentice Hall.

CHAPTER 47
STRESS MANAGEMENT AND EMPLOYEE COUNSELLING

Key Concepts

- Counselling
- Stress

Learning Outcomes
Having read this chapter, you should be able to:

- define stress and list potential sources
- distinguish three categories of stress symptom
- explain what employers can do to help employees suffering from stress
- propose steps an employer could take in order to minimise the possibility of harassment

Stress The physical symptoms of ill-health caused by excessive pressures in the workplace or elsewhere and leading to reduced job performance; how far an individual succumbs to stress is determined mainly by personality, and the extent to which they are confident of their ability to overcome the pressures

Counselling When a counsellor sees an employee in a private and confidential setting to explore a difficulty the employee is having, distress they may be experiencing or perhaps their dissatisfaction with life, or loss of a sense of direction and purpose

Worklife balance Allocation of time and commitment between work and personal life, which reflects the personal needs of the employee

Harassment Conduct which is unreasonable, unwelcome and offensive and which creates an intimidating or humiliating working environment. Harassment is a direct type of discrimination if the victim can show that the behaviour caused injury to feelings

1.   In this chapter we continue with HRM and the theme of employee performance, considering key factors that might reduce an employee's contribution at work. In particular we will focus on stress and related matters. Work associated stress-related illnesses lead to avoidable absences which can impact upon performance. They may also lead to expensive litigation, prosecution and substantial compensation damages. Furthermore, a poor reputation for welfare makes it harder for an organization to recruit, retain and motivate employees.

2.   The literature on the subject of stress at work is large. Stress and counselling are considered in both the HR and OB literature. The HR literature typically focuses on health, safety and welfare (Torrington *et al*, 2009) or health and wellness management (Bratton and Gold, 2007) and performance or absence management, and the law. HR is also concerned with the impact of its health, safety and welfare reputation on other HR activities such as recruitment, selection, retention and development. The OB literature focuses on personality and stress (Buchanan and Huczynski, 2010, see also Martin, and Fellenz, 2010) or organizational change and stress management, (Robbins, Campbell and Judge, 2010). Others discuss stress in the context of conflict at work or in terms of the worklife balance (Mullins 2010). Increasingly, employers are paying greater attention than in the past to the effects of stress on their workers, especially on their key and talented managers.

3.   Employers must consider common law, UK legislation and European Union directives and regulations when dealing with employees. They will consider legislation such as the Health and Safety at Work Act (1974), the EU's working time directive, the working time regulations (1998), the Protection from Harassment Act (1997) and civil law in particular. The employer has a duty of care over its employees and in recent years we have witnessed employers prosecuted for breaching this. Employers must be conscious of stressful working environments and the way they deal with their people. We consider the law in more detail in Chapter 50. Aside from the legal obligations and the business arguments for performance management, there is now a general view in society that employers should take steps to prevent stress and stress related illnesses and promote healthy lifestyles in a more general sense.

4.   In Chapter 21 paragraph 7 we discussed the quality of working life movement. Quality of working life means an individual's overall assessment of satisfaction with their job, working conditions, pay, colleagues, management style, organization culture, worklife balance, and training, development and career opportunities. The quality of working life movements emphasized programmes of organizational design and development dedicated to improving productivity and workers' retention and commitment by bettering the relationship between employers and employees and the work environment. Amongst the new challenges faced by HR is the need to help employees achieve a satisfactory worklife balance; allocation of time and commitment between work and personal life, which reflects the personal needs of the employee. We start the chapter by defining what is meant by the term stress and then consider some of the ways stress may be caused. Next we outline some of the symptoms of stress and finally consider what the individual and the employer can do to help prevent and manage work related stress. Finally, we discuss counselling, in a stress context, as both a management skill and a specialist activity.

47.1 STRESS

5.   What is 'stress'? It is the adverse psychological and physical reactions that occur in individuals as a result of their being unable to cope with the demands being made on them; it is a form of strain provoked in response to the situational demands (stressors – See challenge stressors and hindrance stressors) which typically occur in jobs with high demand. The Health and Safety Executive (2010) define work related stress as the process that arises where work demands of various types and combinations exceed the person's capacity and capability to cope. They argue recent statistics confirm that work related stress is widespread in the UK working population and is not confined to particular sectors or high risk jobs or industries. In a study into occupational stress, 17 000 randomly selected people from the Bristol electoral register were surveyed; approximately 50% responded. The study found that occupational stress was at levels described as 'very' or 'extremely stressful' (highly stressed) for approximately 20% of the working sample that responded. The study concluded that there is now considerable evidence that occupational stress is widespread and can be a major cause of ill-health at work (Health and Safety Executive, 2000). According to the Labour Force Survey in 2008/9 an estimated 1.2 million people were suffering from an illness they believe was caused or made worse by their current or most recent work.

> **Challenge stressors** Stressors associated with work load, pressure to complete tasks and time urgency

> **Hindrance stressors** Stressors that keep you from reaching your goals (red tape, office politics, confusion over job responsibilities)

6.   The Health and Safety Executive (HSE) note that people get confused about the difference between pressure and stress. We all experience pressure regularly – it can motivate us to perform at our best. It is when we experience too much pressure and feel unable to cope that stress can result. The HSE estimates the costs to society of work-related stress to be around £4 billion each year, whilst 13.5 million working days were lost to stress in 2007/08. By taking action to reduce the problem, employers can help create a more productive, healthy workforce and save money. Many organizations have reported improvements in productivity, retention of staff and a reduction in sickness absence after tackling work-related stress. The HSE also note that 'As an employer, you are also required by law to assess the risk of stress-related ill health arising from work activities and take action to control that risk'.

7.   Stress is triggered not by the external problems faced by individuals, but by the way they cope (or fail to cope) with those problems. Thus, most people can cope with a variety of pressures in their life, and many seem to thrive on 'pressure', especially at work. However, once individuals fail to deal adequately with pressure, then symptoms of stress appear. In the short-term these can be manifested in such conditions as indigestion, nausea, headaches, back-pain, loss of appetite, loss of sleep and increased irritability. In the longer-term, such symptoms can lead to coronary heart disease, stomach ulcers, depression and other serious conditions. Clearly the effects of stress, whether triggered by work problems or domestic/social problems, will eventually lead to reduced employee performance at work, increased sickness absence and even to an early death.

47.2 SOURCES AND CAUSES OF STRESS

8.   Respondents of the aforementioned Health and Safety Executive (2000) survey who considered themselves to be stressed at work, cited the following work characteristics as being associated with stress: working long hours, having to work fast, high skill level required, taking the initiative, not being given enough information, high workload, responsibility, frequent interruptions over time, being treated unfairly, no respect from others and inadequate support. Essentially, the results confirm the importance of perceptions of the physical work environment, working hours, job demand and discretion and social support at work in determining reported stress levels.

FIGURE 47.1   Causes of stress.

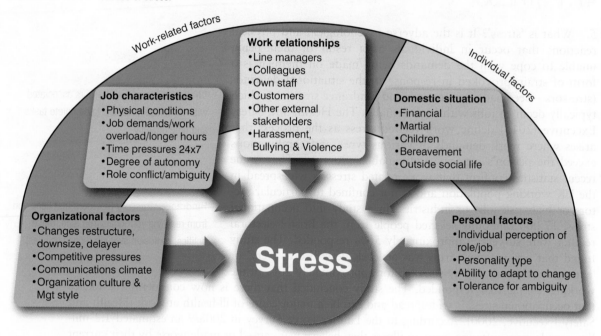

Work-related factors

Work relationships
• Line managers
• Colleagues
• Own staff
• Customers
• Other external stakeholders
• Harassment, Bullying & Violence

Individual factors

Job characteristics
• Physical conditions
• Job demands/work overload/longer hours
• Time pressures 24x7
• Degree of autonomy
• Role conflict/ambiguity

Domestic situation
• Financial
• Martial
• Children
• Bereavement
• Outside social life

Organizational factors
• Changes restructure, downsize, delayer
• Competitive pressures
• Communications climate
• Organization culture & Mgt style

Stress

Personal factors
• Individual perception of role/job
• Personality type
• Ability to adapt to change
• Tolerance for ambiguity

9.   The main sources of stress at work are located in a number of groupings. They may arise from environmental factors, job and organizational factors (including the organization culture), workplace relationships, domestic situation, or personality factors. Examples of factors that have been found to contribute to stress are shown in Figure 47.1:

47.3 INDIVIDUAL DIFFERENCES

Type A and Type B personality profile
A typology of personality types in which Type A individuals are described as always being under time pressure, impatient and having a pre-occupation with achievement

10.   People vary in their ability to handle stress. The perception of any given situation is dependent upon personal attributes including personality and experience. Personality affects the degree to which people experience stress and how they cope with it. One important personality trait in stress is type A personality. Type A and Type B personality profiles are a typology of personality types in which type A individuals (unlike type B individuals) are described as always being under time pressure, impatient and having a pre-occupation with achievement. Those with a type A personality are more likely to suffer stress-related disorders.

47.4 SYMPTOMS OF STRESS

11.   The results of the Health and Safety Executive (2000) study showed that for the highly stressed worker, problems at work interfere with life outside the workplace. The highly stressed groups perceived life in general to be more stressful, consumed more alcohol than they used to and were less likely to do vigorous exercise. High stress levels were also associated with more health problems, especially increased heartburn and indigestion, pains in the chest and depression. However, we should note that stress is not always a bad thing. A certain degree of stress is normal in life; however, if stress is repeated or prolonged, individuals experience physical and

psychological discomfort. Symptoms of stress are typically analyzed under three headings – physiological, psychological and behavioural. Common symptoms are as follows:

Physiological – in addition to short-term reactions such as increased heart beat, tensed muscles and extra adrenalin secretion which are a human being's instinctive reaction to danger, the chronic (i.e. longer term) effects of stress are associated with such unhealthy conditions as coronary heart disease, high blood pressure, indigestion, gastric ulcers, back pain and even cancer.

Psychological – in chronic situations the psychological symptoms of stress tend to become manifest in anxiety states (phobias, obsessions, etc.) and depression. In less serious cases, stress emerges in the form of tension, irritability, boredom and job dissatisfaction.

Behavioural – ultimately the physiological and psychological symptoms lead to generalized changes in behaviour such as loss of appetite, increased cigarette smoking and alcohol consumption and sleeplessness. In the workplace behaviour may take the form of increased absences (flight), aggression towards colleagues (fight), committing more errors than normal and taking longer over tasks. In utterly intolerable conditions, individuals may leave the organization and seek work elsewhere or sink into despair at home. The loss to the community resulting from stress-related conditions is estimated to be substantial.

47.5 COPING WITH STRESS

12.   Strategies for coping with stress can best be analyzed under two headings – personal strategies and organizational strategies. The former include actions individuals can take at work and outside work to increase their ability to cope with sustained pressure and thus avoid the symptoms of stress. The latter include a number of organizational steps that can be taken to reduce the likelihood of stress due to structural and style problems. Individual strategies to reduce workplace stress include physical exercise, hobbies, meditation, group discussions and assertiveness training. Individuals may also seek to develop better time management skills (see Chapter 27) and expand their social support network.

13.   The HSE has designed the Management Standards approach to help employers manage the causes of work-related stress. It is based on the familiar 'five steps to risk assessment' model*, requiring management and staff to work together:

Step 1 Identify the risks – there are six areas of work that can have a negative impact on employee health if not properly managed: demands (workload), control (how much say a person has in the way they do their work), support (sponsorship and access to resources), role (clarity and without conflict), change (management and communication) and relationships (promoting positive working to avoid conflict and dealing with unacceptable behaviour).

Step 2 Decide who might be harmed and how – gather and analyze data from annual staff surveys, sickness absence data and exit interviews, etc.

Step 3 Evaluate the risks – use the results from Step 2, to help you identify hot spots and priority areas. Also, involve employees and consult through focus groups.

Step 4 Record findings – develop and implement action plans. Some examples of popular actions are: giving specific groups of employees more control over aspects of their work; improving communication up and down the management chain, and between groups; job reviews/task analysis and updating a specific policy or procedure shown to have failings. Systems should be implemented locally to respond to any individual concerns; where possible, employees should have control over their pace of work; employees should have a say over when breaks can be taken and consulted over their work patterns; the organization should implement policies and procedures to support employees; and the organization should promote positive behaviours at work to avoid conflict and ensure fairness.

Other employer actions of note may include: changing an individual's job responsibilities; permitting flexible hours, reducing time spent away from home, etc.; improving physical working conditions,

---

*See also the risk management model discussed in Chapter 12 paragraphs 17–20.

providing counselling facilities and/or fitness centres/programmes for their employees. Research suggests that stress at work can be substantially reduced by giving employees greater control over exactly when, where and how they carry out their jobs. Secondly, and this applies in all cases of employee stress, employers can help support employees' ability to cope with the stress.

Step 5 Monitor and review – the actions in your plan to ensure they are having the desired effect in the appropriate timescale.

14.   Managers may sometimes wonder why they have to spend time dealing with employees whose problems are domestically-related, but the fact of the matter is that employees cannot help but bring their personal problems with them to work. Most people are usually too embarrassed to admit that they are having acute problems with their spouse, teenage children or elderly parents. Thus they tend to suppress their anxieties when they come to work, and all too often the first that a manager learns of a problem is either when the employee begins to take increased amounts of sick leave, or when confronted by requests for time off to attend a solicitor's, or a juvenile court or a funeral! Most managers are not, and probably do not want to become, trained counsellors. However, it is important for the well-being of a team that the leader should take sufficient time out to listen to a stressed employee's story, agree that the immediate situation should be taken into account in respect of performance, workload, etc. and propose that the employee seeks professional help. In other words, the manager's job in such circumstances is to reassure himself/herself that the employee's situation is not being allowed to drift, but is being managed, both by the individual concerned and the manager. Before looking more closely at counselling at work, it will be useful to consider one of the known, and unfortunately growing, causes of stress that is work-related – sexual and racial harassment

47.6 HARASSMENT AND DISCRIMINATION IN THE WORKPLACE

15.   Developments in equal opportunities have been one factor in focusing attention on harassment at work, since much of the harassment is sexually or racially motivated. What is harassment? Clearly, it has to do with the individual's right to privacy and dignity at work. If colleagues or managers bring excessive pressure to bear on an individual, which is clearly distressing to that person, then this could constitute harassment. Harassment covers a wide range of offensive behaviour. It is commonly understood as behaviour intended to disturb or upset. In the legal sense, it is behaviour which is found threatening or disturbing. Harassment occurs when, on the grounds of race, disability, sex, sexual orientation, belief or religion, an employer – or their agent such as another employee or a manager – engages in unwanted conduct which has the purpose or effect of violating an individual's dignity or creating an interrogating, degrading, hostile, offensive or humiliating environment for the employee in question.

16.   Any person who is perceived by work colleagues as being different or somehow vulnerable is liable to harassment. The greatest attention has been focused on harassment of a sexual nature, mainly, but not exclusively, inflicted on women by men. However, harassment can be triggered by racial or religious prejudice, membership or non-membership of a trade union, and attitudes towards young persons, the disabled and other minority groups. Harassment can take forms such as: unwanted physical contact, suggestive propositions or language, public jokes, offensive posters and graffiti, isolation or non-cooperation at work, shunning an individual at work and socially ('sending to Coventry'), and pestering a person.

Discrimination Usually refers to unfair treatment of an individual or group on grounds of their sex or race

17.   The consequences for employers in the UK of not taking action against harassment are primarily two-fold: firstly, they stand to be taken to an industrial tribunal (e.g. under sex discrimination/race relations legislation) or to a civil court (e.g. for breach of contract), and the costs of such procedures are high; secondly,

the work performance of their organization is likely to suffer adversely due to workplace tension, higher staff turnover, increased absenteeism and lower morale.

18.   Employers avoid liability for discriminatory harassment if they can prove they took reasonably practical steps to prevent harassment from occurring. The best way an employer can avoid complaints of harassment is by ensuring that harassment does not occur in the first place. The first step is to have in place an equal opportunities policy which, amongst other things, defines harassment and makes it clear to employees that they should not allow it to occur.

47.7 COUNSELLING

19.   Rees and Porter (2008) explore the skills of management, focusing upon counselling in one of their chapters. They discuss a range of work situations in which counselling may be needed: handling appraisals, disciplinary situations and grievances (see Chapter 45) and where employees are experiencing work-related stress. They define counselling as a purposeful relationship in which one person helps another to help themselves. They note that counselling discussions are typically initiated by the person who needs the help; however, there will be occasions when managers need to take the initiative and encourage employees to face up to issues that are having an adverse effect on their work. Several stages of any counselling interview are identified: (1) problem identification; (2) information gathering; (3) checking everything that needs to be said has been said; (4) establishing the criteria for a satisfactory solution; (5) deciding on the appropriate solution; (6) subsequently checking whether or not the solution has worked and (7) evaluating any outstanding problems.

20.   With regard, in particular, to stage five, counselling involves helping people work out their own solutions to problems rather than telling them what to do; we note, however, a continuum of counselling styles dependent upon the counsellor and the counselling situation. The continuum ranges from listening through to recommending. Any counsellor should have good active listening and communication skills and will hold communications with the subject in strict confidence. However, it may sometimes be impossible to treat information confidentially and in such cases the subject should be warned when something cannot be treated confidentially.

21.   In several earlier paragraphs above we have referred to 'the provision of counselling services' for employees. There have been employee counselling programmes for many years; there was such a programme at the Hawthorne plant from 1936 (see Chapter 5 paragraph 6). It is important for employees to have someone to talk to who will listen without judging; who can provide advice. Within the organization there are occupational health nurses, welfare officers, and specialized counsellors.

22.   In essence counselling is a joint activity in which a person seeking help, support or advice in dealing with personal problems (a 'client') shares his or her dilemma with a trained helper (a 'counsellor'). Counselling aims to provide a supportive atmosphere that helps employees find their own solution to problems. Counselling is a skilled activity. Of course, work colleagues can and do provide a level of informal counselling to employees in the course of their daily work. At the very least this boils down to listening to the other person and giving them the opportunity to share their anxieties and fears. However, it may also involve the passing on of quite unhelpful remarks from the one acting as informal counsellor! The message for managers and others in supervisory positions is 'recognize when a problem may require employee counselling, provide immediate support but then facilitate professional counselling arrangements'. The goals of counselling are effectively to enable an individual to handle stress by making better use of their own strengths, insights and resolve. It is of prime importance to recognize that counselling is not intended to do anything to individuals; its role is to enable them to get their problems into perspective and to see what they themselves can do to solve them.

23.   Essentially, counselling is a process in which the counsellor helps the client to:

- identify the problem

- agree what would be the ideal, or preferred, outcome and

- consider ways by which the client might achieve that outcome.

24.   Organizations which provide counselling services for their employees may provide an in-house service using their own trained counsellors, or may hire the services of an external counselling organization. One approach which relies on external assistance is the Employee Assistance Programme, in which an employer contracts a specialist counselling service to provide counselling support for its employees. This usually takes the form of a telephone counselling service which employees can ring at any time of the day or night to seek help for work problems or personal problems. There is usually a limit to the number of occasions that the service can be used by any one employee. Where appropriate the counselling can be of a face-to-face kind in an off-the-job location. Client confidentiality is guaranteed, and the only information that is fed back to the contracting employer is the rate of calls, the type of problems raised and other general information which does not identify individuals in any way, but which does provide important evidence as to the use and costs of the service.

CONCLUSION

25.   In this chapter we focussed on stress and related matters. Work associated stress-related illnesses lead to avoidable absences which can impact upon performance. They may also lead to expensive litigation, prosecution and substantial compensation damages. Furthermore, a poor reputation for welfare makes it harder for an organization to recruit, retain and motivate employees. The Health and Safety Executive (2010) define work related stress as the process that arises where work demands of various types and combinations exceed the person's capacity and capability to cope. The main sources of stress at work are located in a number of groupings. They may arise from environmental factors, job and organizational factors (including the organization culture), workplace relationships, domestic situation or personality factors. Personality affects the degree to which people experience stress and how they cope with it. Symptoms of stress are typically analyzed under three headings – physiological, psychological and behavioural. Strategies for coping with stress can best be analyzed under two headings – personal strategies and organizational strategies. The HSE has designed the management standards approach to help employers manage the causes of work-related stress. It is based on the familiar 'five steps to risk assessment' model, requiring management and staff to work together. Counselling aims to provide a supportive atmosphere which helps employees find their own solution to problems. The goals of counselling are to enable an individual to handle stress by making better use of their own strengths, insights and resolve. Essentially, counselling is a process in which the counsellor helps the client to: identify the problem, agree what would be the ideal, or preferred, outcome, and consider ways by which the client might achieve that outcome.

QUESTIONS

1 Explain the symptoms and causes of job stress and what an organization can do to alleviate them.

2 Define stress and list potential sources.

3 Discuss the symptoms of stress.

4 Explain what employers can do to help employees suffering from stress.

USEFUL WEBSITES

Health and Safety Executive: **www.hse.gov.uk/stress/index.htm** – guidance, see for example **www.hse.gov.uk/pubns/indg430.pdf**, how to tackle work-related stress – a guide for employers on making the management standards work.

UK EAP Association: **www.eapa.org.uk/** - EAPA is the professional body for Employee Assistance Programmes (EAPs). It represents the interests of professionals concerned with employee assistance, psychological health and well being in the UK.

VIDEO CASES

Now take a look at the online video cases – visit the companion website to work through real world business problems associated with the concepts presented within this chapter.

42 Work–life balance and workplace health
Explores work–life conflict and the importance of people in the organization.

REFERENCES

Bratton, J. and Gold, J. (2007) 'Human Resource Management Theory and Practice', Ed. 4. Palgrave Macmillan.

Buchanan, D. and Huczynski, A. (2010) 'Organizational Behaviour', Ed. 7. Financial Times Press.

Health and safety executive, (2000) 'The scale of occupational stress: the Bristol stress and health at work study', Health and safety executive, Crown copyright.

Martin, J. and Fellenz, M. (2010) 'Organizational Behaviour and Management 4e', Ed. 4. Cengage Learning EMEA.

Mullins, L. (2010) 'Management and Organizational Behaviour', Ed. 9. Financial Times Press.

Rees, W. and Porter, C. (2008) 'Skills of Management', Ed. 6. Cengage Learning EMEA.

Robbins, S., Campbell, T. and Judge, T. (2010) 'Organizational Behaviour', Financial Times Prentice Hall.

Torrington, D., Hall, L., Taylor, S.and Atkinson, C. (2009) 'Fundamentals of Human Resource Management: Managing People at Work', Ed. 1. Financial Times Press.

CHAPTER 48
JOB EVALUATION

Key Concepts

- Job evaluation
- Job grading
- Job ranking

Learning Outcomes Having read this chapter, you should be able to:

- explain what is meant by job evaluation
- contrast job evaluation methods

1. In this chapter we continue with the theme of performance management and employee retention by turning our attention to reward management-salary structures in particular. HR practitioners want to ensure that salary (reward) systems are seen to be fair, administered accurately and professionally. In previous chapters we have discussed job analysis, roles and job descriptions along with person specifications. We recognized that roles require different knowledge, skills, abilities and competences and now discuss the means to determine how much each jobholder should be paid. Reward systems are used to attract, retain and motivate employees and as a consequence are typically designed with significant input from HR.

2. There are different types of pay system (methods used by organizations to determine pay): basic rate schemes are clear and tend to be job-based (i.e. the pay rate is based on the job). A grading structure may be developed through a job evaluation scheme, used to allocate jobs to appropriate pay grades or bands. However, these schemes may not offer enough incentive for increased or improved performance. Individual performance may be rewarded through bonuses or commission; group performance may be rewarded through schemes like profit sharing and share options. Collective bargaining between unions and management (see next chapter) is a dominant method of determining pay as is 'custom and practice'. In other cases, management attempt to determine pay in the light of the 'going rate' for their industry or their local market. Whilst this may work reasonably well for the overall level of pay, it does nothing to sort out differentials in pay between different groups of employees.

> **Job evaluation** A technique for determining the size of one job compared with another, and the relationship between the two; job evaluation schemes can broadly be divided into analytical and non-analytical; the technique forms the basis for wage and salary administration

3. There is a general recognition that some jobs are worth more than others because their overall contribution is greater and they carry more responsibility, but measuring these attributes in any kind of objective way is very difficult to achieve in practice (Torrington *et al*, 2009). Most organizations of any size implement some form of grading structure which is used as the basis of determining the basic rate of pay for each job. The traditional approach involves developing a salary structure of groups (see job families and career frameworks), ladders and steps (see scales or points). Typically, different groups have different pay scales. The grade is then allocated a lower and upper annual salary and an employee on that grade will draw a salary dependent upon their point within it. In traditional models, increments within the scale are awarded annually, reflecting individual seniority. Promotion is used to access a different ladder. One of the main tasks associated with the administration of such a system is setting the differential gaps. In doing so, evaluators need to give consideration to the market rate for a particular role, equity and the individual's performance within that role. Job evaluation is the most common method used to compare the relative values of different jobs in order to provide the basis for a rational pay structure. We will explain and evaluate the concept, process and associated methods in this chapter.

48.1 JOB EVALUATION

4. Job evaluation is the name given to a set of methods designed to compare jobs systematically with a view to assessing their relative worth. According to ACAS (2010) job evaluation is a method of determining, on a systematic basis, the relative importance of a number of different jobs; a way of getting a hierarchy of jobs on which to base a grading structure. A job evaluation scheme is a way of systematically assessing individual jobs objectively, whilst avoiding prejudice or discrimination. Job evaluation involves deciding the relative importance of some or all of the different jobs within an organization. Employers carry out job evaluation for a number of reasons such as to resolve problems with the existing system (lack of rationale for current grades); to update the reward system following organizational change leading to new job design; and to overcome or prevent issues over equal pay and equal value.

5.   The purpose and aim of job evaluation is to produce a defensible ranking (hierarchy) of jobs which can be used as the basis for a rational pay structure. Following job evaluation, pay can be based on a rational estimate of the contribution made by individual jobs to the organization in terms of skill, responsibility, length of training and other factors. There are several key points which need to be noted about job evaluation. These are as follows, job evaluation:

- deals in relative positions, not in absolutes

- assesses jobs, not the individuals in them

- is usually carried out by groups

- committees utilize concepts such as logic, fairness and consistency in their assessment of jobs

- will always incorporate some element of subjective judgement and

- job evaluation by itself cannot determine pay scales or pay levels; it can only provide the basic data on which decisions about pay can be taken.

48.2 JOB EVALUATION PROCESS

6.   The job evaluation process may be broken down into a number of activities and steps. The main activities are outlined below:

- Determine which jobs should be included in the job evaluation process.

- Determine who should be involved in the project and the job evaluation committee.

- Gather the data: determine how information about individual jobs will be collected (job descriptions, interviews with job holders, freshly written job descriptions, questionnaires – in recent years there has been increased interest in computer-assisted job evaluation systems which awards scores to each job – see the next stage in the process on the basis of information gathered from job analysis questionnaires).

- Evaluate the job: form an evaluation panel to evaluate the information collected; compare collected job descriptions with factor plans and allocate an appropriate level for each factor (see job evaluation methods below). The **factor plan** is the agreed criteria for evaluating the relative importance of a job. Job characteristics such as skill, responsibility, working conditions and effort are typically broken down into a list of factors. For example, responsibility might include the following factors: safety of others, contact with others, supervision of others – a number of levels are then established for each factor (ACAS 2010).

Factor plan (job) The combined number of factors against which jobs will be evaluated

- Check evaluations to ensure accuracy (use benchmarks or indicative jobs to check evaluations).

- Assign pay to the job: apply the outcomes of job evaluation and create the hierarchy of jobs, grades, job families.

- Determine how appeals will be managed.

- Determine how to deal with employees who move to a lower grade after evaluation (most organizations protect pay in such situations, see **red circling**).

Red circling The term applied to jobs which, as a result of the implementation of a new grading structure, are found to be overpaid but where the existing job holders are pay protected for a period of time

- Implement the scheme (apply the new grading structure and, acting on legal advice, determine whether employees will be paid retrospectively from a specified date.

–   Maintenance: once established, the scheme will need to be maintained effectively. Establish the criteria used to trigger re-evaluation (re-evaluation may be triggered by permanent changes to duties though the whole process may typically be undertaken every ten years or so).

48.3 JOB EVALUATION METHODS

7.   Most job evaluation methods can be divided into two categories: Non-analytical methods and analytical methods. Non-analytical methods take whole jobs, compare them and then rank them. The two most common examples of such methods are:

Job ranking – in this method, basic job descriptions are written for a representative sample of jobs in the total population; evaluators compare the descriptions and then make an initial ranking of the jobs in order of perceived importance, i.e. this is their subjective view of relative importance; the rankings are discussed in an evaluation committee, and eventually a final rank order is agreed; the remaining jobs in the population are then slotted in to the rank order. The advantage of this method lies in its simplicity; the main disadvantage is that, because of the high degree of subjective judgement required, it can only be effective in a relatively simple and clear-cut organization structure.

> **Job ranking** A job evaluation scheme based on job descriptions

Job grading/job classification – in this case, the usual procedure is reversed, for in job grading the pay/salary grades are worked out first, then the broad characteristics of each grade are defined (e.g. in terms of knowledge, skill, etc. expected for each grade); a representative sample of jobs, known as benchmark jobs, is selected as typical of each grade; full job descriptions are written for these jobs; the remaining jobs (usually written up in outline) are then compared with the benchmarks and allocated to the appropriate grade. Like job ranking, this is also a simple method to operate, but it relies heavily on the credibility of the initial salary grades, and does not permit sufficient distinctions to be made between jobs, especially in a relatively complex organization with a wide variety of specialist roles.

> **Job grading** A job evaluation scheme based on an organization's hierarchy of job grading

8.   Non-analytical methods are simple, but crude. In complex organizations it is essential to use analytical methods, as these are the only way of discriminating fairly between jobs which are not at all similar. For example, they could be used to distinguish the relative importance of a systems analyst compared with, say, a management accountant, or a chief architect compared with a head brewer.

9.   **Analytical methods** break jobs down into their component tasks (use job descriptions etc.), responsibilities and other factors, and assess the jobs factor by factor, sometimes allocating points for each factor and sometimes allocating monetary sums to them. A group of benchmark jobs is evaluated in this way, and ranked according to the scores. The remaining jobs in the population are slotted in to this benchmark rank order. Then all the jobs are either allocated to a salary grade, or, if monetary sums were allocated, are allotted a specified total salary. The most commonly used analytical method is Points Rating, where points are allocated to job factors; the method where monetary sums are allocated to the factors is known as Factor Comparison, and is not widely used nowadays. The most commonly used factors in analytical methods are as indicated in Figure 48.1.

> **Analytical (job evaluation)** A method of job evaluation which involves assessing the worth of a job by dividing it into factors

10.   In a **points rating method**, each factor is broken down into degrees or levels, which are allocated points in accordance with an

> **Points rating method** The method of numerically evaluating jobs by the detailed analysis of component job factors. Each factor is defined and is given a range of point values, so that every job can be assessed numerically within the established range

FIGURE 48.1   Analytical methods – typical job factors.

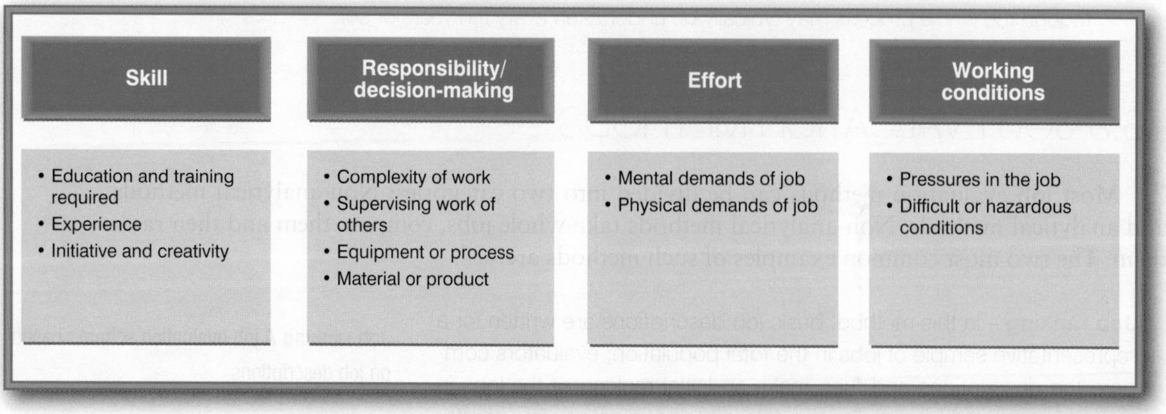

Skill	Responsibility/ decision-making	Effort	Working conditions
• Education and training required • Experience • Initiative and creativity	• Complexity of work • Supervising work of others • Equipment or process • Material or product	• Mental demands of job • Physical demands of job	• Pressures in the job • Difficult or hazardous conditions

agreed weighting. In evaluating manual jobs, a greater weighting may be given to factors such as Effort and Working Conditions, whereas in evaluating white-collar jobs, the greater weighting will tend to be given to Skill and Responsibility. An example of a possible Points Rating matrix for the evaluation of manual jobs is shown in a simplified form in Figure 48.2. In terms of degrees of each factor, 1 represents a minor requirement in the job, whilst 8 represents a major requirement.

11.   The matrix in Figure 48.2 weights the points in favour of the skill factors, physical effort and noisy/dirty working conditions. These are typically the most important factors to be considered in establishing the comparative value of manual jobs. If an example for managerial or senior white-collar jobs had been chosen, there would still have been an emphasis on skill factors, but then responsibility factors would have outweighed effort and working conditions. To help make evaluations as consistent as possible, the various degrees of each factor are described in an accompanying document. For example, if we take Education: 1st degree could equate to 'basic secondary education', 3rd degree could equate to 'GCSE in four subjects' and 6th degree could equate to 'HNC equivalent'; the other two degrees are not required for manual jobs.

12.   Some points rating methods are available in proprietary form. A notable example is the Hay Guide-chart System (Hay Group Guide Chart-Profile Method of Job Evaluation), which is particularly popular with organizations composed of a wide variety of specialist, professional and managerial occupations, although it can also be applied to junior clerical and to manual grades of work. Clients pay for the use of the Hay Guide-charts, the services of their consultants, and for a salary guidance service which enables them to keep up-to-date in the marketplace for labour. The guide-charts form a standardized system of job evaluation, and it is thus possible to see what other organizations are paying for jobs of a particular points total. This feature overcomes one of the major drawbacks of most points methods, which is that whilst they can solve the problem of internal differentials, they cannot link the results into the external labour market or the 'going rate' for the jobs they have evaluated.

48.4 JOB EVALUATION AND THE LAW

13.   The Equal Pay Act 1970, as amended by the Sex Discrimination Acts 1975 and 1986, provides that a woman has the right to equal pay with a man working for the same employer if the woman is employed on work of the same or broadly similar nature to that of her male comparator; or in a job which, although different from that of a man, has been rated as equivalent to the man's job under a job evaluation scheme (ACAS, 2010). Equal pay law – in particular the equal

FIGURE 48.2 Manual jobs – points rating matrix.

Job Factor	Degree							
	1	2	3	4	5	6	7	8
Skill								
1 Education	15	30	45	60	75	90	–	–
2 Experience	20	40	60	80	90	100	–	–
3 Initiative	15	30	45	60	75	90	105	120
Effort								
4 Physical	10	20	30	40	50	–	–	–
5 Mental	5	10	15	20	25	30	35	40
Responsibility								
6 Supervisory	5	10	15	20	25	30	35	40
7 Equipment	5	10	15	20	25			
8 Safety	5	10	15	20	25			
Work Conditions								
9 Hazards	5	10	15	20	25			
10 Noise/Dirt	10	20	30	40	50	–	–	–

value regulations – has important implications for job evaluation. Care must be taken that any job evaluation scheme is non-discriminatory in its effects and is linked to a payment system where employees performing work of equal value are rewarded equally, regardless of their sex. When designing a job evaluation scheme it is particularly important to bear in mind that only analytical schemes are likely to be capable of demonstrating an absence of sex bias. Salary structures should also take account of the national minimum wage (NMW). The national minimum wage (NMW) is a legal right (see National Minimum Wage Act 1998) which covers almost all workers in the UK. It became law on 1 April 1999 to prevent unduly low pay and also to help create a level playing field for employers.

48.5 EVALUATING JOB EVALUATION

14. Job evaluation has the following advantages: it

– provides a rational and defensible basis on which to decide pay in general, and differentials in particular, because it focuses on job content

– provides a rational basis for devising, or improving, grading structures

- reduces the effects of ad hoc or traditional arrangements for pay or grading and

- it encourages management and employees alike to think of jobs in terms of key components.

The full range of advantages can only come from the use of analytical methods, nevertheless there are certain disadvantages of job evaluation. These are:

- implementation of even quite simple methods can be a costly and time-consuming business

- analytical methods, in particular can give the impression that they are completely objective and scientific, but they still rely considerably on human judgement, i.e. subjective influences cannot be ruled out

- whilst job evaluation can provide a rational basis for grade differentials based on job content, it is usually unable to link the resulting pay grades into the labour market itself.

CONCLUSION

15.   There is a general recognition that some jobs are worth more than others since their overall contribution is greater because they carry more responsibility, but measuring these attributes in any kind of objective way is very difficult to achieve in practice. There are different types of pay system (methods used by organizations to determine pay): basic rate schemes are clear and tend to be job-based (i.e. the pay rate is based on the job). A grading structure may be developed through a job evaluation scheme, used to link jobs to appropriate pay grades or bands. One of the main tasks associated with the administration of such a system is setting the differential gaps. In doing so, evaluators will need to give consideration to the market rate for a particular role, equity and the individual's performance within that role. Job evaluation is the most common method used to compare the relative values of different jobs in order to provide the basis for a rational pay structure. Job evaluation is the name given to a set of methods designed to compare jobs systematically with a view to assessing their relative worth. We outlined a job evaluation process and various job evaluation methods. Finally we reviewed job evaluation and the law. When designing a job evaluation scheme it is particularly important to bear in mind that only analytical schemes are likely to be capable of demonstrating an absence of sex bias.

QUESTIONS

1   Explain what is meant by job evaluation.

2   Describe the main activities undertaken as part of the job evaluation process.

3   Contrast job evaluation methods.

USEFUL WEBSITES

The Equality and Human Rights Commission **www.equalityhumanrights.com/** – see advice and guidance/Information for employers/Equal pay/What is job evaluation

CIPD **www.cipd.co.uk/subjects/pay/general/jobeval.htm** – job evaluation factsheet

ACAS **www.acas.org.uk/** - ACAS (Advisory, Conciliation and Arbitration Service) aims to improve organizations and working life through better employment relations – see advisory booklet – job evaluation: considerations and risks

VIDEO CASES

Now take a look at the online video cases – visit the companion website to work through real world business problems associated with the concepts presented within this chapter.

97 Reward management – we were wrong on pay
Morgan Stanley's CEO says compensation for short-term results was a mistake, but the 'war for talent' requires high pay.

REFERENCES

ACAS (2010) 'Job evaluation: considerations and risks', Acas publications, www.acas.org.uk/publications.
Bratton, J. and Gold, J. (2007) 'Human Resource Management Theory and Practice', Ed. 4. Palgrave Macmillan.

Torrington, D., Hall, L., Taylor, S. and Atkinson, C. (2009) 'Fundamentals of Human Resource Management: Managing People at Work', Ed. 1. Financial Times Press.

CHAPTER 49
EMPLOYEE
RELATIONS AND
COLLECTIVE RIGHTS

Key Concepts

- Collective agreements
- Collective bargaining
- Employee involvement
- Employee relations
- Procedure agreement
- Substantive agreement

Learning Outcomes Having read this chapter, you should be able to:

- review perspectives on employee relations
- appraise current trends in union–management relations
- describe the main types of trade union
- explain collective-bargaining
- discuss the various degrees of participation that can be available to employees
- differentiate between employee participation and employee involvement

1. In this chapter we build upon previous work (Chapter 26 communication in organizations and Chapter 23 delegation and empowerment in particular), continuing with themes such as employee retention and performance management and the role of the HR function in maintaining a satisfied, committed and high-performance workforce. We will continue to emphasize important links with strategy and competitive advantage in particular and the changes that have taken place within the organization and its environment. In particular, we consider the social and political context in terms of trade unions and employment legislation and the changing ways employee views become heard by employers (via managers).

2. The chapter commences with the definition of key concepts. We then outline briefly the key trends in the decline of trade unions and the growth in employment law. Following this, in the first main section of this chapter, we discuss (collective) union-management relations. In this section we explain what a trade union is, consider different types and how they negotiate (collective bargaining) with management. Next we consider different forms of employee participation before progressing, in the second main section, to explain the more recent concept of employee involvement as a part of employee relations. Thus the final part of this chapter focuses more on contemporary individual employee and employer relations.

Empowerment A climate where employees are allowed greater freedom, autonomy and self-control over their work, and the responsibility for decision-making

Trade union An organization of employees whose principal purpose is to negotiate with employers about terms and conditions of employment and other matters affecting the members' interests at work. (See also Certified Trade Union)

Employee involvement A participative, employer led, process that uses the input of employees and is intended to increase employee commitment to an organization's success

49.1 KEY CONCEPTS – AN OVERVIEW

3. Several key concepts will be discussed within this chapter, some of which have been discussed previously. In particular we consider employee participation, employee empowerment, employee involvement (EI), communications, industrial relations (IR), employment relations, employee relations, collective bargaining and the strategic aspects of employee relations. There is much confusion over the use of these concepts within the literature. Sometimes terms are used interchangeably; sometimes appropriately and other times in a confusing manner. In many cases, it is necessary to understand the context in which the term is applied. The meaning of certain terms has evolved over time and they can be a source of confusion for students perusing the HR literature.

4. The expression 'employee relations' generally describes all those activities which contribute both formally and informally to the organization of the relationships between employers and their employees. In some instances these relationships are predominantly formalized as a result of collective bargaining between employers and trade unions as to the role, status and working conditions of employees. This aspect of employee relations is often called 'industrial relations'. However, employee relations can refer just as easily to arrangements worked out less formally between local management and their work teams, whether unionised or not. Because of its importance to national economies, employee relations has tended to be the focus of legislation. Thus, procedures such as balloting for possible strike action or the election of union representatives, or for the announcement of redundancies, are contained within legal parameters.

Employee relations Employee relations is an alternative label for 'industrial relations'. It is not confined to unionized collective bargaining but encompasses all employment relationships. It goes beyond the negotiation of pay and benefits to include the conduct of the power relationship between employee and employer

Employment relations Concerned with the relationships between the policies and practices of the organization and its staff and the behaviour of work groups

5.   Employee participation (role and contribution) may be enhanced for a number of reasons: (1) to increase motivation; (2) to minimize potential conflict between employers and employees and (3) to harness collective employee inputs. A keynote about employee participation is that it is often inspired by the workforce or government. By contrast, employee involvement (EI), a more recent concept, tends to be management initiated to secure employee commitment, motivation and loyalty so as to contribute to the achievement of organizational goals and objectives. Leopold and Harris (2009:475) argue the two approaches to be distinct and recommend we avoid using the terms interdependently. To add further confusion, the term employee empowerment overlaps with employee participation and employee involvement, indeed many authors use the terms interchangeably. Empowerment has been used to describe the organizational climate; it has been used in a similar manner to delegation (but is generally not considered to be delegation); it is often associated with authority, control, responsibility, freedom, power, autonomy, discretion and decision-making. Empowerment is also seen as an important enabler for organization design in terms of delayering and creating more flexible, adaptable and responsive organizations. The rationale behind participation and involvement has evolved with time.

6.   An important implication of employee relations is that rule-making is essential if the parties concerned are to contain any conflict within manageable bounds. The main body of rules in employee relations is drawn from the following:

- company/organization rules – these are usually generated by, and enforced by, managers
- collective agreements – jointly agreed rules or practices made by management representatives and employee representatives
- custom and practice – these are the informal rules which arise from the behaviour of managers and employees over a period of time; unlike the other rules just mentioned, these rules are not usually written down
- legal sources – these are the rules arising from statute, judicial precedent, and the common law, so far as they relate to employee relations
- codes of practice – these may be the codes of professional bodies, or those of bodies such as ACAS (the Advisory, Conciliation and Arbitration Service).

Rules affecting employees may be made therefore by management, by management with input from employees or by external bodies. In some cases employees will act collectively through trade unions and in other cases they may act alone.

49.2 TRENDS

7.   Over the last thirty years in Britain there has been a marked shift in employee relations away from the more combative stance of union-led collective bargaining towards a more unified approach to management–employee relationships. This change has been accompanied by a strengthening of individual rights in the workplace, both in respect of the individual's relationships with management, and in respect of union members' rights vis-à-vis their union. The legal system now acts to support individuals in the workplace as well as collective groups represented by a union. The emphasis now is less on producing joint procedures and rules of behaviour, and more on gaining mutual commitment to organizational success within the framework of the law.

8.   Trade union membership in Britain has fallen quite substantially in recent years. In 2006, the rate of union membership (union density) for employees in the UK fell to 28 per cent (Office for National Statistics, 2010). There are regional differences in the proportion of employees who are union members. Union density ranged from 21.4 per cent in the South East to 38.9 per

cent in the North East. The data are derived from the Trade Union Membership 2006 report published by the DTI in 2007. By 2009 the figure had fallen to 25% i.e. one in four employees. The latest trade union membership publication contains annual estimates of trade union densities for employees and all workers from the Labour Force Survey (LFS) for the fourth quarter of 2009. The decline in membership has been due to several factors, including

- fewer people employed in industries with strong tradition of union membership

- where employment growth has occurred, it has been in white-collar areas not usually known for their interest in trade union representation

- demise of the 'closed shop' and similar agreements, whereby individuals had to join an appropriate trade union.

Nevertheless, trade unions still have an important watchdog role to perform, supported by law, to prevent managements from acting in a purely arbitrary fashion. Nowadays it is more likely that groups of employees themselves – as empowered work teams – will contribute to the control of work and its key processes.

49.3 UNION–MANAGEMENT RELATIONS

9.   In this section we consider the relationship of management with employees, through the unions that represent them. Union-management relations address the collective aspects of the employment relationship and focus on the relations between organized employees (represented by a union) and management (Bratton and Gold, 2007). We will discuss the key features of union–management relations (see also industrial relations, employment relations, labour relations). In a non-unionized workplace managers will typically have greater (unilateral) control and flexibility to impose their thinking upon the workforce. However, where a union is recognized there may be a greater need to negotiate before seeking change. Unions may seek control over employee rewards (such as pay), appraisals, training and development. Where management accept the legitimacy of trade unions they may move towards management by agreement. In the case of union acceptance, the organization will typically engage in collective bargaining as a process to regulate the employment relationship, to support their strategy.

10.   There are four notable types of trade union: (1) general unions (represent workers from all industries and companies, rather than just one organization or a particular sector), (2) craft unions (seeks to unify workers in a particular industry along the lines of the particular craft or trade in which they work), (3) industrial unions (workers in the same industry are organized into the same union – regardless of skill or trade), and (4) white-collar unions (a non-manual workers' union covering those in clerical and administrative jobs). Unions may also be affiliated to a larger organization that negotiates with the government, for example the Trades Union Congress (TUC) in the UK. Most trade unions (approximately 60 unions, representing over six million people) are affiliated to the TUC, which is the central confederation of unions in Britain. With the decline in both national collective bargaining and direct government intervention in industrial relations, this body has lost much of its former power, and this is reflected in its corresponding employer bodies, at least so far as their industrial relations influence is concerned.

11.   The role of the TUC today is primarily to represent the interests of employed people in debates and policy discussions on employment and social security matters (e.g. pension's policy) at national, European Community and international levels. The organization's policies are derived from the annual congress of the TUC, whilst the day-to-day operations are administered by a general secretary and staff directed by a general council, composed of a cross-section of independent trade union leaders, who are elected every year.

49.4 TRADE UNIONS IN BRITAIN AND THE WORKPLACE

12.   Essentially, a trade union is an organization of workers, which aims to protect and promote their interests in the workplace, mainly by means of collective bargaining and consultation with employers. Although the last three decades have seen a major change in the emphasis of British employment law from collective rights to the rights of individuals in the workplace, there is still a considerable body of law affecting collective activities, especially those of trade unions. The principal legislation on trade unions is contained in the Trade Union and Labour Relations (Consolidation) Act, 1992 (TULRCA).

> The legal definition of a 'trade union' is stated in the 1992 Act as follows: '. . . an organization (whether permanent or temporary) which either – (a) consists wholly or mainly of workers of one or more descriptions and is an organization whose principal purposes include the regulation of relations between workers . . . and employers or employers' associations; or (b) consist wholly or mainly of – (i) constituent or affiliated organizations . . . or (ii) representatives of such . . . organizations; and in either case is an organization whose principal purposes include the regulation of relationships between workers and employers or between workers and employers' associations . . .'

> Source: Public Sector Information (1992). *Trade Union and Labour Relations (Consolidation) Act 1992*. © Crown Copyright 2002–2008.

13.   Whilst some collective issues are handled by national bodies, such as unions and employers' associations, the majority of collective matters are dealt with in the workplace. In organizations where one or more trade unions are recognized for the purposes of bargaining and/or consulting on behalf of the employees, it is usual for workplace representatives to be appointed by the union members. These may be called 'shop steward', 'staff representative' (rep) or some other agreed term. Such representatives are employees of the organization who fulfil unpaid work on behalf of their trade union colleagues within a framework of rules agreed between the two parties – employer and union members. The work of a representative usually includes the following responsibilities: negotiating local conditions; dealing with members' problems in respect of pay, hours and other relevant conditions of employment; representing members in the course of disciplinary or grievance hearings; acting as a communication channel between members and the employer on relevant matters and acting as a link between the trade union and its members.

14.   Whereas historically the average workplace representative had a considerable amount of power to influence both employment conditions and working methods, the situation today is very different. The combined effects of increased competition, legal restrictions on arbitrary trade union sanctions and more flexible working methods have weakened the power once held by shop stewards and staff representatives.

49.5 COLLECTIVE BARGAINING AND COLLECTIVE AGREEMENTS

Collective agreements The results of collective bargaining are expressed in agreements; these are principally procedure agreements and substantive agreements; they are not legally enforceable in the UK. (See also Procedure Agreements and Substantive Agreements)

15.   Collective bargaining is a system of negotiation involving both management and the union i.e. union representatives and management jointly determine rules belonging to the employment contract. The outcome of union-management negotiations is a collective agreement. **Collective agreements** (or rules made) between employers and employees are usually divided into two categories: procedural agreements and substantive agreements. Substantive agreements deal with the substance of employee relations, i.e. actual terms and conditions of employment (pay, hours of work, holiday entitlements, etc.). Procedural agreements regulate the way in which substantive rules are made and understood and indicate

how workplace conflicts are to be resolved. Matters covered by procedural agreements include negotiating rights for unions; scope of subjects for collective bargaining (i.e. what is negotiable); procedure to be followed in the case of a dispute between the parties and grievance and disciplinary procedures. Substantive agreements are usually re-negotiated every one or two years, but procedural agreements are negotiated only as and when the parties feel the need to change or clarify the rules. Most procedural agreements require either side to give several months' notice of variation or termination of the agreement, whereas most substantive agreements run out automatically at the end of the period concerned.

Substantive agreement A collective agreement dealing with terms and conditions of employment, e.g. wages, hours of work, holidays, etc. (See also procedure agreement)

16. In conducting a negotiation both sides engage in a considerable amount of prior preparation. The relative bargaining power of each side depends upon several issues: the general economic situation; the company's ability to pay; the company's need for particular skills; pay deals struck elsewhere in comparable industries and the negotiating ability of union officials. Much depends on the particular circumstances of a negotiation. For example, when the demand for particular skills is high, the union has the advantage; when the demand for labour is low, then management have the stronger position. This latter situation can be offset, to a certain extent, by a union that is well-organized and not afraid to employ sanctions (i.e. strikes, overtime bans, etc.). The immediacy of the impact of possible sanctions is an important factor here. For example, where union sanctions can bring immediate chaos or disruption to a service, then clearly the union is in a stronger bargaining position than one whose sanctions have no immediate effect whatsoever. In recent years the number of days lost through strikes in the UK is but a mere fraction of what it was decades ago, reflecting changed economic circumstances and a less indulgent legal framework.

17. The tactics employed by each side are those actions which, in the course of the negotiations, can contribute to the achievement of their respective objectives. The issue of tactics can be illustrated by considering a substantive matter – the negotiation of a pay increase. As Figure 49.1 shows, each side in the negotiation has its idea of the ideal settlement – i.e. the lowest possible increase from the management side, and the maximum possible increase from the trade union side. Recognizing the relative bargaining strength of the other side, plus the influence of external factors, each side also has its fallback position. This represents the point beyond which each side is not prepared to retreat. When this point is reached, the likelihood of a breakdown in negotiations is very great, especially if it has not been recognized until too late. One of the skills of experienced negotiators is to be able to recognize when the other side is close to its fallback position, and settle before it is too late, hopefully somewhere near the realistic solution. In the example shown (Figure 49.1), the likely increase will be in the 3–3.5% range.

Collective bargaining The process of negotiating wages and other working conditions collectively between employers and trade unions, it enables the conditions of employees to be agreed as a whole group instead of individually

18. The likely outcome in Figure 49.1 reflects the tight fallback position of the management side, probably set in the light of other settlements, the desire to contain labour costs in a highly competitive situation, and yet wanting to provide some incentive to employees. The union side, in accepting this level of increase, are probably bowing to general economic conditions, in which their members are lucky to be employed. We have described a negotiation but note that at the beginning of this chapter we discussed the decline of trade unions. One consequence of this decline has been a decline in the number of employees whose terms and conditions are determined through collective bargaining.

19. A key element in most procedure agreement is the disputes procedure. The aim of a disputes procedure is to settle disputes speedily, and as near to the original source as possible. Disputes can arise from a failure to agree during the course of negotiations,

Procedure agreement A collective agreement setting out the procedures to be followed in the conduct of management – union relations with particular reference to negotiating rights, union representatives, disputes and grievance procedures. (See also substantive agreement)

FIGURE 49.1 **Anatomy of a pay claim**

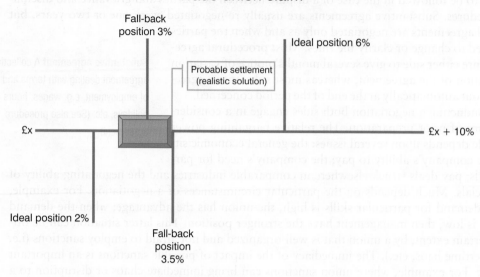

or from a differing interpretation of an existing agreement, or from an issue which has arisen as the result of the implementation of an agreement (e.g. concerning redundancies or dismissals). When they arise, disputes have to be tackled at once, for it is generally in everyone's interests that disputes should be short-lived. Most organizations have two or three stages within their internal dispute procedure, involving progressively more senior managers and union officers. If the dispute cannot be solved internally, then, but only then, can external sources be called upon. These external sources may be in the shape of an ACAS conciliation officer, a mediator or an arbitrator. The difference between these three alternatives is as follows: conciliation is essentially a peace-making service, in which the outsider helps the parties to reach their own decision; arbitration is a settlement-making service, in which the arbitrator makes the decision for the parties and mediation is a halfway approach between conciliation and arbitration, in which the third party makes active suggestions to the disputing parties as to how they might reach a compromise.

20. The law in the UK currently assumes that collective agreements are not intended by the parties to be legally binding, unless certain conditions apply. These are (1) the agreements are in writing and (2) it is stated they are intended to be enforceable contracts. Most collective agreements are still voluntary (i.e. non-binding). However, the terms of all collective agreements may be incorporated into individual contracts of employment, in which case they then become legally binding. This applies especially to the terms agreed in a substantive agreement (i.e. pay, holidays, hours of work, etc.). However, any reference to a 'no-strike' clause in a collective agreement is excluded from an individual contract, unless the agreement states in writing that this condition will be incorporated into the contract. There are other conditions that have to be met before such a clause can be so absorbed into individual contracts. The situation in practice is that few such clauses have been agreed between unions and managements.

49.6 EMPLOYMENT LAW

21. Employment law was absent in Britain for much of the 20th century but became more prevalent in the 1970s and 1980s onwards. As trade unions have declined in power, the law has stepped in to protect employee rights. Laws cover matters such as unfair dismissal, sex discrimination, race discrimination, health and safety, disability discrimination, the minimum wage,

restrictions on working time, age discrimination, trade union recognition, employment relations and data protection.

22.   In the next part of this chapter we outline the main features of current legislation regulating the collective relationships between trade unions and employers. There have been considerable changes to the law on trade unions since the passing of the Industrial Relations Act, 1971. The overall effect of the changes has been to reduce the power of trade unions to influence decisions about employment conditions, and especially working methods, in the workplace. The changes have also enhanced the rights of individuals in the workplace, protecting them from arbitrary behaviour on the part of trade union officials as well as their employers. Individual rights are contained mostly in the Employment Rights Act (ERA), 1996 (see Chapter 50). Collective matters are the concern of the Employment Relations Act, 1999 and the Trade Union and Labour Relations (Consolidation) Act, 1992 (TULRCA). These last two pieces of legislation deal with such key issues as the status of collective agreements, trade disputes, strikes and other employee sanctions, picketing, and balloting. These will be outlined next.

> **Picketing** Trade union activity where groups of workers in dispute with their employers attend at their own place of work for the purpose of peacefully persuading other workers not to leave or enter the premises for work; the persons in attendance are the pickets, and the area they are picketing is called the picket line

49.7 TRADE DISPUTES, PICKETING AND BALLOTS

23.   The definition of a trade dispute is important because it affords certain immunities to the unions and individual members in respect of action they might take during a dispute. Normally, any action taken by one person to induce others to break their contract will be considered a civil wrong (a tort). However, such an action will not necessarily be held to be a tort in the circumstances of a 'trade dispute', which is defined (TULRCA) as follows:

'a dispute between workers and their employer which relates wholly or mainly to one or more of the following . . .:

(a)   terms and conditions of employment . . .;

(b)   engagement or non-engagement, or termination or suspension of employment . . . of one or more workers;

(c)   allocation of work or the duties of employment as between workers or groups of workers;

(d)   matters of discipline;

(e)   a worker's membership or non-membership of a trade union;

(f)   facilities for officials of trade unions . . .;

(g)   machinery for negotiation or consultation, and other procedures relating to any of the above matters, including the recognition by employers . . . of the right of a trade union to represent workers . . .'

Source: Public Sector Information (1992). *Trade Union and Labour Relations (Consolidation) Act 1992.* © Crown Copyright 2002–2008.

24.   The above clauses effectively mean that trade unions and their members can generally be protected from legal liability for tort when involved in a dispute with the relevant employer on matters which are crucial to the conditions under which members are employed. It should be noted, however, that the law restricts the meaning of 'worker' to a worker employed by the employer with whom he is in dispute. It thus precludes action against someone who is not your employer (previously called 'sympathy action').

25.   In order to gain the necessary protection, a union or its members in a dispute have to fulfil the following obligations:

– The employees involved must be employees of the employer at the centre of the dispute.

– The action must not be designed to pressure an employer into recognizing a trade union, or forcing employees to take up union membership, or to exclude suppliers or others on the grounds that they do not recognize or consult with trade unions.

– So far as trade unions themselves are concerned, they must ballot their members prior to any action; such a ballot must conform to laid down conditions, and the union may only take action freely if there is a majority in favour of the specific questions outlined in the ballot.

26.   Ballots should be conducted in secret and proper arrangements made for the correct counting of voting papers. Employers, subject to certain conditions being fulfilled, are obliged to provide facilities on their premises to enable voting to take place properly. Part of the reasoning behind such legal support for ballots is to ensure that trade unions are made accountable to all their members rather than just to their activists.

27.   Picketing refers to actions taken to persuade a person to support a strike by not attending for work. Trade unions and union members will be immune from civil action when picketing so long as certain conditions are fulfilled (TULRCA):

'A person acts lawfully if he attends

(a)   in contemplation or furtherance of a trade dispute. . .

(b)   at a specified place, namely

    i   at or near his own place of work. . .

    ii if he is unemployed and either his last employment was terminated in connection with a trade dispute or if the termination was one of the circumstances giving rise to a trade dispute, at or near his former place of work. . .

    iii if he does not . . . normally work at any one place . . . at any premises of his employer. . .

    iv if he is an official of a trade union, at or near the place of work or former place of work of a member of that union whom he is accompanying and whom he represents. . .

(c)   for the purpose only of peacefully obtaining or communicating information or peacefully persuading any person to work or abstain from working.'

Source: Public Sector Information (1992). *Trade Union and Labour Relations (Consolidation) Act 1992*. © Crown Copyright 2002–2008.

28.   It is important to note that picketing is only permissible at the place of work, and not, for example, at the private residence of an employer. Also the law only protects peaceful actions by the pickets in pursuit of their strike. An official Code of Practice on Picketing is in force, which recommends that there should be no more than six pickets at any one entrance. Such a code does not have the force of law in itself, but may be taken into consideration in any legal proceedings. Action outside what is permitted by the TULRCA may lead to criminal charges against individuals, including fines or imprisonment.

29.   At the beginning of this chapter we discussed the decline of trade unions. One consequence of this decline has been a decline in the incidence of industrial action. We discussed trends and recognized that unions have been weakened both numerically and politically over the past three decades. During this time we have witnessed the rise of the HRM model. Union management relations have evolved and the idea of social partnership advocates the pursuit of mutual gains for both unions and the organization.

49.8 EMPLOYEE PARTICIPATION

30.   Broadly speaking, employee participation is about involving employees in the affairs of the organization; the concept has been discussed in several chapters of this book. However, the extent to which they should be encouraged or indeed permitted to do so is a matter of considerable debate. Figure 49.2 indicates some of the leading alternatives that have been proposed over recent decades. The options are shown on a continuum, since this helps to reflect the various degrees of participation available to employees. They range from participation in the ownership

FIGURE 49.2 Range of alternatives for employee participation.

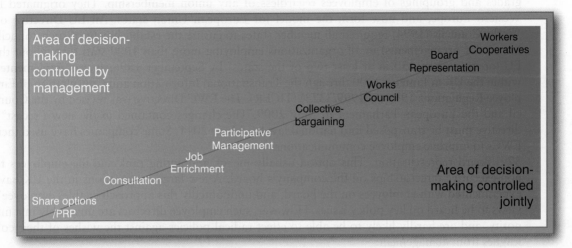

of the organization by means of shareholdings to total employee control through worker cooperatives. Each alternative is described briefly below.

31. Share options/profit-related pay. This option was promoted in the UK as part of the drive to extend the scope and spirit of private enterprise in the economy. The intention was to offer relevant employees the chance to own shares in their company, and thus participate in its financing. There was also an intention to link employee effort to profitability by permitting profit-related elements in total pay. This option does give employees the chance to take a stake in their employer's business, but is scarcely relevant if one considers 'participation' to involve sharing in decisions.

32. Consultation. This can be seen as 'participation' only in the sense that employees are consulted about decisions affecting their working lives. This does not imply that employers need take any notice of employees' views. However, there have been efforts in recent years to give communications with employees a higher profile. Companies that make use of workplace consultative groups (e.g. Quality Circles) are not only engaging in a management-employee dialogue, but in many cases are actively encouraging such consultation in order to improve working methods, quality standards and productivity. This form of consultation comes much closer to real participation in decision-making.

33. Job enrichment. This is 'participation' in the sense that the employee is given greater discretion over immediate work decisions (see also empowerment). It can certainly add to employee motivation by increasing responsibility and job interest. However, it does not offer any opportunity to participate in the major, strategic decisions affecting the organization.

34. Participative management. A participative management style implies that all employees will be encouraged to play a part in the decisions affecting their work. However, in practice this may be no more than a paternalistic attempt to involve employees in day-to-day affairs. Where a radical approach to participation is adopted, then it is likely that employees will be enabled to share in the decision-making process at all levels, including the strategic level.

35. Collective bargaining. As stated above, collective bargaining is less common now. This is not difficult to understand, for when management is in a strong negotiating position due to external economic circumstances, then there is less likelihood they will want to engage in negotiations with their employees, since this restricts their freedom of discretion. Bargaining by its very nature is adversarial, and its outcomes, therefore, depend on the relative power of the parties, and the extent to which compromises can be reached. Consultation by comparison is essentially a passive form of participation.

36. Works Councils. These are joint bodies of managers and employees established to consider and agree key matters affecting employment within the organization. They are not for

union-only employees, as would be the case in collective bargaining, but must be open to all grades and groupings of employees regardless of any union membership. They originated in Western Europe, and now form the model for European Union states. An EU Directive on Works Councils (1994) required all member states to ensure the establishment of such councils (or similar arrangements) in all organizations employing more than 1000 staff throughout the EU (or more than 150 in at least two of the states) by September 1996. It was implemented within the UK in January 2000 through the Transnational Information and Consultation of Employee Regulations 1999 (SI 1999/3323) (TICER). The EWC Directive was revised by the Council and the European Parliament in May 2009. The changes contained in the new ('recast'") directive must be transposed into national law by 5 June 2011. Some companies have used their EWCs to improve employee communications.

37.   Board representation. This option usually means appointing rank-and-file employees to non-executive directorships on the company's board. A few large corporations in the UK have experimented with employees on the board, and undoubtedly this approach enables employee's views to be heard on key policy issues. However, such employee directors are invariably in a minority, and are hardly likely to be able to effect radical policies against the wishes of their colleagues from management.

38.   Workers' cooperatives. This option is the nearest to workers' control. Effectively it means that the business is run by the employees in a totally collaborative way. It has never been a widespread form of business management.

49.9 EMPLOYEE INVOLVEMENT AND RELATIONS

39.   Whereas union-relations address the 'collectivist, dimension of the employment relationship, 'employee relations' first and foremost addresses individual aspects of employer-employee relations. There are four important dimensions of employee relations: communication, involvement, rights and discipline, (Bratton and Gold, 2007). Employee involvement (EI) can either support management directly through performance improvement or indirectly through organizational commitment.

40.   We defined and described employee involvement, contrasting it with employee participation at the beginning of this chapter. Many organizations have moved recently from employee participation to employee involvement. As was noted earlier, employee involvement is seen as management initiated for the purpose of gaining commitment, improving efficiency, productivity and customer service. Whilst many would argue that employee involvement has replaced employee participation as a contemporary HR concept, task participation remains a component of EI.

41.   Communication plays an important role in EI. Managers inform and educate employees through downward communication, typically in the form of corporate newsletters, reports, news on the Intranet, team briefings based on a cascade system and meetings. In addition, EI seeks upward problem-solving through participation schemes (see attitude surveys, suggestion schemes, quality circles and total quality management) that enable managers to draw on employee knowledge of their jobs. EI often extends the range and type of tasks undertaken by employees (see job redesign, job enrichment and team working – see Chapter 21). As has been previously mentioned, such initiatives attempt to increase employee commitment.

42.   EI is also associated with team working which, when associated with empowerment, can lead to greater flexibility (multi-capable workers able to switch between tasks, organize and allocate work), efficiency and responsiveness. Finally, employee involvement is associated with financial involvement. There are a variety of schemes (see for example profit sharing and employee share ownership) which seek to link part of individual employee rewards to the success of their team, department or organization as a whole. Such theories may encourage co-operation and involvement, improving commitment and performance. They may also increase business

awareness, aligning the company goals with individual goals and could be introduced with the objective of reducing or preventing trade union power.

43. Earlier, we made attempts to distinguish between categories of participation (see Figure 49.2). In a similar manner, Marchington and Wilkinson cited in Sisson and Bach (1999), provide a simple stage model which distinguishes between the major categories of involvement, focusing on the extent of influence. Starting with no involvement, where managers make all the decisions, organizations at the other extreme may be controlled by employees. The next stage after no involvement is more about communication and the exchange of information between the employer and employees; information sharing may be witnessed in team briefings, news sheets, attitude surveys and suggestion schemes. Following this, in the next stage (consultation) information may be exchanged through formalized channels and management may make use of information provided by employees before making decisions; it is important to note that there may be, in some situations, a legal duty to consult (see for example over redundancy, pension changes or in the event of one organization being taken over by another). In the next stage, before employee control, there is joint decision-making (codetermination). Generally this stage is less common within the UK where important decisions tend to be made by managers.

CONCLUSION

44. We briefly outlined key trends in the decline of trade unions and the growth in employment law. Following this, we discussed (collective) union-management relations. In this section we explained the term trade union, considered different types of union and how they negotiate (collective bargaining) with management. Next we considered different forms of employee participation before moving on to explain the more recent concept of employee involvement as a part of employee relations. Whereas union-relations address the collectivist, dimension of the employment relationship, employee relations first and foremost address individual aspects of employer-employee relations. There are four important dimensions of employee relations: communication, involvement, rights and discipline. Employee involvement (EI) can either support management directly through performance improvement or indirectly through organizational commitment.

QUESTIONS

1 An important implication of employee relations is that rule-making is essential if the parties concerned are to contain any conflict within manageable bounds. Identify and briefly discuss where the main body of rules is drawn from in employee relations.

2 Explain why trade union membership in Britain has fallen quite substantially in recent years.

3 Identify and explain the main types of trade union.

4 Briefly explain what a trade union is.

5 Briefly explain what is meant by collective bargaining and collective agreements.

6 Define what is meant by employee participation and, with reference to a continuum, discuss the degrees of participation available to employees.

7 What is meant by employee involvement and what is its purpose?

8 What is meant by employee relations and what are the important four dimensions of employee relations?

USEFUL WEBSITES

Office for National Statistics **www.statistics.gov.uk/cci/ nugget.asp?id=4** see Labour Market – Union Membership.
The Confederation of British Industry **www.cbi.org.uk/**
Department for Business, Innovation and Skills **www.bis.gov.uk/** The Department for Business, Innovation and Skills (BIS) is responsible, with the Office for National Statistics (ONS) for publishing the National Statistics on trade union membership.

Central Arbitration Committee **www.cac.gov.uk**
DirectGov Employment Trade unions **www.direct.gov.uk/en/ Employment/TradeUnions/DG_447**
ACAS **www.acas.org.uk**
IPA **www.ipa-involve.com/** The IPA is a British organization delivering partnership, consultation and employee engagement. . .
Trades Union Congress **www.tuc.org.uk**.

VIDEO CASES

Now take a look at the online video cases – visit the companion website to work through real world business problems associated with the concepts presented within this chapter.
60 Managing conflict – mediation to resolve workplace disputes

Using mediation to resolve workplace disputes.
In this case we examine mechanisms by which organizations and workers communicate and resolve conflict within the employment relationship.

REFERENCES

Blyton, P. and Turnbull, P. (2004) 'The Dynamics of Employee Relations', Ed. 3. Palgrave Macmillan.
Bratton, J. and Gold, J. (2007) 'Human Resource Management Theory and Practice', Ed. 4. Palgrave Macmillan.
Hollinshead, G.,Tailby, S. and Nicholls, P. (2003) 'Employee Relations', Ed. 2. Financial Times Press.
Leopold, J. and Harris, L. (2009) 'The Strategic Managing of Human Resources', Ed. 2. Financial Times Press.

Rose, E. (2008) 'Employment Relations', Ed. 3. Financial Times Press.
Sisson, K. and Bach, S. (1999) 'Personnel Management', Ed. 3. Blackwell Publishers.
Torrington, D., Hall, L., Taylor, S. and Atkinson, C. (2009) 'Fundamentals of Human Resource Management: Managing People at Work', Ed. 1. Financial Times Press.

CHAPTER 50
LEGAL ASPECTS OF EMPLOYMENT – INDIVIDUAL RIGHTS

Key Concepts

- Discrimination
- Employee
- Industrial tribunals
- Psychological contract
- Terms of employment
- Unfair dismissal

Learning Outcomes Having read this chapter, you should be able to:

- identify four sources of employment law in England and Wales
- discuss employee rights
- review the key legal obligations placed on employers when addressing employee rights
- explain the role of employment tribunals in enforcing employment rights

> **Employee** A person who carries out work for a person under a contract of service

1.   In the previous chapter we noted the increasing trend of using employment law to protect the individual at work. We also noted employee rights to be an important dimension of employee relations. It is important for managers at any level of responsibility to be aware of the legal framework that applies to the workplace. This chapter outlines a number of the key features of employment law likely to be experienced by a practising manager. When more detailed information is required, managers may refer to specific guides, to the legislation as published from time to time by the appropriate government department or statutory body (e.g. ACAS, Health and Safety Executive, etc.). Our primary purpose here is to alert the reader to consider legal issues at work so that they have a better idea as to when and where they should take expert legal advice or devise policies, change processes, practices and procedures and conduct risk assessments, etc.

2.   The chapter begins with a short consideration of the all-important question of what is, and what is not, employment, and outlines the principal features of the employment contract. The remaining sections of the chapter focus on the following:

- human rights
- individual rights in the workplace
- employment equality law
- health and safety at work and
- employment tribunals.

50.1 EMPLOYMENT LAW

3.   There are four sources of employment law in England and Wales as follows:

The common law – i.e. the 'unwritten law' arising from custom and practice, especially in relation to (a) the contract of employment, and (b) the law of torts (civil wrongs) affecting workplace incidents.

Statute law – i.e. the written law arising from the numerous Acts of Parliament passed by the nation's law-makers, and which is the most far-reaching of the legal influences on the workplace.

Case law – i.e. the decisions of courts and tribunals (in the European Union as well as in Britain itself) in interpreting statutes in particular.

European Union law (historically called European Community law) is a body of treaties, law and court judgements which operates alongside the legal systems of the European Union's member states. It has direct effect within the EU's member states and, where conflict occurs, takes precedence over national law.

50.2 THE EMPLOYMENT CONTRACT

4.   All employees have an employment contract with their employer. A contract of employment is an agreement between employer and employee and is the basis of the employment relationship (see previous chapter); it is an agreement between an employer and an employee which sets out their employment rights, responsibilities and duties. The legal parts of a contract are known as 'terms'. The terms of an employment contract set out what an employer and employee can expect of each other. Contract terms can come from different sources such as: verbally agreed; a written contract, or similar document; an employee handbook; an offer letter; required by law (e.g. minimum wage); collective agreements

> **Terms of employment** The provisions of a persons contract of employment, whether provided for expressly in the contract itself or incorporated by statute, custom and practice or common law etc

(see previous chapter) or may be implied terms (see for example, terms implied by custom and practice). Changes to employment contracts should be done by mutual agreement. Employment contracts may be permanent or of limited duration (temporary or fixed term).

5.   A contract is made when an offer of employment is accepted. A number of rights and duties, enforceable through the courts, arise as soon as this happens. Most employment contracts do not need to be in writing to be legally valid. The Employment Rights Act 1996 requires employers to give most employees a written statement of the main terms within two calendar months of starting work (a written statement of particulars of employment). The statement shall contain particulars of the date when the employment began; the scale or rate of remuneration or the method of calculating remuneration; the intervals at which remuneration is paid (that is, weekly, monthly or other specified intervals); any terms and conditions relating to hours of work, entitlement to holidays, incapacity for work due to sickness or injury, including any provision for sick pay, and pensions and pension schemes; the length of notice which the employee is obliged to give and entitled to receive to terminate his contract of employment; the title of the job which the employee is employed to do or a brief description of the work for which he is employed; where the employment is not intended to be permanent, the period for which it is expected to continue or, if it is for a fixed term, the date when it is to end; and any collective agreements which directly affect the terms and conditions of the employment. Aside from the formal contract of employment, employers should remain conscious of the psychological contract – informal understandings between the employer and employee.

> **Act** A law or piece of legislation passed by both Houses of Parliament and agreed to by the Crown, which then becomes part of statutory law (i.e. is enacted)

6.   A person employed by an organization is either employed under a contract of service, and is therefore an employee, or under a contract for services, and is then an independent contractor. It is only the former which is referred to as the contract of employment. Employees have access to a wider range of legal rights than non-employees. The difference between an employee and a contractor is important. For example if a person is an employee, his employer is liable vicariously for any civil wrongs that the employee may commit in the course of his employment. A civil wrong, or tort, could occur when an employee steals from a customer or injures a member of the public when driving in the course of his or her duties.

> **Psychological contract** An informal understanding between the employer and employee. Unlike the formal employment contract, this has no physical existence. It is a set of expectations held by both employers and employees in terms of what they wish to give and receive from their working relationship (Rousseau and Parks, 1993)

50.3 HUMAN RIGHTS ACT, 1998

7.   Human rights are 'rights and freedoms to which all humans are entitled'. Such rights are not removed when employees go to work. Human rights have been encoded in statute law, in the Human Rights Act 1998. This Act came into force in 2000 and is derived directly from the European Convention on Human Rights. It enables British citizens to obtain redress on human rights matters in UK courts and tribunals, instead of having to refer to the European Court of Human Rights. The Act is an overarching law, which means that other relevant pieces of legislation must be interpreted in the light of its principles. The Act applies *prima facie* to public bodies, such as government departments and local authorities, but its implications stretch much further. In respect of employment matters, the Act affects all organizations that employ people. There are sixteen basic rights protected in the Act, including the right to life, and to liberty and security. The rights most relevant to employers and employees are as follows:

Right to a fair trial – everyone is entitled to a fair and public hearing within a reasonable time by an independent and impartial tribunal established by law. Disciplinary rules within organizations should make clear provision for a right of appeal to an employment tribunal (ET).

Right to respect for private and family life – everyone has the right to respect for their private and family life, their home and their correspondence. Managers need to be aware of possible abuses of this right when monitoring employees' personal telephone calls or emails whilst at work. Clear guidelines will be needed to show staff where the limits are to be set. This is especially important when company rules require behaviour to conform to security and other restrictions on personal communications. Employers do not have an absolute right to contact employees at their home, unless such arrangements form part of the employees' contract of employment.

Freedom of thought, conscience and religion – this right includes the right to change one's beliefs. For employers this right has to be considered in relation to the Race Relations Act, and clearly any exercise by individuals of the basic right must not contravene legislation designed to restrict racial or religious abuse. Managers now need to take more notice of religious beliefs than in the past and ensure that employees are not expected to work on their Sabbath days and major religious festivals. With the increasing provision of retail and other services for twenty-four hours a day, seven days a week, such considerations must be taken into account in setting employment conditions.

Freedom of expression – individuals have the right to hold opinions and receive and impart ideas without interference by a public authority. This right extends to dress codes and personal appearance. Managers now have to review disciplinary rules to ensure that any restrictions on an employee's right of expression are reasonable in the circumstances (e.g. for safety and health reasons).

Freedom of assembly and association – this includes the specific right to join, or not to join, a trade union, and to hold union meetings during working hours. The right to take industrial action is not explicit, but is strongly implied. Most of the implications of this basic right are already well catered for in UK businesses and public sector organizations.

Prohibition of discrimination – access to the rights available under the Act should not be denied on any discriminatory grounds unless they can be justified objectively. The effect of this right is to extend the scope of anti-discriminatory measures to religious and political issues as well as those already in force regarding sex, race and disability discrimination. Any such prohibitions in the workplace have to be seen to be lawful and reasonable.

8.   As a consequence of the Act, all managers in the workplace will have to review their existing grievance, disciplinary and other codes of behaviour. They will also need to review their agreements with recognized trade unions in order to ensure that they conform to the spirit of the human rights legislation. The Act does not give carte blanche to individuals to do or say what they want without any consideration of public unrest or outrage caused by their behaviour. When everyone has rights there have to be arrangements for deciding what is fair when one person's rights conflict with another's. The UK's existing laws affecting employment are still very much in force. The chief difference now is the way in which they are likely to be interpreted by courts and tribunals.

50.4 EMPLOYMENT LEGISLATION – INDIVIDUAL RIGHTS

9.   Aside from legislation specifying general human rights, there is an abundance of legislation addressing employee rights. United Kingdom labour law involves the legal relationship between workers, employers and trade unions. We briefly touched on a selection of relevant laws in the previous chapter and introduced the Employment Rights Act, 1996 when discussing contracts above. Labour law derives primarily from the Employment Rights Act 1996, the Equality Act 2010, the Trade Union and Labour Relations (Consolidation) Act 1992, as well as a multiplicity of European Directives, Statutory Instruments and cases through the UK court system, the European Court of Justice and the European Court of Human Rights.

10.   Labour law can be analyzed as either 'individual labour law' or 'collective labour law'. We discussed collective labour law in the previous chapter and will focus on Individual labour law here. This involves basic rights of people at work. Under the National Minimum Wage Act 1998 every UK worker has the right to a minimum wage, no longer working hours other than those consented to under the Working Time Regulations 1998; the right to leave for child care and the right to request flexible working arrangements under the Employment Rights Act 1996. With regard to discrimination, people should be judged by what they do, and not characteristics; by their colour, gender, sexuality, beliefs, disabilities or age, the Equality Act 2010. The Employment Rights Act 1996 adds that in the event of dismissal, employees have a minimum level of job security, so every employer must give reasonable notice after one month of work, backed by a sufficiently fair reason after one year of work, and with a redundancy payment after two years. Further rights arise if a company is taken over, triggering the Transfer of Undertakings (Protection of Employment) Regulations 2006. These hold that when an employer changes, employees' terms cannot be reduced, even to the point of dismissal, without a good economic, technical or organizational reason. We will consider these matters in more detail next.

> **Regulations** Secondary legislation made under an Act of Parliament (or European legislation) setting out subsidiary matters which assist in the Act's implementation

11.   The UK government has now introduced enabling legislation to provide for a national minimum wage, the National Minimum Wage Act, 1998. The intention is to set minimum hourly rates of pay for 16–17, 18–20 and for workers aged 21 and over. The rates as at October 2010 were £3.64per hour for the younger group, £4.92 for the 18–20 rate and £5.93 for those workers aged 21 and over.

12.   Parental leave is an employee benefit that provides paid or unpaid time off work to care for a child or make arrangements for the child's welfare. Often, the term parental leave includes maternity, paternity and adoption leave. Often the minimum benefits are stipulated by law. Maternity (and paternity rights) stem directly from the Employment Protection Act, 1975, which contained Britain's first such provisions for women employees. The present rights are included in the Employment Rights Act, 1996, as amended by the Employment Relations Act, 1999, the Maternity and Parental Leave Regulations 1999 and the Maternity and Parental Leave (Amendment) Regulations 2001. Employees on Statutory Maternity Leave have their employment terms and conditions protected.

13.   The Employment Rights Act, 1996, allows employees time off work for specified reasons. In some cases, the employer is also bound to pay the employee his normal remuneration during the time off. Apart from certain trade union activities, the principal rights to time off work for individuals include performing certain public duties (e.g. JP, school governor, local councillor), performing safety duties and attending relevant safety representative training and attending for antenatal care. The employer is not obliged to pay employees their normal pay where public duties are concerned.

14.   The Employment Rights Act, 1996, gives employees the right to a minimum period of notice of termination of employment. Currently, these minima are as follows: at least one weeks' notice if employed for between one month and two years; one additional weeks' notice for each further complete year of service up to a maximum of twelve weeks' notice and not less than twelve weeks' notice if employed for twelve years or more. These rights may be extended or waived by agreement, and an employer may offer pay in lieu of notice. Contracts can, of course, be terminated without notice, if the conduct of either party justifies it (see unfair dismissal notes below).

> **Unfair dismissal** A statutory definition of dismissal now part of the Employment Protection (Consolidation) Act, 1978; the Act states that every employee shall have the right not to be unfairly dismissed; remedies for unfair dismissal must be pursued via an industrial tribunal, which may award compensation or reinstatement or re-engagement

15.   Employees have the right to a redundancy payment if they have worked continuously for an employer for at least two years and are being made redundant. The provisions relating to

redundancy originated in the Redundancy Payments Act, 1965. This right does not apply to those over the normal retiring age at the time of the redundancy. The provisions for redundancy pay represent the minimum standard, and many organizations pay substantially more, mainly as a result of collective agreements. Redundancy payments are dependent on employee wage, length of service with the company and employee age. The legal minima are as follows: 0.5 week's pay for each full year of service where the employee is under 22; 1 week's pay for each full year of service where the employee is 22 or above but under 41 and 1.5 week's pay for each full year of service where the employee is 41 or above.

16.   An employee is dismissed when the employer terminates an employee's contract. A dismissal will normally be fair provided the employer had sufficient reason for the dismissal and acted reasonably in so doing. Amongst the commonest reasons for dismissal are misconduct, inability to do the job and redundancy. The concept of unfair dismissal was introduced by the Industrial Relations Act, 1971, and has remained firmly entrenched in subsequent legislation. It now forms an integral part of the Employment Rights Act, 1996 (S. 94) as follows: 'an employee has the right not to be unfairly dismissed by his employer.' Dismissal occurs when an employee has had his contract of employment terminated by his employer, with or without notice; it also refers to the non-renewal of a fixed term contract; and it applies in a situation when, because of the employer's conduct, the employee himself terminates the contract, with or without notice, in circumstances where he is entitled to terminate it without notice (known as 'constructive dismissal').

17.   A dismissal for reasons of lack of capability usually revolves around questions of ill-health or incompetence, and the courts will invariably want to know whether other, more suitable, work has been offered to an employee in one of these situations, for, even if the grounds for dismissal are considered as fair, the employer must still show that it was reasonable to dismiss in the circumstances. A dismissal for reasons of misconduct is very much an issue where 'reasonableness' must be taken into account. ACAS advises against dismissal for a first offence, except in cases of gross misconduct. What constitutes 'reasonable behaviour' by the employer depends upon how tribunals interpret the difference between 'misconduct', 'repeated misconduct' and 'gross misconduct'; it also depends upon what is stated in company rule-books, how previous cases have been dealt with by the company, and the extent to which the ACAS Code has been adhered. A dismissal on the grounds of redundancy requires the employer to show that there is no longer any need for that job in the organization. The job becomes redundant and the employee is dismissed – this at least is the logic of the situation. Such a dismissal can be unfair, however, if the employee is unfairly selected for redundancy in a situation where some jobs are redundant, but other similar jobs are not.

18.   The remedies for unfair dismissal are as follows: (a) an award for compensation, (b) reinstatement (i.e. in the employee's original post), and (c) re-engagement (i.e. in some other post). Most applications relating to unfair dismissal do not reach a tribunal (see below) for decision. About two-thirds are conciliated, i.e. withdrawn or settled out of court.

50.5 EMPLOYMENT EQUALITY LAW

Discrimination Less favourable treatment of a person compared with another person because of a protected characteristic

19.   UK employment equality law overcomes prejudice in the workplace. An important part of UK labour law, it bans discrimination against people based on gender, race, religion or belief, sexuality, disability and age. These different categories were consolidated in the Equality Act 2010. There are also important provisions which deal with discrimination by an employer on the grounds of work status (such as part time worker, fixed term employee, agency worker or union membership). It is constructed from various pieces of legislation which occasionally cover employment issues only, and sometimes are part of a larger equality framework.

20.   In 2006 the government passed the Equality Act, which established the Equality and Human Rights Commission, a body designed to strengthen enforcement of equality laws. The Equality and Human Rights Commission have a statutory remit to promote and monitor human

rights; and to protect, enforce and promote equality across the seven 'protected' grounds – age, disability, gender, race, religion and belief, sexual orientation and gender reassignment. The commission provides guidance to employers on how to comply with equality law and implement good practice in all aspects of employment including recruitment, pay, working hours, managing staff and developing policies.

21.   The primary purpose of the Equality Act 2010 is to bring together lots of different equality laws, which formed the basis of anti-discrimination law in the United Kingdom. This was, primarily, the Equal Pay Act 1970, the Sex Discrimination Act 1975, the Race Relations Act 1976 and the Disability Discrimination Act 1995. It requires equal treatment in access to employment regardless of gender, race, disability, sexual orientation, belief and age. In the case of gender, there are special protections for pregnant women. In the case of disability, employers and service providers are under a duty to make reasonable adjustments to their workplaces to overcome barriers experienced by disabled people. The Act makes equality law simpler and easier to understand.

Duty to make reasonable adjustments Where a disabled person is at a substantial disadvantage in comparison with people who are not disabled, there is a duty to take reasonable steps to remove that disadvantage by (i) changing provisions, criteria or practices, (ii) altering, removing or providing a reasonable alternative means of avoiding physical features and (iii) providing auxiliary aids

22.   Equality law recognizes that bringing about equality for disabled people may mean changing the way in which employment is structured, the removal of physical barriers and/or providing extra support for a disabled worker. This is the duty to make reasonable adjustments. The duty to make reasonable adjustments aims to make sure that a disabled person has the same access to everything that is involved in getting and doing a job as a non-disabled person, as far as is reasonable. When the duty arises, employers are under a positive and proactive duty to take steps to remove or reduce or prevent the obstacles a disabled worker or job applicant faces.

23.   Equality law applies during recruitment, making decisions about workers' hours, whether they can work flexibly or have time off; making decisions about worker levels of pay or determining benefits; making a decision, or taking action following dismissal of a worker, making a worker redundant, retiring someone reaching a particular age or when dealing with a request for a reference from someone who has left the company. As an employer, liability is broad-reaching. For instance – another person employed by you or carrying out your instructions to do something (whom the law calls your agent) may engage in unlawful discrimination, harassment or victimisation and you, as the employer, can be held legally responsible for the unlawful actions of your employees/agent.

Harassment Unwanted behaviour that has the purpose or effect of violating a person's dignity or creates a degrading, humiliating, hostile, intimidating or offensive environment

50.6 HEALTH AND SAFETY AT WORK

24.   All workers have a right to work in places where risks to their health and safety are properly controlled. Health and safety is about preventing employees being hurt at work or becoming ill through work. The Health and Safety at Work etc. Act 1974 also referred to as HASAW or HSW is the primary piece of legislation covering occupational health and safety in the United Kingdom. The Health and Safety Executive is responsible for enforcing the Act and a number of other Acts and Statutory Instruments relevant to the working environment. Statutory instruments are the secondary types of legislation made under specific Acts of Parliament. These cover a wide range of subjects, from control of asbestos at work, diving, escape and rescue from mines, ionising radiation and working at heights.

Occupational health The ongoing maintenance and promotion of physical, mental and social well-being for all workers

25.   Employers have a number of general duties under the act-a selection of which are outlined here. Section 2 states that, 'It shall be the duty of every employer to ensure, so far as is

reasonably practicable, the health, safety and welfare at work of all his/her employees'. Section 3 states the duty of all employers and self employed persons to ensure, as far as is reasonably practicable the safety of persons other than employees, for example, contractors, visitors, the general public and clients. Employers must undertake risk assessments; provide health and safety training; provide employees with any equipment and protective clothing needed, and ensure it is properly maintained; provide toilets, washing facilities and drinking water; provide adequate first-aid facilities; report injuries; and have insurance. Employers must prepare and keep under review a safety policy and bring it to the attention of employees (s.2(2)).

50.7 THE ROLE OF EMPLOYMENT TRIBUNALS IN ENFORCING EMPLOYMENT RIGHTS

26.   Employees who feel their rights have been breached may seek redress through employment tribunals. Employment Tribunals are tribunal non-departmental public bodies in England and Wales and Scotland which have statutory jurisdiction to hear many kinds of disputes between employers and employees. The most common disputes are concerned with unfair dismissal, redundancy payments and employment discrimination.

27.   Where individuals think they have a case against their employer in respect of the various rights available to them under the employment protection and anti-discrimination laws, they may make an application to an employment tribunal for financial compensation or other remedy (e.g. re-instatement, re-engagement, etc.). Tribunals provide for a speedier, cheaper and less complex approach to legal disputes than the ordinary courts. Such tribunals have been active in Britain since the 1960s, and their jurisdiction has been increased substantially over the last fifty years. The typical tribunal is presided over by a legally qualified chairman and two other approved persons, usually one an experienced manager and the other an experienced employee representative. Procedures are considerably less formal than in other courts, and legal representation is not necessary, although it is increasing. Appeals on a point of law only may be made to the Employment Appeal Tribunal, which is presided over by a High Court Judge supported by two lay-members, one representing employers and the other trade unions. Further appeals lie to the Court of Appeal, the House of Lords and the European Court of Justice.

Industrial Tribunals Tribunals set up originally to hear appeals against training levies; their scope has increased considerably since 1971 to include unfair dismissal, sex discrimination, etc. Now known as Employment Tribunals

CONCLUSION

28.   Employees have rights, both as human beings and as people who carry out work for employers under a contract of service. Additionally, the contract of employment is an agreement between employer and employee and is the basis of the employment relationship and rights. Various legal frameworks are used to deter employers from breaching those rights. There is an abundance of legislation specifically addressing employee rights. See for example Employment Rights Act, 1996 and the Equality Act 2010. All workers have a right to work in places where risks to their health and safety are properly controlled. Health and safety is about preventing employees becoming hurt at work or made ill through work. The Health and Safety at Work etc. Act 1974 is the primary piece of legislation covering occupational health and safety in the United Kingdom. Employees who feel their rights have been breached may seek redress through employment tribunals. Employers assure employee rights are not breached through policies, practices, facilities, training, informed decision-making, risk assessments and audits. They seek to develop a value system and organizational culture which develops the employee relationship.

QUESTIONS

1   Identify and discuss the four sources of employment law in England and Wales.

2   Explain what a contract of employment is and list, with reference to the employment rights act 1996, the main contents/terms.

3   Discuss the role of employment tribunal's in enforcing employment rights.

USEFUL WEBSITES

Office of Public Sector Information (OPSI): **www.opsi.gov.uk/ acts.htm** Acts of the UK Parliament.

Directgov: **www.direct.gov.uk/en/index.htm** Delivers information and practical advice about public services

Equality and human rights Commission: **www.equalityhumanrights.com/** Have a statutory remit to promote and monitor human rights; and to protect, enforce and promote equality across the seven 'protected' grounds – age, disability, gender, race, religion and belief, sexual orientation.

Health and Safety Executive: **www.hse.gov.uk** The Health and Safety Executive (HSE) is a non-departmental public body in the United Kingdom. It is the body responsible for the encouragement, regulation and enforcement of workplace health, safety and welfare, and for research into occupational risks in England and Wales and Scotland.

Department for Work and Pensions: **www.dwp.gov.uk** The Department for Work and Pensions is responsible for welfare and pension policy.

REFERENCES

Sargeant, M. and Lewis, D. (2010) 'Employment Law', Ed. 5. Longman.

Torrington, D., Hall, L., Taylor, S. and Atkinson, C. (2009) 'Fundamentals of Human Resource Management: Managing People at Work', Ed. 1. Financial Times Press.

Section Fourteen
Financial Aspects
of Management

CASE STUDY

FINANCIAL ASPECTS OF MANAGEMENT

STREETCAR LIMITED

Car clubs provide a network of readily accessible vehicles, parked in local areas, for hourly or daily rental. Car club members book vehicles via the Internet or by phone. Vehicles may be accessed 24 hours a day, subject to availability. At the end of the vehicle rental period, the car must be returned to the parking space from which it was taken. Car clubs are 'self service' in that cars are picked up from and returned to unmanned locations, and paperwork does not need to be completed for each rental period. Members pay a fee to join a particular car club, and an hourly or daily rate for vehicle usage. The cost of insurance, the congestion charge (where applicable) and an amount of fuel (often 30 miles' worth) is built into the usage charge. Car clubs have grown rapidly in recent years. It is estimated that the national car club fleet increased in size to over 2000 vehicles during 2009, and that there were approximately 100 000 car club members in the UK by the end of 2009.

One such car club is Streetcar, established in 2002 by Andrew Valentine and Brett Akker. After spending 18 months researching the idea, they launched Streetcar in London in April 2004 with just eight cars. It immediately took off, and today the scheme has approximately 1500 cars serving the needs of 80 000 members using over 1100 locations in ten UK cities. Streetcar's mission is to provide a viable mass-market alternative to car ownership across Europe. You can use one for as little as 30 minutes or as long as six months. The cost of usage is based on how long you have the car and how far you drive but unless you are a heavy car user, the annual cost of Streetcar will be dramatically less than owning a car and with lots of the hassle of car ownership removed. It is estimated that owning a car equivalent to Streetcar's VW Golf and driving 5000 miles per year costs £3927. The same trips in a Streetcar would cost just £1400.

Streetcar Limited (Company No. 04525217) now operates as a wholly owned subsidiary of the American company Zipcar, Inc. which retained Andrew Valentine as Finance Officer but appointed its own CEO, Scott Griffith from the USA. As a limited company, streetcar is recognized as a separate legal entity-distinct from its owners. The main advantage of this concerns the limitation of liability of the owners who would not be personally responsible for any debts should the company go bankrupt. However, as a limited company they are subject to various rules, regulations and legislation. They must register the company with companies' house and file accounts (balance sheet and income statement) each year. Extracts of which are provided below:

Streetcar: Simple Balance Sheet 31/12/2009

	THGBP (£'000)
Fixed assets	
Tangible fixed assets	14 033
Current assets	5 037
Stocks	62
Debtors	0
Other current assets	4 975
Total assets	19 070
Shareholders funds	−1 141
Non current liabilities	64
Long term debts	
Current liabilities	10 847
Loans	7 331
Creditors	0
Other Current Liabilities	3516
Total shares	19 070
Funds & Liab.	

Information about the financial position of Streetcar at the end of 2009 is presented in their balance sheet. At the end of 2009, Streetcar had approximately £19 million in total assets. These are broken down into fixed (non-current) assets of approximately £14 million and current assets of approximately £5 million. All of the fixed assets are tangible and the current assets include stock and cash or cash equivalent. The total liabilities for the company also amount to approximately £19 million. This is because the value of assets equals the value of liabilities on the balance sheet. The liabilities are also reported under categories of current and non-current. The most common example of a current liability (those liabilities folding due for repayment within one year) is a bank overdraft or something similar and streetcars has current liabilities in the form of loans (approximately £7 million), and other current liabilities (approximately £3.5 million). Another example is where goods are bought on credit terms and the supplier has not been paid at the balance sheet date. However, we can see from the Streetcar balance sheet that there are no creditors. Clearly there are other types of liability which do not have to be repaid

in full in one year and they are recorded as non-current liabilities. Streetcar owes approximately £9.3 million (long-term debt). The Balance sheet also shows shareholder funds. The owners equity is normally left in the business as long as it is required. The owners equity can be calculated by subtracting the liabilities from the assets. Next we turn our attention to the measurement of profit. The income statement (profit and loss account) for Streetcar is shown below:

Streetcar: SIMPLE income statement (profit and loss account) 31/12/2009

	31/12/2009 THGBP (£'000) Local GAAP	Comments (Notes have been added by the authors and would not normally be shown in the accounts)
Operating revenue/turnover	16 448	
Costs of goods sold	8 483	
Gross profit	7 965	Gross Profit = Revenue − The cost of goods sold (16 448 − 8 483 = 7 965)
Other operating expenses	7 219	
Operating P/L	746	Operating P/L = Gross Profit − Other Operating Expenses
Financial revenue	718	
Financial expenses	179	
Financial P/L	539	
P/L Before tax	1 285	Operating P/L + Financial P/L
Taxation	−1 724	
P/L After tax	3 009	Tax is normally deducted from profit however in this case there was a tax refund and it is therefore added
P/L for period	3 009	

Unlike the balance sheet, the income statement relates to a period of time and summarizes certain transactions taking place over that period, one year in the case of Streetcars. This statement tells you whether or not the company is profitable. It enables us to determine the bottom line, amount of profit made by the company. It does this by summarizing the revenue for the period and deducting expenses incurred in earning that revenue. The revenue relates to the services sold (Streetcar charges members according to how long they use the car). The statement also shows the cost of goods sold (expenses). Examples of costs include wages, car maintenance, purchase of equipment, etc.

The accounts may be used by a variety of stakeholders, internal and external, for a variety of purposes. For example, the income statement may be used by the owners for judging the performance of the business. Investors and Lenders require information to assess risk and select investment opportunities. Financial state

ment analysis for streetcar Limited, using accounting data between 2006 and 2009 reveals that the company turnover has risen from £1 million to £16 million per year and the value of company assets has also been growing significantly. Following a number of years of making a loss, Streetcar Ltd made a profit in 2009. As the company grows, it requires more cars and employees and as a result its expenses and costs also grow. Thus the company must invest in assets and have adequate cash flows to meet its expenses if it is to achieve its mission, grow and return a profit. Investment may come from revenues, lenders or investors. Success will depend not only on customer demand but also prudence in financial management decision making.

Sources:

1 www.streetcar.co.uk
2 http://wck2.companieshouse.gov.uk/546f2ed6362158bc41ef018dc2fa66aa/compdetails

CHAPTER 51
COMPANY
ACCOUNTS

Key Concepts

- Accounting
- Accounting standards
- Annual report
- Balance sheet
- Financial accounting
- Management accounting
- Profit and loss account

Learning Outcomes   Having read this chapter, you should be able to:

- distinguish between financial accounting and management accounting
- describe the principal statements of accounts
- explain how society assures financial statements are reported fairly

Accounting is the recording of financial or money transactions. Accounting is the systematic recording, reporting and analysis of financial transactions of a business

Financial accounting Reporting of the financial position and performance of a firm through financial statements issued to external users on a periodic basis

Management accounting The process of identifying, measuring, analyzing, interpreting and communicating information for the pursuit of an organization's goals

Balance sheet A statement that lists the assets of a business or other organization, at some specified point in time, together with the claims against those assets

Annual report Document detailing the business activity of a company over the previous year, and containing the three main financial statements: Income Statement, Cash Flow Statement and Balance Sheet

1.   As yet, we have not discussed the management of financial resources within the organization, a matter we address in this and the final chapter. The system for recording and summarizing business transactions and activities designed to accumulate, measure and communicate financial information about economic entities for decision-making purposes is termed accounting. **Accounting** refers to the overall process of identifying, measuring, recording, interpreting and communicating the results of economic activity; tracking business income and expenses and using these measurements to answer specific questions about the financial and tax status of the business, i.e. it is a system that provides quantitative information about finances.

2.   Whereas **financial accounting** is the use of accounting information for reporting to parties outside the organization, **management accounting** is concerned with the provisions and use of accounting information to managers within organizations, to provide them with the basis for making informed business decisions thus allowing them to be better equipped in their management and control functions.

3.   In this chapter we outline the accounting system, how financial transactions are recorded and information generated for a range of stakeholders. We start by exploring the differences between management (internal) and financial (external) accounting and then consider financial statements as the information outputs of the accounting process. The three main financial statements (income, **balance sheet** and cash flow) are described as typical components of the company **annual report**. In the final part of this chapter we discuss the importance of assuring financial statements are reported accurately and fairly.

51.1 ACCOUNTING

4.   It is not easy to provide a concise definition of accounting since the word has a broad application within businesses. A simple definition is the recording of financial or money transactions. Accounting is the systematic recording, reporting and analysis of the monetary financial transactions of a business; it is a system that provides quantitative information about finances. Accounting and accountancy also refers to the occupation of maintaining and auditing records and preparing financial reports for a business. Accounting refers to processes involved in providing information about a company's financial situation. This includes recording financial information and compiling it into financial statements for public use in assessing the financial health of a company.

5.   Accounting is typically split into two key branches: financial accounting and management accounting. In simple terms, management accounting can be defined as the provision of information required by management for planning, organizing and control. According to the Chartered Institute of Management Accountants (CIMA), management accounting is 'the process of identification, measurement, accumulation, analysis, preparation, interpretation and communication of information used by management to plan, evaluate and control within an entity and to assure appropriate use of and accountability for its resources'. Management accounting is

concerned with information for management purposes and focuses on the internal running of the organization. Management accountants therefore help with strategy formulation, planning and decision-making and the safeguarding of assets.

6. The key difference between managerial and financial accounting is that managerial accounting information is aimed at helping managers make decisions within the organization. In contrast, financial accounting is aimed at providing information to parties outside the organization. Financial accountancy (or financial accounting) is concerned with the preparation of financial statements for decision makers, such as stockholders, suppliers, banks, government agencies, owners and other stakeholders.

7. Financial accounts are concerned with classifying, measuring and recording the transactions of a business. At the end of a period (typically a year), financial statements are prepared to show the performance and position of the business. The purpose of financial accounting statements is mainly to show the financial position of a business at a particular point in time and to show how that business has performed over a specific period. Financial accounts are geared towards external users of accounting information. To answer their needs, financial accountants draw up the profit and loss account, balance sheet and cash flow statement for the company as a whole.

> **Profit and loss account** A statement that sets the total revenues (sales) for a period against the expenses matched with those revenues to derive a profit or loss for the period

8. The Companies Act 2006 (c 46) is a UK Act of Parliament which forms the primary source of UK company law; part 15 deals with accounts and reports, ss 380–474. Certain companies are required to publish their annual report and accounts; others must file various documents and reports with companies' house.

51.2 THE PROFIT AND LOSS ACCOUNT

9. The profit and loss account is a statement setting the total revenues (sales) for a period against the expenses matched with those revenues to derive a profit or loss for the period, i.e. it describes the trading performance of the business over the accounting period. The profit and loss account also provides a perspective on a longer time-period. The profit and loss account measures 'profit' – the amount by which sales revenue (also known as 'turnover' or 'income') exceeds 'expenses' (or 'costs') for the period being measured.

10. The profit and loss statement presented in the annual accounts is a historical review of the revenue and expenditure activities of the company for the previous financial year. These statements may also be called Income and Expenditure or Revenue Accounts. They may be produced at other intervals during the year (e.g. monthly or quarterly) but in these circumstances the purpose is not to account to shareholders but to provide useful information to management. The conventional way of producing the profit and loss statement is to show gross sales' income (or turnover) less the cost of sales (materials, wages and other direct costs) to produce a gross profit figure, which is further reduced by the deduction of overheads (all the indirect costs of the business – rents, administration, salaries, etc.) to produce a net profit or surplus before tax. It is also usual to include items such as interest received and payable during the year, and exceptional Items (which need to be explained in the notes to the accounts). Non-manufacturing companies omit the cost of sales step in the presentation of their accounts.

11. An example of a profit and loss account, in this case an income and expenditure account, is given in Figure 51.1. The company is a not-for-profit organization limited by guarantee i.e. it has no share capital like public and private limited companies, but is limited by a nominal sum guaranteed by its members. The statutory requirements for presenting the profit and loss accounts only require that the annual figures are consolidated. However, all company accounts supply detailed notes explaining various features of the results, and some companies

FIGURE 51.1 **A small not-for-profit company – income and expenditure account.**

	£'000s
Income	1,152
Administration Expenses	1,919
	(767)
Other Operating Income	316
Operating Deficit	(451)
Interest Receivable	537
Surplus Before Taxation	86
Tax	(22)
Surplus For Year	64

additionally provide a full breakdown of the profit and loss account under their principal income and expenditure headings, as shown in Figure 51.2.

12. By supplying a full breakdown of their consolidated management accounts for the year, and presenting them in the annual report after the statutory accounts, the company enables its members to see exactly where the main sources of income and expenditure arise, as shown in Figure 51.2.

51.3 THE BALANCE SHEET

13. Unlike the profit and loss account, the balance sheet does not serve to review activity over a year (or some other period), but presents a snapshot view of the company at a particular point in time. A balance sheet attempts to state what a company is worth at that time, rather than showing how much money it is attracting over a period of time, which is the role of the profit and loss account.

14. The balance sheet summarizes the assets, liabilities and shareholders' equity of the organization. Assets describe the property owned by the business. Tangible assets include money, land, buildings, investments, inventory, vehicles or other valuables. Intangibles such as goodwill are also considered to be assets. It is normal practice to categorize assets as current or fixed (non current). A fixed asset (capital asset) is a long-term, tangible asset, held for business use and not expected to be converted to cash in the current or upcoming fiscal year, such as manufacturing equipment, buildings, and furniture. Fixed assets are sometimes collectively referred to as 'plant'. Assets expected to be converted into cash within one year are termed current assets. These include assets a company has at its disposal which can be easily converted into cash such as accounts receivable, work in process and inventory.

15. Liabilities are obligations that legally bind an organization to settle a debt; a liability is a financial obligation, debt, claim or potential loss. Liabilities are reported on a balance sheet and are usually divided into two categories: 'current liabilities' the term given to a balance sheet item which equals the sum of all money owed by a company and due within one year (also called

FIGURE 51.2 A small not-for-profit company – consolidated management accounts.

	£'000s	£'000s
Fee revenue		1,152
Operating expenditure		
Wages and salaries	800	
Social security costs	76	
Pensions	56	
Other staff costs	45	
Directors fees and	62	
Rent and services	397	
Travel costs	30	
Publishing and PR	164	
Computer facilities	54	
telephone, insurance and other administrative costs	76	
Legal and audit fees	39	
Depreciation	98	
Projects written off	22	
		(1,919)
		(767)
Other income		
Rents received	244	
Subscriptions received	52	
Interest	537	
Sundry income	20	
		853
Surplus before tax		86
Corporation tax		(22)
Surplus for year		64

Notes: The figures in brackets are negative amounts or deductions. The overall picture here shows that administration expenses are greater than income from the company's operations, but that is because, in this case the company holds large sums of undistributed royalties in a deposit account on behalf of its members, the interest receivable more than makes up for the operating deficit. Indeed at the year end corporation tax is due on the surplus. As the company is not for profit, the excess of income over expenditure is described as surplus rather than profit.

payables or current debt) and long-term liabilities – (non-current liabilities) these liabilities are not expected to be liquidated within a year. They usually include issued long-term bonds, notes payables, long-term leases, pension obligations and long-term product warranties.

16.   The accounting equation relates assets, liabilities and owner's equity:

$$\text{Assets} = \text{Liabilities} + \text{Owner's equity}$$

The accounting equation is the mathematical structure of the balance sheet. A typical example of a balance sheet is given in Figure 51.3 for a public utility in the UK. The figures are based on the company's position as at 31 March 2012. The company shown is a public limited company (i.e. a company with a minimum share capital of more than £50 000, and whose shares are offered to the public).

FIGURE 51.3 Balance sheet.

Electricity Company Plc Balance sheet as at 31st of March 2012	
FIXED ASSETS	£m
Tangible assets	525
investments	55
CURRENT ASSETS	580
Stocks	10
Debtors	220
Investments	15
Cash and short-term deposits	36
	281
CREDITORS: (amounts falling due within one year)	251
NET CURRENT ASSETS:	30
TOTAL ASSETS LESS CURRENT LIABILITIES	610
CREDITORS: (amounts falling due after more than one year)	15
PROVISION TO LIABILITIES AND CHARGES	40
NET ASSETS	555
CAPITAL AND RESERVES:	
Called up share capital	122
Profit and loss account	425
Other	8
	555

Note: NB The tangible assets referred to in the accounts include the electricity network, land, buildings, vehicles and equipment. The provisions for liabilities and charges include sums set aside for restructuring following privatization and pensions.

51.4 CASH FLOW STATEMENTS

17.   The income statement, discussed previously, differs from a cash flow statement because the income statement does not show when revenue is collected or when expenses are paid. In financial accounting, a cash flow statement is a financial statement that shows a company's incoming and outgoing money (sources and uses of cash) during a specified time period (often

monthly or quarterly). The statement shows how changes in balance sheet and income accounts affected cash and cash equivalents, and breaks the analysis down according to operating, investing and financing activities. As an analytical tool, the statement of cash flows is useful in determining the short-term viability of a company, particularly its ability to pay bills.

18. The balance sheet is a snapshot of a firm's financial resources and obligations at a single point in time, and the income statement summarizes a firm's financial transactions over an interval of time. These two financial statements reflect the accrual basis accounting used by firms to match revenues with the expenses associated with generating those revenues. The cash flow statement includes only inflows and outflows of cash and cash equivalents; it excludes transactions that do not affect cash receipts and payments directly. The cash flow statement is intended to provide information on a firm's liquidity and solvency. An example of a cash flow statement is given in Figure 51.4, which is based on the reported accounts of a large public transport undertaking.

FIGURE 51.4 Large transport Plc – group cash flow statement

large transport PLC-group cash flow statement (year ending 31st of March 2012)	
	£m
Net cash flow from operating activities	718
Returns on investment and servicing of finance	
Interest received	27
Interest paid	(150)
Net cash outflow from returns on investment etc	(123)
Capital expenditure	
Purchase of tangible fixed assets	(2,189)
Sale of tangible fixed assets	55
Capital element of finance lease receipts	14
Capital grants received	63
Loans to joint ventures	(32)
Net cash outflow from capital expenditure	(2,089)
Equity dividends paid	(124)
Management of liquid resources	
Disposal of short-term investments	474
Financing	
Issue of ordinary share capital	3
New loans	1,065
Net cash inflow from financing	1,168
Increase/(decrease) in cash	24

Notes: Any enterprise involved in large-scale infrastructure projects, such as here, requires considerable purchase of fixed assets. It needs to raise substantial sums from loans and share issues, and is likely to receive government grants for certain activities with a strong element of social responsibility. In the present example, where the company was once in public ownership, it can be seen that income from operating activities is greatly out of step with the capital requirements of the business. It will take years to build up the contribution made to the business by the income it receives from operations. At the year end the company showed an increase of £24m in its cash holdings compared with a net decrease of £15m reported in the previous year.

51.5 GOVERNANCE

Accounting standards Rules for preparing financial statements

International Financial Reporting Standards (IFRS) International accounting standards, designed to harmonize reporting standards in different countries, which are gradually supplanting national accounting standards

Auditor Professional accountant appointed by a company to prepare its annual accounts in accordance with applicable regulatory rules, and from an independent perspective

19.   Management has a responsibility to ensure that financial information is fairly prepared, in accordance with relevant reporting requirements (see Accounting standards and Reporting Standards (IFRS)). To meet this responsibility companies introduce internal controls – procedures or systems designed to promote efficiency or assure the implementation of a policy or safeguard assets, avoiding fraud and error, etc.

20.   Organizations employ auditors to assure control systems are working and typically outsource the auditing of financial statements to third-party (independent) auditors to ensure that financial statements are a fair representation of the financial position of the organization. However, the responsibility for adopting sound accounting policies, maintaining adequate internal control and making fair representations within financial statements rests with management. The auditors must obtain, through audits, reasonable assurance that the financial statements are free of error. When company account, financial statements are prepared, management make assertions about them. For example, they assert whether assets included in the balance sheet actually exist and whether all transactions and accounts that should be represented in the financial statements are included (completeness). Similar assertions are made about the value of assets and other issues concerning how the statements were prepared. Auditors make use of the financial statements and management assertions when conducting audits.

21.   We discussed corporate governance in Chapter 12 (see paragraphs 15–16). Corporate governance is an area that has developed very rapidly in the last decade; much of the recent emphasis has arisen from high-profile corporate scandals, globalization and increased investor activism. Corporate governance deals with the ways in which suppliers of finance, to commercial organizations, assure themselves of getting a return on their investment. Previously we discussed the importance of assuring financial statements are reported fairly. Corporate governance consists of the set of processes, customs, policies, laws and institutions affecting the way people direct, administer or control an organization. According to the Institute of Chartered Accountants, in England and Wales corporate governance is commonly referred to as a system by which organizations are directed and controlled. It is the process by which company objectives are established, achieved and monitored.

22.   Corporate governance is concerned with the relationships and responsibilities between the board, management, shareholders and other relevant stakeholders within a legal and regulatory framework. Corporate governance aims to protect shareholder rights, enhance disclosure and transparency, facilitate effective functioning of the board and provide an efficient legal and regulatory enforcement framework.

CONCLUSION

23.   The system for recording and summarizing business transactions and activities designed to accumulate, measure and communicate financial information about economic entities for decision-making purposes is termed accounting. Accounting refers to the overall process of identifying, measuring, recording, interpreting and communicating the results of economic activity; tracking business income and expenses and using these measurements to answer specific questions about the financial and tax status of the business, i.e. it is a system providing quantitative

information about finances. Whereas financial accounting is the use of accounting information for reporting to parties outside the organization, management accounting is concerned with the provision and use of accounting information to managers within organizations, to provide them with the basis for making informed business decisions that will allow them to be better equipped in their management and control functions.

24. We need accounting and its products such as an organization's annual report as a platform upon which to build many decisions and activities. Organizations must follow specific rules and formats of presentation for their annual reports and financial statements. The key accounting event for any organization is the publication of the annual report which records the organization's (financial) performance over a book year. Whilst the balance sheet tends to remain somewhat of a mystery to those who are not accountants, the profit and loss account and the cash flow statement can be useful for many people in management as an indication of how well a business is progressing over the course of a year. Most managers, however, are more accustomed to dealing with finance at an operational level, i.e. at the level of department and section budgets, and it is to these aspects of finance that we turn in the next chapter.

Finance A branch of economics concerned with resource allocation as well as resource management, acquisition and investment; deals with matters related to money and markets

QUESTIONS

1 Distinguish between financial accounting and management accounting.

2 What is a profit and loss account and how might this help a range of stakeholders in either the management of or investment in a business?

3 Compare and contrast the profit and loss account with the balance sheet. What is the accounting equation?

4 Compare and contrast the profit and loss account (income statement) with the cash flow statement. How might the cash flow statement help the finance director at Streetcar limited?

5 What mechanisms exist to ensure that financial information is fairly prepared and reported?

USEFUL WEBSITES

Companies House **www.companieshouse.gov.uk/** – The main functions of Companies House are to: incorporate and dissolve limited companies; examine and store company information delivered under the Companies Act and related legislation; and make this information available to the public.

CIMA **www.cimaglobal.com** – The Chartered Institute of Management Accountants

Institute of Chartered Accountants/England and Wales **www.icaew.co.uk**

REFERENCES

Berry, A. and Jarvis, R. (2006) 'Accounting in a Business Context', Ed. 4. Cengage Learning EMEA.

Institute of Chartered Accountants in England and Wales (ICAEW), (1999) 'Implementing Turnbull: A Boardroom Briefing', ICAEW.

McLaney, E. (2006) 'Business Finance: Theory and Practice, 7/E', Financial Times Prentice Hall.

Weetman, P. (2010) 'Management Accounting', Ed. 2. Financial Times Press.

Wood, F. and Horner, D. (2010) 'Business Accounting Basics', Financial Times Press.

CHAPTER 52
BUDGETS, FORECASTS AND BUSINESS PLANS

Key Concepts

- Budget
- Business plan
- Capital budgeting
- Net present value (NPV)

Learning Outcomes Having read this chapter, you should be able to:

- evaluate the purpose of budgeting in organizations
- discuss the process for developing budgets
- describe the key contents of a typical business plan
- apply investment appraisal techniques such as NPV and IRR

Budget Statements of desired performance expressed in financial terms; typically a financial plan to manage the spending and saving of money

Revenue centre (income centre) is a unit such as a sales section within an organization where income is accumulated and identified with a specific project or organizational entity; the manager is held accountable for the revenue generated by the subunit

Profit centre A part of an organization that directly adds to its profit/run as a business with profit objectives; it is a subset of the business for which senior managers want to track income and expenses

Cost centres A unit which serves other parts of the organization (e.g. HR, IT, accounts, etc.) and which is allocated a budget based on the costs of operating the service at an agreed level; cost centres account for related expenses – they add to the cost of an organization, but only indirectly add to its profit

1. In this chapter we explore financial planning and control mechanisms and techniques for allocating financial resources. Today practically every type of organization practises some form of budgetary control. Budgets are used to implement strategy (see Chapter 17) by managing tactical issues and the allocation of resources to attain goals. The process of budgeting was briefly referred to in Chapter 28 (Control). We noted in that chapter that a budgetary control system is laid on the foundations of strategy (goals), forecasts, sales and production budgets, capital expenditure and cash budgets, and departmental/unit budgets. All these subsidiary budgets are integrated to form a master budget for the organization, which becomes in effect a projected profit and loss statement and balance sheet.

2. Budgets are statements of desired performance expressed in financial terms. They represent the tactical or operational end of business activities, and can be applied to different organizational contexts in which individual managers are given responsibility for a particular unit of operation, which typically may be a revenue centre, cost centre or profit centre. The essential features of these three responsibility centres are as follows:

> A revenue centre (income centre) is a unit such as a sales section within an organization where income is accumulated and identified with a specific project or organizational entity; the manager is held accountable for the revenue generated by the subunit

> A cost centre is usually a unit which serves other parts of the organization (e.g. HR, IT, accounts, etc.) and which is allocated a budget based on the costs of operating the service at an agreed level; **cost centres** account for related expenses – they add to the cost of an organization, but add only indirectly to its profit

> A profit centre is a part of an organization that adds directly to its profit/run as a business with profit objectives; it is a subset of the business for which senior managers want to track income and expenses.

52.1 BUDGETS

3. Budgets, quite simply, are plans expressed in numerical terms, usually in financial terms. They indicate how much should be spent, by which departments, when, and for what purpose (Thompson and Martin, 2005). All budgets should be prepared against the backcloth of wider organizational plans. They are, after all, a means to an end, which is the achievement of the organization's business or service objectives. Indeed, they are themselves specific and often quantified goals. Budgets are used to anticipate future costs and revenues, prioritize and control spending, and ensure that expenses do not exceed available funds and revenues.

4. A number of budget types may exist within an organization such as capital budgets used to allocate resources for investment in buildings, plant and equipment; sales budgets (forecast) reflecting the flow of funds into the organization and revenue or expenses budgets which concern the operating costs to be incurred when creating products and delivering services. Organizations devise budgetary processes to help with planning and control. In overall terms the process of developing budgets can be summarized as shown in Figure 52.1 Budget development process.

FIGURE 52.1   Budget development process.

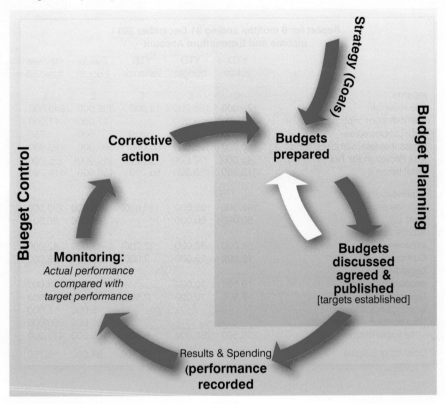

5.   Most budget planning embraces a period of one year or less, and some budgets are of a 'rolling' nature, i.e. they are amended each month or quarter in the light of what has transpired during the previous monthly or quarterly period. This ability to amend and adapt budgets, as well as to take other corrective action, is the essence of budgetary control.

6.   When management discuss results and spending (see Figure 52.1) and performance against budget, they usually work from management reports, which have been prepared by their accountants (or management accountant in a large organization) using accounting information systems. Such reports show budgeted revenues and costs for the period or year to date (YTD), actual revenue and costs to date and the variances between them. This gives management the opportunity to judge whether the variances are significant, and if so, what to do about them. An example of such a management report is given in Figure 52.2, which is based on a fee-earning service industry in publishing. A feature of these particular accounts is the column dedicated to the revised forecast for each item.

7.   In the report in Figure 52.2 it is clear to the company's senior managers (using other information at their disposal) that budgeted fee income for the year as a whole will not be realized, even though the year to date figure exceeds budget. The revised forecast is substantially lower than budgeted and this fact should be the focus of management questions. Why the absence of the expected high revenue for the final quarter of the year? There may be quite acceptable reasons for the situation, in which case these reasons can be offered. If there are no satisfactory explanations, then management will need to take some fairly strong corrective action by the start of the next financial year, given that overall expenditure is forecast to be slightly higher than budget and the operating surplus considerably lower than originally budgeted. The point is that by having regular reviews of actual progress against budget targets, the management of an

FIGURE 52.2 An example of a management report

Report for 9 months ending 31 December 2011 Income and Expenditure Account					
	YTD actual	YTD budget	YTD variance	Full Yr budget	Revises forecast
Income:	£	£	£	£	£
Fee revenue	175,000	160,000	15,000	335,000	240,000
Member subscriptions	3,000	3,000	-	11,000	11,000
Publications sales	500	300	200	500	750
Gross interest-members' fund	180,000	120,000	60,000	160,000	220,000
less Provision for Tax	(45,000)	(30,000)	(15,000)	(40,000)	(55,000)
Total Income	313,500	253,300	60,200	466,500	416,750
Expenditure:					
Salaries etc	145,000	135,000	(10,000)	185,000	190,000
Rent etc	60,000	60,000	-	80,000	80,000
Administration expenses	34,000	32,000	(2,000)	42,000	42,000
Computer	12,000	15,000	3,000	20,000	18,000
Legal and accountancy fees	10,500	10,000	–	14,000	14,000
Directors fees	7,500	10,000	2,500	12,500	12,000
Contingency item	–	–	–	5,000	5,000
Depreciation (at year end)	–	–	–	50,000	50,000
Total Expenditure	268,500	262,000	6,500	409,500	411,000
Operating Surplus	45,000	(8,700)	53,700	57,000	5,750

organization is in a position to take corrective action, where necessary, before the situation becomes out of control.

52.2 CASH FLOW FORECASTS

8.   Trading businesses, whether selling goods or services, need to know that they have enough cash available to fund their immediate operating expenses such as wages/salaries, rent, telephone charges, etc. If sufficient funds are not available from internal sources, then borrowings must be made – usually in the form of a bank overdraft (i.e. credit on the firm's current account). The usual way of keeping track of the cash position is to prepare a cash flow forecast. This is essentially a budget which sets out the estimated receipts and payments of the business on a month-by-month basis over a period of one financial year. The net cash flow figure and balance for each column is expressed as a positive or negative sum. Thus it is easy to see at what stages of the year it may be necessary to borrow in order to finance the operating costs of the business. An outline example of a cash flow budget is shown at Figure 52.3.

9.   The cash flow budget in Figure 52.3 is a working document, unlike the cash flow statement referred to in the previous chapter, which is an end-of-year summary of the total cash position in the company concerned. As a working document, the cash flow budget is intended to provide a detailed (e.g. month-by-month) picture of the movement of funds in and out of the organization. A sufficiency of cash is vital for every business – it is literally the lifeblood of the system. Even if a business is actually and potentially profitable, it cannot survive without sufficient cash (liquidity), and there have been numerous businesses which have collapsed because, even though profitable and with a good product, they have experienced a 'cash crisis' and have been unable to meet their debts.

FIGURE 52.3 An outline example of a cash flow budget.

Outline of a Cash Flow Budget					
Month	**Jan**		**Feb**		**Mar**
	Budget £	**Actual £**	**Budget £**	**Actual £**	**Budget £**	**Actual £**
Cash sales						
Cash from debtors						
Sale of assets						
Loans received						
Total Receipts (a)						
Payments:						
Cash purchases						
Payments to creditors						
Wages/Salaries						
Rent/rates						
Repairs etc.						
Insurance						
Telephone						
Postage						
Stationery						
Transport						
Loan repayment						
Interest						
Bank charges						
Professional fees						
Other						
VAT payable (or refunded)						
Total Payments (b)						
Net Cash Flow (a–b)						
Opening Bank Balance						
Closing Bank Balance						

52.3 INVESTMENT APPRAISAL

10. Financial management involves making decisions about investment, sources of finance and how to manage the financial resources of organizations most efficiently. Earlier we discussed capital budgeting – the process of analyzing and selecting various proposals for capital expenditures. The organization must establish mechanisms for developing, screening and selecting projects in

Capital budgeting The process of analyzing and selecting various proposals for capital expenditures

which to invest. Investment decisions generally concern outlays of cash, the acquisition and development or use of assets and speculation i.e. risk and reward. Capital budgeting techniques enable managers to compare different investment alternatives so that they can make informed choices about where the organization should invest its scarce resources.

11.   Investment decisions are important for all organizations. Organizations must raise finance (money) from various sources (internally and externally, from revenues, banks and other investors) which is then invested in assets such as plant, machinery and systems. Cash flows out of the organization when investments are made; however, the purpose of investment is to increase value and ultimately cause cash to flow into the organization. There is normally a time lag between flows and the organization must choose the most appropriate opportunities in which to invest i.e. those that will increase shareholder wealth.

12.   The overall process of investment appraisal is based upon the rational economic decision-making process (refer back to Chapter 19). Once business objectives/goals have been set in the strategy making process, investment opportunities and needs can be identified. Data are then assembled about costs and benefits associated with the investment opportunities (CBA, cost benefit analysis). It is rarely possible to fund all investment opportunities, or in some cases some opportunities may seek to tackle the same problem. It is therefore necessary to choose the projects in which to invest. These are then implemented and monitored.

13.   Investments are made to help the organization achieve its goals. Since there may be many ways to achieve goals there are often many initiatives and assets (such as new IT systems, new products, new factories, etc.) in which to invest to attain such goals. Investment opportunities arise in many ways either intentionally or by chance. Once an idea emerges it must be evaluated. To do this, the organization must describe the problem to be overcome by the investment, quantify the benefits of the investment and explain why investment is necessary to attain goals. Numerous quantitative approaches for evaluating investments are available such as, net present value (NPV), internal rate of return (IRR), payback period and pay-off tables – some of which are discussed below. The main goal of such techniques and investment appraisal is to assess the profit (increase in wealth) for a given period.

14.   The net present value (also called discounted cash flow) measures the worth of a stream of cash flows (or savings), taking into account the time value of money. For example, imagine an organization wants to invest in a new production system that will either reduce costs or improve sales – each year for the next five years. The concept is based on the idea that money today is worth more than money in the future. The net present value (NPV) is a logical, quantitative, practical evaluation procedure that evaluates opportunities which seek to maximize shareholder wealth. The net present value of an investment is calculated by using a discount rate (typically the rate at which money is borrowed at e.g. 10%) and a series of future payments (negative values) and income (positive values).

15.   The calculation of NPV involves three simple yet nontrivial steps. The first step is to identify the size and timing of the expected future cash flows generated by the project or investment and costs incurred (investment costs). The second step is to determine the discount rate or the estimated rate of return for the project. The third step is to

Cost benefit analysis The assessment of resources used in an activity and their comparison with the value of the benefit to be derived from the activity. Choice and evaluation of competing solutions should take account of net present value and changing price levels

Net present value (NPV) An investment appraisal technique that determines the amount of money an investment is worth, taking into account its cost, earnings and the time value of money

Internal rate of return (IRR) The internal rate of return (IRR) is the discount rate which delivers a net present value of zero for a series of future cash flows. it is a discounted cash flow (DCF) approach to valuation and investing

Payback period An investment appraisal technique that assesses how long it takes for initial cash investment to be repaid from cash receipts generated by the investment

calculate (typically using a spreadsheet) the NPV using the equations shown below:
The net present value is calculated using the following formulae

$$NPV = \sum_{i=1}^{n} \frac{Values}{(1 + rate)^i}$$

16.   £1000 is worth more now than it is one or more years into the future, i.e. we would not lend some person or entity that amount now and expect the same amount back one year later because of risk, inflation and interest foregone. The fact that money has a 'time value' makes investment appraisal more complicated. We need to be able to make comparisons between money now and money that may be paid out or flow into the company at some point in the future. In order to work out the value of a future cash sum we need to discount the sum by the amount of interest we could have earned over the period concerned and calculate the present value of the sum. For example, imagine a software company will be paid £1 000 000 in one year – what is the present value of the receivable? The present value of a future amount of income is: Present Value = (Future Value)/(1 Discount Rate). If we assume the interest (discount) rate to be 10% then the present value of £1 000 000 = 1000 000/ 1.1 = £909 091. That is to say that if we had £909 091 today and invested it with a bank offering 10% interest we would turn our £909 091 investment into £1 000 000 over 1 year.

17.   There are other techniques to evaluate investment opportunities. Many decisions involve a choice of whether to accept or reject a single investment opportunity. The internal rate of return may be used to help with such decisions (it can be calculated using Microsoft Excel). IRR is sometimes referred to as 'economic rate of return (ERR)'. The internal rate of return for an investment is the discount rate which makes the present value of the income stream total zero; the interest rate received for an investment, consisting of payments (negative values) and income (positive values) that occur at regular periods. In general, if the IRR is greater than the project's cost of capital, or hurdle rate, the project will add value for the company. To find the internal rate of return:

IRR is defined by the equation:
$$NPV(C, t, IRR) = 0.$$

18.   In other words, the IRR is the discount rate which sets the NPV of the given cash flows made at the given times to zero.

Example

Year/Cash Flow : 0(−100); 1(+30); 2(+35); 3(+40); 4(+45)

$$IRR = -100 + \frac{30}{[(1+i)^1]} + \frac{35}{[(1+i)^2]} + \frac{40}{[(1+i)^3]} + \frac{45}{[(1+i)^4]}$$

$$IRR = 17\%$$

19.   As a decision tool, the calculated IRR should not be used to rate **mutually exclusive** projects, but only to decide whether a single project is worthy of investment. IRR is closely related to NPV, the net present value function. The major difference is that whilst net present value is expressed in monetary units, the IRR is the true interest yield expected from an investment expressed as a percentage.

Mutually exclusive Options may be seeking to solve the same problem and competing with each other

20.   In many cases, an organization will consider numerous investment options. In some cases the options may seek to solve the same problem and compete with each other to the extent that only one of the options should be selected (mutually exclusive). In other cases, options may compete with each other for internal capital i.e. the company may have a limited amount of money (the budget) to spend. When there are a number of non-mutually exclusive alternatives considered, various ranking criteria, such as return on investment (ROI) or more general cost benefit ratios provide a basis for evaluation.

21.   The rate of return (ROR) or return on investment (ROI), or sometimes just return, is the ratio of money gained or lost on an investment relative to the amount of money invested. ROI is usually expressed as a percent rather than a decimal value. To calculate ROI, the benefit (return) of an investment is divided by the cost of the investment; ROI = (Gain from investment) − (cost of investment)/cost of investment Or ROI = (Annual revenue) − (Annual costs) / Initial investment Or % ROI = (benefits / costs) × 100 Or (Total benefit − total costs)/total costs = _ × 100 = ROI.

22.   Another way of looking at ROI is to calculate how many months it will take before benefits match costs and the investment pays for itself. This is called the payback period: payback period = costs / monthly benefits. The payback technique simply asks how long will it take for the investment to pay for itself out of the expected cash inflows. Proposals are typically ranked in order of highest ROI first and are selected until total initial investment exceeds a budget. Benefits can be quantified as revenues or cost savings. In either case, they should be converted to present values in order to take account of the time value of money. Ratios greater than '1' generally indicate that a proposal should be adopted if sufficient resources exist to support it.

23.   Many decisions involve a choice amongst several mutually exclusive alternatives. When only one alternative can be selected from many, the best choice can usually be identified by evaluating each alternative according to some criteria. The NPV or IRR may be used to choose between competing projects/choices. For decisions involving multiple criteria, simple scoring models are often used. The scoring model is a qualitative assessment of a decision alternatives value, based on a set of attributes. For each decision alternative, a score is assigned to each attribute (which might be weighted), and the overall score as a basis for selection.

24.   Financial decision-making is easy when only a single choice can be made (take it or leave it), i.e. if there is only one alternative (Hobson's choice). However, rather than only one alternative, most of the time a set of choices exist. It is also relatively easy to make decisions when the precise outcome of the decision is known. However this is rarely the case with contemporary management business decisions. Such decisions normally involve highly uncertain outcomes. Many decisions involve a selection from a small set of mutually exclusive alternatives with uncertain consequences; i.e. we are unsure what the benefits will be. In this scenario we must also define the outcomes, or events, that may (savings and revenues) occur once a decision is made and over which the decision maker does not have control. These outcomes provide a basis for evaluating risk associated with decisions. A useful tool for making decisions under uncertain conditions is the pay-off table; a payoff table is a tool for organizing what is known about each alternative.

52.4 BUSINESS PLANS

Business plan A document that summarizes how an entrepreneur will organize a firm to exploit an opportunity, along with the economic implications of exploiting that opportunity

25.   The budgets and forecasts that have been described above are, of course, examples of business plans, and those principally interested in using them are the managers of the business. However, the expression 'business plan' has particular meaning for small and medium-sized enterprises and here the main interested parties are (a) owners and (b) lenders and investors.

26.   Entrepreneurship is the process of starting new businesses, generally in response to opportunities. Entrepreneurs typically spot opportunity and then set up in business operation in order to seize that opportunity. Before starting out they will research the opportunity thoroughly and examine what they must do in order to bring the idea into reality. Many new businesses are created every year. Many of these are destined to fail within the first two years, and one of the key reasons is that they have failed to produce a viable business plan for their operation. Most

lenders will insist that the entrepreneur presents and defends an initial business plan before agreeing even to consider lending money for a business start-up.

27.   The business plan is a written document that summarizes how an entrepreneur will organize a firm to exploit an opportunity, along with the economic implications of exploiting that opportunity. There are a number of templates for creating the business plan but their content tends to follow a similar structure. Barringer and Ireland (2010) suggest the following key sections: cover page, executive summary, table of contents, company background information, industry analysis (size, growth rate, sales projections, industry structure, etc.), market analysis (competitor analysis by behaviour), marketing plan (overall marketing strategy and the marketing mix), management team and company structure, operations plan (location, facilities and equipment, etc.), product (or service) design and development plan, financial projections and appendices.

28.   In planning a budget, appraising an investment or creating a business plan, managers or owners make a number of assumptions about the future. Sales revenue, for example, can only be estimated on (a) the number of units likely to be sold, and (b) the sale price per unit, and these factors in turn depend upon others such as anticipated demand for the product and the prices being charged by competitors. Direct costs are variable depending on the level of production, and so assumptions have to be made about the size of output in order to reach some estimate of the likely additional direct costs for given levels of production. Overheads are more predictable, but still depend on assumptions about the number of staff, size of premises and other resources thought to be required to sustain the business as a whole. With the advent of computer spreadsheets, it is easier for firms to consider different scenarios for their business, asking 'what if?' questions, e.g. 'what would be the effect on gross profit if we increased production by 1000 units per month?' 'What would be the effect on overheads of an increase in full-time clerical staff by two?'

29.   Once a new business has completed the difficult but necessary process of preparing draft budgets and forecasts, it achieves a number of important benefits:

- The owners or managers will have a number of performance indicators against which to pit their resources.

- These indicators will set the parameters for profitability and cash flow on a month by month basis for the first year.

- The very process of trying to estimate likely sales and costs (both direct and indirect) enables owners and managers to think through their assumptions and test them in discussion.

- The resulting draft budgets will form the basis for discussion with the banks and other financing bodies about funding support, overdraft facilities, etc.

- The owners can be satisfied they have a viable basis for their new business.

CONCLUSION

30.   In this chapter we explored financial planning and control mechanisms and techniques for allocating financial resources. Budgets are statements of desired performance, expressed in financial terms. They indicate how much should be spent, by which departments, when and for what purpose. All budgets should be prepared against the backcloth of wider organizational plans. Budgets are used to anticipate future costs and revenues, prioritize and control spending, and ensure that expenses do not exceed available funds and revenues. A generic Budget development process was presented. Next we noted that businesses need to know they have enough cash available to fund their immediate operating expenses such as wages/ salaries, rent, telephone charges, etc. The most usual way of keeping track of the cash position is to prepare a cash

flow forecast. This is essentially a budget which sets out the estimated receipts and payments of the business on a month-by-month basis over a period of one financial year.

31.   Investment decisions are important for all organizations; the purpose of investment is to increase value and ultimately cause cash to flow into the organization. Once business objectives/ goals have been set in the strategy-making process, investment opportunities and needs can be identified. Data are then assembled about costs and benefits associated with the investment opportunities (CBA, cost benefit analysis). It is rarely possible to fund all investment opportunities, or in some cases some opportunities may seek to tackle the same problem. It is therefore necessary to choose the projects within which to invest. Numerous quantitative approaches for evaluating investments are available such as, net present value (NPV), internal rate of return (IRR), payback period and pay-off tables. The main goal of such techniques and investment appraisal is to assess the profit (increase in wealth) for a given period.

32.   Budgets and forecasts are examples of business plans. However, the expression 'business plan' has particular meaning for small and medium-sized enterprises and here the main interested parties are (a) owners and (b) lenders and investors. The business plan is a written document that summarizes how an entrepreneur will organize a firm to exploit an opportunity, along with the economic implications of exploiting that opportunity.

QUESTIONS

1 Discuss the contents of a 'business plan' and evaluate the purpose of each component.

2 Evaluate the purpose of budgeting in organizations. In your answer you should comment on a number of budget types that may exist within an organization.

You should also describe a generic budget development process.

3 Explain the role of investment appraisal within organizations and discuss how the net present value technique can help improve the quality of investment decisions.

USEFUL WEBSITES

Institute of Financial Services **www.ifsis.org.uk**

VIDEO CASES

Now take a look at the online video cases – visit the companion website to work through real world business problems associated with the concepts presented within this chapter.

16 The Welly Boot Box: starting up – This case documents the challenges of starting up a new (simple) company with a single product. However, it enables the exploration of many start-up related business issues and theories such as the business plan, the value chain and value configuration, the fragmentation of the value chain and outsourcing production to low-labour cost countries (globalization), disintermediation

and the use of the web as a sales channel. Additionally, marketing concepts are considered, particularly the use of PR as a means to promote sales in a cost efficient manner. Case-study users may pick and mix their preferred concepts for discussion and activity.

68 Choices in systems acquisition – Tedia Case Study
This case outlines the activities and events surrounding the acquisition of a software system by a chemicals manufacturer. Different acquisition methods and the acquisition process are considered.

REFERENCES

Barney, J. and Hesterly, W. (2009) 'Strategic Management and Competitive Advantage: International Edition', Ed. 3. Prentice Hall.

Barringer, B. R. and Ireland, D. (2010) 'Entrepreneurship: Successfully Launching New Ventures: Global Edition', Ed 3. Pearson Higher Education.

McLaney, E. (2006) 'Business Finance: Theory and Practice, 7/E', Financial Times Prentice Hall.

Thompson, J. L. and Martin, F. (2005) 'Strategic Management', Ed. 5. Cengage Learning EMEA.

APPENDIX

1. Graduates have to demonstrate a systematic understanding of key aspects of their field (management in this case) and must be able to use established techniques of analysis and enquiry. Post graduate students must demonstrate understanding and a critical awareness of current problems; be at the forefront of their field; and show a comprehensive understanding of management techniques. Amongst the common assessment methods used are coursework and exams, both of which typically require the student to write essays. In this appendix we aim to provide advice to help you in such tasks. Whilst there is a difference between an academic essay and business report, they are both forms of essay. Consequently, the advice will also help practising managers write internal business documents, especially reports.

2. At this stage we might ask how course examiners distinguish between different levels of work. How do they assess a diploma student, a first, second or third year undergraduate or a postgraduate? How will you be assessed? It is important to note first and foremost that a quality assessment will only seek to test whether the student has attained the specified learning outcomes for the course in question. These are normally specified in module or programme specifications or any other forms of course description. It is therefore essential that as a student, studying management, you are familiar with the learning outcomes for your course. You should constantly remind yourself of these.

3. So perhaps a more pertinent question would be, how do tutors design teaching, learning and assessment instruments with the various levels (undergraduate, postgraduate etc) in mind? It is common for textbook authors and tutors to categorize learning in levels. Many educators make use of Bloom's Taxonomy – a classification of learning objectives within education. Thinking skills may be categorized as lower order through to higher order. Using a stage model, we might start at the bottom with a focus on the knowledge we expect somebody to remember. Memory recall is generally regarded as a lower order thinking skill and this is followed by comprehension for which students are expected to understand various theories, concepts and phenomena. Moving up the order of thinking skills, next we might expect students to be able to apply their knowledge and understanding in different contexts. Case studies are typically used to help people learn how to apply business knowledge. Knowledge, comprehension and application are often associated with the first two years of study at undergraduate level. In the final year and at postgraduate level, students are expected to be able to analyze business problems. This represents a higher order thinking skill as does synthesis and evaluation.

4. You will often hear the term critical thinking associated with higher order thinking skills. Critical thinking is not a matter of accumulating information. A person with a good memory and who knows a lot of facts is not necessarily adept at critical thinking. A critical thinker is able to deduce consequences from what he/she knows, and can make use of information to solve problems, and to seek relevant sources of information to inform him/herself. Critical thinkers understand the logical connections between ideas; can identify, construct and evaluate arguments; can detect inconsistencies and common mistakes in reasoning; solve problems systematically and identify the relevance and importance of ideas.

5. A crucial part of critical thinking is being able to give reasons, whether it is to support or to criticize a certain idea. To be able to think critically, it is very important to identify, construct, and evaluate arguments. To give an argument is to provide a set of premises as reasons for accepting the conclusion. Arguments can be used to support viewpoints (to convince). To become a decent critical thinker it is necessary to develop the habit of giving good arguments to support the claims made. Giving good arguments is one of the most important ways to convince other people that certain claims should be accepted. For example,

consider the implementation of a new computer-based information system. Managers may argue about whether they should invest in such a system; they may also argue about which specific system should be chosen. Arguments will be informed by the relative strengths and weaknesses or advantages and disadvantages associated with each option.

6. Textbook authors and tutors operationalize levels of thinking through the use of specific verbs in the learning outcomes. These words (verbs) indicate the approach or style expected for the piece of writing. Examples of verbs used for the different levels of thinking are shown below:

KNOWLEDGE: arrange, define, duplicate, label, list, memorize, name, order, recognize, relate, recall, repeat, reproduce, state

COMPREHENSION: classify, describe, discuss, explain, express, identify, indicate, locate, recognize, report, restate, review, select, translate

APPLICATION: apply, choose, demonstrate, dramatize, employ, illustrate, interpret, operate, practice, schedule, sketch, solve, use, write

ANALYSIS: analyze, appraise, calculate, categorize, compare, contrast, criticize, differentiate, discriminate, distinguish, examine, experiment, question, test

SYNTHESIS: arrange, assemble, collect, compose, construct, create, design, develop, formulate, manage, organize, plan, prepare, propose, set up, write

EVALUATION: appraise, argue, assess, attach, choose compare, defend, estimate, judge, predict, rate, core, select, support, value, evaluate

7. Look for these verbs typically found in learning outcome and assessment question text and use them to understand what the assessor expects from the student. Students should also focus upon content/information key words in the essay or assignment question. These words indicate the areas upon which the essay will focus. These key content words should guide student research. Finally, consider the delimiting words accompanying any exam or assignment question. These are words that may limit your research to a particular place, time or group; the word length of the essay; the scope of information that is required, the resources used and the time allowed for the essay.

8. For example, consider the following question: 'Write an individual report (4–5000 words) which critically appraises and discusses the challenges and issues with regard to information, knowledge, HR and technological resources, commenting on sources of competitive advantage, suggested organization design, coordination and control measures.' The operational word(s)/verbs are 'critically appraise and discuss' indicating a need to demonstrate a higher order of learning. Content words include 'the challenges and issues with regard to information, knowledge, HR and technological resources, commenting on sources of competitive advantage, suggested organization design, coordination and control measures'. Finally, the delimiting words are, 'challenges and issues; Individual report (4–5000 words)'.

WRITING ACADEMIC ESSAYS

9. What is an essay? The academic essay is generally written in response to a question. There is a requirement to present a point of view (expressed in a thesis statement) that is informed by study. The aim is to develop support argument(s) for the thesis proposed. Most people follow an essay writing process similar to that portrayed in Figure 53.1.

10. Analyzing the question, aim to develop a clear understanding of what the student is expected to do. Make sure there is an understanding of what issue/problem has to be addressed. Analyze the wording of the question (see Para 6–8 above) carefully to gain an understanding of what is being asked. When analyzing the question, think about the levels of learning and the learning outcomes discussed above.

11. It is helpful to think of an essay as having four main parts: 1) the introduction will explain the academic problem as seen by the student, and outline how the student intends to handle it. It tells the reader what to expect, and what to look for. 2) The body or content of the essay will contain the points the student wishes to make, with supporting arguments and evidence. It must show the reader the student knows the subject. This is done by explaining the subject to the reader. It should also present the evidence for the essay's argument; 3) the conclusion and 4) the bibliography – the list of books and other sources used for the essay. The bibliography should relate to references in the essay.

12. An essay should have its correct title written in full at the start of the piece of work. Every aspect of the essay title needs to be addressed by the essay. Reproducing the title at the start of the esaay also helps to focus the essay. Students should not just write around a subject in a general way. It is really important to spend time thinking about what the essay title means, and how best to answer it. Analyzing helps respondents see what is wanted.

13. The introduction should explain the academic problem, as viewed by the student, and outline how it will be addressed. Next outline the purpose and aims of the essay – the reader should know what it is the student is trying to accomplish. It may be appropriate to include background on any organization/company discussed. In some essays there will be an expectation for the writer to state the main argument he/she intends to make. It may help to think of the argument as having a statement and a demonstration. The statement of the argument is made in the introduction. The demonstration of the argument is done in the body of the essay. The body of the essay presents the evidence for the statement. Finally, in the last part of the introduction students should tell the reader what to expect, and what to look for, i.e. outline the structure of the essay. Authors call this signposting.

14. The body of an essay is the largest part of the essay and contains the points the writer wishes to make, in greater detail than the introduction (because points are being explained) and with the evidence for the points. It must show the reader the student knows the subject. This is best done by explaining the subject (in your own words) to the reader. It is a fatal mistake to think 'the marker already knows this subject. I will discuss it without explaining it.' The marker is

FIGURE 53.1 **Essay writing process**

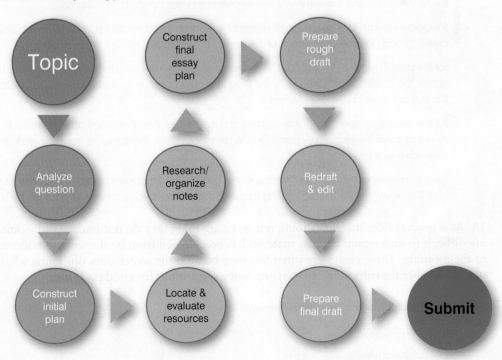

looking for evidence that students know the subject. Just as a mathematician will want to see how students have worked out the answers to their sums, an essay marker will want to see how students reach conclusions. It should also present the evidence for the essay's argument. In most cases, it is not sufficient to simply state your personal opinion in an academic essay. The assessor will want evidence to be provided of the student having read widely around the subject area. This is achieved by citing the work of other business scholars. Most academic writing requires the student to stand back and analyse unemotionally, as an objective onlooker.

15. In most academic essays, the assessor is looking for demonstration of knowledge and understanding. This is not achieved by simply quoting, verbatim, the work of others. Similarly, there is often an expectation to demonstrate wider reading by citing the work of others. This is normally done by paraphrasing the work of others, creating a précis of what they have said. Their work then needs to be cited and a reference included at the end of the essay, when appropriate.

16. The final part of the essay, before the references and bibliography, is the conclusion. This section should not contain any new material. If the essay's argument has been stated in the introduction, the conclusion can be just a brief summary of the main points. If it is found that the conclusion includes important points not already fully covered, serious consideration should be given whether these points need including in the introduction, or omitting from the essay entirely. In the last sentence, sum up the arguments briefly and link them back to the title, where appropriate. The conclusion is followed by the references and bibliography. These may then be followed by the appendix. Generally, it is best not to swamp the reader with material in an appendix. If anything is included in the appendix, make sure to reference it in the main body of the essay.

CHECKING AN ESSAY

17. The essay writing process referred to earlier in this chapter contains the later stage of reviewing and redrafting the essay. Students must read over their essays several times in order to achieve perfection. Often the following will need checking:

- that the introduction describes the body of the essay accurately. The structure of the essay should follow the outline and the summary should describe precisely what the essay says.

- for logical argument: Is an argument present? Is it stated in the introduction? Is the argument followed through logically in the body of the essay? Is it recapped within the conclusion?

- for the use of evidence to back up the argument. Evidence may take the form of references to an author the student is interpreting. Is the argument supported by quotations and other references to the authors to which the essay refers?

- for the accurate presentation of quotations and references. Are quotations clearly identified? Do the references use the Harvard system? Do the references allow the reader to trace the work and page to which they refer?

- for grammatical accuracy and correct spelling. Run the spellchecker if using a word processor, then read the essay through for the spelling mistakes that a spellchecker misses, and for its grammar.

18. As a general rule, students should not write anything they do not understand. Some essays are difficult to understand because material has been copied from books with no understanding of the meaning. These essays are often too long because the writer does not know what to cut out. Remember the rules about plagiarism. Some suggestions for good essay writing:

- Develop a personal essay writing strategy.

- Focus on the essay title.

- Do multiple drafts.

- Do not pad. Try to ensure that everything included is relevant to the essay title.

- Include other opinions. Show different sides to the question have been considered by discussing points of view that contradict your own.

- Show understanding of the material read.

- Write simply.

- Use technical terms correctly.

- Fully reference all material used.

- Plan to finish the essay ahead of time.

19. Finally, where figures and/or tables are used, ensure they are labelled appropriately (see for example 'Figure 53.1 essay writing process') and they are referred to in the text, e.g. 'Most people follow an essay writing process similar to that portrayed in Figure 53.1'.

EXAMINATION TECHNIQUE

20. Factors affecting exam performance include: subject knowledge; exam preparation and practice; experience of the subject; writing skills; use of time and attitude and approach. The better the subject is known, the easier it is to recognize what is significant – and to understand what must be included and what can be omitted when revising and when writing exam answers; identify links and connections between different aspects of the subject; and recognize which schools of thought are relevant to which exam questions.

21. It is rarely easy to write a good narrative answer to an examination question. This is particularly true in the field of Management Studies where the quality of the discussion of a topic is as important, if not more important, than the quantity of facts that can be raised to support the arguments. It is also worth recognizing that in most cases there is no one correct answer. The important thing is for the student to convince the examiner of the reasonableness of their particular solution/argument. Nevertheless, it is possible, with practice, to develop a technique to improve the way the more popular questions that occur in examinations are tackled. Part of the aim of this book is to help students with both the technique and the practice.

22. For all written exams, exam success is affected by style – using a clear, easy to read, writing style; vocabulary – having the vocabulary to express oneself quickly, succinctly and accurately; composition – using well structured, reasoned argument and technical writing skills – using grammar, punctuation and spelling accurately in order to express the case more clearly, and to ensure the examiner remains focused on the quality of the argument presented and not on writing errors. Remember, in the case of most business exam questions there is a requirement to write an essay (see above). However, it is unlikely students will be allowed to have their books or a computer with them!

23. Through exam practice students may gain a sense of how much they can write in a short time; this helps students to revise more efficiently, recognizing the importance of selecting the most essential material. Respondents must learn to work quickly in planning, writing and checking answers; improve at becoming focused quickly; discover what they really know and what they only half–remember; check answers after the event – and judge the quality of their answers.

AT THE START OF THE EXAMINATION

24. Read the instructions on the paper and follow them. Make quite sure how many questions must be answered. Mark off the questions that seem to be the easiest, i.e. Those which trigger plenty of ideas the moment they are considered. Make an appropriate allocation of time for each question, then select the first question.

TACKLING THE QUESTIONS

25. Read each question carefully. It will be worth it! Ask , 'Is there more than one question?' 'What is the examiner getting at?' 'What issues are raised by the question?' Now make a rough answer plan, jotting down key points that come to mind, and rearranging them into some kind of order. This will take perhaps five minutes, but allows students to proceed with confidence to write a satisfactory answer. If the question is set out in a particular sequence, answer it in the same sequence. Where opinion or comment is asked for by the examiner, don't be afraid to say what you think, so long as you can point to some evidence or other source of opinion to back up your assertions. Always try to keep to the point. Identify the issues raised in each question and build an answer around them. Do not go off at a tangent, for there will be precious few marks awaiting you at the end. Remember that neat writing and tidy layout always create a good impression with examiners. It helps them in their task, and may earn an extra mark or two. The final task is to read through the answer quickly and make any amendments or last–minute additions.

TOWARDS THE END OF THE EXAMINATION

26. Students must ensure they move on to the final question even if the previous one is incomplete. More marks tend to be earned at the beginning of an answer than towards the end, so it is wise to make a start, however brief. If you are desperately short of time (as a result of bad planning) then write down brief notes or headings for the examiner. If you do have time to spare at the end of the examination, it is worth looking to see if you can add any further relevant points to your completed answers.

AT THE END OF THE EXAMINATION

27. Check that your answer sheets are correctly numbered and collated.

WHAT GETS GOOD MARKS?

28. Examiners may assess work using criterion-based or normative marking. Criterion-referenced assessment judges how well a learner has performed by comparison with predetermined criteria. Norm-referenced assessment judges how well the learner has done in comparison with the norm established by peers. Most universities and colleges tend to make use of criterion-referenced marking. Assessors will typically follow a previously written marking scheme when scoring an essay. Such marking schemes vary in detail and will also rely upon the judgement of the particular assessor. Marking may be said to be objective or subjective. Marking multiple-choice exam questions for a statistics paper would tend to be at the objective end of the spectrum. Marking a critical analysis essay is more likely to include greater aspects of subjective marking.

29. Good marks are not always associated with the amount of study time allocated. In order to get good marks students should thoroughly analyze the question and make sure the question is answered. Students should be aware of the learning outcomes and know exactly what is expected of them. Institutions often provide students with general criteria applicable to essays, reports and aspects of projects and dissertations. This is a valuable resource to help guide expectations and should be used when self-marking drafts of essays. Example grade criteria for a second year undergraduate are provided below:

POOR FAIL: No serious attempt to address the question or problem, and/or manifests a serious misunderstanding of the requirements of the assignment and acutely deficient in all aspects.

FAIL: Work in this range attempts to address the question/problem but is substantially incomplete and deficient; the work may be severely under/over–length and/or fails to grasp the nature of the topic matter. Content, analysis, expression, structure and use of sources will be very weak or missing.

BORDERLINE/WEAK PASS: Adequate work that attempts to address the topic and demonstrates some understanding of the basic aspects of the subject matter; the topic is researched using mainly books and Internet resources. The student attempts to use and/or present references/bibliography according to convention (e.g. Harvard) and a basic attempt to follow directions regarding organization, structure, use and flow of language, grammar, spelling, format, diagrams, tables etc.

GOOD PASS: As above plus work that demonstrates understanding of the topic area with some attempt to discuss material; the student presents evidence of research in the topic area extending beyond key texts; satisfactory presentation and/or use of references/bibliography according to convention; a satisfactory attempt to follow directions regarding organization, structure, use and flow of language, grammar, spelling, format, diagrams, tables etc.

VERY GOOD PASS: As above plus a very good, well presented piece of work covering much of the subject matter and which is clearly and coherently written. Good attempt to consider and evaluate the material presented; evidence of research in the topic area and satisfactory use of sources and references and good organization, structure, use and flow of language, grammar, spelling, format, diagrams, tables etc.

EXCELLENT PASS (typically over 70 or 80% – distinction or merit pass): Very good work which is clearly written, well argued and covers the subject matter in a thorough, thoughtful and competent manner. Contains some originality of approach, insight or synthesis; good evidence of research and good use of source material. Good use and presentation of references; very good presentation, organization, grammar, spelling, punctuation, diagrams and tables; excellent work which contains relevant material and shows analysis, originally or creativity of approach and a clear, well articulated understanding of the subject matter; wide research incorporating up to date, relevant original material. Accurate citation and use of references; and excellent with few or no errors in organization, structure, grammar, spelling, punctuation, use of diagrams and tables.

FINAL NOTES

30. The above techniques can be thoroughly employed in this book by working through the Practice Questions, making use of the Outline Answers (available at the student website) and asking your tutor or lecturer to comment on what you have written.

REFERENCES

Cottrell, S. (2008) 'The Study Skills Handbook', Ed. 3. Palgrave MacmillanMcMillan, K. and Weyers, J. (2007) 'How to write Essays & Assignments', Prentice HallPrice, G. and Maier, P. (2007) 'Effective Study Skills: Essential skills for academic and career success', Prentice.

Glossary

360-Degree Appraisal Performance assessment of a person by the key people or groups with whom they interact. May include external people or groups such as customers

7-s Model A model for organizational analysis and dynamics including components: strategy, structure, systems, style, staff, shared values and skills

Accountability This is the ultimate responsibility which managers cannot delegate. While managers may delegate authority, they remain accountable for the decisions and actions of their subordinates

Accounting Is the recording of financial or money transactions. Accounting is the systematic recording, reporting and analysis of financial transactions of a business

Accounting Standards Rules for preparing financial statements

Act A law or piece of legislation passed by both Houses of Parliament and agreed to by the Crown, which then becomes part of statutory law (i.e. is enacted)

Actor–Observer Effect When we judge others we tend to assume that failure is due to their lack of ability rather than caused by the situation

Adaptive System In general, an adaptive system has the ability to monitor and regulate its own performance. In many cases, an adaptive system will be able to respond fully to changes in its environment by modifying its behaviour

Adhocracy A type of organization design which is temporary, adaptive and creative, in contrast with bureaucracy which tends to be permanent, rule-driven and inflexible

Adjourning When a group disperses after goals have been met

Administrative Controls Formalized standards, rules, procedures and disciplines to ensure that the organization's controls are properly executed and enforced

Advertising A paid-for form of non-personal communication that is transmitted through mass media (television, radio, newspapers, magazines, direct mail, outdoor displays and the Internet)

Analytical (Job Evaluation) A method of job evaluation which involves assessing the worth of a job by dividing it into factors

Annual Report Document detailing the business activity of a company over the previous year, and containing the three main financial statements:
Income Statement, Cash Flow Statement and Balance Sheet

Application Forms (Blanks) Usually sent out to jobseekers who respond to some kind of job advertising. The form or blank is a template for the presentation of personal information that should be relevant to the job applied for. This ensures that all candidates provide the desired range of information in the same order of presentation to facilitate comparison and preparation of a short-list for further selection procedures

Appointed Leader A leader who influences others by virtue of their position

Appraisals Appraisals rate individuals on quasi-objective criteria or standards deemed to be relevant to performance. Traditional appraisals rated individuals on a list of qualities, primarily work-related attitudes and personality traits. See also 'Performance assessment'

Area Structure The organization is structured according to geographical areas

Assertiveness The capacity to express our ideas, opinions or feelings openly and directly without putting down ourselves or others

Assessment Centres Centres used to provide information on candidates for jobs. They typically consist of multiple evaluations including job-related simulations, interviews and psychological tests

Asynchronous Communication The sending and receiving of messages in which there is a time delay between the sending and receiving; as opposed to synchronous communication

Attribution Theory The way in which individuals make sense of other people's behaviour through attributing characteristics to them by judging their behaviour and intentions on past knowledge and in comparison with other people they know

Auditor Professional accountant appointed by a company to prepare its annual accounts in accordance with applicable regulatory rules, and from an independent perspective

Authority The right to make particular decisions and to exercise control over resources

Automation The use of control systems (such as numerical control) and information technologies (such as CAD, CAM and robotics) reducing the need for or enhancing human intervention and leading to enhanced productivity

Autonomous Work Groups A work team with delegated responsibility for a defined part of an organization's activities with the freedom to organize its own resources, pace of work and allocate responsibilities within the group

Balance Sheet A statement that lists the assets of a business or other organization, at some specified point in time, together with the claims against those assets

Basic Assumptions A term used by Schein to refer to the origins of values and cultural artefacts in organizations. Basic assumptions are shared and deeply embedded presuppositions about issues such as whether human beings do or should live for the moment (immediate gratification) or see their activities as a means to a future end or goal (deferred gratification)

Batch Manufacturing A type of manufacturing process where items are moved through the different manufacturing steps in groups, or batches

Batching The process of producing large quantities of items as a group before being transferred to the next operation

Behavioural Control A form of control based on direct personal supervision which is responsive to the particular needs of the tasks, the abilities of the manager and the norms of the organization

Behaviouralism An approach to job design that aims to improve motivation hence performance by increasing job satisfaction

Belief System (Formal) The explicit set of organizational definitions that senior managers communicate formally and reinforce systematically to provide basic values, purpose, and direction for the organization

Biodata Scoreable information about a job applicant

Boston Matrix (Also called the BCG Matrix, the Growth-Share Matrix and Portfolio Analysis)

Brand A name, term, design, symbol or any other feature that identifies one seller's good or service as distinct from those of other sellers

Branding The process of creating and developing successful brands

Break-Even Analysis The technique of comparing revenues and costs at increasing levels of output in order to establish the point at which revenue exceeds cost, that is the point at which it 'breaks-even'

Budget Statements of desired performance expressed in financial terms; typically a financial plan to manage the spending and saving of money; A financial plan to manage the spending and saving of money

Bureaucracy Describes a form of business administration based on formal rational rules and procedures designed to govern work practices and organization activities through a hierarchical system of authority. (See Standardization, Centralization, Formalization, Specialization)

Business Ethics The accepted principles (beliefs and values) of right or wrong governing the conduct of business people

Business Information System Specific information system used to support business

Business Model The organization's essential logic for consistently achieving its principle objectives- explains how it consistently makes money, highlights the distinc-

tive activities and approaches that enable the firm to succeed — to attract customers and deliver products and services profitably

Business Plan A document that summarizes how an entrepreneur will organize a firm to exploit an opportunity, along with the economic implications of exploiting that opportunity

Business Process A specific ordering of work activities across time and place, with a beginning, an end and clearly identified inputs and output

Business Process Reengineering (BPR) The redesign of business processes in an effort to reduce costs, increase efficiency and effectiveness and improve quality. BPR is characterized as radical rather than incremental in its approach to change and broad rather than narrow in its organization impact

Business Strategy Describes how the organization competes within an industry or market

Capabilities What the organization can do

Capability The capacity for a team of resources to perform some task or activity

Capital Budgeting The process of analyzing and selecting various proposals for capital expenditures

Centralization The degree to which the authority to make certain decisions is located at the top of the management hierarchy

CEO (Chief executive officer) the highest-ranking executive or administrator in charge of management; the singular organizational position that is primarily responsible for carrying out the strategic plans and policies of an organization

Challenge Stressors Stressors associated with work load, pressure to complete tasks and time urgency

Change Agent Any person seeking to promote, further, support, sponsor, initiate, implement or help to deliver change within the organization

Change Implementers The persons who put the change plan into practice and take steps to assure the change vision is realized – make change happen

Change Model An abstract representation describing the content or process of changes

Channel Cannibalization The decrease in sales through an existing channel due to the introduction of a new channel

Channel Richness The amount of information that can be transmitted during a communication episode

Charismatic Authority Authority derives from the 'rulers' personal qualities

Charismatic Leadership The ability to exercise leadership through the power of the leader's personality

Classical Approach The organization is thought of in terms of its purpose and formal structure and this approach aims to identify how methods of working can improve productivity. Emphasis is placed on the planning of work, the technical requirements of the organization, principles of management and the assumption of rational and logical behaviour

Classical Approach to Management The organization is thought of in terms of its purpose and formal structure and this approach aims to identify how methods of working can improve productivity. Emphasis is placed on the planning of work, the technical requirements of the organization, principles of management and the assumption of rational and logical behaviour

Classical Decision Theory A theory which assumes that decision-makers are objective, have complete information and consider all possible alternatives and their consequences before selecting the optimal solution

Coalition Building The forming of partnerships to increase pressures for or against change

Code of Ethics A set of ethical-behaviour rules developed by organizations or by professional societies

Collective Agreements The results of collective bargaining are expressed in agreements; these are principally procedure agreements and substantive agreements; they are not legally enforceable in the UK. (See also Procedure Agreements and Substantive Agreements)

Collective Bargaining The process of negotiating wages and other working conditions collectively between employers and trade unions, it enables the conditions of employees to be agreed as a whole group instead of individually

Combined Code A set of principles of good corporate governance and provides a code of best practice aimed at companies listed on the London Stock Exchange

Communication The activity of conveying information

Communication Climate in an Organization The prevailing atmosphere, open or closed, in which ideas and information are exchanged

Communications Essentially the process by which views and information are exchanged between individuals or groups; usually refers to the system of communication in use, but can also mean personal skills of communication

Company's Memorandum and Articles of Association The documents needed to form a company – In the U.K., a company must draw up a Memorandum of Association to document and record details of the firm. The memorandum provides basic information on a business or association in the United Kingdom and with the Articles of Association, forms the company's charter or constitution. The memorandum may be viewed by the public at the office in which it is filed

Competence Work related knowledge, skill or ability held by an individual

Competency-Based Approach The development of a list of abilities and competencies necessary to perform successfully a given job, and against which the applicant's performance can be assessed

Competitive Advantage Used interchangeably with 'distinctive competence' to mean relative superiority in skills and resources

Competitive Dynamics How one firm responds to the strategic actions of competing firms

Competitive Strategy Competitive strategy is concerned with the basis on which a business unit might achieve competitive advantage in its market

Computer Integrated Manufacturing (CIM) A term used to describe the integration of computer-based monitoring and control of all aspects of a manufacturing process, often using a common database and communicating via some form of computer network

Computer-Aided Design (CAD) Software Software that allows designers to design and 'build' production prototypes, 'test' them as a computer object under given parameters, compile parts and quantity lists, outline production and assembly procedures and then transmit the final design directly to milling and rolling machines

Computer-Aided Manufacturing (CAM) Software Software that uses a digital design such as that from a CAD system to directly control production machinery

Concurrent Feedback Information which arrives during our behaviour and which can be used to control behaviour as it unfolds

Configuration The shape of the organization's role structure – the structures, processes and relationships through which the organization operates

Consumer Movement A diverse collection of independent individuals, groups and organizations seeking to protect the rights of consumers

Content Theories of Motivation These theories attempt to explain those specific things which actually motivate the individual at work and are concerned with identifying people's needs, the strength of those needs and the goals they pursue in order to satisfy those needs

Contingency Approach An extension of the systems approach that implies organizational variables (e.g. strategy, structure and systems) and its success or performance is dependent upon environmental influences (forces). There is, therefore, no one best way to structure or manage organizations; rather it must be dependent upon the contingencies of the situation

Contingency Approach to Organization Structure A perspective which argues that an organization, to be effective, must adjust its structure in a manner consistent with the main type of technology it uses, the environment within which it operates, its size and other contextual factors

Contingency Theory of Leadership A view which argues that leaders must alter their style in a manner consistent with aspects of the context

Continuous Change Organizational changes that tend to be ongoing, evolving and cumulative

Control Ensuring plans are properly executed; assuring the organization functions as planned

Controlled Performance Setting standards, measuring performance, comparing actual with standard and taking corrective action if necessary

Controlling Ensuring plans are properly executed; assuring the organization functions as planned

Cooperative Business organizations owned and operated by a group of individuals for their mutual benefit

Core Competence Those capabilities fundamental to the organization's strategy and performance

Core Values Core values are the principles that guide an organization's actions

Corporate Culture Defined by Bower as 'the way we do things around here'. Trice and Beyer elaborated this as: 'the system of . . . publicly and collectively accepted meanings operating for a given group at a given time'. Hofstede describes corporate culture as 'the psychological assets of an organization, which can be used to predict what will happen to its financial assets in five years time'

Corporate Governance The system used to control and direct a company's operations

Corporate Social Responsibility A concept whereby organizations consider the interests of society by taking responsibility for the impact of their activities on all stakeholders, including the environment

COSO ERM Framework The COSO (Committee of Sponsoring Organizations of the Treadway Commission) Enterprise Risk Management-Integrated Framework published in 2004 defines ERM as a . . . process, effected by an entity's board of directors, management and other personnel, applied in strategy setting and across the enterprise, designed to identify potential events that may affect the entity, and manage risk to be within its risk appetite, to provide reasonable assurance regarding the achievement of entity objectives

Cost Benefit Analysis The assessment of resources used in an activity and their comparison with the value of the benefit to be derived from the activity.
Choice and evaluation of competing solutions should take account of net present value and changing price levels

Cost Centre A unit which serves other parts of the organization (e.g. HR, IT, Accounts, etc.) and which is allocated a budget based on the costs of operating the service at an agreed level; Cost centres account for related expenses – they add to the cost of an organization, but only indirectly add to its profit

Counselling When a counsellor sees an employee in a private and confidential setting to explore a difficulty the employee is having, distress they may be experiencing or perhaps their dissatisfaction with life, or loss of a sense of direction and purpose

Critical Path The longest sequence of activities through a project network, it is called the critical path because any delay in any of its activities will delay the whole project

Cross Cultural Competence An individual's effectiveness in drawing on a set of knowledge, skills and personal attributes in order to work successfully with people from different national cultural backgrounds at home or abroad

Cultural Artefacts Phenomena accessible to the senses, including architecture, myths, rituals, logos, type of personnel employed and so on, which signify the values in an organization's culture

Cultural Distance Cultural distance aims to capture the overall difference in national culture between the home-country and affiliates overseas. As the cultural distance increases, the difficulties facing business processes overseas also increase

Culture Shared ways of thinking and behaving (Uniformity)

Culture Shock Psychological process affecting people living and working abroad that may affect their work performance

Customer Relationship Management (CRM) The entire process of maximizing the value proposition to the customer through all interactions, both online and traditional. Effective CRM advocates one-to-one relationships and participation of customers in related business decisions. Uses technology-enhanced customer interaction to shape appropriate marketing offers designed to nurture ongoing relationships with individual customers within an organization's target markets

Customer Satisfaction When an exchange meets the needs and expectations of the buyer

Customer Service Customer satisfaction in terms of physical distribution, availability, promptness and quality

Cybernetic System A system with reference to the components and operation of feedback control (see self-regulation)

Data Raw facts

Database A system or programme in which structured data is stored

Decision Commitment of resources

Decision Making The process of making choices from among several options

Decision Support System (DSS) A computer-based information system that combines models and data in an attempt to solve semi-structured problems with extensive user involvement

Decision Tree A diagram showing the sequence of events, decisions and consequent actions that occur in a decision making process

Decision-Making Approach An approach to management that focuses on managerial decision-making and how organizations process and use information in making decisions

Delayed Feedback Information which is received after a task is completed, and which can be used to influence future performance

Delegation A distinct type of power sharing process that occurs when a manager gives subordinates the responsibility and authority for making certain decisions previously made by the manager

Design (Structure) Purpose The primary purposes of design are to divide and allocate work and then coordinate and control that work so that goals are met

Development Anything that helps a person to grow, in ability, skills, confidence, inter-personal skills, understanding, self-control and more

Diagnostic Control System Formal information systems used to monitor organizational outcomes and correct deviations from preset standards of performance

Diamond of Competitive Advantage Configuration of four sets of attributes (factor conditions, demand conditions, supporting industries and inter firm rivalry) which, in Porter's theory, determine a nation's competitive advantage

Differentiation The degree to which the tasks and the work of individuals, groups and units are divided up within an organization

Digital Organization An organization where nearly all significant business processes and relationships with customers, suppliers and employees are digitally enabled and key corporate assets are managed through digital means

Direct Distribution Channels Distribution channels in which products are sold directly from producers to users

Direct Marketing The use of non-personal media, the Internet or telesales to introduce products to customers, who then purchase the products by mail, telephone or the Internet

Disciplinary Procedure A set of rules or guidelines for dealing with instances of bad behaviour or rule-breaking amongst employees; the most common sanctions are warnings, suspensions and dismissals

Discrimination Usually refers to unfair treatment of an individual or group on grounds of their sex or race. Less favourable treatment of a person compared with another person because of a protected characteristic

Disintermediation The process of doing away with 'middlemen' from business transactions

Distribution Channel Interlinked stages and organizations involved in the process of bringing a product or service to the consumer or industrial user

Diversity All the ways in which we differ

Division of Labour An approach to job design that involves dividing a task down into relatively small parts, each of which is accomplished by a single person

Divisional Structure A design whereby an organization is split into a number of self-contained business units, each of which operates as a profit centre

Domestic Exporter A strategy characterized by heavy centralization of corporate activities in the home country of origin

Duty to Make Reasonable Adjustments Where a disabled person is at a substantial disadvantage in comparison with people who are not disabled, there is a duty to take reasonable steps to remove that disadvantage by (i) changing provisions, criteria or practices, (ii) altering, removing or providing a reasonable alternative means of avoiding physical features and (iii) providing auxiliary aids

E-Business Using Internet technologies as the platform for internal business operations, electronic commerce and enterprise collaboration

E-Commerce All electronically mediated information exchanges between an organization and its external stakeholders (see sell-side and buy side e-commerce)

Economic Order Quantity (EOQ) The order size that minimizes the total cost of ordering and carrying inventory

Education Formal learning outside (and often before entering) the workplace

Effectiveness Doing right things

Efficiency Doing things right

Employee A person who carries out work for a person under a contract of service

Employee Engagement Refers to the individual's involvement and satisfaction with as well as their enthusiasm for work

Employee Involvement A participative, employer led, process that uses the input of employees and is intended to increase employee commitment to an organization's success

Employee Relations Employee relations is an alternative label for 'industrial relations'. It is not confined to unionized collective bargaining but encompasses all employment relationships. It goes beyond the negotiation of pay and benefits to include the conduct of the power relationship between employee and employer

Employee Resourcing Resourcing is the process by which people are identified and allocated to perform necessary work. Resourcing has two strategic imperatives: first, minimizing employee costs and maximizing employee value to the organization; secondly, obtaining the correct behavioural mix of attitude and commitment in the workforce

Employment Relations Concerned with the relationships between the policies and practices of the organization and its staff and the behaviour of work groups

Empowerment A climate whereby employees are allowed greater freedom, autonomy and self-control over their work and the responsibility for decision-making

Enterprise Resource Planning (ERP) Systems Large, integrated, computer-based business transaction processing and reporting systems. ERP systems pull together all of the classic business functions such as accounting, finance, sales and operations into a single, tightly integrated package that uses a common database

Enterprise Risk Management A framework of methods and processes used by organizations to manage their risks and take opportunities related to the attainment of their objectives

Enterprise System An information system that integrates information from all functional areas of an organization with the goal of providing a more whole or complete information resource for the organization

Environmental Determinism A perspective which claims that internal organizational responses are wholly or mainly shaped, influenced or determined by external environmental factors

Episodic Change Organizational changes that tend to be infrequent, discontinuous and intentional

Equity Theory A theory of motivation which focuses on people's feelings of how fairly they have been treated in comparison with the treatment received by others

European Quality Award (EQA) A quality award organized by the European Foundation for Quality Management (EFQM), it is based on the EFQM excellence model

Expectancy Theory A process theory which argues that individual motivation depends on the valence of outcomes, the expectancy that effort will lead to good performance, and the instrumentality of performance in producing valued outcomes

Experiential Learning Learning from doing

Exports Goods and services produced by a firm in one country and then sent to another country

Extrinsic Motivation A form of motivation that stresses valued outcomes or benefits provided by others, such as promotion, pay increases, a bigger office desk, praise and recognition

Factor Plan (Job Evaluation) The combined number of factors against which jobs will be evaluated

Factors of Production Resources, such as land, labour and capital used to produce goods and services

Feedback (In the Context of Interpersonal Communication) The processes through which the transmitter of a message detects whether and how that message has been received and decoded

Filtering A sender's manipulation of information so that it will be seen more favourably by the receiver

Finance A branch of economics concerned with resource allocation as well as resource management, acquisition and investment; deals with matters related to money and markets

Financial Accounting Reporting of the financial position and performance of a firm through financial statements issued to external users on a periodic basis

Financial Control In financial control the role of the centre is confined to setting financial targets, allocating resources, appraising performance and intervening to avert or correct poor performance

Five Forces Framework Identifies the five most common threats faced by firms in their local competitive environments and the conditions under which these threats are more or less likely to be present; these forces are the threat of entry, of rivalry, of substitutes, of buyers and of suppliers

Flexible Manufacturing Systems Two or more computer controlled machines or robots linked by automated handling devices such as transfer machines, conveyors and transport systems. Computers direct the overall sequence of operations and route the work to the appropriate machine, select and load the proper tools and control the operations performed by the machine

Flow Chart A pictorial summary that shows, with symbols and words, the steps, sequence and relationship of the various activities involved in the performance of a process

Flow Shop Processes Organized around a fixed sequence of activities and process steps, such as an assembly line to produce a limited variety of similar goods or services

Force-Field Analysis A process of identifying and analyzing the driving and restraining forces associated with a change

Formal Communication Formal communication involves presenting information in a structured and consistent manner. Such information is normally created for a specific purpose, making it likely to be more comprehensive, accurate and relevant than information transmitted using information communication. An example of formal communication is an accounting statement. See Informal communication

Formal Management Controls A firm's budgeting and reporting activities that keep people higher up in a firm's organizational chart informed about the actions taken by people lower down in the organizational chart

Formal Organization The collection of work groups that has been consciously designed by management to maximize efficiency and achieve organizational goals

Formalization The degree to which instructions, procedures, etc. are written down

Forming The initial formation of a group and the first stage in group development

Forward Vertical Integration A firm incorporates more stages of the value chain within its boundaries and those stages bring it closer to interacting directly with final customers

Functional Business System A system designed to support a specific primary activity of the organization

Functional Leader A person who leads by action rather than by position

Functional Structure The organization is structured according to functional areas such as finance, marketing and HR

Gantt Chart A graphical tool used to show expected start and end times for project activities, and to track actual progress against these time targets

Gender All human societies divide themselves into two social categories called 'female' and 'male' (this does not exclude other categories). Each category is defined on the basis of varying cultural assumptions about the attributes, beliefs and behaviours expected from males and females. The gender of any individual depends on a complex combination of genetic, body, social, psychological and social elements, none of which is free from possible ambiguity or anomaly. Traditionally, sexual differences have been used to justify male-dominated societies in which women have been given inferior and secondary roles in their working lives

Gender Discrimination Many countries, including all members of the EU, have sex discrimination and equal pay legislation. However, informal psychological and organizational barriers continue to bar the progress of women. The processes of occupational segregation and sex-typing of jobs continue so that women tend to be concentrated at the base of most organizational hierarchies in jobs which are less prestigious and lower paid than those favoured by men

Gender Legislation It is often illegal for a company to make employment decisions based on someone's sex or, more appropriately, gender (i.e .male or female). If a man is promoted over a woman the woman who did not get the promotion may have a claim for sex discrimination

Generic Business Strategies Another name for business-level strategies, which are cost leadership and product differentiation

Generic Routes to Competitive Advantage Cost leadership, differentiation and focus; not mutually exclusive

Glass Ceiling Expression used to denote a subtle barrier to women's promotion to senior posts in an organization, and usually implying that it is kept in place by men's innate prejudice against women in senior management positions

Global A form of international organizational design where foreign subsidiaries are modelled on the parent companies' domestic approach

(replication) – standardization and centralization are emphasized in order to achieve integration

Global Strategy Assumes a single market and offers a standard product(s) to meet customer needs wherever they are located

Globalization Growth and integration to a global or worldwide scale

Globalization of Production Trend by individual firms to disperse parts of their productive processes to different locations around the globe to take advantage of differences in cost and quality of factors of production

Goal Theory A theory of motivation that is based on the premise that people's goals or intentions play an important part in determining behaviour

Goals guide people's responses and actions and direct work behaviour and performance, leading to certain consequences or feedback

Governance Framework The governance framework describes whom the organization is there to serve and how the purposes and priorities of the organization should be decided

Grievance Concerns, problems or complaints that employees raise with their employers

Group An association of two or more individuals who have a shared sense of identity and who interact with each other in structured ways on the basis of a common set of expectations about each other's behaviour

Group Cohesiveness The extent to which members of a group interact, co-operate, are united and work together effectively. Generally, the greater the cohesiveness within a group, the more rewarding the experience is for the members and the higher the chances are of success

Group Dynamics The behavioural interactions and patterns of behaviour that occur when groups of people meet

Halo (or Horns) Effect The bias introduced when attributing all of the characteristics of a person to a single attribute i.e. drawing a general impression or making a judgement about an individual on the basis of a single characteristic. When this is positive it is a 'halo' effect, when negative a 'horns' effect. The perception of a person is formulated on the basis of a single favourable or unfavourable trait or characteristic and tends to shut out other relevant characteristics of that person

Harassment Unwanted behaviour that has the purpose or effect of violating a person's dignity or creates a degrading, humiliating, hostile, intimidating or offensive environment. Conduct which is unreasonable, unwelcome and offensive and which creates an intimidating or humiliating working environment. Harassment is a direct type of discrimination if the victim can show that the behaviour caused injury to feelings

Hawthorne Studies A series of studies exploring aspects of group working within the Western Electric Company in the USA during the late 1920s and early 1930s

Hierarchy of Needs A theory of motivation developed by Maslow which states that people's behaviour is determined by their desire to satisfy a progression of physiological, social and psychological needs

Hindrance Stressors Stressors that keep you from reaching your goals (red tape, office politics, confusion over job responsibilities)

HR System A set of distinct activities, functions, policies and processes that are directed at attracting, developing, and maintaining the human resources of an organization

Human Relations Approach A school of management thought which emphasizes the importance of social processes at work (emphasizes the informal organization)

Human Resource Management A philosophy of people management based on the belief that human resources are uniquely important to sustained business success. An organization gains competitive advantage by using its people effectively, drawing on their expertise and ingenuity to meet clearly defined objectives. HRM is aimed at recruiting capable, flexible and committed people, managing and rewarding their performance and developing key competencies. See also 'Hard HRM', 'Soft HRM'

Human Resource Planning (HRP) A process which anticipates and maps out the consequences of business strategy on an organization's human resource requirements. This is reflected in planning of skill and competence needs as well as total headcounts

Human Resource Strategy Overall plan for staffing, developing and rewarding employees and outsourced human resources tied to business objectives

Hygiene Factors Aspects of work which remove dissatisfaction but do not contribute to motivation and performance, including pay, company policy, supervision, status, security and working conditions are known as hygiene or context factors

Imports Goods and services produced in one country and bought in by another country

Industrial Tribunals Tribunals set up originally to hear appeals against training levies; their scope has increased considerably since 1971 to include unfair dismissal, sex discrimination, etc. Now known as employment tribunals

Informal Communication This describes information that is transmitted by informal means, such as casual conversations between members of staff. The information transmitted in this way is often less structured and less detailed than information transmitted by formal communication. In addition, the information may be inconsistent or may contain inaccuracies. Furthermore, the information may also include a subjective element, such as personal opinions. See formal communication

Informal Management Controls Include a firm's culture and the willingness of employees to monitor each others behaviour

Informal Organization The network of relationships between members of an organization that form of their own accord on the basis of common interests and friendship

Information Data that has been processed (sorted, summarized, manipulated, filtered) so that it is meaningful to people

Information System A set of people, procedures and resources that collects, transforms and disseminates information in an organization – accepts data resources as input and processes them into information products as output

Information Technology The hardware and software that are used to store, retrieve and manipulate information

Inputs The resources introduced into a system for transformation into outputs

Integration The required level to which units in an organization are linked together, and their respective degree of independence (Integrative mechanisms include rules and procedures and direct managerial control)

Intermediary Brings together buyers and sellers

Internal Analysis Identification of a firm's organizational strengths and weaknesses and of the resources and capabilities that are likely to be sources of competitive advantage

Internal Rate of Return (IRR) The internal rate of return (IRR) is the discount rate which delivers a net present value of zero for a series of future cash flows. It is a discounted cash flow (DCF) approach to valuation and investing

International Financial Reporting Standards (IFRS) International accounting standards, designed to harmonize reporting standards in different countries, which are gradually supplanting national accounting standards

International Operations Process by which the firm makes and delivers its goods or services across national borders

International Organization Any organization that engages in international trade, investment or offers products or services outside their home country

International Trade The purchase, sale, or exchange of goods and services across national borders

Internationalization The gradual process of taking organizational activities into other countries

Internet An international network of computers, cables and satellite links that enables individuals to communicate worldwide through their personal computer or workplace server

Intranet Internal, in-company Internet networks for routine communications, fostering group communications, providing uniform computer applications, distributing the latest software or informing colleagues of marketing developments and new product launches

Intuitive Decision Makers Cognitive style that describes people who approach a problem with multiple methods in an unstructured manner, using trial and error to find a solution

Job The set of tasks an individual performs

Job Analysis The determination of the essential characteristics of a job in order to produce a job specification/description. The process of job analysis is that of gathering and analyzing job-related information. This includes details about tasks to be performed as part of a job and the personal qualities required to do so. Job analysis can provide information for a variety of purposes including:

determining training needs, development criteria, appropriate pay and productivity improvements. For resourcing purposes, job analysis can generate job and personnel specifications

Job Characteristics Model A model of job enrichment based on the need to incorporate a number of core job dimensions (skill variety, task identity, task significance, autonomy and feedback) into the design of a job

Job Description A statement of the overall purpose and scope of a job, together with details of its tasks and duties; the description is a product of job analysis

Job Design Involves determining the specific job tasks and responsibilities, the work environment and the methods by which the tasks will be carried out to meet the goals of operations

Job Enlargement The horizontal increasing of job responsibility, i.e. by the addition of tasks of a similar nature to be distinguished from job enrichment

Job Enrichment The process of vertically increasing the responsibilities of a job, by the addition of motivators, e.g. more discretion, improved job interest, etc.

Job Evaluation A technique for determining the size of one job compared with another, and the relationship between the two; job evaluation schemes can broadly be divided into analytical and non-analytical; the technique forms the basis for wage and salary administration

Job Grading A job evaluation scheme based on an organization's hierarchy of job grading

Job Ranking A job evaluation scheme based on job descriptions

Job Rotation The moving of a person from one job or task to another, in an attempt to add variety and help remove boredom. It may also give the individual a holistic view of the organization's activities and be used as a form of training

Job Satisfaction An attitude or internal state which is associated with the working environment and working experiences. In recent years it has been closely associated with improved job design and work organization and the quality of working life

Job Shop A type of (flexible) manufacturing process used to make a wide variety of highly customized products in quantities as small as one

Job Simplification An approach to job design based on a minimization of the range of tasks into the smallest convenient size to make the job efficient and cost effective

Jobbing Processes Processes that deal with high variety and low volumes, although there may be some repetition of flow and activities

Just-In-Time (JIT) Methods of managing inventory (stock) whereby items are delivered when needed in the production process instead of being stored by the manufacturer

Kaizen Japanese term for continuous improvement

Key Result Area Term used especially in management by objectives; refers to those areas of a person's job that make the biggest impact on end results
(See also Management by Objectives.)

Knowledge What people understand as a result of what they have been taught or have experienced. Knowledge may then be applied to solve problems

Lateral Communication Communication within an organization which exist between individuals in different departments or sections, especially between individuals on the same level

Leadership The process of influencing others to understand and agree about what needs to be done and how to do it, and the process of facilitating individual and collective efforts to accomplish shared objectives

Lean Production A term commonly used to refer to just-in-time production

Learning The development of knowledge

Learning Organization An organization skilled at creating, acquiring and transferring knowledge, and at modifying its behaviour to reflect new knowledge and insights

Limited Company A corporation with shareholders whose liability is limited by shares

Line Relationship The links, as shown on an organizational chart, that exist between managers and staff whom they oversee directly

Logistics The management of both inbound and outbound materials, parts, supplies and finished goods

Machine Bureaucracy A type of organization which possesses all the bureaucratic characteristics. The important decisions are made at the top, while at the bottom, standardized procedures are used to exercise control

Maintenance The activity of caring for physical facilities so as to avoid or minimize the chance of those facilities failing

Management Coordinated activities (forecasting, planning, deciding, organizing, commanding) to direct and control an organization

Management Accounting The process of identifying, measuring, analyzing, interpreting and communicating information for the pursuit of an organization's goals

Management By Objectives An approach to management which aims to integrate the organization's objectives with those of individuals; it involves the reduction of overall objectives into unit and individual objectives; in the UK the approach is associated with John Humble. (See also Key Result Area)

Management Development A systematic process for ensuring that an organization meets its current and future needs for effective managers; typical features include manpower reviews, succession planning, performance appraisal and training

Management, Principles Of 14 elements of what being a manager involved, developed by Fayol

Managing Diversity The management of diversity goes beyond equal opportunity and embodies the belief that people should be valued for their differences and variety. Diversity is perceived to enrich an organization's human capital. Whereas equal opportunity focuses on various disadvantaged groups, the management of diversity is about individuals

Market Segment A market segment is a group of customers who have similar needs that are different from customer needs in other parts of the market

Market Segmentation Approach Designing product and service offerings around consumer demand

Market Surveys Structured questionnaires submitted to potential customers, often to gauge potential demand

Market Test An experiment in which a product is made available to buyers in one or more test areas, after which purchases and consumer responses to its distribution, promotion and price are measured

Marketing The processes associated with the transfer of goods from and the relationships between producer and consumer – it is also concerned with anticipating the customers' future needs and wants – marketing involves researching, promoting, selling and distributing products or services

Marketing Audit A systematic examination of the marketing function's objectives, strategies, programmes organization and performance

Marketing Communication The diffusion of persuasive information about a product aimed at key stakeholders and consumers within the target market segment

Marketing Concept The philosophy that an organization should try to provide products that satisfy customers' needs through a coordinated set of activities that also allows the organization to achieve its goals

Marketing Information Systems A system incorporating ad hoc and continuous market and marketing research surveys, together with secondary data and internal data sources, for the purpose of decision making by marketers

Marketing Intelligence Information about buyer needs and competitor activities compiled, analyzed and/or disseminated in an effort to provide insight and assistance in decision-making

Marketing Mix The tactical 'toolkit' of the marketing programme; product, place/distribution, promotion, price and people variables that an organization can control in order to appeal to the target market and facilitate satisfying exchange

Marketing Objective A statement of what is to be accomplished through marketing activities – the results expected from marketing efforts

Marketing Orientation A marketing-oriented organization devotes resources to understanding the needs and buying behaviour of customers, competitors' activities and strategies, and of market trends and external forces – now and as they may shape up in the future; interfunctional coordination ensures that the organization's activities and capabilities are aligned to this marketing intelligence

Marketing Plan The written arrangements for specifying, implementing and controlling an organization's marketing activities and marketing mixes

Marketing Research The process of gathering, interpreting and disseminating information to help solve specific marketing problems or take advantage of marketing opportunities

Marketing Strategy A plan indicating the opportunities to pursue, specific target markets to address, the types of competitive advantages that are to be developed and exploited and maintenance of an appropriate marketing mix that will satisfy those people in the target market(s)

Mass Processes Processes that produce goods in high volume and relatively low variety

Master Production Schedule (MPS) The important schedule that forms the main input to material requirements planning, it contains a statement of the volume and timing of the end products to be made

Material Requirements Planning (MRP) A planning process (usually computerized) that integrates production, purchasing and inventory management of interrelated products

Matrix Management A system of management operating in a horizontal as well as vertical organization structure, where, typically, a manager reports to two superiors – one a departmental/line manager and the other a functional/project manager

Mcgregor's Theory X and Theory Y Theory X managers consider workers as lazy and having to be driven to achieve performance. Theory Y managers consider workers enjoy the experience of work and have a desire to achieve high performance. McGregor believed that managers managed their staff on the basis of these beliefs, irrespective of actual employee approach to work

Mechanistic System A rigid system of management practice and structure which is characterized by a clear hierarchical structure, specialization of task, defined duties and responsibilities and knowledge centred at the top of the hierarchy

Mission Statement A mission statement is a statement of the overriding direction and purpose of an organization

Monochronic Concentrating on one task at a time

Motivating Activating the driving force within individuals by which they attempt to achieve some organizational goal

Motivation A driving force that encourages an individual to behave in particular ways as they seek to achieve a goal

Multidomestic Organization An organization that trades internationally as if the world were a collection of many different (country) entities

Multinational The multinational (multidomestic) is a collection of national companies that manage their businesses with minimal direction from headquarters – decentralization is emphasized to achieve differentiation and a local response

Mutually Exclusive Options may be seeking to solve the same problem and competing with each other

Need for Achievement (NACH) A general concern with meeting standards of excellence, the desire to be successful in competition and the motivation to excel

Need for Power (NPOW) The desire to make an impact on others, change people or events and make a difference in life

Net Present Value (NPV) An investment appraisal technique that determines the amount of money an investment is worth, taking into account its cost, earnings and the time value of money

Niche Strategy A firm reduces its scope of operations and focuses on narrow segments of a declining industry

Noise Factors extraneous to the communication process which interfere with or distract attention from the transmission and reception of the intended meaning

Nonverbal Communication Gestures and facial expressions which convey meaning within a particular linguistic context

Norming The third stage of group development during which members of the group establish guidelines and standards and develop their own norms of acceptable behaviour

Objectives Objectives are statements of specific outcomes that are to be achieved

Occupational Health The ongoing maintenance and promotion of physical, mental and social well-being for all workers

Open System Considers the organization's structures, systems, processes and external environment to be interrelated and able to affect one another

Organic System A fluid and flexible system of management practice and structure which is characterized by the adjustment and continual redefinition of tasks, a network structure of control, authority and communication and where superior knowledge does not necessarily coincide with positional authority

Organization Development A systematic process aimed at improving organizational effectiveness and adaptiveness on the basis of behavioural science knowledge; typical stages in an OD programme include analysis, diagnosis, action plans and review, an external third party assists the process. (See also Change Agent)

Organizational (Corporate) Culture A set of values, beliefs, goals, norms and rituals that members of an organization share

Organizing Determining activities and allocating responsibilities for the achievement of plans; coordinating activities and responsibilities into an appropriate structure

Organizing By Function A way of structuring a marketing department in which personnel directing marketing research, product development, distribution, sales, advertising and customer relations report to the top-level marketing executive

Organization A group of people with a common purpose who work together to achieve shared goals (see formal organization and informal organization)

Organization Theory The study of the structure, functioning and performance of organizations and the behaviour of groups and individuals within them (see also organizational behaviour)

Organizational Behaviour The study of the structure, functioning and performance of organizations and the behaviour of groups and individuals within them

Organizational Change The alteration of organizational components (such as the mission, strategy, goals, structure, processes, systems, technology and people) to improve the effectiveness or efficiency of the organization

Organizational Design The design of an organization patterns its formal structure and culture. It allocates purpose and power to departments and individuals. It lays down guidelines for authoritarian or participative management by its rigidity or flexibility, its hierarchical or non-hierarchical structure

Organizational Routines/Competences When firm-specific assets are assembled in integrated clusters spanning individuals and groups so that they enable distinctive activities to be performed, these activities constitute organizational routines and processes

Organizational Structure The way in which the interrelated groups of an organization are constructed

Output Control A form of control that is based on the measurement of outputs and the results achieved. This form of control serves the needs of the organization as a whole and is used when there is a need for quantifiable and simple measures of organizational performance

Outputs The completed products or services of a system

Packaging The development of a product's container and label, complete with graphic design

Pareto Law A general law found to operate in many situations that indicates that 20 per cent of something causes 80 per cent of something else, e.g. 20% of effort in one area gains 80% of the results

Partnership When you go into business with someone else (more commonly associated with professional services such as accountants, solicitors and doctors)

Payback Period An investment appraisal technique that assesses how long it takes for initial cash investment to be repaid from cash receipts generated by the investment

Perception A mental process used to manage sensory data

Perfectly Competitive Industry When there are large numbers of competing firms, the products being sold are homogeneous with respect to cost and product attributes, and entry and exit are very low cost

Performance Appraisal The process of assessing the performance of an employee in his job; appraisal can be used for salary reviews, training needs analysis and job improvement plans, for example

Performance Assessment One of the many people-management techniques which 'classify and order individuals hierarchically' (Townley, 1994, p.33). Modern assessment is often focused on competences. See also 'Appraisals'

Performance Management Any system for improving management effectiveness by means of standard-setting, appraisal and evaluation; combines informal day-to-day aspects with formal appraisal interviews and goal-setting. A continuous process for improving the performance of individuals by aligning actual performance with that desired (and with the strategic goals of the organization) through a variety of means such as standard-setting, appraisal and evaluation both informally, day-to-day, and formally/systematically through appraisal interviews and goal-setting

Performance Standard An expected level of performance against which actual performance can be compared

Performance Targets Performance targets relate to the outputs of an organization (or part of an organization), such as product quality, prices or profit

Performing The fourth stage of group development during which the group concentrates on the performance of the common task

Person Culture A form of culture where the individual is the central focus and any structure exists to serve the individuals within it. Individuals have almost complete autonomy and any influence over them is likely to be on the basis of personal power

Person Specification A list of the knowledge, experience and skills necessary for a person to be able to perform a particular job

Personal Sellings The task of informing and convincing customers to purchase through personal communication

Personnel Management The specialist management function which determines and implements policies and procedures which affect the stages of the employment cycle

Picketing Trade union activity where groups of workers in dispute with their employers attend at their own place of work for the purpose of peacefully persuading other workers not to leave or enter the premises for work; the persons in attendance are the pickets, and the area they are picketing is called the picket line

Place or Distribution Is essentially about how you can place the optimum amount of goods and/or services before the maximum number of members of your target market, at times and locations which optimize the marketing outcome, i.e. sales

Place/Distribution Variable The aspect of the marketing mix that deals with making products available in the quantities desired to as many customers as possible and keeping the total inventory, transport and storage costs as low as possible

Planning The formalization of what is intended to happen at some time in the future; concerns actions taken prior to an event, typically formulating goals and objectives and then arranging for resources to be provided in order to achieve a desired outcome

Points Rating Method The method of numerically evaluating jobs by the detailed analysis of component job factors. Each factor is defined and is given a range of point values, so that every job can be assessed numerically within the established range

Policy A guiding principle designed to influence decisions, actions, etc.

Polychronic Dealing with several tasks at once

Post-Modern Organization A networked, information-rich, delayered, downsized, boundary-less, high-commitment organization employing highly skilled, well-paid, autonomous knowledge workers

Postmodernism A more recent view of organizations and management that rejects a rational, systems approach and accepted explanations of society and behaviour. Postmodernism places greater emphasis on the use of language and attempts to portray a particular set of assumptions or versions of the 'truth'

Power The ability of individuals or groups to persuade, induce or coerce others into following certain courses of action

Power Culture A form of culture that depends on a central power source that exerts influence throughout the organization

Practice An accepted method or standardized activity

Predetermined Motion–Time Systems (PMTS) A work measurement technique were standard elemental times obtained from published tables are used to construct a time estimate for a whole job

Prejudice Prejudice is an attitude, usually with negative feelings, that involves a pre-judgement about the members of a group

Price Variable The aspect of the marketing mix that relates to activities associated with establishing pricing policies and determining product prices

Principle-Centred Leader A leadership type based upon morals and ethical principles

Procedure Agreement A collective agreement setting out the procedures to be followed in the conduct of management–union relations, with particular reference to negotiating rights, union representatives, disputes and grievance procedures. (See also Substantive Agreement)

Process Consultation An approach to organization development in which the role of the consultant is to facilitate understanding of how to explore problems and find workable solutions

Process Control Systems. These systems deal with the large volume of data generated by production processes

Process Theories of Motivation These theories look at motivation as the outcome of a dynamic interaction between the person and their experiences of an organization and its management. Such processes depend critically on the sense individuals make of their experiences at work

Procurement The act of getting possession of something from a supplier

Product Development A strategy of increasing sales by improving present products or developing new products for current markets

Product Differentiation Refers to one way in which firms can maintain their competitive advantage; they differentiate their product, in ways that appeals to the customer, from all others on the market

Product Liability Involves holding a firm and its officers responsible when a product causes injury, death or damage

Product Life Cycle The four major stages through which products move: introduction, growth, maturity and decline

Product Portfolio The variety of products manufactured or supplied by an organization

Product Portfolio Analysis A strategic planning tool that takes a product's market growth rate and its relative market share into consideration in determining a marketing strategy

Product Structure The organization is structured according to related products or services

Production Process The way that businesses create products and services

Production Run Completion of all tasks is associated with a production order

Productivity Economic measure of efficiency that summarizes the value of outputs relative to the value of inputs used to create them

Profit and Loss Account A statement that sets the total revenues (sales) for a period against the expenses matched with those revenues to derive a profit or loss for the period

Profit Centre A part of an organization that directly adds to its profit/run as a business with profit objectives; it is a subset of the business for which senior managers want to track income and expenses

Profit-and-Loss Centres Profits and losses are calculated at the level of the division in a firm

Promotion Communication with individuals, groups or organizations in order to facilitate exchanges by informing and persuading audiences to accept a company's products

Promotional Mix The combination of five key communication tools: advertising, sales promotions, public relations, direct marketing and personal selling

Psychological Contract An informal understanding between the employer and employee. Unlike the formal employment contract, this has no physical existence. It is a set of expectations held by both employers and employees in terms of what they wish to give and receive from their working relationship (Rousseau and Parks, 1993)

Psychometric Tests Written tests that assess a person's aptitude and personality in a measured and structured way. Such tests are often used by employers as part of their recruitment and selection processes

Public Limited Company (PLC) A limited company whose shares may be purchased by the public and traded freely on the open market and whose share capital is not less than a statutory minimum (for the UK a company registered under the Companies Act (1980) as a public company)

Publicity Non-personal communication in news-story form about an organization and/or its products that is transmitted through a mass medium at no charge

Purchasing The organizational function, often part of the operations function, that forms contracts with suppliers to buy in materials and services.

Push Strategy Information is just 'pushed' by the seller toward the buyer

Quality Degree to which a set of inherent characteristics fulfils requirements

Quality Assurance The specific actions firms take to ensure that their products, services and processes meet the quality requirements of their customers

Quality Circles These are meetings of group of workers committed to continuous improvement in the quality and productivity of a given line of production

Quality Management Refers to systematic policies, methods and procedures used to ensure that goods and services are produced with appropriate levels of quality to meet the needs of customers

Quality Management System (QMS) A systematic approach to proactively managing quality based on documented standards and operating procedures. The best known QMSs are those based on the ISO9000 series of quality standards

Quality of Working Life An individual's overall assessment of satisfaction with their job, working conditions, pay, colleagues, management style, organization culture, work-life balance, and training, development and career opportunities

Quality Standard A framework for achieving a recognized level of quality within an organization. Achievement of a quality standard demonstrates that an organization has met the requirements laid out by a certifying body

Rational Model of Organization A perspective which holds that behaviour within an organization is not random, but that goals are clear and choices are made on the basis of reason in a logical way. In making decisions, the objective is defined, alternatives are identified and the option with the greatest chance of achieving the objective is selected

Rational–Economic Concept of Motivation Motivational theory suggesting employees are motivated by their economic needs

Rational-Legal Authority Authority derives from a person's office/ position as bounded by the rules and procedures of the organization (see also legitimate authority)

Readiness for Change A predisposition to welcome and embrace change

Recruitment Locating, identifying and attracting capable applicants

Red Circling The term applied to jobs which, as a result of the implementation of a new grading structure, are found to be over paid but where the existing job holders are pay protected for a period of time

Regulations Secondary legislation made under an Act of Parliament (or European legislation) setting out subsidiary matters which assist in the Act's implementation

Reinforcement The encouragement of particular behaviours through the application of positive and/or negative rewards

Relationship Marketing Places emphasis on the interaction between buyers and sellers, and is concerned with winning and keeping customers by maintaining links between marketing, quality and customer service

Representative Participation A system in which workers participate in organizational decision making through a small group of representative employees

Resistance to Change The desire not to pursue change

Resource-Based View of Strategy The resource-based view of strategy: the competitive advantage of an organization is explained by the distinctiveness of its capabilities

Responsibility An obligation placed on a person who occupies a certain position in the organization structure to perform a task, function or assignment

Revenue Centre (Income centre) is a unit such as a sales section within an organization where income is accumulated and identified with a specific project or organizational entity; the manager is held accountable for the revenue generated by the subunit

Rivalry The act of competing – a quest to secure an advantage over another

Robot A programmable machine designed to handle materials or tools in the performance of a variety of tasks

Role A set of actions and activities that a person in a particular position is supposed to perform, based on the expectations of both the individual and surrounding people

Role Ambiguity The degree of ambiguity in the minds of individuals forming the role set as to exactly what their respective roles should be at any point in

Role Conflict The simultaneous existence of two or more sets of role expectations on a focal person in such a way that compliance with one makes it difficult to comply with the others

Role Culture A form of culture that is based on logic and rationality and relies on the strength of the functions of specialists in, for example, finance or production. The interactions between the specialists is controlled by procedures and rules

Role Set The collection of persons most immediately affected by the focal person's role performance, who depend upon the focal person for their own role performance and who therefore have a stake in it

Sales Promotion An activity or material that acts as a direct inducement by offering added value to or incentive for the product to resellers, sales people or consumers

Sarbanes–Oxley Act A law defining acceptable accounting practices including audit and control of financial information

Scheduling A term used in planning and control to indicate the detailed timetable of what work should be done, when it should be done and where it should be done

Scientific Management A school of classical management theory, dating from the early twentieth century, based on the application of work study techniques to the design and organization of work in order to maximize output – increased productivity (to find the 'one best way' of performing each task); it is a form of job design theory and practice which stresses short, repetitive work cycles; detailed, prescribed task sequences; a separation of task conception from task execution; and motivation based on economic rewards (see also Taylorism, after Frederick Taylor who was influential in founding its principles)

Segmentation The process of grouping customers in heterogeneous markets into smaller, more similar or homogeneous segments – customers are aggregated into groups with similar needs and buying characteristics

Segmentation Variables or Bases The dimensions or characteristics of individuals, groups or businesses that are used for dividing a total market into segments

Selection Screening job applicants to ensure the most appropriate candidates are hired

Self-Actualization The need for personal fulfilment, to develop potential, to become everything that one is capable of becoming

Self-Esteem How we evaluate ourselves

Self-Serving Bias A situation whereby individuals attribute success to their abilities and failure to the situation

Semi Structured Decisions Decisions where only part of the problem has a clear-cut answer provided by an accepted procedure

Sex Discrimination Discriminatory or disparate treatment of an individual because of his or her sex

Sexism The belief or attitude that one gender or sex is inferior to or less valuable than the other

Situational Approach A viewpoint that emphasizes the importance of the environmental situation in determining (organization) behaviour

Situational Leadership An approach to determining the most effective style of influencing

Social Identity Part of the self-concept which comes from our membership of groups

Social Perception The process of interpreting information about another person

Socio-Technical System A sub-division of the systems approach which is concerned with the interactions between the psychological and social factors, and the needs and demands of the human part of organization and its structural and technological requirements

Sole Trader A type of business entity which legally has no separate existence from its owner (the limitations of liability benefited from by a corporation, and limited liability partnerships, do not apply to sole traders) – the simplest form of business

Span of Control A measure of the number of employees who report to one supervisor or manager

Specialization The degree to which an organization's activities are divided into specialist roles

Sponsorship The financial or material support of an event, activity, person organization or product by an unrelated organization or donor

Staff Relationship A link between workers in advisory positions and line employees – Staff employees use their specialized expertise to support the efforts of line employees who may choose to act on the advice given

Standardization The degree to which an organization lays down standard rules and procedures

Stereotypes Stereotypes are formed when we ascribe generalizations to people based on their group identities and the tendencies of the whole group rather than seeing a person as an individual

Stereotyping Judging someone on the basis of one's perception of the group to which that person belongs

Storming The second stage of group development which involves members of the group getting to know each other and putting forward their views.

Strategic Choice The process whereby power-holders within organizations decide upon courses of strategic action

Strategic Decision Making Determining the long-term objectives, resources and policies of an organization

Strategic Management Process A sequential set of analyses that can increase the likelihood of a firm's choosing a strategy that generates competitive advantages

Strategy Strategy is the direction and scope of an organization over the long term, which achieves advantage in a changing environment through its configuration of resources and competences with the aim of fulfilling stakeholder expectations

Strategy as Position A means of locating an organization in its environment (choice of niche). It can be considered in relation to competitors or simply with respect to markets or an environment at large. Strategy is creating situations where revenues may be generated and sustained

Stress The physical symptoms of ill-health caused by excessive pressures in the workplace or elsewhere and leading to reduced job performance; how far an individual succumbs to stress is determined mainly by personality, and the extent to which they are confident of their ability to overcome the pressures

Structure The structure of an organization is the way in which employees are formally divided into groups for co-ordination and control

Structured Decisions Decisions that are repetitive, routine and have a definite procedure for handling them

Styles of Leadership Suggests that successful leadership is about the style of behaviour adopted by the leader, usually described as falling within an autocratic–democratic scale

Substantive Agreement A collective agreement dealing with terms and conditions of employment, e.g. wages, hours of work, holidays, etc. (See also Procedure Agreement)

Sub-System One part of numerous interdependent elements that comprise the wider system

Succession Planning A process through which senior-level openings are planned for and ultimately filled

Supply Chain A network of manufacturers and service providers that work together to convert and move goods from the raw materials stage through to the end user. These manufacturers and service providers are linked together through physical flows, information flows, and monetary. All of the activities related to the acceptance of an order from a customer and its fulfilment. In its extended format, it also includes connections with suppliers, customers and other business partners

Supply Chain Management The management of all activities that facilitate the fulfilment of a customer order for a manufactured good to achieve satisfied customers at reasonable cost

Sustained Competitive Advantage A competitive advantage that lasts for a long period of time; an advantage that is not competed away through strategic imitation

SWOT Analysis Summarizes the key issues from the business environment and the strategic capability of an organization both of which are most likely to impact upon strategy development

Symbols Symbols are objects, events, acts or people which express more than their intrinsic content

System A set of elements connected together which form a whole, thereby possessing properties of the whole rather than of its component parts

Systems Approach A management approach which is focused on the total work of the organization and the interrelationships of structure and behaviour and the range of variables within the organization. The organization is viewed within its total environment and emphasises the importance of multiple channels in interaction

Systems Theory The study of the behaviour and interactions within and between systems

Systems Thinking A holistic approach to analysis that focuses on the way a system's constituent parts interrelate and how systems work over time and within the context of larger systems

Talent Management A strategic and integrated approach to developing a skilled and competent workforce, involving targeted recruitment, development and training

Tall Hierarchical Structure An organization that has narrow spans of control and a relatively large number of levels of authority

Task Culture A form of culture which is task or job oriented and seeks to bring together the right resources and people and utilizes the unifying power of the group

Taylorism An approach to management based on the theories of F.W. Taylor. See also 'Scientific management'

Team Implies a small, cohesive group that works effectively as a single unit through being focused on a common task

Team-Role A pattern of behaviour, characteristic of the way in which one team member interacts with another, where performance facilitates the progress of the team as a whole

Telecommunications The exchange of information in any form (e.g., voice, data, text, and images) over networks

Terms of Employment The provisions of a person's contract of employment, whether provided for expressly in the contract itself or incorporated by statute, custom and practice or common law, etc.

Theory Z The management style (characteristic of many Japanese companies) that combines various aspects of scientific management and behaviouralism; the characteristics include long-term employment, development of company-specific skills, participative and collective decision-making and a broad concern for the welfare of workers

Tight Control Severe limitations applied to an individual's freedom

Time and Motion Studies Measurement and recording techniques which attempt to make operations more efficient

Time Management Refers to a range of skills, tools, and techniques used to manage time when accomplishing specific tasks, projects and goals

Time Study A term used in work measurement to indicate the process of timing (usually with a stopwatch) and rating jobs, it involves observing times, adjusting or normalizing each observed time (rating) and averaging the adjusted times

Total Quality Management (TQM) A quality approach that emphasizes a continuous process of improvement, through the involvement of people

Trade Union An organization of employees whose principal purpose is to negotiate with employers about terms and conditions of employment and other matters affecting the members' interests at work. (See also Certified Trade Union)

Trademark Legal designation indicating that the owner has exclusive use of a brand

Traditional Authority Authority based on the belief that the ruler had a natural right to rule. This right is either God-given or by descent and tradition. The authority enjoyed by kings and queens would be of this type

Training Any intervention aimed at increasing an individual's knowledge or skills

Training & Development The design and delivery of workplace learning to improve performance

Traits Approach to Leadership Assumes leaders are born and not made. Leadership consists of certain inherited characteristics, or personality traits, which distinguish leaders from followers. Attention is focused on the person in the job and not the job itself

Transactional Change Changes to components of the organization such as the structure, systems and processes

Transformational Change A fundamental change impacting upon the whole organization (the leader, mission, strategy and culture)

Trigger of Change Any disorganizing pressure indicating that current systems, procedures, rules, organization structures and processes are no longer effective

Triple Bottom Line Reporting Corporate reporting focusing on social and environmental aspects of the company, in addition to traditional financial information

Type A and Type B Personality Profile A typology of personality types in which Type A individuals are described as always being under time pressure, impatient and having a pre-occupation with achievement

Unfair Dismissal A statutory definition of dismissal now part of the Employment Protection (Consolidation) Act, 1978; the Act states that every employee shall have the right not to be unfairly dismissed; remedies for unfair dismissal must be pursued via an industrial tribunal, which may award compensation or reinstatement or re-engagement

Unstructured Decisions Unstructured decisions tend to involve complex situations, where the rules governing the decision are complicated or unknown. Such decisions tend to be made infrequently and rely heavily on the experience, judgement and knowledge of the decision maker

Value Analysis A term used to describe an analytical approach to the function and costs of every part of a product with a view to reducing costs whilst retaining the functional ability; sometimes known as value engineering

Value Creation Performing activities that increase the value of goods or services to consumers

Value Engineering An approach to cost reduction in product design that examines the purpose of a product or service, its basic functions and its secondary functions

Value Perspective A quality perspective that holds that quality must be judged, in part, by how well the characteristics of a particular product or service align with the needs of a specific user. Value is often described in terms of quality and cost i.e. value = higher quality for lower cost (price)

Value System The supply chain within which an organization's value chain is located i.e. includes producers, suppliers, distributors and buyers

Vertical Communication Communication flows up and down the management hierarchy

Virtual Organization Uses information and communications technology to operate without clearly defined physical boundaries between different functions

Visioning Mental process in which images of the desired future (goals, objectives, outcomes) are made explicit motivators for action

Vrio Framework Four questions that must be asked about a resource or capability to determine its competitive potential: the questions of value, rarity, imitability and organization

Work Study A term describing several techniques for examining work in all its contexts, in particular those factors affecting economy and efficiency, with a view to making improvements; the two most common techniques of Work Study are Method Study and Work Measurement. (See also Method Study and Work Measurement)

Work–Life Balance Allocation of time and commitment between work and personal life, which reflects the personal needs of the employee

INDEX